EXPERIENCING ART
AROUND US

EXPERIENCING ART AROUND US

Thomas Buser

University of Louisville

WEST PUBLISHING COMPANY

Minneapolis/St. Paul   New York   Los Angeles   San Francisco

Copyedit:	Cheryl Drivdahl
Composition:	Parkwood Composition, Inc.
Cover Image:	Mary Cassatt, [American, 1845–1926] *Summertime: Woman and Child in a Rowboat*, 1984. Oil on canvas. © 1986 Terra Museum of American Art, Daniel J. Terra Collection. Chicago.
Art:	Randy Miyake Illustration; Vantage Art, Inc.
Maps:	Carto-Graphics
Art Research:	Lindsay Kefauver, Visual Resources; Carole Frohlich, The Visual Connection.
Index:	Terry Casey

West's Commitment to the Environment

In 1906, West Publishing Company began recycling materials left over from the production of books. This began a tradition of efficient and responsible use of resources. Today, up to 95 percent of our legal books and 70 percent of our college and school texts are printed on recycled, acid-free stock. West also recycles nearly 22 million pounds of scrap paper annually—the equivalent of 181,717 trees. Since the 1960s, West has devised ways to capture and recycle waste inks, solvents, oils, and vapors created in the printing process. We also recycle plastics of all kinds, wood, glass, corrugated cardboard, and batteries, and have eliminated the use of Styrofoam book packaging. We at West are proud of the longevity and the scope of our commitment to the environment.

Production, Prepress, Printing, and Binding by West Publishing Company.

Copyright 1995   By WEST PUBLISHING COMPANY
610 Opperman Drive
P.O. Box 64526
St. Paul, MN 55164-0526

Printed in the United States of America

01 00 99 98 97 96 95 94   8 7 6 5 4 3 2 1 0

Library of Congress Cataloging-in-Publication Data

Buser, Thomas.
    Experiencing art around us / Thomas Buser.
        p.   cm.
    Includes index.
    ISBN 0-314-02698-3
    1. Art.   2. Visual perception.   I. Title.
N7425.B87   1995
701'.1--dc20   93-45250
                                                          CIP

CONTENTS IN BRIEF

CONTENTS

Contents

Art is all around us. Splendid works of art from all over the world are on display in numerous museums and galleries, outstanding sculpture stands in public places, and impressive architecture graces our cities and countryside. Good design and visual self-expression appear not only in traditional forms like painting but also in the layout of our urban and suburban environment, in handcrafted pieces and commercial products, and in advertising, photography, and film.

A textbook can only introduce us to the abundance of art around us—we have to find it ourselves. Art that we can actually see is almost always better than a textbook illustration or classroom slide. Reproductions alter the size of every work of art or architecture. They distort color. They flatten brushwork and texture in two-dimensional art forms and obscure the feeling for mass and void in three-dimensional forms. They give little or no feeling for scale. They allow only the camera's point of view.

Unless we learn to confront actual objects, art can remain merely theoretical or abstract—something to which we can remain indifferent. A work of art is incomplete without our active participation and reaction. For example, sculpture must be experienced in three dimensions, usually from different angles. Architecture must be walked through and lived in for a while. The experience of art is part of living, and our goal should be nothing less than to open our mind to new modes of seeing and to enrich our thinking and feeling. Neglecting the direct experience of art closes us to new discoveries.

Why Study Art?

People learn at least three important things from the study of art. First, they learn facts. Educated people should know something about the art of ancient Greece, and what a Rembrandt painting looks like or be familiar with the functions of African sculpture. They ought also to know the meaning of the terms used to discuss art and the materials and techniques that artists use. A solid grasp of this information provides a framework on which to build further knowledge and understanding of art.

Second, as with a foreign language, people not only acquire the vocabulary of art, they also learn the rules of grammar—the principles governing art. To experience art, people must see how shapes and lines and colors work and how they are put together by the artist into meaningful communication. People ought to appreciate how paint is put on a surface, how solid materials are shaped into sculpture, and how space is enclosed for living. A knowledgeable viewer remains sensitive to the range of possibilities within an art form and stays open to the experiments of artists who expand the art media.

Like mastery of a new language, artistic awareness opens up new worlds of experience that were once incomprehensible. Understanding the language of art means comprehending other ways of seeing and other ways of looking that come from different places and different times. Moreover, training in the principles and practices of art sharpens our perceptions of the visible world. It enables us to form critical judgments about actual buildings, pictures, movies, and all other types of visual communication in addition to the examples studied in a classroom.

Third, every mature person ought to be able to enjoy art. The experience of art goes beyond the fun of learning something new and the satisfaction of accomplishment. For centuries people have felt that art offered a distinct kind of human experience, different from other forms of awareness. One of its essential characteristics was enjoyment—even when the subject matter was tragic or disturbing—because the insights and revelations of art can be emotionally exciting. In learning about art and how to experience art, it would be a shame to miss the joy that art has to offer.

Structure of This Book

Experiencing Art around Us is divided into five parts, each of which takes a different approach to the study of art. The approaches are theoretical (part I), formal (part II), technical (part III), historical (part IV), and institutional (part V). Constantly illustrated and demonstrated with actual works of art, the approaches build a solid foundation for a lifetime of experiencing art.

Part I, "The Nature of Art," explores a number of fundamental conceptual issues. The first chapter answers the question What is art? by discussing the major theories of art, emphasizing the theory that art is a form of symbolic communication. The second chapter discusses the most common categories of subject matter and their significance to society. The third chapter examines how styles of art express personality, culture, and history, and how different people use the analysis of styles.

Part II, "The Visual Elements," takes an in-depth look at essential formal elements, such as line, light, and space. Much attention is given to the visual elements and the principles of design because an understanding of them will function throughout a lifetime of appreciating art. The visual elements play a key role in every form of art, from a small pencil sketch to the design of a large city.

Part III, "The Visual Arts," examines the principles, materials, techniques, and expressive potential of a range of artistic media.

Part IV, "A History of World Art," shows how art expresses the culture of different peoples and times, in a survey of world art from early cave paintings to contemporary performance pieces.

Part V, "The Art World," uses a new and timely approach to understanding art in the modern world. Chapter 20 probes the business of art in the institutions that influence the creation of art. The chapter investigates the role of the art market, museums,

galleries, collectors, and critics in the production of art. It also discusses conservation, artists' training, and careers in art.

Illustrations

Experiencing Art around Us is illustrated by 665 different works of art, three-fourths of which are reproduced in full color. Every effort has been made to ensure that the vast majority of the illustrations appear on the text page on which they are discussed. Forty line drawings illustrate various concepts and techniques. Forty-eight architectural plans and drawings, all originally rendered for this text, provide an overview of structures and places. Three major time lines and eight maps help students place artistic developments into a historical context.

Features of the Text

Each chapter contains distinctive pedagogical features that enliven the presentation of the material and help foster student comprehension. Several of these features are new to this type of textbook. The features include extended captions to selected works of art, boxed discussions of individual artists at work, summation boxes near the end of each chapter, and a list of key terms and concepts. Following each of the first four parts of the text is a critical analysis of the same work of art, *Summertime: Woman and Child in a Rowboat*, by the American painter Mary Cassatt.

Themes of the Text

Each feature of this text was devised to support four broad pedagogical themes that appear throughout *Experiencing Art around Us*:

1. In-depth analyses of selected works help students develop critical evaluation skills.
2. Students benefit from exposure to a wide diversity of artistic works from throughout the world.
3. Art is best studied within the cultural context in which it was made.
4. A true understanding of art comes from examining the creative process in individual artists and in a wide variety of media, including the latest technology.

Acknowledgments

For the development of this text I have many people to thank, including Charles Grawemeyer, who encouraged my teaching this course many years ago. For their many years of patience and encouragement, my wife and children have earned my constant thanks. I also thank Gail Gilbert, Kathy Moore, and the staff of the Bridwell Art Library for all their help; my colleagues at the Allen R. Hite Art Institute for their suggestions about teaching art and their generous answers to my questions; and my students over the years, who have been my greatest inspiration and my best critics.

At many stages in the development of the text, professors in the front lines of art education all over the United States gave their advice. I was always stimulated by their insights, prodded by their criticism, and encouraged by their kind words. All showed themselves to be thoughtful, concerned, and provocative teachers of art. Everyone who reviewed the manuscript left a mark on the text. I am indebted to the following scholars and instructors:

Ingrid Aall
California State University, Long Beach

Simon Anderson
School of the Art Institute of Chicago

Judith Andraka
Prince George's Community College

Charles Boone
College of DuPage

Bill Buchanan
Western Carolina University

Sandra L. Burwell
Indiana University of Pennsylvania

Edwin L. Clemmer
Adams State College

Harold D. Cole
Baldwin-Wallace College

Norma Coret
University of Nebraska at Omaha

William Derrevere
Tulsa Junior College

Keith Dills
California Polytechnic State University, San Luis Obispo

William Disbro
Jamestown Community College

Suzy Grey
Lindsey Wilson College

Sally Hagaman
Purdue University

Eugene R. Harrison
Eastern Illinois University

Martha Holmes
Fort Hays State University

William L. Hommel
University of Central Oklahoma

Eugene Hood
University of Wisconsin— Eau Claire

Gene Isaacson
Rancho Santiago College

Charles W. Johnson
Modlin Fine Arts Center

Arnold Leondar
Tarrant County Junior College

Lisa Lockman
University of Mississippi

Wil Martin
University of Texas—Pan American

Jacquelyn McElroy-Edwards
University of North Dakota

Lynn Metcalf
St. Cloud State University

Henry Michaux
South Carolina State University

Anita Monsebroten
University of North Dakota

Gary M. Nemcosky
Appalachian State University

Barbara Kerr Scott
Cameron University

Ron Seitler
Bergen Community College

Michael Stone
Cuyahoga Community College

Candace Stout
Texas Tech University

Sally Struthers
Sinclair Community College

Barbara Teague
University of Monticello

Grant Thorp
East Central University

Monica Blackmun Visona
Metropolitan State College of Denver

W. (William) Thomas Young
University of New Orleans

The staff of West Publishing Company has been unfailingly kind and generous and supportive. My biggest debt of gratitude is owed to Robert Jucha, my indefatigable editor, the instigator of this project, and its gentle but persuasive guide at every stage. For the handsome design of the text, the reader may thank Production Editor Ann Rudrud and Administrative Editor Kent Baird, whose expertise helped make the material a pleasure to look at and use. Behind the skillful and easy layout of each page lies a tremendous amount of work with text and illustrations. Many thanks also to Developmental Editors Diane Colwyn and Angela Barnhart, and to Promotion Manager Amelia Jacobson. All these people at West can take pride in another job well-done.

I am also very grateful for the keen eye of Copy Editor Cheryl Drivdahl, who did wonders to make the text clear, consistent, and cogent. Art researchers Lindsay Kefauver, of Visual Resources, San Francisco, and Carole Frohlich, of The Visual Connection, Gloucester, Massachusetts, did an excellent job of obtaining many of the handsome and revealing photographs. The smooth cooperation of all these people helped make my work look good.

THE NATURE OF ART

1

WHAT IS ART?

The Attraction of Art

Each year thousands of people stop to examine Vincent Van Gogh's painting *Sunflowers* (FIG. 1-1) in the Philadelphia Museum of Art. The experience usually makes most of them feel happy. The vivid yellow colors, the tumble of round shapes, and the lushness of the thick paint seem calculated to cause delight. Indeed, whenever art truly engages someone, its images and shapes and colors please the imagination with a complex tangle of feelings and associations. The thoughts and emotions and memories that come rushing together at the encounter may even cancel out the humdrum concerns of everyday existence and transport people outside themselves for a while. Time will seem to stand still as they grasp something different from everyday events.

While examining art like Van Gogh's, people sometimes experience a charge of emotion or they feel possessed by some magic. They can see things in a new light and may be filled with wonder at the revelation. Some have called the experience a natural high. Art's revelation can treat people to a delightful surprise, like the joy they feel on the discovery of something or on meeting an old friend. They feel happy when tangible images and shapes give them new insights into their experience and the world around them. Plainly, if these things happen, Van Gogh's *Sunflowers* is no ordinary reproduction of a bouquet of flowers.

Not all artists set out to please their audience as did Van Gogh when he painted *Sunflowers*. Some artists intend their work to disturb, provoke, and challenge their viewers. For example, Lucas Samaras, since the late 1960s, has been taking twisted, fragmented, and distorted photographs of himself (FIG. 1-2) that are both shocking and ludicrous. These grotesque images express the deep anxieties of modern life lived alongside unspeakable atrocities and reflect as well the crass exhibitionism of the public media. Nevertheless, the provocations and challenges of art like Samaras's can be an essential part of the pleasurable satisfaction that many viewers get from the experience of art. Whatever the explicit subject matter—whether tragic or comic or in between—the experience of art can be like the stimulating pleasure of encountering another person. It is like the satisfaction people have when something works well, when the pieces all fit and everything comes out right.

FIG 1-1 VINCENT VAN GOGH [Dutch, 1853–1890], *Sunflowers*. 1888. Oil on canvas, 36 3/8 × 28 5/8 in. (92.4 × 72.7 cm). Philadelphia Museum of Art. Mr. and Mrs. Carroll S. Tyson Collection.

3

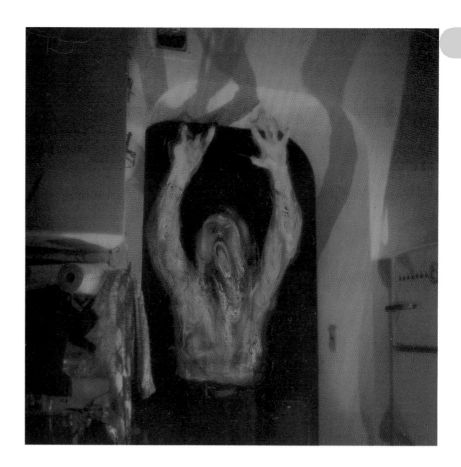

FIG 1-2 LUCAS SAMARAS [American, 1936–], *Photo-Transformation.* February 9, 1974. SX-70 Polaroid, 3 × 3 in. Courtesy PaceWildenstein, New York. Photo by D. James Dee.

Lucas Samaras came to America from Greece in 1948 at age twelve. As a child he had witnessed death and mutilation in World War II and the Greek Civil War. Working as a painter and having tried acting briefly, Samaras discovered the common Polaroid SX-70 camera and immediately began taking photos of himself. He also discovered that in the few moments the Polaroid image takes to develop, the material is soft enough to manipulate manually. Thus he can handle the photograph as freely as a painter adjusts wet oil paint on a canvas. With the supposedly factual material of a photograph, Samaras reveals very subjective and highly charged emotions. His audience can readily admire his artistry and the shocking frankness of his self-revelation.

The pleasurable experience of art is, simply, a good and valuable thing. Like love and friendship, art is something almost everybody would like to understand and experience. Many consider art to be one of the most important things in life—something that defines human nature. Many people cherish the experience of art as something they would not like to do without for long. Like many of the best things in life, the pleasure of art is valuable in itself and needs no further justification.

Aesthetic Theories

Despite the intrinsic value of this experience called art, for centuries the inquisitive Western mind has wanted to isolate and explain it. Unfortunately, no one has ever come up with an entirely satisfying explanation. At different times and in different places, people have proposed all kinds of answers to the question, What is art? There is even a branch of philosophy, called **aesthetics,** that attempts to define the artistic experience. Also, professional psychologists have investigated the personality of artists and the reactions of people experiencing art. With so many new definitions of art continually put forward and so many old ones rejected, artists themselves are often a bit reluctant to answer the question, What is art?

Many of the older definitions of art, analyzing the characteristics of the objects made by artists, asserted that artists create a special class of objects that are inherently beautiful. These definitions usually stated that artists create a thing of beauty by combining a representation of something **real** and a conceptual **ideal.** In other words, artists make a special kind of object for our contemplation by depicting in it what they actually see (the real) and, at the same time, also depicting something they know or imagine (the ideal). For example, Van Gogh both painted actual sunflowers and depicted in them the idea that they were potent life-forms bursting with the energy of the sun. By combining the real and the ideal, artists are capable of transforming something very specific into a universal truth, even though the words *real* and *ideal* may be seen as philosophical opposites if not contradictions by definition.

The discussion of these two facets of art—the copying of reality joined to the interpretation of an imaginative aspect—goes back in time at least as far as the ancient Greek philosophers Aristotle and Plato. The question that has plagued this tradition is, How can artists possibly get the two together?

Aristotle

Aristotle, in the fourth century B.C., taught that the fundamental principle of art was the imitation of nature, or **mimesis** (pronounced mim-*eh*-sis), and his idea has been repeated whenever artists like to work from models of any kind and like to copy or reproduce what they see before them. The school of mimesis maintains that creating a work of art is like holding a mirror up to nature, because the artist accurately reflects what he or she sees.

Belief in Aristotelian mimesis waned in the Middle Ages when the concern for earthly reality became less important, but returned in full force in the Renaissance. As in the studio of the famous French painter Jacques-Louis David (FIG. 1-3), for centuries Western art students practiced and perfected their skills in representation with years of training in copying the model. It was only a little over one hundred years ago that mimesis fell out of favor in the West when art there became increasingly less representational. Mimesis lost its importance about the same time that photography began to preserve, with machinelike speed and precision, the external appearances of nature.

But, to be fair, Aristotle meant more than mere copying when he called art an imitation. For instance, in his *Poetics* he did not hesitate to lay down rules that restrict the making of art through imitation.[1] When it comes to writing a play, he insisted that the drama have just a few characters participating in a single action that takes place in about a day's time. Moreover, he stated that art is not supposed to reproduce ordinary people. Serious art is supposed to imitate men and women whose character is ethically superior to that of ordinary people and, by doing so,

FIG 1-3 LÉON-MATHIEU COCHEREAU [French, 1793–1817], *Interior of David's Studio*. 1814. 35 7/16 × 41 5/16 in. (90 × 105 cm). Paris, Louvre. Bridgeman Art Library/Art Resource, New York.

FIG 1-4 ANGELICA KAUFFMANN [SWISS, 1741–1807], *Zeuxis Selecting Models for His Picture of Helen of Troy.* Annmary Brown Memorial Museum, Providence, Rhode Island.

FIG 1-5 RAPHAEL [Italian, 1483–1520], *Galatea.* 1513. Fresco. Rome, Palazzo della Farnesina. Scala/Art Resource, New York.

demonstrate goodness, beauty, and truth. Art, Aristotle said, is more philosophical and of graver import than history because art deals with such universal issues as beauty and goodness and truth.

Aristotle never made it clear how an artist, in practice, reconciles the imitation of reality with the reproduction of these philosophical ideals. However, to illustrate how an artist goes about depicting the idealized image of the perfectly beautiful woman while imitating reality, the ancients told a story. In the story an artist named Zeuxis searches to find the most beautiful legs, the most beautiful nose, the most beautiful arms on various women. As Angelica Kauffmann imaged the story in her painting *Zeuxis Selecting Models for His Picture of Helen of Troy* (FIG. 1-4), the artist in the his studio is choosing and measuring the parts before he puts them all together.

In another explanation of Aristotle's theory, the artist creates the most beautiful woman by constantly correcting and improving nature, wherever it is found, according to an image carried in the artist's mind. The Renaissance painter Raphael gave this explanation to a friend when he was asked where he found such a beautiful model for the nymph Galatea in his painting *Galatea* (FIG. 1-5). "In order to paint a beautiful woman," he said, "I should have to see many beautiful women . . .; but since there are so few beautiful women and so few sound judges, I make use of a certain idea that comes into my head." The idea in Raphael's head was probably formed by looking not only at many beautiful women but also at many examples of Greek and Roman sculpture, which were being rediscovered during the Renaissance.

Plato

Plato questioned the theory of imitation because he believed that all of nature is already an imitation of higher ideals and that if art only copies nature it will not capture these higher ideals. According to Plato, an ideal is an archetype that exists in a state of absolute perfection. For example, we recognize that a particular chair is a chair because there exists an idea of what constitutes perfect chairness. Plato believed that such ideas are real and that material things exist because they participate in and imitate those universal ideas. If art is supposed to be an imitation of nature, then art is an imitation of what is already an imitation and thus twice removed from true reality. True reality—and true beauty—consists in the everlasting and immutable ideals.

If Plato's theory is correct, who needs art! In fact, Plato banished art from his ideal republic.

But Plato also described art in more positive terms as a form of **inspiration.** According to him, artistic inspiration can change one's perception of reality just like inebriation or like madness. (Unfortunately, alcohol and madness may debilitate a person, whereas artistic inspiration usually leads to the vigorous creation of something.) Plato compared the creation of art to madness because inspiration lifts artists out of themselves and takes possession of them. The inspired artist participates in a transcendent reality and is not governed by earthly rules. Plato's description of the inspired poet in his dialogue *Ion* has long been applied to every artist: "The poet is a light and winged and holy thing, and there is no invention in him until he has been inspired and is out of his senses. . . . God takes away the minds of poets, and uses them as his ministers. . . . These beautiful poems are not human, or the work of man, but divine and the work of God; the poets are only the interpreters of the gods by whom they are severally possessed."[3] Since the divine is acting through the artist, the divine becomes one with the artist, and thus the artist is able to combine the real and the ideal. Through divine inspiration, imitation of the ideal in art is not secondhand but immediate.

Few Western artists living today talk about being possessed by the gods, but a lot of them speak about something happening inside them when their creative juices are really flowing. Time can stand still and the world around them seems to go far away as their imagination takes hold.

Yoruban Aesthetics

Different cultures around the world explain the nature of art in their own terms. For example, Yorubans, who live in Nigeria, would probably agree that the small *Twin Memorial Figure* (FIG. 1-6), carved by the Yoruban sculptor Ogunremi, embodies their concept of beauty in art.

FIG 1-6 OGUNREMI [Yoruban, ?–1933], *Twin Memorial Figure (Ere Ibeji)*. Wood, 10 7/8 in. (27.6 cm) high. From Igbomina, Oro district, Ijomu, Agbegi compound. Courtesy James and Barbara Sellmon, Richmond, Virginia.

Although the Yoruban sculptor of this figure clearly interpreted *imitation* differently than would a Greek or Renaissance artist, Yorubans believe that their carved figures resemble an individual subject—but in a moderate way. Too close a resemblance would not be art; neither would total abstraction. This moderation is perhaps the expression of a certain ideal of human personal behavior found in Yoruban society. Yorubans believe that someone should act in life with coolness, composure, even with a certain detachment. Consequently, Yoruban artists dislike emotions or violence in the facial expressions and gestures of their sculpture. And also because of their desire for coolness and moderation, the Yorubans, like most African carvers, prefer symmetry—the clear delineation of parts arranged equally on either side of an upright central axis. Moreover, what also produces harmony or beauty in the Yoruban imagination is the contrived similarity or repetition of the body parts. We can see this readily in the *Twin Memorial Figure*, in the repetition of the elongated shape of the head, the breasts, and the protruding buttocks and knees, all arranged in parallel diagonals.

Psychological Theories

Modern psychobiology has demonstrated that Plato's description of the artist's feeling of being possessed may have a basis in biology. Research has shown that the two halves of the human brain operate differently. Although the functions of the two halves cannot be entirely separated, the left half of the brain normally controls language, and it analyzes information logically, in a step by step fashion, over a period of time. The **right half of the brain,** on the other hand, "thinks" visually. It intuits things spatially—seeing how parts fit into place to form a whole. The right brain therefore does not have much sense of the passage of time, because time requires left brain sequencing. Intuition and perception of the overall pattern of things, take hold of a person.

Western education and Western culture stress verbal, left brain thinking. But when a Westerner shifts to the right brain modality, she or he experiences a pleasurable new form of awareness—an awareness similar to what Plato referred to as divine inspiration. Still, not all right brain activity automatically becomes art. Nor does the biology of the brain fully explain how an

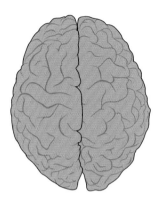

The hemispheres of the brain.

artist actually creates a work of art that will capture her or his personal right brain experience. It does not explain how an artist may successfully fabricate and communicate this kind of visual consciousness to the viewer.

Modern psychologists have also attempted to explain the difference between the real and the ideal in art. They call those who tend to depict what they see before them **perceptual artists** and those who tend to depict what they have stored in their imagination **conceptual artists.** A person categorized as a perceptual artist, from a psychological point of view, has trained the hand to obey the mind's eye so that the hand can form the strokes to mimic what the artists sees "out there." A perceptual artist has to learn to use the right half of the brain and to think spatially. A perceptual artist has to notice edges and intervals and relationships between parts and relationships to the whole. To draw representationally involves learning the conventions for drawing and takes practice, but for anyone who is ordinarily coordinated, it is not very difficult to do a competent job of it. Acquiring the skill to draw competently is on about the same level of difficulty as learning to play golf or to drive a car. Of course, as with playing golf or driving, some people can draw more readily or more easily than others.

The psychologists' use of the term **conceptual** antedates the Conceptual Art movement of the 1970s and is rather different in meaning. In their definition, conceptual artists depict what is in their mind. These artists are not abnormal, as it might first seem. On the

FIG 1-7   ANDY WARHOL [American, 1930–1987], *Blue Marilyn*. 1964. Silkscreen ink on synthetic polymer paint on canvas, 20 × 16 in. (50.8 × 40.6 cm). Princeton University Art Museum.

The entertainment media both reflect and help create what the general public considers to be beautiful men and women. Andy Warhol frequently appropriated images of the icons of American popular culture like Elvis Presley and Marilyn Monroe to play on the ambiguity of their images. In Blue Marilyn *Warhol took a publicity photo from Monroe's film* Niagara *and made a high-contrast photo-emulsion stencil from it. He printed her black silkscreen image on top of flat areas of bright color. By using someone else's reproduction of the real actress for his image of her, the artist attempted to stand aloof from personal expression. Yet the garish colors proclaim that Warhol depicted not the "real" Monroe but the dazzling concept of her created by Hollywood. And even the original photo was not the real Monroe.*

contrary, creating art by visualizing concepts is a quite natural way of proceeding. If asked to draw an eye, for example, 99 percent of us would likely draw the concept of an eye. It would probably look like the old CBS logo, a more-or-less symmetrical or almond-shaped affair. In short, the drawing would eliminate lots of details and simplify the shape. We would tend to depict the eye seen directly from the front; few would draw an eye in profile or from an odd angle, the way we typically see one. Thus we would draw what we conceive an eye to look like—we would draw the standard image or concept we have of it in our mind.

The perceptual-conceptual distinction does not solve the Ancient Greeks' problem of how to depict the beautiful human body, but it certainly confirms that we carry something like Plato's ideal forms in our mind, however they got there—whether we come by them instinctively or have to learn them. If we were to carve a statue or paint a picture of what a beautiful man or a beautiful woman should look like, the visual concepts that we have developed over years of lived experience would certainly shape the end result. For example, Yoruban artists operate with the concepts developed by the traditions of their own society; American artists have to work within a tradition that includes vast amounts of conditioning by the movies and advertising. In the light of that conditioning, the twentieth-century American painter Andy Warhol in his *Blue Marilyn* (FIG. 1-7) makes some wry comments on the popular image of the beautiful woman.

It is surprising how strong an influence mental images and visual concepts exert on what we see. In

Chapter 1: What Is Art?

actual practice, artists often combine perceptually and conceptually derived art. They imitate nature and at the same time they use their imagination either to make things up or to adjust and improve and transform what they see.

Theory of the Artist as An Outsider

Since the early nineteenth century many people have defined an artist as an inspired seer or prophet who saw things that ordinary people did not or could not. This late form of Platonic inspiration gave to the artist a godlike power to penetrate reality, to see hidden meanings, and to unify matter and spirit through art. When an artist challenged commonly accepted beliefs and behavior, the artist was treated as a rebel, an outsider who did not fit in society. Misunderstood and tormented, the inspired artist would make art that was necessarily disturbing, ahead of its times, and in violation of all the rules. Vincent Van Gogh and modern **avant garde** artists—leaders and inventors of new art—have filled this definition of an artist. Until their work was absorbed into the mainstream, the public often condemned it as primitive, raw, and brutal. Non-western artists, it was believed, practiced this art of pure inspiration and pure creativity because they were thought to be innocent and free of rules and conventions.

Since the 1970s inspired and visionary art has been discovered among a distinct group called **outsider artists.** They are usually self-taught artists who through their cultural isolation stand apart from the institutions and standards of the art establishment. In theory, their work has not been influenced by the external art world. They seem instead to obey an inner voice and are seldom aware of art outside their own; they may not even consider themselves artists or their own work as art. Some of them still practice **folk art**—traditional arts and crafts that were passed down within the confines of a minority culture. Some are separated from mainstream society by their race, gender, or social class. Some of them lack formal education; some are eccentric or even mentally unbalanced. Untouched and unspoiled by mainstream artistic culture, they are said to create innocently, spontaneously, and honestly. Through their inspiration they achieve authentic art because their only concern is to discover its magic power.

Bessie Harvey, an outsider artist who lives in rural Tennessee, has visions of spirits living in trees, as is evident from her piece *Tribal Spirits* (FIG. 1-8). Deeply religious, Harvey feels that trees have souls that praise God, and in their wood she sees faces that plead to her to let their spirits come out. In *Tribal Spirits* Harvey has attached around the main stem several pieces of wood that she has transformed with beads and shells into heads. The conflicting sizes and shapes of the different people and the antagonism in their facial expressions are relieved and reconciled by the smooth-necked bird that starts to soar above them. She decorates the whole with bright paint that operates like magic dust on her sculpture. Her ability to embody her vision of living wood and to make her inspiration present in the work defies conventions yet communicates its message with startling power.

FIG **1-8**   BESSIE HARVEY [American, 1928–], *Tribal Spirits*. 1988. Wood and mixed media, 45 × 26 × 20 in. Dallas Museum of Art.

Text continues on page 14.

10

Vincent Van Gogh (1853–1890)

VINCENT VAN GOGH [Dutch, 1853–1890], *Self Portrait Dedicated to Paul Gaugin*, 1888. Oil on canvas 19 1/4 x 23 1/2 in. (49.4 x 60.3 cm). Fogg Art Museum, Harvard University Art Museums, Cambridge. Bequest—Collection of Maurice Wertheim, Class of 1906.

*V*INCENT VAN GOGH was named after his uncle Vincent, a successful art dealer in The Hague; his father was a minister of the Dutch Reformed Church in a series of small towns in Holland. In other words, art and religion were the two family businesses, so to speak, and Van Gogh tried them both.

He worked for his uncle first in The Hague and then in the company's branch office in London.

Van Gogh could read, write, and speak English fairly well. He loved to read—he was probably one of the most well-read painters of the nineteenth century. He also loved to take long walks through the countryside—walks that sometimes became pilgrimages that would last for days.

After a frustrated love affair, Van Gogh became enthusiastically religious for several years. At one point he lived as a missionary among wretchedly poor coal miners in a remote rural district in Belgium, until the religious authorities, disapproving of his zeal in sharing the conditions of the poor, dismissed him.

Typically, whatever Van Gogh did throughout his life, he did it with passion, throwing his whole being into the pursuit. His intensity often made it difficult for him to get along with other people. Yet, at the same time, he was able to analyze and articulate the state of his soul in an extraordinarily revealing series of letters that he wrote over the years to his younger brother Theo, who also became an art dealer and worked in Paris. Theo supported Vincent through many years of poverty, with a regular allowance and with additional money for expenses whenever Vincent pleaded for it in a letter.

In his *Self Portrait*, Van Gogh distorted his own image, not because he had disturbed vision but because he wanted to make a statement. As an indication of his healthy mind when he painted, Van Gogh wrote in quite explicit terms about the distortions he made. In the painting he had tried to make himself look Japanese at a time when a Japanese style was fashionable among young painters. He lucidly explained to his friend Paul Gauguin, to whom he dedicated this portrait, that he "aimed at the character of a simple Bonze [monk], worshipping the Eternal Buddha."[4] To convey the idea that a painter was a religious person, a seer, and a visionary, Van Gogh made it appear that he had shaved his head as do Buddhist monks. The green brush strokes circling around his head like a halo give him a spiritual look. The intensity of the painting builds out from his blue-and-green slanting eyes.

In 1886 Van Gogh arrived at his brother's apartment in Paris, after struggling to be a painter for five years. During his early years as an artist in

Continued on next page.

Holland and in Antwerp, Belgium, he had been especially attracted to landscape and to scenes of peasant life with somber figures in dark colors. In Paris he learned to brighten his palette with the light colors of the Impressionists, and he became friendly with the young painters around Georges Seurat who were experimenting with the expressive potential of color. Van Gogh soon realized that he could never be an exact realist like an Impressionist because he saw nature too intently through the eyes of his own temperament. Since the contemplation of even ordinary things aroused nearly ecstatic feelings in him, he needed to give freer scope to his imagination. Instead of trying to reproduce the exact color of what he had before his eyes, like some "delusive realist," he wrote his brother in the summer of 1888 that he used "color suggesting some emotion of an ardent temperament."[5] Van Gogh started his paintings with a study of a motif from nature, but the works of art eventually struck a balance between the imitation of nature and the expression of his imagination.

He often painted in a kind of passionate fury, at a fever pitch, and with a frenzy for thick paint. Sometimes, growing impatient with the tricks of painterly illusion, he squeezed paint straight from the tube onto the canvas to make his point. Painting became a release for his pent-up emotions, yet he stated that he wanted to paint pictures that would soothe and make people happy, not disturb them. He wanted to produce something consoling in order to make life more bearable.

He often painted in a kind of passionate fury. Sometimes he squeezed paint straight from the tube onto the canvas. He wanted to paint pictures that would soothe and make people happy.

Doctors then and now disagree on a diagnosis of the illness that troubled Van Gogh. He suffered frequent episodes of poor health, during which he could not paint and did not paint. After two years in Paris, he moved in 1888 to the warmer, sunnier south of France for his health. In Paris he had become very familiar with Japanese prints, and he hoped to find in the south a second Japan where he could investigate Japanese art from nature. He also hoped to establish a small artists' colony, but when Gauguin came to live with him, they quarreled. In an infamous incident, Van Gogh cut off his earlobe.

In the few years he spent at Arles and then at Saint-Rémy, both in southern France, Van Gogh produced his most characteristic, his most famous work. Attracted by the bright light and color of Arles, he painted ordinary people and ordinary things with extraordinary intensity. He painted the fruit trees flowering in the spring, bouquets of sunflowers and landscapes with reapers cut-

The south of France, where Van Gogh lived during his most productive years as an artist. Photo by Michael Busselle/Tony Stone Images.

ting grain under the hot sun of late summer. He painted portraits of the postman and his family, and interiors of his bedroom and a sinister-looking cafe at midnight.

When his health broke and he began experiencing prolonged seizures, Van Gogh committed himself, in early 1889, to an asylum in Saint-Rémy, where he was allowed to paint between his attacks. In his confinement, when he regained his clearness of mind, he sometimes copied black-and-white prints of Rembrandt or Delacroix into full-colored paintings; sometimes he painted the fields visible through the bars of his window. Anxious about the ever-more-frequent recurrence of his illness, he made even bolder expressions of his feelings about nature. In *Two Poplars on a Road through the Hills*, painted at Saint-Rémy, each brush stroke is like a broad, thick mosaic tile fitted into place. Every color is heightened and every stroke and every shape twists with energy. The trees tilting to the right seem to be walking up the hill—their instability sets everything in motion. Depressed by the increasingly frequent breakdown of his health, Van Gogh finally shot himself in 1890.

Since Van Gogh sold only one painting in his lifetime and received scant critical recognition, it is tempting to consider him a martyr to his art. It has also been said that he risked his life for his art by devoting himself totally to its creation. In actuality, he feared that his illness was destroying his creative powers. Painting helped keep him reason-

VINCENT VAN GOGH [Dutch, 1853–1890], *Poplars at Saint-Remy.* 1889. Oil on canvas, 24 1/4 × 18 in. (61.6 × 45.7 cm). The Cleveland Museum of Art, Bequest of Leonard C. Hanna, Jr., 58.32

ably happy and sane. He wrote from the hospital in September 1989, "I am working like one actually possessed, more than ever I am in a dumb fury of work. And I think that this will help cure me."[6] Beyond his wildest dreams, his paintings are now admired by millions of people who take great pleasure in seeing them.

Popular Theories

In the last few generations, the ancient Greek concern for imitation joined with an ideal of transcendent beauty has often been corrupted and debased into the popular belief that art should look realistic and pretty. The ideal of truth has been reduced to mere realism and that of beautiful has been reduced to prettiness. There are several things that art does not have to be, and realistic and pretty are two of them. Nevertheless, a lot of people expect art to look very much like the thing it represents, and they want art that is always charming and enjoyable to look at.

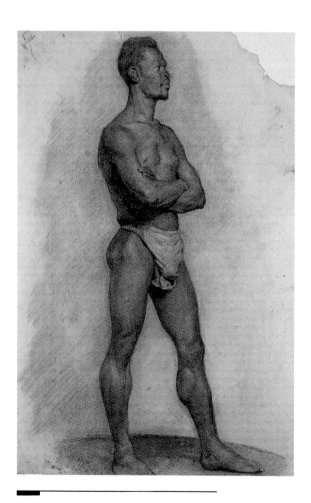

FIG 1-9   PABLO PICASSO [Spanish, 1881–1973], *Standing Male Nude.* 1896–1897. Charcoal and crayon on light tan paper, 18 5/8 x 12 1/2 in. (47.3 × 31.8 cm). Museu Picasso, Barcelona.

Realism

People often say, about a painting, things like, "Those flowers look so real you can almost touch them!" or "Isn't it amazing how he paints those little details!" The thing they like best about the image is its realism, since realism is their fundamental criterion of artistic merit. Unfortunately, it may be their only criterion. Even back in ancient times, some critics set a high priority on a realism that was so convincing that it deceived the eye. The Greeks had another story about Zeuxis, that he painted fruit so realistically the birds flew into the wall to peck at it. Zeuxis's achievement exhibited great skill, not necessarily great art.

Whether birds can actually be so deceived or not, art can never be truly real, because all art is indeed an imitation, a fiction, an illusion, a make-believe. Art is rarely made of the same materials as the thing depicted. Paintings and drawings are flat-two-dimensional things, governed by a series of conventions of representation. Statutes are usually lifeless and colorless; they usually do not move. Dogs and cats and even birds are seldom interested in the illusion of reality in a work of art, since viewing art takes more imagination than animals possess. Of course art is no substitute for the real thing. Still, it is amazing how we humans can suspend our disbelief and react to art as though it were the real thing—especially at the movies. The sudden appearance of the killer makes us jump. Our heart beats faster during the chase scene or at the love scene, even though it is only flickering light on a screen.

What many people demand of art is that it be realistic looking, that it have the appearance of a photograph even though photographs themselves are not real since they capture only a portion of what the eye can perceive. Insisting on realism, many people demand that art not be distorted from normal proportions and relationships. They require a certain accuracy. The more detail there is, some people assume, the better the work of art. Since art is merely a skill, according to these people, the more hard work that appears to have been applied, the better. All these strictures narrow the range of art and fail to grasp its essence.

It is sometimes assumed that an artist who paints in a nonrealistic fashion, like Picasso, must be incompetent or lazy. Picasso's extraordinary skills at rendering reality throughout his career refute that assertion; he made the accurate and natural drawing of *Standing Male Nude* (FIG. 1-9) from a studio model at the age of fifteen or sixteen. Others contend that artists who distort their images in any way must need glasses or some other medical treatment or psychological help. Doctors often fall into this last logical trap when they try to diagnose the illnesses of artists like Leonardo da Vinci or Vincent Van Gogh in order to explain the way they paint. These doctors implicitly assume that if an artist were healthy, he or she would paint realistically.

To challenge realism as the basis for art we might also ask the question that philosophers have been asking for centuries: What is this reality that artists are supposed to imitate? Is it the superficial appearance of things? Some have said that the fundamental reality is an ideal or something spiritual, whereas others claim that it is only what we know through our physical senses. Still others are sure that our sense perceptions give a distorted view of reality—at least, the way things appear real to one person may not be the way things appear real to another. The interests and the background of a person profoundly affect the way a person "sees" things. If perceptions vary, we have no way of knowing if our mind is giving us a true picture of people or objects "out there." Modern science tells us about the reality of atomic and molecular structures, which our unaided senses cannot perceive. It tells us about laws of nature that are operating on a cosmic level beyond common experience. Our emotional and psychological life colors, if not controls, everything we see or do. What indeed is the reality that artists should reproduce?

Realism in History

There were probably only a few times in the history of art when artists deliberately tried to be realistic and nothing else. Even their efforts call the notion of pure realism into question. Perhaps the ancient "no-nonsense" Romans, who had great veneration for their ancestors, strove to get as accurate a reproduction of the face as possible when they had their portraits carved (FIG. 1-10). At least, it has been said that they intended unadulterated realism. Some of their scowling faces look quite real, we might assume, although no one can provide the original face for comparison.

FIG 1-10 [Roman], *Portrait of a Man.* Late first century B.C. Marble, 14 1/2 in. (36.8 cm) high. Metropolitan Museum of Art, New York. Rogers Fund, 1912.

Fig 1-11 Gustave Courbet [French, 1819–1877], *The Source of the Loue.* c. 1864. Oil on canvas, 42 1/2 × 54 in. (107.9 × 137.2 cm). Albright-Knox Art Gallery, Buffalo. George B. and Jenny R. Matthews Fund, 1959.

Fig 1-12 S. J. Akpan [Nigerian, c. 1940–], *Portrait of a Man in Coat and Tie.* 1989. Cement and acrylic paint, 75 9/16 in. (192 cm) high. Musée d'Art Contemporain, Lyon.

But maybe they also carved so many wrinkles and such gaunt cheeks into the face to impress people with their ruggedness and stern character. The Roman head may be an exaggeration of reality. In either case, it was an artistic choice—not an artistic necessity—to produce such craggy portraits.

When the work of the French painter Gustave Courbet was rejected by the jury of a government-sponsored exhibition, he set up his own pavilion nearby and nailed over the door a sign that read Realism. Courbet became the leader of a mid-nineteenth-century style that we now call Realism. He declared that he would paint only familiar subjects that he could actually see and would celebrate their material existence in large paintings. But examining his painting *The Source of the Loue* (River) (Fig. 1-11), we can see that his work was not very detailed or photographic looking. In fact, he applied the paint with a knife in a thick, pasty, rough texture. Many of his early viewers complained that his Realist paintings were not highly finished and that they were crudely painted. What *was* real in his painting was the thick texture and the material reality of the paint, which paralleled the rough and solid materialism of the rocks.

The appearance of precise realism still plays a role in contemporary art. Some artists living around the world, like S. J. Akpan of Nigeria (Fig. 1-12), have made life-sized statues of people so detailed, colored, and textured that it is easy to be fooled into thinking they are real, for a second, as were Zeuxis's birds. Outside his workshop Akpan also has hung a sign; his reads Natural Authentic Sculptor. Akpan's works serve mainly as funeral monuments that are unveiled several years after the person's death in a "second burial" ceremony. Or his statutes might decorate the outside of a hotel or shop to attract customers. The realism effects a surrogate presence and startles the viewer into admiring the artist's skill in refining the intractable medium of cement. Akpan's realism is more than mere imitation; it questions our perceptions of reality and makes everyday reality seem strange and fresh.

FIG 1-13 DON EDDY [American, 1944–], *New Shoes for H.* 1973. Acrylic on canvas, 44 × 48 in. (111.8 × 121.9 cm). Cleveland Museum of Art.

Likewise, a number of late-twentieth-century painters have adopted a style called Photo-realism, which results in the precise realism of an ordinary photograph. In fact, Don Eddy adapted his painting *New Shoes for H* (FIG. 1-13) from black-and-white photographs that he took. Very often Photo-realist painters project a colored slide of some image onto their blank canvas and paint what they see projected there. As the name implies, these artists do not copy "reality" but instead copy the distinctive look of photographs, especially their uniformity and luminosity. Eddy, like some other Photo-realists, goes out of his way to depict highly reflective surfaces like the shop window in *New Shoes for H.* The window, the city street in front of the window, and the display behind the window are all sharply focused so that the difference between what is reality and what is illusion becomes blurred. Eddy gives us far more than what is popularly meant by realistic.

FIG 1-14 *Starving child in Somalia, 1992. Photo by Peter Turnley for Black Star.*

Prettiness

In addition to wanting art to be "realistic," many people are concerned that art be "pretty." These people often remark, for example, "I only want to look at pleasant things" or "There's already too much ugliness in this world" or "Isn't that cute! It's darling!" They want only happy endings at the movies; they want only to be entertained.

The problem with insisting that all art be pretty is that doing so limits art to one kind of expression. Because human experience is much richer than the cute and pleasant, art should be free to reflect life in all its richness. It would be nice if everything in life were pleasing, but some of the most important things are not so nice. Birth and death can be rather painful; so can falling in or out of love. Who is to stop an artist from saying something truthful about these or any other aspects of life that she or he finds meaningful? News photos are often not very pretty—photos of the starvation in Somalia, for example, shocked the United States in the early 1990s (FIG. 1-14). And yet these ugly images can inspire moral indignation and the call for action. Our response to them demonstrates the potential for even ugly visual images to move us deeply.

Theories Based on the Functions of Art

The liveliest debate about the nature of art in the last one hundred years or more has been about not what makes something beautiful but whether art has any purpose. Although many artists of the twentieth century have produced work that challenges and provokes the public, they would probably claim that their art serves no useful function outside art itself. To have art serve a purpose, they believe, would destroy an artist's freedom and creativity, and the artist would no longer produce art. Artists who feel that the essence of art lies in perfecting its purely formal properties rather than in serving a purpose are said to adhere to the doctrine of **art for art's sake.** In a way they define art as the experience of experiencing art. Such artists certainly believe art is an important human activity, although they might be reluctant to say why.

Many of the same artists, who express disinterest in whether their art has a good or bad effect on people, also become indignant when anyone censors their work because it might have a harmful effect on the public. Such conflicts between the public good and the artist's freedom of expression present all artists with a dilemma. Do artists have to claim that their work is useless and without influence in order to maintain their freedom?

Despite this quandary, examples of the usefulness of art stretch way back into the past and continue in the present. The religions of the world have always used art to make visible unseen powers. *Kukailimoku* (FIG. 1-15), a fierce-looking Hawaiian wood carving of the Polynesian war god, clearly embodies the god's powers and makes his invisible spirit very real. His stubby powerful limbs and torso declare agressiveness. His teeth are bared in a cavernous mouth and his enlarged eyes flare like a headdress. The skilled carver got the maximum power from the wood with deep and precise cuts and with a few solid masses that are large in scale relative to the whole figure. When Polynesians erected huge wooden images of their gods, like *Kukailimoku*, on stone platforms, the effect must have been overwhelming.

All through the past, it was also believed that gods, saints, and heroes on public display would teach lessons in moral virtue. Authorities, therefore, usually wanted art under the control of the state or the church so that only uplifting themes would be treated and so that vice would be exposed and the rewards of virtue demonstrated. For many years the former Soviet Union tried to foster a realistic art that would be good for the people. Soviet bureaucrats called it Socialist Realism, and S. V. Gerasimov's *Collective Farm (Kolkhoz) on Holiday* (FIG. 1-16) is one example of the style. Soviet art was supposed to inspire factory workers to produce more trucks and mothers to produce more healthy babies; it was meant to inspire patriotism and love of country, and government officials did not allow artists to depict anything critical or unpleasant. The government was also afraid that giving individuals artistic freedom might undermine the ideology of the state.

FIG 1-15 [Polynesian], *Kukailimoku.* From Hawaii. Wood, 30 in. (76.2 cm) high. British Museum, London.

FIG 1-16 SERGI V. GERASIMOV [Russian, 1885–1964] *Collective Farm (Kolkhoz) on Holiday.* 1939. Oil on canvas. Novosti Photo Library.

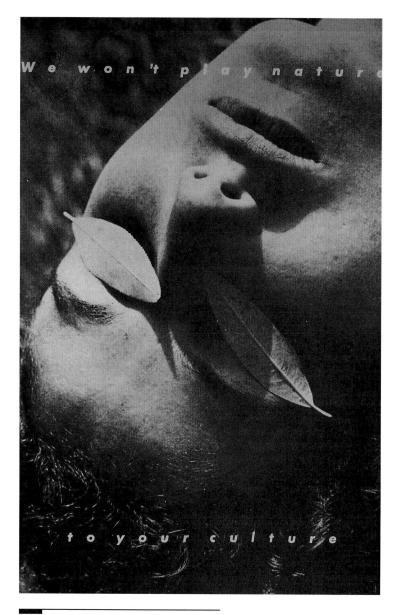

We won't play nature

to your culture

FIG 1-17 BARBARA KRUGER [American, 1945–], *Untitled (We Won't Play Nature to Your Culture).* 1983. Black-and-white photograph, 73 × 49 in. (185.4 × 124.5 cm) (framed). Ydessa Hendeles Art Foundation, Toronto.

In the last several decades, many artists, rejecting art for art's sake, have devoted their work to contemporary causes such as equal rights or AIDS in order the change the moral behavior of their audience. Barbara Kruger has dedicated her art to exposing the signs and symbols that determine power and establish gender roles in contemporary society. She creates photomontages the size of small billboards, like *Untitled (We Won't Play Nature to Your Culture)* (FIG. 1-17), out of old photographs and inscriptions printed in block letters across the image. The cryptic and provocative statement "We won't play nature to your culture" rejects the practice of the male-dominated art world to treat women as art objects controlled by the male gaze. It rejects the inferior role assigned to female nature compared with the male development of high culture. Ironically, the woman in the photograph covering her eyes with "nature"—two small leaves—refuses to look at anything but nature itself. Kruger's work is not an illustration with an explanatory text but, like a catchy advertising campaign, a visual totality of word and image that persuades.

The theory that art is an instrument to instruct or improve morals also goes back to ancient times. Aristotle thought that the actors in a play reveal a moral purpose by their actions or by whatever will disclose their character. To disclose character, painters and sculptors have to work not with speeches but with poses and gestures and facial expressions—with body language. Plato, who could understand art as devine inspiration, thought of music as the prime example of how art has a moral effect. He thought that listening to divinely inspired music that has rhythm, grace, and harmony will bring those same good dispositions of grace and harmony into the soul and consequently educate a youngster in good moral behavior. In Plato's thinking, the moral nature of art lies in its formal properties. A harmonious style produces good behavior, a bad style produces bad behavior.

The different approaches to morality in art devised by Plato and Aristotle continue to be debated to the present day. On the one hand, censors and modern moralists look at what is going on in a painting or a statute or a film and condemn the work if the actions of the characters do not meet the moral standards of the community. On the other hand, many modern artists and critics focus on the inspired rhythms and harmony—the formal properties of the same work—and declare that they are good for us or good in themselves and not harmful to moral behavior. Sometimes the debate is resolved by judging whether the artistic intention outweighs the scandalous content. These issues of morality and censorship are not easy to resolve and they are complicated by our strong tradition of freedom of expression. The issues would never be so hotly debated if everyone agreed that art has no purpose.

Theories Based on Comparisons between the Arts

For a long time artists and critics defined art by relating it to literature, specifically poetry. The Roman poet Horace once said, "*Ut pictura poesis,*" "A poem is like a picture"—which, since the phrase is a simple equation, we can interpret it to mean, "A picture is like a poem." Following this idea, artists not only painted pictures or carved statues that told stories, they created works of art that were like epic or lyrical or tragic poetry. They tried to obey the rules laid down for literature. Long ago, in the seventeenth and eighteenth centuries especially, critics tended to praise paintings that told a story with a moral message, as did literature, and to denigrate paintings, like landscapes, that merely copied nature.

Just as our vocabulary distinguishes between the uncommon art of *poetry* and the everyday use of *language*, so too many people distinguish a difference between the **fine arts** as opposed to the **applied arts** or crafts. The fine arts are those produced to be enjoyed for their own sake, whereas the applied arts perform some function. However, the distinction is quite difficult to maintain. Until the twentieth century most art served a function, and architecture almost always serves a practical function. Conversely, a craft object, like a finely wrought Shaker chair (FIG. 1-18), made for a useful purpose, may express as much formal and cultural significance as any work of painting or sculpture displayed in a museum of fine art.

FIG 1-18   [American], side chair. C. 1850. Courtesy Shakertown at Pleasant Hill, Kentucky.

The United Society of Believers in Christ's Second Appearance, commonly called Shakers, established separatist religious communities throughout the northeastern United States, where they manufactured chairs and other household goods for their own use and for sale to the outside world. They did not invent the slat-backed chair with a woven seat but rather refined its design according to their religious beliefs of simplicity, practicality, and lack of worldliness. The only decoration on the chair is the egg like pommels at the top. The slats have a gradual curve along the top and a straight edge along the bottom. The high back contrasts with the broad seat. The plain uprights of the chair, gracefully tapered at the ends, are as elegant and delicate as possible.

Fɪɢ 1-19 Wᴀssɪʟʏ Kᴀɴᴅɪɴsᴋʏ [Russian, 1866–1944], *Fragment 2 for Composition VII*. 1913. Oil on canvas, 54 1/2 × 39 1/4 in. (87.6 × 99.7 cm). Albright-Knox Art Gallery, Buffalo. Room of Contemporary Art Fund, 1947.

Other artists and theorists, following Plato, have tried to understand the visual arts by comparing them to music. Wassily Kandinsky, for example, when he painted *Fragment 2 for Composition VII* (Fɪɢ. 1-19), believed he could produce a heightened spiritual effect by intensifying the musical elements in his painting. Just as music has the elements of rhythm, harmony, and melody, so too the visual arts have a rhythm of lines, a harmony of forms, and melodious colors. Both the visual elements and the corresponding musical elements would therefore elicit the same emotional or even the same mental and physical reaction in a person. But this comparison involved more than just these similarities. It was also believed that certain lines or shapes or colors correspond to certain musical sensations because of the phenomenon of **synaesthesia.** According to this theory, one sense organ in the body will respond to the stimulus of another. A certain sound, for example, might cause a person to experience a certain color. Kandinsky believed that synaes-

thesia had a basis in human physiology and that individual sounds had an exact equivalent on the color scale. In the act of painting *Fragment 2* he made himself aware of these musical relationships.

At the beginning of the twentieth century the ideas of synaesthesia and the correspondences between the arts were commonly used to explain nonrealistic tendencies in modern art. Since music could be played and enjoyed without words or stories, painting and sculpture could likewise ignore the representational content, even do without it altogether, and express instead the inner life of the artist.

Symbolic Communication Theory

In modern times the discussion about art has concerned not so much what kind of object qualifies for the category of art but what sort of experience the artist and viewer have when they create or when they see art. Viewers, through the medium of art, must re-create something like the artist's experience for themselves. Focusing on the experience of art makes clear that, fundamentally, art is a form of communication. Artists, in making a work of art, create something for somebody else to see and share. The study of this communication between the artist and the viewer through the medium of the artist's signs and symbols has been called **semiotics.**

A work of art, then, is like a sign written in its own distinctive, visual language. Communication through a sign system or language presupposes that both the sender and the receiver of the message understand the same basic language system. Although a good part of the language of art seems to come naturally to most people, very often the receiver has to learn more of the visual language for communication to take place. The culture of the artist, for example, may use different signs from those used by the culture of the viewer. And sometimes contemporary artists revise the visual language of their culture and invent something new. In this case, the feeling often arises that the artist is ahead of the times.

Visual art or any living system of communication between peoples is never a static affair with rigidly set signals and inviolable rules. Both the senders and the receivers operate within a fluid context in which the significance of the visual signs is constantly changing. The language of art, in short, is not set in concrete. To a great extent, the vital and dynamic context surrounding the visual language gives the art-signs their meaning, just as the meaning of a spoken language is derived from its immersion in the surrounding culture.

But art is also a **symbolic communication.** Art is not a mere sign substituting for something else, like an element of Morse code or an algebraic letter in an equation. A sign on a highway that reads Boston 5 Miles tells us directly and unequivocally the distance that lies ahead; an illustration in an anatomy textbook tells us directly and exactly where each part of the body is located and what it should look like; the picture of a rose in a botany textbook describes a certain kind of flower and no other. But artistic imagery conveys a different kind of information. The signs in art operate like symbols or metaphors. A symbol has to be understood here in a broad sense, as a sign that stands for a rich kind of meaning, a meaning textured with memories and colored with emotions. It goes beyond the catalog or traditional visual symbols like a halo standing for sainthood or a skull for mortality. The symbols of art include lines, colors, textures, shapes—every means of visual expression and significance.

To understand this interpretation of *symbolic*, let us take as an example the line of poetry, by Robert Burns, "My love is like a red, red rose." The word *rose* is a symbol—a simile, to be exact—for the poet's girlfriend. The poet is not telling us that his loved one has a red face, has thorns, and smells; no, the poet means that the beloved is delicate, precious, lovely, and in possession of all the other good qualities we associate with roses. The personal experience that we have of roses is transferred to the beloved. Moreover, the repetition of the word *red* intensifies those qualities and that experience.

By this simile the poet does not tell us the facts about the beloved—facts such as height, age, weight, religion, and so forth. Instead, to describe the beloved, the poet banks upon our having had a personal experience of roses, and of people, that we share with him. The language of the poetry calls up that personal experience in us. The information we get about the loved one from the poem is built upon our personal experience.

Because poetry and all art are based upon each person's experience, communication through the symbolism of art can be compared to the "knowledge" we have of other people in friendship. We may know some facts about friends, but mostly we have intuitions and feelings about them and memories of things we have lived through together. The most important "facts" we know about our friends often come in curious shapes—a smile, a walk, a turn of phrase—and are always charged with emotions. The symbolism of art, in this broad sense, communicates this kind of lived experience in layers of meaning interwoven with emotional associations.

FIG 1-20 FRIDA KAHLO [Mexican, 1907–1954], *Self-Portrait with Monkey*. 1938. Oil on Masonite, 16 × 12 in. (40.6 × 30.5 cm). Albright-Knox Art Gallery, Buffalo. Bequest of A. Conger Goodyear, 1966.

Let us explore the symbolic communication of a visual example, Frida Kahlo's *Self-Portrait with Monkey* (FIG. 1-20), by analyzing some of the signs or visual symbols in the painting. We immediately focus on Kahlo's dark, penetrating eyes, framed by thick V-shaped eyebrows, and her pursed red lips. She has turned her face to the side, but the eyes, brows, and lips almost seem to move forward and thus increase the intensity of her riveting expression. The unnatural length of her elegant neck and the pulled-back hair help to accentuate the face. In addition to the expression of her face, Kahlo communicates much more emotion-charged information about herself in the rest of the painting. A black-haired monkey, wearing a leash, puts its arm around her neck. Kahlo also wears a collar—a strange piece of bent wood. A leafy background tends to push her face forward. For some unknown but disturbing reason, Kahlo exaggerates the veins and hairy texture of the leaves, the hairlike growths on the white branches, the monkey's hair, and her own facial hair. Without investigating the fascinating biography of the painter, we sense a tense and forceful personality.

This interpretation may not be what another viewer sees in Kahlo's self-portrait or even what the artist herself precisely intended. Interpretations differ because the experience that the poet-artist has and the experience that the reader-viewer has may not be exactly the same. Experience is personal, since all people have a different personal history, even if they belong to the same general culture. The differences between people is one of the reasons why art, which conjures up personal experience, could never be a direct, one-to-one form of communication like the highway sign.

The point is that art communicates information that is something like personal knowledge—a many-layered mixture of thoughts and emotions. And to some extent the depth of that information has to do with the amount and quality of experience that the artist and the viewer have accumulated. That is why an adult probably gets more out of a Shakespeare sonnet than a twelve-year-old does—because the adult likely brings more experience to the interpretation.

The experience of art does not require a particular class of objects. Almost any material in any size or shape can give us the experience of art, provided that

Fig 1-21 Marcel Duchamp [French, 1887–1968], *Fountain*. 1917. As photographed by Alfred Stieglitz and published in *The Blind Man*, no. 2 (May 1917). Ransom Humanities Research Center, University of Texas at Austin.

No work of art in the twentieth century seems to have caused more discussion about the nature of art than Marcel Duchamp's Fountain. *In 1917 Duchamp challenged every accepted definition of art by submitting the piece as the work of an unknown artist, R. Mutt, to a New York City exhibition of independent artists that had advertised that it would accept every work submitted. The exhibition committee excluded Duchamp's work, however, not just because they thought it indecent but because they questioned whether it was art. Nevertheless, in* Fountain *Duchamp boldly asserted that art is whatever the artist says is art, even a ready-made object that he had found in the plumbing supply outlet of the J. L. Mott Iron Works company. Art, he declared, resides in the intention of the artist. But his assertion does not explain everything. If a professional plumber had displayed a urinal in a nearby shop and called it art, the historic results would not have been the same. Because Duchamp was an* established artist (the identity of R. Mutt soon became known) and because Fountain was intended to be seen in an art gallery, the public was asked to experience Fountain as art. For better or for worse, the viewer was asked to appreciate its visual symbols (its lines, shapes, texture, and color) along with its preposterous subject matter—especially now that, turned on its side, signed, and labeled, the object in Fountain was dissociated from its practical function.

we view it symbolically. Theorists were investigating the wrong thing when they were searching for objects that combined the right amount of the real and the ideal, or the right amount of representation and imagination. Art lies not in the thing itself, but in the intention of the artist and the viewer to see something as art, as Marcel Duchamp demonstrated radically in his *Fountain* (Fig. 1-21). Since artist and viewer can turn on the artistic faculty at any time, perhaps we have been asking the wrong question. Perhaps we should be asking not What is art? but When does art happen?

As stated at the beginning of this chapter, the communication of the shapes and emotions of our lived experience through art usually makes us happy. The pleasure of art comes about because the visual arts communicate something like the "knowledge" we have of persons—an awareness of the world of people and things derived from associations and feelings. As art reveals an inner self-knowledge and discloses the hidden relationships between things in the world, we are treated to some delightful surprises, to amazing discoveries, stimulating feelings, and remarkable insights. Discoveries and insights inevitably tickle the soul—or perhaps make it cry. Art ranks alongside love and friendship as one of the nicest ways to get to know life.

WHAT IS ART?

Aesthetic Theories

Aristotle   Art is imitation or mimesis.

An artist should only imitate ethically superior characters to demonstrate universal ideas.

Plato   Imitation is too removed from true reality.

Art is inspiration, or possession by the divine.

Yorubans   Art is moderate imitation.

Art is cool, detached.

Psychological Theories

Left brain, right brain theory   The left brain controls language, logic, and sequencing; the right brain controls art, intuits spatially.

Perceptual process   Art represents what the eye sees.

Conceptual process   Art depicts what the mind knows.

The Artist as Outsider Theory

Avant garde artists   Inventors of new art whose work is often condemned as primitive until it is absorbed into the mainstream.

Outsider artists   Artists whose work has not been influenced by the external art world.

Folk art   Traditional arts and crafts that are passed down within a minority culture.

Popular Theories

Realism   Art is the same as reality.

Artists who paint in a nonrealistic fashion must be incompetent or ill.

Prettiness   Art cannot be ugly.

Theories Based on the Functions of Art

Art for art's sake   Art has no function but to serve as art itself.

Religion   Art instructs, inspires, makes the invisible visible.

Morality   Art provides models for behavior.

Art inspires by its good style.

Theories Based on Comparisons between the Arts

Art as poetry   The rules of literature apply to art.

Art as music   Art affects correspondences between the senses.

Symbolic Communication Theory

Communication   Art consists of visual signs between artist and viewer.

Symbolic Communication   Art is analogous to the multileveled experience of a person in friendship.

Key Terms and Concepts

aesthetics	folk art	real
applied arts	ideal	right half of the brain
art for art's sake	inspiration	semiotics
avant garde	mimesis	symbolic communication
conceptual artists	outsider artists	synaesthesia
fine arts	perceptual art	

SUBJECTS AND THEIR USES IN ART

FIG 2-1 [Seneca Iroquois, Native American], *Rim-Dweller.* 1920–1925. Basswood mask, 11 in. (27.9 cm) high. Allegheny Reservation, New York, private collection. Photo by Peter T. Furst.

Iconography

When we first see the Seneca Iroquois mask *Rim-Dweller* (FIG. 2-1), most of us feel compelled to find out what it is about and whom the carving represents. We hope the few words in the title or on the label will help explain what we see or direct our attention to what we should see. We are curious to know all that the work of art represents and what the message is supposed to be. After all, works of art are usually about *something,* and we would like to know what that something is. We might even feel disappointed when the label tells us only that the mask is *Rim-Dweller.*

In the jargon of art criticism, we call the subjects and the symbols of works of art their **iconography.** The Greek roots of the word mean "picture writing," as though images are hieroglyphics that have to be deciphered. The concepts of iconography and style (discussed in chapters 3 to 7) are both useful tools for analyzing and discussing art. Through **style** we examine the formal properties of works of art—things like lines, color, shapes, mass, and texture—and the ways artists employ these properties. If iconography includes everything that answers the question *What* is it? style takes in everything that answers the question *How* is it done? Style and iconography are very much like the terms *form* and *content,* used frequently in literary analysis. Concerned viewers may also want to know *why* the style and iconography are what they are, or what they mean.

Significance

A word of caution: The iconography, or content or subject matter, of a work of art is only part of its meaning, or **significance.** A simple description of the iconography does not carry the sum total of the significance of a work of art. To interpret the iconography properly, one needs to understand the historical, social, economic, and psychological factors that conditioned it. Even after understanding the iconography of some work and even after appreciating how it has been done (its style), we still have a third stage to perform: we must decide how iconography and style combine and interpret each other. The interaction between iconography and style reveals the significance of the piece.

In many ways the style clarifies the iconography and the iconography manipulates the style. Together they produce something more than, and something different from, the mere addition of subject matter and form. In this instance, one plus one equals three. The significance does not equal the simple sum of style and iconography because the accomplished work of art offers a new way of seeing and opens up alternative levels of interpretation.

To most of us the Iroquois mask of *Rim-Dweller* (FIG. 2-1) probably appears distorted and amusing when we first see it. The mouth, eyes, and nose are larger than normal human features. The nose is twisted and the eyes are askew. Deep ridges are cut into the surface of the face. But when we learn about the iconography of the Iroquois mask, its style starts to make sense. In fact, the artist has embodied the significance of the work in the carving of the mask. The mask represents Rim-Dweller, the grandfather of all the grandfathers, the great spirit who lives at the edge of the world. Rim-Dweller's face was twisted when it collided with a moving mountain—the collision transforming him into a beneficent spirit. Now we can not only see why the nose and eyes are twisted but also feel in the circular lines of the face the force of the impact and sense Rim-Dweller still staggering from the blow. The hair to one side of the face accentuates the feeling of being off-balance. Perhaps there is even a hint of a kindly grandfather who helps cure diseases and drives away misfortune. The iconography and style interact with each other so that the significance of the mask is really the fusion of style and iconography, which opens up the work to interpretation.

Categories of Iconography

The titles given by artists, museums, or art books to many works of art do not often provide a lot of infor-

FIG 2-2   CLYFFORD STILL [American, 1904–1980], *1947-H-No. 3*. 1947. Oil on canvas, 91 × 57 1/4 in. (231.2 × 145.4 cm). San Francisco Museum of Modern Art. Gift of the artist. Photo by Ben Blackwell.

mation about iconography. Some titles like *Still Life with Fish* or *Landscape with Cows* merely indicate the obvious. Other titles may read *Landscape at Such-and-Such*, a place few people recognize, or *Portrait of So-and-So*, a person few people have known. All these labels chiefly indicate the general category to which the subject belongs: still life, a grouping of small objects; landscape, a nature scene; portrait, a representation of a certain person. Other categories include the nude, religious and mythological art, personification and allegory, fantasy, and subjects drawn from everyday life, or genre (pronounced *zhahn-ruh*). Works of art fall into these iconographic categories very often because they serve certain functions connected with a category. However, not every work of art can be pigeonholed into a simple category, and its category by no means fully explains the iconography of a work.

Fig 2-3 Shelton Jackson "Spike" Lee [American, 1957–] *Malcolm X.* 1992. Denzel Washington as Malcolm X. Warner Bros. Photo courtesy The Kobal Collection.

Fig 2-4 Emanuel Leutze [German, 1816–1868], *Washington Crossing the Delaware.* 1851. Oil on canvas, 12 5/12 × 21 1/4 ft. (3.78 × 6.48 m). The Metropolitan Museum of Art, New York. Gift of John Stewart Kennedy, 1897 (97.34).

But it is surprising that there are so few customary iconographic categories for visual images.

At times a traditional iconographic category is only the springboard for the artist's fantasy, and the artist produces something totally unexpected out of that category. A picture titled *Landscape of My Mind* might look like a still life. In modern times, just to be provocative, an artist might give a work an arbitrary title derived from the name of a mountain in New Hampshire or from a phrase in a book or from a chance encounter with a friend. These unfathomable, subjective associations in a title force us to look a little harder and longer at the piece to comprehend the visual significance. Modern artists might label a piece *Composition 29* or even *Untitled* to make us look at the work and not at the title. The American painter Clyfford Still (Fig. 2-2) labeled everything he did with a simple code number, sometimes adding the date of execution.

Narrative Art

Religious, mythological, and genre subjects often function as inspiring examples of courage and virtue, and tell a part of a story that in actuality has a beginning, a middle, and an end. Even though many events in religion and myth are legendary and not necessarily factual, critics since the Renaissance have called these storytelling pictures **history paintings.** Religious and mythological storytelling also appears in drawings, prints, photographs, films, and sculpture, but no one has come up with another term for referring to these dramatic images of significant human events. History painting declined at the end of the nineteenth century when it was scorned by the early modern movement as too "literary." However, the tasks of history painting have blossomed in the movies, where biblical subjects and historical events, like the life of Malcolm X (Fig. 2-3), are frequently visualized.

Within the category of narrative art, some artists try to re-create actual events in secular history, as in *Washington Crossing the Delaware* (Fig. 2-4). The

The Tale of Genji *describes Japanese
court life and the intrigues of the
aristocracy of Kyoto. Lady Shikibu
Murasaki's long novel implies subtle
relationships at court, very often
through nuanced descriptions of
flowers and costumes and the
calculated adjustment of painted
screens in a room. This illustration to*
The Tale of Genji *shows just this sort
of restrained and intimate narrative. It
is early morning—the ladies-in-
waiting, at the top and bottom on the
left, are still asleep. On the right, in
the cramped space behind a folding
screen and a blue silk curtain, a
gentleman, returning from a
rendezvous with another woman, tries
to console his weeping lover. The
masklike heads of the figures, who
wear mounds of heavy, starched
clothing, do not express much
personality or emotion because the
decorum and etiquette of court life
are the important elements. Instead,
the awkward space at the right
conveys the mood of the story.*

ancient Sumerians, Assyrians, and Egyptians, and
many more recent cultures around the world, have
also recorded victorious battles and other important
historical events in art, generally as propaganda to
enhance the power of the state. Other narrative artists
illustrate scenes from great works of literature like
Shakespeare's *Hamlet* or Lady Shikibu Murasaki's
eleventh-century Japanese novel *The Tale of Genji*
(FIG. 2-5). However, compared with the great number
of religious and mythological history paintings, only a
small percentage of history paintings illustrate secular
fact or literature.

The dramatic arrangement of the human figure in
history painting will sometimes appear in other categories as well. Small-scale mythological or biblical figures inhabiting a landscape painting may tell a story,
producing a mixture of categories that might be called
a historical landscape. Thomas Eakins, in his painting

FIG 2-6   THOMAS EAKINS [American, 1844–1916], *The Gross Clinic*. 1875. Oil on canvas, 96 × 78 in. (234.8 × 198.1 cm). Jefferson Medical College, Jefferson University, Philadelphia.

The Gross Clinic (FIG. 2-6), transformed a group portrait of Dr. Samuel Gross and his colleagues into a history painting by depicting the doctor in the midst of surgery on a young man's leg while he lectures to his medical students. Although each face reproduces the likeness of an individual, the dramatic lighting, the intense expressions, and the gesture of the patient's mother, who hides her face, also give the impression that a significant event is taking place.

As Eakins does so well in *The Gross Clinic*, history painters are expected to illustrate events with appropriate actions and expressions that will tell the story clearly and convincingly. Because of the difficulty of inventing appropriate actions and expressions and because of the nobility of its aims, European critics for many centuries considered history painting the highest kind of art. In effect, the nobility of the subject

matter determined how someone judged whether one work of art was better than another. As a consequence, the iconographic categories of art were frequently listed in a hierarchical order, with the best kind of art ranked according to the seriousness of the subject matter. In contrast, few Western critics today would maintain that certain iconographic categories are essentially better than others. Furthermore, since iconography is considered only a part of the art experience, it would be misleading to assume that employing one category automatically produces better works of art.

The standard iconographical categories are few in number perhaps because the visual arts are limited in the kinds of subject matter that they can normally treat. The visual arts do not handle very well many subjects that are popular in other media. For example, most works of fiction develop a situation through time with a series of episodes—as do love stories in which boy meets girl, girl loses boy, and so forth. But, except in the film medium and except in mythological images of the loves of the gods, like Raphael's *Galatea* (FIG. 1-5), where Galatea is attracted by the music of her unseen lover, few artists tell a love story.

Many modern paintings with narrative potential, like Philip Pearlstein's *Male and Female Nudes with Red and Purple Drape* (FIG. 2-7), appear, upon examination, rather uneventful. The few everyday props and the immobility of the figures in Pearlstein's painting weaken the initial impression that they are part of a narrative. By cropping their image at the edge of the frames, Pearlstein draws attention to their lines and shapes on the surface of the canvas. In other words, Pearlstein treats his models in the same way that a modern abstract painter would arrange shapes.

The Nude

Although artists seldom depict love stories, they often dwell on the sensuous appeal of the male or female body. For centuries in the West, the unclothed human figure in art—the **nude**—has been considered the prime example of how to do something "beautiful," with the result that it has almost become an iconographic stereotype of something artistic. Very often artists call their nude figure Venus or Aphrodite or Eve or Hercules or the Dying Gladiator or The Dance—names that fit the categories of mythology and allegory. But the main emphasis of the work is really the

FIG 2-7 PHILIP PEARLSTEIN [American, 1924–], *Male and Female Nudes with Red and Purple Drape.* 1968. Oil on canvas, 75 1/4 × 75 1/2 in. (191.2 × 191.8 cm). Hirshhorn Museum and Sculpture Garden, Smithsonian Institution, Washington, D.C. Gift of Joseph H. Hirshhorn. Photo by John Tennant.

beauty and grace and sensuousness of the human body.

It should not surprise us that the nude has been a prime topic in the visual arts. What else is as important to people, especially those in Western culture, as their own body? What other object in nature possesses the same range of emotional and psychological expression and moral attitude? And how can an artist show the body if it is covered up?

The Ancient Greeks were the first to celebrate the nude figure in major works of art like Polyclitus's nude *Spearbearer* (FIG. 2-8). Certain aspects of Greek culture explain why many Greek statues are nude. Nudity was more common in ancient Greece than in modern society: Greek men exercised in the nude and they competed in games like the Olympics in the nude. To them nudity was a sign of civilization, not a sign of shame; only barbarians wore pants. In Greek thought, man was the measure of all things, the focus of the universe, and the only subject truly worthy of study. He should use his reason, his highest faculty, to control his animal instincts and to discover the essential laws of nature. (Females had little part to play in the public life and thought of ancient Greece.)

FIG 2-8 POLYCLITUS [Greek, fifth century B.C.], *Spearbearer (Doryphoros).* Roman copy after a bronze original, original c. 440 B.C. Marble, 78 in. (198 cm) high. Minneapolis Institute of Arts.

Polyclitus expressed these high ideals in his nude figure *Spearbearer*—a heroic and perfected athlete or warrior at the peak of his powers with his intellect fully in control of his body. No emotion disturbs his concentration; no individualized traits spoil the general perfection of his body. Through work like this the Greeks made the nude in art represent humankind's aspirations for a well-ordered existence—an ideal, not an actual reproduction of reality. Polyclitus achieved the ideal perfection of the human figure by means of numerical proportions. The dimensions of his *Spearbearer*'s anatomy were determined by whole number ratios such as 2:1 or 3:1, so that, for example, the fingers were in proportion to the palm of the hand, the palm of the hand to the forearm, the forearm to the upper arm, and all parts to each other throughout the entire body. Polyclitus's point was not that these numbers represented the average size of the hand, arm, or head in human beings but that the interrelated numbers represented norms—what a head or chest or leg ought to be—since the constancy of numerical pro-portions embodied universal truths and thus an ideal beauty.

For a long time the Greeks never depicted the female nude. For instance, the goddesses of the Parthenon, including *Three Goddesses* (FIG. 2-9), and other female statutes from the golden age of ancient Greece, the fifth century B.C., were usually fully covered. Nevertheless, for the Parthenon statues the sculptor Phidias devised clothing that appears so light and transparent that it clings to the figure in some places and in fact reveals the body underneath. The interplay of bodily form and material texture actually seems to enhance sensuousness. Then, in the fourth century B.C. an Athenian sculptor named Praxiteles carved *Aphrodite of Knidos* (FIG. 2-10), a statute of a nude Aphrodite, the goddess of love and passion, and placed it in her temple on the island of Knidos. Its beauty reportedly drove some men wild.

Twentieth-century standards of female beauty are very different from those portrayed in the Greek Knidian Aphrodite, who has broad shoulders and

FIG 2-10 PRAXITELES [Greek], *Aphrodite of Knidos*. Roman copy after a fourth-century-B.C. original. Marble, 80 in. (203.2 cm) high. Rome, Vatican Museums. Alinari/Art Resource, New York.

FIG 2-11 [Indian], *Yakshi (Tree Goddess)*. Early Andhra period, first century B.C. From the East Gate of the Great Stupa at Sanchi, India. Photo courtesy ACSAA, University of Michigan, Ann Arbor.

broad hips and a big, almost masculine frame. The discrepancy between our fashions and the Greeks' ideals exists in part because Praxiteles constructed his female figure by regularizing its proportions. In *Aphrodite* the distance between the breasts is the same as the distance between a breast and the navel. The same measurement controls the distance between the navel and the groin. As a consequence, the breasts on Greek statutes often do not seem to be organic parts of the body, since they are separated too much. Furthermore, the Greek artist conceived the goddess as grand, imposing, and larger-than-life.

The ancient Greeks established in the West the possibility that male and female nudity in art stands for a heroic and idealized existence.

Whereas the Greeks eventually gave roughly equal emphasis to the attractiveness of the male and female bodies, artists and patrons since the Renaissance have more often emphasized the female nude as seen by the male gaze, which turns it into an object of desire.

Although some cultures reserve nudity for only certain undesirable types such as prisoners, victims, or the inhabitants of hell, other cultures accept nudity in the depiction of the human figure as a matter of course—without the connotations of Greek nudity. Alongside Buddhist art in India, there often appear very sensuous and appealing nude representations of popular gods of fertility—the male god called Yaksha and the female called Yakshi. The famous *Yakshi* (FIG. 2-11) serves as a carved stone bracket on the East Gate of the Great Stupa (Shrine) at Sanchi (see FIG. 16-27). Her limbs are entwined in a fruit-filled tree, and she strikes the tree trunk with her left foot in the belief that the touch of a beautiful woman will cause the tree to blossom. Her whole body twists in voluptuous, sinuous S-curves. She welcomes the visitor to the austere Buddhist stupa with the promise of the pleasures of the senses. The frank sensuality of the Yakshi differs from the reserved and ideal sensuality of the Parthenon goddesses.

FIG 2-12 *Hall of Bulls.* C. 13,000 B.C. From Lascaux cave, Dordogne, France. Photo courtesy Gallery of Prehistoric Art, New York.

Religious Art

Works of **religious art** like the Iroquois mask and the Greek and Indian sculpture make tangible the gods, goddesses, and spirits, the beliefs and hopes of a people. This crucial role dates back to the very beginning of art. Anthropologists theorize that Stone Age cave dwellers drew animals on the walls deep within the earth, as in *Hall of Bulls* (FIG. 2-12) at Lascaux, France, to secure the well-being of the community in this life or in the future by controlling, through art, the forces that were beyond human powers. They speculate that the animals were depicted there in order to obtain magical power to ensure success in the hunt or to ensure the propagation of the herds. The prehistoric painters may have realized that visual images, which can create a presence and stir emotions, have a natural magic that makes them the immediate ally of religion.

The broad category of religious art likely abounded in every ancient culture, since almost every civilization before the modern era was permeated with religion's sense of the mysterious—much more so than is the secular Western society of today. When many natural events received supernatural explanations, religion used to be a much more integral part of everyday life. The arts, with their powerful resources to stimulate the imagination, served religions all over the world. The first impulse toward the visual arts in most societies seems to have been to use the magic of images to reach unseen forces to control their power or solicit their help.

Their pervasive religious function raises a special problem about enjoying religious works. As they are now displayed for our aesthetic pleasure, many reli-

FIG 2-13 [Bamana People], male and female antelope figures (Chi Wara dance headdresses). Late nineteenth– early twentieth century. Wood, brass tacks, string, cowrie shells, iron, quills; male, 38 1/2 in. (97.8 cm) high; female, 31 1/2 in. (79.8 cm) high. From Mali, Africa. Art Institute of Chicago. Ada Turnbull Hertle Fund (1965.6-7).

The Chi Wara association teaches the cooperation of Bamanan men and women in food production. Only the men, however, participate in the initiation rites in which the male and female Antelope Dance headdresses are worn. Roy Sieber, an authority on African art, explained the meaning of the performance:

The animals carved on the headdress are composites of different species of antelopes. To the Bamana, these forest animals, with their grace and strength, embody the ideal qualities of champion farmers. The male is the sun, and the female is the earth; the fawn on the female's back symbolizes human beings. The fiber costumes worn with these head-dresses represent water. As there must be a union of sun, earth, and water for plants to grow, there must be cooperation between men and women possessing the requisite physical and moral qualities to ensure that agricultural processes . . . take place on schedule to ensure a successful harvest.[3]

gious objects have been disconnected from the context where they once elicited spiritual power. The Iroquois mask *Rim-Dweller* (FIG. 2-1), now in a private collection, once functioned in the living religious life of the Iroquois people. Such masks continue to be carved and worn by members of the Society of Faces in dances during the great midwinter rites and other festivals, to cure disease and purify the Iroquois houses. The masks are respected by the Iroquois people for their spiritual power. The striking *Antelope Dance Headdresses* (FIG. 2-13), made by the Bamana people of Mali, Africa, and now on display in the Art Institute of Chicago, were actually worn in ritual dances to praise and honor the heroic creator of agriculture, *Chi Wara.* Exquisitely wrought medieval *reliquaries* (containers or shrines for storing sacred relics),

Dancers wearing headdresses. Photo by Eliot Elisofon. Photographic Archives, National Museum of African Art, Washington, D.C.

FIG 2-14 Follower of Eilbertus [German], *Arm Reliquary.* C. 1180. Gilt silver over oak core, champlevé enamel; 20 in. (50.8 cm) high. From Lower Saxony, Hildesheim, Germany. Cleveland Museum of Art. Gift of John Huntington Art and Polytechnic Trust (30.739).

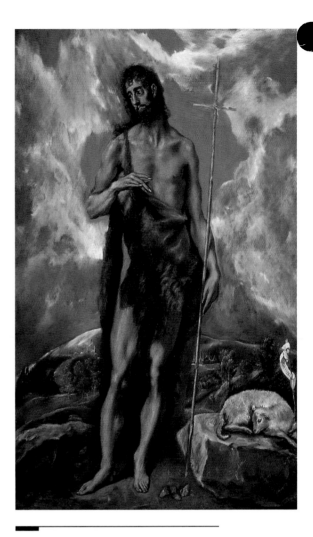

FIG 2-15 EL GRECO (Doménikos Theotokópoulos) [Spanish, 1541–1614], *Saint John the Baptist.* 1597–1603. Oil on canvas. The Fine Arts Museums of San Francisco. Museum purchase, gift of various donors.

like the silver gilt and enamel *Arm Reliquary* (FIG. 2-14), now in the Cleveland Museum of Art, once contained the bones or other sacred remains of a saint who was venerated by the faithful in hopes of obtaining answers to their prayers. Lovely statutes of the Virgin and Child, now in a museum, once stood in a church where they inspired mothers to pray for the health and safety of their children.

All these works lose something when they are isolated in private collections and museums and appreciated merely as pieces of art. In fact, groups of people have protested that their sacred objects do not belong in such displays and have demanded that they be returned to where they came from. Some groups of

Native Americans want objects housed in museum collections returned to them because of the sacred character of these objects—even though the museums bought or received the items in good faith years ago. In recent years some of their requests have been honored.

The interpretation of religious iconography is not always easy, even though the religious objects may once have had mass appeal. In the Christian tradition of religious art, artists frequently made images of saints who wear halos to indicate their heavenly status. They usually hold a symbol or an attribute by which people can identify who they are. In the painting *Saint John the Baptist* (FIG. 2-15), by the Spanish artist El Greco, St. John is accompanied by a lamb because John iden-

Part 1: The Nature of Art

Fig 2-16 Andres Serrano [American, 1950–], *Blood Cross*. 1985. Cibachrome, silicone, plexiglas, wood frame; 40 × 60 in. (101.6 × 152.4 cm). Photo courtesy Paula Cooper Gallery, New York.

Andres Serrano, a New Yorker whose family comes from Cuba and Honduras, deliberately made his poster-sized photograph of a small Plexiglas cross filled with animal blood on Good Friday. Looming against a dramatically lit background, Blood Cross symbolizes for the artist not only Christ's sacrifice but also all the blood shed because of the introduction of Western religion into the Americas.

Serrano has made a series of works that combine conventional religious images with essential bodily fluids like blood and milk. Blood Cross has a companion composition called Milk Cross, *which symbolizes both the nurturing role of religion and also its white purity when it helped squelch native cultures in America. Serrano's simple raw images send a powerful new jolt of electricity through traditional Christian iconography.*

tified Jesus Christ with the words, "Behold the lamb of God."[1] In medieval art, a young knight dressed in a suit of armor and lancing a dragon at his feet can be identified by these attributes as St. George, who supposedly rescued a princess by his heroic deed. There was a time when almost everyone in the West knew these saints and their attributes. Now even Westerners probably have to look them up in a specialized dictionary of symbols.

Many people in America, even if they never went to church or synagogue, probably know the story of *Adam and Eve* and the story of the *Nativity* (Christ's birth at Bethlehem), the *Adoration of the Shepherds*, the Visit of the *Three Magi (Wise Men)*, and the *Crucifixion*. Since the religious iconography of these events still forms part of the general culture, contemporary artists like the photographer Andres Serrano can bank on the public's awareness of their meaning as he transforms them into a personal exploration like *Blood Cross* (Fig. 2-16). Artists in the past could presume that the audience for whom they worked knew the religious stories mentioned in the Bible as well as in the legendary material that for centuries expanded the biblical narrative. For example, the Bible never says that there were three wise men, only that there were three gifts—gold, frankincense, and myrrh.

FIG 2-17 GIAMBOLOGNA (Giovanni da Bologna) [Italian, 1529–1608], *Mercury.* 1564. Bronze, 24 11/16 in. (62.7 cm). Vienna, Kunsthistorisches Museum. Alinari/Art Resource.

FIG 2-18 HAESEMHLIYAWN [Tsimshian, Native American], *Totem Pole.* C. 1865. Cedar wood. Gitwancool, Upper Skeena River, British Columbia. Photo by Peter T. Furst.

A totem pole like this very old one represents the ancestors of the family and the spirits who will help them. The lowest part of the pole is pierced by a large hole surrounded by twelve small human figures. It probably served as a passageway to and from the house and represents the "hole-through-the-sky," the cosmic hole through which the ancestor emerged into the present world or traveled to obtain religious knowledge and ritual items. Near the top of the pole, a migrating wolf is taking away Ligi-ralwil. Below that appears a grizzly bear splitting open while a wolf bites his entrails. The figures on the totem pole do not narrate the entire story but rather symbolize or identify the myth of when the animal's spirit and gifts were transferred to the ancestor.

Mythological Art

The once familiar characters from Greek and Roman **mythology**—stories about the gods and goddesses, and heroes and heroines of an ancient culture—now pose problems for the modern viewer. Not many people today could identify the flying male nude in FIG. 2-17 as the god Mercury, the messenger of the Greek gods. The winged feet and winged hat are the attributes that identify the figure. Mercury sometimes carries the *caduceus* (pronounced kah-*doo*-see-us), a winged magic wand intertwined with snakes. The caduceus became a symbol of healing and is still used to identify the medical profession.

In previous centuries Greek and Roman classical authors, who described their gods, were a fundamental part of almost every Western person's education, at least among the upper classes. It was common to assign a moral message to the Greek myths, and many mythological works have one. To interpret these messages, educated people read the Latin poet Ovid's *Metamorphoses,* a popular source that used to be called the painter's Bible. Today we probably have to look up the stories of Hercules or of Niobe and her children in an encyclopedia.

Other cultures also have an elaborate set of mythological symbols, characters, and stories that appear in their art and also need identification and explanation for us to appreciate their significance. At least since the early nineteenth century, the Tsimshian and other people living on the northwest coast of North America have carved totem poles (FIG. 2-18) with stacked animal and human forms that can only puzzle the average outside viewer. The poles were originally erected immediately in front of the door to the communal house. Totem poles are like heraldic devices that identified a family by illustrating the animals and human figures who founded the family's noble lineage. More important, the totem pole advertised the rights and privileges that linked the family to these supernatural powers.

Personification and Allegory

In modern times personifications and allegories seem like strange forms of subject matter until we realize that some common examples still exist. A **personification** is a human figure that stands for a virtue or some other abstract concept. For instance, the giant statute in New York harbor, of a classically draped woman who holds up a torch, stands for liberty (FIG. 2-19). The blindfolded woman carrying a sword and a set of balanced scales personifies justice. This personification often stands as a reminder of the principle of justice in courtrooms and courthouses. The gods of Greece and Rome often personify virtues or ideas: Venus means beauty or love; Mars is the god of war. Apollo, the sun god, represents culture and is the embodiment of male physical beauty.

Artists and patrons in the Middle Ages, and in the Renaissance too, were especially fond of personification. The statutes of biblical David by the Renaissance sculptors Donatello (FIG. 17-8) and Michelangelo (FIG. 17-18) are often said to personify the city of Florence, defiant in the face of larger enemies. Some modern advertising campaigns try to carry on the tradition of personification. Think of the Pillsbury Dough Boy or Big Boy (FIG. 2-20), Colonel Sanders or Mr. Clean. The first two do not stand for a virtue or an ideal but merely identify the product. The second two—the amiable colonel and the powerful Mr. Clean—might suggest qualities inherent in the product.

An allegory is very much like a personification, in that it stands for an idea; in fact, figures involved in an allegory are often personifications. Strictly speaking, however, an **allegory** means two or more personifications performing some action that has a conceptual or moral message. For example, two figures fighting one another might represent virtue overcoming vice. Allegory is an old method of narration that nearly dis-

FIG 2-19   FRÉDÉRIC-AUGUSTE BARTHOLDI [French, 1834–1904], *Liberty Enlightening the World.* 1871–1886. Copper sheets beaten into large forms (repoussé technique) over structural framework designed by Alexandre-Gustave Eiffel [French, 1832–1923]; pedestal by Richard Morris Hunt [American, 1827-1895]; 151 ft. (46.02 m) high. New York Harbor, Liberty Island. Photo: National Park Service.

FIG 2-20   Big Boy logo. Photo © 1989 Stephen Farley.

Fig 2-21 Robert Colescott [American, 1925–], *Knowledge of the Past Is the Key to the Future: Matthew Henson and the Quest for the North Pole.* 1986. Acrylic on canvas, 90 × 114 in. (228.6 × 289.6 cm). Phyllis Kind Gallery, New York and Chicago.

In his work Robert Colescott does not paint traditional allegorical figures so much as historical characters who have become stereotypes in the West for virtue and achievement. The black Matthew Henson, who fought alongside the white Robert C. Peary to reach the North Pole in 1909, was all but forgotten when Peary received international fame and glory for his achievement. In this painting, Colescott depicts several other historical figures as blacks, thereby reversing racial stereotypes. In the upper left, Salome presents King Herod with the head of a black John the Baptist. In the lower foreground, an Elvis type embraces an enchained slave. Jesus Christ, in the upper right, is half black and half white. The painting provokes questions like What if Jesus were the product of an interracial marriage?—as was Colescott himself. Colescott's mixing of the races in history may not teach a lesson for the future, but it exposes, through ironic humor, the absurdity of stereotyping.

appeared in modern times, although political cartoonists in the cold war era employed it when they portrayed Uncle Sam confronting the Russian bear. This form of iconography has made a surprising comeback in contemporary works where artists like Robert Colescott (Fig. 2-21) use a very personal kind of allegorical figure to confront issues of public concern.

Genre

Some artists deliberately avoid high-minded iconography taken from the Bible, mythology, or military history and prefer to depict scenes from everyday life, or **genre.** Emanuel de Witte's genre painting *Interior with a Woman Playing a Virginals* (Fig. 2-22) appears to illustrate daily life in a prosperous Dutch home in seventeenth-century Holland. The Dutch in that period were among the first to exploit this kind of iconography by showing ordinary domestic life and lively tavern scenes. The appearance of genre iconography probably indicated that the ordinary life of the middle and lower classes was gaining in importance.

FIG 2-22   EMANUEL DE WITTE [Dutch, 1617–1692], *Interior with a Woman Playing a Virginals.* C. 1660. Oil. Montreal Museum of Art. Photo by Brian Merrett.

Everything in this large and well-appointed home is neat and tidy, except for the clothes and sword draped across the chair placed diagonally on the left. They belong to a military officer, barely visible in the bed, for whom the woman plays her music. Very likely the implied liaison between them was illicit. The sensuousness and sinfulness suggested in the foreground (bed, clothes, and music) contrast with the symbols of moral cleanliness in the distance (the pump and bucket and the industrious maid).

Just as mythological or biblical iconography can tell a story, so genre subjects may tell a story, usually one with a moral message. The objects within seemingly innocuous and realistic genre pictures often have symbolic meanings or make reference to proverbs that deliver a moral message. On closer examination, for example, de Witte's *Interior* also teaches a lesson about clean living. Non-Dutch critics, who frequently missed the moral message, often found genre subjects the worst kind of art because they were so matter-of-fact and down-to-earth. These critics denigrated genre artists, who they thought merely copied what went on around them.

In the eighteenth century, during the Age of Reason, genre scenes became vehicles for social satire. For example, the English artist William Hogarth published several series of satirical engravings, such as *The Harlot's Progress* or *The Rake's Progress* (FIG. 2-23), genre subjects with a moral intent. In them Hogarth exposed and ridiculed the vices of high society so that they might be avoided and public morality might be improved—although it is unlikely that his engravings had the effect on society he desired.

FIG 2-23   WILLIAM HOGARTH [English, 1697–1764], *He takes possession,* plate 1, from *The Rake's Progress,* New York, Metropolitan Museum of Art. Harris Brisbane Dick Fund, 1932 (32.35.[28]).

The Rake's Progress, in eight separate scenes, tells the story of the misadventures of Tom Rakewell. In the first scene, plate I, Tom drops out of college when he inherits bundles of money from his miserly old father. While being measured for new clothes by a tailor, Tom spurns his pregnant sweetheart, Sarah Young, and sets out upon a life of lavish spending, carousing, and gambling.

Fig 2-24 SOPHIE RIVERA [American], *Woman and Daughter in Subway.* C. 1982. Silver gelatin print, 16 × 20 in. (40.6 × 50.8 cm). Courtesy the artist.

Moralizing genre is still prevalent today, although it has primarily shifted from painting and printmaking to photography and TV. Despite the great relaxation of the rules of public morality in modern times, many TV sitcoms deal with ordinary family life while developing an instructive moral. Photographers likewise have extended genre iconography into the twentieth century, since they often capture scenes of everyday life in their work. The photographer Sophie Rivera, for example, has documented the life of the Puerto Rican minority in New York in a series of photographs taken on the subway. Her *Woman and Daughter in Subway* (FIG. 2-24) captures not just the commonplace event of a subway ride but also the innocence of the child and the pride and fierce protectiveness of the mother.

Sometimes the artist seems to go too far, especially with genre subjects, by trying to make the viewer feel emotions for iconography that may not deserve them. Sometimes the artist tries to make the viewer feel emotions for the wrong reasons. This kind of art is labeled **sentimental.**

In sentimental art, the means used to arouse our feelings are usually exaggerated. Many people would call Adolphe William Bouguereau's (pronounced Booger-oh's) *Indigent Family* (FIG. 2-25) sentimental. Even after taking into account the different responses of different individuals, it can be argued that the emotions aroused by the work's sentimentality do not represent a normal or proportionate reaction to the subject. The artist tugs at our heartstrings with an image of pathetic-looking children that is sure to catch our sympathy. But because our sympathy is aroused for false reasons, our sentimental reaction ignores the root causes of the problem the artist has depicted. Both Rivera's *Woman and Daughter* and Bouguereau's *Indigent Family* have appealing children, but the attitude of the mother on the subway—a mature and healthy human reaction—undercuts the potential sentiment in the photographer's work.

Fig 2-25 William Bouguereau [French, 1825–1905], *Indigent Family.* 1865. Oil on canvas, 48 × 60 1/4 in. (122 × 153 cm). City Museum and Art Gallery, Birmingham, England.

In the nineteenth century, when there was no system of government welfare to support a mother with dependent children, the death of a husband often spelled disaster for a woman. The artist wanted the viewer to have sympathy with this mother who was forced to beg for charity. However, William Bouguereau was afraid of upsetting his middle-class audience by showing a family that was genuinely starving and homeless. Instead, he made them appealing and attractive. Their features are full and smooth and clean. Their clothes are clean and made of a silky material. In front of grand and noble architecture, he arranged them in a pyramid that resembles the classical composition of traditional images of the Madonna and Child. Consequently, we are attracted to this lovely group for the wrong reasons. The sympathetic emotions that the work arouses are false. A critic in 1865 rightly called it middle-class sentimentality.

Portraits

Except for religious subjects, artists have probably made more **portraits,** or representations of an individual, than any other kind of iconography. Even now, when the ordinary job of portrait making has been taken over by the photographer, painters and sculptors are still copying the likeness of other people and of themselves. Portraits are plentiful because people instinctively want to examine their self-image and to record and preserve what they look like. Friends have used portraits to keep the memory of someone dear to them alive. Moreover, a portrait may be used to expose or interpret the character of an individual, as in a propaganda portrait promoting someone as a courageous leader. Whenever we interpret someone's personality in a portrait, however, we must remember that artists continue to express themselves even when they copy someone else's likeness. So it is not always easy to tell if the characterization in a portrait derives from the sitter's personality or is a reflection of the personality and background of the artist.

FIG 2-26 [Egyptian], *Methethy, a Palace Official,* detail of head. Old Kingdom, mid-third millenium B.C. Wood with gesso and paint, 31 5/8 × 6 3/8 × 15 15/16 in. (80.3 × 16.2 × 40.5 cm). Nelson-Atkins Museum of Art, Kansas City, Missouri. Purchase of Nelson Trust (51-1).

Artists have not always made exact likenesses of individuals. The ancient Egyptians made rather formal portraits of people, but most of them seem very much alike until we learn to recognize subtle interpretive differences. In the Egyptian piece *Methethy* (FIG. 2-26), it takes some close examination and comparison with other statues to see the face as a portrait. The intensity of the inlaid eyes and the weak mouth and chin help make Methethy an individual. In contrast to Egyptians, ancient Greek artists were generally satisfied with portraying only standard character types such as youth, wise old man, or aged woman even when they were representing an individual. Most sculptors in West Africa seem to have wanted only generalized and abstracted representations of individuals.

The ancient Romans, however, specialized in distinctive, particularized portraiture (FIG. 1-10), perhaps because Rome was, in the beginning, a society of rugged individuals. The Romans in their culture also stressed the importance of a person's family and the family's distinguished ancestors. It was close to a religious duty for the Romans to keep in their home exact replicas of the faces of their ancestors.

Although European artists in the subsequent Middle Ages seldom depicted the exact features of a person, because spiritual reality was more important to them, portraits again became popular in the Renaissance when individual achievement on earth was once more prized. In general, it takes a certain degree of awareness of the worth of an individual for a society to begin to want to make portraits. Having one's portrait made is usually an ego trip.

Portrait artists are generally expected to flatter the individual sitter or at least portray the individual at her or his best. We still expect as much when we pay a professional photographer to take our portrait. A skilled portrait artist can also use artistic means to reveal the sitter's personality, although not every artist in the past has tried to depict what the modern age is interested in—the psychological character of an individual.

Artists may have first attempted to expose psychological character when they examined themselves and did self-portraits. Self-portraits are painted because it is always cheaper to look in the mirror than to hire a model. More important, when artists are committed to expressing themselves, revealing their inner life, or examining their role as creator in works of art, they might naturally want to examine their own persona, in a self-portrait. Frida Kahlo was an artist with such a commitment who did numerous self-portraits, including *Self-Portrait with Monkey* (FIG. 1-20). So did Van Gogh (see p. 11), and so did Rembrandt (see p. 79). Alice Neel painted her self-portrait (FIG. 2-27), sitting on the edge of a striped chair in the nude, paintbrush in hand, when she was eighty years old. She did not spare us a sardonic view of her sagging flesh, although she painted her head, glasses on, upright and alert. Her head appears at the very top of the canvas, against the violet color of the background that vibrates through the stripes of the chair and the contours of her body.

Portraits come in all shapes and sizes. A bust-length portrait, like Kahlo's *Self-Portrait*, which includes the head and shoulders, obviously concentrates on the features of the face. Other types of portraits include half length, from the waist up; three-quarter length, from the knees up; and full length. Occasionally artists portray a profile view of the face, like the relief portraits of presidents on coins, a tradition that goes back to the profile portraits of emperors on ancient Roman coins. A group portrait is possible in any portrait length, and it depicts several people together, usually members of a family, as in John Singer Sargent's *The Daughter's of Edward D. Boit* (FIG. 2-28) and Alice Neel's *The Family* (FIG. 2-29), or members of an organization. The type of portrait, whether bust, half length, full length, and so forth, is one of the first decisions the artist has to make, before she or he starts.

Half length portraits are popular, but full-length, full-sized portraits can be special and grand. They are relatively rare because not only does the artist need a large piece of canvas or a large quantity of bronze or a

FIG 2-27   ALICE NEEL [American, 1900–1984], *Nude Self-Portrait*. 1980. Oil on canvas, 54 × 40 in. (138.5 × 102.6 cm). National Portrait Gallery, Smithsonian Institution, Washington, D.C. Art Resource, New York.

big block of marble for producing one, but also the owner needs a rather palatial residence in which to display the finished work. In imitation of the full-length state portraits of kings and queens, it became fashionable about one hundred years ago for millionaires in America to commission full-length portraits for their grand estates. Furthermore, commemorative portraits of national heroes and heroines in public places tend to be full-length statutes.

Most portraits include the hands, which may be doing or holding something significant, and also include a good bit of the clothing, or costume, that someone is wearing. Often the costume counts for more than does the sitter's rather bland or stereotyped face. In older societies with strict divisions between the social classes, it was generally more important to all concerned that the costume indicate the person's social status than that the artist capture subtle facial features. The setting and the objects in the room also help reveal character or even the sitter's profession.

In the group portrait, *The Family*, twentieth-century portrait specialist Neel has father, mother, and daughter sitting close together in a circular grouping on the same sofa, all harmonized in variations of warm brown accented by violet. Their three slightly enlarged heads—serious and intent—all slump forward on their hunched shoulders. Neel has the ability to expose the character lying beneath the surface appearances and to make her sitters represent the times in which they live.

In the past women artists often concentrated on making portraits because they lacked the training needed to depict the human figure in a variety of poses and actions as in history paintings. On moral grounds women were officially excluded from instruction in art schools and academies, where, until the mid–nineteenth century, most of the nude models were male. They continued to be excluded even when most artists' models became female. This meant that women often never learned how to draw the human figure properly and were thus at a disadvantage when it came to more ambitious religious or mythological iconography. Their lack of training in history painting, which the art world at one time considered to be the greatest artistic achievement, is a major reason why so few became famous artists years ago. However, it does

FIG 2-29   ALICE NEEL [American, 1900–1984], *The Family (John Gruen, Jane Wilson, and Julia).* 1970. Oil on canvas, 58 × 60 in. (147.3 × 152.4 cm). © The Estate of Alice Neel. Courtesy Robert Miller Gallery, New York

not follow that portraits or any other subjects are necessarily feminine iconography. It would be hard to specify a strictly male or female iconography.

Landscapes

Like the sense of individual worth needed for portraiture, a certain respect for nature is required for **landscape art,** or works in which the major focus is on nature. Although Roman artists practiced landscape painting, the other-worldly attitude of the Middle Ages produced few earthly landscapes. Renaissance artists once again began painting landscapes because of a new respect for this world and in part because the Romans had done it.

Asian cultures have appreciated views of nature in art for a much longer time because of their unique history and religious beliefs. Western biblical religion

places human beings at the head of nature. Chinese Taoist religion stresses atunement and identity with nature, and Chinese Ch'an Buddhism encourages the cultivation of quiet and openness to moments of illumination. In these Eastern religions a man or a woman is not superior to nature but plays a small part in the scheme of creation. For centuries Chinese artists have striven to capture the spirit of nature through close study of each of its details. The forms of nature are boiled down to their essence and skillfully reproduced by the artist with a distinctive dash that animates everything. A Chinese landscape invites the mind to travel from place to place through nature and to find at each resting spot food for contemplation and consolation for the return to real life. The distinct Chinese culture gives life to a distinct style of painting.

In the first half of the tenth century, when Li Ch'êng painted *A Solitary Temple Amid Clearing Peaks* (FIG. 2-30), no major artist in Europe was painting landscapes. In fact, no significant European artist would care enough about nature to paint a true landscape for another four hundred years. In Li Ch'êng's landscape the mind's journey begins with the little figures emerging down the path and across the wooden bridge in the lower left. Another figure enters the gates of the monastery. Partially glimpsed steps lead up to the pagoda on the hill, from which one can contemplate the steep mountains across the mist-filled valley or contemplate the jagged silhouettes of dark trees against the light mist. The tall format of Li Ch'êng's landscape, painted on a silk hanging scroll, presupposes more space to the left and right, and the empty area above the mountains suggests limitless space beyond. The Chinese artist does not allow us to take in the whole panorama at once—in fact, different parts of the landscape are seen from different points of view.

Until the nineteenth century, artists in the West seldom painted landscapes directly from nature; landscapes were almost always created in the artist's workshop from conceptions about nature or, at best, from sketches made outdoors. Furthermore, until the nineteenth century the painting of landscapes was not generally held in high regard. People thought the landscape painter was merely copying nature and not doing anything very original. To justify the painting of landscape by elevating the theme, artists frequently made

FIG 2-31 CHILDE HASSAM [American, 1859–1935], *Afternoon Sky, Harney Desert.* 1908. Oil on canvas, 20 1/8 × 30 1/8 in. (51.1 × 76.5 cm). Portland Art Museum. Gift of August Berg, Henrietta E. Failing, Winslow B. Ayer, William D. Wheelwright, I. N. Fleischner, estate of D. P. Thompson.

nature the setting for some biblical or mythological event. These landscapes usually depicted a golden age when men and women lived a simple life close to nature and gods walked the earth. Such landscapes illustrated not nature in the raw but an idealized image of what nature should be like.

Since about the mid–nineteenth century, many artists have adopted a fresh approach to landscape painting and attempted to reproduce nature just as it appears. They have actually taken their paints outdoors and tried to capture a small corner of nature as it impressed them at the time. The direct approach to nature of artists like the American Impressionist Childe Hassam (FIG. 2-31), whose view of the Harney Desert in Oregon shows only flat land and broad sky, does not often result in grand compositions or strong

emotional associations. Instead, artists like Hassam are able to find delight in simple things, in the variety of textures, in the play of sunlight, and in the ordinary. None of the actual scenes that they paint would probably have caught our attention without the intervention of the artist's sensitivity.

Artists depicting landscape today are no longer permitted such innocence about nature now that we realize how fragile and imperiled the ecology is. Some contemporary artists like Neil Jenney cannot help but express concern about the environmental crisis and the threat of apocalypse when they take up the tradition of landscape painting. In *Meltdown Morning* (FIG. 2-32) Jenny views a woodland, the symbol of the once great North American wilderness, through an enormous slit, as though from a bunker. The heavy dark

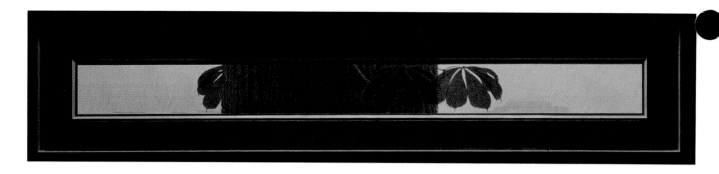

FIG 2-32 NEIL JENNEY [American, 1945–], *Meltdown Morning*. 1975. Oil on panel, 25 3/4 × 112 1/2 in. (65.4 × 285.8 cm). Philadelphia Museum of Art. Purchase of Samuel S. White III and Vera White Collection (by exchange) and funds contributed by Daniel W. Dietrich Foundation in honor of Mrs. H. Lloyd Gates.

frame with its bold lettering visually threatens the delicate light, the fragile leaves, and the pale blue sky.

Still Lifes

A **still life** can be any deliberate grouping of small inanimate objects; they almost never have people in them. Like landscapes, still life compositions have had limited appeal to sculptors. In addition to the artful arrangement of the objects in a still life, the nature of the objects can be of some interest because the objects chosen may symbolize or otherwise express some significance.

Still life became a specialty among a considerable number of Flemish and Dutch painters of the seventeenth century, many of whose works depict a rich display of food that signified abundance, perhaps even excess. Other Dutch artists painted a plain table set with simple foods, as did Pieter Claesz. in *Breakfast Still Life* (FIG. 2-33) (the Dutch commonly ate ham and bread and beer and fish for breakfast or other light meals). Sometimes the pictures of food or other objects contain hidden meanings usually relating to the passing of time and the transience of sensory pleasures in life. The meal in the still life might be partially eaten so that it looks as though the people suddenly left the table in disarray. A skull on the table is the clearest indication of the theme of *vanitas* (vanity)—the reminder that all things must pass away.

Still life iconography attracted Cubist artists in the second and third decades of the twentieth century, and in the 1960s a movement called Pop Art once again rejuvenated the form. Pop Art added a new twist to the iconography of still life by depicting common modern objects and popular images from advertising and other mass media. For example, a Campbell Soup can by Andy Warhol (FIG. 19-7) fits the still life category, even though it is an arrangement of only one item. The amusing images of Pop Art also make the serious point that meaningful iconography should now come from popular culture and from the mass media that saturate our imagination.

Fantasy Art

Within the limits of their culture, it has always been possible for artists to depict a **fantasy,** an illusion or a vision of something that exists only in their imagination. Landscapes before the nineteenth century were often not a reconstruction of an exact place but an imaginative combination of hills and valleys, trees and streams actually experienced in different locations and at various times by the artist. In many cases the visual reenactment of a traditional mythological, religious, or historical event came fresh from the artist's imagination—unless the artist was merely following a prototype—since few artists were there when the event happened. Hieronymus Bosch's *Garden of Earthly*

52

Part 1: The Nature of Art

FIG 2-33 PIETER CLAESZ. [Dutch, 1597 or 1598–1661], *Breakfast Still Life.* 1641. Oil on panel, 27 7/8 × 39 in. (70.8 × 99.1 cm). Frances Lehman Loeb Art Center, Vassar College, Poughkeepsie, New York. Gift of Mrs. Lloyd Williams, in memory of her father, Daniel Cottier.

Delights (see p. 55) contains a most vivid fantasy of biblical hell. Modern mass media, especially the movies and television, constantly churn out a seductive kind of fantasy, not only in science fiction and thrillers but in images of supposedly real life showing violence without consequence to anyone, wealth without work, or sex without personal involvement.

Many modern painters and sculptors like to work even more explicitly from their imagination and visualize even their more bizarre or weird mental images or fantasies. They like to change and distort reality and recombine it, if for no other reason than to stress how much our imagination creates what we call reality. The twentieth-century movement called Surrealism especially encouraged artists to depict the images of their dreams and the fantasies of their subconscious mind. The Surrealists in fact believed that dreams captured the truth of things and the meaning of life better than the rational mind. They liked to explore the psyche by illustrating the illogical and chance juxtaposition of very disparate things. Salvador Dali's small Surrealist painting *The Persistence of Memory* (FIG. 2-34) illustrates a fantastic dream where enlarged watches melt and are devoured by ants. The crazy objects in the picture are sharply focused and brightly lit, characteristics that weirdly exaggerate their reality.

FIG 2-34 SALVADOR DALI [Spanish, 1904–1989], *The Persistence of Memory.* 1931. Oil on canvas, 9 1/2 × 13 in. (24.1 × 33 cm). Museum of Modern Art, New York. Given anonymously. Photo © 1994 The Museum of Modern Art, New York.

FIG 2-35 WILLEM DE KOONING [American, 1904–], *Woman IV.* 1952–1953. Oil, enamel and charcoal on canvas, 59 × 46 1/4 in. (149.9 × 117.5 cm). Nelson-Atkins Museum of Art, Kansas City, Missouri. Gift of William Inge (56-128).

Dali painted everything, real or imagined, in the same precise technique and in the same bright light, to convince us that, as in a disturbed dream, these impossible things can actually happen.

Very often, when illustrating a fantasy, the Surrealists and other modern artists will continue to work in the traditional iconographical categories, such as landscape, portrait, or still life. Dali's *Persistence of Memory* could be classified a landscape, but its disruption of the normal expectations of a landscape painting is an essential part of its Surrealistic message.

Abstract and Nonobjective Art

Many of the old categories of iconography are thriving in modern art. Only history painting has been neglected, and even it has reappeared in photography and the movies. However, a large portion of modern art, especially **abstract art,** which emphasizes the formal properties of art, appears to be without iconography or has iconography that seems impossible to comprehend. Sometimes the viewer can recognize people or things in abstract works—or can recognize at least small parts of people or things. This fragmentation and distortion of reality can occasionally be explained by modern art's emphasis on strong emotional expression that exaggerates some aspects of reality to convey the artist's feeling about them. In other cases abstract artists like to strip appearances bare and reduce things to their essences so that the underlying forms of things stand out clearly. In still other instances modern artists choose as their subject the actual creative process of art, which they make explicit, often at the expense of a lucid iconography. Their work focuses on the making of art and even the changing appearance of the work over time.

Even identifiable objects or fragments of objects in abstract art are not always reliable clues to the meaning of the work. Modern artists often confess that they merely used a subject as an initial impulse to make an arrangement of forms or to express themselves in their work and that the iconography of the subject had little significance for them. The painter Willem de Kooning, for example, painted a series of brutally twisted women, including *Woman IV* (FIG. 2-35), in

Text continues on page 58

Hieronymus Bosch (c. 1450–1516)

VERY LITTLE of the iconography of the painting *The Garden of Earthly Delights* by Hieronymus Bosch can be found in the Bible. This fascinating piece is a *triptych*, three separate wooden panels hinged so that the left and right "wings" can fold over to conceal and protect the painting.

The Garden of Earthly Delights illustrates in three stages the religious history of humankind, which Bosch sees as a relentless journey into hell. The left panel depicts the creation of Eve in the Garden of Eden. The square central panel shows life on earth as a garden of lust in which men and women devote themselves only to the sinful pleasures of the flesh. However charming their activities may look to us today, the late-medieval mentality considered deriving

HIERONYMUS BOSH [Flemish, c. 1450–1516], *The Garden of Earthly Delights.* C. 1505. Oil on wood; central panel, 86 5/8 × 76 3/4 in. (220 × 194.9 cm); each wing, 86 5/8 × 38 1/4 in. (220 × 97.2 cm). Prado Museum, Madrid.

Continued on next page

HIERONYMUS BOSH [Flemish, c. 1450–1516], *Self-Portrait*. C. 1505. Copy of the original. Bibliothéque Municipale d'Arras, France. Scala/Art Resource, New York.

pleasure from sex sinful. Lust was the first sin of Adam and Eve after the Fall, and the cause of numerous other sins. It is apparent from the position of the hell scene on the right that as the result of their actions, all men and women will be eternally tormented in hell. There is no heaven in Bosch's last judgment.

The thrust of Bosch's message is clear, but the details of his iconography have puzzled and fascinated observers from practically the day it was painted. In the panels men and women engage in bizarre activities on earth and in hell. Strange animals and stranger monsters populate the landscapes. Animals transform themselves into human shapes or combine in endless mutations with insects. The land itself, whether paradise, earth, or hell, produces exotic vegetablelike rock formations. The punishments in hell are grotesque and nightmarish. What sort of person produced these weird images? Was he a fanatic given to hallucinations?

Unfortunately, very little is known about Bosch, except that he led an

HIERONYMUS BOSH [Flemish, c. 1450–1516], *The Garden of Earthly Delights*, detail of center panel, lower-left section. C. 1505. Prado Museum, Madrid. Scala/Art Resource, New York.

unremarkable existence in the town of 'sHertogenbosch in the Netherlands, where he grew up, worked, married, and died. Although his family name was Van Aken—his grandfather came from Aachen, Germany—he has always been referred to by the abbreviated name of his home town, Bosch. Since grandfather, father, and uncles were all painters, Bosch learned the family trade. We also know that Bosch belonged to the Brotherhood of Our Lady, a respect-

ed and orthodox religious group that maintained, in the town's cathedral, a richly decorated chapel with a miracle-working image of the Virgin. However, since *The Garden of Earthly Delights* belonged to the nobleman Hendrick III of Nassau, it can be assumed that this intricate painting was created for an audience of sophisticated aristocrats rather than for public consumption in a church.

Each of the panels is divided into three sections—a foreground, a middle ground with a body of water, and a background with distant hills. In effect, the same terrain is the setting for the three events, as though the earth is gradually transformed from paradise into hell. The Garden of Eden and the Garden of Earthly Delights are bright and colorful; hell is dark. In this work Bosch employed an unorthodox manner of painting for his day, laying down directly a layer or two of paint and then dabbing on a few highlights and finishing touches. Instead of painting in carefully planned multiple layers like his contemporaries, Bosch worked as though he were in a hurry to get his fantasies down as quickly as possible.

Our fascination with Bosch may increase when we examine the details. In the foreground of a lush landscape, Jesus Christ, the creative Word of God, introduces the newly created Eve to Adam, who awakes from sleep. Bosch hints that their sinful passions are first aroused even in Eden. The lush landscape of this paradise is filled with life, including some unusual animals like a giraffe, an elephant, a unicorn, and a three-headed bird. Bosch would have known about such animals from medieval bestiaries that listed the fabulous animals of far-off lands. The thin pink Fountain of Life, made of vegetable forms, rises in the center of the pond. Out of the circular base of the fountain peers an owl—the bird of evil magicians and of secular knowledge, and a bird of the night—a premonition of the evil to come.

The middle of the central panel contains a circular pool where women bathe. Around them dozens of men ride and cavort on a great variety of animals, which probably symbolize their base instincts. Through this merry-go-round

of human beings, Bosch conveys the perpetual carnival of male-female sexual attraction. Among the foreground groups of men and women, some engage in obvious sexual activity; many more pick fruit, offer each other fruit, or eat fruit, especially oversized strawberries. In fact, one early commentator called *The Garden of Earthly Delights, The Strawberry Plant*. Strawberries and other fruit symbolize short-lived sensual pleasures. Bosch seems to be illustrating, throughout the garden, figures of speech, plays on words, sayings, and proverbs that were popular in his day. For example, some men carry fish because the Netherland word for fish was once slang for the male sex organ.

While the fires of hell explode with volcanic force in the background of the right wing, the nearer parts of hell are filled with exquisite torments tailored to an individual's sin. Most of the instruments of torture are common things enlarged to nightmarish proportions. People are impaled on or harassed by musical instruments—a lute, harp, *hurdy-gurdy* (stringed instrument), woodwind, drum, or bagpipe—because the sensuous delights of music led to the sin of lust. A giant pair of ears emerges from the fires of hell like a battle tank ready to grind down its victims. Monsters attack gamblers and drinkers, in the lower left corner, for their sinfulness. Perhaps the most fascinating image of the right panel is the centrally placed white Tree Man, whose face almost seems to be a portrait. On his hat, sinners eternally parade to the music of the sexually symbolic bagpipe. His cracked-open egg body reveals inside an infernal tavern scene. As if in a bad dream he stands on legs made from dead tree trunks that rest on boats standing on a frozen lake.

HIERONYMUS BOSH [Flemish, c. 1450–1516], *The Garden of Earthly Delights,* detail of right panel, center section, including Tree Man. C. 1505. Prado Museum, Madrid. Scala/Art Resource, New York.

Even without understanding all the allusions and symbolic references of Bosch's iconography, the transformations and incongruity of his imagery still express to every viewer the pervasion of the laws of nature and a world turned upside down through evil.

FIG 2-36 VICTOR VASARELY [Hungarian-French, 1908–], *Orion.* 1956–1962. Paper on paper mounted on wood, 82 1/2 × 78 3/4 in. (209.6 × 200 cm). Hirshhorn Museum and Sculpture Garden, Smithsonian Institution, Washington, D.C. Gift of Joseph H. Hirshhorn Foundation, 1966. Photo by Lee Stalsworth.

To an unsophisticated, literalistic eye, Victor Vasarely's work may appear only to be rows of small circles and squares. But as soon as one realizes that the "topic under discussion" is the perception of color and space, the work begins to reveal its meaning. Light-and-dark contrasts and color contrasts make some circles or squares come forward and others recede. Light and color, in short, create movements in and out of space. It is possible to spend a considerable amount of time examining the work to experience the variety of effects, to contemplate the activity of the human imagination, and to feel how the work expresses modern sensibilities.

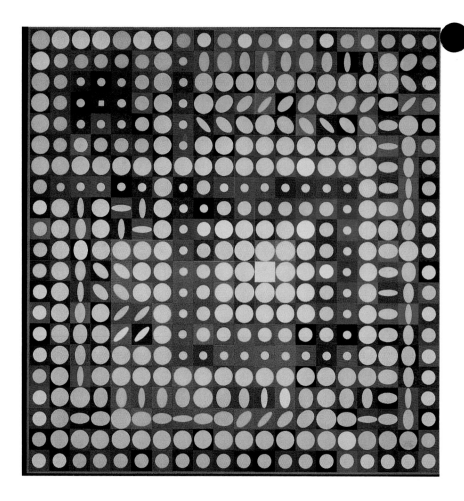

order to express himself in the dynamic act of painting, but he maintained that he was saying nothing derogatory about the subject of women in his art. Despite his assertion, the iconographical meaning of *women* has evolved since the 1950s, and, having had our consciousness raised in recent decades, we can scarcely look at his painting with the same indifference to the subject as he did. Clearly our own visual and cultural background affects the way we see and understand an artist's iconography.

The general term **abstract art** includes any work that fragments, simplifies, or distorts reality so that the formal properties of lines, shapes, and colors come to the forefront of our consideration. Works that have no recognizable objects in them whatsoever, like Wassily Kandinsky's *Fragment 2 for Composition VII* (FIG. 1-19), should strictly be designated **nonobjective.** Whether their work is merely abstract or totally nonobjective, many modern artists say that the lines, the colors, or the arrangement of masses themselves are the subject of their work—that the painting or

statute is about itself or concerned with the process of making of art. What they often mean is that the work of art depicts the very experience of visual perception—the experience of space, the experience of shape, or the experience of color, as in Victor Vasarely's *Orion* (FIG. 2-36), where the alterations of light and color change our perception of three-dimensional space. It may be stretching the term *iconography* to include the phenomena of visual perception and artistic creativity as other possible categories. Nevertheless, the basic experience of visual reality can furnish an eminently suitable subject for art because visual experience is such an important part of our existence. Indeed, anything having to do with human psychology fascinates a great many people in the twentieth century and moves them at their core.

The formal properties of a work are also sometimes said to "symbolize" certain feelings or mental states or to represent the artist's mind and emotions. The analogy between art and music (discussed in chapter 1) has helped convince numerous artists that shapes and col-

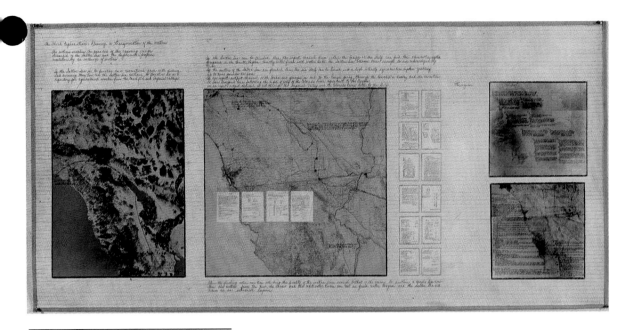

FIG 2-37 HELEN MAYER HARRISON and
NEWTON HARRISON [American], *The Fifth
Lagoon, Second Version, Third Explanation:
Planning a Transformation of the Waters.*
1978. Photographs, oil, graphite, printed
maps, and ink on canvas; 36 × 75 in. (91.4
× 190.5 cm). Ronald Feldman Fine Arts,
New York.

ors, like sounds and rhythms, have significance and
that a completely abstract and nonobjective art is
therefore possible. However, feelings and mental states
do not have exact classifications, and an artist's symbolism of forms to represent feelings may be very personal and subjective. We can never know precisely
what a particular color or line means to an individual
artist. Still, we can bank on our own experience of
these visual elements as well as on our common
human makeup to understand this sort of visual "symbolism." Once we experience for ourselves that
abstract art or nonobjective art possesses a legitimate
iconography, we can let our imagination and feelings
run free, let the work speak to us on its own terms, and
enjoy its insights into the psyche.

Protest Art

In some art since the 1970s, recognizable imagery has
returned in a stimulating new way. Expanding on the
iconography of Surrealism, Pop Art, and Photo-
realism, this new imagery rejects their cool and aloof

detachment, for a profound commitment to political,
social, and personal problems. The iconography is no
longer secondary to formal concerns but is once again
of profound importance to many contemporary artists
who want their art to say something about racism, sex-
ism, politics, the AIDS epidemic, or the environmental crisis. Robert Colescott's *Knowledge of the Past Is the
Key to the Future: Matthew Henson and the Quest for the
North Pole* (FIG. 2-21) and Neil Jenney's *Meltdown
Morning* (FIG. 2-32) are two examples of this trend.

In many areas of contemporary art, the politically
and morally committed iconography of these artists
has rejuvenated painting and sculpture and stimulated
new experimental media. For years Helen Mayer
Harrison and Newton Harrison have developed real
and ideal environmental projects such as *The Fifth
Lagoon, Second Version, Third Explanation: Planning a
Transformation of the Waters* (FIG. 2-37), which concerned the Salton Sea in southern California. Pioneers
of ecological art, they have made biological ecosys-
tems the subject of their work. Their proposals are like
stories that usually take the form of drawings, charts,

FIG 2-38 E. FAY JONES [American, 1921–], and Associates, *Thorncrown Chapel.* 1980. Eureka Springs, Arkansas. Courtesy Photos by John.

Thorncrown Chapel *is a pilgrimage chapel, a place for mediation, set across a steep slope deep in the Ozark Mountains. Constructed mainly of two-by-fours that crisscross over a tall space, the building has narrow wooden beams that mimic the slender trees that surround it. Whereas the spiky cross-pieces under the broad roof symbolize the crown of thorns from Christ's passion, the openness of the chapel and the immediacy of nature suggest more pantheistic mediations. The unusual architecture of the chapel successfully achieves a sacred space for a certain kind of religious inspiration. It also banks on certain things that more traditional church architecture often employs: light, open space, and dazzling structural design—all calculated to produce awe and reverence.*

photographs, diagrams, and maps installed in a museum display and sometimes in city hall. They use the power of art to transform the attitudes and the imagination of people in order to stimulate awareness and concern for the environment. In the process, the concerns embodied in their iconography have stretched the nature of art.

Architecture

The art of architecture obviously does not fit iconographic categories of representation such as landscape, portrait, or still life. Nevertheless, since iconography concerns the subjects and symbols of art and their significance, we can still ask the question about a building, What is it? As with all iconography, a complete answer to this question includes an explanation of why the building was built and what use it serves.

Ordinarily, the question What is it? would elicit a simple response such as It's a Christian church or It's a Greek temple or It's a Japanese house. House, church, school, hospital, fortress, factory, and office tower are all **building types.** A building type is identified partially by its use and partly by its conventional size and shape, which approach those of other buildings of the same type. To a great extent, the use or function that a building serves conditions the size of its rooms, the shape of its walls, and so forth. Different societies in different places and in different times have felt different needs for residences, places of worship, or commercial facilities and have developed building types of their own.

In general, in American culture a home needs a comfortable and conveniently organized set of relatively small rooms that serve a variety of needs, and a church or synagogue usually has to have at least one large assembly room. A factory needs unencumbered space for efficient operation or perhaps exacting climate controls for manufacturing delicate electronics. These different needs in a society tend to create similar kinds of buildings.

Considerable pressure also exists in modern society, as in past societies, that buildings symbolize their function through their appearance. They are expected to resemble a building type. Houses should look comfortable and feel welcoming like other traditional houses;

FIG 2-39 CHARLES MOORE [American, 1925–1993], with Allen Eskew and Malcolm Heard, Jr., of Perez & Associates, and Ron Filson, *Piazza d'Italia*. 1976–1979. New Orleans.

office towers should not only have efficient work spaces but also convey by their design and materials the impressive status desired by their corporate owners; churches should convey a religious feeling through either the splendor of their materials or the symbolism of their light and space. The architect E. Fay Jones, by most accounts, has achieved such a feeling in the unusual yet modest architect of his *Thorncrown Chapel* (FIG. 2-38).

Various styles from the history of architecture can also have symbolic meaning. Architects, especially in the nineteenth century, have often revived past styles of architecture because they wished to add the values and ideas associated with those styles into their new construction. Many architects in the nineteenth century insisted that contemporary churches should con-

form to a medieval Gothic type of architecture so that they would symbolize continuity with the age of faith. Government buildings in America are frequently designed in a classical Greek or Roman style so as to symbolize the ideals of the ancient civilization in the new democracy. In the 1970s and 1980s a new movement in architecture, called Post-Modernism, made a point of adopting certain aspects of past architecture and of *vernacular* (popular) architecture for their symbolic content. Charles Moore's *Piazza d'Italia* (FIG. 2-39) in New Orleans not only restores the classical language of columns and arches to modern architecture but also adopts the color and neon lights of a contemporary theme park. The architect felt that both of these were architectural symbols that people could empathize with.

CATEGORIES OF ICONOGRAPHY

Narrative art	Storytelling religious, mythological, or historical subjects are used in narrative art.
The nude	The nude emphasizes the sensuous attraction of the human body.
	Greeks made nudity an ideal state of existence.
Religious art	Religious art was the early and fundamental embodiment of humankind's deepest concerns.
	Religious works often show obscure characters and stories.
	Religious art played a vital role in a community.
Mythological art	Mythological art depicts Greek and Roman gods or the legends of a culture.
Personification and allegory	Personification and allegory use human beings to symbolize virtues or ideas.
Genre	Scenes of the everyday life of ordinary people are called genre.
	Genre often has a moralizing intent.
Portraits	Portraits emphasize the importance of the individual.
	The different types of portraits include bust, half-length, three-quarter length, and full length.
	Portraits often provide an ambiguous expression of the sitter's character.
Landscapes	
Chinese	Chinese landscape art is based on the atunement of human beings and nature.
Western	Western landscapes were often idealized.
	Nineteenth-century Western artists discovered the beauty of the ordinary in nature.
Still lifes	A still life is the deliberate grouping of small inanimate objects.
	Still lifes were frequent in Cubism and Pop Art in the twentieth century.
Fantasy art	Fantasy art depicts an illusion or vision from the imagination.
	Fantasy is essential to Surrealism.
Abstract and nonobjective art	Abstract and nonobjective artists use their work to express emotions, reduce forms to their essences, reveal the process of art, focus on visual perception, and symbolize feelings or mental states.
Protest art	Protest art emphasizes political and social concerns.
Architecture	Architecture is identified by building types.
	Architectural styles can have symbolic meaning.

Key Terms and Concepts

abstract art

allegory

building types

fantasy

genre

history painting

iconography

landscape art

mythology

nonobjective

nude

personification

portraits

religious art

sentimental

significance

still life

style

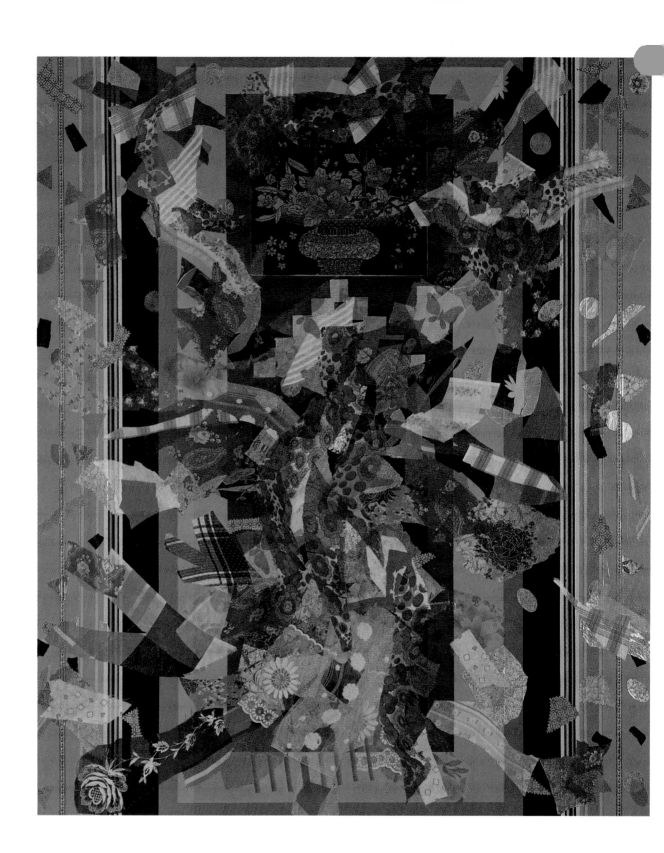

3

STYLES AND CULTURAL EXPRESSION

Style

Miriam Schapiro's painting called *Personal Appearance #3* (FIG. 3-1) has a distinctive **style.** The term *style* signifies the way an artist renders the visual elements of a piece, whether in a representational work or in an abstract work. In her art Schapiro combines straight-edged geometric areas of paint with irregularly shaped pieces of highly patterned cloth pasted to the canvas. She organizes these shapes into a composition that resembles both quilts and modern abstract painting. *Personal Appearance #3* has an underlying symmetry even as the cloth patches explode with energy from the central axis.

Schapiro's style, like every artist's style, is made up of visual elements such as lines, shapes, textures, and colors arranged and presented in a certain way in the work of art. The formal elements of style, and also the media that help shape the style, make their presence felt in art because style is not merely a means to an end; that is to say, style is not the illustration of an idea or a subject. Schapiro's style, for instance, is the very embodiment of the visual significance of the work. Since Schapiro and other successful artists spend a lifetime trying to develop their style, style lies at the heart of an individual's creativity. Even when a conservative society makes rigid demands on an artist to conform to an accepted style, the artist still must work years to attain mastery of that style.

For several decades, Schapiro has developed much the same style throughout all her work. There is a **style constancy** in the way she presents the visual elements. Her style differs from that of other artists because she has found satisfaction, consistency, and success through her chosen means to express her personality and her cultural background. Artists develop an individual style because each one of them is trained in a certain way, sees only certain examples to follow, and is filled with certain ideas, habits, and ambitions. Schapiro had struggled for years to formulate a style that would demonstrate her feelings of being a female artist in a male-dominated art world. Joining the feminist movement in 1970, she felt encouraged to liberate her painting to express herself in what she considers a female style. Her use of shapes that remind us of quilts—traditionally a medium of female expression—in *Personal Appearance #3* is one example of that focus.

FIG 3-1 MIRIAM SCHAPIRO [American, 1923–], *Personal Appearance #3.* 1973. Acrylic and fabric on canvas, 60 × 50 in. (152.4 × 127 cm). Marilyn Stokstad Collection. Courtesy Steinbaum Krauss Gallery, New York. Photo by Robert Hickerson.

Countless examples illustrate the point that different artists have a different **personal style.** Among the artists called Abstract Expressionists in New York in the 1950s, it is easy to see the difference in personal style between, for example, Jackson Pollock's layered filigrees of splattered paint in *Cathedral* (FIG. 3-2) and Lee Krasner's ordered patterns in thick layers of paint in *Noon* (FIG. 3-3). Even though both artists, who were married to each other in 1945, came to share the same aesthetic of covering the whole field of a painting with a dispersion of color and emphatic paint, their styles are readily identified with their personality. Krasner created a single, overall texture of circles and dabs of thick paint on small canvases, different from Pollock's thin lines and splatters. Pollock and Krasner shared an approach, but their styles were different.

Personal Style

Style, especially for the past several centuries in the West, can be an expression of personality. An artist

FIG 3-4 FITZHUGH LANE [American, 1804–1865], *Owl's Head, Penobscot Bay, Maine*. 1862. Oil on canvas, 16 × 26 in. (40.6 × 66 cm). Museum of Fine Arts, Boston. Bequest of Martha C. Karolik for the Karolik Collection of American Paintings, 1815–1865.

FIG 3-5 ALBERT PINKHAM RYDER [American, 1847–1917], *Moonlight Marine*. 1870–1890. Oil on panel, 11 3/8 × 12 in. (28.9 × 30.5 cm). Metropolitan Museum of Art, New York. Samuel D. Lee Fund, 1934.

Albert Pinkham Ryder lived a reclusive life in New York City, painting only a few small pictures very slowly. His iconography came from the Bible, Shakespeare, or the operas of Richard Wagner, but his style came from his inner vision. He once said he carried the idea for some of his paintings around in his mind for five years before he began to put them on canvas. Then he would spend the next ten or more years painting and repainting his image, reducing it to a few essential shapes while building up a thick layer of paint. His works ripened and grew thick and heavy in his ongoing search for the expression of his inner reality.

tends to choose the formal elements that suit what she or he feels and thinks. A visual style operates something like the artist's distinctive handwriting when it reveals her or his character. An assertive, aggressive person might adopt—consciously or unconsciously—a bold and flashy handwriting. A shy, retiring person might adopt a small and hesitant handwriting. An assertive, aggressive artist might use a big, bright, bold style. A calculating, cerebral artist probably feels comfortable with a controlled and rationalized style.

The relationship between style and personality is not a difficult connection for us to make, since we often form judgments about someone's personality based on the style of music that person plays or the clothes he or she wears. We understand immediately the significance of their styles when the Wall Street businessman dons a dark business suit and when the rock star dresses in leather and lace.

Two artists, whether separated in time and place or not, will probably treat the same iconography in two different personal styles. For instance, two nineteenth-century American artists, FitzHugh Lane and Albert Pinkham Ryder, painted the same subject, sailing ships, only decades apart, with very different results. In Lane's *Owl's Head, Penobscot Bay, Maine* (FIG. 3-4), the special luminosity of the sky and the hyperreal pre-

cision of the details freeze the silent moment before us. In Ryder's *Moonlight Marine* (FIG. 3-5), built-up layers of paint reduce the boat and clouds to dark bloblike forms in stark contrast to the moonlit sky. The curved shapes add to the feeling of the boat riding the waves. Through their styles the painters produce quite different images of a transcendent spirit pervading nature.

FIG 3-7 PABLO PICASSO [Spanish, 1881–1973, *Mother and Child*. 1921. Oil on canvas, 56 1/2 × 64 in. (143.5 × 162.6 cm). Art Institute of Chicago. Gift of Maymar Corporation, Mrs. Maurice L. Rothschild, Mr. and Mrs. Chauncey McCormick; Mary and Leigh Block Charitable Fund; Ada Turnbull Hertle Endowment; through prior gift of Mr. and Mrs. Edwin E. Hokin, 1954.270. Photograph © 1994. All Rights Reserved.

FIG 3-6 PABLO PICASSO [Spanish, 1881–1973], *Three Musicians*. 1921. Oil on canvas, 80 × 74 in. (203.2 × 188 cm). Philadelphia Museum of Art. A. E. Gallatin Collection.

An artist's choice of a style is not solely a personal matter because not every style is possible at every moment. The culture in which an artist lives sets limits on what the artist can do. Moreover, within those cultural possibilities, most artists work with some consistency in a certain style of art for years, just as people usually maintain a certain style of life on a regular basis. One artist may try to copy another's style, but most of us value the original, personal creation more.

Individual Style Phases

People change, of course, and artists may change their style. Critics often speak of an artist's mature, or fully developed, style as opposed to the tentative style of her or his early work. Searching to express herself, Miriam Schapiro first tried a number of styles. When she arrived in New York in the mid-1950s, she painted in an Abstract Expressionist style, and in the late 1960s she even experimented with computer-aided drawing.

Picasso changed his style a number of times, especially in his twenties when he tried something new every few years. The most striking contrast between

FIG 3-8 ROBERT KUSHNER [American, 1949–], *Fish Gate.* 1979. Acrylic on fabric, 99 × 171 in. (251.5 × 434.3 cm). Holly Solomon Gallery, New York.

Picasso's different styles occurred in the 1920s when he painted *Three Musicians* (FIG. 3-6) in an abstract Cubist style of harsh geometric shapes and at the same time *Mother and Child* (FIG. 3-7) in an almost classical style of swollen figures. Picasso's virtuosity in juggling two styles at once is exceptional. Despite his many styles, critics have observed a degree of consistency within each new phase of his development and there are relationships between one style and the next.

Because of the consistency between style and personality, it is possible to identify on the basis of style alone the artist who produced a piece. It is possible to identify another never-before-seen Schapiro, Pollock, or Picasso by recognizing that its style is similar to that of a work known to be by the same artist. In fact, on the basis of style alone, it has been possible to reconstruct a body of work by an artist based on only a few certain examples of the artist's style. The situation arises because there is often not enough documented information about older works of art to prove who did them.

Regional or Group Style

Even though Miriam Schapiro's painting *Personal Appearance #3* (FIG. 3-1) embodies her personal style, many elements of her work are similar to the general style pursued by a contemporary group of artists centered in New York. This **group style** has been called Pattern Painting, Pattern and Decoration, or simply P&D. In addition to Schapiro, a number of artists in the 1970s—Robert Kushner (see *Fish Gate*, FIG. 3-8) and Joyce Kozloff (see *Homage to Robert Adam*, FIG. 3-21), among others—all incorporated in their work ornamental designs of popular and folk origin. They sought the repetition of rich and brightly colored textures in reaction to the spare abstractions of many leading painters at that time. Clearly, a group of people in one place may practice pretty much the same style—especially when compared with the style of other people in a different place.

FIG 3-9 [African, Yoruban; Nigeria], *Mother and Child for Sango.* Late nineteenth century. Wood; beads, 17 × 5 5/8 × 6 1/2 in. (43.2 × 15.2 × 16.5 cm). Seattle Art Museum. Gift of Katherine White and the Boeing Company. Photo by Paul Macapia.

Since artists perceive things from the point of view of their surroundings, they routinely absorb the conventions and assumptions of their context and environment. So in addition to expressing a personality, style can also express a regional character. Historians sometimes speak of a **regional style** embodying the spirit of a whole people. Consider, for example, how people around the world dress differently from Americans. The style of clothing each people wears reveals more than just differences in climate. The clothes may demonstrate a national tradition and a national personality that includes a whole set of religious beliefs, customs, ways of thinking and perceiving, and so forth.

A Regional Style in African Art

Groups of artists in certain regions around the world can be distinguished by the common style they share. For example, to the casual Western observer, most pieces of African art might look alike at first glance. But after having examined the characteristics of the Yoruban style of wood sculpture in *Twin Memorial Figure* (FIG. 1-6), it is relatively easy to recognize *Mother and Child* (FIG. 3-9) as another example of Yoruban art. In *Mother and Child,* the woman, a worshiper of Sango, the thunder god, holds an offering bowl as she carries her child on her back. She sits on a small support. It is clear that both Yoruban sculptors preferred conical and ovoid masses when they carved. The heads and breasts, and arms and legs in both *Twin Memorial Figure* and *Mother and Child* lie in the same diagonal direction. The different body parts have a formal consistency about them and an appealing rhythm in their composition—the long curved line of the chin in *Mother and Child,* for example, is answered by the bend of arms.

The Yorubans live mainly in the plains of southwestern Nigeria. The Ijo people, a much smaller group, live in the watery delta of the Niger River, not many miles away. When the work of one Ijo carver, *Personal Shrine* (FIG. 3-10), is compared with the Yoruban *Mother and Child,* the difference in style between the two groups of people is obvious. The Ijo personal shrine represents a man sitting on the back of a guardian spirit (*ejiri*), probably in the shape of a cat-like animal. To ensure his well-being, the man is about to pour a libation from the cup he holds in his right hand. Like most African works of art, this personal altar of the Ijo has bilateral symmetry as well as a consistency among the forms throughout the work. But in contrast to the Yoruban delight in diagonals, curves, and ovals, the Ijo sculptor carved forms that are squared off. Masses are blocklike, and they join one another at right angles. Even the gaping mouth of the spirit is a square.

We would have to examine many more pieces to appreciate the full range of the Yoruban or Ijo style of sculpture. Nevertheless, after we have studied just two examples, it would seem virtually impossible that a Yoruban sculptor could have carved the personal shrine of the Ijo.

Period Style

Style can also be a fairly accurate indicator of time. Imagine, for example, the style of clothing worn by people around the time of the Civil War. Give or take a few years, we could probably date a picture of people wearing that kind of clothing by its style—a style no longer in use. To be sure, we are free to go to a supplier of theatrical costumes, rent a hoop skirt or a stovepipe hat, and wear such clothing today. But the social pressure to conform to more contemporary styles would be hard to bear. People might even question our sanity because of the evident clash between style and time in our life. Since artists' styles, like clothing styles, generally change from one period of time to another, the **period style** employed at a certain point marks that period of time and no other.

Any kind of style may be theoretically possible at any time, but all the possibilities never appear at once. Despite the precedents for her style in the work of Henri Matisse (d. 1954) and in traditional fabric crafts, Miriam Schapiro's style belongs to the time in which she was painting and to no other. Her style emerged in the 1970s when the feminist movement surged and artists were revolting against excessive abstraction. Not only does the cultural context of a particular time determine to a great extent the possibilities open to an artist, an artist would also find it virtually impossible to stand totally apart from the time in which he or she lives. It is impossible to imagine Schapiro painting in her style alongside Rembrandt in seventeenth-century Holland, for example.

Fig 3-10 [African, Nigerian; Western Ijo], *Shrine (ejiri)*. Wood, paint, 25 1/2 in. (64.8 cm) high. Metropolitan Museum of Art, New York. Michael C. Rockefeller Memorial Collection, gift of the Mathew T. Mellon Foundation, 1960. (1978.412.404)

FIG 3-11   L. MURRAY DIXON [American, d. 1949] The Marlin Hotel. 1939. Miami Beach, Florida. Photo © Scott Frances/ESTO.

FIG 3-12   FRANK LLOYD WRIGHT [American, 1867–1959), writing desk and chair designed for the Johnson Wax Administration Building, Racine, Wisconsin. C. 1936. Manufactured by Cassina USA, Inc. Enameled steel, cherry, and brass, 39 in. (99 cm) high. Photo courtesy Cassina USA, Inc.

People often speak of the **spirit of the time** (or *zeitgeist* in German) influencing an artist to work in a particular style. It sometimes seems that the air people are breathing makes a style appear simultaneously in architecture, sculpture, painting, and interior design. The modernistic Art Deco style, popular in the 1920s and 1930s, occurred everywhere—on a building facade in Miami, Florida (FIG. 3-11); in office furniture for Racine, Wisconsin (FIG. 3-12); in a coffee service designed in New York City (FIG. 3-13); and in a clock designed in Pasadena, California (FIG. 3-14). Although the spirit of the time appears tangibly in

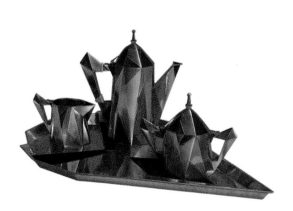

FIG 3-13   ERIK MAGNUSSEN [Danish, 1884–1961], *"Cubic" Coffee Service*, designed for the Gorham Manufacturing Company. 1927. Silver, with patinated, oxidized, and gilt decoration; coffee pot, 9 1/2 in. (24.1 cm) high. Museum of Art, Rhode Island School of Design; Gift of Textron, Inc. Photograph by Cathy Carver.

FIG 3-14   KEM WEBER [American, 1889–1963], Digital Clock/Zephyr Clock. C. 1933. Brass and copper, 3 1/2 in. (8.9 cm) high. Lent by John P. Axelrod. Museum of Fine Arts, Boston.

such works of art and, like the Art Deco style, can be documented, it is hard to determine exactly what this force is. The elements building a cultural environment are numerous and complexly interwoven. They include works of art themselves, as well as perhaps a thousand different concrete objects, traditions, assumptions, words, and examples. No one single social condition, like the economic system or the class structure, determines the style of a particular period.

Art History

Since art is not a static thing but changes from one period to the next, it has a history. For several centuries **art history** has entailed not just the biographies of artists and the documentation of their work, but also the record of ever-changing iconography and styles. Even a seemingly straightforward symbol like the halo in Christian art has undergone continuous transformation over time, from a glowing light to a thin gold ring seen in perspective. Style has a history as well, since at no point in time have artists worked in exactly the same style as artists at another time. Even when the goal of art was to follow very carefully the example of a prototype, differences between the work of different generations can be observed. For example, Elon Webster carved another unmistakable image of *Rim-Dweller* (FIG. 3-15) about fifteen years later than the Iroquois mask of the same spirit illustrated in figure 2-1. Both artists were probably following the same prototype or set of conventions—an oval face, twisted nose and eyes, large curved mouth, and deep curved lines—but the differences in style, especially in the mouth, are quite pronounced.

Each style of art expresses its own time because it grows out of the context in which it lives. Studying the history of art means exploring how iconography and style might express the economic and political systems, the ethical values, the religious beliefs, the social hierarchies, the symbolic thought processes, the gender roles, the sexual practices, the ethnic identity, and the modes of visual perceptions of an age because all these elements condition the artists living at that time. Since the values and mentality that produced a work of art in another time are always different from our own, we must interpret that work using information about the culture that produced it.

FIG 3-15   ELON WEBSTER [Onondaga Iroquois, Native American], *Rim-Dweller.* 1937. Wooden False Face mask. Cranbrook Institute of Science, Bloomfield Hills, Michigan.

FIG 3-16 [Roman], Maison Carrée. C. 20 B.C. Nîmes, France. Giraudon/Art Resource, New York.

FIG 3-17 THOMAS JEFFERSON [American, 1743-1826], Virginia State Capitol. 1785–1789. Richmond, Virginia. Photo from the Virginia State Library and Archives.

We can postpone an examination of the history of art until we have thoroughly discussed and understood the formal elements of style, but no such separation in real life is possible. Line, space, mass, and color in art appear only through styles in historic time, not in the abstract. The very understanding we have of these elements today is itself historically conditioned.

Two different artists, separated in time, cannot practice the same style because the conditions of the first are not those of the second. Some artists have tried to revive past styles, but their imitations are never quite the same as the original. On a trip through Europe, Thomas Jefferson was so fascinated by the Roman temple called *Maison Carrée* at Nîmes, France (FIG. 3-16), that he consciously imitated it in his design for the Virginia State Capitol in Richmond (FIG. 3-17). By the similarity of style Jefferson wanted to draw the symbolic connection between heroic Rome and the ideals of the new democratic Republic in America. But of course the styles of the Roman temple and the state capitol building are different: the structures are made from different materials, Jefferson used a different kind of column, the columns do not go around his building, and the wide-open interior of the classical temple had to become government meeting rooms and offices on several floors in the state capitol. Jefferson's reference to a Roman style is unmistakable, but the style looks different and has a different meaning in the new context.

The history of art does not imply that artistic worth progresses—or even declines—over time. Instead, the basic assumption of the history of art is that a style is relative to the culture that produced it. Each culture is happy, so to speak, with its own style. The style is meaningful to those sharing the culture at that time. It is unlikely that ancient Egyptian sculptors wanted to be Greek sculptors but were unable to, or that tenth-century Chinese painters wanted to be Americans. Moreover, contemporary art historians do not assume that there are absolute standards of art that all cultures are striving to achieve. They do not claim that universal rules of beauty were discovered by the ancient Greeks and that some periods of time achieve these standards, and others do not. They also make no dogmatic judgments about which style is best, since doing so might imply that one culture is better than another.

While examining the relationship of a style to its culture, historians of art also like to consider the changes in style from one period to the next. **Style change** is a crucial issue because developing artists normally create their own style by redefining and reshaping the forms of art that they have learned until something new is born. A new generation scarcely ever reinvents all of art from scratch; instead, artists frequently work out a new style because they are dis-

FIG 3-18 [French], Beauvais Cathedral, nave and choir. 1247– . France. Foto Marburg/Art Resource, New York.

FIG 3-19 LUDWIG MIES VAN DER ROHE [American, 1886–1969] and PHILIP JOHNSON [American, 1906–], Seagram Building. 1956–1958. New York. Photo by Ezra Stoller, © Esto.

satisfied with the now irrelevant style before them. In other words, an artist's creativity transforms the style he or she was given. This is why critics often speak about the influence of one artist on another—not because artistic creativity is a mechanical affair but because the inventive and creative part of the new style stands out by contrast with what went before.

Consequently, the history of art often compares one style with another not to point out how one style is better than the other but to bring out the distinct character and the creativity of each. Compare, for example, the Gothic cathedral of Beauvais in medieval France (FIG. 3-18) with a glass-and-steel office tower, the Seagram Building, from the twentieth century (FIG. 3-19). The architects of both structures enjoyed soaring heights and both built a structural skeleton that supports large areas of glass—but for entirely different reasons. Each building is ingenious and sophisticated in its own terms. However, the

jagged pinnacles and mysterious light and space of the cathedral are the product of an age of religious faith when the entire community shared the same spiritual beliefs. The sleek lines and efficient spaces of the skyscraper are made possible by an age of technology, an age of economic power, and urban density.

This method of comparative analysis does not decide that one building is better than the other or that one culture is better than the other. They are just different. Of course, personally, you may prefer one building or one culture to another. That is a matter of **taste**—the result of your own background and education.

The history of art, like every human endeavor, possesses a certain amount of bias. Feminist art historians have protested for several decades that male historians left the contribution of women artists out of the history of art. Perhaps as a result, historians recently have discovered a number of woman artists, like Artemisia

FIG 3-20 [Bwete Kotan], *Reliquary Guardian Figures (Mbulu Ngulu).* Nineteenth or twentieth century. Larger figure: wood, with copper, brass and iron; height: 18 7/8 in. (48 cm). Smaller figure: wood with copper, brass and ivory; height 13 1/4 in. (33.5 cm). From Gabon and Ivory Coast, Africa. Photograph by Bobby Hansson.

Gentileschi or Mary Cassatt, who contributed significantly to the culture of their time. But because of the numerous obstacles that women faced to become artists, it is unlikely that anyone will discover female artists to compare to Michelangelo in the sixteenth century or Rembrandt in the seventeenth century, for example. Feminist art history has had perhaps a more profound effect in expanding the kinds of art that contribute to defining the culture of a period. Many art forms, like quilt making, that have traditionally been female forms of expression are now finding their rightful place in the history of culture.

The Uses of Art History

Studying style as an expression of a culture can be considered one use for art. Defining a culture through its art can be serious business. For example, in modern times, the nations of the world make great efforts to preserve their own artistic heritage within their borders because it helps to identify themselves as a people. Italy, for example, has laws preventing the export of Italian art so that the Italian people themselves will not lose all their artistic inheritance to wealthy foreigners. Preserving a national heritage also promotes tourism. And satellite regions dominated by the political or economic power of a neighboring country will often exploit the history of their own art to emphasize their indigenous and independent culture.

Historians in general "use" art to expand the story of civilization. Professional historians often examine the art of the past as a means to understand the character of some former culture. Whenever written records about a culture are scanty or nonexistent, archaeologists unearth the ruins of buildings and fit together broken pieces of pottery, sculpture, and other artifacts to tell us something about these vanished people.

Even in modern times, the artistic style identified with a time, place, and people may reveal more about a culture than do lists of military battles and the names of kings and politicians. The history of styles may reveal fundamental things about a culture's attitude toward life, feeling for nature, or religious thinking—fundamental things that might otherwise remain a mystery. For example, the Kota people who live in Gabon and Zaire in Africa made reliquary guardian figures (see FIG. 3-20) that were inserted into a basket or box containing the skulls and bones of ancestors. When the lower part of the figure was concealed within the basket, the basket looked a bit like the body of the figure. The Kota revered the relics of chiefs, religious leaders, and other important people whose powers they wanted to preserve. The guardian figures would keep away evil spirits and the uninitiated from the powerful relics and thus ensure fertility, health, and prosperity to the living.

The guardian figures in FIG. 3-20 are entirely in one plane; only the oval faces protrude somewhat beyond the flat curving forms of the hair or headdress. The round eyes keep a watchful gaze. All other human features have reached a high degree of abstraction by which the sculptor avoided the reproduction of living appearances and rather evoked a spiritual meaning. Respect for the spirits of ancestors was undoubtedly a strong force in Kota society.

Text continues on page 80

Rembrandt van Rijn (1606–1669)

*R*EMBRANDT spent a lifetime revising and developing his style, and yet each stage in his career seems to manifest the coherent growth of his personality. Examining the parallel paths of the development of his style and the evolution of his personality has been a fascinating aspect of Rembrandt studies.

Rembrandt van Rijn—his family adopted the name because they owned windmills on the Rhine (Rijn in Dutch) River in Leiden, Holland—first embraced the style of the Amsterdam artist Pieter Lastman, with whom Rembrandt studied for six months. As a young artist back in his hometown of Leiden, Rembrandt painted in imitation of Lastman small biblical scenes such as *Judas Returning the Thirty Pieces of Silver.* Small-scale figures wearing exotic costumes and a mysterious space give the painting an Oriental flavor.

Unlike Rembrandt, who never left Holland, Lastman had been to Italy, where biblical and mythological art reigned supreme. Lastman must have impressed young Rembrandt with the importance of history painting. When a well-educated Dutch connoisseur—(an expert in judging art)—saw Rembrandt's *Judas*, he praised the artist's ability to express vivid emotions through the gestures and facial features of his biblical characters. Ambitious and eager, Rembrandt aimed for success at the highest level of art.

Although Rembrandt painted portraits of his family in Leiden, his first important portrait commission came from Amsterdam, the bustling cosmopolitan metropolis of the New Dutch Republic. Rembrandt received this commission from the Amsterdam merchant Nicholaes Ruts, whose portrait now hangs in the Frick Museum in New York. In Rembrandt's painting of him,

REMBRANDT VAN RIJN [Dutch, 1606–1669].
Judas Returning the Thirty Pieces of Silver.
1629. Oil on wood, 31 5/16 × 40 3/16 in.
(79.5 × 102 cm). England, private collection.

Continued on next page

REMBRANDT VAN RIJN [Dutch, 1606–1669].
NICHOLAES RUTS. 1631. Oil on wood, 46 ×
34 3/8 in. (116.8 × 87.3 cm). Frick
Collection, New York.

REMBRANDT VAN RIJN [Dutch, 1606–1669].
The Night Watch. 1642. Oil on canvas,
142 15/16 × 172 1/16 in. (363 × 437 cm).
Rijksmuseum, Amsterdam.

Ruts, who grew wealthy through trade with Russia, wears a fur coat and a Russian-style fur hat. He seems to be in the act of turning toward us to offer us a piece of paper. His intent eyes and the naturalness of every texture make the man come alive before us.

At age twenty seven Rembrandt moved permanently to Amsterdam, where his lifelike portraits soon became very much in demand. In 1634 Rembrandt married Saskia van Ulenborch, the daughter of a well-to-do and well-respected family. Flush with his newfound status and wealth, Rembrandt bought a large house in Amsterdam and began collecting and dealing in paintings, prints, and other art objects.

However, he was not a very lucky or a very cautious investor, so debt hung on him like a weight during the last twenty years of his life.

Very early in his career Rembrandt also became aware of the work of several other Dutch artists who had been to Italy and had returned with a style based on strong and dramatic contrasts of light and dark. He adopted the style as his own. It became Rembrandt's life-long goal to develop a style that would convey interior feelings and spiritual drama through variations of light and dark, especially in the many religious works he painted throughout his career.

Unfortunately for Rembrandt, there was little call for religious painting in

seventeenth-century Holland. The Calvinist churches did not commission religious art, and so artists had to sell religious art, if they chose to paint it at all, on the open market just like any other iconographic type. Holland, which had just won its independence from Spain, was booming economically with merchants and professional people who had the wealth to buy landscapes, still lifes, and genre subjects for their homes and to commission portraits of themselves and their family.

Rembrandt painted one of his most famous works, *The Night Watch*, in his style of dramatic light-and-dark contrasts. *The Night Watch* depicts the militia company of Captain Frans

Banning Cocq, who, front and center, gives orders to his lieutenant Willem van Ruytenburch, dressed in yellow, to muster the men in front of a monumental gateway.

The painting brought Rembrandt fame for many generations because it hung on public display in the militia company's indoor shooting range just a few doors down from where Rembrandt once lived. *The Night Watch* is a group portrait of about sixteen people in the guise of a dramatic event. Several men are inspecting, cleaning, and loading their firearms as drums roll, dogs bark, and children scamper about. Bright spotlights seem to illuminate the captain and lieutenant, the little girl, and other figures as they emerge out of the darkness into light. The contrasts add to the drama and movement of the painting. Despite the painting's popular title, the action happens during the day. The appearance of night was the result of Rembrandt's preferred style of light-and-dark contrasts and of the dirty varnish that once darkened the painting.

Over the years, through the 1640s, 1650s, and 1660s, Rembrandt continued to refine his style by making the contrasts between light and dark more subtle and by introducing mysterious half-lights that elicit psychological interpretation from the viewer. Because he continued to use light and dark to penetrate the psyche of a person, long after most other artists dropped such dramatic contrasts, Rembrandt's less-than-flattering portraits eventually became no longer fashionable.

Rembrandt penetrated beneath the surface and examined his own personality as an artist in *Self-Portrait*, now in Washington, D. C. Rembrandt, with shadowed, troubled eyes, seems worn

REMBRANDT VAN RIJN [Dutch, 1606–1669]. *Self-Portrait.* 1659. Oil on canvas, 33 1/16 × 26 in. (84 × 66 cm). National Gallery of Art, Washington, D.C.

and weary although he was only fifty three at the time. Throughout his career Rembrandt conducted "experiments" in the revelation of character in many self-portraits, trying out on himself different costumes, poses, and facial expressions. He made about one hundred of these studies over a forty-year career. Taken together, his self-portraits not only reveal how he grew old but also, we like to think, expose his spiritual development as though they are an intimate diary.

Living beyond his means and falling into debt, Rembrandt had to sell his house and auction his belongings in 1657–58. Rembrandt's loss of popularity and other personal problems—his wife and infant children died—may have deepened his personality, and it is tempting to trace the direct effect of these circumstances on his work. Throughout his career Rembrandt's style evolved from the small Italianate history paintings, his lifelike portraits, and his dramatic light-and-dark contrasts, to his moody and introspective late works. The phases of his style remain a fascinating and enigmatic revelation of a single personality reacting to the circumstances around him.

The history of styles provides more than a tool of historical research; it offers a way of appreciating art. Through it we learn to have a sensitivity and an empathy for art by people whose culture we do not share. When we learn about the style of a certain culture, we can also begin to understand the creative possibilities within that style. This understanding stretches the imagination and adds meaning and enjoyment to what we see. The insights we have into the style of a certain period can illuminate every new work of art from that period that we run across. When we see another piece in the style of Pattern and Decoration—for example, *Homage to Robert Adam* (FIG. 3-21), by Joyce Kozloff—we are able to appreciate its essential qualities rapidly if we are familiar with that style through the work of Miriam Schapiro (see *Personal Appearance #3,* FIG. 3-1). When we see the characteristics of a familiar period style in a newly discovered work, we are able to place the work in its historical context and add rich mental and emotional associations to the pleasure of experiencing it.

An Artistic Heritage

The cultural heritage of most English-speaking peoples stretches back several thousand years to the origins of European civilization. Other civilizations are older and perhaps richer, but it was European culture that shaped North American laws and institutions, ways of thinking and religious beliefs, attitude toward nature and science, and forms of art. Now that an international culture is rapidly spreading over the globe and everyone is becoming a citizen of the world, it is essential that we understand and appreciate the cultures of all peoples. Onto North America's European heritage are being grafted profound influences from Latin America, Africa, Asia, and native America. For example, James Luna's work called *The Artifact Piece* (FIG. 3-22) makes a devastatingly ironic comment about Native Americans in American society by adopting the standard techniques of a museum display. Out of this amalgamation of cultures has developed a visual language that most artists at present attempt to speak.

One of the most important lessons that the history of art has to teach is the genuine realization of **cultural diversity.** The lesson gets taught whenever art history comes to grips with different styles from diverse cultures. Art is not, as some claim, a completely universal language, because it is relative to the culture that produced it. The history of art assumes that different cultures all merit an equal footing. It also reveals that our own culture is, like others, timebound. It is not a constant or an absolute. It is changing at this very minute through the influence of new ideas and different peoples from around the world.

Although art is not a universal language in a simpleminded sense, common elements lie in the very nature of making art. In drawing, painting, sculpture, and architecture, each new generation faces similar tasks in delineating objects and arranging shapes, putting paint on a surface, shaping solid material, or enclosing space for living. The very nature of a surface, a solid, or a space affords certain possibilities of artistic activity and establishes norms to some extent. Since the origins of art, human beings seem to have had the same physical visual and mental equipment for organizing visual information and for forming perceptions. Despite the diversity of ways of seeing in different cultures over the course of time, the psychology of human seeing suggests some universal approaches and principles (which are discussed in chapters 4 through 7).

Media

The **medium** (tools and materials) and the techniques that an artist employs contribute greatly to the appearance of a finished work of art. Artists spend time learning the tools of their trade, the characteristics of the materials, and the techniques that will produce the effects they seek. With practice, they develop a feel for their medium. They try to become aware of the permanence of the materials they use and what they can and cannot do with the medium. Many artists today also enjoy experimenting with new techniques and manipulating traditional materials into new forms.

But no costly materials, clever skills, or painstaking efforts can substitute for the artist's imagination. The most important part of any medium is the artist's vision that controls the tools and materials and develops a personal, group, or period style. Most artists do not simply play with the medium for its own sake to see what tricks can be performed. Tools and materials are subordinate to the artist's creativity. The artist's

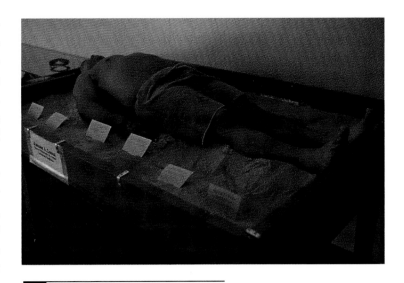

FIG 3-22   JAMES LUNA [American, 1950–], *The Artifact Piece.* 1986. Installation and performance at the Museum of Man, San Diego.

James Luna puts his own body on display by lying on an exhibition table where he has also placed other "artifacts" such as his school diplomas, his divorce papers, and so forth. The artist is protesting that American Indians are treated as objects in American society even though they too are flesh and blood and lead a life very much like that of other Americans.

materials—whatever they may be—take on meaning when the artist transforms them into symbols rich with life.

The more common media include drawing, printmaking, painting, sculpture, crafts, design, architecture, photography, and film (all discussed in chapters 8 to 15). We want to learn about the artist's tools and materials to open our eyes to the variations within them, to the range of inherent possibilities, to normal expectations of the quality of the artisanship, and to the experiments of modern artists who are expanding the media. A little knowledge of the tools and materials will not turn us into professional artists, but ought to help us understand how artists approach their work and to appreciate the character and expressive potential of each medium. Awareness of the media helps us see art more clearly and enjoy the artist's achievements more fully.

SUMMATION BOX

STYLE

Personal style	A personal style embodies an artist's vision, expresses a personality, and identifies an individual.
Regional or group style	A group usually shares the same style.
	A regional style embodies the spirit of a people.
Period style	Styles are timebound.
	Not every style is possible at any time.
Art history	Art has a history because style is timebound.
	Art expresses the values and mentality of a certain time.
	Changes in style can reveal an artist's creativity.
	Art historians often use a method of comparative analysis.
The uses of art history	Art history is used to define a culture, to expand history, and to aid appreciation.
An artistic heritage	Art teaches cultural diversity.
	American art has entered a world culture.
Media	Media include the tools and materials of the various forms of artistic expression.

Key Terms and Concepts

art history	period style	style
cultural diversity	personal style	style change
group style	regional style	style constancy
medium	spirit of the time	taste

CRITICAL ANALYSIS I

Is it Art?

It is hard to imagine that in 1894, when Mary Cassatt's *Summertime: Woman and Child in a Rowboat* was painted, some people would have questioned whether it was art. They may have demanded, as Aristotle once did, characters of a higher type, performing an inspiring action. The woman and child, however, seem to be ordinary people performing an inconsequential summertime activity. Their image is not particularly idealized or heroic, and the figures scarcely possess the proportions of Greek sculpture, although they appear handsome and well dressed in the casual clothes of the period.

In the mid-1890s, critics subscribing to a Platonist view might have complained that the painting was merely an imitation of reality, something that a photograph could have done better. However, the piece is far from being photographically or mechanistically realistic in a number of ways: the loose brushwork roughly sketches the image; the color seems more varied and intense than in reality; and the surface of the water seems to tip up unnaturally, especially toward the top of the canvas. Many of the unreal elements in the painting may legitimately be charged to the artist's imagination. As a member of the Impressionist movement, Cassatt liked to paint directly from aspects of nature that she could see before her. In fact, she wrote in 1894 in a letter to a friend that "going out in a boat to study the reflections of the water, on the bay here has made me seasick."[1] Nevertheless, it is unlikely that the two subjects (and the ducks!) held that precise pose in a boat on a sunny day for the hours that Cassatt must have

Mary Cassatt [American, 1845–1926], *Summertime: Woman and Child in a Rowboat*. 1894. Oil on canvas, 42 × 30 in. (106.7 × 76.2 cm). Terra Museum of American Art, Chicago.

taken to paint the canvas. Her realism was more likely assembled, like Zeuxis's idealism, from piecemeal observation.

If art is understood as communication through a visual symbolism of lived experience, the painting *Summertime* without question succeeds as art. Most of us have been mesmerized by looking at water on a hot summer day and can share the experience of the two boaters with the artist. Cassatt vividly brings to our imagination the light and color that dance on the water in the sun. To appreciate the picture, we need not know the facts of the situation—the air temperature, the exact location, or the size of the boat. Instead, Cassatt arouses in us sensations we have experienced and opens our eyes to delightful perceptions of color, light, and space we might otherwise have missed in a casual glance at the scene. When we work at looking as intensely as she did, so that the painting works its magic on us, it is art.

What theory of art did the artist herself believe in? Cassatt never published a statement or submitted to an interview about her aesthetic beliefs. Her many letters reveal little along these lines. We might assume, nevertheless, that her own understanding of the nature of art was close to that of the other Impressionists who recorded the startling light and color in the world around them. In one letter, in the midst of writing about her rose garden, Cassatt exclaimed, "There is nothing like making pictures with real things."[2] Like many of the Impressionists, she was challenged to make something beautiful out of the offbeat and the ordinary. To demonstrate the point, she once chose a decidedly homely servant girl and had her pose in an awkward position. The result was *Girl Arranging Her Hair*, in which Cassatt's skillful placement of the lines and shapes and the harmony of the colors transformed even something "ugly" into art.

Even this brief search for Cassatt's opinions about art raises the questions, Can we trust the artist's own opinion to be a valid analysis of her own art? And why should it matter to us what the artist thought? Should we judge the artist's work on the basis of her aesthetics or on our own or on a mix of the two? In the briefest of answers to those questions it may be said that although it is always helpful to investigate the artist's intentions, it will always be impossible to see with another person's eyes exactly what that person sees. Even though we value art because it helps us see what another culture saw, each culture must ultimately experience art for itself.

Iconography

The objects depicted in Cassatt's *Summertime* are easily listed: a woman, a young girl, a boat, two ducks, and water. The

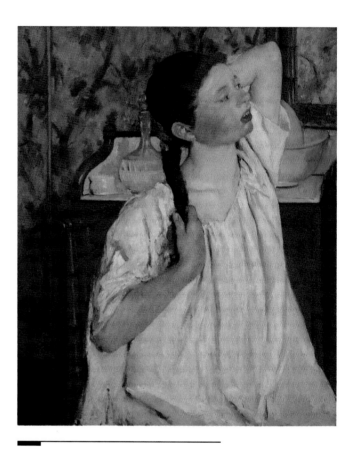

Mary Cassatt [American, 1845–1926], *Girl Arranging her Hair.* 1886. Oil on canvas, 29 1/2 × 24 1/2 in. (75 × 62.3 cm). National Gallery of Art, Washington, D.C.

event depicted by Cassatt is easily surmised: the two figures are enjoying a relaxing boat ride in the summer sun. Perhaps they have fed the ducks to attract them. However, the woman and child seem to be staring instead at the water, mesmerized by the light dancing on the surface on this bright and lazy day. Since the faces of the two figures are somewhat obscured, it is unlikely that the painting is a portrait. Much more likely, the painting should be categorized as a genre subject, illustrating a commonplace event devoid of overt symbolism or moral message.

Equally interesting is what Cassatt does not depict: the sky, the shoreline, and any other landmark are omitted. Also left out is the oarswoman or oarsman whose weight must be balancing the boat while the woman and child lean over the edge. The artist deliberately concentrated instead on the figures staring at the water. We may imagine that the woman

Octave Tassaert [French, 1807–1874], *An Unfortunate Family or Suicide*. 1850. Oil on canvas, 45 1/2 × 30 in. (115 × 75 cm). Musée d'Orsay, Paris.

and child are mother and daughter, although they do not interact with each other and, in fact, Cassatt's models were probably not related.[3] Young and old, they are drawn together primarily by their fascination with the water.

The clothing of the woman—a long-sleeved dress and gloves—is the only part of the iconography that places the scene at a certain period of time—about the mid-1890s. The awareness of a time through the iconography allows us to speculate on the significance of the activity of the woman and child in the context of the society in which they lived. We know from other evidence that women and children of the middle class, as these appear to be, in general led rather

sheltered lives. They were allowed only nonstrenuous leisure time activities and recreations like boating, although some were beginning to ride bicycles and play tennis. From some people's point of view, an awareness of the social context may add a note of wistfulness to this picture of the genteel activity allowed the two women.

Style

Cassatt developed her personal style in association with a group of artists called the Impressionists who made their mark in the history of art at the end of the nineteenth century. To examine the style of Cassatt's *Summertime*, let us compare it with another painting of two women, by Octave Tassaert, *An Unfortunate Family or Suicide*, painted a generation or two earlier in 1850. Tassaert's painting is also a genre piece, but it tells a moralizing story of an impoverished mother and daughter huddled in an attic room. The mother implores an image of the Madonna and Child pinned to the wall, while the daughter collapses in her lap. The title *Suicide* probably describes not the self-inflicted death of the daughter but the effect of the social system that would force a widow and her daughter to live—and die—by sewing. The light coming through the skylight in the snowy roof to illuminate the figures suggests the influx of divine grace as symbolized in older religious paintings. Otherwise, murky shadows fill the colorless room. The solid figures enact their roles in the tragic drama on the small, but carefully constructed stage space of the room. *An Unfortunate Family* barely escapes sentimentality because it plays upon a strong emotional reaction to get its serious message across.

By contrast, Cassatt's painting is almost devoid of sentiment. Some of Cassatt's earliest critics praised the refreshing lack of this emotion in her many paintings of women and children. Her work lacks dramatic action and a deep stage-like setting. *Summertime*, set out-of-doors, avoids opaque shadows. Patches of bright color appear everywhere and call attention to themselves, unlike the muted shading of *An Unfortunate Family*. In fact, the surface of Cassatt's painting seems rather flat, especially since the water appears to be tilted up. Cassatt as a painter apparently wanted to draw more attention to the color, light, and paint than to the iconography.

THE VISUAL ELEMENTS

4

LINE, SHAPE, AND MASS

Line

Why is it that when we look at Figs. 4-1 and 4-2, we cannot help imagining two different personalities? When Henri Matisse and Max Beckmann depicted their own features, the results looked very different even though neither one of the artists exhibited much facial expression. The differences in our response to the self-portraits of Matisse and Beckmann cannot be attributed to vast variations in the iconography, since the basic subject—the human head—is the same. Each drawing basically describes essential physical fea-

tures; that is to say, each artist rendered eyes, mouth, chin, and the shape of the head with adequate visual information so that we recognize the body parts for what they are. To some extent the differences result from the different implements the two artists employed to draw their head. Nonetheless, since the visual information comes to us through **lines**—marks made to form the design on the surface—the heads look different because the lines the two artists made are quite different.

FIG 4-1 HENRI MATISSE [French, 1869–1954], *Self-Portrait*. 1968. Lithograph, 9 × 7 1/4 in. (22.9 × 18.5 cm). Bibliothèque Nationale, Paris.

FIG 4-2 MAX BECKMANN [German, 1884–1950], *Self-Portrait*. 1920. Drypoint, 7 11/16 × 5 3/4 in. (19.5 × 14.6 cm). Collection of the Grunewald Center for the Graphic Arts, UCLA. Gift of Mr. and Mrs. Stanley I. Talpis.

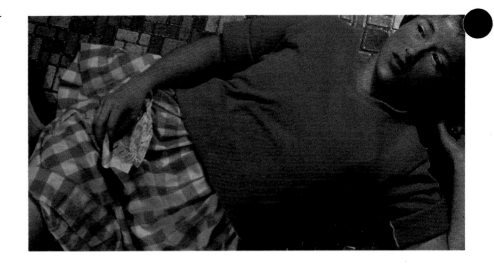

Fig 4-3 Cindy Sherman [American, 1954–], *Untitled*. 1981. Color photograph, 24 × 18 in. (61 × 121.9 cm). © Metro Pictures no. 6.

Matisse used continuous, curvy lines; Beckmann used short, jagged, broken lines. Because the lines in each work have a different character, the feelings that we have about these portraits are very different. Matisse seems serene, almost jovial; Beckmann seems intense and troubled. Perhaps the personality of each artist prompted the artist to use those particular lines. But whether we know anything about the artist's personality or not, the lines themselves speak to us and communicate thoughts and feelings beyond mere information about the shape of the eyes, mouth, or chin of the subject.

Whether imitating nature or creating a nonobjective work, a visual element such as line does not simply illustrate the artist's imagination; the elements become the concrete embodiment of the artist's imagination. Line is the first of the traditional seven elements of design that embody and express an artist's vision. Those seven visual elements are line, shape, mass, value, color, texture, and space.

General Characteristics

Quality. In art, lines can have a personality, whereas in Euclidean geometry, a line is an abstraction signifying a series of locations on a plane. The theoretical line in geometry has no thickness or any other feature. In art, lines can be thick or thin, jagged or smooth, broken or continuous. Straight lines seem regular and assuring in contrast to broken and jagged lines, which create a tense feeling because of their

irregularity. Because we sense these different qualities, they seem to express a personality or character. For instance, John Hancock expressed himself in the bold lines of his famous signature—in lines so resolute and determined that the name of the first person to sign the Declaration of Independence has become a synonym for *signature*.

All lines can instinctively produce in us emotional effects. They soothe the soul or they excite our interest. We read into lines some of the same kinds of feelings and attitudes we have toward different people.

Movement. The artist Paul Klee, who called line "the most primitive of elements," understood line as essentially **movement** because for him a line was "a point that sets itself in motion."[1] To Klee a point was a dynamic thing, full of potential and capable of generating lines of motion. To illustrate his idea, we have, at the end of the twentieth century, a tool that Klee did not have at the beginning of the century—namely, a computer graphics program. Generating lines from the point of a cursor across a screen with the emphatic motion of a handheld mouse somehow captures his idea a bit more strikingly than moving a pencil across a page.

Fig 4-4 Georges Seurat [French, 1859–1891], *Study for Le Chahut,* 1889. Oil on canvas, 21 7/8 × 18 3/8 in. (55.6 × 46.7 cm). Albright-Knox Art Gallery, Buffalo. General Purchase Funds, 1943.

Georges Seurat believed that an artist should achieve harmony in a work of art by expressing a dominant emotion through the use of the appropriate light, color, and lines. To simplify things for himself, Seurat condensed and subsumed all possible emotions under three categories: gay, calm, and sad. Seurat then devised the dominant light, color, and lines that would produce each of these three emotions. To express gaiety, for example, an artist should use predominantly bright light, warm colors like yellow or orange or red, and lines that rise above the horizon. In a letter he wrote in August 1890, Seurat explained his formula for emotional expression, in very terse language:

Gaiety of value *is the light dominant; of* hue, *the warm dominant; of* line, *lines above the horizon.*

Calmness of value is the equality of dark and light; of hue, of warm and cool; and the horizontal for line.

Sadness of value is the dark dominant; of hue, the cool dominant; and of line, downward directions.[2]

In Le Chahut *Seurat not only painted numerous lines that rise above the horizon, he also employed a color scheme in which warm colors, such as orange and yellow, dominate and add to the vibrant gaiety of the dance.*

Lines may also be thought to move because they make the eye move. They create paths that the eye can follow. Cindy Sherman, for example, carefully arranged the lines in her photograph *Untitled* (FIG. 4-3) to move the viewer's eye between her head and the letter and thereby suggest another layer of meaning. From the artist's point of view, lines are sources of energy that not only construct and organize the forms but also draw our attention and introduce movement into works of art that otherwise seem frozen and stand perfectly still.

Direction. If lines have movement, they also have direction: they go up or down, or they move diagonally or constantly change direction in curves. These directions have significance because the mind's eye, moving along a line, is always judging the direction and position of a line and projecting emotional states onto the line's location.

The emotions communicated by lines are subjective and relative to the context of the lines. Nevertheless, the Post-Impressionist painter Georges Seurat tried to establish strict guidelines for the emotions that the formal elements like line convey and tried to embody his theory in a few of his paintings. In his *Le Chahut,* for which he painted the preliminary work *Study for Le Chahut* (FIG. 4-4), Seurat wanted to express the dominant emotion of gaiety. *Le Chahut* illustrates a popular high-kicking dance of the same name in a French café music hall. To Seurat, horizontal lines expressed calmness, and lines that fell below the horizon expressed sadness. To illustrate gaiety, according to Seurat, an artist should use lines that rise above the horizontal. Since the subject of *Le Chahut* is a happy one, rising diagonal lines dominate the composition. The legs and skirts rise above the horizontal, and so do the lips, eyes, and mustache of the dancers and musicians.

FIG 4-5 EDVARD MUNCH [Norwegian, 1863–1944], *The Scream*. 1893. Oil on canvas, 33 × 26 1/2 in. (83.8 × 67.3 cm). Oslo, Kommunes Kunstsamlinger, Munch-Museet.

The Scream has become one of the best known expressions of the anxiety and desperation of modern life. Edvard Munch once elaborated on the event he visualized so graphically: "I stopped and leaned against the balustrade, almost dead with fatigue. Above the blue-black fjord hung the clouds, red as blood and tongues of fire. My friends had left me, and alone, trembling with anguish, I became aware of the vast, infinite cry of nature."[3] The figure in the foreground, a portrait of the artist, raises his hands to his ears to shut out the cry of nature. But the writhing lines in the sky and the land already resonate in the twisted shape of his body. By contrast, the straight lines of the fence, keeping him from the abyss below, skewer his throbbing form. The steep perspective distances him from the ghostlike shapes on the left.

Although Seurat's three categories of the emotional effects of line direction might be a bit mechanical and simplistic, they reflect some of the emotions we feel in lines, since they refer to basic physical experience. In general, horizontal lines are said to be calm and serene, like a solid floor or a flat horizon. Vertical lines are elevating because they mimic our feeling of standing up, and they follow the growth of trees and plants rising toward the sun. If horizontals symbolize the earth, verticals can also express our feeling for strength and resolution. Diagonal lines (think of mountain slopes and children's slides) seem more dynamic and exciting because they move in two directions at once—up or down, and across. They can convey action and motion. Curved lines seem to flow like water or like musical melody, and visually express a feeling of constant change and of gracefulness.

The interaction of two or more lines arouses feelings because of other physical associations. A combination of horizontal and vertical lines looks ordered and stable, like people standing on the earth or like the steel framework of a building. Lines that meet at a ninety-degree angle give a sense of regularity. Lines may intersect and conflict with one another like crossed swords, or they may meet at obtuse angles and create blunt corners. Lines may come together to form sharp angles that communicate a spiky feeling, as they do in Beckmann's *Self-Portrait*. Straight diagonal lines may clash with sinuous curved lines, as they do in Edvard Munch's famous *The Scream* (FIG. 4-5), where they express the anguish of the lonely, howling figure.

The problem with a psychological interpretation of lines is that by definition, emotional associations always contain a subjective, nonrational element. Curved lines may look graceful and melodic to one person and sinister to another person, as in *The Scream*. Furthermore, the effect of a line depends on the context in which the line appears and on its relationship to other lines. For instance, in Umberto Boccioni's painting *Dynamism of a Soccer Player* (FIG. 4-6) several "dynamic" diagonal lines cross through the canvas. But Boccioni communicated the movement and energy of the athlete mostly by the repetition of numerous short curved lines that tumble around the center of the composition—even though curved lines are usually characterized as graceful and melodic. Although it is hard to go much beyond generalizations in discussing the emotional quality of lines, art has always depended heavily for its interpretation on the psychological properties of lines.

Specialized Lines

Contour Lines. From the simple drawing of Henri Matisse's head in his *Self-Portrait* (FIG. 4-1) to the sophisticated representation of reality in Raphael's *Alba Madonna* (FIG. 4-7), artists' images depend on lines—especially contour lines—to create the appearance of a face, an apple, an abstract shape. Many of the lines in Cindy Sherman's photograph *Untitled* (FIG. 4-3) and Georges Seurat's *Study for Le Chahut* (FIG. 4-4) are contour lines. A **contour line** surrounds the edge of a form, limiting the form and distinguishing one area from another. It indicates where the form breaks off and another form begins, and in this way implies some space or room until the eye comes to the next area. The lines in a child's coloring book usually consist of contour lines.

When Raphael began painting *The Alba Madonna*, he first drew the contour lines of the figures on the surface to be painted. He then filled in these outlines with

FIG 4-6 UMBERTO BOCCIONI [Italian, 1882–1916], *Dynamism of a Soccer Player.* 1913. Oil on canvas, 76 1/8 × 79 1/8 in. (193.4 × 201 cm). Museum of Modern Art, New York. The Sidney and Harriet Janis Collection.

FIG 4-7 RAPHAEL [Italian, 1483–1520], *The Alba Madonna.* C. 1509. Oil, transferred from wood to canvas, 37 1/4 in. (94.6 cm) in diameter. National Gallery of Art, Washington, D.C. Andrew W. Mellon Collection.

color, fundamentally in the same way that children try to keep each colored crayon mark within the lines in a coloring book. If artists apply the paint thinly enough, sometimes their lines underneath the paint are still visible. In Matisse's head, where contour lines are actually drawn, they are a **convention,** a device of representation that we all accept. In reality there is no line under anyone's chin or along the tip of anyone's nose. We have learned to understand contour lines as the limit of a form, even though they themselves seldom really exist in nature. These lines represent the edge of what one can see as those forms turn around through space.

Architectural and Sculptural Lines. Cubelike solids and rectangular planes have distinct edges, of course, but not dark lines around them. Thus, by convention, one can also speak of the linear contours of the three-dimensional forms of sculpture or architecture or even furniture—the line of a statue's back or the roofline of a building or the S-curve of the cabriole (pronounced *kah*-bree-ole) leg of a Queen Anne–style chair (Fig. 4-8).

Horizontal and vertical lines dominate in architecture because of our natural desire for a building's stability. The vertical lines of classical columns and the soaring lines of modern office towers lie perpendicular to the horizontal line of the ground and to the horizontal transverse beams of the structures themselves. In many buildings perpendicular window frames or curved arches create lines that express the character of the edifice. The intersection of walls at the corners of buildings normally produces stable right angles. The exceptions have their own character: circular walls may expand rather than enclose the interior space; zigzag walls can produce great energy; walls that flow gradually into the curved vaulting above them may lift our spirit to a higher plane.

Architecture also has rooflines—the angular pitch of gables, the jagged points of Gothic spires and pinnacles, the swelling curves of domes. The series of long vaults of the Kimbell Art Museum (Fig. 4-9) in Fort Worth, Texas, by Louis Kahn, presents a rhythmic curved shape apparent both outside and inside the

Part II: The Visual Elements

FIG 4-9 LOUIS KAHN [American, 1901–1974], Kimbell Art Museum, Fort Worth, Texas. 1966–1972.

The cycloid curve is created by rotating a point on a circle.

building. The contour of these vaults is not strictly semicircular but a lower, more elastic, cycloid curve, formed by tracking and tracing a point on a circle as the circle was rotated along a straight line. The horizontal pause between each curve on the roofline also helps effect the elegance of the design.

Drapery Folds. In sculpture the eye is often attracted to the rhythmic lines of drapery folds. **Drapery** is art jargon for the loose garments arranged on figures in sculpture and painting. Flowing garments or drapery is not usually of great interest today, but a considerable amount of sculpture in the past was draped. The tubular folds and parallel crevices of the drapery often flow in a single direction when they gather at specific points or hang loosely across the surface. Drapery may flow from point to point or flutter free of the figure.

Sharp or soft, curved, wavy, angular, or straight, the lines of drapery folds allow the sculptor to display motion in the body or simply express the excitement latent in the figure. The sculptor of *The Ascension of Christ* (FIG. 4-10) at Vézelay, France, graphically visualized drapery folds not as the bending of real cloth but as energetic patterns of lines that swirl about the figure and express the exhilaration of the event. While Christ stretches his long arms to each side and shifts his long legs flat to the right, the narrow parallel lines of the drapery folds curve and sway in distinct patterns across and around the figure. The lower edge of his robe, especially, ripples with movement. On the hip, knee, and arms the folds swirl like small whirlpools flinging out lines of energy. The flat pattern of lines does not decorate the Christ figure but transforms him into an ecstatic heavenly being.

Fig 4-10 [French], *The Ascension of Christ.* 1120–1132. Detail from the tympanum over the central portal of the narthex of La Madeleine. Vézelay, France. Foto Marburg/Art Resource, New York.

Fig 4-11 Rembrandt van Rijn [Dutch, 1606–1669], *Old Bearded Man Looking Down.* Etching; plate, 4 5/8 × 4 1/8 in. (11.7 × 10.5 cm). Rijksprentenkabinet, Rijksmuseum, Amsterdam.

Hatching. Unlike the deliberate simplicity of a contour drawing in Henri Matisse's *Self-Portrait* (Fig. 4-1), artists also have linear conventions to indicate variations of light and dark. In his etching *Old Bearded Man Looking Down* (Fig. 4-11), Rembrandt drew a series of close, parallel lines to indicate the darker parts of forms—a technique called **hatching.** Sometimes two series of parallel lines crisscross on top of one another to create a particularly dark area—a technique called **cross-hatching.** In fact, Rembrandt depicted his old man with nothing but hatching and cross-hatching. By varying the closeness and the character of hatched lines, he suggested various degrees of darkness and the distinctive qualities of light in an area. The contour of the man's back nearly disappears in the dark, whereas the bright light obliterates the contour of his forehead and left arm. Without this latter contour, the effect of the light is intensified on the man, lost in his thoughts and dozing in the sun.

In Rembrandt's *Old Bearded Man* each series of hatched lines lies in the same, usually diagonal direction. In other works the parallel lines of hatching may curve around each form, just as a series of bracelets encircles a wrist. Hatched lines, for example, curve around George Washington's face and neck on the dollar bill. This kind of form-following hatching can accentuate the roundness of a shape and even characterize its texture.

FIG 4-12 GUERCINO (Giovanni Barbieri) [Italian, 1591–1666], *Mars and Cupid.* Pen and ink (bistre), 10 1/16 × 7 3/16 in. (25.6 × 18.3 cm). Oberlin College, Ohio. Allen Memorial Art Museum. R. T. Miller, Jr. Fund, 1958.

Calligraphic Lines.   In Guercino's drawing *Mars and Cupid* (FIG. 4-12), many of the lines do not define the precise contour of the form. Many of the curved lines are so animated and decorative that they create surface patterns and merely enhance the forms. Such lines are called **calligraphic** in the sense that they look like the elegant flourishes of fancy handwriting like that in "Elegance of Taste" (FIG. 4-13), in Thomas Tompkin's *The Beauties of Writing*—a little something more than what is necessary to describe the form. We enjoy calligraphic lines for their decorative aspect, for their virtuosity and stylishness, and for the energy they generate.

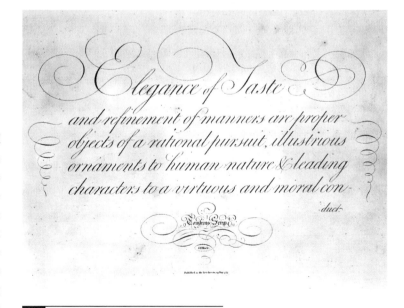

FIG 4-13   "Elegance of Taste," in Thomas Tomkins, *The Beauties of Writing.* 1777. 11 × 17 1/2 in. (28 × 44.5 cm). Victoria and Albert Museum, London.

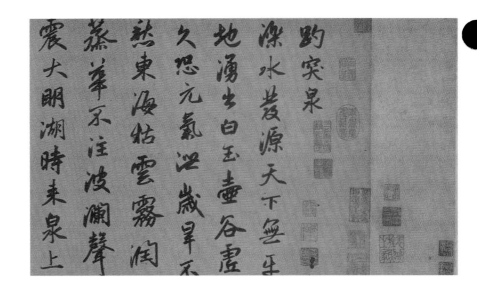

FIG 4-14 CHAO MENG-FU [Chinese, 1254–1322], running script *(hsing-shu)*, part of *Pao-t'u Spring Poem* handscroll. Yüan dynasty. Ink on paper. National Palace Museum, Taipei, Taiwan, Republic of China.

The Chinese have a special reverence for calligraphy. As children, Chinese are instilled with respect and appreciation for the art of writing. Like any handwriting, Chinese calligraphy may express a person's character through the quality of the lines. Using a brush for writing allows the Chinese calligrapher greater variety in the shape and personality of each character's lines. Brushed lines easily swell and taper. Chinese characters have more meaning and associations connected with them than the independent letters of the Western alphabet. Also, Chinese calligraphy has a history of styles, just as painting or sculpture does, and the various styles of calligraphy may be appreciated as expressions of the historical culture that produced them. In his calligraphy, Chao Meng-fu combined the elegance of linear movement with a strength that is embodied in the angles and the thickness of the lines. His style strikes a classical balance between elegance and strength.

In the East, to write the characters of their languages, the Chinese and Japanese have long employed a tradition of calligraphy, which has developed into an art form of its own. The landscape painter Chao Meng-fu illustrated a classic style of Chinese calligraphy in part of his *Pao-t'u Spring Poem* handscroll (FIG. 4-14).

Implied Lines. The human eye can also imagine lines in places where no lines may exist. Despite the numerous wavy contour lines that ripple around them, the arms and shoulders of the figure in *Archer* (FIG. 4-15), a charcoal drawing by Tintoretto, form a diagonal line almost parallel to the arrow. The torso and leg of Tintoretto's archer also form a curve very similar to the curve of the bow. His body takes on the very shape of his weapon.

But there is in reality no straight line to the arms and shoulders of Tintoretto's archer and no single curve in the torso and leg. The eye, always at work with the brain, likes to simplify many irregular forms and disjointed shapes and treat them as a line that moves in one direction. In spite of a very wiggly contour line, we can generalize and read the archer's whole arm as a single line. These **implied lines** appear in the figure because the mind's eye straightens out the twisty contour line to make one continuous line or it observes the general direction in which the undulations are moving. Or perhaps the human eye senses the central axis of the limb, functioning like an imaginary line running down the middle of the form, as in the legs of the dancers in Georges Seurat's *Study for Le Chahut* (FIG. 4-4). However we look at it, the mind's eye schematizes the body part or parts and sees them as a single simple line.

Simplifying irregularities into comprehensible lines works not just with body parts. The outline of a hill in a landscape painting might be very irregular and disjointed and yet seem to flow in a steady diagonal direction. We perceive these implicit lines because our mind prefers to see a unified whole before it experi-

Part II: The Visual Elements

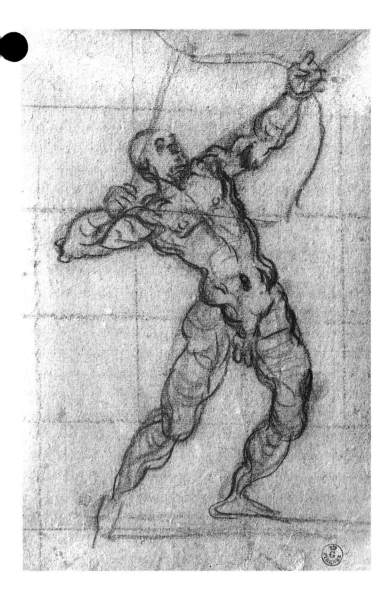

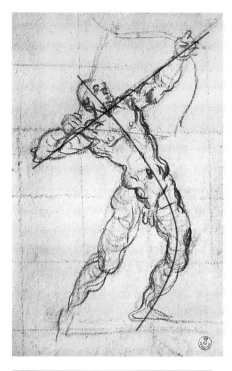

FIG 4-15 TINTORETTO (Jacopo Robusti) [Italian, c. 1518–1594], *Archer.* Charcoal, 12 11/16 × 8 1/8 in. (32.2 × 20.7 cm). Florence, Uffizi Gallery.

ences the individual parts. This idea was developed as part of **Gestalt psychology** in the early twentieth century. The German word *gestalt* means forms, pattern, or shape. Gestalt psychologists observe that people are much more likely to see complete and unified patterns, such as single lines, than fragments and parts. A broken circle will thus be seen as a circle sooner than it will be perceived as a series of disconnected arcs.

The exchange of glances between John the Baptist and the Christ Child and Mary in Raphael's *The Alba Madonna* (FIG. 4-7) also creates a diagonal line parallel to the one formed by Mary's left leg and forearm. Call this imaginary line between an eye and the object of its

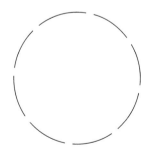

A series of arcs perceived as a circle.

FIG 4-16 [Japanese], *Guardian Figure.*
Kamakura period, 1185–1333. Wood,
66 5/16 in. (168.5 cm) high. From Shiga
Prefecture, Japan. The Cleveland Museum of
Art. Leonard C. Hanne, Jr., Fund, 72.158.

glance an **eye-line.** Eye-lines create movement because they establish another kind of path for the viewer's eye. It is common experience that just as people tend to look in the direction someone is pointing, someone's glance draws our attention along the imaginary line of its direction.

Figural Movement Lines. Since we readily see the limbs of the human body as lines, the gestures and attitudes of the human figures in a work of art make forceful linear roadways for our eyes. The alignment of the limbs, head, and torso create lines for our eyes to follow. It is only natural that we have strong sympathy for human movements. We feel in our own body the movements that others make with theirs. Staying within the confines of the front plane, the Japanese sculptor of *Guardian Figure* (FIG. 4-16) arranged the lines of the arms, legs, and trunk to act like a diagram of threatening violence. This figure is one of a pair of life-sized guardians that were positioned at the entrance to a shrine, to frighten off evil spirits. The guardian makes a terrifying face, knots all his muscles, and, feet spread apart, threatens intruders with his hand and fist. His anatomy is rendered in deeply cut knobs and tendons that emphasize the lines of his limbs and trunk. Even more than our eye, our body can empathize with the movement of the figure.

These explicit and implicit eye-moving lines generated by the human body help explain the prevalence of dramatic gestures in history paintings and other traditional kinds of figural art where the characterization of individuals and the entire narrative had to be expressed clearly and forcefully through the poses of the human figures. Some poses and gestures come to most human beings naturally: laughing and crying seem to generate similar body movements all over the world. Other motifs, like shaking hands or waving good-bye, developed as conventions in an individual society. Often we have to learn the body language of distant cultures in order fully to appreciate their lines. With some awareness of the significance of the body language of Hindu culture, for example, we can have a better feel for the strong lines of the sculpture of *Shiva Nataraja, Lord of the Dance* (FIG. 4-17) in the Cleveland Museum of Art.

FIG 4-17 [Indian], *Nataraja: Shiva as King of Dance.* Chola period, eleventh century. Bronze, 43 7/8 in. (111.4 cm.) high. The Cleveland Museum of Art.

Nataraja is a manifestation of Shiva in Hindu religion. Shiva and Vishnu are the two important members of the Hindu trinity. In this sculpture Shiva Nataraja is dancing within the circle of the sun, from whose rim flames shoot forth. The circle also represents the cosmos. Shiva tramples the Demon of Ignorance under one foot. Hindus consider the universe to be the light reflected from the limbs of Shiva as he dances within the circumference of the sun. Shiva also periodically destroys the universe so that it might be created again.

Hindu sculptors add arms to Shiva whenever additional attributes are given to the god. In this example, while the forward hands perform the ritual of the dance, a third hand holds a small drum and the fourth a flame. One leg crosses over the body of Shiva and parallels the movement of the arm. The trunk and the other leg create a zigzag line similar to the W-configuration of the one pair of outstretched arms. The violence of the dance expresses the awesome power of the beautiful god, exquisitely poised and balanced within the circle.

Contrapposto. The lines created by the pose and gestures of the human figure do not always signify an instant in a repeated movement like a dance or represent the acting out of a story as in a speechless drama. Often the pose is an end in itself. It may merely display the human body handsomely or at most convey some sense of character. The classical Western tradition has preferred stationary poses, developed by the ancient Greeks, whose lines only imply movement or the potentiality of movement within the human figure. Movement may be indicated without suggesting running or jumping or even walking. The posed figure is not necessarily changing location.

FIG 4-18 [Greek], Riace Bronze Warrior.
460–450 B.C. Bronze, silver teeth and
eyelashes, copper lips and nipples, 73 in.
(185.4 cm) high. Archeological Museum.
Reggio Calabria, Italy. Alinari/Art Resource,
New York.

Whereas the dancing *Shiva* in FIG. 4-17 displays
very striking movement through its linear configuration, the Greek bronze warrior from Riace, Italy, in
FIG. 4-18 displays movement in the human body by a
device called **contrapposto.** The Italian word means
"counterpositioning." The bronze warrior, while
maintaining his balance, twists and turns in a three-
dimensional manner. By contrast, Shiva's more violent movements do not break a flat plane.

Contrapposto usually entails the contrast between
parts of the human body by placing them in positions
that are different from one another. Either one part
turns in one direction and a related part turns in
another, or one part is up and the other is down. The
Riace Bronze Warrior has simply shifted his weight to
one leg so that that leg is tensed, and the other leg is
relaxed. One arm is up and the other is down. From
the rear we notice that one buttock is up and the other
down. Shifting the weight to one leg throws the hip
out and creates a slight spiraling curve throughout the
entire body from toe to head. The statute is almost a
textbook illustration of how the body can move by
alternately tensing and relaxing groups of muscles.

Compositional Lines. The lines of body movements in many older works not only express the feelings of individual figures, they also help move the eye
along lines that convey the essence of the drama.
When Giotto told the story in his *Lamentation* (FIG. 4-
19), he surrounded the dead body of Christ with
mourners, all of whom direct our attention to Christ
by their glances. The mourners focus also on Mary,

Christ's mother, who looks directly into her son's face. The tightly knit web of eye-lines created by the glances of the figures intensifies the drama. Since Giotto always concentrated on human reactions, the setting did not much interest him. In *Lamentation* the hill behind the figures looks more like a piece of cheese than a rock formation. Nevertheless, its obvious diagonal line leads our eye to the center of interest in the lower-left corner—the embrace of Christ and Mary. St. John's out-flung arms parallel the same diagonal movement toward Christ. Except for these diagonals, most of the lines in the painting are stable and somber horizontals and verticals—especially the verticals at the left and right, framing the composition. The symbolic dead tree at the right lines up with the verticals of the disciples below, both lines running parallel to the frame.

In Leonardo da Vinci's *The Last Supper* (Fig. 4-20), the diagonal lines of the architecture, as rendered in perspective, all point to the figure of Christ in the center. Christ stretches his arms out on the table and forms an equilateral triangle, a very stable configuration. The apostles surrounding him are in turmoil because he has announced that one of them is about to betray him. Their expressions and gestures embody various kinds of emotion such as surprise, anger,

FIG 4-19   GIOTTO [Italian, c. 1266–1337], *Lamentation.* C. 1305. Fresco. Arena Chapel, Padua, Italy. Scala/Art Resource, New York.

FIG 4-20   LEONARDO DA VINCI [Italian, 1452–1519], *The Last Supper.* 1495–1498. Santa Maria delle Grazie, Milan. Scala/Art Resource, New York.

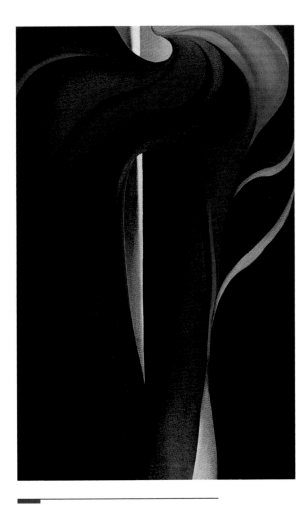

When Georgia O'Keeffe painted flowers, she came so close to them that their lines and shapes often extend beyond the edge of the canvas. By enlarging and then distilling the essence of the jack-in-the-pulpit, O'Keeffe showed us a pattern of tall, tapering shapes and S-curves we might never have seen ourselves. She once wrote that although everyone likes and admires flowers, "still—in a way—nobody sees a flower—really—it is so small— we haven't time—and to see it takes time like to have a friend takes time . . . . So I said to myself—I'll paint what I see—what the flower is to me but I'll paint it big and they will be surprised into taking time to look at it."[4]

puzzlement, and pain. Most of the apostles move away from Christ; the angle formed by the contours of Christ and Judas puts a wedge of space between them. The apostles at either end of the table, by the lines of their gestures and glances, move our eye back to the center of the controversy again. Thus all the lines of the setting and of the figures contribute to a single focal point and a single dramatic moment. As Giotto and Leonardo have demonstrated, gestures and poses are one of the ways that lines move the eye to discover what is important in a composition.

Shape and Mass

Shape

In Georgia O'Keeffe's painting *Jack-in-the-Pulpit, No. 5* (FIG. 4-21), some of the S-curved configurations may be considered either thick lines or thin shapes. As lines swell to a certain thickness, we become more aware of their two-dimensional character. This awareness transforms them into shapes. **Shapes** are areas of the surface of a work of art that have a distinct form. If any line is wide enough, we might easily call it a shape. If their surface is taken into account, many of the sinuous lines that vibrate throughout the landscape in Edvard Munch's *The Scream* (FIG. 4-5) seem to swell into snakelike shapes. Piet Mondrian may be said to have painted either black lines or black barlike shapes across his canvas in *Diamond Painting in Red, Yellow, and Blue* (FIG. 4-26).

Sometimes we recognize an area of a work of art as a shape because it is bound by a contour line like the shape of Max Beckmann's head in his *Self-Portrait* (FIG. 4-2). In other words, a line that comes around and closes in on itself creates a shape out of the surface, whether the shape be a circle, a rectangle, or something more amorphous. Distinctions between light areas and dark areas may break a surface into separate shapes, like the shape of a cast shadow on a wall. Finally, differences in color, as in O'Keeffe's painting *Jack-in-the-Pulpit, No. V,* or differences in pattern or texture can also distinguish areas one from another and create shapes.

Mass

In three-dimensional art media, such as sculpture and architecture, recognizable and distinguishable shapes

FIG 4-22 DAVID SMITH [American, 1906–1965], *Cubi XVII*. 1963. Stainless steel, 108 in. (274.3 cm) high. Dallas Museum of Fine Arts. The Eugene and Margaret McDermott Fund.

FIG 4-23 [Indian], Dancing couple. Andhra period, early second century A.D. Granite, over–life-sized. From the facade of the Chaitya Hall, Karle, India. Borromeo/Art Resource, New York.

have solid, three-dimensional **mass** taking up real space, not simply an area of a surface. Although the masses of sculpture and architecture correspond to the shapes of two-dimensional media, they are not exactly the same. For instance, David Smith, in his sculpture *Cubi XVII* (FIG. 4-22), strictly speaking welds together not square and rectangular shapes but cubic and cylindrical masses. In a drawing a head might have an oval shape—and only the appearance of mass; in a piece of sculpture a head probably has an actual egg-shaped mass. In a drawing a bent leg might be a curved shape; in a piece of sculpture it becomes a cylindrical mass protruding into space at the knee. In an architectural plan the walls of an old stone building are black lines; in actuality the walls and vertical columns of a building have thickness and substance and fill up space—they have mass.

Unlike the two-dimensional shapes of drawing and painting, the masses in sculpture and architecture may bulge out, lie flat, or break at a sharp angle as in a cube or a pyramid. Curving gently or protruding to a point, the swelling of a mass expresses its character. The Indian sculptor who carved the two dancers (FIG. 4-23) into the living rock at Karle certainly understood sculptural form as mass. The dancers flank the doorway of an enormous pillared hall cut into the hillside. Their relaxed bodies still flush from their exercise and their chests raised to inhale the air, this prince and princess pause to welcome the worshiper. Their faces, his broad shoulders, her breasts and hips, everything the sculptor carved is conceived as a rounded mass, filling but not crowding the framework of the relief. The full masses of their bodies burst with vitality and health.

Chapter 4: Line, Shape, and Mass

FIG 4-24 [Olmec], Las Limas sculpture.
C. 800 B.C. Greenstone, 21 5/8 in. (55 cm)
high. Veracruz, Mexico, Museo Regional de
Veracruz. Photo by Michael Zabe Thirriat.

FIG 4-25 JOAN MIRÓ [Spanish,
1893–1983], *Personages with Star.* 1933. Oil
on canvas, 78 1/4 × 97 1/2 in. (198.8 ×
247.7 cm). Art Institute of Chicago.

Kinds of Shapes and Masses

In Georgia O'Keeffe's painting *Jack-in-the-Pulpit, No. V* (FIG. 4-21), and in David Smith's abstract sculpture *Cubi XVII* (FIG. 4-22), the shapes and masses are easy to recognize, since they are distinct and obvious. But even in representational works of art, simple shapes and masses can be distinguished within the forms of reproduced nature. Since an imaginary triangular line can be inscribed around the figure of Christ in *The Last Supper* (FIG. 4-20), the entire figure may also be considered a triangular shape. The Olmec sculptor who carved the seated figure holding a child in his lap (FIG. 4-24) apparently understood the head, torso, and limbs as swollen cylindrical masses perpendicular to one another. These representations of "hidden" shapes and masses within nature reveal that the artist sees relationships and order underlying reality.

Shapes and masses have some of the same characteristics as lines. Like lines, they have directions and make pathways for the eye. Except for circles and squares, and spheres and cubes, most shapes and masses have a longitudinal axis that establishes a primary direction for the eye. The shapes in O'Keeffe's *Jack-in-the-Pulpit, No. V* establish strong curvilinear movements. Whereas the masses at the top of Smith's *Cubi XVII* lie in diagonal directions, the masses in the Olmec figure remain strictly horizontal or vertical.

Different shapes and masses have different emotional characteristics. Compare the shapes in O'Keeffe's painting with the shapes in Joan Miró's *Personages with Star* (FIG. 4-25). In O'Keeffe's piece smooth-edged consistently curved shapes flow out beyond the canvas on all sides. O'Keefe's shapes are simple, sleek, and regular. In Miró's painting black, white, and red curving blobs float against a somberly colored background. Many of the shapes resemble distorted heads, arm, legs, and even breasts. They seem playful and dreamy.

In a work of art shapes and masses can be small or large, delicate or overpowering; they can be many or

Part II: The Visual Elements

few, repetitious or isolated. When straight or curved shapes in modern art are bounded by precise contours and resemble regular geometric forms like the square, circle, or triangle, they are often called **hard edged.** They can also resemble the irregular shapes of biological organisms like a cell or tiny animal. Some critics have called the shapes in Miró's painting **biomorphic.** These shapes suggest a dramatic life of personal relationships in the biological world, or, better still, a dramatic life of biological relationships in the personal world.

The Format

In Helen Frankenthaler's painting *Lush Spring* (Artist at Work, p. 108) the irregularly contoured shapes line themselves up, for the most part, around the perimeter of the canvas. Since the center space remains almost empty, Frankenthaler's shapes repeat and reinforce the rectangular format of the canvas. In many a painting or drawing the shapes likewise tend to arrange themselves parallel to the edges of the canvas or the paper. In fact, the shape of the surface worked on by the artist often influences the internal lines and shapes in a variety of ways. As an artist proceeds, the shape of the format exerts a kind of magnetic force on the composition.

Most canvases or pieces of drawing paper are rectangular in shape, and the lines and shapes within the typical rectangular format are often in effect defined by their relationship to the edges. The edges, like *x* and *y* axes, act as the reference lines for even the diagonals and curves in a composition. The lines and masses of architecture and sculpture also often conform to the overall configuration of the work. The rectangular shapes of windows usually align themselves with the main masses of the building. In a similar way, the shape of a block of stone sometimes influences the masses a sculptor carves in the work. The consistency between the format and the internal forms of a composition usually appeals to both artists and viewers.

The painter Piet Mondrian once attempted to defy the influence of the format in a series of diamond-shaped canvases including *Diamond Painting in Red, Yellow, and Blue* (FIG. 4-26). In most of Mondrian's other paintings, the lines, squares, and rectangular shapes run parallel to the edges of his canvas.

FIG 4-26 PIET MONDRIAN [Dutch, 1872–1944], *Diamond Painting in Red, Yellow, and Blue.* C. 1925. Oil on canvas on fiberboard, 56 1/4 × 56 in. (142.8 × 142.3 cm). National Gallery of Art, Washington, D.C. Gift of Herbert and Nannette Rothschild.

Occasionally, as in *Diamond*, Mondrian tilted the canvas forty-five-degrees to create a more dynamic, diagonally oriented format. As a result, the frame seems to be continually cutting the painted lines and the shapes, which implicitly go beyond the framework. We seem to be looking through a diamond-shaped porthole at a small part of a reality, unrelated to the frame and extending far beyond the frame.

Not all canvases are square or rectangular, however, and not all sculpture is carved from a rectangular block of stone. In painting and low-relief sculpture, circular shapes, or **tondos,** were once popular, especially in the Renaissance. Circular formats are inherently unstable, and tend to roll since they do not have a dominant axis. To counteract this inclination, artists may place strong horizontal or vertical lines or solid-looking

Text continues on page 111

Helen Frankenthaler (1928–)

*W*HEN HELEN FRANKENTHALER paints, she often steps or crawls on her hands and knees inside the painting. Like Jackson Pollock, she paints on large pieces of canvas, spread on the floor, which can be worked on from all four sides. By approaching her work this way, she really identifies no top or bottom to the canvas.

Unlike Pollock, who drips and splatters paint, Frankenthaler pours paint onto the canvas, moves it around with a sponge or her hands more often than with a brush, and lets it soak in and stain the canvas. The flooding color may grow dark and opaque as it pools in spots, or the same color may grow thin and transparent and even fade away as it washes over another part of the canvas. Light and dark, opaqueness and transparency can be modulated within the same shape by her technique. Sometimes, as in *Lush Spring*, Frankenthaler will add strokes of thick paint over the stained passages.

Frankenthaler saw an exhibition of Pollock's painting in 1951 and visited his studio on Long Island a number of times. His work struck her as a revelation. She had grown up amid the art museums and galleries of Manhattan and had studied art at Bennington College in Vermont, where she developed a late-Cubist style. It was not Pollock's technique of splashing and dripping paint that amazed her but the

openness and boldness of his approach and the overall design floating in space that he achieved.

In October 1952, after weeks of sketching and of painting watercolor

HELEN FRANKENTHALER [American, 1928–], *Lush Spring*. 1975. Acrylic on canvas, 93 × 118 in. (236.2 × 299.7 cm). Phoenix Art Museum. Museum purchase with Matching Funds provided by COMPAS and the National Endowment for the Arts.

Frankenthaler paints spontaneously. She works with the accidental flow of the paint, adjusting her next moves and allowing the shapes to grow and evolve.

Helen Frankenthaler in her studio, 1969. Photo by Ernst Haas.

landscapes in Nova Scotia, Frankenthaler stained a canvas for the first time with shapes of oil color. The shapes of her painting, Mountains and Sea, preserved the feeling of wooded cliffs against the blue ocean. For years her work reflected a landscape she had seen or an experience from life, although the titles were usually added after the paintings were finished.

Frankenthaler's technical innovation was in transferring the methods of watercolor painting to oil painting on canvas. She washed the oil paint, thinned with turpentine, across the canvas. And because the canvas was raw and unprimed, the paint soaked in and stained it. The light and the texture of the canvas material come through the transparent paint. The painted form does not sit on the surface; it becomes part of the surface so that it appears very flat and yet of mysterious spatial ambiguity like a cloud in the sky. For exam-

ple, the transparent, washed-in shapes of *Lush Spring* float around the rectangle, interlock, and frame a center of mysterious depth.

At first Frankenthaler added drawn lines to her painting, but they gradually disappeared from her work, leaving only a sea of colored shapes. Frankenthaler seldom overlaps her irregular, nongeometric shapes. Very often the shapes do not even touch because channels of unpainted canvas separate them. Only the optical phenomenon of size or color contrast or the contrast of light and dark effectively pushes and pulls the shapes in and out through space.

Frankenthaler paints spontaneously although without the splashing and slashing of most expressionistic styles. She works with the accidental flow of the paint, adjusting her next moves and allowing the shapes to grow and evolve. Although different areas of color frequently define different shapes, colors

Continued on next page.

HELEN FRANKENTHALER [American, 1928–], *Mountains and Sea*. 1952. Oil on canvas, 86 5/8 × 128 1/4 in. (220 × 325.8 cm). National Gallery of Art, Washington, D.C. On extended loan from the artist.

often change imperceptibly one into another within the same shape because of Frankenthaler's flooding technique.

Around 1960 Frankenthaler began priming the canvas and switched to water-based acrylic paints to avoid the fading of oil paint and to achieve larger and more solid and more defined shapes. She began adding the thick paint visible in *Lush Spring* in the early seventies. Her method is to try everything and experiment with new shapes, new color combinations, new textures. Nine times out of ten the experiment fails, she admits, and she rips up and trashes the canvas. When a painting works, she often crops the canvas lying on the floor, to achieve the final composition. Her shapes thus usually extend beyond the edge of the finished painting, unlike those in *Lush Spring*, which echo the rectangular framing edge.

Frankenthaler fights constantly against easy solutions and successful habits. Admired and respected for a lifetime of achievement, she is still growing as an artist.

FIG 4-27   [Aztec], *Coyolxauhqui*. C.
1400–1500. Stone, about 132 in. (335.3 cm)
in diameter. From the Great Temple of
Tenochtitlán. Mexico City. Photo by David
Hiser/Photographers/Aspen.

*Discovered in 1978, this great circular
relief lay at the foot of the twin
pyramids that once stood in the heart
of Tenochtitlán (Mexico City). In
Aztec mythology, Coyolxauhqui, the
moon goddess, was killed and
dismembered by her brother
Huitzilopochtli (pronounced weet-
zeal-oh-poch-tlee), the god of the sun,
because she had killed their earth
mother. The enormous image of this
macabre event confronted the
thousands of sacrificial victims whose
blood would spill down the steps of
the Aztec pyramid.*

shapes in the circular composition to help stabilize it
visually. To stabilize his tondo *The Alba Madonna* (FIG.
4-7), Raphael built a strong triangular configuration
out of the three figures. Other artists may play with the
instability of the circular form and build a dynamic
composition out of circular or radiating shapes. The
dismembered body in *Coyolxauhqui* (pronounced ko-
yol-*show*-kee) (FIG. 4-27) seems to revolve around the
large stone tondo format because of the repetition of
similar forms and short diagonal lines.

The second half of the twentieth century saw a
movement, led by the American artist Frank Stella,
toward irregular formats, or **shaped canvases.** In
Agbatana III (FIG. 4-28) and in many of Stella's other
works, it is as though the shapes within the painting
determine the shape of the work's format, instead of
the format influencing the shapes as is traditional.
Whenever the shape of the canvas calls attention to
itself, a painting starts to take on a sculptural quality.
In this way shaped canvases, especially as they grow
more three-dimensional, frequently combine the arts
of painting and sculpture into one work.

FIG 4-28   FRANK STELLA [American,
1936–], *Agbatana III*. 1968. Fluorescent
acrylic on canvas, 120 × 180 in. (305 ×
457 cm). Oberlin College, Ohio, Allen
Memorial Art Museum. Ruth C. Roush Fund
for Contemporary Art and National
Foundation for the Arts and Humanities
Grant, 1968.

Figure-Ground Relationship

Some shapes psychologically seem to be more important than others in a work of art. In general, the figures or objects in the foreground tend to dominate the shapes in the background. The figures in Giotto's painting *Lamentation* (Fig. 4-19) attract our interest more than the pieces of earth and sky visible between them. This phenomenon of perception is called the **figure-ground relationship.** Gestalt psychology also investigated this tendency to perceive a form or a pattern as a figure against a background. The popular Dutch printmaker M. C. Escher took delight in toying with the figure-ground phenomenon in his woodcut *Day and Night* (Fig. 4-29). At the top of his print a flock of dark birds flies over the daytime landscape on the left, and a flock of light birds flies over the nighttime landscape on the right. Toward the center we may perceive the shapes either way, depending on how we adjust for ourselves the figure-ground relationship. The ambiguity of the shapes as they transform themselves from ground into figure makes the transition between night and day.

The figure-ground phenomenon of visual perception can mislead us about the relative importance of shapes. Although artists often characterize the leftover shapes in the background as **negative shapes,** they nevertheless still consider them to be shapes. Sometimes the background is blank, as in numerous portraits, but usually behind the figure is a setting in which the shapes, although they may seem subordinate psychologically, play an important role in the overall design and effectiveness of the work. Amateur photographers may discover this importance only when their prints are developed and they realize that there was a telephone pole in the background that now appears to be growing out of the subject's head. Many artists contend that negative shapes in a composition are just as important visually as the positive shapes in the foreground. Escher's woodcut demonstrates the principle that an artist should care about every shape.

Since many modern artists are convinced that all the shapes, both positive and negative, are vital and that in sculpture both the masses and the space around them have meaning, they try to do away with the figure-ground relationship. They diminish the importance of the traditional figure against the ground by treating all the shapes in the work equally. In Frank Stella's *Agbatana III* (FIG. 4-28) and in Valerie Jaudon's *Yazoo City* (FIG. 4-30), the artists do away with the figure-ground distinction completely. Even the little wedges and triangles occurring in between the interlaced pattern in Jaudon's painting assert themselves as legitimate shapes and rise to the surface of the canvas. Most modern artists like Jaudon and Stella demand that each and every shape function equally in the design so that each shape can be appreciated in its purity.

FIG 4-30 Valerie Jaudon [American, 1945–], *Yazoo City*. 1975. Oil on canvas, 72 × 72 in. (1829 × 182.9 cm). Courtesy Sidney Janis Gallery, New York.

Key Terms and Concepts

biomorphic	eye-line	mass
calligraphic	figure-ground relationship	movement
contour line	Gestalt psychology	negative shapes
contrapposto	hard edged	shaped canvases
convention	hatching	shapes
cross-hatching	implied lines	tondos
drapery	lines	

LINE

General characteristics

Quality	Thick, thin, jagged, smooth, broken, and continuous lines express character.
Movement	Lines make the eye move.
Direction	Lines that go up or down, move diagonally, or are curved convey feelings.

Specialized Lines

Contour lines	Contour lines surround the periphery of a form.
	Contour lines are an artistic convention.
Architectural and sculptural lines	Architectural and sculptural lines also have quality, movement, and direction.
Drapery folds	The folds and crevices of cloth create lines.
Hatching	Parallel lines indicate dark areas.
Calligraphic lines	Elegant flourishes, called calligraphic lines, are used to enhance forms.
Implied lines	The eye may imagine lines where none actually exist.
Figural movement lines	The eye has strong sympathy for the lines of the human body.
Contrapposto	Contrapposto is a device that uses contrasting directions of the body to portray movement.
Compositional lines	Compositional lines can guide the eye to the essence of the work.

SHAPE AND MASS

Shape	A shape is an area of surface with a distinct form.
Mass	A mass is a solid, three-dimensional form.
Kinds of shapes and masses	Shapes and masses also have quality, movement, and direction that can all effect feeling.

THE FORMAT

The format often influences the internal lines, shapes, and masses.

FIGURE-GROUND RELATIONSHIP

Negative and positive shapes define the figure-ground relationship.

LIGHT AND COLOR

FIG 5-1 J. M. W. TURNER [British, 1775–1851], *Slave Ship (Slavers Throwing Overboard the Dead and Dying, Typhoon Coming On)*. 1840. Oil on canvas, 35 3/4 × 48 1/4 in. (90.8 × 122.6 cm). Museum of Fine Arts, Boston. Henry Lillie Pierce Fund. © 1994. All rights reserved

Light

In Joseph Mallord William Turner's painting *The Slave Ship* (FIG. 5-1) the light of the sun becomes the leading actor in a tragic drama. Since the typhoon swirls around the light and seems to emanate from it, the sun appears to operate as the agent of divine vengeance that causes the cataclysm and punishes evil. Throughout the painting light cuts through, flings, and churns the blood-stained darkness. Turner's painting reveals that light itself can be much more than a mere source of illumination—that it can have meaning and be an active agent in a composition.

Turner first titled his painting *Slavers Throwing Overboard the Dead and Dying—Typhoon Coming Up.* He had read about a slaveship called the *Zong,* whose captain had ordered the sick and dying thrown overboard in order to collect insurance. There was an epidemic on board, and the ship had been insured only for losses at sea, not for losses of life through disease. As Turner imagined the scene, the small, spindly ship struggles against crashing waves and is about to be engulfed by the storm. The captain has already thrown the diseased slaves into the sea. In the foreground, fish that look like freshwater piranhas devour the slaves' manacled limbs. Although we might interpret the light as divine vengeance, Turner himself, in a poem he wrote about the painting, emphasized the irony that the storm, which had prompted the captain's evil deed, would also dash the captain's hopes for high profits. Significantly, the burning golden sunset stains the clouds and water blood-red.

At times throughout history the sun has been worshiped as a god, and it symbolizes divinity in religions around the world. The sun, in fact, is the ultimate source of energy, heat, and light on earth; it makes life on earth possible. Light also makes seeing possible. The separation of light from dark was one of the first acts of creation in the Hebrew Bible, and it can be the primary act of creation for the artist. Primitive feelings about light and dark lie deep inside us. Light in our culture expresses goodness, clarity, intelligence, and fullness. Darkness is evil, mystery, ignorance, and emptiness. The contrast between light and dark not only creates forms and describes space in art, it generates feelings, energy, and drama.

Value

Color is usually an integral part of light, but an important distinction between light and color exists and the difference can be easily demonstrated. Charles Sheeler's powerful photograph called *Wheels* (FIG. 5-2) is in black and white. Black-and-white photography reproduces not just black and white but a wide range of grays in between. Thus, photographic film in a camera can instantly translate the light-filled colors of nature into a seemingly infinite number of lights and darks, without color, to reproduce solid reality. Also, it is possible to adjust a color television set until all the color disappears, without removing the image from the screen. In both examples the image remains legible without color—we can still recognize what it is; but an image cannot exist without distinctions between light and dark. An all-white, an all-black, or a solid green surface without variations of light and dark would not signify very much.

It is clear then that light reflected from objects has two quite different properties: "lightness" and color.

116

The first property has to do with the amount of light reflected from the surface of an object. The technical name for this relative lightness or darkness of some area is **value.** The color of an object, a property distinct from its value, has the technical name **hue.** Hue is what we most often mean by the word *color*—that is to say, hue is what we mean by names such as *red*, *green*, and *blue*. With value and hue, a surface can be dark or light and, at the same time, red or green.

Scientists say that light belongs to a whole series of electromagnetic energy waves radiating through space like radio waves, x rays, and cosmic rays. The human eye can tune in to only a small number of these wavelengths. Technically speaking, a hue is a certain wavelength of light, a small part of the energy scale.

Light Source

The variations of light and dark on an object in nature—its values—depend upon the location of a source or sources of light at a certain distance from the object. The sun, fires, and electric lightbulbs are common **light sources.** Rooms are often lit by a combination of natural and artificial light, but artists have traditionally depicted what they see as if it were illuminated by a single light source. Two or more light sources are possible, but the simplicity and consistency of a single source make the job of rendering light and dark surfaces easier.

The light in most premodern paintings usually comes from the upper-left corner. Since most people are right-handed, artists usually sit with the light source at their left so that their right arm does not cast a shadow across their work (see *The Interior of David's Studio*, FIG. 1-3). In portraits, this means that the sitter usually turns to the viewer's left to face the light coming from the left.

Light usually comes into a painting from somewhere up above, just as sunlight most often comes from above. Occasionally, for special effects, an artist will use a more unusual light source, such as the light of dawn and of sunset, which strikes the earth from an unusual angle for a few moments each day. Some landscape painters make a specialty of those rare times of day. In *The Slave Ship* (FIG. 5-1) Turner looked directly into the low-lying sun and into its light blazing across the sky and sea. Notice that the shadows created by the waves fall toward the viewer. A cloudy day presents a

FIG 5-3   MARY CASSATT [American, 1845–1926], *Lydia Crocheting in the Garden at Marly.* 1880. Oil on canvas, 26 × 37 in. (66 × 94 cm). Metropolitan Museum of Art, New York. Gift of Mrs. Gardner Cassatt, 1965 (65.184).

special challenge to a landscape painter, since the entire overcast sky becomes the light source and diffuses the light on things evenly from almost every direction. In Mary Cassatt's painting of *Lydia Crocheting in the Garden at Marly* (FIG. 5-3) there are almost no shadows and no changes between light and dark in Lydia's face. Almost every colored surface in the painting has the same middle value—except the slash of light in the bonnet and scarf that accents the face.

If the light source were placed behind some subject, the interruption of the light might turn the subject into a **silhouette,** or a likeness consisting only of an outline that has been darkened or filled in solid. (In the mid–eighteenth century the French minister of finance Étienne de Silhouette began cutting profile portraits of people out of black paper; hence the term *silhouette.*)

The light in many Surrealist paintings comes from the front or from the side, casts very sharp shadows, and helps make the scene seem strange. The strong source of light coming from the right front in Yves

FIG 5-4   YVES TANGUY [American, 1900–1955], *Indefinite Divisibility*. 1942. Oil on canvas, 40 × 35 in. (101.6 × 88.9 cm). Albright-Knox Art Gallery, Buffalo. Room of Contemporary Art Fund, 1945.

ELEANOR PARKE CURTIS, silhouette bust of George Washington. Nineteenth century. Hollow cut, cardboard, mounted on black cloth and canvas. Metropolitan Museum of Art, New York. Gift of Mrs. S. W. Oakey, 1879 (79.6).

FIG 5-5   ARTEMISIA GENTILESCHI [Italian, 1593–1653], *Judith and Maidservant with the Head of Holofernes*. C. 1625. Oil on canvas, 72 1/2 × 56 in. (184 × 142 cm). Detroit Institute of Arts. Gift of Mr. Leslie H. Green.

Unlike other women artists of her time, Artemisia Gentileschi developed the necessary skill to depict the human figure in action because her father, Orazio Gentileschi, also a prominent artist, gave her adequate training. Judith, an outstanding Old Testament heroine, cut off the head of Holofernes, the enemy of the Israelites. Artemisia Gentileschi, who painted the event several times, probably felt sympathetic toward the iconography of a heroic woman. In the Detroit painting, Judith and her servant seem startled by a noise they hear outside the tent. They both stop and look up. Judith raises her left hand either to quiet her servant or to shield her eyes from the glare of the candlelight. Her hand casts a sinister patch of dark shadow across her face. Gentileschi exploited the brightness and harsh shadows of candlelight to fill the air with menace and dramatic tension.

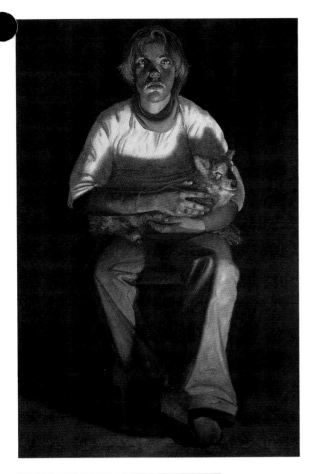

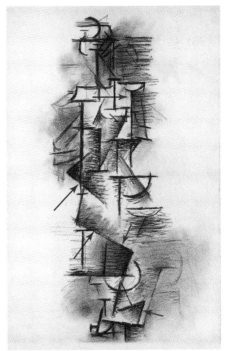

FIG 5-7   PABLO PICASSO [Spanish, 1881–1973], *Nude.* 1910. Charcoal on paper, 19 1/16 × 12 5/16 in. (48.4 × 31.3 cm). Metropolitan Museum of Art, New York. Alfred Stieglitz Collection, 1949 (49.70.34).

The arrows indicate how the light comes from many different directions.

FIG 5-6   ALFRED LESLIE [American, 1927–], *Portrait of Donna Kaulenas.* 1976. Oil on canvas, 108 × 72 in. (274 × 183 cm). Courtesy of the artist.

Tanguy's *Indefinite Divisibility* (FIG. 5-4) put every object in sharp focus and casts sharp shadows on the ground. By contrast, Tanguy's featureless landscape dissolves into the sky. The sharp light gives the strange "people" and machines made from what looks like dried bones and weathered rock an uncanny reality.

The source of illumination can even come from some artificial source visible within the picture. When the artist Artemisia Gentileschi painted *Judith and Maidservant with the Head of Holofernes* (FIG. 5-5), she set the scene at night and cleverly depicted the source of light to set the mood of stealth and suspense. Sometimes, for symbolic reasons, the Christ child in a Nativity scene becomes the light source and all the other people and things in the painting are lit consistently from his direction. The light source in a painting or drawing might even be underneath an image. The painter Alfred Leslie experimented with such an unusual light in his *Portrait of Donna Kaulenas* (FIG. 5–6). Just as it does when children shine a flashlight under their

chin to make a scary face, light from underneath creates rather weird illumination. Leslie's light source, located in the lower right, casts sharply defined shadows across the subject—including the shadowy outline of the sitter's pet. The shadow of the sitter's nose falls across her right eye! Coming from underneath, the light illuminates unusual places like the neck and chin and the skin under the eyes and the eyebrows. The extraordinary light source allowed the artist to reverse the conventionally expected formulas for painting the figure.

As soon as the modern movement in Western art abandoned the idea that a work of art had to be a reproduction of nature, many artists dropped the idea of using a consistent light source coming from a single direction, and felt free to light their forms in unorthodox ways. For example, Picasso, in the charcoal drawing *Nude* (FIG. 5-7), made the geometrical facets of Cubism appear to overlap and tilt in one direction or the other by means of contrasts of light and dark. He placed the lights and darks as though the light was

coming from one source in one place, then from another source in another place. Picasso seems to have changed the source of light with each observation of a shape in space. The source of light becomes relative to the depiction of the shape. This treatment is typical of Cubist lighting, which is sometimes said to be irrational in the sense that the artist has not simplified, unified, or "rationalized" the light sources.

Architects are also very concerned with sources of light and the quality of light these sources produce in their buildings. The placement and the size of the windows allow an architect to adjust the natural light within. Buildings are frequently sited in relationship to the sun as a source of not only light but also heat. The ancient Roman Pantheon has only one source of light, the circular, unglazed "skylight" in the center of the dome (see FIG. 16-18). It spreads an even illumination throughout the interior while it projects the shimmering disc of the sun on the floor or wall. Medieval buildings incorporated large windows high above the central area of their Gothic-style cathedrals (see FIG. 16-35), then filled the windows with dark colored glass that suffuses the interior with colored light that creates a mysterious atmosphere. In modern architecture plate glass can be substituted for walls to open a building so that little distinction remains between outdoor and indoor light. Philip Johnson's famous all-glass house (FIG. 5-8), whose only walls are the surrounding woods, teems with light. And of course the contemporary architect has countless possibilities with modern electrical sources of light.

Chiaroscuro

Images are formed in the eye by differences between light and dark. This text will call *any* contrast between light and dark **chiaroscuro** (the Italian word means "light-dark"), although many people reserve the term for pronounced contrasts.

Every change from light to dark—be it gradual or abrupt—suggests volume or spatial depth to our eye, so the term *chiaroscuro* often refers to the space-creating quality of light and dark in a painting or drawing. In architecture, too, changes in light and dark help us understand the spatial organization of a building and help make its masses look solid. The curving external wall of the ancient Roman Colosseum (FIG. 5-9) is penetrated by deep and dark tunnellike openings whose shadowy depths accentuate the solidity of the building.

Modeling. In one common type of chiaroscuro, light from a single source causes a gradual change in light and dark across rounded surfaces like a face, an arm, or a leg. This effect is called **modeling.** The painter Georges Seurat drew his *Seated Boy with Straw Hat* (FIG. 5-10) with almost nothing but the technique of modeling. Modeling gives the impression that part of the arm or leg is turned toward the light and part of it is turned away from the light. Modeling, in short, suggests that the form turns through space. Light and dark are thus used like modeling clay to build a solid three-dimensional form.

Not every culture in the world nor every period of Western culture adopted the technique of modeling and the solid, statuesque look it produces. The Japanese artist Kitagawa Utamaro, for example, when he depicted *Three Celebrated Beauties* (FIG. 5-11), did not employ modeling because he did not have Western concerns for the illusion of weightiness. Utamaro did not want dark smudges to mar the perfect complexions of these women or detract from the elegance of the curved lines throughout the composition. Although the three women at first look identical, Utamaro portrayed three distinct people—Toyohina, Okita, and Ohisa—who are characterized by subtle differences in the noses, the eyes, the mouths, and the way they hold their head.

Cast Shadows. Do not confuse the darks on the underside of modeled arms and legs with **cast shadows.** Reserve the word *shadow* for the dark shapes projected onto another surface by an object that intercepts the light. In short, restrict it to mean a cast shadow like the ominous ones made by the objects in Yves Tanguy's painting *Indefinite Divisibility* (FIG. 5-4). Cast shadows may reveal not only the direction of the light but also the quality of the light. A fuzzy, faint shadow means a diffused, soft light; a sharp and distinct cast shadow results from a strong and focused light source—inexplicably too strong and too sharp in Tanguy's painting.

Tenebrism. Baroque artists at the beginning of the seventeenth century developed a style of painting with such strong contrasts of light and dark that it has

FIG 5-10 GEORGES SEURAT [French, 1859–1891], *Seated Boy with Straw Hat.* 1882. Conté crayon drawing, 9 1/2 × 12 1/4 in. (24.1 × 31.1 cm). New Haven, Connecticut, Yale University Art Gallery. Everett V. Meeks Fund.

FIG 5-11 KITAGAWA UTAMARO [Japanese, 1753–1806], *Three Celebrated Beauties.* 1792–1793. Woodblock print, 14 11/16 × 9 7/8 in. (37.3 × 25.1 cm). Museum of Fine Arts, Boston. Spaulding Collection. © 1994. All rights reserved.

become known as **tenebrism** (the Latin word *tenebrae* means "gloomy darkness"). Artemisia Gentileschi, one of the finest Tenebrist painters in Italy, made the chiaroscuro of her depiction *Judith and Maidservant with the Head of Holofernes* (FIG. 5-5) a source of exciting drama. The Tenebrist style of painting can be very dramatic because by emphasizing the space-creating property of chiaroscuro it pushes the sharply illuminated parts of the painting out of the darkness into the light and seemingly into the viewer's presence.

Reflected Light. When modeling a form in light and dark, a painter will often add a little touch of white to the light part to show where the light is most intense and where it might be actually reflected from some surface. The area of the brightest light is called the **highlight.** Highlights not only reveal something about the strength of the light source, they also reveal the nature of the surface that reflects the light, since different surfaces reflect light differently.

It would seem logical that as a rounded form turns away from the light, it should get darker and darker until the deepest dark is met. But artists often observe in the darkness **reflected lights,** lights bouncing off other objects, that retard the progressive darkening of modeled forms. Amazingly, the darks may appear luminous. Hendrik Terbrugghen's *Boy Singing* (FIG. 5-12)—to a great extent a dark silhouette against a light background—is painted in a patchwork of light and dark streaks. But Terbrugghen's darks are transparent, light filled, and seldom opaque. Terbrugghen did not indicate the source of this secondary light; instead, the light-filled ambiance of the room seems to reflect light into the shadows. Reflected lights are easily observed in summer on the shadowy underside of objects surrounded by water, or in the winter on the underside of objects surrounded by snow. These lights often keep the darks of a modeled form from growing so dark that they merge with the darks of other surfaces and thereby obscure the contours of the form.

Light reflected from sculpture has a variety of characteristics. Polished white marble captures the most subtle shadows, whereas polished bronze appears glossy and accentuates the light. Marble is also slightly translucent—that is to say, light can penetrate a short way through the surface before it is reflected. Chisel marks left by a sculptor in a stone carving mute, or soften, the surface light; lumpy clay surfaces fragment, or break apart the light. Modern sculptors exploit the gleam of polished aluminum and the hidden shadows of rusty steel.

Value contrasts in sculpture telegraph to the eye the swelling of masses and the hollow depth of voids between the masses. These contrasts are especially important in our awareness of relief sculpture. Sculptors often carefully calculate their masses and voids to catch light and to create darks. The forms of Gianlorenzo Bernini's *The Ecstasy of St. Teresa* (FIG. 5-13) seem to be conceived, in major part, for the sake of the patterns of light and dark that they create. To catch light and create deep pockets of shadow—and to express the saint's ecstasy—Bernini deliberately bunched and wrinkled the heavy, coarse cloth of her habit. In fact, Bernini placed a window directly above his statute so that light would shine down on the figure from above and produce strong contrasts of light and dark in the drapery folds. Light and dark no longer merely define forms; they have a life of their own.

Color

The palette of a typical artist during the Renaissance held only eight or ten colors before they were mixed, and these painters seldom made use of vivid contrasts. Modern artists, however, have available dozens of colors. They have at their disposal broader technical means, an expanded science of color, and perhaps a greater appreciation for color. In fact, the world we live in seems to grow more and more colorful. Vivid color now bombards us on television and in photography, clothing, furnishings, interiors, paints, advertising, and of course art.

A color, or hue, is a wavelength of light—an "electric energy" that strikes the eye. Like value, hue is a property of light, not strictly speaking a property of an object. For instance, if a room contains only a red light source, most of the objects in the room will appear red. To be even more exact, hue is a perceptual response, in the visual cortex of the brain, to certain wavelength stimulations.

FIG 5-13 GIANLORENZO BERNINI [Italian, 1598–1680], *The Ecstasy of St. Teresa.* 1645–1652. Santa Maria della Vittoria, Cornaro Chapel, Rome. Scala/Art Resource, New York.

FIG 5-14 MARK ROTHKO [American, 1903–1970], *Orange and Lilac over Ivory*. 1953 or c. 1961. Oil on canvas, 116 x 94 in. (294.6 × 238.8 cm). Hood Museum of Art, Dartmouth College, Hanover, New Hampshire.

To celebrate the energy of color, Mark Rothko painted large horizontal rectangles of color that hover on the surface of enormous vertical canvases. In his painting *Orange and Lilac over Ivory* (FIG. 5-14) his rectangles have soft, fuzzy edges that make the color areas slightly insubstantial. Color alone creates his shapes. The vibrant patch of orange on top dominates the composition and seems to move aggressively forward. Although it is painted opaquely, traces of yellow radiate from underneath its edges. Rothko made the pale lilac rectangle on the bottom much larger to compensate for the aggressiveness of the orange. Still, it seems cool and retiring compared with the orange. Since

Rothko loosely brushed a layer of lilac over a lighter ivory color visible underneath, the lilac rectangle seems misty and therefore appears mysterious.

Rothko used color to express his feelings, and he expected viewers to have something like a religious experience when they are surrounded by his floating colors. In art and in life, the perception of color both delights the mind and excites the emotions. But the eye is no passive receiver. The eye, the mind, and the emotions filter, coordinate, distort, and interpret the colored energies they confront. Seeing color is a very human, a very personal affair.

Color in Different Cultures

Presumably, the eye mechanism for seeing color remains the same from place to place and from time to time, although it does vary somewhat between genders, since far more males are color-blind than females. Nevertheless, the perception of an individual color can be rather subjective. For instance, cultural conditioning influences the way we enjoy color. Statistically, most adults in the United States, Canada, and Western Europe prefer the color blue. People in Spain and some South American countries like red best. Children everywhere also prefer red. The Japanese choose white as their favorite color, black second, and yellow third. The Japanese are more concerned with whether a given color is glossy or dull than whether it is yellow, red, or blue. Europeans in the Middle Ages saw only three colors in the rainbow—red, a yellow green, and a dark color—although they could paint in all the colors of the rainbow. Many African languages do not distinguish between reds and browns and yellows, yet they are concerned with whether a color is wet or dry, hard or soft, rough or smooth, loud or quiet, happy or sad. When women of the sub-Saharan region of West Africa paint murals on the mud walls of their homes (FIG. 5-15), they traditionally employ only the colors black, white, red, and yellow. Since these colors are abundantly available in the earth where they live, their availability may have conditioned the artists' color sense.

In previous centuries color was called the sensual part of art because it was thought that color assaulted the emotions directly and had no rules. Some critics even implied that too much attractive color was immoral because it seduced the viewer too easily. Line, on the contrary, was good and was considered the intellectual part of art because there were rules for lines to obey. Later, in the twentieth century, scientists developed more theories about color than the science of line ever had.

The Art of Color

Color can get a bit technical because there exists a complex physics of light and an elaborate chemistry of **pigments,** or substances that impart color. Nevertheless, we can approach color only as an artist does, not as a scientist, and try to keep the technicalities to a

FIG 5-15 DIOCOUNDA, ASSA, and DIANNA CAMARA [Soninke], wall painting. C. 1988–1989. Buanch, Mauritania, Africa. Photo by Margaret Courtney-Clarke.

Wall painting in West Africa is a communal activity, often accomplished under the leadership of an expert in the art. The mothers of these women taught them to use the zigzag pattern for a festive occasion. The Soninke women of southwestern Mauritania paint with their fingers. They obtain their pigments from the earth near the Senegal River area and grind them into a powder themselves. Pigments are seldom mixed. In addition to using the traditional white, black, yellow ocher, and red earth colors, women of the twentieth century have adopted imported washing blue as a native color. Green is conspicuously absent from most of the wall paintings of these arid regions.

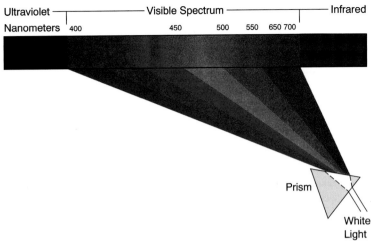

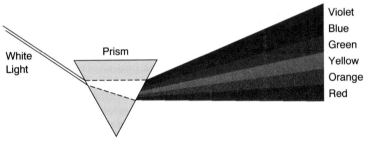

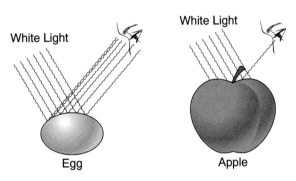

Why an egg looks white and an apple looks red.

minimum. Art—even the art of color—is far from an exact science, since the psychology of visual perception can be quite subjective. What the painter, as well as the viewer, has to see and feel most of all is the relationship of one color to another. Artists worry most about how one color acts upon another and how the colors work together as a whole, not whether such-and-such a green is essentially better than such-and-such a red.

The Spectrum

White light is the presence of all colors, a fact that can be demonstrated by shining a light through a prism. When white light is beamed through a triangular prism, the prism bends the different light waves at different angles into a **spectrum**—all the visible colors, arranged by the size of their wavelengths, from red, which has a long wavelength, to violet, which has a short wavelength. There are actually some colors beyond the spectrum that the eye cannot see: we call them *infrared*, the long waves at one end of the spectrum, and *ultraviolet*, the shorter waves at the other end of the spectrum.

Different pigments absorb, or subtract, different wavelengths of light. A white surface, like the shell of an egg, looks white because it has no pigment and thus reflects all the wavelengths of white light, producing in the eye the sensation of white. An apple looks red because the pigments on its surface absorb all the other wavelengths of light and only reflect a red wavelength. If pigments of every wavelength are mixed together, they absorb all the wavelengths of light and the result looks black.

The Color Wheel

Artists have found it helpful to bend the linear spectrum around into a circle called the **color wheel.** The British scientist Sir Isaac Newton, who discovered the spectrum in the seventeenth century, also turned it into the color wheel. On the color wheel, instead of being at opposite extremes, red and violet lie next to one another. A circular spectrum better describes our perception of the continuous flow of hues, and it establishes oppositions across the diameters.

It is easy to construct the color wheel, so easy that people can do it in their head and carry the visible

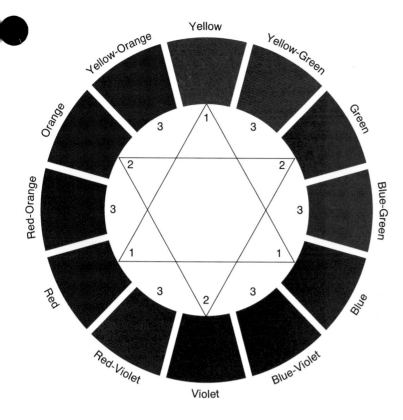

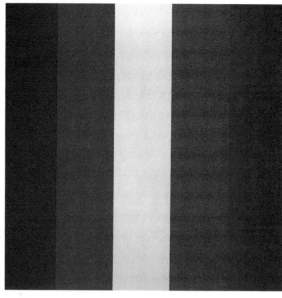

FIG 5-16 ELLSWORTH KELLY [American, 1923–], *Five Panels: Red Orange White Green Blue.* 1968. Oil on canvas, 120 × 120 in. (304.8 × 304.8 cm). Norton Simon Museum, Pasadena, California. Museum Purchase, Fellows Acquisition Fund.

spectrum around with them as part of their mental equipment. The German poet Goethe, who wrote extensively about color, made his color wheel in the same way most commonly used today. To construct the color wheel, first draw or simply imagine an equilateral triangle. On the tips of the triangle place the **primary colors,** which are red, yellow, and blue. These are called primary because they cannot be formed by mixing other colors and, theoretically, all other colors can be formed by combining them. Then draw another equilateral triangle, upside down, on top of the first one, to form a six-pointed star. On the three points of the second triangle, place the **secondary colors:** green, violet, and orange. These are called secondary because they can be created by mixing two primaries. Red and yellow make orange, so be sure to place orange on the tip of the triangle between red and yellow. Blue and yellow make green, and red and blue make violet, so place them accordingly. Finally, connect the six points of the star with a circle so that the essential features of the spectrum are now distributed in their correct order on the color wheel.

Artists seldom use all the primary and secondary colors of the color wheel in significant amounts in a single painting—unless they have some reason for the riot of color. Perhaps to make a case for pure, strong color, the American artist Ellsworth Kelly, in the 1960s, did a series of paintings, including *Five Panels: Red Orange White Green Blue* (FIG. 5–16), reproducing in large areas of opaque flat paint the primary and secondary colors of the spectrum. However, Kelly seldom admitted purple into his painting series unless he wanted to reproduce the complete spectrum. Orange does not appear frequently in his paintings either. Kelly seems to feel that yellow, red, blue, and green are the fundamental colors. Significantly, nineteenth-century physiologist Ewald Hering called these four colors the psychological primaries. They are the colors the eye recognizes as distinct, the colors the eye cannot infer from other colors. The eye, for example, can detect red in orange, but cannot detect yellow or blue in a true green.

It takes some concentration to perceive the central white panel of Kelly's *Five Panels* as the ground on which the colors are painted. Its equality with the colored panels in terms of size, shape, and treatment asserts its positive presence. The two primary colors red and blue appear, left and right, on the outside panels. The two related secondaries orange and green come next to them. In the middle panel, where we

FIG 5-17 MICHELANGELO [Italian, 1475–1564], *Mathan*. 1508–1512. Fresco. Rome, Sistine Chapel. © 1994 Nippon Television Network Corporation, Tokyo.

At the top of the wall above one of the windows of the Sistine Chapel, Michelangelo illustrated Mathan, an ancestor of Christ, sitting in a rather contrived pose. Michelangelo painted the background lilac and colored Mathan's tights green and violet. Mathan rests on a yellow ocher, or yellow orange, cushion—his hair is the same orange color—and a red ocher, or red orange, cloak is draped around his left arm and leg. The colors are close to the triad of the secondary colors, although the color orange is split into its neighbors, yellow orange and red orange. Michelangelo applied the same few colors—plus blue—among all the ancestor figures in the chapel, juxtaposing violet and yellow in one figure, orange and green in another.

Michelangelo modeled in light and dark with color. The dark values of Mathan's green tights, for instance, became strokes of violet, not dark green. As a consequence, Michelangelo's shadows glow with color. The combination of unmixable colors in one area resembles, to some extent, the shot, or iridescent color of cloth woven with two colors of thread. Michelangelo's bold blocks of color build big masses and betray the hand of a sculptor.

might logically expect yellow, as in the spectrum, Kelly has used white. He forces us to see white as a primary color. A number of color theorists do indeed call white a passive primary—and black a passive secondary. Kelly harbors no symbolism or philosophy to justify his reduction to basics. He simply enjoys confronting the viewer with strong color.

With the exception of Kelly, artists seldom paint with the three primaries—red, yellow, and blue—in equal amounts, since the results run the risk of looking too much like a comic strip. Nevertheless, the Dutch artist Piet Mondrian painted with the triad as a matter of principle—because he wanted to use only the fundamental colors plus black and white and sometimes gray. He wanted color at its most basic, so that its purity would speak universal truths. In his paintings (see FIG. 4-26) areas of these colors, varying in size and devoid of color contrasts, were balanced to express a dynamic equilibrium.

Combinations of the secondary colors—violet, green, and orange—seem to be rather common, perhaps because the employment of this triad seems more sophisticated than that of a combination of primaries. For example, Michelangelo painted the figure of Mathan (FIG. 5-17) on the Sistine Chapel ceiling in a clever arrangement of secondary colors. In terms of synaesthesia (one sense organ responding to the stimulus of another), an arrangement of secondary colors produces a slightly acidic, lemon-lime taste in the mouth, or perhaps it sounds like a minor key in music.

The color wheel can be filled with a great number of colors between the primaries and secondaries, although after a while the human brain finds it hard to distinguish between small changes of hue. We would also find it hard to come up with meaningful new names for them. But if we fill the gaps between the six points of the star with just one more hue, created by the mixture of a primary and a secondary, the result is called the **tertiary colors.** Some people call them intermediate colors. Mix orange and red, and the result is red-orange. Mix blue and green, and the result is blue-green.

In *Destiny* (FIG. 5-18), Henri Matisse overlapped, on the right, a rectangle of red-violet on a rectangle of blue-green, two tertiaries in high contrast. A white shape appears in a window of blue and yellow, both primary colors. On the left, the same red-violet intersects a rectangle of black. Behind them lies the same red-violet, lightened in value to a pink. The curved

Part 2: The Visual Elements

FIG 5-18   HENRI MATISSE [French, 1869–1954], *Destiny, [Le Destin]*. plate 16 from *Jazz*. (Paris, Editions Tériade, 1947). Pochoir, printed in color, double sheet: 16 5/ 8 × 25 5/8 in. (42 × 65 cm). The Museum of Modern Art, New York. The Louis E. Stern Collection. Photograph © 1994 The Museum of Modern Art, New York.

black shape on the left resembles the profile of an African mask, which watches the white shape on the right, distilled from the image of a couple embracing. *Destiny* comes from a series of twenty plates of a limited edition book Matisse called *Jazz*. He made the original illustrations by cutting colored papers with a scissors. Cutting the papers reminded Matisse of jazz music, and he also felt it was like drawing with color. Instead of filling in an outline drawing with a brush, Matisse used scissors to make shapes immediately in pure color.

Complementary Colors

The color wheel enables us to see which colors are close to one another, like red and violet, and also which colors are far apart. Colors that are directly opposite one another on the color wheel provide the greatest color contrast. They are called **complemen-**

tary colors because they contain or complete the triad of primary colors—for example, the primary red is opposite the secondary green, which contains the primaries yellow and blue. Placed near one another, they accent each other; one complementary color makes the other seem more vivid. But if a painter mixes equal portions of complementary colors, the result is usually a muddy gray.

It is easy to remember complementary relationships. If we use just the primaries and secondaries from

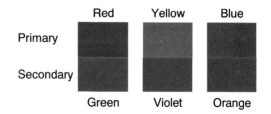

Fig 5-19 Ernst Ludwig Kirchner [German, 1880–1938], *Self-Portrait with Model*. 1910 or 1926. Oil on canvas, 58 5/8 × 39 in. (148.9 × 99.1 cm). Hamburg, Kunsthalle.

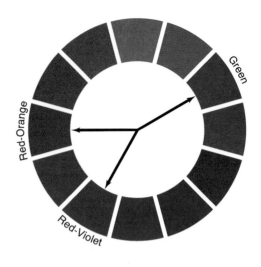

Split Complementaries

the color wheel, the opposite of red is green, so red and green are complementary colors. Yellow and violet, and blue and orange are the other basic complementary pairs.

Since complementary pairs accent one another by definition, Ernst Ludwig Kirchner could achieve the loudest possible color in his *Self-Portrait with Model* (Fig. 5-19) with complementary contrasts. Carrying a brush dipped in deep red, the aggressive-looking artist, turning from his model to confront the viewer, wears an orange robe with big bold blue stripes. Another complementary pair of colors, red and green, decorates the background. Kirchner's favorite model, Dodo, sits sullenly behind him. The delicate pale blue of her dress clashes with, or is incompatible with, the intense complementary colors around her. Contrasting colors are often said to clash when they have very different values.

As vivid as they are, complementary contrasts can be found in nature. Orange-stained clouds at sunset look especially striking when they are seen against the blue of the sky. Many flowers, like the violet, have parts that contrast one with another in complementary color combinations. Like nature, artists usually save complementary contrasts for their boldest color effects.

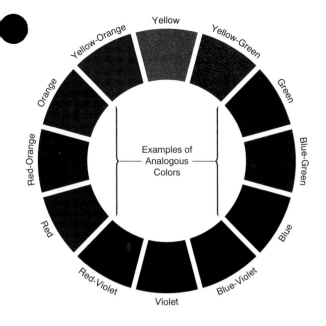

Examples of
Analogous
Colors

Yellow
Yellow-Orange
Yellow-Green
Orange
Green
Red-Orange
Blue-Green
Red
Blue
Red-Violet
Blue-Violet
Violet

FIG 5-20 MILTON AVERY [American, 1893–1965], *Clear Cut Landscape*. 1951. Oil on canvas, 31 × 43 1/2 in. (78.7 × 110.5 cm). San Francisco Museum of Modern Art. Gift of Women's Board.

A complementary pairing does not have to be exact. Sometimes an artist will match one color not with its opposite but with the two tertiaries adjacent to the opposite. A green placed next to some orange-red and some red-violet might produce a more sophisticated complementary contrast than simply a green with a red. This combination is called a *split complementary*.

Analogous Colors

Artists often paint with a combination of colors that are near one another on the color wheel. These are called **analogous colors,** or adjacent colors. Red, red-orange, and orange constitute a sample of analogous colors. Since every other color on the color wheel is a tertiary, every group of analogous colors has to contain at least one tertiary.

Nature is filled with analogous color combinations. Foliage in summer is colored with yellow-greens, greens, and blue-greens, and foliage in autumn is colored with yellow-orange, orange, and red-orange. In his painting *Clear Cut Landscape* (FIG. 5-20), the artist Milton Avery employed a color scheme of green, blue, and blue-violet—close to a series of three analogous colors on the color wheel. Avery did not spoil the serenity of his simplified landscape with even the

slightest touch of an opposite color. The lavender purple foreground and the yellow-green clump of trees in the middle offer the strongest color contrast, although both colors are considerably lightened so that the contrast is muted. Avery sometimes rubbed off some of his paint so that his color areas are thin and transparent and the contours of his interlocking shapes are airy.

Values of Color

Some colors are naturally higher in value than others. A pure yellow usually looks lighter than a true violet. Orange is usually lighter than red or green. Because of this, Michelangelo could model his figure of Mathan from the Sistine Chapel (FIG. 5-17) in different colors.

Any individual color can itself be lightened or darkened—that is changed in value—by the addition of white or black to the pigment. Theoretically, this does not change the wavelength of the hue and its position on the spectrum. Enough white added to red eventually makes us name the red *pink*; baby blue has a fair amount of white in it. Adding white to make a color lighter produces a **tint** of that color. Adding black to darken the same color produces a **shade** of that color.

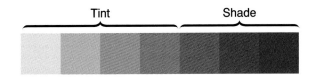

Tint   Shade

Intensity

Full intensity   Full intensity

Primary   Neutral   Secondary

Mixing some of the complement to any color will also produce a shade of that color. Brown can be a shade of orange (orange with some black in it), or the shade can be achieved by adding some dark blue to orange. Chocolate brown will have more dark red in it. Artists often prefer to create shades by adding the complement, rather than by adding black, because the complementary mixture results in a richer color of a darker value.

Intensity

Color has a third characteristic, in addition to hue and value. Colors may vary also in terms of *intensity* or *brilliance* or *saturation* or *purity*—all these words have been used to describe this characteristic. **Intensity** is one of the few fundamental principles of art that is somewhat slippery to grasp. It refers to the quality or purity of a hue—the redness of a red, the blueness of a blue. An intense red is fully saturated with redness. A pigment color becomes more intense as it approaches the true spectrum color.

A spectrum hue of full intensity can be reduced in intensity or neutralized by mixing it with its complement. For example, if you add a touch of green to a puddle of red, the red will become less intense. Add more green, and the red will become even less intense. Finally, add enough green, and the combination will probably become a dark gray, a **neutral** color fully reduced in intensity. Theoretically, when mixed together in equal proportions, complements of full intensity should become black because one complementary color has totally absorbed or subtracted the wavelength of the other complementary color.

So-called **earth colors** result from the mixing of secondaries. A mixture of violet and orange produces a reddish earth. A mixture of orange and green produces yellow ocher. A mixture of green and violet produces olive green. These combinations mimic the colors of minerals found naturally in the earth. Artists, ever since cave men and women began to paint, have used the colors of nature with great success. The Soninke women of Mauritania use earth colors to paint their walls (see FIG. 5-15), and the Navajo women who wove the serape in figure 5-21 in the mid–nineteenth century used only natural dyes.

Navajo women wove this wool shawl in traditional colors of white, red, and blue. The blue came from the indigo plant—the same deep blue once used to dye blue jeans. The red came from the cochineal insect that lives on the cactus in the Southwest. The creamy white was undyed wool. The woman sometimes also used wool dyed black.

The weavers made an intriguing pattern of horizontal lines and zigzags, visual ambiguities abound. The horizontal bands change into a new pattern when they appear beneath the red diamond shapes and zigzags. The bands of color cut into the diagonal zigzags andproduce blurry serrated edges instead of straight lines. When the serape was worn with the short edge pulled around the shoulders, the effect of the pattern would still be visible.

Contrasts

Complementary colors placed side by side intensify one another because of a phenomenon known as simultaneous contrast. **Simultaneous contrast** is the ability of a color to induce in its neighbor the opposite in value and hue. It is simultaneous contrast that enhances the vivid combination of complementary colors in Ernst Ludwig Kirchner's *Self-Portrait with Model* (FIG. 5-19). In this piece the blue is inducing more orange into the orange and making it more lively, and vice versa.

We experience something like the effect of simultaneous contrast by staring at a green, orange, and black American flag for thirty seconds, then looking at a blank space to see the true red, blue, and white colors and values of the flag. This experience is called *successive contrast* because it happens in separate moments of time. Simultaneous contrast involves similar processes in the eye, but it works instantaneously.

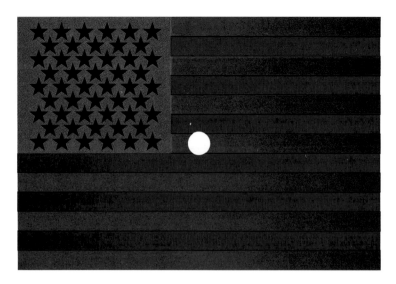

Stare at the dot in the center of the flag for at least thirty seconds. Then quickly turn your eyes to a white paper or a white wall. The flag should appear in its usual colors, which are complementary to those shown here.

Orange	Blue-Green	Red

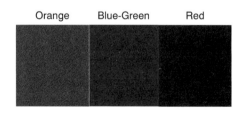

Green	Red-Violet	Yellow

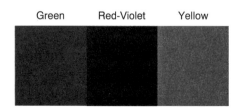

Simultaneous Contrast

Let us first consider how simultaneous contrast induces the opposite value. Placing a dark color next to a light color will make the light color seem lighter and the dark color seem darker. A central stripe that remains the same value will appear to change when contrasted with different backgrounds.

Simultaneous contrast also induces the complementary hue in the color next to it. The opposite of red is green, and red will induce the appearance of green in the color next to it. If the color next to the red is a neutral gray, the gray will look greenish. Simultaneous contrast will make an actual weak green look more intensely green next to some red.

Artists frequently use a touch, or an **accent** of a complement to enliven otherwise monotonous or even dull colors. Edward Hopper's very simple composition of a plain hallway and a distant room, *Rooms by the Sea* (FIG. 5-22), was largely painted with related colors: yellow, green, and blue. The shaft of light on the wall is tinged with the pale yellow of the hall floor and of the sun. The shaded part of the wall is tinged with a cool blue. The rug inside the room is green, the mixture of yellow and blue. However, the chair against the far wall is a red-orange. Not only does the color accent of the chair contrast with the complementary green of the rug next to it but also the red enlivens the whole painting, including the pale grays of the wall. The striking red accent on the left also balances the mysterious door on the right, which opens directly onto a vast sea.

Since simultaneous contrast will induce the opposite hue in an adjacent color, the appropriate simultaneous contrast can push a tertiary color more toward one part of the pair. A blue-green will look more bluish next to some orange; the same blue-green will look more greenish next to some red. A red-violet will look closer to a red when placed next to some green; the same red-violet will look closer to a violet when placed next to a yellow.

Psychology of Color

Although the enjoyment of color is universal and color theory has all kinds of names and technicalities to it, color remains a very emotional and subjective element. Our awareness of color is partially conditioned by our culture, but color also affects us intu-

Fig 5-22 Edward Hopper [American, 1882–1967], *Rooms by the Sea*. 1951. Oil on canvas, 29 × 40 1/8 in. (73.7 × 101.9 cm). Yale University Art Gallery, New Haven, Connecticut. Bequest of Stephen Carlton Clark.

itively and probably arouses primitive instincts. Our psyche reacts in different ways to colors in part through subjective associations and in part through cultural conditioning, and the two are often hard to separate. Black and white, for example, remind us intuitively of night and day, darkness and light; their association with evil and good is likely the result of culture. Red reminds us instinctively of fire and blood; it can also symbolize love, passion, martyrdom, danger, revolution.

Vincent Van Gogh often loaded the colors of his paintings with strong emotional and symbolic significance. Since the message of these colors is extremely subjective and personal, it is hard for everyone to feel exactly the same about them. Soon after Van Gogh painted his *Night Café* (Fig. 5-23), he wrote in a letter to his brother that it was "one of the ugliest I have done." He revealed that he had tried to show by means of color "the terrible passions of humanity" and "to express the idea that the café is a place where one can ruin oneself, go mad or commit a crime."[1] He spoke of the complementary contrast of blood red and green and the clash of analogous colors: blue-green, green, yellow-green, and sulfur yellow. These colors clash because they are of contrasting values. About a month later Van Gogh wrote that, in contrast to those in

Fig 5-23 Vincent Van Gogh [Dutch, 1853–1890], *The Night Cafe*. 1888. Oil on canvas, 28 1/2 × 36 1/4 in. (72.4 × 92.1 cm). Yale University Art Gallery, New Haven, Connecticut. Bequest of Stephen Carlton Clark.

FIG 5-24 VINCENT VAN GOGH [Dutch, 1853–1890], *The Bedroom.* 1888. Oil on canvas, 28 3/4 × 36 in. (73 × 91.4 cm). Art Institute of Chicago. Helen Birch Bartlett Memorial Collection (1926.417). Photo © 1994. Art Institute of Chicago.

Night Café, the colors of his *Bedroom* (FIG. 5-24) suggest rest or sleep. However, the combination of violet, red, yellow, lemon green, scarlet, green, orange, blue, and lilac in the painting of his bedroom does not necessarily transmit restfulness to the eye. Although we may be impressed with the depth of his feeling about color expressed in his letters, those associations remain, in the final analysis, personal.

There exists, however, a universal tendency to feel that some colors are warm whereas other colors are cool. Colors that are near red on the color wheel are considered **warm colors**—think of red-hot fire. Colors that are near blue on the color wheel are considered **cool colors**—think of cool blue water. Warm colors seem more exciting; cool colors seem more relaxing. Scientists have demonstrated that exposure to red light increases the heartbeat and that exposure to blue light slows it down. For artists the designation of warm and cool depends on the contrasting relationship between any two colors. A violet might be cooler than an orange, because it has blue in it, and the same violet might be warmer than a green, because it has red in it. The warm-cool distinction helps to create stimulating color contrasts because warm colors seem warmer next to cool colors and cool colors seem cooler next to warm colors.

Peter Paul Rubens frequently exploited warm-cool contrasts in his art. In his *Holy Family with Infant St. John and St. Elizabeth* (FIG. 5-25), for example, Rubens enhanced the dark blue sleeve and luminous red dress of the Madonna through contrasts of values and the warm-cool relationship. He also enlivened the sensuous appeal of his flesh areas with cool darks and warm lights. Rubens painted the bright and warm flesh tones of the figures with a thick layer of opaque paint, then he painted over that, the shadows, and the modeling in a thin veil of cool blue-gray. He painted his figures over a warm reddish brown underpainting, most visible at the bottom of the panel. In many places—in the slate blue robe of St. Joseph, for example—he applied over the underpainting a fluid layer of dark color, thin enough to let the lighter underpainting show through. Thus, throughout the painting, dark colors are transparent and light colors are opaque. Splashes of bright red on the flesh of the two children indicate light and color reflected from the mother's dress.

136

Part 2: The Visual Elements

Whereas Rubens used warm and cool colors to model the substantial forms of his figures, Raphael, in his *The Alba Madonna* (FIG. 4-7), used them to create the illusion of depth in the landscape. The warm-cool contrast produces three-dimensionality because warm colors seem to project forward and cool colors seem to recede. Based on this space-creating property, landscape painters during the Renaissance developed a formula for setting out the colors in a landscape. Features closest to the viewer, like rocks or a dirt road, were painted a warm brown. Trees in a middle distance were usually a cooler green, and distant hills were a still cooler blue. In Raphael's landscape the distance hills are green and the sky is blue. In Mark Rothko's painting *Orange and Lilac over Ivory* (FIG. 5-14) the orange rectangle seems to move forward, and the lilac square beneath it seems to retreat.

Some artists paint by using only **local color**—that is, the colors they know the objects to be without any regard for temporary or accidental effects. They color an apple with a single red hue, modeling the hue with some white for the lights and black for the darks. Grass might be painted in a single green hue, and the sky will be painted blue. Painting with local color was once standard practice. The French artist Nicolas Poussin, in such paintings as his *Madonna of the Steps* (FIG. 5-26), observed the tradition of local color whenever he confined each hue within the contour lines of the drawing. Poussin did not necessarily use fewer or less intense colors than Rubens, but his rational approach to painting led him to reject Ruben's display of coloristic effects, such as color reflections, transparent veils of one color over another, and warm-and-cool contrasts within a single area.

Rubens may be said to have painted with what is known as **optical color**—color as the eye sees it, with all the subtleties of reflected colors, filtering atmosphere, colored lighting, and simultaneous contrasts. Optical-color artists might paint an apple with touches of different red hues. They might use green for the modeling of the darks, a touch of blue reflected from the tablecloth, and a highlight of yellow reflecting the golden sun. When Rubens, in his painting *Holy Family*, captured the reflections of the red dress on the skin of the children and when he used blue for the shadows of flesh, he was employing optical color.

FIG 5-25 PETER PAUL RUBENS [Flemish, 1577–1640], *Holy Family with Infant St. John and St. Elizabeth.* C. 1615. Oil on panel, 46 × 35 1/2 in. (116.8 × 90.2 cm). Art Institute of Chicago. Major Acquisitions Fund 1967.229.

FIG 5-26 NICOLAS POUSSIN [French, 1594–1665], *Madonna of the Steps.* 1648. Oil on canvas, 28 1/2 × 44 in. (72.4 × 111.8 cm). Cleveland Museum of Art. Leonard C. Hanna, Jr., Fund.

FIG 5-27 CLAUDE MONET [French, 1840–1926], *Rouen Cathedral, West Facade, Sunlight*. 1894. Oil on linen, 39 1/2 × 26 in. (100.3 × 66 cm). Washington, D.C., National Gallery of Art, Chester Dale Collection.

Separate brush strokes of different hues are visible in a single area in Rubens's painting. Instead of producing dead areas of bland color with no visual interest, the optical-color artist declares that nature itself is full of reflections, colored light, and vivid contrasts.

A Brief History of Color in Modern Art

The French Impressionists, at the end of the nineteenth century, made painting with optical color extremely popular. Claude Monet, for example, observing the subtleties of color on the facade of Rouen Cathedral, recorded his sensations in numerous separate brush strokes to produce *Rouen Cathedral, West Facade, Sunlight* (FIG. 5-27). The Impressionists left it to the eye of the viewer to mix the many dabs of different colors in any area. These artists were part of a revolution away from transcribing nature as a system of boundary lines—in other words, drawing—and toward reproducing nature as patches of color. Although they originally devised their technique in order to be true to nature, their dabs of color took on an independent life. As in Monet's painting, color asserts itself.

The Impressionists tried to reproduce natural light by raising the values of all their colors. They painted in what has been called a *high key*, or a light range of values. They kept their color sensations unmixed on the canvas because combining colors would muddy and darken them. Dabs of complementary colors appear side by side in their work so that simultaneous contrast can go to work and intensify the colors. The broken or separated brush work and the juxtaposed colors help re-create the scintillation of natural sunlight.

Chiaroscuro as a design element faded from the Impressionists' imagination. Some of them rejected the use of black altogether, since they found light and color even in shadows. They decided that since sunlight tends to color areas with tinges of yellow and orange, simultaneous contrasts should induce into the adjacent shadows tinges of violet and blue. Many Impressionists delighted in exaggerating the effect.

Fig 5-28 Georges Seurat [French, 1859–1891], *The Channel at Gravelines: Petit Fort-Philippe.* 1890. Oil on canvas, 28 7/8 × 36 1/2 in. (73.3 × 92.7 cm). Indianapolis Museum of Art. Gift of Mrs. James W. Fesler, in memory of Daniel W. and Elizabeth C. Marman.

The Impressionists painted intuitively and seldom spoke about color theory. By the time of the last Impressionist exhibition in 1886, Georges Seurat and his Neo-Impressionist followers were turning Impressionist intuition into a rationalized system, splendidly illustrated in Seurat's painting *The Channel at Gravelines: Little Fort-Phillipe* (Fig. 5-28). When he painted this landscape outdoors in the summer light, Seurat was also studying the latest findings of science about optics and color and devising a technique called **Divisionism** or Pointillism to make the application of color scientific. In Divisionism colors were strictly separated and applied in a methodical series of touches of the brush according to Seurat's color theory (see chapter 4).

The Neo-Impressionists would paint only with the pure colors of the natural light of the sun. They removed earth colors, neutrals, and avoided mixing colors on their palette. Only the eye was allowed to add one color to another and thus mix colors optically. Seurat's landscape seems to strike a balance between warm colors like yellow and orange, and cool colors like blue. Blue dots predominate in the sky, blue green dots in the water, and rose and yellow in the sidewalk. The dominance of the light values of the landscape contrasts with the dark frame that he painted around it. In the balance of colors and of values he likely wanted to express the harmony and serenity of a summer day. Like an Impressionist, Seurat recorded a moment in time, but then he fixed it permanently with a feeling of equilibrium. Whereas his unmixed and intense dots of color are combined by the eye, they are too small for the eye to perceive them individually at a distance. To a great extent, the eye mixes and perceives the complementary colors as a light gray—as a luminous haze enveloping the deserted land on a still, hot summer afternoon.

FIG 5-29 PAUL GAUGUIN [French, 1848–1903], *Day of the God (Mahana no atua)*. 1894. Oil on canvas, 26 5/8 × 35 5/8 in. (67.6 × 91.5 cm). Art Institute of Chicago. Helen Birch Bartlett Memorial Collection (1926.198).

Unlike the Impressionists, who painted their immediate perceptions of nature, Paul Gauguin sought to evoke in his work underlying spiritual truths. In the upper two-thirds of this canvas, where a mysterious religious ritual seems to be taking place, the colors tend to be pale, with a good deal of white in the sky and with the sand painted pink. The bottom third of Gauguin's canvas, which probably represents a sacred pool, has far more striking color contrasts. The strong colors most likely symbolize spiritual realities.

Since the Middle Ages colors had seldom been applied so flatly in Western art. The shapes in the pool can in no way be interpreted as reflections of the land above. Many of the bloblike forms are yellow, shifting to orange on the right. The "shadow" *of the rock on the left is an intense red. All the primary and secondary colors are present—although there is little violet. Whatever symbolic significance Gauguin may have had* *for his colors, his example freed color from the restrictions of representing reality.*

At about the same time, also in the late 1880s, Paul Gauguin started to apply colors flatly, without modeling (see *Day of the God [Mahana no atua]*, FIG. 5-29), like the Japanese artists he admired (see *Three Celebrated Beauties*, FIG. 5-11). Gauguin, in his work and in his words, encouraged artists to intensify and exaggerate the colors they found in nature. In fact, Gauguin often used colors for personal symbolic reasons and arranged colors to create visual harmonies and "music"—regardless of the natural color of the object depicted. The theory of the correspondence between painting and music, embodied in synaesthesia, encouraged his free use of color. It was at this time too that Vincent Van Gogh explored the emotional and symbolic potential of color (see *Night Café*, FIG. 5-23, and *Bedroom*, FIG. 5-24). For Van Gogh color became a means of expressing his feelings directly.

By the beginning of the twentieth century, color, freed from the description of nature and allowed to express feeling, took on a dynamic life of its own. André Derain, Henri Matisse, and several other French painters asserted themselves in basic, bright patches of color applied so boldly that critics named them Wild Beasts, or *Fauves*, in 1905. Derain, in *The Turning Road (L'Estaque)* (FIG. 5-30), seems to have used color for the delight of it. Painted in the summer of 1906, *The Turning Road* burns with an array of hot analogous colors: red-orange, red, red-violet, and violet. The spots of cool dark green or dark blue make strong complementary contrasts. The yellow road complements the violets. In this picture, Derain came under the spell of Gauguin, whose South Pacific work had recently appeared in a Paris exhibit. But instead of the exotic "harmonies" of Gauguin's colors, Derain substituted loud and brash complementary contrasts and artificial heat. Color transforms a fairly traditional landscape composition into subjective expressionism.

Even more than Derain and perhaps more than any

other artist of the twentieth century, Matisse set an example of an artist dedicated to the enjoyment of rich color (see his *Destiny,* Fig. 5-18). The intense hues, strong contrasts, and large simple areas of color in much twentieth-century painting all bear the hallmark of Matisse.

Although Picasso eliminated all but earth colors from his early exploration of Cubist space, most twentieth-century artists have relished color. Wassily Kandinsky investigated the psychology of individual colors and likewise affirmed the analogy between color and music (see Fig. 1-19). He painted thoroughly abstract compositions containing patches of color, separated from and independent of the lines in the pictures. In the second half of the twentieth century Josef Albers, as a painter, teacher, and author, impressed on artists the relativity and the complexity of color relationships and made the perception of color the very theme of his work (see *Homage to the Square,* p. 143). In the 1960s

Color Field Painting, Hard-Edge Abstraction, and Minimal Art exploited large, simple areas of flat color in large-sized abstractions. Mark Rothko, Ellsworth Kelly, Frank Stella, and Helen Frankenthaler in New York belonged to a group of Color Field Painters. Another group of Color Field Painters worked in Washington, D.C. The Minimalists among them reduced their work to the raw experience of color. Also in the 1960s Pop Artists like Andy Warhol (see Fig. 1-7) often employed luminous and intense, almost fluorescent colors.

A portion of the general population may not like the distortion and abstraction of modern art, but many enjoy its colorfulness. Many contemporary artists still delight in intense colors, strong complementary contrasts, and the emotional and spiritual significance of colors. Unquestionably, the artistic revolution in color has opened our eyes to color as never before.

Josef Albers (1888–1976)

W HEN Josef Albers painted, he sat at a table in a modestly sized room. On the table before him lay a piece of Masonite, not a canvas. He preferred the hard surface of a panel because it did not move as he applied the paint.

Joseph Albers at Black Mountain College, August 1944. Photo © the Estate of Hans Namuth.

In the series of paintings he began in 1949 called *Homage to the Square*, Albers designed three or four squares nesting inside one another. He used a ruler to outline the squares in silverpoint (a drawing tool with a silver tip), since the marks of an ordinary graphite pencil would have smeared when he painted over them. Then Albers merely filled in the spaces between the lines that he had measured, painting each square a different color. He deliberately chose an arrangement of simple regular shapes so that the relationships between and among the colors would stand out.

Albers painted with a palette knife, with colors squeezed directly from the tube. He systematically marked down on the back of the panel the name of the colors and the name of their manufacturers. He almost never mixed colors. As he spread the paint between the drawn lines with his small knife, he was careful not to let the knife strokes show. He once likened his application of paint to making sandwiches. Albers applied the color thinly in one coat over a white underpainting so that the white underneath showed through. His red or blue or brown color thus appears translucent and luminous.

In this series Albers paid homage to color. In other words, it is the relationship between the colors that matters, not the repetition of square shapes. In each work in the series he generally painted the inner and outer squares in contrasting colors, whether the contrast was between values or between hues or between both. The intervening square or squares form an ambiguous transition between the center and the periphery. The intervening color can often be seen as the mixture of the two others on either side of it or as a third color veiling part of the inner square and part of the outer square. Thus the colors can be seen as either opaque or transparent. Colors seem to change their character because of their interaction with an adjacent color. In short, we may perceive them in different ways. By means of his arrangement of colored squares Albers caused us to participate in the creation of his art.

JOSEF ALBERS [American, 1888–1976], *Study for Homage to the Square.* 1950. Oil on Masonite panel, 20 5/8 × 20 1/2 in. (52.4 × 52.1 cm). Yale University Art Gallery. Gift of Anni Albers and the Josef Albers Foundation, Inc.

Albers was a provocative teacher. He showed his students that human perceptions provide various explanations for ever-changing problems. He made them see for themselves by making them think for themselves.

The *Homage to the Square* painting in the Yale University Art Gallery, one of the earliest in the series, is also one of the most colorful. At first the painting seems to have four different, randomly chosen colors: yellow, orange, blue, and blue-green (or aquamarine). The outer two colors may be described as cool and have a tendency to recede; the inner two colors are warm and seem to project forward. The spatial effect of this warm-cool contrast contradicts the appearance that the colors are nested one within the other, with the smallest square farthest back in space. The yellow square—luminous, intense, spatially ambiguous—gains a special presence. Starting with the yellow square, the colors are also arranged in contrasting values: light, dark, light, dark. Because of simultaneous contrast, the intense orange makes the dull blue square seem bluer.

Like many other artists in the twentieth and earlier centuries, Albers supported himself by teaching in art schools and university art departments. Before coming to America, he taught at the Bauhaus, a famous progressive school of art in Germany in the 1920s and early 1930s. There he taught the preliminary course in basic materials and basic design. He came to the United States when the Nazis declared modern art degenerate and closed the school. In the mid-1930s he began teaching at Black Mountain College near Asheville, North Carolina, and after that he taught for some time at Yale University in Connecticut.

Albers was a provocative teacher. He did not lecture his students and tell them what to think. Rather, he presented them with problems for which they were to find solutions. He showed them that human perceptions provide various explanations for ever-changing problems. He made them see for themselves by making them think for themselves. He presented a thoughtful approach to art, in contrast to an approach stressing the exploitation of self-expression, intuition, and individuality.

Albers also wrote an influential book, *The Interaction of Color,* published in 1963. Through teaching, speaking, writing, and the example of his own art, he made generations of artists see color and learn how to use it. Albers even believed that an awareness of the interaction of color alerted the mind to changes and shifting relationships in life. In his life and in his art, he was always teaching.

LIGHT

Value	The relative lightness or darkness of some area is its value.
Light source	Light sources may be above, within, behind, or underneath the subject, diffused, or irrational.
Chiaroscuro	Chiaroscuro is any contrast between light and dark, produced by modeling, cast shadows, Tenebrism, or reflected lights.

COLOR

Hue	A hue is a wavelength of light.
Color perception	The perception of color can be culturally conditioned.

Color Relationships

Primary	The primary colors are red, yellow, and blue.
Secondary	The secondary colors are green, violet, and orange.
Tertiary	A tertiary color is a mix of a primary color and one of its adjacent secondary colors.
Complementary	Complementary colors are opposites on the color wheel.
Analogous	Analogous colors are adjacent to each other on the color wheel.

Values of Color

Tint	A lightened color is called a tint.
Shade	A darkened color is called a shade.

Intensity

The saturation or purity of a hue is called its intensity.

Contrasts

Simultaneous contrast	A simultaneous contrast induces the opposite in value and hue.
Accent	An accent is a touch of a complementary color.
Warm-cool contrast	A warm-cool contrast has psychological effects.

Part 2: The Visual Elements

Key Terms and Concepts

accent
analogous colors
cast shadows
chiaroscuro
color wheel
complementary colors
cool colors
Divisionism
earth colors
highlight

hue
intensity
light sources
local color
modeling
neutral
optical color
pigments
primary colors
reflected lights

secondary colors
shade
silhouette
simultaneous contrast
spectrum
Tenebrism
tertiary colors
tint
value
warm colors

6

SURFACE AND SPACE

Different Realities

Romare Bearden built his work titled *Black Manhattan* (FIG. 6-1) around a duality found in most works of art—a division between the tangible surface of the art object and the visual effects produced by the imagination. In this work Bearden combined large areas of very flat color, like the orange and blue shapes at the top, with other colors roughly applied with the brush. The roughly applied paint has a texture, a quality of the surface that calls attention to the physical presence of the paint. The large orange and blue areas appeal to our eyes differently, since they have a smooth, plain texture.

In other parts of *Black Manhattan* Bearden added pieces of photographic reproduction, like the black-and-white fire escapes and the faces of some of the figures (other figures have a flat, masklike silhouette for a face). The photographic areas give the impression of three-dimensional space lying beyond the surface. The contrast of textures, the juxtaposition of flat and three-dimensional objects, and the sudden shifts in scale probe the differences between reality and illusion. The combinations and contrasts declare that Bearden's work is not an illustration of a Black neighborhood in Manhattan but a complex memory of various sensations of it.

With few exceptions, works of art have a physical reality with a texture to them, as well as an illusion of something else. On the one hand, they almost always offer a tangible surface or a solid mass—an object that might be touched. On the other hand, they present something for the mind to imagine beyond the dimensions and the shapes of the object: a space and a surface quality are two such possible illusions. In contemplating texture and space in a work of art, the mind delights in the interplay between the tangible actuality and the imaginary.

Real and Apparent Texture

As part of their visual appeal, shapes and masses can have textures that are rough, irregular, or smooth. **Texture** refers to the real or apparent quality of the surface. A conspicuous texture calls attention to the surface and often makes us aware of the material from which it was made. We may enjoy the feel of the texture even though we never touch the surface. Texture, adding a richness to forms, may simply delight the eye.

In architecture, texture plays a crucial role. A wall in any building has a different appeal depending on whether it is made out of rough-cut stone, marble

FIG 6-1 ROMARE BEARDEN [American, 1914–1988], *Black Manhattan.* 1969. Collage and synthetic polymer on board, 25 1/2 × 21 1/4 in. (64.8 × 54 cm). Schomburg Center for Research in Black Culture, Art and Artifacts Division; New York Public Library; Astor, Lenox, and Tilden Foundations. Photo by Manu Sassoonian.

The Pueblo people have lived at Taos for a thousand years in houses made of adobe, a Spanish word for sun-dried brick. The word adobe also applies to the buildings built with these bricks and to the clay from which they are made. Workers commonly covered adobe brick walls by hand with mud. Since the Pueblo Indians stacked their rooms on top of one another in an irregular steplike fashion, ladders are needed to reach the upper levels of their houses.

With suitable care, adobe is permanent in the dry climate of the Southwest, where the interior of a house built from it stays cool. The texture of adobe walls reflects the surrounding earth from which it was made and retains something of the personal touch of the builder.

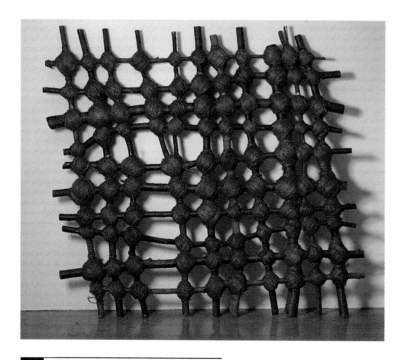

FIG 6-3 JACKIE WINSOR [Canadian, 1941–], *Bound Grid*. 1971–1973. Wood and hemp. Courtesy Paula Cooper Gallery, New York.

veneer, red brick, plate glass, or some other substance. The material may be rich and warm like polished wood, or harsh and brutal like poured concrete. We know just by looking that each surface would feel different if we touched it. Building materials also may influence environmental systems such as acoustics, ventilation, heating, and cooling. Sleek modern glass walls offer poor insulation against heat and cold and usually prevent natural ventilation. In contrast with the flawlessly smooth machine-made panels on the walls of many modern buildings, the adobe buildings of the Pueblo Indians at Taos, New Mexico (FIG. 6-2), have a rugged texture, an appealing irregularity, and a human touch.

The texture of pieces of sculpture may vary from that of polished brass to that of porous clay and rusty iron. Texture comes to the fore in any art form involving textiles. Jackie Winsor has made intriguing pieces of sculpture, like *Bound Grid* (FIG. 6-3), from rope, raw wood, tree branches, cement, or bricks that are bound, nailed, or coiled together in an almost primitive way so that the texture of the raw material stands out. Since we can seldom touch and carry works of sculpture, texture often becomes an important clue to the character of the sculptor's material, its weight, and its solidity. The sculptor may also control the play of light with variations in texture.

In two-dimensional art works, texture can be both real and imagined. The artist may produce a rough or smooth surface in the very application of the medium. In some works—in Raphael's painting *The Alba Madonna* (FIG. 4-7), for example—nothing breaks the polished finish of the paint to call attention to the smoothness of the surface. If we do reflect on the unblemished quality of the surface, it may signify to us the skillfulness of the artist. In other works—in the paintings of Monet or Van Gogh, for example—the application of paint creates a consistently rough surface that draws attention to the paint itself. We become aware of the artist using paint as paint. In the work of artists whose brush strokes create a distinctive texture, we can enjoy the richness of the surface and, at the same time, we can see the illusions that the brush strokes create. In many works of art the contrast of textures, like a contrast of colors, stimulates visual interest in the shapes that the artist has created.

Texture often occurs when an artist draws with the paintbrush. In such cases, the texture of the brush strokes can disclose the virtuosity of the artist and the very creative act of making art. The texture of Willem de Kooning's *Woman IV* (FIG. 2-35) gives a very graphic account of the artist's energetic gestures while painting.

A textured surface may be produced in other ways. Twentieth-century artists like Romare Bearden (see FIG. 6–1), who paste different material on the surface, take obvious delight in the contrast of differently textured shapes. Sometimes an artist will add thickeners or granular material to the paint itself to produce a textured surface. Paul Klee first constructed a textured surface out of roughly applied plaster before he began painting his *Vocal Fabric of the Singer Rosa Silber* (FIG. 6-4). Reinforcing the rough texture with the illusion of flimsy patches of cloth that Klee painted on the surface, the overall texture is a visual pun on the meaning of a "vocal fabric," or musical texture. (The letters are the singer's initials, and the five vowels, the more melodious part of the voice.) Sometimes the canvas or paper itself has a rough surface with a distinctive character that the artist may exploit. For his drawing *Seated Boy with Straw Hat* (FIG. 5-10) Georges Seurat deliberately chose a rough-textured paper so that his crayon

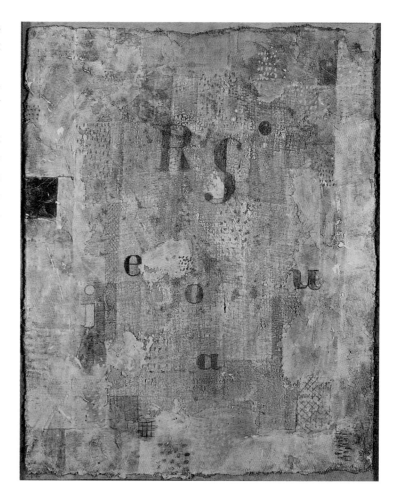

FIG 6-4　PAUL KLEE [Swiss-German, 1879–1940], *Vocal Fabric of the Singer Rosa Silber.* 1922. Gouache and plaster on canvas, 20 1/4 × 16 3/8 in. (51.4 × 41.6 cm). Museum of Modern Art, New York. Gift of Mr. and Mrs. Stanley Ressor.

FIG 6-6 JUAN GRIS [Spanish, 1887–1927], *Still Life with Poem.* 1915. Oil on canvas, 31 3/4 × 25 1/2 in. (80.6 × 64.8 cm). Norton Simon Collection, Los Angeles.

FIG 6-5 WILLIAM M. HARNETT [American, 1848–1892], *The Old Violin.* 1886. 38 × 24 in. (96.5 × 61 cm). National Gallery of Art, Washington, D.C. Gift of Mr. and Mrs. Richard Mellon Scaife in honor of Paul Mellon.

The American painter William M. Harnett specialized in still life paintings with objects arranged on some vertical surface like an old door. More than the accuracy of his brush strokes, it is the painting's lights that convince the eye about the material of any surface. The wood of the violin reflects more light than the wood of the door. Notice as well the soft transparent shadow cast by the fold of the sheet music, and notice the subtle modeling of the letter (addressed to the artist himself). Harnett's use of light attempts to trick the eye into believing that his painting is a real door in the wall. The viewer must be careful not to open the door; the bottom hinge is broken.

would not easily fill in the pitted surface. The irregularity of the paper helps produce a grainy soft light as the crayon hits the top of the hills and leaves the valleys empty.

Texture can also be merely implied through a purely visual illusion called **trompe l'oeil** (pronounced trohmp *loy*). Viewers today, as in the nineteenth century, are often fascinated with the illusions of natural materials in William M. Harnett's still life painting *The Old Violin* (FIG. 6-5). Artists like Harnett have the ability to reproduce for the eye the material of any object in nature, and the eye may be fooled into believing that the represented material has the same surface texture in the painting or drawing that it does in nature. To fool the eye about texture, the artist must not only reproduce the exact color and design of the material but also observe how the surface reflects light. Light reflections, more than anything else, give the eye clues about the nature of the material and thus the texture of the reproduced surface. An expert still life painter like Harnett re-creates the texture of wood, metal, fruit, or stone with sensitive observations of

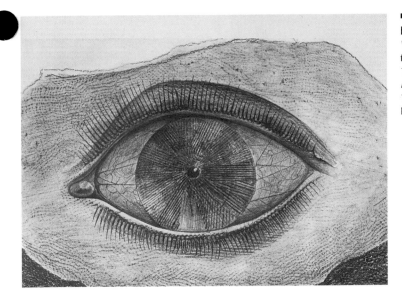

FIG 6-7   MAX ERNST [German, 1891–1976], *Wheel of Light, (Lichtrad)*. Collotype, after frottage, printed in black, composition: 10 1/2 × 17 in. (26.6 × 43.2 cm). In *Histoire Naturelle* (Paris, Galerie Jeanne Bucher, 1926), plate 29. Museum of Modern Art, New York. Gift of James Thrall Soby.

how light reflects from those different surfaces. Textures re-created through the luster of the materials are, of course, only an illusion.

Another kind of implied or imaginary texture is produced by patterning. To produce a texture this way, the artist Juan Gris filled a few of the shapes in his painting *Still Life with Poem* (FIG. 6-6) with rows of small circles. These circles are so regular and small that we ignore them as shapes and imagine instead that the larger shapes have a texture like a screen. We imagine that if we were to rub our fingers across the surface it would feel rough. Whenever a small-scale configuration is repeated with the regularity of a pattern over an extended area, the eye will ignore the lines and shapes of the configuration and believe instead that the area has a texture.

The Surrealist artist Max Ernst invented a drawing and painting technique he called **frottage** (pronounced froh-*tazh*), which means "rubbing," to let texture itself stimulate his imagination. In *Wheel of Light (Lichtrad)* (FIG. 6-7), one of a series of illustrations to a book of Surreal science, he placed his paper on top of ordinary materials like floorboards, rough sackcloth, or tree leaves and rubbed the paper to produce textures. The textures then freed his imagination to create hallucinatory images. Frottage transforms ordinary material into a new reality. For instance, in *Wheel of Light* it transforms the veins of a leaf into the blood vessels of the eye to suggest a disturbing similarity between life-forms.

The Illusion of Space

In his painting called *The Staircase Group: Raphaelle and Titian Ramsay Peale I* (FIG. 6-8), Charles Willson Peale created another kind of illusion on the surface of the canvas when he depicted **space,** or the imagined area behind the surface. The artist not only explored the two dimensions of height and width in his painting, he also conjured up a third dimension of space that seems to extend back beyond the surface. From inside the painting, two of his sons, painted in the

scale of life, look out and seem to beckon the viewer to climb the stairs with them. When *The Staircase Group* was first exhibited in the statehouse in Philadelphia, Peale hung it in the frame of a doorway, as though the doorway led into the painted staircase; in other words, the door frame served as the picture frame. In addition, the artist placed a wooden step, built out into the room, at the base of the painting. The deception is reported to have fooled George Washington, who bowed politely to the painted figures as he passed by.

Many Western artists over the centuries have attempted, like Peale, to create a three-dimensional illusion in their work, perhaps because the Western world itself loves to explore and conquer space. From Christopher Columbus to modern astronauts, Western culture has been continually attracted to the challenge of conquering deep space. Likewise, many Western artists, from the Renaissance until the modern period, have tried to deny that the two-dimensional surface they work with is flat. Like magicians, they have created the illusion of a substantial, three-dimensional world out of the lines and layers of paint they apply. For centuries they have treated the flat surface of a picture—the **picture plane**—as though it were a window through which viewers can see another world spread out before them. And if, like Alice in Wonderland, a viewer could eat the right amount of mushrooms, he or she would become the right size to step over the frame and walk around through this "window world." No painting can fool anyone for very long into thinking it has three-dimensional reality, but few paintings demonstrate so explicitly as Peale's *The Staircase Group* the idea that a painting is a window—or in this case a doorway—into a world lying behind the canvas.

Space and Time

Of course we cannot enter into the painting and climb the stairs with the Peale brothers. We must view the painting from a fairly static point in front of it. There are, however, kinds of art in which the viewer actually does move through space. If Peale had built the staircase as part of a work of architecture, we indeed could follow his invitation to climb the stairs and move through space. If Peale had been a filmmaker, no doubt his camera would have moved through space up the stairs and we would see in a short while what was at the top of the stairs. If Peale had carved statutes of his sons, we might well be encouraged to walk around the group to examine it from all sides. In architecture and sculpture, space in a work is normally a physical reality, not an illusion as it is in painting. Space may be an illusion on a movie screen, but through the camera's eye the viewer can move through it. Since it normally takes movement to see these three kinds of art, it therefore takes a period of time for architecture, film, and many kinds of sculpture to unfold like a performance of music.

Sculptural masses take up space in the real world, and the empty spaces between the masses establish voids. Voids also result from the concavities in the masses themselves. In traditional figural sculpture, limbs that extend out into space incorporate the volume of space surrounding the statue into the work. Extended limbs and centrifugal movements may charge not just the space around the statue but even the viewer's space, so that the work acquires a kind of living presence. Being near a work such as Rodin's *Thinker* (FIG. 18-9), one can feel an emanation of the sculpture into the space around it as it looms overhead. Photographs of the *Thinker* cannot capture the sensation. However, the sculptors of ancient Egypt (see FIG. 16-7), Michelangelo (see p. 184) and many other sculptors avoided gaps between the limbs of their figures and never extended their limbs into space. Their figures seem to be still confined within the original mass of the block of stone.

Some sculptors of the twentieth century, inspired by the Cubist sculpture of Picasso, have realized the potential of thin planes to segregate and defines volumes of space. These planes have almost no mass and act like mere membranes that confine or subdivide space. In *Constructed Head No. 2* (FIG. 6-9) Naum Gabo created a work of almost pure space in which the surrounding space flows freely into the sculpture. Trained as an engineer, Gabo understood that the strength of an object and the volume of space it took up were not to be identified with the solidity of the mass. A sturdy modern bridge, for example, could be constructed of an openwork steel structure, rather than a solid mass of stone. In *Constructed Head No. 2* the intersecting flat planes that structure a human bust open up and "measure" the space of the head. The cells of "empty" space become the primary element in

FIG 6-9 NAUM GABO [American, 1890–1977], *Constructed Head No. 2*. 1916. Galvanized iron, 17 3/4 in. (45 cm) high. Dallas Museum of Art. Family collection.

the sculpture. Furthermore, the surrounding space easily invades the inner space so that the two become one environment. Think how the surrounding environment would invade the inner space if the work were submerged in water. The open structure of Gabo's head expresses the modern awareness of the continuity of all reality.

Many pieces of sculpture require that viewers move through space in order to appreciate their forms. (Most paintings do not require this kind of physical activity on the part of viewers.) By changing viewpoints, observers can better understand the swelling of every mass, the placement of each mass in space, and the thrust of cavities. By moving about a piece of sculpture, viewers may see new forms emerge and will often find that the relationships between the masses and voids change. Observers continually re-create the work as they move in the space about it. Even if a statute is intended to be seen and appreciated from

without the illusion of a window. Inspired by their example, many twentieth-century Western artists have closed the pictorial window, or shattered the artistic mirror that was once held up to reflect nature. Many modern abstract paintings and drawings scarcely suggest an Alice-in-Wonderland adventure beyond the frame. Nevertheless, modern artists in Europe and America have never completely squelched their instinct that from the very first brush stroke, the flat two-dimensional surface of the work takes on a third dimension. A great deal of modern art delights in the interplay between a very evident two-dimensional design and the persistent illusion of three-dimensional space.

For the most part, other cultures, although they might show the viewer the correct proportions of figures or objects, have avoided a three-dimensional appearance to their two-dimensional works of art. They take pains not to represent human beings or things as if they were merely copying reality. These artists prefer to create by investing people and things with a spiritual reality. Rather than denying the flat surface, they affirm that they are working in two dimensions. Their flat images insist that they are decorating a surface. Something in the philosophy or religious beliefs of many cultures dictates that their artists avoid imitating the optical appearance of reality. For them, art is rather a language to make invisible powers visible.

Ancient Egyptian artists typically tried to keep things as flat as possible (see FIG. 6-10). Whether they were depicting a landscape, food, flowers, animals, or the human figure, they spread the object out in one flat plane. It took some doing to arrange the human figure two-dimensionally so that it would not contradict the plane of the surface. The hard part, the necessary part, was to depict each feature of the body to its best advantage and in its most characteristic shape on the plane. Egyptian artists kept things flat because the permanence of the form was important to them and they did not wish to give the appearance of a fleeting perception. Just as most of their art that has survived comes from decorated tombs, so it was meant to last for eternity.

To illustrate the human figure the way they wanted, the Egyptians developed a series of conventions, that is, certain techniques of representation that all

only one point of view, the sculptor still usually leads viewers' eyes around the work by manipulating the lines and masses so that they appreciate the spatial projection of the forms and grasp the three-dimensionality of the masses.

Architectural spaces come in all sizes and shapes: the enormous interior of ancient Roman buildings like the Pantheon (FIG. 16-18), the low tunnel-like space of the Kimbell Art Museum (FIG. 4-9), the exalted heights of a Gothic cathedral like Chartres (FIG. 15-1). As we move through space in architecture, from one room to another, the sequence of open areas may be static or fluid. Space may be measured and rationally ordered, or intuitive and free-form. But the only way to experience space in architecture is to be surrounded by it and to take the time to walk through it.

Space in Different Cultures

Modern Western artists are very much aware that other cultures have represented reality in their art

Egyptian artists generally agreed upon and employed. To a great extent, Egyptian artists kept to these conventions for several thousand years. When an Egyptian depicted the human figure, an eye had to be clearly and unmistakably a typical eye; a foot had to be clearly and unmistakably a typical foot. Because their civilization cherished regularity and permanence, not progress, they chose to depict the stable concept of an eye or foot, rather than an arbitrary view recorded at a certain moment.

According to their conventions, an Egyptian artist always depicted the head in profile, but the eye frontally, just as we would if asked to picture the concept of the eye. The almond-shaped eye on the side of the head thus appears to stare straight out at the viewer. Their conventions also required that the Egyptians display two shoulders—two broad shoulders in males—frontally. Even though the figure might be reaching across to touch or to hold something, the movement does not draw the shoulder out of the flat plane. Although the Egyptians spread out the shoulders, the waist had to be in profile and the legs and feet were in profile too. The figure in fact had two left feet, because the arch and big toe appeared the same on each foot. In sum, the ancient Egyptians went to some trouble to keep the essential features of a human being two-dimensional in conformity with the surface.

Crafts traditions around the world usually show respect for the surface of the objects being made. The decoration of most pieces of pottery or textile does not try to transform the surface into the illusion of something else. Although the motifs decorating a Zuni jar in the Cleveland Museum (FIG. 6-11) are derived from birds, their transformation by the Zuni into circular and triangular lines moves our eye around the jar. The designs painted on the jar decorate two areas—the small indented neck and the high-shouldered wide body. A daggerlike design of stylized feathers thrusts around the neck. Circular motifs—derived centuries earlier from the rainbird, whose cries were believed to foretell rain—reinforce the circular mass of the jar's body. As a number of curved lines join to form sharp points, the interrupted motion seems to snap across the surface. The eye, exploring the design, is led around the jar and thus experiences its mass. The painting enhances the configuration of the jar rather than contradicts it.

FIG 6-11 [Native American, Zuni Pueblo], Zuni jar. Late nineteenth century. Earthenware with slip decoration, 10 3/16 × 14 5/8 in. (25.9 × 37.1 cm). From Zuni Pueblo, New Mexico. Cleveland Museum of Art. Gift of the Smithsonian Institution (23.1082).

Methods of Spatial Projection

Westerners in general used to think that other cultures were primitive, or undeveloped. In fact, except for classical Greek and Roman art, any art produced before about 1500 was once considered to be primitive. Imperialistic Westerners assumed that if only these people knew what Westerners knew, they would see the error of their ways. The word *primitive* often implied that these people were not intelligent enough to discover the secret for themselves. The secret of reproducing reality, according to the common prejudice, was a thing called perspective. If a primitive artist could only master the mysteries of perspective, he or she could make beautiful, professional-looking pictures with the appearance of real space.

That arrogant attitude rested on a number of fallacies about the superiority of one culture over another. Also, it is misleading to imply that the plunging lines of a perspective drawing are the only way to get

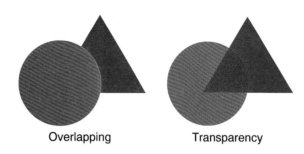

Overlapping   Transparency

a three-dimensional look. Even in the Western tradition, artists use a half dozen other ways to make a picture seem as if some space exists behind the surface. In fact, a sense of three-dimensional space can also be achieved by overlapping of shapes, positioning, the diminishing size of objects, foreshortening, chiaroscuro, atmospheric perspective, and warm-and-cool color contrasts.' In any art work these alternative devices, alone or in combination, produce space as well. Furthermore, many styles of art have existed for centuries by emphasizing only one of them or the other.

Overlapping and Positioning

Overlapping is probably the fundamental method of spatial projection. If one thing gets in the way of a second thing and obscures part of it, then it must be in front of the second thing. When the violin obscures a part of the sheet music in William M. Harnett's painting *The Old Violin* (FIG. 6-5), we judge that the violin is in front of the sheet music. If a triangle cuts off part of a circle, we judge that the triangle is in front of the circle. If, however, the circle and triangle intersect and both shapes remain complete, we have no way to judge which shape is in front of which. The shapes seem to be transparent and their spatial relationship is ambiguous.

Strange as it may sound, too much overlapping can be confusing and runs the danger of obscuring the person or thing that lies behind the foreground shape. An artist has the freedom to rearrange reality so that the items in front do not entirely obscure the items in back. And a photographer likewise has the freedom to find the right camera position or move the subjects into the desired position, if possible.

The absence of overlapping can also have some significance. As a rule, the important person in a composition must never be obscured by a subordinate, otherwise she or he might not look so important. Imagine

an official portrait of the president of the United States with some unknown person standing in front of the president.

Overlapping seems so natural that we might find it hard at first to imagine doing without it. However, cave painters in Europe fifteen thousand years ago apparently ignored overlapping or at least ignored its potential (see FIG. 2-12). They usually kept each animal separate from each other. The animals on some cave ceilings look at first like a herd in a landscape, but on further inspection it becomes clear that the animals were not painted from a consistent point of view as though the observer were standing in the meadow with them. Sometimes the cave artist did paint one image of an animal on top of another, but the animals do not really overlap. Instead, they merely intersect, since the one underneath shows through. It has been speculated that for the artist who painted the second one on top of the first, the first animal simply did not exist anymore, perhaps because it had been created at an earlier time for a ritual that was now over.

Some cultures avoid overlapping at all costs. Sixteenth-century Persian artists kept people and things from overlapping by placing them one above the other. Even the floor tiles in 'Abd Allah Mussawwir's small painting *The Meeting of the Theologians* (FIG. 6-12) go straight up the surface. These Persian artists had a convention for indicating depth by an object's **position** on the surface. According to their convention, whatever was higher up in the picture was understood to be farther back. The relationship between the parts of the image should be read like a road map. We can tell on a map of California that San Francisco is at some distance from Los Angeles because it is closer to the top of the map. We can tell that the teacher wearing the blue and orange robes in *The Meeting of the Theologians* is at the back because he sits nearer the top of the picture.

Diminishing Size

It is also part of our everyday experience that the farther away things get from us, the smaller they appear in our field of vision. By using the technique called **diminishing size,** or reducing the size of one form relative to the size of another in a painting, drawing, or relief sculpture, an artist can create the illusion of depth. A tree may appear to be in the distance of some work because it is much smaller than the people,

FIG 6-12 'ABD ALLAH MUSSAWWIR [Persian, Bukharam; active mid sixteenth century], *The Meeting of the Theologians.* Uzbek Shaybanid dynasty, c. 1540–1550. Watercolor on paper, 13 × 9 in. (33 × 22.9 cm) (sheet), 11 3/8 × 7 1/2 in (28.9 × 19.1 cm) (image). Kansas City, Missouri, Nelson-Atkins Museum of Art.

This small painting of a madrasa, *or religious school, describes a considerable amount of deep space by the location of people and things up and down the symmetrical design. At the bottom appears a street scene. As a theologian approaches the doorway, two beggars hold out their hands for alms. In the room behind the door, seven theologians sit on a floor that rises straight up the page. Behind them, in what appears to be another room or an alcove, a* mullah, *or teacher, instructs a young man. We may even imagine that the figures appearing in the "windows" above them reside in deeper space. Nevertheless, the figures toward the top of the page are the same size as the figures in the street at the bottom.*

whereas, in reality, the reverse is true—trees are normally bigger than people. The columns in the painting *The Annunciation* (FIG. 6-13, next page), by the anonymous Master of the Barberini Panels, for example, get progressively smaller as they move away from the observer. Notice, however, that the figures in *The Meeting of the Theologians* (FIG. 6-12) do not diminish in size as they go up the surface—that is to say, back in space.

The amount that an object should diminish in relationship to its intended position in space can be determined by the rules for perspective. Therefore, some people might claim that diminishing size is actually a part of linear perspective. However, in many paintings and drawings, diminishing size operates without the receding lines of a perspective scheme. Most landscape painters, for example, do not use perspective to set out the receding space of irregular nature. They diminish the size of objects in space from observation and intuition. Diminishing size can work as a space creator independently of perspective, and many artists employ it without a perspective drawing.

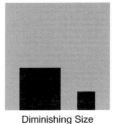
Diminishing Size

Position

Diminishing Size and Position

FIG 6-13 Master of the Barberini Panels [Italian], *The Annunciation*. C. 1450. Tempera, and possibly oil, on panel, 34 1/2 × 24 3/4 in. (87.6 × 62.9 cm). Washington, D.C., National Gallery of Art, Samuel H. Kress Collection.

Linear Perspective

The painter known as the Master of the Barberini Panels very clearly demonstrated in *The Annunciation* (FIG. 6-13) the Italian Renaissance invention of **linear perspective**—a scheme for creating the illusion of three-dimensional space, in which parallel lines that move away from the viewer are drawn not as parallels but as diagonals that converge and meet at some point. If the lines that move away from the viewer, like the pavement lines in *The Annunciation*, are genuinely perpendicular to the picture plane, they are called **orthogonals.** The picture plane is the imaginary window or surface perpendicular to the line of vision on which the image appears to be inscribed.

Linear perspective reproduces our everyday experience that the parallel lines of highways or railroad tracks appear to merge in the distance. It is most easily demonstrated in images, like *The Annunciation*, that have buildings and pavement, or roads or tabletops in them, because the regular parallel lines of these items make the perspective scheme clear.

The system of perspective was invented in the early fifteenth century by the architect Filippo Brunelleschi, who wanted a method of rendering buildings in space. Renaissance artists like the Barberini Master were fascinated with the concept as soon as Brunelleschi invented the rules, because the perspective space within the painting operates something like a chessboard or three-dimensional graph paper upon which objects can be located in space in a rational way. In *The Annunciation* the exact lines of the perspective create a serene and ideal setting for the religious event depicted.

When the artist stands, as the Barberini Master did for *The Annunciation*, so that the parallel lines of the objects in the picture are considered to be exactly perpendicular to the picture plane, then the lines of perspective will meet at a single point called the **vanishing point.** This arrangement, called **single-point perspective,** or one-point perspective, usually places the vanishing point in the center of the composition.

To add a little visual interest, the Master of the Barberini Panels placed the figures of Mary and the angel to the right of the central axis and positioned the single vanishing point of the perspective to the left, almost exactly underneath the white dove of the Holy Spirit.

Very few pictures use such a rigid system of perspective for creating the third dimension as does *The Annunciation*. Most painters, in fact, avoid single-point perspective because the space seems very contrived. Single-point perspective requires a special, almost an ideal, point of view. The artist and viewer must assume that everything in nature lines up precisely and rigidly so that all the lines fall into place.

In our actual experience, we observe objects in space from a constantly shifting point of view, as David Hockney cleverly illustrated in the assembled photographs of his mother titled *Mother I, Yorkshire Moors, August 1985* (FIG. 6-14). His procedure of taking numerous shots of his subject and then assembling them imitates the actual experience that we have of reality. Confronted with reality, the eye moves rapidly back and forth across any subject and focuses on one aspect of it after another over a period of time. Our experience of the subject is a composite of a succession of rapid eye movements and shifting viewpoints. Through Hockney's composite photograph, his mother's expression seems to change as we take the time to move from one segment of her image to another, just as his camera did.

Instead of single-point perspective, many paintings and drawings employ an angular kind of perspective, called **two-point perspective,** like that in Edward Ruscha's *Standard Station, Amarillo, Texas* (FIG. 6-15), in which the vanishing points lie to the sides of the composition. Notice the plural word *points*. If objects are turned at an angle and are not strictly perpendicular to the picture plane, they should have two vanishing points, one for each set of parallel lines visible on the sides of the object. If the parallel lines lie at a rather slight angle relative to the picture plane, the vanishing points may lie well beyond the limits of the artist's composition. In practice, all vanishing points lie on the picture's horizon line, which is determined by the position of the eyes of the artist. The higher the artist's eye level, the higher the horizon line.

Even though many Chinese painters liked to depict extensive landscapes, Far Eastern cultures never chose

FIG 6-14 DAVID HOCKNEY [English, 1937–], *Mother I, Yorkshire Moors, August 1985.* Photographic collage, 18 1/2 × 13 in. © David Hockney.

FIG 6-15 EDWARD RUSCHA [American, 1937–], *Standard Station, Amarillo, Texas.* 1963. Oil on canvas, 65 × 124 in. (165 × 315 cm). Dartmouth College, Hanover, New Hampshire, Hood Museum of Art.

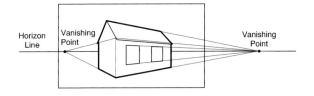

FIG 6-16 CH'I SHAN WU CHIN [Chinese], *Streams and Mountains without End.* (Detail). Northern Sung dynasty, early twelfth century. Handscroll, ink on silk, 13 13/16 × 83 7/8 in. (35.1 × 213 cm). Cleveland Museum

to pursue the same methods of perspective as those employed in the West. In Ch'i Shan Wu Chin's *Streams and Mountains without End* (FIG. 6-16) landscape features do not fall into places assigned by a single point of view, as dictated by the rules for linear perspective. In fact, we are not meant to take in all of nature at one glance. Our eye is supposed to wander through the landscape from one feature to another, and, although some things do overlap other things, we really "read" each part independently of the others. Chinese landscapes, such as this one, which is nearly eighty-four inches long, were often painted on a scroll that allowed the viewer to see only one part at a time as the painting was gradually unrolled from one end at the same time that it was wound up on the other.

Foreshortening

When Uncle Sam points his finger out in space toward us in the famous World War I poster *I Want You* (FIG. 6-17), by James Montgomery Flagg, most people would say that his arm is foreshortened. Strictly speaking, the same rules apply to **foreshortening** as to one-point perspective, but the word *foreshortening* is usually reserved for parts of the body and other irregularly shaped things that appear to go forward or back in

space. An artist usually creates a linear perspective scheme with a vanishing point to draw the lines of a building, a table, or chair. But it would be too cumbersome to use one-point perspective for something like an extended arm that has no straight lines. Instead, artists usually practice drawing the human figure for a long time in order to develop the knack of placing limbs intuitively in foreshortening.

Although in Flagg's poster Uncle Sam's intense stare and the directional lines of his arm toward the viewer have an emotional impact, too many foreshortened arms or legs jutting out at the viewer will seem awkward. Surprisingly, little foreshortening appears in most paintings and drawings of the human figure.

Chiaroscuro

In addition to perspective, the Master of the Barberini Panels demonstrated that light and dark can also establish a spatial relationship (see *The Annunciation*, FIG. 6-13). Chiaroscuro, which is any change between light and dark, can appear to us as the result of a change in the direction of the shape of an object and consequently suggests a movement into depth. If one

FIG 6-17 JAMES MONTGOMERY FLAGG [American, 1877–1960], *I Want You.* Poster. Library of Congress, Washington, D.C.

FIG 6-18 TORII KIYONAGA [Japanese, 1752–1815], *Interior of a Bathhouse.* Edo period, 1785. Oban, diptych; ink and color on paper as mounted, 15 1/4 × 20 in. (38.7 × 51 cm). Museum of Fine Arts, Boston. William Sturgis Bigelow Collection, by exchange.

side of a box receives light, the other, darker side that does not receive light appears to go off in another direction. When light gradually changes to dark in the modeling of a human figure's torso, arm, and leg, the torso and limbs appear rounded, solid, and three-dimensional.

Modeling and perspective transformed Western art in the Renaissance, since they gave to images the appearance of solid bodies existing in space. Many modern artists have turned their back on that tradition by adopting the example of pre-Renaissance art or art from other cultures. For example, many Impressionists and Post-Impressionists greatly admired Japanese wood-block prints, like Torii Kiyonaga's *Scenes in a Woman's Bathhouse* (FIG. 6-18), which they imitated in their own art. They observed that the Japanese did not employ modeling nor did they depict cast shadows, but instead they delighted in large areas

of flat color. Western artists also noticed that in their prints Japanese artists employed an angular perspective in which parallel lines do not meet at a vanishing point. The lines of the floorboards remain parallel in what is known as **isometric projection.** The different rules gave the Eastern artist a freedom to develop linear patterns on the surface and exploit areas of bold color.

Atmospheric Perspective

Despite the similar name, atmospheric perspective has little to do with linear perspective. **Atmospheric perspective,** or aerial perspective, conveys to us three-dimensional space not by means of converging lines but through our experience that distant objects change their appearance because of the intervening atmosphere. In George Caleb Bingham's *Fur Traders Descending the Missouri* (FIG. 6-19) a morning mist

Chapter 6: Surface and Space

Fig 6-19 George Caleb Bingham [American, 1811–1879], *Fur Traders Descending the Missouri.* C. 1845. Oil on canvas, 29 × 36 1/2 in. (73.7 × 92.7 cm). Metropolitan Museum of Art, New York. Morris K. Jesup Fund, 1933 (33.61).

Consequently, in Bingham's *Fur Traders* the early morning sun tints the filtering atmosphere red.

Things at a distance also appear fuzzy and out of focus even to the sharpest eyes. No one can expect to see every leaf on every distant tree; things just get too small. Moreover, the air in between gets in the way and blurs distant things. In Bingham's *Fur Traders* the mist rising from the Missouri River almost completely obscures the distant riverbank. Even on the clearest of days the intervening air lessens the sharpness of distant objects.

Finally, the contrast between light and dark on distant objects gets narrower than the contrast of light and dark on similar objects in the foreground. This aspect of atmospheric perspective is often the hardest to understand, although it is *the* essential element of the effect. The foreground of any landscape probably contains bright highlights as well as deep darks. In the forward parts of a painting, the lights are the lightest and the darks are the darkest in value—consequently, the contrast between light and dark is the strongest in the foreground. In the distance, not only are landscape features bluish and hazy, the contrast between light and dark on those features is also not very great. In the distance, the darks become lighter and the lights become a little darker. Both the lights and the darks approach a middle value. In Bingham's *Fur Traders* strong lights and strong darks appear in the shirts of the man and boy in the foreground. Very little contrast occurs, however, between light and dark in the clumps of trees in the distance behind them.

Warm-Cool Color Contrasts

Recall that a **warm-cool color contrast** can produce a spatial effect. Warm colors like red, orange, and yellow on the color wheel tend to come forward; cool colors like green, blue, and blue violet tend to recede. The warm earth tones of a dirt road in some landscape painting might underscore the road's near location; majestic blue purple mountains seem definitely at a distance because of their cool colors. Paint a room red, and the walls seem to come closer and the room seems to get smaller.

The appearance of depth caused by a particular color in a painting often depends on the contrast with a cooler or warmer color. A red does not always appear to come forward exactly eight inches; its relative dis-

rises into the cool air to obscure the banks of the Missouri River. The three figures, including the black fox, stare at the viewer, who represents the rare intruder passing their canoe in this wilderness. There are no diagonal lines receding into the distance. Nevertheless, the atmosphere gives the impression of a deep space because distant objects in the painting change in terms of color, distinctness, and light-dark contrasts.

Color changes in atmospheric perspective happen because we live inside a gas called air. We usually consider air to be invisible, but as we know from looking at the sky, it normally has a bluish tint to it during the day—because blue light rays from the sun are scattered in the atmosphere. When enough air interposes itself between us and some distant object, we see the object through a colored filter, as it were. The intervening air causes a color shift. Distant wooded mountains usually appear blue, and they appear distant because they seem blue. At dawn and dusk, since the light of the sun travels through more atmosphere, sunlight is red.

ance depends on whether it is contrasted with a hot violet or a cool green. The more the contrast, the more the spatial push and pull.

Space in Modern Art

Artists seldom employ at any one time all the seven devices to create a spatial illusion. Artists, throughout history, have seldom wanted to create too much deep space in their work anyway—a little modeling, overlapping, and a little foreshortening or atmospheric perspective suited most painters just fine—because deep perspective tends to direct too much attention to the background. After the early Renaissance, deeply receding space was only fashionable during the Baroque period—the seventeenth and early eighteenth centuries in Europe. Jacob van Ruisdael's baroque landscape *Wheatfields* (FIG. 6-20) rushes the eye deep into space as a road and several rugged paths converge in a giant inverted V-shape on a clump of trees on the horizon. In the sky, which takes up two-thirds of the canvas, sodden clouds are foreshortened and seem to recede endlessly over the horizon. Unchecked in their horizontal movement, the wheatfields spread left and right beyond the composition—giving the impression that Ruisdael's painting is only a section of a panorama of the flat Dutch countryside. A man, a woman, and a child on the road suggest that the viewer too should "take a walk" through the land and enjoy the vastness of nature.

By the end of the nineteenth century, Western artists began to challenge the idea that a painting was a mirror of nature or a window behind which one could take a stroll. A French artist, Maurice Denis, told painters in 1890 to "remember that a picture before it is a war horse, a naked woman, or some anecdote, is essentially a flat surface covered with colors arranged in a certain order."[1] Even before that date, Western artists began to look to distant cultures to find out how those peoples called attention to the arrangement on the surface by de-emphasizing the spatial projection. They became fascinated with so-called primitive arts of other cultures—African, Japanese, preclassical Greek. Rejecting the Western tradition that they had been taught in the conservative art academies, they turned their back on perspective, modeling, and atmospheric perspective. For at

FIG 6-20   JACOB VAN RUISDAEL [Dutch, 1628 or 1629–1682], *Wheatfields*. C. 1670. Oil on canvas, 39 3/8 × 51 1/4 in. (100 × 130.2 cm). Bequest of Benjamin Altman, 1913 (14.40.623). New York, Metropolitan Museum of Art.

this time a number of artists felt that Western civilization was decaying, that it was corrupt and about to die. Pictorial practices like perspective represented the exhausted values of an established society. These traditional practices produced mere illustration, not art, contended some artists who wanted to make a new beginning.

The rejection of deep space—one of the great revolutions in Western art—developed rapidly over a few generations at the end of the nineteenth and beginning of the twentieth centuries. By the opening years of the twentieth century, an artist like Henri Matisse could insist that paintings were primarily decorations on a surface. Also at that time, Pablo Picasso and Georges Braque developed Cubism—an entirely new system for achieving a small amount of three dimensional space seen from a changing rather than a single fixed point of view. Few artists in the twentieth century have escaped the impact of Cubism, since it has significantly changed the way an artist sees and represents forms in space.

Pablo Picasso (1881–1973)

*T*HE SON of a professor of art, Pablo Picasso possessed extraordinary talent. As a teenager he could draw like Raphael (see FIG. 1-8). In a sense, he spent his life taming the slickness of his gifts and channeling them into a modern idiom.

Picasso, ca. 1913. Archive Photos.

In 1990 Picasso left his home in Barcelona, for Paris, where he permanently settled in 1904. Endowed with a strong visual memory, Picasso absorbed many different styles in his early years as an artist. For several years during his so-called Blue Period, the first of many such stages, he painted attenuated beggars, starving children, and the homeless, entirely in blue. The color, associated with the blue sky and the blue sea, was a natural poetic symbol of the beyond and of longing. Picasso next chose to portray poor, itinerant acrobats, jugglers, and clowns, during his Rose Period. The mood of these circus paintings is as somber as the art of the Blue Period.

Finally, Picasso labored for six months in 1907 over his breakthrough painting *The Women of Avignon (Les demoiselles d'Avignon)*. In it he took up the painter Paul Cézanne's challenge to reconcile the flat plane of the canvas with the solid forms of nature. The strongly expressive shapes of African art also spurred Picasso's imagination in the new direction. He then turned *Les demoiselles d'Avignon* to the wall of his studio for years, showing it only to a few friends, most of whom were stunned. He left the painting not so much because he considered the work unfinished as because he had gotten ahead of himself. He spent the next two years with his friend Georges Braque developing the implications of *Les demoiselles d'Avignon* into the style of Cubism.

Even Cubism went through successive stages, beginning first with the period of Analytic Cubism where the figure in a painting like Picasso's *Man with a Pipe* is fragmented into hundreds of intersecting planes. Picasso seems to have been analyzing his subject from different points of view and fragmenting the object into myriad planes and facets. The space in *Man with a Pipe*, created by the overlapping of flat geometrical planes, is shallow—only a few inches deep, so to speak. Value contrasts and cast shadows in this kind of early Cubism also contribute to a slight impression of three-dimensional space.

However, in Cubism it is usually difficult to tell which shape is on top of which. Many of the intersecting planes penetrate one another, making the shallow space ambiguous and relative to one's point of view. Seen from one point of view, a dark parallelogram might look as though it overlaps a light patch. Seen from another point of view, the same light patch belongs to a larger triangle that overlaps the parallelogram. Light sources coming from different directions contribute to the ambiguity of the space created by the overlapping and intersecting facets. *Man with a Pipe* also contains letters of the alphabet integrated into the composition. Their presence adds another level to the ambiguity of the three-dimensional space. Looking at a Cubist painting like *Man with a Pipe* is an endless mind game about the relativity of our perception of space.

Within a few years' time there followed the period of Synthetic Cubism, where the flat planes were the result of

PABLO PICASSO [Spanish, 1881–1973], *The Women of Avignon (Les demoiselles d'Avignon)*. June–July 1907. Oil on Canvas, 96 × 92 in. (243.8 × 233.7 cm). Museum of Modern Art, New York. The Lillie P. Bliss bequest.

PABLO PICASSO [Spanish, 1881–1973], *Man with a Pipe*. Summer 1911. Oil on Canvas, 35 3/4 × 27 7/8 in. (90.8 × 70.8 cm). Fort Worth, Texas, Kimbell Art Museum. Photo by Michael Bodycomb, 1987.

collage or were painted to look like collage. **Collage** (pronounced cole-*azh*), from the French word for pasting, is the gluing of forms upon a surface. Starting in 1912, Picasso and Braque reduced the facets of Cubism to larger, simpler flat planes. The synthesis of a fewer,

larger shapes in Picasso's *Guitar* (see next page) seems to build a more monumental composition. The shapes either look like pieces of colored paper that Picasso cut out and pasted on the surface, or actually were pasted-on materials. Because of collage, they do not

recede behind the picture plane but come out from it. The space in the new painting seems to lie in front of the surface instead of behind it. Picasso also introduced color into Cubism, so that the contrast of warm and cool color sometimes adds to the spatial illusion.

Continued on next page.

It would seem that Picasso had in his imagination from the beginning a picture of the general design he wanted to achieve.

After World War I Picasso worked in a representational and classical style (see *Mother and Child*, FIG. 3-7) at the same time that he was painting in a colorful synthetic Cubist vein (see *Three Musicians*, FIG. 3-6). The Surrealists in the 1920s adopted Picasso as one of their own, and in the late 1920s and in the 1930s he made Cubism into a vehicle of aggressive self-expression with deep-lying symbolism. His experiments culminated in the distorted and twisted figures of *Guernica* (FIG. 18-34).

Picasso worked constantly, preferably at night. He made little distinction between his working space and his living space—the rooms where he lived were cluttered with his paintings and ceramics, his tools and equipment, and various props that he collected.

When Picasso painted he often propped up the smaller canvases on a tabletop. He began by laying out the essential structure or armature of the composition with a few lines or shapes. It would seem that he had in his imagination from the beginning a picture of the general design he wanted to achieve. He then began to paint over this basic structure a series of experiments, changes, and adjustments—

repainting, erasing, and developing forms on the canvas. His father taught him to pin pieces of paper over parts of the canvas to try out new visual ideas rapidly. Picasso once said that when he painted he did not seek, he found. He meant that in many changes on the canvas he was not groping in the dark for solutions but looking for the forms that were the equivalent of the vision he had from the start. An untiring worker, Picasso had a fertile imagination that never stopped creating and searching for new means of expression.

PABLO PICASSO [Spanish, 1881–1973], *Guitar. 1913.* Charcoal, wax crayon, ink, and pasted paper; 26 1/8 × 19 1/2 in. (66.4 × 49.5 cm). Museum of Modern Art, New York. Nelson A. Rockefeller bequest.

SUMMATION BOX

TEXTURE	
Real texture	Real texture is the actual physical quality of a surface owing to the nature and treatment of the material.
	Real texture can be rough, irregular, smooth.
	Real texture calls attention to the surface; it adds richness and appeal; it delights the eye.
Apparent texture	Apparent texture is imagined or implied texture; an illusion.
	Apparent texture imitates the appearance of a natural material.
	The effect of apparent texture depends on light reflections.
	Apparent texture is also produced by a patterning.

SPACE	
Sculpture	In sculpture, masses take up space and move through space.
	Voids also create space in sculpture.
	Some sculpture may charge the surrounding space.
Architecture	Space is an essential experience of architecture.
	Architecture unfolds in time as the viewer moves in space.
Painting	Western painting often creates an illusion of a three-dimensional world behind the window of the picture plane.
	Painting in other cultures usually respects and affirms the flat surface.
	Methods of spatial projection include overlapping, positioning, diminishing size, linear perspective, foreshortening, chiaroscuro, atmospheric perspective, and warm-cool color contrasts.
	Space in modern art is influenced by art from around the world.
	Cubism reproduces space as seen from multiple points of view; it fragments space.

Key Terms and Concepts

atmospheric perspective	linear perspective	space
collage	orthogonals	texture
diminishing size	overlapping	trompe l'oeil
foreshortening	picture plane	two-point perspective
frottage	position	vanishing point
isometric projection	single-point perspective	warm-cool color contrast

PRINCIPLES OF DESIGN

Design

When we look at Alvin Langdon Coburn's photograph *The Octopus, New York* (FIG. 7-1), the first thing we notice is the series of curved lines radiating from the circular "body" on the right. The awareness of what the photograph actually represents probably comes second to our attention. The imagination of the photographer, who decided to take this picture from the top of a tall building, has transformed the snow-covered city park into another dimension where the viewer is free to fantasize and see everyday reality in a new way. Coburn imagined that the dark shape in his photograph resembled an octopus. Not everyone may think of an octopus, but on a fundamental level, instead of walkways and trees and snow-blanketed lawns, everyone on first viewing likely sees the photograph primarily as a design of lines, shapes, and value contrasts. Coburn's unusual photograph emphasizes what every work of art contains: a unifying system among the visual elements—a **design** that imposes its coherence on the image and transforms the subject so that it is seen in a new way.

Perspective, overlapping, and the other devices of three-dimensional projection can give intelligibility and coherence to the space *behind* the surface of a work. Another set of principles organizes the forms as they appear *on the picture plane*, the imaginary front surface of the image on which artists select, arrange, and organize the visual elements of a work of art into a design. Like the "octopus" design in Coburn's photograph, this design holds the elements together and makes the visual elements in the work of art different from the masses, shapes, lines, light, color, texture, and space of everyday existence.

Unity

One reason a design transforms visual reality is because with it, both three-dimensional spaces and two-dimensional elements, like lines and colors, work together and form a **unity.** Artists usually try to achieve unity in the broadest sense—a wholeness and a completeness so that the art object coheres, so that

FIG 7-1   ALVIN LANGDON COBURN [American, 1882–1966], *The Octopus, New York*. 1912. Photograph. George Eastman House, Rochester, New York.

FIG 7-2   LEONARDO DA VINCI [Italian, 1452–1519], *Study for the Composition of the Last Supper.* C. 1495. Red chalk, 10 1/4 × 15 1/2 in. (26 × 39.4 cm). Accademia, Venice. Alinari/Art Resource, New York.

it works. In a unified piece, the design dominates the individual parts; there is agreement or congruity among all the elements; nothing superfluous is let in; nothing distracts. As a general rule, only something that is organized and directed tends to be satisfying and has the power to make its visual point efficiently and effectively. The design is often the primary clue to the viewer that the artist, out of the tangle of possible visual information, has captured something meaningful. The design makes us stop and look and think and enjoy.

A unified and coherent design gives shape to the visual inspiration that possesses an artist. As artists compose their work, they remain true to their artistic intuition through an integrated design that gives their intuition shape. However, without a coherent design, their visual statements communicate less forcefully, if at all, and their imaginative energy is dissipated. It would be sad if an artist had a profound vision or inspiration but could never express it in a coherent form. In fact, many artists would say that the form of a work *is* their vision. Another sort of artist may be born with incredible skill and facility, but even that talent has to be cultivated and purposefully directed to be any good. And if an artist tries to make art out of an experience or a vision that is fragmented, incomplete, or con-

fused, no doubt that artist will produce a design that is equally fragmented, incomplete, or confused.

In a visual design an artist can pull together all the basic components of art—lines, shapes, mass, value, color, texture, and space—to make a meaningful work of art. Artists may have a master plan for their art object from the moment they start work, or they work out a design as they go along.

Before painting his *Last Supper* (FIG. 4-20) Leonardo da Vinci made numerous preliminary drawings for the arrangement of elements and for individual figures. It is immediately obvious that his early sketch *Study for the Composition of the Last Supper* (FIG. 7-2) differs significantly from the finished painting. For example, the left side of the table lies in the lower-right corner of the paper. Most of the poses were changed; the figures are not symmetrically organized into four groups of three; and in the sketch Judas sits on the near side of the table and Christ feeds him bread soaked with wine. The clarity and perfection of the finished painting were things Leonardo had to work out. Even Jackson Pollock, who spontaneously splattered and dripped paint (see *Cathedral*, FIG. 3-2), said he had a general idea of what he was about before he began, and in practice he would readily discard a canvas if the painting got out of his control. One way

Fig 7-3 Elizabeth Murray [American, 1940–], *Can You Hear Me?* 1984. Oil on canvas, 106 × 159 in. (269.2 × 403.9 cm). Dallas Museum of Art. Foundation for the Arts Collection. Anonymous gift (1985.4 A-E.FA).

or the other, whether a work is planned beforehand or worked out along the way, organizing visual elements in a meaningful way is what the artistic right side of the brain likes to do.

Principles of Design

Artists strive to bring unity and focus to their vision by means of certain **principles of design.** Despite the freedom that artists enjoy, over the years experience has taught them that these principles—dominance, consistency with variety, rhythm, proportions, scale, and balance—work. Perhaps we should not consider these six principles binding rules so much as rules of thumb. They are guidelines and directions based on artists' intuition and the "facts" of visual perception. Artists absorb them through their training and apply them only with sensitivity. Since many good artists frequently challenge and break the rules, these principles of design only head the artist toward the effect intended and at the same time open up the work of art for the viewer.

Dominance

Among the several ways to unify a design, one simple way is to use **dominance,** or to make some aspect of

the arrangement the main focus. The subject matter often determines what will be dominant, and it is up to the artist to control the visual elements so that the main subject will be emphasized. People who pay an artist to have their portrait made generally expect that their image will dominate the composition. In portraits of single figures—including religious "portraits" of sacred persons—the person is usually placed near the middle of a design and thus becomes the obvious, dominant form.

The main motif in any work may also be made dominant by receiving the brightest illumination, the main linear movements, the strongest color, the most detail, the most striking contrast, a prominent location in space—anything to draw attention to it. In nonrepresentational or nonobjective art, a certain line or shape, a certain light or color, a certain value contrast or color relationship may be the main goal of the work. If so, that particular visual element ought to dominate the design. In Elizabeth Murray's *Can You Hear Me?* (Fig. 7-3) a number of contrasts are at work—(between straight and curved lines, between the colors orange and blue, and between painted shapes and shaped pieces of canvas)—but visually the contrast of the large, bright yellow-green and orange proturberance to the right dominates the piece.

FIG 7-4 ERICH HECKEL [German, 1883–1970], *Two by the Sea (Zwei am Meer)*. 1920. Woodcut, 7 × 5 5/16 in. (17.8 × 13.5 cm). Los Angeles County Museum of Art, The Robert Gore Rifkind Center for German Expressionist Studies. Purchased with funds provided by Anna Bing Arnold, Museum Acquisition Fund, and deaccession funds.

FIG 7-5 [Ohio Hopewell], falcon-effigy platform pipe. 200 B.C.–A.D. 100. Pipestone and river pearl, 2 1/8 × 3 1/4 in. (5.4 × 8.3 cm). Columbus, Ohio Historical Society.

Consistency with Variety

Another fundamental principle of design requires that a work of art possesses **consistency with variety.** Line, shape, mass, value, color, texture, and space achieve unity in a work of art whenever they exhibit some sort of **consistency,** or agreement. Consistency helps integrate the work when most of the lines or shapes resemble one another in some way, when the value contrasts are treated in a uniform way, or when the color contrasts establish homogenous relationships. If the visual elements share common characteristics, we feel visually assured, satisfied, and confident that we will find a direction to our perceptions.

Perhaps the most common way to achieve consistency is through repetition. In Erich Heckel's *Two by the Sea* (FIG. 7-4), for example, the artist employed the same sharp triangular shape both in the figures and in the setting. The consistent use of this shape unifies the figure and ground into a coherent visual statement about a return to a primitive nature. In another example, *Seated Boy with Straw Hat* (FIG. 5-10), by Georges Seurat, the artist modeled the figure consistently with the same sort of strong yet soft value contrasts throughout. Such consistency helps unify a work by pulling its parts together and by making explicit relationships among the elements that the casual observer would have missed. In contrast, inconsistencies such as a color that clashes unnecessarily or a mistake in perspective in a work that tries for correct perspective are disturbing and distracting.

Also, artists usually strive to obtain consistency in the brushwork, the pencil stroke, the manner of carving, or the general **handling,** or treatment, of any medium. The Hopewell Indians did so when they carved the stone pipe in FIG. 7-5 in the form of an alert little falcon: they consistently polished all parts of the bird into streamlined tubular masses into which they inscribed a regular pattern of lines for feathers. Painters usually try to apply the paint in much the same way across the entire surface. At one extreme, some artists consistently try to hide their brushwork. Other artists make a point of displaying their brushwork. In any case, artists ordinarily do not change their method of painting in midstream—except for a good reason.

Of course, consistency must be tempered with **variety,** or differences. A work would look too static, dull, and monotonous if all the shapes or all the colors were exactly the same. It must have a certain variety to attract the imagination and keep the eye interested. In music, variations on a theme enhance the theme. Consistency and variety in art not only resemble theme and variation in music, they also resemble the philosophical idea of a universal norm in which different individual instances participate.

For the sake of variety and in contrast to its many straight lines and angles, Heckel introduced a few broad curves across his *Two Figures on the Shore*. In contrast to the predominantly curved shapes of Alvin Langdon Coburn's *The Octopus, New York* (FIG. 7-1), the large vertical shape of the office tower's shadow cuts across the snowy park. In his painting called *Smaragd Red and Germinating Yellow* (FIG. 7-6), Hans Hofmann covered most of the surface with thick rough paint applied with a broad brush or a palette knife. Most of the patches of paint are consistently irregular in shape with contrasting colors underneath breaking through. The title of the work reflects that characteristic: *Smaragdos* means emerald in Greek; emerald red is a contradiction. For variety, the large yellow rectangle in the lower left is quite different from almost all the broken patches of paint. Although thickly painted, it has fairly precise and regular edges, uniform color, and the greatest luminosity, or brightness, of all the colors in the painting. The variety among the shapes of *Smaragd Red* forces us to notice the prominent regularity of the one and the rich irregularity of the other. In a sculptural example, *Cubi XVII* (FIG. 4-22), David Smith welded together a number of similar stainless steel boxes, but for variety and contrast the rectangular boxes are of different sizes and tilt in different directions and are balanced on a cylindrical post.

In traditional figural pieces, older critical theory liked to see the attitudes and movement of all the figures consistent with the theme of the work, and at the same time it liked to see a variety in the characterization of the different people. For example, if an artist chose to illustrate a biblical event, such as the Last Supper, all the people the artist depicted were supposed to be doing something integrally connected with the event. However, the figures were expected to display variety—differences perhaps between young and old and differences of personality to show that the

FIG 7-6   HANS HOFMANN [American, 1880–1966], *Smaragd Red and Germinating Yellow.* 1959. Oil on canvas, 55 × 50 in. (139.7 × 127 cm). Cleveland Museum of Art. Contemporary Collection (60.57).

and across the canvas intersect in a thick, dense web as the car speeds by through space. Dark vertical lines that seem to come closer to us at a steady rhythm, capture the Doppler effect of the speeding car's roaring engine. The rhythms of this painting not only create a complex pattern, they visualize speed and the reality of light and sound.

As in music, rhythm in visual works has a beat or an emphasis that repeats itself at regular intervals. The idea of rhythm in art combines the movement of lines and shapes with the notion of repetition. Architecture critics often speak of the steady rhythm of the vertical columns down the length of a Gothic cathedral (see Chartres, FIG. 15-1) or similar building. Their repetition suggests movement. The curving arcs in Balla's *Automobile Speed + Lights + Noises* increase the tempo of the rhythm as they get gradually closer.

Proportions

Dominance, consistency with variety, and rhythm are appropriately vague and intuitive principles of design. To establish a more solid basis for good design, some theorists have devised concrete and complicated rules based on a system of **proportions,** or the relationships of parts to one another or the whole. Their proportions usually involve mathematical relationships or ratios. An advantage of numerical ratios is that they generate, through a numerical progression or relationship, all the measurements in a work, once an initial measurement is established. One shape—a room in a building, for example—might be a square (1:1); the next shape a rectangle (1:2); the next shape a longer rectangle (1:3); and so forth. When these ratios govern the intervals of the entire piece as well as the dimensions of individual forms, they undoubtedly produce an integration and orderliness by relating the parts one with another.

The ancient Greeks believed strongly in controlling the design of architecture, sculpture, and probably painting through proportions. They realized that numerical proportions governed musical harmony, and they believed that such ratios reflected the principles by which the universe was constructed. In the Renaissance, architects again used ratios to determine the proportions of the parts of their buildings. The Renaissance architect Leon Battista Alberti believed in the universal validity of proportions and employed them in his work (see the facade of Santa Maria Novella in

artist understood human nature and the moral implications of the event. In his *Last Supper* (FIG. 4-20) Leonardo da Vinci, through the gestures and expressions of the twelve Apostles and Christ, varied each reaction to Christ's accusation so that the figures reveal thirteen distinct personalities.

Rhythm

Sometimes, when the visual elements in a work of art repeat themselves, they seen to flow steadily through an image and—to borrow another term from music— they create a **rhythm** across the picture plane. The curved lines and shapes in Umberto Boccioni's *Dynamism of a Soccer Player* (FIG. 4-6), create a forceful rhythm revolving around the center of the canvas. Another Italian painter, Giacomo Balla, was fascinated with the power and speed of modern means of transportation.

In his *Automobile Speed + Lights + Noises* (FIG. 7-7) Balla also demonstrated that by repeating the lines and fragments of Cubism in a sequence or rhythm he could visualize motion. *Automobile Speed + Lights + Noises* represents an automobile at night racing across the picture, by turning the movement of the car into lines and planes. The curving lines stand for the spinning wheels, the glaring lights, and the forward thrust of the automobile. Large curves arcing from top to bottom

Fig 7-8 Leon Battista Alberti [Italian, 1404–1472], facade of Santa Maria Novella, Florence. Completed 1470. Scala/Art Resource, New York.

Leon Battista Alberti's facade, covering the front of an older church with a new Renaissance design, employs a system of proportions governing the size and placement of every part of his arrangement. It is as tall as it is wide; in other words, the facade as a whole is in a ratio of 1:1. This basic square is divided in half by the cornice that runs horizontally underneath the circular window, giving two parts that are each in a ratio of 1:2. The lower part of the facade, divided in half vertically by the line between the door panels, is of course formed by two squares, each one exactly one quarter of the entire surface and therefore in the ratio of 1:2:4. The top story of the facade has the same dimensions as one of the two lower quadrants. The top story itself is divided in half at the horizontal line immediately above the capitals of the striped pilasters—the flat vertical supports. The central part of the lower story—the door and the two flanking columns—is one-and-one-half times as high as it is wide and thus in the ratio of 3:2. The height of the intermediate zone between the first and second stories is half the width of the door, for a ratio of 3:2:1.

The delightful pattern of light and dark inlaid marble, covering the facade, is also governed by the same whole number proportions. Just as, in music, simple numerical proportions control the progression from one chord to another, so too Alberti's proportions harmonize the dimensions of one part of the building in relationship to another.

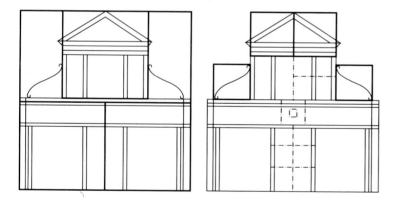

FIG. 7-8). In his famous treatise on architecture, *De re aedificatoria* (1452), he coined a classic definition of beauty as "the harmony and concord of all the parts achieved in such a manner that nothing could be added, or taken away, or altered, except for the worse."[1] Many artists would still agree with Alberti's definition because to them to change one thing in a successful composition would be to upset the whole work.

Chapter 7: Principles of Design

175

Rather than using a set of proportional measurements involving whole numbers, some people have been fascinated by the ratios of the golden section to determine the dimensions of design elements and their relationships to one another. A shape whose sides are related according to the golden section can often be found in nature and is said to be very pleasing to the eye.

The **golden section** is the relationship between two unequal entities such that the smaller is to the larger as the larger is to the whole. To illustrate, subdivide the line AB at C so that AC becomes the smaller segment and CB becomes the larger segment:

$$A \quad C \quad B$$

The golden section is created when the smaller line, AC, is related to the larger line, CB, just as the larger segment, CB, is related to the whole line, AB. In other words,

$$\frac{AC}{CB} = \frac{CB}{AB}$$

It is not all that difficult to draw two lines in the relationship of the golden section. First draw a rectangle ABDE whose long side is twice that of the short side (AB = 2 × AE). Using the short side AE as the radius of a circle whose mid point is E, find the point of intersection F on the diagonal of the rectangle EB. Then use the rest of the diagonal FB as the radius of a circle whose mid point is B. Where this circle intersects line AB at C will subdivide lines AB into the golden section, so that AC is to CB as CB is to AB.

In actuality, the ratio between short and long segments in the golden section is approximately 5:8, or more exactly .618. (The number .618 is only part of an irrational number—an unending decimal.) As a principle of design in art, the golden section can adjust the size of one element relative to another, since it can generate a series of relationships approximating the number series 5, 8, 13, 21, 34. . . . For example, an architect could design for a building a variety of windows whose width and height are constantly in the relationship of the golden section.

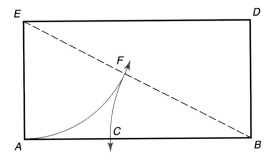

Scale

Proportions imply the perfecting of the shapes of nature and of art by applying to them some universal mathematical rule that is always valid. A **scale** is something different. Although a scale may use numerical ratios also, the word *scale* refers primarily to the relationship between the artistic image and the object in reality that it imitates. A drawing of a small building, for example, might be governed by a mathematical scale in which one foot equals one inch, or a scale of 12:1. Such a scale is a convenient tool. Nothing is suggested about the universal validity of this scale for all drawings.

Artistic representations can vary in scale. A miniature painting is on a small scale; a mural painting is usually on a large scale. Consistency of scale is important because, beyond the question of what ratio is used, small-scale works and large-scale works often have a different style. Most small-scale works, like a Rembrandt drawing or the paintings of Paul Klee (see *Vocal Fabric of the Singer Rosa Silber*, FIG. 6-4), are meant to be viewed up close in somewhat intimate circumstances. They tend to have intricate detail, small shapes, or delicate colors. Most large-scale works, like a mural or like Anselm Kiefer's painting *The Hierarchy*

FIG 7-9 ANSELM KIEFER [German, 1945–], *The Hierarchy of Angels*. 1985–1987. Oil, emulsion, shellac, acrylic, chalk, lead propeller, curdled lead, steel cables, band-iron, and cardboard on canvas; 134 × 220 1/2 × 21 1/2 in. (340.4 × 560.1 × 54.6 cm). Walker Art Center, Minneapolis. Gift of Penny and Mike Winton, 1987.

The phrase hierarchy of angels *refers to the ordering of the nine ranks of angels in heaven according to the sixth-century Christian writer called Dionysius the Areopagite. In Anselm Kiefer's work, the celestial orders are represented ironically by heavy stones suspended at the bottom of the painting from steel cables. In the context of Kiefer's other works, we know that the heavenly weights and the propeller symbolize Nazi bombing in World War II, which ravaged the land. Only destruction reigned when these heavenly messengers brutally tried to establish order.*

of *Angels* (FIG. 7-9), are meant to be seen at a distance in a somewhat public setting. They tend to have large, simple shapes and bold colors. Only in the presence of Kiefer's work—over eighteen feet high—does the menace of the surface and the weight of the rocks strike home. Most works of art cannot be arbitrarily translated from one scale to another. A miniature cannot be easily made into a mural, and vice versa. The loss of scale is one of the greatest disadvantages to examining art in textbook illustrations.

Despite the importance of a consistent scale, many Pop Artists distort the scale of everyday items to great effect. The sculptor Claes Oldenburg has made a clothespin, an electrical plug (see FIG. 19-8), and other household objects on a giant scale. The reversal of scale makes us appreciate the shapes of these common items as never before. The painter Chuck Close has specialized in enlarging snapshots of heads into an enormous scale, as in *Big Self-Portrait* (FIG. 7-10). When it is exhibited in a gallery, it is hard to focus on and comprehend an image so large. In Close's hands, a simple snapshot becomes disturbing and exciting.

Different scales are not easily mixed in the same work—unless the artist intends to produce a fantasy or

a Surrealistic dream. The Surrealist painter René Magritte, in a painting titled cryptically *The Birthday* (Fig. 7-11), filled an ordinary room with an enormous rock painted in a vastly different scale from the room. The discrepancy in scale irrationally conflicts with the realism of the painting. Variations in the scale can make other positive points of emphasis. In **hieratic representation** the important people in a work of art—perhaps the king or the goddess—are depicted in a larger scale than subordinate individuals, in order to symbolize their significance. In traditional forms of representation, idealized figures are often depicted in a larger-than-life-sized scale. The exaggerated scale makes them look heroic and grand. The religious figures in Ruben's *Holy Family* (Fig. 5-25) appear to be larger than life, especially the Christ child, who has the build of an infant Hercules. Rubens no doubt felt that the dignity of the Lord God Almighty demanded the change in scale.

The relationship between the size of the shapes in a work and the format of the work seems also to affect the sense of scale. The figures in Ruben's painting fill up the rectangle of the panel. The tight relationship between the figures and the format makes the figures seem large in scale and consequently heroic. In Audrey Flack's still life *Wheel of Fortune (Vanitas)* (Fig. 7-12) the objects are fairly large shapes relative to the confines of the canvas. This relationship magnifies their scale and transforms them from common things into something significant.

Balance

Most artists employ "rules" that are more general and more intuitive than mathematical proportions to unify their creation. To organize the elements and to achieve a satisfying unity, most artists simply consider whether the work before them is balanced. **Balance** means the stability that comes when, as with a seesaw, the visual elements on one side visually seem to "weigh" as much as those on the other. An artist might want an unbalanced work of art in order to convey a sense of tension or anxiety, but such pieces are rare. In fact, it is possible for an artist to express tension and anxiety by means of imbalance because we instinctively expect equilibrium. The imbalance frustrates our expectations.

As a general rule, to see if a work of art is balanced, artist and viewer can draw an imaginary line down the

FIG 7-12 AUDREY FLACK [American, 1941–], *Wheel of Fortune (Vanitas).* 1977–1978. Oil over acrylic on canvas, 96 × 96 in. (243.8 × 243.8 cm). Photo courtesy Louis K. Meisel Gallery, New York.

A vanitas *still life is a group of inanimate objects that symbolize the transience of life and the vanity of frivolous and sensuous pursuits. This type of iconography has a long tradition, which Audrey Flack* rejuvenated with popular contemporary imagery. The skull, the hourglass, the calendar page, and the burning candle symbolize the passage of time. The jewelry, the mirrors, the lipstick, the grapes, and the wine represent ephemeral sense pleasures. The tarot card and the die allude to the fickleness of fortune. Poignantly, the portrait in the upper-left corner is the artist's daughter.

To paint her large still life composi-tions, Flack first arranges the actual objects in a balanced, unified design in her studio, before she begins to paint. She then takes photographs of her arrangement and paints from a slide that has been projected onto a canvas mounted on a wall. Her procedure eliminates the need for a linear sketch but does not bypass the need for a design that fills and balances her square canvas.

FIG 7-13 JAMES MCNEILL WHISTLER [American, 1834–1903], *Arrangement in Gray and Black, No. 1: The Artist's Mother.* 1871. Oil on canvas, 57 × 64 1/2 in. (144.8 × 163.8 cm). Paris, Musée d Orsay. Art Resource, New York.

Although this painting is popularly known as Whistler's Mother, *James McNeill Whistler titled it* Arrangement in Gray and Black *because he wanted to stress the artistic aspects of his work. The organizing of colored shapes mattered more to him than the subject matter, although the colors themselves have been neutralized to an almost uniform gray. The lines of the floor barely recede: the entire image seems as flat as a Japanese print. Every part of the painting—the drapes, the pictures on the wall, the figure—can be read as rectangular shapes running parallel to the edges of the canvas.*

Whistler's mother sits in strict profile, far to the right of the piece, her head positioned carefully between the two pictures. On the right Whistler balanced the shape of the woman and her detailed and psychologically interesting head with the large rectangular area of the decorated curtain and the picture on the wall—most of which falls to the left of the center. The intriguing asymmetry of the picture, rather unusual for a portrait, makes Whistler's mother seem frozen in the formal world of art.

middle of the piece and try to judge if the visual stimulation on the left side "weighs" the same as the visual stimulation on the right side. James McNeill Whistler painted his famous portrait *Arrangement in Gray and Black, No. 1: The Artist's Mother* (FIG. 7-13) almost as a demonstration of balance. "Weight," of course, is a metaphor for the total effect, or stimulation, of the visual elements. The actual physical weight of the objects represented plays a negligible role in this kind of visual balance. The artist and the viewer must decide how much each element stimulates, and also how much all the elements stimulate in combination.

Visual balance also has little to do with arranging equal *quantities* of elements. In other words, it has little to do with placing the identical *number* of people or things on one side of the imaginary line and the same number on the other. Balancing has more to do with feeling than with numbers. Because "weighing" the various visual elements must always be a matter of intuition, no rules can ever exist to calculate the rela-

tive stimulation of things that are as different as colors and lines. The determination that so much light blue "weighs" as much as so many curved lines can only be done by intuition.

Relationships among forms are important for establishing a balance. Visual elements that are farther from the imaginary central axis increase in visual weight, just as a child at the end of a seesaw can exert more weight than someone closer to the center. Any element near the edge, like the fragment of picture frame in the corner of Whistler's painting, pulls the eye farther to one side. Linear movements in directions relative to the central axis stimulate the eye to one side or the other. Contrasts of value or of color attract the eye too, more than an equal patch of either value or either color alone. The size of a color affects its psychological stimulation. Textured shapes—the drape on the left of Whistler's painting, for example—or complicated shapes attract the viewer more than do plain and simple surfaces. With experience and practice in looking, one gets a feel for the weight of visual stimulation.

Symmetrical Balance.

The most obvious way to obtain a balance is, of course, to have the same kind of stimulation on one side of a work as on the other—in other words, **symmetry.** Symmetry means that the formal elements on one side resemble the formal elements on the other side, but reversed, as in a mirrored image. Many good-looking things are symmetrical. The facades of buildings are often quite symmetrical, since symmetry reflects our desire for stability in architecture. And the human body is, in general, naturally symmetrical. In carving the human figure, the Buli Master (see the chief's stool in FIG. 7-14) and many other African sculptors adhered to bilateral symmetry in their work.

Asymmetrical Balance.

Western artists often take the risk to strike an asymmetrical form of balance, as James McNeill Whistler did in his *Arrangement in Gray and Black, No. 1: The Artist's Mother* (FIG. 7-13). In **asymmetry** the visual elements on one side are rather different from those on the other side. In Audrey Flack's still life painting *Wheel of Fortune (Vanitas)* (FIG. 7-12) almost nothing on one side of the painting resembles the items on the other, although circular shapes are everywhere. The artist's sensitivity to line, value, shape, color, and space has to decide when totally different elements are equal. Because asymmetry is a bigger gamble, an asymmetrical balance usually has a bigger payoff and is a little more exciting to look at than a symmetrical work.

Landscape painters often create an asymmetrical picture with an attractive deep vista on one side balanced by foreground shapes on the other. Although Mary in Titian's so-called *Gypsy Madonna* (FIG. 7-15) stands nearly in the center of the painting and the

FIG 7-14 BULI MASTER [BaLuba], chief's stool. Wood, 21 in. (53.3 cm) high. British Museum, London.

FIG 7-15 TITIAN [Italian, c. 1488–1576], *The Gypsy Madonna.* C. 1510. Oil on wood, 25 3/4 × 32 7/8 in. (65.5 × 83.5 cm). Kunsthistorisches Museum, Vienna. Photo by Erich Lessing.

FIG 7-16   GEORGE CALEB BINGHAM [American, 1811–1879], *The Jolly Flatboatmen.* 1877–1878. Oil on canvas, 26 1/16 × 36 3/8 in. (66.2 × 92.4 cm). Terra Museum of American Art, Chicago. Terra Foundation for the Arts. Daniel J. Terra Collection (1992.15).

Because of the inscribed triangle, this composition is almost symmetrical— the left side is nearly a mirror image of the right. The poses of the men balance one another too. The two men sitting on the left and the right strike the same pose, although the direction of their contrapposto is different. The pose of the fiddler approximates that of the boy beating the skillet as a drum. The pose of the jolly dancer in the center corresponds to that of the man lying on his back watching him. It is as though, for each pair of men, George Caleb Bingham studied the same model from two different points of view. Bingham demonstrated that he could find classical principles of design through contrapposto even on the American frontier.

group of the Mother and Child forms a stable triangular shape in the center, almost everything else is asymmetrically arranged. The Christ child stands on a small parapet to the right. The cloth of honor, a drapery that was traditionally spread behind royalty, has been shifted to the right. In the distance on the left and beyond another low parapet lies a peaceful landscape with gently rolling hills. The spatial recession of the work, beginning with the parapet and the child Jesus on the right, moves diagonally back through the Mother to the light on the distant horizon on the left. Titian's new kind of balance, harmonizing nature and human beings, is one of the pleasant seductions of this lovely painting.

Composition

When artists apply the principles of design, they organize and unify the visual elements into a structure, or **composition.** A composition is like a scaffolding of lines or shapes or contrasts of the elements across the picture plane or embedded in a three-dimensional

work. The unifying principles build a structure over the whole. Through such a compositional framework, the artist takes the raw material of reality and makes clear its underlying structure, or the artist makes up a design for this raw material to create a structure for it.

Whether the artist is working with reality or with nonrepresentational shapes, masses, and spaces, the structural design holds things together and helps form a unified composition. George Caleb Bingham's *The Jolly Flatboatmen* (FIG. 7-16) has a clear-cut compositional structure. The boat, musicians, and dancers form a triangle on the picture plane even though the lines and shapes of this triangle exist at various depths within the image. The perspective in Emanuel de Witte's painting *Interior with a Woman Playing a Virginals* (FIG. 2-23) leads the eye through three rooms and out the far window. But de Witte also composed his picture like a quilt of rectangular shapes forming a series of parallel and perpendicular lines lying on the picture plane. The two figures of Michelangelo's *Pietà* (p. 183) form a very stable pyramidal mass.

Text continues on page 187.

Michelangelo (1475–1564)

W E DO NOT KNOW who taught Michelangelo how to carve marble. When he was a grown man and people began to call him a divinely inspired genius, he liked to think of himself as self-taught. A genius did not need the standard five-year apprenticeship of an artisan to become an artist. Since the husband of Michelangelo's wet nurse was a stonemason, Michelangelo said he absorbed the tools of his trade along with her milk.

MICHELANGELO [Italian, 1475–1564], *Pietà*. 1498–1500. Marble, 68 1/2 in. (174 cm) high. St. Peter's, Rome. Alinari/Art Resource, New York.

Although he was apprenticed at age thirteen, in April 1488, to the Florentine artist Ghirlandaio, Michelangelo probably practiced only drawing and painting in Ghirlandaio's shop. About a year later he was doing something quite different. He had been invited to become a member of the household of the leading family of Florence, the Medici. In their extensive art collection, curated by a bronze sculptor named Bertoldo di Giovanni, he studied and copied classical sculpture. These ancient stones were Michelangelo's true master. From them he learned the pagan love of the nude human body—its sensual appeal and its abilty to express emotion through its torsions. Furthermore, living with the Medici, he dealt with people who were interested in art on a more sophisticated and intellectual level than that of most Florentine artists running a shop. The Medici probably taught him to appreciate art like Plato, as divine inspiration and as the embodiment of

higher ideals. Without the demands of a traditional apprenticeship, Michelangelo was free to experiment. He was perhaps telling the truth when he said he taught himself to be a sculptor.

During those years in Florence, Michelangelo also heard the fiery sermons of the Dominican preacher Girolamo Savonarola, who condemned the immorality of his time. Whether he was affected by Savonarola's preaching or not, Michelangelo often displayed deep religious feeling in his work. In fact, Michelangelo only grew more pious and more earnest in his faith as he grew older. Most people see in all of Michelangelo's work an expression of frustrated conflict. Very likely the fundamental conflict within him was between his pagan love of the beauty of human flesh and his belief in the sinfulness of human nature—the result of his

faith in God. Two of his earliest works, the classically nude *David* (FIG. 17-18) and the compassionate *Pietà*, symbolize the two poles of his troubled nature.

A major work of art in the Renaissance, like the David or the *Pietà*, usually began as a business deal between the patron and the artist. The contract Michelangelo signed for the *Pietà* in 1498 specified that he was to finish the

Continued on next page.

MICHELANGELO [Italian, 1475–1564],
Awakening Slave. 1520–1523? Marble.
Galleria dell'Accademia, Florence.
Alinari/Art Resource, New York.

signed the contract, he must have had a rough idea of what he intended to do. In fact, Michelangelo had already spent several months in Carrara, Italy, overseeing the quarrying of the stone. Throughout his career as a sculptor, Michelangelo spent a great deal of time in the quarry—sometimes months, sometimes years, sometimes longer than he actually spent carving the statues of a commission.

The *Pietà* and the David are highly polished and finished. Their precision and perfection reveal Michelangelo's virtuosity in carving marble. They are also two of the few pieces of sculpture that Michelangelo ever finished. Most of his work in stone he left incomplete. In some cases he was distracted by new work that a powerful patron like a new pope insisted that he carve first. But the basic responsibility probably lay with Michelangelo himself. Again and again he agreed to undertake enormous commissions, involving dozens of statues, which he contracted to complete in impossibly short periods of time. Out of jealousy and an awareness of his own greatness, he refused to collaborate with other artists or to farm out the pieces of a large-scale work.

Some of Michelangelo's statues, in their unfinished state, reveal his manner of carving a block of marble. *Awakening Slave*—one of several unfinished prisoners or slaves that belonged to an enormous tomb for Pope Julius II,—is an example. Before carving any statue, Michelangelo may have made rough models in wax or clay to work out his ideas. He made preliminary drawings too, in which the hatch marks that modeled the drawing imitated the striation that he would make with his chis-

Michelangelo never intended that any of his works be seen in an unfinished state. Nevertheless, the figures still trapped in the stone that surrounds them seem to symbolize his belief that the spiritual soul is trapped in the material of the body.

el. Above all, he developed a powerful concept of the figure concealed within the stone. Michelangelo then made a full-scale drawing on the surface of the block before he began to carve. Even when Michelangelo was carving a figure in the round, he worked on the block as though he were making a relief. Instead of first roughing out the major masses of the figure from all four sides, he carved the block from one side. A friend compared the way the figure emerged from the stone to the process of pulling a body gradually up out of a tub of water. The most forward parts emerged first, while the rest was still encased in the block.

In his incomplete *Awakening Slave*, after an unskilled assistant rough cut the stone, Michelangelo himself used a chisel with teeth or claws that left markings like the network of hatching lines in his ink drawings. Through them we see the traces of his carving as he

work in one year and was to be paid 450 ducats (perhaps the equivalent of several thousand dollars today). He was to be given another 150 ducats before he began. Michelangelo actually took about three years to finish the *Pietà*. Since the marble block for the *Pietà* had already been quarried when Michelangelo

MICHELANGELO [Italian, 1475–1564], *Nude Youth (Ignudo)*. 1509–1512. Fresco. Sistine Chapel ceiling, Rome. © 1994 Nippon Television Network Corporation, Tokyo.

worked the stone and shaped the forms. The stages of his procedure are still visible: from the uncut block and the rough shaping of the stone, to his habit of bringing certain parts that interested him to a degree of finish, while ignoring other parts and leaving them rough. Perhaps Michelangelo was unable to complete these statues because he lost interest in them when he solved the artistic problem they represented.

Michelangelo never intended that any of his works be seen in an unfinished state. Nevertheless, the figures still trapped in the stone that surrounds them seem to symbolize his belief that the spiritual soul is trapped in the material of the body. The figures seem to carry the weight of the stone.

Pope Julius II had Michelangelo stop work on his tomb in order to paint the ceiling of the Sistine Chapel in the Vat-

ican. When Michelangelo painted the figure *Nude Youth (Ignudo)* on the chapel ceiling, he thought of him as a statue carved from a block of stone around whom the rectangular shape of the block could still be inscribed. Michelangelo also posed the limbs of the figure in a tightly controlled pattern in which parallels, perpendiculars, and forty-five-degree angles govern the position of the body parts. The upper-right arm, right thigh, and lower-left leg of the figure are approximately parallel. The central axis of the trunk and the lower-right leg are parallel. In between these lines, limbs move at forty-five-degree angles. This very strict pattern of lines lends structural support to the twisting figure. It is a wonder that Michelangelo could make such a contrived pose look so relaxed and graceful.

Continued on next page.

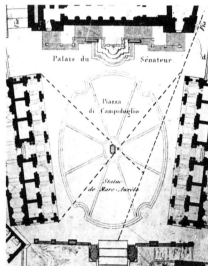

Michelangelo's plan of Capitoline Hill, Rome. Engravings by Etienne Dupérac. Foto Marburg/Art Resource, New York.

MICHELANGELO [Italian, 1475–1564], (left) Capitoline Hill, Rome. Begun 1538. Engraving by Etienne Dupérac. Staatliche Graphische Summlung, Munich.

In addition to being a sculptor and painter, Michelangelo was also an accomplished poet and architect. While completing the basilica of St. Peter (FIG. 17-20), Michelangelo also redesigned the ancient Capitoline Hill in Rome to make it once again the civic heart of the city. He began by making the equestrian statue of the Roman emperor Marcus Aurelius the central focus of his urban design. (At the time it was believed that the statue represented Constantine, the first Christian emperor.)

When Michelangelo started this project in 1538, the Capitoline Hill was an irregular, muddy area spotted with older medieval buildings. Michelangelo made one of these buildings, the Senators' Palace, the imposing backdrop of the plaza by setting a grand double staircase in front of it and redesigning its facade. Another medieval building lay at an awkward angle in front of the Senators' Palace. Michelangelo turned that irregularity into an advantage by designing another building, now a museum, across the plaza at exactly the same angle so that the two symmetrical buildings frame the open area at the top of the hill. For the new building and for the restored older building, Michelangelo designed a monumental architecture in which giant pilasters, or rectangular columns, rise through two stories and support the grand entablature, or horizontal members, at the top. Each building is imposing yet carefully integrated into the unified design of the Capitoline Hill. Although Michelangelo died before most of the work on the Capitoline project was accomplished, it was successfully completed according to the engraved design made from his plans.

In the midst of creating a composition, artists are very unlikely to refer explicitly to a set of principles of design to determine their next step. Through continual observation and practice, principles of design have, more likely, become so internalized that they seem instinctive. Moreover, these principles function simultaneously in an artist's creativity. Whether in the planning stage or in the middle of creation, artists are continually adjusting the elements in their work toward a unified composition.

SUMMATION BOX

PRINCIPLES OF DESIGN

Six principles of design are used to achieve unity or a wholeness:

Dominance	The main subject or main element is emphasized.
Consistency with variety	The visual elements resemble one another without monotony.
Rhythm	The repetition of elements creates a steady flow like a musical beat.
Proportions	Whole number ratios or golden section ratios organize forms.
Scale	The visual elements conform to a large or small scale.
Balance	The visual elements on the right "weigh" the same as the elements on the left.

COMPOSITION

A composition is the result of an artist's design—an arrangement of visual elements into a coherent structure.

Key Terms and Concepts

asymmetry	golden section	scale
balance	handling	symmmetry
composition	hieratic representation	unity
consistency	principles of design	variety
design	proportions	
dominance	rhythm	

CRITICAL ANALYSIS II

Mary Cassatt [American, 1844–1926], *Summertime: Woman and Child in a Rowboat*. C. 1894. Oil on canvas, 42 × 30 in. (106.7 × 76.2 cm.). Terra Museum of American Art, Chicago.

Line and Shape

The woman in Mary Cassatt's painting *Summertime: Woman and Child in a Rowboat* looks down at the water and establishes an imaginary vertical line between her eye and the duck. This eye-line is paralleled by the basically vertical lines of the upright child. The child's eye-line parallels the diagonal tilt of the woman's shoulder. Contour lines are visible around the forms of the figures, but throughout most of the painting Cassatt did not so much fill in between the contours as create a network of short wavy lines by means of the large interwoven brush strokes of color. The straight eye-lines conspicuously intersect the curves of the boat and of the woman's arms. The same sort of curve in the shape of the boat is repeated in the shapes of the hats and of the ducks.

Light and Color

Water is one of the favorite motifs of Impressionist painters because its dancing ripples and reflections encourage the painter to separate colors into quickly applied touches of unmixed paint. In the water that rises to the very top of the canvas, Cassatt set down reds and greens, oranges and blues—complementary combinations that would instantly turn muddy gray if they were mixed.

She also used dark colors—especially in the water under the boat—as a foil for the light clothes of the woman and child in order to help give some impression of the cloth's luminosity in bright sunlight. Light reflected from the water softens modeling and brightens shadows everywhere. Cassatt applied her colors in rather irregular brush strokes. In contrast to other Impressionists who laid down paint systematically, she seems to have enjoyed the expressionistic potential of her colors.

Texture and Space

The vigorous, visible brushwork throughout the painting creates a rich texture for the eyes. *Summertime* shows no linear perspective and very little modeling to indicate deep space and solid bodies residing in space. However, the forearm of the woman, the shoulders of the girl, and the white duck are foreshortened. The most remarkable feature of the spatial construction of *Summertime* is the two points of view from which the composition is seen. The water is observed from such a high vantage point above it that the horizon line lies beyond the frame at the top. The water can thus become a consistent background for the figures, and the placement of the figures and ducks comes close to the space-by-position scheme seen in the Persian *Meeting of Theologians* (FIG. 6-12). The profile figures, the boat, and the ducks, however, are observed from a point of view more or less perpendicular to them. The combination of separate viewpoints in one image, although derived from the example of Japanese prints (see Kiyonaga's *Scenes in a Woman's Bathhouse*, FIG. 6-18), looks forward to the shifting points of view of Cubist space.

Principles of Design

Cassatt took the risk of an asymmetrical balance by shifting the two main figures and the boat in her *Summertime* to the right. Still, the figure of the woman is nearly in the center of the composition. Although the contour line of the boat also directs the viewer's eye out of the picture toward the right,

the vertical curve of the girl's back helps to curb that visual movement. The girl's glance to the left also counterbalances the visual stimulation of her form on the right. The value contrast between the little white duck and the dark blue-green water is an important counterweight to the larger shapes on the right. The very active color contrasts in the bottom half of the painting balances the human interest, value contrasts, and curving shapes of the top half. Although the balanced composition is carefully calculated, the asymmetry gives the impression of a casual glimpse of a fragment of reality.

THE VISUAL ARTS

A Comparison

To understand the nature of drawing, let us compare the drawing of the Countess d'Haussonville (FIG. 8-1) with the painted portrait of her (FIG. 8-2), both by the prominent French artist Jean A. D. Ingres (pronounced ahng-gr). The drawing is a **study** for the painting, in which the artist explored a part or an aspect of his work to resolve any problems in rendering that segment. In his drawing Ingres ignored the setting and the composition of the finished painting. The faint treatment of the arms and the head indicates that the artist has already settled on the countess's pose and is seeking instead to resolve the problems of her dress. In fact, Ingres reworked the area of her waist a second time on the right of the drawing. Neither solution seems to have satisfied Ingres, for the dress in the painting—especially the sleeve—is still somewhat different from the drawing.

Other differences between the two works are more fundamental and underscore what is meant by draw-

FIG 8-1 *(left)* JEAN A. D. INGRES [French, 1780–1867], *Countess d'Haussonville.* 1845. Graphite and black chalk, 14 1/4 × 7 3/8 in. (36.4 × 18.7 cm). Frick Museum, New York.

FIG 8-2 *(above)* JEAN A. D. INGRES [French, 1780–1867], *Countess d'Haussonville.* 1845. Oil on canvas, 53 1/2 × 36 1/4 in. (139 × 92 cm). Frick Museum, New York.

FIG 8-3 [Anasazi] 1050–1250 and earlier. Petroglyphs. Newspaper Rock, Utah. Photo © 1992 Navaswan, FPG.

The Basic Art

Drawing can be considered the basic art for several reasons. One is that drawing is probably the first art medium that almost all human beings practice. Sometime between the ages of eighteen months and twenty-four months, most of us suddenly realized that some scribble we are making represented a person like Mommy or Daddy. Drawing was our first experience of art—our first experience of a visual symbol standing for something else.

Drawings are also among the earliest and most sophisticated works of art that men and women produced in history, and they appear among the earliest kinds of art found in many cultures around the world. In addition to the drawings in European caves (see FIG. 2-12), drawings by prehistoric peoples appear on rock walls in Australia and in America—especially in the Southwest. The abundant rock art in the Southwest consists of paintings and more commonly **petroglyphs,** which are drawings made by pecking or cutting a design into the stone face of a natural rock or cliff (see FIG. 8-3). The two roots of the word mean rock cutting.

For the last several hundred years, the Western art world has treated drawing as the basic art in another sense. Drawing has been the primary means by which the tradition of art is passed from generation to generation. It has been the chief means of instruction because learning to draw sharpens observation, increases perception, and releases self-expression. The low cost of drawing materials and the ease of making corrections and alterations encourages experimentation and creativity in the developing artist. In short, drawing has become the chief means for the education of the artistic imagination.

In many ways, drawing is the art form on which all others build. The first creative impulses of a painter or sculptor are commonly expressed in drawings. Painters and sculptors are likely to work out their visual ideas, at least partway, in the less costly and less intractable medium of drawing before tackling their preferred medium. Architects and even photographers are commonly trained to draw, if for no other reason than to condition their perceptual skills and develop their creative potential. Compared with architecture and

ing. The painting displays full color. The drawing disregards areas of color in exchange for explicit black contour lines that create shapes. Sensitive lines are also an integral part of Ingres's painting, but the lines in the painting are essentially the limits of the areas of color.

Especially in the case of Ingres, who claimed that line was the essential element in art, the drawing has attractions not present in the painting. The drawing makes the artist's assurance and simplicity in depicting the contours of the arms more evident than in the painting. The sketchier lines of the dress, which demonstrate the artist's striving to perfect the forms, records his creative impulses and his sensitive adjustments. The drawing documents the process of creation, whereas the painting is so highly finished that it obliterates all preliminary stages. Since the Renaissance, many collectors have felt that the artist's awe-inspiring power of creativity was often best preserved in drawings. Consequently, even preliminary working sketches like Ingres's study for *Countess d'Haussonville* have been avidly collected and admired.

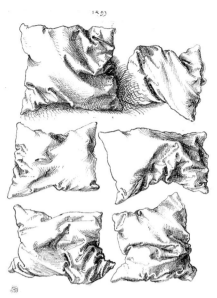

FIG 8-4 ALBRECHT DÜRER [German, 1471–1528], *Self-Portrait at Age Twenty-Two* and *Pillow Exercise*. 1493. Pen and ink, 11 × 8 in. (28 × 20.3 cm). Metropolitan Museum of Art, New York. Robert Lehman Collection, 1975 (1975.1.862).

Because Albrecht Dürer looked at himself in a mirror to make this self-portrait, his left hand—held closer to the mirror—is larger than his head. His pen lines, scratching the paper, are abrupt and turn in every direction. To reproduce dark areas and accentuate the roundness of forms, Dürer curved the hatching and cross-hatching and varied the thickness of the line and the frequency of the hatch marks.

*Underneath his self-portrait on the front side of the page, or **recto,** Dürer practiced depicting the masses of a pillow with hatch marks. Then, on the reverse side, or **verso,** he tossed the* pillow six different ways and repeated the drawing exercise six more times, curving the hatching along with the folds of the pillow. Art students today still practice Dürer's drawing *exercise—usually by trying to reproduce the masses and dark values of several crumpled pieces of paper.*

sculpture, drawing is a more spontaneous medium, allowing architects and sculptors to visualize possibilities rapidly and to find their way to solutions.

A Definition

In most cases, to draw means to make marks on a surface in order to delineate something. It usually means to make lines and with those lines to make shapes. As we saw in comparing Ingres's two works of the Countess d'Haussonville (FIGS. 8-1 and 8-2), lines and shapes are usually more explicit in a drawing than in a painting. The use of explicit lines is one of the conventions that helps define drawing. Drawings usually begin and often end with contour lines—those imaginary lines around the edges of forms in nature or the boundary lines of any sort of shape.

The lines of a drawing are stated clearly and explicitly. Through them we can almost sense the artist's state of mind and emotional attitude, because in a drawing we experience immediately whether the artist used lines that are thick or thin, long or short, broken or smooth, harsh or delicate. Drawn lines also have direction and guide the eye. The movement of the eye along a line often repeats the very stroke made by the artist in the drawing.

The art of drawing is also defined by the tools the artist employs. Traditionally, certain instruments like a pencil, a pen, chalk, or charcoal produce only drawings when they are the chief agents in a work of art. Some tools, however, produce several different kinds of art. For example, artists can use paintbrushes—dipped very likely in ink—to make drawings as well as to make paintings. In many cases it is only the artist who decides that his or her work is a drawing or a painting.

In addition to lines, drawings can also depict values, and the art of drawing has established several conventions for the representation of values. In his *Self-Portrait* (FIG. 8-4) the twenty-two-year-old Albrecht Dürer demonstrated that the parallel lines of hatching can darken a form and that the thickness of contour lines can also imply darker areas.

Artists also may rub the surface with their pencil, chalk, or charcoal to model a form in light and dark,

FIG 8-5 ANNIBALE CARRACCI [Italian, 1560–1609], *Triton Sounding a Conch Shell*. Black chalk on blue paper, 15 1/4 × 9 1/2 in. (38.7 × 24.1 cm). Metropolitan Museum of Art, New York. Rogers Fund, 1970 (1970.15).

or simply smear the contour line with their finger to achieve modeling. In the study *Triton Sounding a Conch Shell* (FIG. 8-5), made in preparation for a mural, Annibale Carracci often blurred the chalk lines, probably with his fingers, to model the dark undersides of ribs and muscles. Notice also how faint he left the contour line of the shoulder to indicate that it is exposed to the strongest light. We can still see in the drawing the first lines that Carracci made with the chalk as he searched for the right shape and adjusted the undulating contour to depict the anatomy of the sea creature. We can also feel in his lines a vibrancy that almost shakes the figure. The human figure can be drawn in many ways, but Carracci developed a classical technique that served as a model for generations to come.

To achieve value contrasts in drawings, diluted ink may also be spread across the surface. After Giovanni Battista Tiepolo made the small sketch *Holy Family* (FIG. 8-6), he then brushed diluted ink across patches of the drawing for light-and-dark contrasts. Whether the different values are created by lines or by rubbing the drawing instrument or even by brushing ink across the surface, the play of light and dark is an integral part of the drawing medium.

In most of these conventions for light and dark, the drawing medium is optically mixed with the lightness of the paper. In fact, a fundamental convention of drawing is that the artist usually leaves a considerable amount of the surface blank—unlike the technique of most forms of painting, which tends to cover the whole surface with paint. Most often the white of the paper is visible throughout a drawing, both in the figures that might be the draftsperson's main interest and in the background. By convention we do not hesitate to understand one part of the white paper as a human figure and another part of the same paper as the sky in a drawing. By contrast, in painting artists normally fill up these different positive and negative shapes with areas of different colors.

Drawings usually lack color. Traditionally, most drawing media have been monochromatic, limited to black, gray, red, or brown. Even if numerous colors are available, most artists probably use only two or perhaps three colors at a time in any drawing. Full-color drawings that fill the entire surface with colors are possible, but not common, and of course they blur the distinction between drawing and painting. Soft-colored chalks called pastels are normally considered to be drawing instruments. When they are used to produce a work with the rich colored surface of a painting, the result might be considered both a painting and a drawing.

Functions of Drawing

Drawings are made for a variety of reasons. Many are created as completely finished artworks in themselves. Artists also might draw as an experiment to increase their ability in general or as an experiment to complete a work in another medium, as did Ingres. Even though these drawings may seem to be lesser art forms, they are often appreciated as works of art in themselves. Outside the visual arts, preliminary studies are seldom so highly regarded. Scholars may be interested in the manuscripts of famous authors in order to explain their novels, but seldom is the reading public expected to appreciate the manuscript as art. Not so with a drawing. The incompleteness of its composition and its subordinate function does not detract from its quality as art.

Artists commonly make at least four kinds of drawings: drawings on paintings; drawings as studies; drawings as final works; and illustrations, cartoons, or caricatures.

Drawings on Paintings

Traditionally, before they begin to paint, artists draw the outline of their subject on the surface to be painted, whether the surface is a canvas or the wall of a building. If the paint is applied thinly enough on top of the preliminary drawing, the drawn lines may show through and become part of the finished work. Very often, contour lines in finished paintings are reinforced or painted as distinct lines, as Alice Neel did in her *Nude Self-Portrait* (FIG. 2-27). A painter may also draw lines directly on the surface of a painting, as Giacomo Balla did in his *Automobile Speed + Light + Noises* (FIG. 7-7).

Sometimes artists in the act of painting leave such visible brush strokes on a canvas that they seem to be drawing instead of painting. In this way, the visible evidence of the creative gesture—which is prevalent in the art of drawing—becomes a main theme of the painting. American Abstract Expressionist painter, Franz Kline, drew perhaps the boldest painted lines

FIG 8-6   GIOVANNI BATTISTA TIEPOLO [Italian, 1696–1770], *The Holy Family.* Brown ink and wash drawings, 12 × 8 1/8 in. (30.5 × 20.6 cm). Los Angeles County Museum of Art. Gift of Cary Grant.

FIG 8-7 FRANZ KLINE [American, 1910–1962], *Buttress*. 1956. Oil on canvas, 46 1/2 × 55 1/2 in. (118 × 141 cm). Museum of Contemporary Art, Los Angeles. The Panza Collection. © 1995 Estate of Franz Kline/VAGA, New York.

ever on his large canvasses. Made with house paint-brushes, Kline's big strokes slash across the canvas in his *Buttress* (FIG. 8-7). The raw sweeps of paint visualize for us the directness and spontaneity of creation and the energy of Kline's action as he painted. Kline's paintings seem like excerpts from an ink sketch that has been magnified dozens of times. His paintings, which indeed often began as brush-and-ink drawings on paper, are evidence that he made no distinction between painting and drawing. We may appreciate his paintings in much the same way that Chinese collectors appreciated the sweeping, expressive lines of calligraphy.

Drawings as Studies

Artists customarily make drawings to study different aspects of a work of art to be executed in another medium. They might make several drawings of a model in order to determine the poses of the figure in their final work, as did Antoine Watteau in his *Two Studies of the Head and Shoulders of a Little Girl* (FIG. 8-8). The French artist Watteau drew continually, studying models in a great variety of casual poses, and when he wanted to make a painting, he referred to his collection of drawings. The features of the little girl, studied in two different poses in this drawing, appear in paintings he made about two years later.

In preparation for a painting, an artist might make a separate drawing of the perspective to make sure of the spatial relationships. The artist might study the landscape or the clothing, as did Ingres for his portrait of the Countess of d'Haussonville (see FIG. 8-1). In addition to sketches of individual figures, an artist might make rough drawings of the entire composition, as did Leonardo da Vinci when he recorded his preliminary conception of his *Last Supper* (FIG. 7-2).

If the artist is satisfied with one of these studies and the drawing suits the purposes of the larger work, the artist might want to transfer it to the other medium. In the past the most common method of transfer was to draw a grid of lines over the study and a corresponding but larger grid on the other surface. The grids made the copying of the drawing much easier. A grid scoring the drawing for transfer to another medium is visible in Tintoretto's *Archer* (FIG. 4-15). Entire compositions, established in a finished drawing, could be transferred this way. A modern artist would more likely use a projector to transfer a drawing to a larger scale.

Not only painters but sculptors, architects, and theater designers make studies for their work in another medium. Some architects' drawings have an expressiveness that goes beyond the need to illustrate the dimensions of the building. Louis Kahn's sketch for a gallery in his Kimbell Art Museum (FIG. 8-9) reveals the architect's feelings for the space, lines, and light of his building rather than rigidly analyzes the structure. Stage designers and costume designers often make drawings that express more than what is necessary for theatrical assistants to translate their conceptions into reality. These utilitarian drawings may then take on artistic qualities.

FIG 8-8   ANTOINE WATTEAU [French, 1684–1721], *Two Studies of the Head and Shoulders of a Little Girl.* C. 1716–1717. Red, black, and white chalks on buff paper, 7 3/8 × 9 5/8 in. (18.7 × 24.4 cm). Pierpont Morgan Library, New York.

Antoine Watteau has earned the reputation as one of the ablest draftspersons of all times and he himself may have esteemed his drawings more than his paintings. Contemporaries praised the freedom of execution, the lightness of touch, the delicacy of the contour lines in his drawings. To achieve his graceful style, Watteau drew mostly in red chalk, never in pen and ink, but he is most famous for drawings, such as this one, in three chalks—à trois crayons, in French.

In the pose on the left, where the girl looks into the light, white chalk renders the highlights on her forehead, cheek, and mouth. In the pose on the right, where the girl looks away from the light, her face is covered with translucent shadow. The drawing gives the impression that the artist captured spontaneous and natural attitudes with ease and charm.

FIG 8-9   LOUIS KAHN [American, 1901–1974], perspective of gallery interior for Kimbell Art Museum. 1967. Charcoal. University of Pennsylvania and Pennsylvania Historical and Museum Commission.

FIG 8-10 CHRISTO [American, 1935–], *Running Fence (Project for Sonoma and Marin Counties).* 1976. Pencil, pastel, charcoal, pencil, engineering data, and topographical map; two parts—15 × 96 in. (38.1 × 243.8 cm) and 42 × 96 in. (106.7 × 243.8 cm). © 1976 Christo. Collection Jeanne-Claude Christo, New York. Photo by Harry Shunk.

The environmental artists Christo and Jeanne-Claude are well-known around the world for wrapping in fabric famous landmarks, like the Pont Neuf, a bridge in Paris, and tying them with rope into packages. They also draped fabric across a landscape, as when they surrounded an island in Biscayne Bay, Florida, with fabric floating on the water. Their packages conceal and then reveal the land or structure in a new light. The fence in California, cutting across the landscape, accentuates its undulations and its openness.

Over the months and years that it takes to devise and fund a project, Christo makes hundreds of drawings in preparation. Some of the projects are never realized and remain only on paper. Even the completed works are temporary, since the building or landscape, once wrapped, is soon returned to its previous state. All that remains of their art are the excellent drawings, such as this one, as well as photographs and models, that document their work. Christo's drawings and early works are the sole source of income financing their art.

Running Fence, Sonoma and Marin Counties, California, 1972–76. Height: 18 ft. (5.5 m.) Length: 24.5 mi. (40km). Photo by Jeanne-Claude.

The completed project.

Artists can make studies at any time, with or without a specific work in mind. Many artists draw constantly to study anatomy, foreshortening, or perspective. They draw to record people, places, and other visual **motifs** (recurrent themes or designs employed in artist's work) that they have experienced. And they draw to stimulate the imagination.

Drawings as Final Works

The heading "Drawings as Final Works" describes the intention of the artist in making a drawing, not the quality of the drawing. In the past, artists made portrait drawings not as studies for paintings but as finished works of art. Portrait drawings, which are less expensive than paintings or sculpture, sometimes lend themselves to more intimacy and characterization than the formal portraits of the times. It was common, too, for artists to make drawings of interesting geographic features or of famous pieces of architecture as finished works. Before the age of photography, people were interested in such drawings as reproductions of faraway places or as records of their travels.

In the late twentieth century artists are as likely as ever to produce independent finished drawings, whether original compositions or reproductions of particular places or things. Many artists make finished drawings because they prefer the scale of drawings, they like the directness of a drawing medium, or they want to experiment. Some modern artists specialize in drawing; other artists will devote themselves to the art of drawing exclusively for a long period of time. For example, Vija Celmins concentrated for some time on making finished drawings, such as *Untitled (Ocean)* (see p. 202), which she exhibited and sold as completed works of art. In another example, Christo makes finished drawings to document his large-scale projects such as his *Running Fence (Project for Sonoma and Marin Counties)* (FIG. 8-10).

Illustrations, Cartoons, and Caricatures

Since drawings can be photomechcanically reproduced in the mass media, they often appear as illustrations in books or magazines. One common form of illustration appears in **cartoons**—the often humorous drawings in most daily newspapers and in magazines. Cartoons come in all styles, from the simplicity of *Peanuts* to the elaborate drawings of many dramatic, noncomic strips. Perhaps the only common denomi-

FIG 8-11 JACK OHMAN [American, 1960], caricature of President Bill Clinton. 1994. *Oregonian. © 1994 Tribune Media Services.*

nator among them is their popular appeal. Cartoonists have developed an interesting set of drawing conventions, such as balloons for speech and auxiliary lines indicating movement.

A **caricature** exaggerates prominent or characteristic features of well-known individuals or common types for either satirical effect or social commentary. Caricatures can be made in any medium, but most often they are drawings. And since they tend to make public statements, caricatures frequently appear in the mass media. Political cartoonists every day create caricatures of presidents and prominent government leaders. They exaggerate Richard Nixon's nose, Jimmy Carter's teeth, Ronald Reagan's hair and wrinkles, George Bush's sunken cheeks, Bill Clinton's full cheeks, hair, and nose (see FIG. 8-11). A caricature may also satirize a class of individuals such as an overstuffed capitalist, and caricature consequently runs the risk of reinforcing stereotypes. A good caricaturist has a keen eye for telling features and a knack for making the distortions in drawing plausible.

Text continues on page 204

Chapter 8: Drawing

Vija Celmins (1939–)

OR ABOUT fifteen years, from the late 1960s to the early 1980s, Vija Celmins concentrated on making drawings. Her medium was the simple drawing pencil, which comes in a variety of hard or soft leads.

She usually covered the drawing paper with a ground of white acrylic paint, perhaps to make the paper more sensitive to the pencil's touch and to make the luminous white of the paper more permanent. Celmins drew not with lines but with minute and subtle value contrasts.

During those years Celmins focused on three main subjects: the ocean, the desert, and the night sky. In *Untitled (Ocean)*, working from her own photographs, she expressed the infinity of the ocean not by sweeping the horizon in a vast panorama but by looking down upon a segment of the water and painstakingly observing the myriad shapes of the ripples on the choppy sea. The overall pattern of small waves covers the entire surface except for a small white border.

What appears as a pattern, however, has no repeating elements. Every ripple is different—a seemingly ordered chaos of shapes and an infinite series of variations. Nor does the texture that Celmins wove across the surface have a dominant dramatic feature, a climax, a beginning or an end. The same sort of ruffling

waves appear from one end of the paper to the other. The silvery gray of her light and dark pencil strokes is the perfect medium for capturing the enormous range of values in a black-and-white photograph. Just as the single eye of the camera can freeze thousands of wave movements in sharp focus, Celmins

VIJA CELMINS [American, 1939–], *Untitled. (Ocean)* 1970. Pencil and acrylic on paper, 12 3/4 × 17 1/2 in. (32.4 × 44.5 cm.) Collection of the Modern Art Museum of Fort Worth, Texas. Purchase of Benjamin J. Tillar Memorial Trust.

*Celmins
has the need
to examine reality
as closely as possible
and to fix its image
in her memory
through her art.*

captured each shadow and each reflected light.

Even as a student Celmins possessed great technical ability and the diligence to reproduce nature with exactitude. She has the need to examine reality as closely as possible and to fix its image in her memory through her art. But trompe l'oeil (fooling the eye) has never been her goal. The aim of her drawing is thinking. When we look at her ocean, she wants us to think about space and to think about the process of making art. Her space is exact and distinct and yet it has no precise location. Because it has no temporal or human references, this one specific area of ocean is timeless and universal. From a distance, the sameness and vastness of

the image stand out. Up close, each stroke of the pencil forming the illusion of reality is visible. The industrious pencil of the artist lovingly enriches the commonplace on earth.

A stretch of rock-and-pebble-strewn desert afforded Celmins the same contrast of the finite and the infinite. In *Untitled (Irregular Desert)* a repetitious and overall pattern of small and large shapes is dispersed over the surface, and the infinite variety of sizes and shapes extends implicitly beyond the borders. A low-lying light source rakes across the surface, casting shadows toward the upper left. Celmin's drawing is factual yet somehow strange and mysterious. Nevertheless, our awareness that she has reproduced a photograph keeps the

image one step removed from reality. It keeps the desert impersonal and checks us from projecting feelings of awe or sublimity upon nature.

Although her drawings of the night sky, which celebrate the rich blackness of a very soft pencil, reproduce observatory photographs of the stars, she herself photographed the desert sands in Death Valley and the ocean from a pier in Venice, California, where she lived for nearly twenty years. In 1980 Celmins moved to New York, where she took up painting again, transferring her ocean, desert, and night sky to canvas. Although her motifs work well on canvas, we no longer feel the intimacy of drawing.

Paper

Drawings are made most frequently on paper. But they have also been made on wood, cloth, skin, clay, or rock walls. Chinese artists frequently drew on expensive silk. In the West in ancient times and throughout the Middle Ages, artists drew on **parchment,** made from the skin of animals such as sheep, goats, or calves. Very fine lambskin, kidskin, or calfskin is called **vellum.** Parchment must be primed, or rubbed with pumice, ground bone, or chalk to smooth it and to prepare it for drawing. Anything done on parchment today signifies something treasured and rare, as when we refer to a college diploma as a sheepskin.

Paper is made from the matted fibers of rags or of woodpulp, soaked in water and then pressed to varying degrees of smoothness or roughness. Rag paper lasts much longer than paper made from wood pulp because the longer and stronger rag fibers contain more stable cellulose. The Chinese invented paper in the second century A.D.; Islamic peoples in Samarkand learned the secret of papermaking in the eighth century; and the invention arrived in Europe through Islamic Spain in the twelfth century. However, the use of paper became common in Europe only in the fifteenth century.

For many centuries after that, the paper that artists used was dyed blue or an earth red or green, since it was hard to produce paper that had an even white tone to it. Annibale Carracci's drawing *Triton Sounding a Conch Shell* (FIG. 8-5) is on blue paper; Antoine Watteau's paper for *Two Studies of the Head and Shoulders of a Little Girl* (FIG. 8-8) is tan. Artists, like Watteau, often take advantage of the color of the paper and use it as a middle value, applying white chalk to the drawing for lighter values and black chalk for darker values.

Drawing Tools

For a variety of reasons, artists use many different tools or media to make drawings. Over the years new drawing implements have been invented and old implements refined. Different tools seem to satisfy different artistic needs and to determine to some extent what the finished product will look like. Most artists, in making a drawing, develop the potential latent in the medium, but it is amazing what certain artists are able to do within the restrictions of the resources they have adopted. It is as though the unlikely medium challenges them.

Perhaps the essential drawing implement is the artist's hand. The hand develops the skill to move the tool to create the lines that embody the artist's vision. Popular wisdom maintains that drawing skill lies in a person's ability to draw a straight line. But a ruler makes a straight line better than anyone can freehand. Instead, it is more important that the hand be able to vary a line by moving it around, by applying and releasing pressure, by turning and tilting the drawing implement.

Even the way the tool is held affects the character of the lines. In the West, artists tend to hold all drawing implements the way they hold a pencil: on an angle between the first three fingers, with the heel of the hand resting on the surface. This method encourages downward strokes of the implement moved mainly by the fingers. Many artists will also hold the drawing tool with the shaft running under the hand and nearly parallel to the surface, especially when they want broader strokes to render values. In the East, a Chinese or Japanese artist holds the brush upright between the first two fingers and the back of the third. The hand is poised free of the surface. This position allows movement in all directions and greater control in twisting and turning the brush to vary the line.

The drawing media are often divided between those that are dry and those that are liquid. Each medium possesses its own inherent characteristics that artists learn to exploit and expand upon. A liquid medium may or may not be easier to apply then a dry medium; for instance, a simple pencil may flow across the paper more freely than a steel-tipped pen filled with ink. It is always possible to combine different

FIG 8-12 PABLO PICASSO [Spanish, 1881–1973], *The Bathers.* 1918. Pencil on cream paper, 9 × 12 1/2 in. (23 × 31.9 cm). Fogg Art Museum, Cambridge.

media in one drawing. The ultimate criteria are that the medium be at the service of the artist and that it encourage creativity.

Some common drawing tools are pencil, metalpoint, charcoal, chalk, pastel, pen and ink, brush and ink, and modern inventions.

Pencil

Professional artists and amateurs alike draw with **pencils,** which commonly consist of graphite encased in wood. In *The Bathers* (FIG. 8-12) Picasso made a virtue of the simplicity of an ordinary pencil line. Once committed to a contour line, Picasso seldom lifted the pencil from the page until the contour intersected with another line. He kept a steady pressure on the pencil and established each form with a single delicate line. The economy of his line seems like a modern equivalent of the linear simplicity of classical Greek vase painting (see FIG. 16-16).

All kinds of pencils are available, some of them hard (H-pencils) and some of them soft (B-pencils): well over a dozen degrees of hardness or softness are produced commercially. The common "lead" pencil is actually made of graphite mixed with clay to determine the degree of hardness. In the late seventeen hundreds a Frenchman named Nicholas-Jacques Conté sheathed a thin shaft of graphite and clay in wood to invent the pencil as we know it. The thin tip of any pencil lends itself to an essentially linear style, although rubbing with the side of the pencil and the variations of pencil hardness can achieve values. The average pencil produces a gray color, somewhat shiny, although a wide variety of colored pencils are also available. The common pencil tends to be a reserved medium, since it seldom lends itself to bold effects. Artists will frequently use pencil in the preliminary stage of a work and then go over the sketch with a stronger medium like ink.

FIG 8-13 JAMES GRUBOLA [American, 1950–], *Available Light Series: Lauriston Place*. C. 1990. Silverpoint, 8 3/4 × 12 in. (22.2 × 30.5 cm). Artist's collection, Louisville, Kentucky.

Metalpoint

A few artists today—James Grubola, who drew *Available Light Series: Lauriston Place* (FIG. 8-13), is one of them—still draw with a tool, somewhat like a "mechanical pencil," designed to hold a hard metal shaft. The metal shaft, or any stylus of metal, makes so-called **metalpoint** drawings. Although the medium now is rare, the use of metalpoint was common in the Middle Ages, and in the Renaissance many artists made masterful metalpoint drawings. Painters frequently made compositional drawings on their panels in metalpoint because metalpoint lines would not smear when painted over. The metal may be gold, copper, tin, lead, or most commonly, silver. None of these metalpoints will leave marks on a paper unless the surface is made hard and abrasive with a grit—traditionally bone dust.

All the metalpoints, including **silverpoint,** create thin, faint gray lines that are impossible to erase. Pressure on the metalpoint scarcely increases the width or darkness of the lines. Some of the metallic lines tarnish with age: silver will turn faintly brown.

Silverpoint drawings appear soft, subtle, and delicate; each line is calculated, isolated, and clean. A silverpoint drawing requires precision and restraint—the very opposite of what quick sketches demand—and a silverpoint draftsperson must have infinite patience.

Charcoal

A favorite artist's medium is charred wood, or **charcoal.** Cave-dwelling men and women must have discovered it when they rubbed burnt sticks on the rock wall. Art students use charcoal all the time to make rapid sketches that quickly explore different points of view. The boldness of charcoal also makes it suitable for working on a large scale. Soft sticks of charcoal make a fairly thick, dark line, and the side of the stick can create broad tonal passages that are rich and velvety. Charcoal is dry, coarse, and granular; it smudges easily. Consequently, it can be rubbed to create blurred lines and shading. Since charcoal can be erased and smudged, it must be secured with a spray of fixative to preserve the drawing.

FIG 8-14 KÄTHE KOLLWITZ [German, 1867–1945], *Self-Portrait Drawing*. 1933. Charcoal on brown laid Ingres paper, 18 3/4 × 25 in. (47.6 × 63.5 cm). National Gallery of Art, Washington, D.C. Rosenwald Collection.

Käthe Kollwitz demonstrated the freedom and range of charcoal lines and values in her *Self-Portrait* (FIG. 8-14). When she drew this picture of herself—in profile, without a mirror—she was being persecuted by the Nazis because she had championed the poor and oppressed in her art. With a stick of charcoal she made a fairly sharp image of her profile, deep eyes, determined mouth, and poised hand. She easily blended the soft charcoal to produce fuzzy gray variations. It is common for an artist, when doing a portrait study, to make a precise face and then roughly sketch in the rest. Kollwitz did this, then, with the side of the charcoal stub she made a thick black zigzag line, as strong as the coil spring of an automobile, between her head and her hand. Few lines so loudly shout defiance.

Chalk

Chalks make soft, fuzzy lines, like those from charcoal but usually not as dark. A chalk line has a softness to it, and a transparency that allows the light of the paper to show through. Chalk is more permanent than char- coal, since it cannot be as easily erased. In addition to black, artists since the fifteenth century have also drawn with red and white chalk, sometimes in combi- nation, as Antoine Watteau did in his *Two Studies of the Head and Shoulders of a Little Girl* (FIG. 8-8). These red, white, and black chalk colors are naturally found in the earth.

In the eighteenth century the same French manu- facturer who invented the pencil compounded fairly hard chalk with an oily material so that it would adhere to the surface even better. His chalks are known, con- fusingly, as **Conté crayons.** Georges Seurat used a black Conté crayon to produce the smooth, rich value con- trasts in his *Seated Boy with Straw Hat* (FIG. 5-9).

Although the French word **crayon** has been applied to manufactured chalks, it signifies to most of us the colored wax sticks made for children. The main ingre- dient of these crayons is paraffin. Wax crayons are sel- dom employed as an artist's medium, however, because the pigments are not always permanent and because the crayons are not very flexible. It is nearly impossi- ble to blend the colors of crayons.

FIG 8-15 ROSALBA CARRIERA [Italian, 1675–1757], *Allegory of Painting*. C. 1720. Pastel, 17 3/4 × 13 3/4 in. (45.1 × 34.9 cm). National Gallery of Art, Washington, D.C. Samuel H. Kress Collection.

Rosalba Carriera not only made the use of pastel fashionable in the eighteenth century, she also established in her work models of lightness and charm that became standards for the Rococo style. Antoine Watteau visited with Carriera twice when she made a much-publicized sojourn in Paris in 1720–21. A glance at his Two Studies of the Head and Shoulders of a Little Girl *(FIG 8-8) shows that their art has much in common.*

Carriera was highly praised in her day for the liveliness of her figures, for their grace of expression, and for the beauty of her colors. The turn of the head, the poised fingers, the sidelong glance, and the luminous color in this drawing confirm that praise. The features of the face seem too idealized to be a portrait of an individual. The soft modeling of the face, the blurred contours, and the delicate shadows around the upturned mouth remind us of Leonardo's Mona Lisa *(FIG 17-15), which Carriera could have seen in Paris. The broader application of pastel on the girl's dress creates the illusion of a fluffy,* transparent material. Deft touches of pastel as highlights make the hair silky, the earrings sparkly, and the lips moist.

Pastels

Renaissance artists such as Leonardo da Vinci knew about **pastels,** but it was the Venetian artist Rosalba Carriera who first made them a popular medium in the early eighteenth century (see *Allegory of Painting*, FIG. 8-15). These colors are almost pure pigments, lightly bound together by a gum into chalklike sticks. They have a fine texture and are dry because they contain no oil. Thus they preserve the brilliance of the pigment with no oil to darken them, but they crumble easily and require a grainy paper with some tooth to hold the pastel. The dry pigment on the surface of the paper is very fragile; therefore, it must be preserved carefully with a fixative that will not affect its matte (nonglossy) texture. Nevertheless, unlike oil paint, pastel is easy to handle and allows artists to express themselves directly in full color.

Pastels are sold in a wide variety of hues and in many tints and shades of those hues. With this considerable range of color, artists like Carriera and Edgar Degas were induced to create works of art that have the appearance of paintings, like Degas's *The Dancers* (FIG. 8-16). Compared with most oil paints, however, pastel colors appear more luminous, although frequently they are pale. (Deep darks are also quite possible in the medium.) Pastels have a delicacy, a blurred, velvety quality, even when the artist is attempting a sharp definition of reality.

Despite their reputation for delicacy, the prominent Impressionist painter Degas made robust and exiting work with pastels. After 1895 Degas switched from oil paints to pastels to achieve a luminous and richly textured and richly colored surface without the problems inherent in layers of oil paint. Pastels require no drying time and so Degas could change and rework his drawings immediately. Pastels allowed him to unite drawing and color. In his drawing *The Dancers* he applied the pastels in parallel strokes that run, for the most part, down the page. Degas also applied the colors in layers, one color over another. This application was made possible by spraying the preliminary layers with a fixative, whose secret Degas never divulged. His color scheme emphasizes juxtaposed orange and violet with some green—the triad of secondary colors. Unmixed and layered, his pastel colors anticipate the vivid color of early-twentieth-century painting.

Pen and Ink

A pen filled with liquid ink held in the nib (point) produces decisive and clear lines. The calligraphic lines in Guercino's drawing of *Mars and Cupid* (FIG. 4-12) were made with pen and ink. The stark dark-against-light of pen and ink produces pure lines of bold energy or fluid elegance. Whether the line of an ink pen appears thick or thin depends on the size of the point, the angle at which the flattened nib is held, and the pressure applied by the hand.

Quill pens are taken from the wing feathers of large birds like the goose or swan, or of smaller birds like the raven or crow. A quill pen fairly glides across the paper and produces a fluid line. To create the distinctive quivering line in his *Holy Family* (FIG. 8-6) Giovanni Battista Tiepolo must have used a quill pen with a point that glided over the paper like a skater on ice. His wiggly line records his spontaneity, and we marvel at this magic mark that produces so much with so little, so quickly and so easily. Because it is soft and pliable, the tip of the quill needs frequent recutting to produce clear and fluent lines. Soft and light, quills respond readily to the touch to create smooth, flexible lines.

Pens cut from a hollow reed were common in the ancient world. A **reed pen** makes broad, bold lines that have considerable character. Since a stiff reed pen does not slide easily over the surface, it tends to create rather harsh, angular lines and does not permit the artist to show off in a fluent way. Since a reed pen releases its ink more rapidly than a quill, it also tends to make lines that are short and choppy. Van Gogh

FIG 8-16 EDGAR DEGAS [French, 1834–1917], *The Dancers*. C. 1899. Pastel on paper, 24 1/2 × 25 1/2 in. (62.2 × 64.8 cm). Toledo Museum of Art.

FIG 8-17 VINCENT VAN GOGH [Dutch, 1853–1890], *Cypresses*. 1889. Pencil, quill, and reed pen, brown and black ink on white paper, 24 1/2 × 18 in. (62.2 × 45.7 cm). Brooklyn Museum of Art.

liked the challenge of the reed pen and revived its use to great advantage. In his drawing *Cypresses* (FIG. 8-17) he copied one of his own paintings of cypress trees to send an image of it to his brother Theo in Paris. The lines of the drawing and the variety of textures they produce attempt to imitate the colors in the oil painting. With the reed pen Van Gogh was able to draw thick, powerful lines. Curved lines are everywhere and they constantly are turning into patterns. But the knots and swirls of the trees give them an extra force as they surge above the horizon, into the sky, and beyond the top border.

Artists in the nineteenth and twentieth centuries have preferred to draw with opaque black India ink. In previous centuries the ink that filled an artist's pen tended to be brown or turned brown in time. Among the brown inks were **bistre,** made from wood soot, and **sepia,** made from secretions of the cuttlefish or squid. The warm tones of sepia were popular in the late-eighteenth and early-nineteenth centuries.

The challenge with ink is that an artist cannot erase lines made with it. Because of the stubbornness and boldness of the medium, artists often make their ink drawings over a preliminary pencil sketch.

Brush and Ink

Artists sometimes draw with another liquid medium, **brush and ink.** One of the advantages of the brush as a drawing tool is that the line it makes can go from surprisingly thin to rather thick with the same stroke of the brush. Lines in a brush drawing have a telltale swelling and tapering look—the result of a push-and-pull action—as seen in Diego Rivera's drawing *Mother and Child* (FIG. 8-18). By manipulating the brush, Rivera could cause the black line to swell and thicken. By gradually raising the brush, Rivera made his line thin and tapering. The thickening of the lines models the forms to some extent. The simplicity and strength of his lines befit the strength and simplicity of his subject.

FIG 8-18 DIEGO RIVERA [Mexican, 1886–1957], *Mother and Child*. 1936. Ink drawing on paper, 12 1/8 × 9 1/4 in. (30.8 × 23.5 cm). San Francisco Museum of Modern Art. Albert M. Bender Collection. Photo from Schopplein Studio.

The Chinese and Japanese prefer to use the brush above all other drawing media and have developed a tradition of technical facility and visual sensitivity to brush drawing. In *Bamboo* (FIG. 8-19) the Chinese artist Wu Chen used a brush to depict a few sprigs of bamboo, a plant that symbolizes for the Chinese the human ideal to remain steadfast and yet pliant to the winds of adversity. The brush is perfectly suited to reproducing the thin tapering leaves of the plant. With deceptive ease Wu Chen articulated the direction and location of each leaf and the natural growth of the plant, without falling into a stereotyped pattern. Diluted, paler ink creates the effect of atmospheric perspective. The expression-filled lines of the bamboo branch are matched by the expressionistic style of the calligraphy running down the left side of the page.

Western artists most often use the brush not to draw lines, but to apply a wash to a pencil, pen, or chalk drawing. A **wash** is ink diluted with water and then brushed or washed in like watercolor. Giovanni Battista Tiepolo used wash in his pen-and-ink drawing of *Holy Family* (FIG. 8-6). The white of the paper, showing through the veil of diluted ink, mixes with the dark ink to provide smooth and diffused value contrasts. Values achieved with wash are smoother than the textured appearance of hatching and cross-hatching. Wash renders atmosphere superbly.

In the Baroque era, when artists could imagine objects solely in terms of light and dark, some artists like Gianlorenzo Bernini made drawings almost entirely by means of wash. In *St. Jerome Kneeling before the Crucifix* (FIG. 8-20), over a light charcoal sketch, Bernini drew with a brush not the contours of the figure but the value contrasts. He washed or flooded areas with diluted transparent ink. The values that he washed in do not, strictly speaking, model the figure. That is to say, they do not primarily produce the sensation of solid three-dimensional masses. Rather, the wash records the subtle lights and darks that flicker across the surface of the ecstatic saint. These lights and darks may change at any moment. No doubt Bernini made sketches like this for his marble Saint Teresa (FIG. 5-13) as he tried to imagine not so much the solid forms of the saint but the dynamism of light and dark as she swoons in ecstasy.

FIG 8-19 WU CHEN [Chinese, 1280–1354], *Bamboo*. 1350. 16 7/8 in. (42.9 cm) high. Taipei, Taiwan, National Palace Museum.

FIG 8-20 GIANLORENZO BERNINI [Italian, 1598–1680], *St. Jerome Kneeling before the Crucifix*. Brown ink wash over charcoal, 6 1/8 × 8 3/4 in. (15.6 × 22.2 cm). London, Courtauld Institute of Art. Witt Collection (4752).

Modern Inventions

Felt-tipped pens come in every color, including fluorescent colors, although the colors may not be very permanent. They leave a transparent mark that seems to stain the paper. The lines of ball-point pens, of a consistent thickness and darkness, may be extremely continuous, since the pens do not ordinarily run out of ink. Computers can be programmed to make drawings as the operator moves a mouse or other electronic device. A typical computer graphics program, such as the one used to create the illustration in FIG. 8-21, allows considerable variety in the quality of the lines, even the possibility of imitating drawings made by a can of spray paint.

Drawings are usually intimate works of art that are normally meant to be held in the hand. Even when they are exhibited, under glass, in the subdued light of a museum gallery, they are meant to be seen up close. We are asked to become familiar with the formal properties of a drawing more than in most finished paintings or pieces of sculpture. We scan the lines and values of a drawing for their expressive potential while the drawing reveals to us the artist's creative process.

FIG 8-21 TOM LOCHRAY [American, 1959], *Carribean Islands* (detail). 1994. 3 × 9 in. (7.7 × 23 cm). Adobe Illustrator 5.5

Key Terms and Concepts

bistre	metalpoint	recto
brush and ink	motifs	reed pen
caricature	parchment	silverpoint
cartoons	pastels	study
chalks	pen and ink	vellum
charcoal	pencils	verso
Conté crayons	petroglyphs	wash
crayon	quill pens	

DRAWING

Characteristics	Drawing is the first art of children.
	Drawing was one of the earliest arts in prehistoric times.
	Drawing is a chief means of art instruction.
	Drawing is a chief means for visual study and for creative stimulation.
Definition	To draw means to make lines and to render values.
Functions	Artists commonly make four kinds of drawings: drawings on paintings; drawings as studies; drawings as final works; and illustrations, cartoons, and caricatures.
Tools	A drawing tool is anything that makes a mark. Some common tools are illustrated below.

Pencil

Silverpoint

Charcoal

Chalk

Pastels

Brush and Ink

Pen and Ink

Felt-tipped Pens

Computer Graphics

Silverpoint drawing by Mary T. Walter, Computer Graphics by Tom Lochray. All other drawings by Tracy Turner.

9

Frank Stella's *Giufà e la berretta rosa* (*Giufà and the Pink Cap*) (FIG. 9-1) is an example of the complex and creative nature of printmaking in the modern world. Traditionally, a **print** is any impression onto a piece of paper made by ink applied to a plate, a slab, a block, or a stencil that in some form holds an image. Stella, who won fame as a painter of shaped canvases and a maker of mixed-media works, produced his print in collaboration with Tyler Graphics, one of several groups around the United States that offer their technical skill and their well-equipped workshops to painters and sculptors who want to make prints. Stella claims that he knows very little about printmaking! Unlike the relatively bare studios of most painters, a printmaking workshop is normally filled with worktables, machinery, tools, and chemicals necessary for the printmaking processes. The special techniques and skills of printmaking attract people who like the challenge of working with materials and who like making things.

Giufà e la berretta rosa is printed on a specially made, enormous piece of paper over six feet high. To make the print, Stella and his collaborators used a variety of techniques. The grooves and ridges made on the metal plates to hold the ink were cut with tools or etched (cut) with acid. The plate itself was divided into pieces with a jigsaw so that parts of it could be inked separately; in fact, jigsawed pieces were reassembled and printed differently from the original design. Perhaps the most exciting part of the creative process was that Stella used a computed-aided design (CAD) system to develop a three-dimensional model of his image so that it could be turned, adjusted, and changed from a variety of angles on the screen. The computer printout was enlarged and transferred to the metal plate through a photographic process. Skill,

FIG 9-1   FRANK STELLA [American, 1936–], *Giufà e la berretta rosa*. 1989. Computer-generated imagery; relief, aquatint, engraving, and etching on white TGL handmade paper, 77 3/4 × 58 in. (197.5 × 147.3 cm). Printed and published by Tyler Graphics Ltd., Bedford, New York. Photo by Steve Sloman.

technology, collaboration, and the constant exploration of new possibilities are all vital parts of the current printmaking scene.

The Nature of Printmaking

A clear-cut definition of **printmaking** is difficult because we also call photographs made on light-sensitive paper prints and speak of prints made by laser jets, xerography, and a number of other new technologies that are now being incorporated into the art of printmaking. All these technologies are capable of producing multiple copies of the same image. Nevertheless, although Frank Stella's print *Giufà e la berretta rosa* (FIG. 9-1) exists in a number of copies, each one of them is considered an original work of art because each one is the result of the artist's hand and creativity.

Prints have served many purposes. Long before the invention of photographic reproduction, printmaking arose in the West chiefly to provide inexpensive devotional images for the generally illiterate masses. Many precious early prints simply reproduced original paintings or statues, which then became more widely known. Some artists had prints made of their own work to advertise their talents. Many other visually exciting prints were produced for educational purposes. For example, John James Audubon's series *Birds of America* illustrates hundreds of birds, including the cardinal (FIG. 9-2), in their natural setting. Albrecht Dürer's *Apocalypse* series, which includes *The Four Horsemen* (see FIG. 9-4), visually interprets a fascinating book of the Bible. Francisco Goya's *Hunting for Teeth* (see FIG. 9-14), from his *Caprichos* series, attempts to uproot vice and instruct the public in virtue. Some prints, whatever their subject, were produced as independent works of art from the start. Since the late 1800s many of the functions of printmaking to reproduce and to illustrate have been taken over by modern methods of photomechanical reproduction. In modern times printmaking as an artist's medium has come to the fore.

Printmaking has traditionally been considered a graphic medium like drawing, since it often concentrates on delineating objects with lines. In the past the results often looked a great deal like drawings. Unlike unique drawings, however, most fine art prints are produced in an **edition** (total number printed) of about twenty to a hundred **impressions** (single copies). In a

FIG 9-3 MARY FRANK [American, 1933–], *Two Walking Figures.* 1982. Monoprint, 23 3/4 × 35 1/4 in. (59.7 × 88.9 cm). New York, Midtown Payson Galleries.

number of the printmaking media, a limited number of impressions can be made in an edition before the device from which a print is made starts to break down. When artists stop making impressions of their print, they usually cancel the plate by damaging the image so that no more impressions can be taken from it. The printmaker will then mark each impression in pencil with a number like 15/40, meaning that this sheet is the fifteenth impression from an edition of forty.

Some printmakers, however, occasionally make **monotypes** (also called *monoprints*), or single impressions, by simply pressing paper to a newly painted surface. A monotype is really a hybrid combination of printmaking and painting. To produce a monotype, the artist paints or draws an image in paint or printer's ink on a smooth, nonabsorbent surface like zinc, plastic, or glass. The single impression is transferred to paper by rubbing the back of paper that has been laid on the plate or sometimes by running the plate and paper through a press, as was the case for Mary Frank's monoprint *Two Walking Figures* (FIG. 9-3). The Impressionist painter Edgar Degas made numerous monotypes, and the medium was revived by American artists in the 1960s and 1970s. Since it demands

This famous print comes from a series of fifteen that Albrecht Dürer published illustrating St. John's Book of Revelation, or the Apocalypse. In it Dürer illustrated St. John's vision in the Bible when the Lamb broke the first of the seven seals (Revelation 6:1–8). Death, riding a sickly, pale horse, tramples a bishop who soon will be swallowed by the jaws of Hell. Next to him the dominant, burly Famine, swinging an empty pair of scales, rides a black horse. War, on a red horse, wields a great sword. Pestilence gets ready to shoot his bow. Three of the horses fly in rank over the earth, knocking down all before them. Then the pale horse of Death stumbles over the fallen mass of men and women.

spontaneity—all of the ink or paint must remain wet for printing—monotype tends to produce a free and painterly kind of print in which the transfer to paper creates a special luminosity not found in ordinary painting or other kinds of printmaking.

Relief

The oldest method of printmaking is the **relief** process, in which the design to be printed is raised from the surrounding surface of a block. Ink is then applied to the raised part. A relief can be made from the surface of different sorts of materials—wood, linoleum blocks, potatoes, or rubber, for example. The ordinary typewriter with raised type does relief printing, although the ink is printed through a ribbon, not applied to the raised surface of the type.

After ink is applied to a relief block with a roller, the impression is made by applying light pressure on the back of paper that has been laid over the block. Printmakers usually press the paper into the ink with a **baren,** a rounded pad about five inches in diameter. Something like the back of a wooden spoon or a smooth doorknob can also be used. It is possible to run the block through the rollers of a press, although too much pressure could damage the relief.

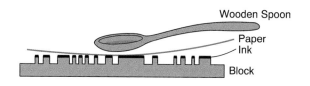

Woodcut

A common and very old type of relief printing is the **woodcut,** in which a design is drawn on a wooden block and the part of the block *not* to be printed is cut away with wood-carver's tools such as knives, gouges, and chisels. The design is left raised in relief above the cutaway part.

The German artist Albrecht Dürer elevated the art of the woodcut to a medium of artistic expression that no one had previously imagined possible. Undoubtedly, Dürer first made a drawing of *The Four Horsemen* (FIG. 9-4) on the wooden plank before he cut away the "white" parts, or negative areas. Although some printmakers have other technicians carve the design they have drawn, Dürer probably cut his own blocks, since his demands from the medium were quite high. For instance, his lines vary in length and width and density. In Dürer's new technique, contour lines and hatching lines are difficult to distinguish one from another, since his shapes are often formed by contrasting values. Many lines serve two functions at once—defining forms and defining values.

A good-quality wood is a must for such a woodcut so that delicate lines can be cut. The types used for this purpose range from soft woods like pine to hard fruitwoods like cherry. Artists have also deliberately printed from rough, grainy, and knotted woods, which may supply their own texture to the print. Edvard Munch let the wood grain appear in his print *The Kiss* (FIG. 9-5).

Woodblock prints first became popular in the fifteenth century in Europe, especially for religious images. For only a few cents, even illiterate poor people could have a crude image of a saint to pin to the wall of their home. Also, until the advent of the printing press with movable type, illustrated block books like the *Art of Dying* and the *Pauper's Bible* spread throughout Europe. In block books, the illustrations and the text were cut from the same block. By the end of the fifteenth century, Dürer and other artists became interested in making woodcuts of high quality. Soon other forms of printmaking supplanted the woodcut in artists' concerns. In modern times, Paul Gauguin, Munch, and members of the German Expressionist movement called Die Brücke (The Bridge) revived the art of the woodcut by returning to

FIG 9-5 EDVARD MUNCH [Norwegian, 1863–1944], *The Kiss*. 1902. Color woodcut, 18 3/8 × 18 7/8 in. (46.7 × 47.9 cm). Museum of Modern Art, New York.

its unsophisticated origins as a direct and forthright medium.

Colored Woodcuts

Colored inks are available for relief printing, but to produce a multicolored print, separate blocks must be used to print each color. Yvonne Jacquette's woodcut *Times Square (Overview)* (p. 220) was printed from ten separate blocks to which seventeen colors were applied to reproduce the flickering lights for which New York's Great White Way is famous. At the time of printing, each new block must be carefully aligned, or *registered*, with the colored areas of the preceding impression on the paper.

Text continues on page 222

Yvonne Jacquette (1934–)

*Y*VONNE JACQUETTE has specialized for years in aerial views of cities taken from the top of tall buildings, as in her woodcut *Times Square (Overview)*, or views of the land taken from an airplane, as in her etching *Skowhegan II*. She chose the high point of view in order to raise and eliminate the horizon line. Without a horizon the objects depicted in her work do not rush away into space but are flattened across the surface of her design or move across the surface.

For example, the curved lines of the highway, dam, and embankment in *Skowhegan II* assert their autonomy as a design scheme.

The result of her overhead observation is full of paradoxes. Features in her work are seen at a distance, but they do not recede into space because of the lack of perspective. Her views take in a grand and considerable expanse of city or land, but from a distance they seem

YVONNE JACQUETTE [American, 1934–], *Times Square (Overview)*. 1987. Woodcut printed in seventeen colors, 22 3/4 × 28 in. (57.8 × 71.1 cm). Edition 38. Courtesy Experimental Workshop, San Francisco.

miniature and toylike. She is a realist who imitates what she sees, but the work itself emphasizes a patterning and an abstract design. The city or the land is radically shaped by a thriving modern civilization, but for the most part people are absent, invisible, or antlike. The artist is airborne and detached from earth, but finds beauty in the commonplace on earth and enjoys the energy of modern life.

Jacquette also specializes in night views of the city, whether New York, Tokyo, or Washington. In these, her real subject is the lights—the street lamps, the automobile headlights, and the neon signs. In *Times Square* the tapestry of colored lights pulsates across the surface, symbolizing the lively energy of the city. In all her drawings, paintings, and prints Jacquette creates a web of dots and dashes—strokes that represent forms in reality and also create a self-conscious texture along the surface. The interplay of flatness and depth and the ambiguity of our perception of her colored lights set up a fascinating tension for the viewer.

Jacquette frequently exhibits the same subject matter rendered in painting, drawing, pastel, small-scale fresco, and printmaking. As a printmaker, she

YVONNE JACQUETTE [American, 1934–],
Skowhegan II. 1987. Etching, aquatint;
29 7/8 × 22 3/8 in. (75.9 × 56.8 cm).
Edition 35. Photo courtesy Crown Point
Press, San Francisco.

Yvonne Jacquette in her studio. Photo
courtesy Crown Point Press, San Francisco.

has published monotypes, lithographs, etchings, aquatints, and woodcuts. She works ordinarily from rapid pastel sketches made flying over the site, which are then photographed and eventually projected through a slide onto canvas, drawing paper, or a printing plate, where the essentials of the design are traced. Her imagination works equally well in each medium.

In modern times, the woodcut has been associated with the Expressionist movement, whose artists used this very old and basic printing technique to express their feelings in jagged cuts, scratches, and slashes across the wood. Even the Neo-Expressionist movement of the 1980s saw a widespread resurgence of woodcutting because of its potential for immediacy and self-expression. But just as Jacquette's compositions resemble the flattened space of Japanese ukiyo-e prints, so too her technique follows their tradition. To make *Times Square*, she sent drawings to the studios of the Experimental Workshop in San Francisco, where, under her supervision, its staff of printmaking technicians did most of the carving of the ten blocks that constitute the work. Nevertheless, the finished print still gives the impression that the woodblocks were attacked and gouged by the same personal hand that paints with dots and dashes on canvas. The irregular cutting of each block achieves a flickering quality to the light, and the multiple layers of color, which seem to have been printed deliberately off register, produce a hazy aura around the lights.

Born in Pittsburgh, and raised in Stamford, Connecticut, Jacquette graduated from the Rhode Island School of Design. She lives in New York and spends the summers working on an old farm in Maine. To achieve a successful career with her style of aerial observation, she had to overcome her fear of flying.

Fig 9-6 Ugo da Carpi [Italian, c. 1480–between 1520 and 1532], *Saturn.* Chiaroscuro woodcut. Museum of Fine Arts, Boston. Bequest of W. G. Russell Allen.

The colored woodcuts that were popular in sixteenth-century Europe became known as **chiaroscuro woodcuts** because the several colors printed on them imitate different values rather than local colors. In other words, the inks of chiaroscuro woodcuts tend to be different values of the same color instead of strongly contrasting colors. In his chiaroscuro print of the winged god *Saturn* (Fig. 9-6), Ugo da Carpi printed three blocks, each with a different color, for the value changes as well as the contour lines. The difficulty of designing and printing chiaroscuro woodcuts make them rare.

In the East, Japanese woodblock printmakers employed a range of colors in their prints. In the eighteenth and nineteenth centuries in Japan woodcuts were considered popular rather than high art. The Japanese call them **ukiyo-e** or "pictures of the floating world." "The floating world" refers to the entertainment district of Edo (modern Tokyo) with its famous courtesans and actors. *The Great Wave off Kanagawa* (Fig. 9-7), filled with surging curved lines, is perhaps the most famous print by Katsushika Hokusai, a creative and energetic artist who made tens of thousands of designs for woodcuts.

Japanese artists like Hokusai seldom cut their own woodblocks, which were made of cherry. Instead, craftspeople who had years of training cut the wood usually in separate blocks for the printing of each color, as done

in the West. Very likely, a third set of specialists printed the blocks. Instead of rolling on the ink, they brushed onto the block a water-based ink that would soak into the tough rice paper used for the finished print. With a brush, they might blend colors right on the wood relief of the block. For example, whereas three separate shades of blue were used for the water of *The Great Wave*, the ink for the sky was brushed and blended on the block to reproduce indistinct clouds and the dark horizon.

Linocut

In the late 1950s and early 1960s Pablo Picasso cultivated a method of color relief printing called **linocut.** His multicolored linocut *Still Life with Cherries and Watermelon* (Fig. 9-8) employed a process that carves images out of linoleum instead of wood. The soft linoleum, without any grain, is easily cut with a knife or other tool in any direction. After Picasso printed an entire linoleum block with one color, he cut away a portion of the block before he printed this block a second time in another color, covering over parts of the first color. He then cut away another portion of the same block before he printed a third color, and so on, until a very small portion of the relief was left to print the final color on top of all the others. He practiced what can be called a reduction method of color relief printing.

FIG 9-8   PABLO PICASSO [Spanish, 1881–1973], *Still Life with Cherries and Watermelon*. 1962. Linocut 23 3/8 × 28 11/16 in. (59.4 × 72.9 cm). The Metropolitan Museum of Art, New York. The Mr. and Mrs. Charles Kramer Collection, Gift of Mr. and Mrs. Charles Kramer, 1979.

Pablo Picasso, who made more than twenty-five hundred prints in his lifetime, constantly experimented with new techniques to expand their range. Still Life with Cherries and Watermelon is printed from three linoleum blocks, or linoblocks, in eight colors. Picasso first printed almost the entire page in yellow from a block in which only the white of the lightbulb had been cut away. On a second block, which Picasso printed in brown, he cut away the lines that in the final print appear yellow. Picasso then, in stages, continued to eliminate areas of relief from this second block so that areas of the colors that had already been printed would show. In short, he created his print by progressively destroying his linoblock.

Wood Engraving

Blocks of wood, like those available at a lumber store, are usually planks with a grain that runs along their length. Small blocks for printmaking can also be made by cutting across the grain of boxwood or maple trees. Turkish boxwood is preferred. A number of such cross-grained, or end-grain, blocks can be glued together to form a larger block.

The printmaker can cut into these end-grain blocks more easily in all directions. The relief carved out of end-grain blocks is also stronger and can withstand more pressure. This method of relief printing, called **wood engraving,** was widely used in the nineteenth century for book, magazine, and newspaper illustrations because the blocks could hold up under the pounding of a mechanical printing press where thousands of impressions are possible.

A prolific illustrator of books, Thomas Bewick, revived and popularized the technique of wood engraving at the very end of the eighteenth century. He illustrated his most famous work, *History of British Birds*, with many small profiles of birds in a rustic setting. To depict the duck in this series (FIG. 9-9), Bewick started from the "black" surface of the woodblock and then gouged out "white" lines to create the image. He seldom developed contour lines with his method, but rather his white lines produced an amazing variety of light and shade to build form and to re-create textures.

Unfortunately for us, printmakers started calling Bewick's process wood engraving, even though it is a form of relief printing, not engraving. Perhaps the confusion arose because the wood engraver often uses a pointed tool called a graver. When photomechanical processes killed the commercial aspects of wood engraving about the end of the nineteenth century, wood engraving was again resuscitated as an attractive art medium.

Boxwood cut across the grain (end grain).

FIG 9-10 CLARE ROMANO [American], *Night Canyon.* Collagraph (four colors), 22×30 in. (55.9 × 76.2 cm). Collection of the artist.

The essential feature of wood engraving is that instead of cutting out the areas between the lines, the wood engraver cuts white lines into the "black" surface of the block. Since the raised surface is printed, the end result is still a form of relief printing. Only the wood engraver's attitude toward the image—light into dark—and a part of the procedure is different. Instead of cutting away the spaces in between lines that have already been drawn on the block, a wood engraver works directly at creating the image by cutting white lines into the block. The wood engraver draws the image as he or she engraves, instead of merely eliminating unwanted wood from a line drawing.

Collagraph

Rather than by carving, a relief may also be created on a plate by gluing diverse materials to the plate in order to build a raised surface. By attaching pieces of sandpaper or cardboard, fabric, plant leaves, or flat metal to cardboard, metal, or plastic sheets, printmakers produce a **collagraph.** The name *collagraph* was invented for this modern process because in effect the printmaker fabricates a collage on the surface of the plate. Printmakers like Clare Romano, who produced *Night*

Canyon (FIG. 9-10), enjoy the collagraph because of its inventiveness and its almost surreal transformation of materials. The raised surface of the "collage" on the plate may be inked and printed like that of other relief plates, or the ink may be forced between the raised areas, which then are wiped clean. To pick up the ink lying at these low levels, the paper must be pressed down to meet the ink by the rollers of a printing press, as in the method called intaglio.

Intaglio

The Italian word **intaglio** (pronounced in-*tal*-yo) means "carving or indentation." In intaglio, the printmaker cuts the surface of a printing plate where she or he wants black lines to appear, instead of cutting away the white spaces, as in the relief process. Deeper incisions make thicker, darker lines. When the plate is printed, ink the consistency of mayonnaise is smeared on it and forced down into the furrows cut in the metal. Colored inks can be applied to separate sections of the intaglio plate, or separate plates may be inked in different colors. The surface of the plate is then carefully wiped clean, leaving the ink in the furrows, before it is placed on the bed of an intaglio press. Dampened paper is laid over the plate and both are

Fig 9–11 Albrecht Dürer [German, 1471–1528], *Adam and Eve.* 1504. Engraving, 9 3/4 × 7 9/16 in. (24.8 × 19.2 cm). Minneapolis Institute of Arts. Christina N. and Swan J. Turnblad Memorial Fund.

covered with felt blankets. Several hundred pounds of pressure supplied by the rollers of the press force the paper into the furrows and into contact with the ink.

In a genuine intaglio print, the lines of the image are raised slightly above the surface of the paper because the roller pressed the paper into the troughs. Because of the pressure applied during printing, the plates are made of metal, usually copper or zinc, or pos-

sibly plastic. The edges of a metal intaglio plate are always beveled so that they do not cut the paper.

There are two major forms of intaglio: engraving, which includes drypoint, and etching, which includes aquatint. Although they both achieve the same basic result—a metal plate with grooves in it for ink—the two processes are really quite different.

Engraving

Engraving, the older printmaking process, began in the fifteenth century. Albrecht Dürer, as is evident in his *Adam and Eve* (Fig. 9-11), became a brilliant exponent of the engraving technique also. Dürer's *Adam and Eve* illustrates the ideal man and woman according to the classical canon of proportions devised in antiquity. The figures both stand frontally like statues in classical contrapposto and are placed symmetrically to the left and right of the Tree of Life, represented as a mountain ash. Dürer cut incredibly delicate lines

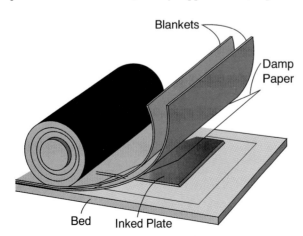

Blankets

Damp Paper

Bed   Inked Plate

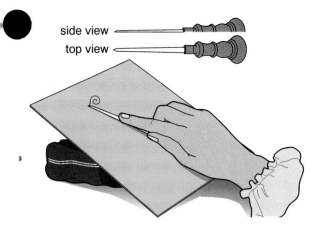
side view
top view

Fig 9-12 Mary Cassatt [American, 1845–1926], *Baby's Back.* 1889–1890. Drypoint, 9 3/16 × 6 7/16 in. (23.3 × 16.4 cm). Library of Congress, Washington, D.C.

into the intaglio plate. His lines not only model the forms but reproduce the appearance of textures—skin, bark, foliage, fur. Values range from the stippling that subtly models the flesh to the deep dark hatching of the forest.

Engravings are made by directly cutting grooves into the plate by hand with a tool called a **burin.** A burin is about the size of a small screwdriver, with a steel tip that has a diamond-shaped profile at a forty-degree angle. The cutting is done with the sharp tip of the lower point of the diamond.

The hard part of engraving is to apply just the right pressure in just the right direction so that the engraved line is of the desired thickness, length, and location. In general, one arm, holding the burin, applies the pressure, while the other arm turns the plate to achieve the direction in the line. In a sense, one arm pushes the plate into the burin. Engraving results in a precise line that tends to swell as the burin bites deeper into the metal. Value contrasts are achieved by hatching and cross-hatching.

Engraving scarcely tolerates mistakes and corrections. The only recourse is to scrape away part of the surface of the plate to remove an unwanted line and then rub, or burnish the area smooth again.

Because of the strength of the V-shaped engraved trough, engravings can be published in large editions. Yet the training necessary to be a competent engraver is so tedious and the process so arduous that few modern printmakers practice the art, except in combination with other techniques.

Drypoint

An artist can make lines on a metal plate just by scratching the surface directly with a sharp diamond-tipped or carbide steel needle. This simple method is

called **drypoint.** Mary Cassatt used drypoint exclusively for her print *Baby's Back* (Fig. 9-12), where the unforgiving metal point shows her creative process and her skill. The metal removed by the drypoint needle forms a burr at the side of the trough. Because the burr catches most of the ink, drypoint lines tend to be soft and fuzzy. Close cross-hatching in drypoint can

Fig 9-13 James McNeill Whistler [American, 1834–1903], *Little Venice,* from *Twelve Etchings,* or *The First Venice Set.* 1879–1880. Etching on laid paper, trimmed to plate mark, 7 3/16 × 10 7/16 in. (18.3 × 26.5 cm). University of Michigan Museum of Art, Ann Arbor. Bequest of Margaret Watson Parker.

produce velvety blacks. However, drypoint scratches are usually rather shallow and the burr does not hold up well after only a few dozen impressions under heavy pressure.

Rembrandt and other printmakers often employed drypoint on top of previously etched plates to add the richness of drypoint lines. By itself, drypoint tends toward short, jagged, spontaneous lines, an effect that Max Beckmann exploited in his *Self-Portrait* (FIG. 4-2). Cassatt's image in *Baby's Back* has the simplicity and spontaneity of a pencil sketch; in fact, several tentative sketch lines scratched in the plate were never "erased." But drawing in drypoint takes more time, effort, and skill than drawing with a pencil because of the resistance of the metal plate. Cassatt's needle made very sparse, short lines. In only a few places, very close hatching produced rich blacks, accenting the weight of the child in contrast to the lightness of the mother's arm. Although the delicate drypoint lines suggest that Cassatt captured a fleeting impression, the juxtaposition of the two faces is an intriguing calculation.

Etching

Etching is a more versatile process than engraving or drypoint. Brute pressure does not cut the lines. Instead, acid—usually nitric acid—does the cutting. This acid—like many printer's inks—is a toxic material that is dangerous to handle, inhale, and dispose of. Printmakers have learned that they must take ade-

quate safety precautions in the pursuit of their art.

To make an etching, the zinc or copper plate is first coated with a black tarlike "paint," an acid-resistant liquid called **asphaltum.** Rosin and other acid-proof coatings may also provide the resistive coating, or ground. After the ground dries, a drawing is made in the asphaltum by scratching the surface with a stylus or other sharp tool. The marks in the asphaltum lay bare the metal underneath. Making marks in the asphaltum for an etching is a lot easier than gouging out the actual metal with a burin for an engraving. Etched lines tend to be long and fluent, since the etching needle never scratches or runs out of ink like a pen. If the printmaker makes a mistake, the unwanted line can be removed simply by covering it over with more asphaltum.

Acid bites into the plate where the metal surface beneath the asphaltum has been exposed. A short immersion time will produce thin, faint lines; a longer time will produce thicker, deeper lines. Some of the lines can also be covered over with an acid-proof varnish or with more asphaltum after an initial acid bath. When the plate is returned to the acid, the lines that remain exposed will be etched deeper and the lines that have been covered will remain relatively thin.

James McNeill Whistler's etching *Little Venice* (FIG. 9-13) illustrates the freedom, delicacy, sketchiness, and atmosphere that are possible with etching. Whistler drew this image of the city directly onto the plate while he was positioned on an island across the lagoon. Confident in his art, he was unconcerned that the city appeared in reverse when printed—as does every impression pressed to a printing plate. He envisioned the city as a thin line floating between the water and sky. His etching needle made small, delicate lines that keep the image as simple as the nearly empty space above and below.

Whistler did not immerse his plate in an acid solution but applied the acid and moved it around with a feather in order to control the biting of the plate more carefully. Sometimes Whistler did not wipe the surface of the plate thoroughly clean of ink before printing so that a thin film of ink left on the plate would print as a glowing atmosphere.

A plate to be etched may also be covered with a **soft ground,** which is asphaltum mixed with petroleum jelly so that it will remain soft and sticky. A variety of materials and textured surfaces can be pressed into the soft ground to expose the metal plate under the ground. Fabrics, cork, or lace can be used to make a textured impression. The acid will then bite these patterns and textures into the plate. It is possible to reproduce the fuzzy quality of a pencil line in soft ground by placing a sheet of tracing paper over the plate and drawing on the paper with a pencil. This will remove the sticky soft ground from the plate where the pencil has touched the paper.

Aquatint

Within the etching process, printmakers can also achieve a gray tone—instead of using hatching for darker values—by means of a process called **aquatint.** To produce aquatint, printmakers dust or spray an area of the plate with fine acid-resistant particles. If the printmaker dusts the plate with rosin powder, the plate must be heated to attach the rosin to it. The acid then etches the metal plate around each particle of rosin, which will print as a tiny white dot.

After Francisco Goya etched the copper plate for his *Hunting for Teeth* (FIG. 9-14), he added aquatint. Goya applied aquatint of varying values to all parts of the plate except where the light of the moon hits the dead man's arm, the woman's hands and handkerchief, and parts of the woman's dress. After he covered the clouds and several other lighter parts, Goya let the acid bite the aquatint still more to get a darker night sky. He then burnished, or smoothed out, some of the aquatint—on the woman's face, the man's body, the

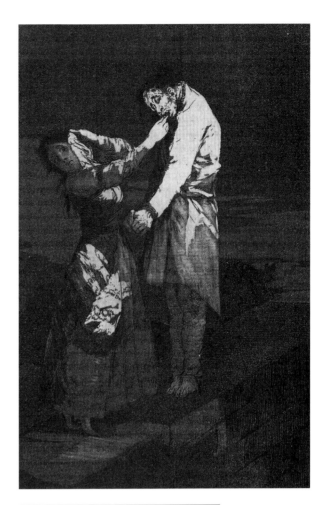

FIG 9-14 FRANCISCO GOYA [Spanish, 1746–1828], *A caza de dientes (Hunting for Teeth),* plate 12, from *Los Caprichos.* 1799. Etching, burnished aquatint and burin, 8 9/16 × 5 15/16 in. (21.7 × 15.1 cm) (plate). Art Institute of Chicago. Clarence Buckingham Collection (1948.110/12).

During the Age of Reason, Francisco Goya produced satires of Spanish society, especially in his Los Caprichos *series. In* Hunting for Teeth *Goya satirized the foolish superstition of a woman who believes that she needs the tooth of a hanged man for a witch's love potion. The well-dressed woman stands on her tiptoes at the top of a high wall in the dark of night to yank the teeth from the corpse. She holds a handkerchief to her face to avoid the sight of the dead man. Like William Hogarth (see* The Rake's Progress, *FIG. 2-23), Goya shared the Enlightenment's belief that the mere exposure and ridicule of vice would improve society.*

Drypoint	Engraving	Smooth Bite	Rough Bite

Inked Plate

patch under the woman's feet. The subtle manipulation of aquatint recreated a spooky predawn darkness, perfectly suited for the woman's grotesque folly.

Comparison of Methods

Experts can tell by looking at a print whether the lines were produced by engraving, etching, or drypoint. Each method digs a trough in a slightly different way. Each kind of trough tends to produce a slightly different quality of line. Drypoint raises a distinctive burr that prints a textured line. A burin cleanly removes a V-shaped piece of metal and produces engraving's precise line. Since acid's bite eventually undermines the ground, the darker lines of an etching may have an irregular edge.

Many printmakers, always experimenting for new effects, like to combine techniques, mixing line etching, soft ground, aquatint, and drypoint on a single plate. The Mexican printmaker José Guadalupe Posada, during his lifetime, made prints in an unusual relief etching process. As a printmaker Posada published thousands of illustrations for popular songs, games, storybooks, and broadsides—cheap single sheets like *Skeleton of the Fashionable Lady (La calavera catrina)* (FIG. 9-15) that were sold to the general public. To make a relief etching, Posada used acid to cut away areas of a zinc plate but then inked the unetched, raised areas of the plate—as one normally would for a relief, not an intaglio. By this method he could draw directly and rapidly on a zinc plate with a greasy ink that, together with some rosin, would resist the deep biting of the acid. The simple and robust lines he drew transferred directly into the print. Furthermore, a metal relief plate, unlike a woodcut, could withstand the printing of hundreds of impressions.

FIG 9-15 JOSÉ GUADALUPE POSADA [Mexican, 1851–1913], *Skeleton of the Fashionable Lady (La Calavera Catrina).* 20th century. Engraving on zinc, 4 5/16 × 6 1/8 in. (11 × 15.6 cm). The Harry Ransom Humanities Research Center, The University of Texas at Austin.

Skeleton of the Fashionable Lady (La calavera catrina) *is one of a series of prints depicting the skeletons of various public characters published for sale on November 2, The Day of the Dead. (Calavera means "skull" and, by extension, "skeleton.") Mexicans remember the souls of the dead on that day, but they also use the occasion for witty and macabre comments about death. In this piece by Posada the grinning skeleton wears a very fashionable broad-brimmed hat bordered with a dangling fringe and festooned with feathers and flowers. The ludicrous image makes fun of both life and death.*

Lithography

Lithography, was invented in 1798 in Germany by Aloys Senefelder. Lithography is called a *planographic* process because the design stays on the flat surface plane. It is neither raised in relief above the surface plane nor cut below the plane as in intaglio. Instead, lithography involves a chemical reaction based on the principle that oil and water do not mix. The chemical reaction makes the smooth surface of a block of limestone accept ink in places where the artist wants ink and reject ink in places where the artist wants empty white spaces. Not every kind of limestone works. In fact, only stone from certain quarries in Bavaria works well, and those quarries have been nearly exhausted. Sheets of zinc or aluminum may now be substituted, but most artists prefer working on the old stones.

The French caricaturist Honoré Daumier produced over four thousand lithographs in his career—most of them satires of French society and wry comments on the human condition. In one print from a series called *The Public at the Salon* (FIG. 9-16), with direct and bold strokes, Daumier captured the eagerness with which the Parisian public crowded around their favorite paintings at the Salon, the annual exhibition of the Art Academy. The boy pleads with his father, "Let me look a little longer, papa! The torments of poor Count Egmont trouble me deeply!" (Egmont is the subject of a play by Goethe.) The father replies, "You ought to have pity on the torments of your unfortunate father who has broken his arms holding you up in the air!"

To make a lithograph, artists usually begin by drawing on the stone with a greasy lithographer's crayon or with **tusche,** which comes in solid or liquid form and may be brushed on like ink or applied with a pen. Lithography thus appeals to artists in media other than printmaking because they can draw or paint freely on the stone. Lithography will capture the freshness of sketched lines and subtle value changes immediately because its responsive process can make multiple impressions of the artist's direct drawing. No other printing technique is so immediate.

Lithographer's crayons and tusche contain grease, which will repel water during the lithographic process. After the drawing or painting is completed on the stone, the stone is chemically treated with gum arabic and very diluted nitric acid so that the image is securely bound to the stone and so that the *unmarked* surface of the stone will absorb water. Finally, the whole stone is cleaned with a solvent like turpentine. At this point the visible image has disappeared from the surface of the stone. Before ink is rolled over this surface, the printmaker wipes the stone with a wet sponge. The part that has absorbed water will repel the printer's ink; the part that has been marked with greasy crayon or tusche has repelled the water and so will now accept and retain ink. In a lithographic press, a scraper forces the paper against the ink. The process of wetting and inking the stone can be repeated numerous times, since lithography plates do not break down.

In the nineteenth century the American firm

FIG 9-16 HONORÉ DAUMIER [French, 1808–1879], *The Public at the Salon.* Lithograph. Bibliothèque Nationale, Paris.

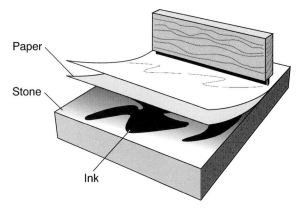

Paper
Stone
Ink

Currier and Ives produced thousands of popular lithographs of everyday events, familiar places, and newsworthy disasters. One example is *American Winter Scenes, Evening* (FIG. 9-17), by Nathaniel Currier and James Merritt Ives. Most Currier and Ives prints were colored by hand, but because lithography can produce areas of vivid flat color as well as subtle chiaroscuro, multicolor lithography has been popular with painters who turn to printmaking. A separate block must be prepared for each color.

FIG 9-17 NATHANIEL CURRIER [American, 1813–1888] and JAMES MERRITT IVES [American, 1824–1895], *American Winter Scenes, Evening.* 1868. Color lithograph, 8 3/4 × 12 9/16 in. (22.2 × 31.9 cm). Scala/Art Resource, New York.

Screen Printing

Prints can also be made from stencils. Thousands of years ago a few cave dwellers made "prints" of their own hands on the cave wall by this method. For centuries cloth and wallpapers have been decorated with stenciled designs. Stencils are commonly used for lettering, although the center will fall out of zeros or any other closed forms unless it is attached to the stencil. This problem can be solved by attaching the stencil to a screen of porous material like silk that will stabilize all parts of the design and let the ink or paint flow through the open areas. The process is then called **silk screening** or **screen printing.**

Modern artists have developed the technique of screen printing into a major activity. For example, Andy Warhol and other Pop Artists in the 1960s rejuvenated screen printing and helped transform it from a commercial medium to an art medium (see Warhol's

Blue Marilyn, FIG. 1-7). Artists like Richard Anuszkiewicz who use strong, unmodulated color are attracted to screen printing. The intense red-orange lines of Anuszkiewicz's silk-screened plate from William Blake's *The Inward Eye* (FIG. 9-18) contrast sharply with the green, blue-green, and blue of the background. The series of thin lines produces rapid changes in simultaneous contrast that cause the colors to vibrate, disturb the eye, and force the eye to move. In other words, the optical sensations induce kinetic sensations. The intense colors of modern inks made these visual vibrations possible. The nested lines may be read as the illusion of spatial projection into the print or as rectangular pyramids projecting out from the print.

To hold a stencil in screen printing, a fabric like silk, nylon, or polyester is stretched across a rigid frame, one side of which is attached with hinges to a flat surface. The word **serigraphy** was coined in the late 1930s to distinguish fine art printing through a screen of silk from commercial activity. (*Seri* in Latin means "silk".) Nevertheless, several fabrics other than silk are now commonly used in the art of screen printing.

The stencil blocks parts of the porous screen and leaves parts of it open so that ink may be forced through it and print the image. Stencils can be made of paper or plastic film glued or taped to the fabric. Stencils can also be painted directly onto the screen

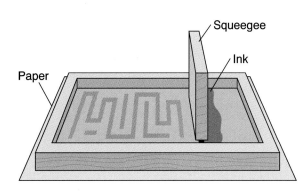

Squeegee

Ink

Paper

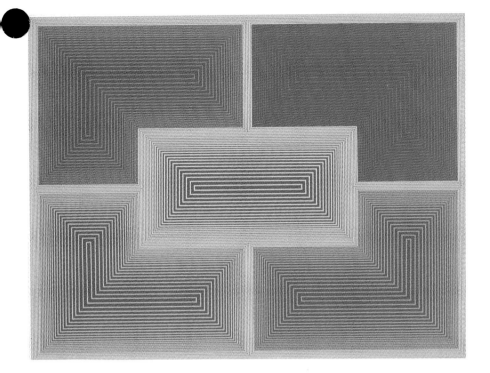

FIG 9-18 RICHARD ANUSZKIEWICZ [American, 1930–], plate 3 from William Blake, *The Inward Eye* (Baltimore: Aquarius Press, 1970). Silk screen, 25 3/4 × 19 7/8 in. (65.4 × 50.5 cm). Museum of Modern Art, New York.

© 1995 Richard Anuszkiewicz/Licensed VAGA, New York, NY

COLLECTING PRINTS

Although framed prints can hang on a wall to decorate an interior space, they are normally collected to be examined like drawings within arm's length on an intimate and personal level, since their imagery and forms are usually on a small scale. Frank Stella's large *Giufà e la berretta rosa* (FIG. 9-1) is of course an exception. Prints are sometimes sold in a portfolio or in a book form. When a museum puts its prints on exhibition, they will be displayed for only a short time. Too much exposure to light will make the ink fade and even damage the paper. Because of the economics of supply and demand, prints seldom cost as much as paintings. And since prints are pressed into pieces of paper, storing them does not take much room. Even a person of moderate means could assemble a small collection of good-quality prints.

The print buyer ought to be aware that an original print, produced by hand as a work of art, is quite different from a photomechanical reproduction of an artist's painting or drawing—a reproduction of Leonardo da Vinci's *Mona Lisa,* for instance. True, many modern artists incorporate photography into their paintings, drawings, and prints, and photographers themselves normally print copies of their work. Yet most responsible artists are reluctant to have someone simply take a photograph of their work, reproduce it in a high-speed, motorized press, and call the reproduction an original.

A photomechanical process can turn out thousands of copies of the original artwork so that the volume of the reproduction dilutes considerably whatever value the copies might have had. Even if few in number and signed by the artist, they remain photographic copies of the original, which is kept by the artist or a museum. Hand-printed works like relief or intaglio prints are much superior in quality to a photoreproduction of the *Mona Lisa,* not only because they are harder to make but because, above all, they are products of the artist's creativity, not of a machine's efficiency. Each print is an original, not a copy of an original. Because the printmaker's plates are really the printmaker's tools, they are not the original work of art—the print itself is.

FRANK STELLA painting with stop-out varnish on etched magnesium plates for *Guifa e la berretta rossa* (see fig. 9-1), with assistance from Kenneth Tyler. Photo by Marabeth Cohen-Tyler.

with a variety of materials. Even photographic images can be printed onto a screen coated with a photo emulsion.

The ink is pushed through the stencil onto the paper with a squeegee. Creamy screen inks are usually opaque, although they can be made transparent, and they come in a full line of colors.

Screen printing is a basically simple process, with relatively inexpensive equipment. Yet it lends itself to multicolor printing, is open to a variety of approaches, and therefore is the printmaking process most like painting.

Contemporary Printmaking

Printmaking as an art form is flourishing in the twentieth century. Artists like Frank Stella are quite likely to combine techniques in a single print, as in *Guifà e la berretta rosa* (FIG. 9-1). Artists experiment constantly to push the limits of printmaking, and never has the medium enjoyed such freedom. Yet, of all the current art forms, this one seems to be the most technical and the one most tied to skill. Despite its technicalities, many artists enjoy the challenge of mastering the craft and working through the difficulties.

At the same time, collaboration between artists from other media and printmaking technicians commonly occurs, since it frees the artist from technical concerns and often expands the medium further. Many famous painters and sculptors including Stella have taken advantage of the extensive equipment and expert technical assistance of craftspeople working at fine art publishing companies where they can turn their creative ideas into prints. Yvonne Jacquette's colored woodcut *Times Square (Overview)* (see p. 220), for example, was printed with the collaboration of the Experimental Workshop of San Francisco. Richard Anuszkiewicz's silk screen from *The Inward Eye* (FIG. 9-18) was printed in collaboration with the Aquarius Press of Baltimore. With such printmaking expertise behind them, prints designed by famous painters like Andy Warhol, Frank Stella, or Ellsworth Kelly can reproduce and extend the style and imagery of an artist's painted work with great success.

RELIEF

Woodcut	A woodcut is the earliest relief process. In this type of printing, the design is drawn on wood and the rest is cut away.
Chiaroscuro woodcut	Several woodblocks are used to produce value contrasts in a chiaroscuro woodcut.
Linocut	For a linocut, linoleum is used instead of a woodblock.
Wood engraving	For a wood engraving, a cross section block of wood is cut with engraving tools instead of a knife.

COLLAGRAPH

A collagraph results when a "collage" on a plate is printed as a relief or intaglio.

INTAGLIO

Engraving	For an engraving, a burin is used to cut lines into a plate.
Drypoint	A drypoint is produced when a needle is used to scratch lines on a plate.
Etching	For an etching, the design is drawn into an acid-resistant ground and then cut in an acid bath.
Aquatint	An aquatint results when the etching process is used to achieve varying tonal qualities.

LITHOGRAPHY

For a lithograph, the design is drawn on polished stone; it prints because the oil in the drawing medium does not mix with water.

SCREEN PRINTING

To produce a screen print, ink is forced through a stencil attached to a screen.

Key Terms and Concepts

aquatint	etching	screen printing
asphaltum	impressions	serigraphy
baren	intaglio	silk screening
burin	linocut	soft ground
chiaroscuro woodcuts	lithography	tusche
collagraph	monotypes	ukiyo-e
drypoint	print	woodcut
edition	printmaking	wood engraving
engraving	relief	

FIG 10-1   WINSLOW HOMER [American,
1836–1910], *Guide Carrying a Deer*. 1891.
Watercolor on paper, 14 × 20 in. (35.6 ×
50.8 cm). Portland (Maine) Museum of Art.
Bequest of Charles Shipman Payson
(1988.55.10). Photo by Benjamin Magro.

The American artist Winslow Homer painted the same Adirondack mountain scene first in a watercolor called *Guide Carrying a Deer* (FIG. 10-1) and then in an oil painting titled *Huntsman and Dogs* (FIG. 10-2). Only in the watercolor **medium,** or mode of artistic expression, could Homer brush the paper rapidly to nail down a creative impulse before the moment passed or distractions intervened. Only in this medium could he dab the brush across the paper to achieve soft, grainy texture, transparent light, and a luminous sky. In the watercolor the brilliant autumn foliage around the feet of the guide becomes dancing pools of transparent and opaque color. The oil painting on canvas, typically, is more than twice the size of the watercolor on paper and for that reason alone perhaps more imposing. The composition is somewhat different, especially owing to the addition of the dogs, but the painting medium alters the appearance of the scene even more. The sky is a more ominous steely gray; the woodlands are dark and opaque and much more somber, even with a few touches of autumn foliage. At the loss of spontaneity, the mood is intensified.

Pictures are painted in a number of different ways, depending on the kind of paint used. Oil, watercolor, and other kinds of paint have unique characteristics and are applied differently. Not every artistic effect is possible from any one painting medium. And the same artist might paint the same subject in different manners because different painting media are employed.

The medium does not control the artist in a deterministic fashion. Some artists, challenged by the limitations of a medium, extend the medium's possibilities beyond the ordinary. Artists usually choose a medium because they want to paint in the manner suitable for that medium. The relationship between medium and style or the precedence of one over the other is another chicken-and-egg question.

J. M. W. Turner, the painter of *Slave Ship* (FIG. 5-1), once said that "painting is a rum thing." *Rum* is British

FIG 10-2   WINSLOW HOMER [American, 1836–1910], *Huntsman and Dogs.* 1891. Oil on canvas, 28 × 48 in. (71.1 × 121.9 cm). Philadelphia Museum of Art. William L. Elkins Collection.

The deer carcass slung across his shoulders, the young hunter sets his boot triumphantly on the stump. His heroic stance makes an ironic contrast with the deforested and burned land around him. Only the bloody carcass of the dead animal remains; the hunter has probably killed the deer for a few dollars for the skin and antlers.

Contemporary critics commented on the look of brutality on the young man's face. Winslow Homer perhaps underscored his savagery with the addition of the leaping and barking dogs. Modern critics have related Homer's painting to the late-nineteenth-century interpretation of Darwin's The Descent of Man *touting the survival of the fittest. Homer suggested that, with his inhumane cruelty, destruction, and irresponsible way of pursuing prey, the huntsman belongs to a lower, savage state of human development, and that modern man has not yet evolved to a very high state of civilization.*

FIG 10-3 GILBERT ("MAGU") LUJAN [American 19?–], *Our Family Car.* 1985–1986. Photo by Tom Vinetz.

slang for odd or queer. Turner probably meant that for all the high-flown principles and profound ideas connected with art, a painter still has to dab on paint and get dirty, use the tricks of the trade, fudge and make do. The application of paint can be a messy affair. It can also be the most creative part of an artist's activity, since an artist discovers new and significant imagery and styles through the medium.

Vehicles and Supports

The media of painting do not necessarily differ from one another because of the **pigments,** which are dry powdery substances that produce the different colors, or because of the tools used to apply the colors. They differ because of the **vehicle,** which is the liquid that suspends the pigments. Some vehicles, because of their chemistry, limit the kind and number of pigments that can be used. If they are a fluid, vehicles allow brushing of dry pigments. Vehicles also bind the pigments and cause the pigments to dry and adhere to a surface. They range from water to oil, from wax to eggs and to plastics. Some vehicles change the color of pigments, if only slightly. Even if someone has never held a paintbrush, she or he can probably readily imagine that vehicles act and handle differently and have different possibilities.

Many of us may think of painting primarily as applying oil paint to canvas, and most of the paintings in most museums are probably oil on canvas. But oil paintings are not by any means the oldest form of painting, and perhaps most artists working today no longer use oils. Paintings are not always done on canvas either. Wood has always been a favorite **support**— the surface to which the paint adheres—and countless pictures have been painted on wooden panels. Today an artist might use a hardboard: Masonite is a common brand. Wood feels solid beneath the brush, whereas canvas on a stretcher flexes to the touch of a brush. Wood tends not to soak up paint as canvas might. The weave of a canvas has a texture that painters may or may not want to exploit in their work.

Artists also paint on plaster walls and on copper plates, slate, or paper. The Chicano artist Gilbert ("Magù") Lujan, who has painted murals along the streets of Los Angeles, painted a 1950 Chevy, *Our Family Car* (FIG. 10-3), with a scene of two Chicano youths pointing to and considering their future.

On most common supports, an artist might have to size the raw surface, usually with a thin coating of glue, to seal it, to render it less absorbent, and to keep the paint from making the support dry out and decay. An artist then applies a preliminary coating, called a **ground,** so that the support will uniformly receive the paint. **Gesso,** the traditional ground for a wooden support, contains plaster of Paris or white chalk, and glue. The ordinary ground for canvas is gesso or a white paint, which increases the luminosity of colors applied to it.

The nineteenth-century English painter William Turner and the French Impressionists Claude Monet and Auguste Renoir painted on canvases with a white ground because they wanted light-filled colors. In the preceding two or three centuries, when artists were more concerned with the manipulation of light-and-dark contrasts, or chiaroscuro, artists preferred to paint on a colored ground, usually a gray or a reddish brown. Rubens and Rembrandt, who usually worked on a nonwhite ground, sometimes let the color of the ground appear in the finished painting, since it could provide a middle value where it was needed.

FIG 10-4 [Roman], *Portrait of a Man.* C. 117–161. Encaustic on panel, 15 1/2 × 7 5/8 in. (39.4 × 19.4 cm). From Fayum, Egypt. Metropolitan Museum of Art, New York. Rogers Fund, 1909.

Encaustic

In ancient Roman times artists frequently painted in a medium called **encaustic.** The vehicle in this type of painting is hot beeswax, which is applied to a wooden support. Most of the surviving examples of this type of painting are panels from a region of Egypt called the Fayum, where the dry desert climate has preserved them remarkably well; *Portrait of a Man* (FIG. 10-4) is one. These encaustic panels are all portraits that were buried with mummies. The ancient Roman artists in the province of Egypt achieved remarkably lifelike results in the medium.

FIG 10-5 JASPER JOHNS [American, 1930–], *Painting with Two Balls.* 1960. Encaustic and collage on canvas with objects, 65 × 54 in. (165.1 × 137.2 cm). Collection of the artist. Photo courtesy Leo Castelli photo archives.

Jasper Johns once explained why he revived the encaustic technique. "It was very simple," he said. "I wanted to show what had gone before in a picture, and what was done after. But if you put on a heavy brushstroke in paint, and then add another stroke, the second stroke smears the first unless the paint is dry. And paint takes too long to dry. I didn't know what to do. Then someone suggested wax. It worked very well; as soon as the wax was cool I could put on another stroke and it would not alter the first."[1]

John's Painting with Two Balls *appears at first to be a repetition of Willem De Kooning's style of Abstract Expressionism. However, the emotional self-expression embodied in the slashes of paint is undercut by the deliberate gap in the painting, held apart by two actual balls (a pun for masculinity), and by the matter-of-fact stenciled lettering at the bottom. The primary colors, red, yellow, and blue, predominate. Johns seems to have been interested in merely displaying the colors, rather than in exploiting their psychological effects. Color, language, and sculptural form act upon one another in this work to produce a refreshingly strange experience.*

The main requirement of encaustic painting is to keep both the paint and the panel hot so that the wax can be brushed. Encaustic has a little flexibility, since it is possible to rework the paint once it has been applied, if the surface is kept warm. Traditionally, a heat source was passed over the completed panel to fuse and smooth the colors—hence the Greek word *encaustic,* which means "burned in." The twentieth-century American painter Jasper Johns revived the encaustic medium precisely because it does not allow colors to mix on the canvas. *Painting with Two Balls* (FIG. 10-5) is one example of his work in this medium.

Mural and Fresco

The ancient Greeks and Romans also painted **murals,** that is to say, pictures on walls or ceilings where they become part of the architectural decoration. In the Renaissance, mural painting became the highest form of artistic achievement. Although it is possible to detach a mural from the wall and transport it, most American museums do not have examples of great mural painting from the past by Giotto or Michelangelo because these are still in their original location. Some ancient Roman mural paintings, especially from

Pompeii and Herculaneum—cities that were buried by an eruption of Mount Vesuvius in A.D. 79—have been excavated and moved to safer locations. Murals from a *cubiculum* (bedroom) in a *villa* (country house), including the one in figure 10-6, were uncovered from the ashes of Mount Vesuvius in 1900, and three years later these remarkable paintings were brought to the Metropolitan Museum of Art in New York. Today it is unlikely that Italy or any other government would allow such treasures to leave the country where they were found.

In the mural in figure 10-6, the Roman artist in effect painted away the walls of the room by converting the bedroom into an airy loggia open to the outside. On closer inspection, however, it is clear that the artist has not treated the viewer to a single, unified panorama sweeping around the room. Instead, between each pair of columns, the artist has painted a separate view. One section illustrates a rustic garden, another shows a temple precinct, another looks over the rooftops of a city, and so on. It has been suggested that the sections mimic the backdrops used in theatrical productions.

Diego Rivera and other painters in Mexico in the first half of the twentieth century revived mural painting with great success (see *The Fertile Earth*, FIG. 18-33). In the United States, during the Great Depression in the 1930s, mural painting was revived by the Works Progress Administration's Federal Art Project and the Treasury Department's Section of Painting and Sculpture. They put artists to work painting thousands of murals in post offices, courthouses, and other government buildings in Washington, D.C., and throughout the country. Ethel Magafan's *Threshing* (FIG. 10-7), for the Auburn, Nebraska post office, illustrates the kind of popular imagery that the government encouraged artists to employ in a mural project. Her regional iconography and simple style lend dignity to farm labor while they extol the value of hard work at a time of economic hardship. The government art programs during the Depression not only gave employment to hundreds of artists on relief, they sought to bring the benefits of artistic culture to small-town America and to create a new national spirit in the process.

FIG 10-6   [Roman], cubiculum from a villa at Boscoreale. C. 50 B.C. Fresco, about 96 in. (243.8 cm) high. Metropolitan Museum of Art, New York. Rogers Fund, 1903.

FIG 10-7   ETHEL MAGAFAN [American, 1916–], *Threshing*. 1938. Oil on canvas. Auburn, Nebraska. Photo courtesy Nebraska State Historical Society.

DIVISION OF THE BARRIOS & CHAVEZ RAVINE

FIG 10-8 JUDY BACA [American, 19?–], *Division of the Barrios,* detail from *The Great Wall of Los Angeles.* 1983. Tujunga wash, 13 × about 2,500 ft. (4 × about 762 m). Los Angeles, California. Photo courtesy SPARC, Venice, California.

Judy Baca formed the Citywide Mural Project, through which she directed

about 150 murals. She selected young people from the ethnic communities of Los Angeles to execute the murals. Some of the muralists were juvenile offenders who were given the choice of reform school or mural painting. The creation of The Great Wall was a learning experience because through

it the different groups learned to think positively about their own culture and to reject stereotypes of other groups. This section of the wall shows the division of a Chicano community in Los Angeles when a freeway cut through the neighborhood.

More recently mural painting has resurged in urban America. Artists in many cities, especially Los Angeles, El Paso, and Philadelphia, have covered the embankment walls along streets and the sides of multistoried buildings with gigantic murals whose themes and styles are often quite popular. These works frequently embody the political messages of individuals and groups in ethnic neighborhoods. Inspired by Rivera, José Clemente Orozco, and David Alfaro Siqueiros, the Chicano activist Judy Baca organized and directed *The Great Wall of Los Angeles* (see FIG. 10-8), a mural painted on the walls of a flood channel in the suburban San Fernando Valley. A half mile

long, perhaps the longest mural in the world, *The Great Wall* tells the story of California from the point of view of those normally left out of the history books.

The fashion for outdoor urban murals and graphics coincided with the spread of spray-painted graffiti on walls and subway cars—a kind of "popular" art form. The tradition of outdoor billboard advertising also lurks behind the movement. Unfortunately, outdoor painting of any kind has little chance of surviving the elements for very long.

Because of the persistent dampness of a climate, some indoor murals are painted in oil on a canvas that is then attached to a wall. Where the wall can be kept

FIG 10-9 GIOTTO [Italian, c. 1266–1337], *The Nativity.* C. 1305. Fresco. Scrovegni Chapel, Padua, Italy. Alinari/Art Resource, New York.

Work patches over Giotto's Nativity.

dry, murals have traditionally been painted in **fresco.** The Italian word *fresco* means "fresh." In true fresco, water-based paints are applied to fresh, or wet, plaster so that the pigment soaks into the plaster. Since the paint actually becomes part of the wall when the plaster dries, fresco is a very permanent kind of painting. The colors are matte, not glossy. They stay bright for hundreds of years, and as long as the wall lasts, the fresco lasts.

Since true fresco must be painted on *wet* plaster, an artist can work on only a small portion of the wall where the plaster was freshly applied beforehand. A normal area of a mural for a day's work might be about one or two square yards, although the size depends on the complexity of the painting. Some days a frescoist might complete only a head, for example. In Giotto's fresco *The Nativity* (FIG. 10-9) the breaks between one day's work on fresh plaster and the next are visible on close inspection.

Fresco painting takes a lot of preparation, since artists have to have the entire composition worked out before they get started on an individual patch of plaster. Many artists, in whatever medium, make prelimi-

nary sketches beforehand so that they have some sense of where they are headed, but a frescoist also makes **cartoons**—drawings on paper in the same scale as the mural—so that at least the essential lines of the composition and the proportions of the figures can be traced and transferred to the wall. (The same word, *cartoon,* was applied to humorous drawings centuries after it was first used to describe full-scale preliminary drawings for frescoes.)

The vehicle for carrying the pigments in fresco is water. The lime of the plaster, changing to calcium carbonate when it dries, binds the pigments in the wall. Since some pigments will not combine chemically in this medium, the colors of fresco are limited. In *The Nativity* Giotto's blue pigment would not mix with the lime in plaster, and so he had to paint it on the dry plaster. As a consequence, the blue of the sky and of Mary's robe has almost all flaked off. (Blue pigment was also problematic for another reason: for a long time it was very expensive because it was ground from semiprecious lapis lazuli. Artists used it sparingly. If a patron wanted a lot of blue in a painting, he or she had to pay the artist extra for it.)

Chapter 10: Painting

In the 1980s and 1990s conservators cleaned Michelangelo's Sistine Chapel frescoes and discovered surprisingly bright color once again under the accumulated dirt. The cleaning of the Sistine ceiling caused outrage among some art historians who could not believe that Michelangelo wanted such stark, unmodulated color. They complained that in removing the centuries of grime, the restorers had also removed veils of paint that Michelangelo had applied to the dry fresco. The technical evidence weighs in favor of the result produced by the restorers of the Sistine frescoes. However, restorations of any kind will continually arouse controversy because they involve fundamental aesthetic issues such as, What were the original intentions of the artist? Should every work be stripped of every touch that is not by the artist's hands? Can contemporaries ever possibly restore a work without imposing their own point of view on it?

Michelangelo's frescoes before restoration. Scala/Art Resource.

Michelangelo's frescoes after restoration. © 1994 Nippon Television Network Corporation, Tokyo.

Egg Tempera

Distinct from murals, most artists produce **easel paintings**—works intended to be hung on a wall, whether they were painted on an actual easel or not. When European artists in the fourteenth and fifteenth centuries wanted to create an individual easel painting, they worked on a carefully prepared wooden panel. Wooden panels assembled from several planks and as high as ten to twelve feet were common in Giotto's day. The wood had to be dried, aged, and possibly carved with a frame. Then it was sized to seal it and primed with many coats of gesso so that it would accept paint as desired. The surface became like polished marble.

When Italian Renaissance artists in the fourteenth and fifteenth centuries painted an easel painting, they mixed their pigments with egg yolk, a medium that is called **egg tempera.** If their panels have received decent treatment over the years, five- or six-hundred-year-old egg tempera paintings like Benozzo Gozzoli's *Virgin and Child with Angels* (FIG. 10-10) usually have colors that are still well preserved and fresh. Egg tempera is quite a permanent medium. Not only is the painted surface of Gozzoli's tempera panel still intact, the colors are still brilliant and bright. The vibrating boldness of the alternating red and blue colors of the six-winged seraphim contrasts with the careful modeling of the flesh and the delicacy of the precisely rendered details, such as the jewels sewn to the Madonna's dress. The contrast and the decorative patterning of the whole design give an otherworldly quality to the painting.

A problem with the egg tempera medium is that it dries as fast as a film of egg yolk dries on a breakfast plate and is just as stubborn to remove. An artist applies it in short strokes because of the rapid drying time, and by the time the artist comes back to the panel with the next brush stroke, the preceding one has already dried. Little blending is possible, and the only way to remove a mistake is by scraping it off. Every stroke has to be placed deliberately with small brushes.

Egg tempera is transparent, since it does not cover well and what is underneath shows through. Therefore, the paint has to be built up in layers. At the start of an egg tempera painting, the artist makes an accurate drawing on the gesso ground. The artist then works out the modeling, often in a cool green preliminary layer, before filling in the local colors.

An egg tempera painting, like a fresco, takes careful preparation and planning, but the finished product, like Gozzoli's *Virgin and Child*, can have rich color and details. Sometimes the background of an old egg tempera painting is gold in color because actual gold leaf was once applied to the panels. The artist-craftsperson also might have attached semiprecious stones to the surface or stamped the surface with a

FIG 10-10   BENOZZO GOZZOLI [Italian, 1420–1497], *Virgin and Child with Angels.* C. 1460. Tempera and gold leaf on wood panel, 25 1/2 × 20 in. (64.8 × 50.8 cm). Detroit Institute of Arts.

Christina Olson, who lived near Andrew Wyeth in Maine in the house at the top of the hill, was crippled with polio as a child. Although Wyeth observed Christina and her house many times, he never asked her to pose in the field for the painting. Despite the realistic appearance of his style, the image is essentially the artist's fantasy, which the minute details drive deep into the mind.

The artist raised the horizon so that the flat field of the painting is filled with the color of the dry grass. The small size of the house, a shape wedged between the horizon and the top border, exaggerates the distance between the figure and the building. Her glance up at the house creates a strong diagonal tension. The sky is one flat color in contrast with the faded lobster shell pink of her dress. In light of the artistic contrivance in the painting, it is no wonder that Wyeth considers himself an abstractionist.

leather-working tool to make decorative patterns. Thieves have long since removed the jewels and the gold in most cases.

One contemporary artist, Andrew Wyeth, has revived the egg tempera process and has made quite a reputation for himself in the medium. His painting *Christina's World* (FIG. 10-11) has been widely reproduced. Wyeth uses a traditional egg tempera technique, mixing dry, powered mineral pigments with fresh egg yolk and a little water. Wyeth deliberately chose egg tempera because the patience demanded by the medium put a brake, he said, on his inherent messiness. The weeks and months it takes to paint a panel like *Christina's World* also allow him to whittle his composition down to its essence.

Oil Painting

By the time of Leonardo da Vinci and Raphael, around the year 1500, Italian artists started using oil as the vehicle for painting, and they soon started using canvas as the support. Actually, Netherland artists, like Jan van Eyck (see *The Arnolfini Wedding*, FIG. 17-5), were working with an oil vehicle several generations earlier. **Oil**—usually linseed oil—as a vehicle has the advantage that it can combine with a great range of pigments taken from all sorts of elements. Oil-based paint offers a greater variety of colors than fresco or egg tempera. And unlike other media, oil paint dries slowly so that its colors can easily be blended with one another right on the canvas. The best feature about painting with oil is its great flexibility. Oil paint can be laid on thick or thin. It can be made opaque or transparent.

The flexibility of the medium also allows artists to sketch in oil paint with the freedom of a drawing medium to display their virtuosity, creativity, and individuality. First Venetian artists like Titian, then Rubens and many other artists dabbed and swirled oil paint on a panel or canvas, and the dabs and swirls often became the finished product.

Rubens painted the preliminary oil sketch *St. Gregory Nazianzus* (FIG. 10-12), portraying the saint fighting Heresy (the monster in the lower left), for one of thirty-nine ceiling panels that decorated the Jesuit Church in Antwerp, Belgium. Because the final painting was to be placed on the ceiling, Rubens drew the figure of the saint seen from below in steep foreshort-

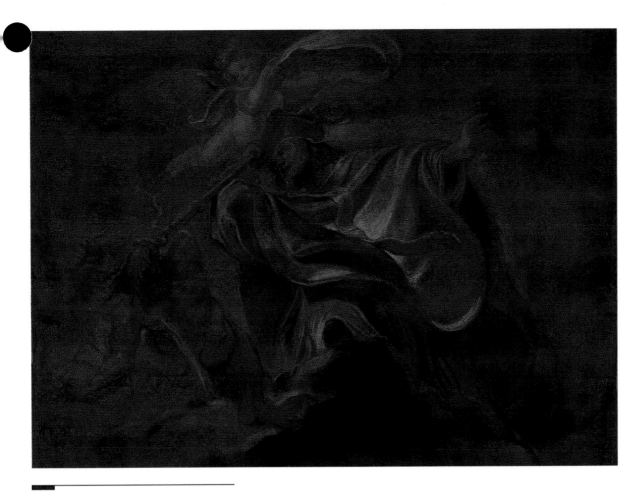

FIG 10-12 PETER PAUL RUBENS [Flemish, 1577–1640], *St. Gregory Nazianzus.* C. 1620. Oil on wood, 19 3/4 × 25 3/4 in. (50.2 × 65.4 cm). Albright-Knox Art Gallery. Buffalo. George B. Matthews Fund, 1952.

ening, lunging forward on a cloud and stabbing Heresy with his bishop's crosier, or staff. His robes, swirling in loops and undulations, accentuate his action. Over a colored underpainting, Rubens let thin oil paint flow freely in some places, dabbed thicker patches of paint in others, and drew contour lines with the brush. A fire in the church unfortunately destroyed Ruben's ceiling paintings, but in all likelihood the vigor of his oil sketch more obviously illustrates his creative imagination and his dexterous hand at work than did the finished painting.

Artists can apply oil paint to the canvas opaquely or they can apply it in thin, transparent layers called **glazes.** In glazing, the paint underneath, usually lighter in value, shines through the translucent upper layer and gives the color a luminous quality. Van Eyck, one of the first artists to use oil paints with regularity, employed glazes to make his colors especially brilliant

and shiny like enamel. Light penetrates his paintings and is reflected back from the white ground through the colored glazes.

A layer of opaque oil paint can also cover over unwanted parts of a painting. However, sometimes because of chemical changes with aging, the opaque

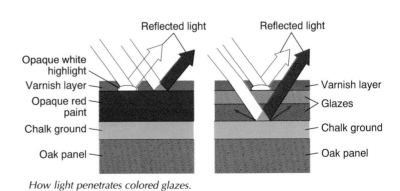

How light penetrates colored glazes.

Chapter 10: Painting

FIG 10-13 VINCENT VAN GOGH [Dutch, 1853–1890], *Sunflowers,* detail of FIG. 1-1. 1889. Oil on canvas, 36 1/4 × 28 7/8 in. (92.1 × 73.3 cm). Philadelphia Museum of Art.

FIG 10-14 JOAN MITCHELL [American, 1926–], *A Few Days II (After James Schuyler).* 1985. Oil on canvas, 87 × 78 3/4 in. (221 × 220 cm). © The Estate of Joan Mitchell. Photo courtesy Robert Miller Gallery, New York.

layer grows transparent and reveals a **pentimento,** the ghostlike figure or shape underneath that the artist wanted hidden. (*Pentimento* in Italian means "repentance.")

Susan Rothenberg (see *For the Light* and *Night Ride,* p. 249) and many other artists like to lay paint directly on the support, without glazing. The technique of direct painting is sometimes called ***alla prima,*** which in Italian means "at the first." In other words, the artist achieves the desired effect right away in the first layers of paint, instead of gradually working toward an image by applying layer after layer of transparent paint. Artists for centuries had employed the *alla prima* technique for oil sketches. By the end of the nineteenth century, they were taking advantage of the sketch technique of *alla prima* for finished paintings. The early Impressionists used *alla prima* to demonstrate that the creativity of their work was immediate and spontaneous and in direct contact with nature.

When paint on the surface of a canvas appears thick and somewhat three-dimensional, it is called **impasto.** Van Gogh liked to apply paint in an impasto manner in order to make his intense feelings about things an actuality on the canvas (see the detail of *Sunflowers* in FIG. 10-13). In his impatience, he sometimes used paint squeezed directly from the tube. (Tubes for paint were invented in the mid-1800s.) Artists have also used their palette knife to spread thick paint on the support for the impasto effect.

Another oil painting technique involving thickish paint is called **scumbling.** In scumbling, the artist drags brush strokes of wet paint over the dry layer of paint underneath, as Joan Mitchell did on her canvas *A Few Days II (After James Schuyler)* (FIG. 10-14). Scumbling creates a kind of open-textured brush stroke of opaque paint that still lets the color underneath appear. Usually a light color is scumbled over a dark one.

Opaque, transparent, *alla prima*, impasto, and scumbling are some of a variety of ways an artist can apply oil paint. With the openness and freedom of these techniques artists readily leave the marks of their personality in applying oil paint. Oil can be a very expressive medium.

Text continues on page 252

Part III: The Visual Arts

Susan Rothenberg (1945–)

*W*HEN Susan Rothenberg paints a picture, such as *For the Light*, she tacks a large canvas on the wall of her studio, dips a paintbrush in a can of paint-stained water or turpentine, and begins by drawing an outline of a figure on the canvas. At times the images in her paintings result from random studies that she made in drawings; at times the images result from "doodling" directly on canvas.

She then starts to stab and stroke the canvas with a controlled and assertive freedom. The surface becomes layered with countless energetic brush strokes that often "correct" the initial drawing. In the process of painting, the image becomes fixed and embedded in the rough and emotional texture of her brushwork.

Like many painters who express themselves in a direct and vigorous application of paint, Rothenberg frequently steps back from the canvas or sits for some time with the canvas to reflect on what is happening. Sometimes her paintings relate to things she has seen or experiences she has felt; sometimes they go off in an unknown direction and become truly mysterious to the artist herself. Rothenberg has compared her pictures to prayers asking to fulfill the wants of daily life. Through painting she can sublimate and exorcise her demons and put the world together the way she wants.

For five years, from 1974 to 1979, Rothenberg painted horses almost exclusively. She produced her first horse impulsively, as a "doodle" that immediately seemed right for her. In her mind she had the vague desire to paint some-

SUSAN ROTHENBERG [American, 1945–], *For the Light*. 1978–1979. Acrylic and flashe on canvas, 105 × 87 in. (266.7 × 22.1 cm). Collection of Whitney Museum of American Art, New York. Purchased with funds from Peggy Danziger (79.23).

Continued on next page.

Susan Rothenberg in her studio.
Photo by Brigitte Lacombe.

thing simple, magical, and universal like the prehistoric cave paintings of animals. Despite the serendipitous beginning, Rothenberg soon realized that her horse was a surrogate for the human figure. But her life-sized, powerful animals represent living spirits without the specifics of age, sex, or personality that accompany nearly every depiction of human beings.

Rothenberg first painted horses in profile, then horses posed frontally, and then dismembered parts of the horse as she pulled away from her fascination with the animal. In *For the Light*, the horse gallops toward the viewer, but its motion is stopped by the bone in its

way. The horse's outline has grown to such thick and rugged dimensions that it can be read as the silhouette of another ghostlike horse looming behind it. Rothenberg likes to think of such forms as "bands," halfway between lines and shapes.

The white horse in the painting, with its abnormally small head, seems spectral also. Despite the strong diagonal movement of its powerful forms, the lack of modeling keeps the image flat and the identical expressionistic treatment and lack of color of both the horse and the background keep the image embedded in the surface of the canvas. The ambiguity of our perception keeps

the level of tension in the painting high.

Rothenberg painted in water-based acrylic paints in the 1970s, then switched to oil paints in the 1980s. In the early 1970s she often brought her newborn baby into the studio, and realized that it was easier and safer to wash up with water in order to care for her daughter. In 1981 she switched to oil paints just to shake up her procedures and to see what it was like to work with oil. She liked the way the brush moved in oil paint, and compared the consistency of acrylic paint to yogurt and of oil paint to stiff butter. With oil paint, she found herself using smaller, shorter,

SUSAN ROTHENBERG [American, 1945–], *Night Ride.* 1987. Oil on canvas, 93 × 110 1/4 in. (236.2 × 280 cm). Collection of Walker Art Center, Minneapolis. Walker Special Purchase Fund, 1987.

The staccato slashes of light throughout the dark painting eliminate the difference between figure and ground by dissolving the figure into streaks of light across the surface.

denser, and choppier brush strokes. The new brushwork enabled her to capture light, light reflections, and movement.

In the 1980s the human figure appeared in Rothenberg's work. At first she painted body fragments like a head and hand, then complete figures that still look like disembodied spirits. *Night Ride* depicts a figure in motion, not by the vigor of its contour but by the Futuristic, rhythmic repetition of its brushwork. Her later paintings have a denser, more compact layering of choppy brush strokes. The staccato slashes of light throughout the dark *Night Ride* eliminate the difference between figure and ground by dissolving the figure into

streaks of light across the surface.

When Rothenberg was growing up in Buffalo, she had a firsthand familiarity with the Abstract Expressionists and other modern painters in the splendid collection of the Albright-Knox Art Gallery. As an undergraduate at Cornell University, she majored in sculpture, which she flunked, and then painting, earning a bachelor of fine arts degree in 1967. In 1969, on a trip to Canada, she detoured on a whim to New York City, where she immersed herself in the art scene.

Perhaps the most vital influence on her work from those early years in New York came through her participation in

dance and performance art. From performance she grew to understand art as an activity and a process. The energy and assurance of her horse paintings of 1974–75 first attracted favorable critical attention and the interest of collectors and dealers who had had their fill of spare abstraction. She became one of the few female painters associated with the male-dominated Neo-Expressionist movement in the early 1980s. Rothenberg now lives in New Mexico, where she has finally learned to ride a horse.

FIG 10-15 KENNETH NOLAND [American, 1924–], *Trans Flux*. 1963. Acrylic on canvas, 10s × 164 in. (259.1 × 416.6 cm). Collection of the artist. © 1995 Ken Noland/ Licensed VAGA, New York, NY

Acrylic

Oil paints dry too slowly to suit some artists. They can also crack, especially if the vehicle contains too much oil. Oil pigments can yellow or darken or undergo chemical changes because of the slow drying time. Several more modern vehicles, commonly referred to as **acrylics,** seem to have solved many of these problems. For example, acrylic paints probably will not yellow or become brittle. They seem to have many of the advantages of oil paint and few of its drawbacks. Since World War II, modern artists have more and more converted to the use of these paints.

Acrylic paints are a liquid form of plastic. Chemically, acrylics are synthetic resins; most of them are vinyl polymers. The vehicle for acrylic paint is the plastic resin mixed with water. When the water dries, the plastic hardens, and more water cannot remove it.

Acrylic paints seem to be quite permanent, although they have survived only a half century so far. They dry about as fast as a brush stroke of water, which is slow enough for the artist to blend the paints on the canvas to some extent, and fast enough for the artist to paint another layer on top without much waiting. Oil paints are still probably superior for subtle value gradations and extensive blending on the canvas. Acrylic paints, applied directly without additives, tend to be matte, opaque, and even in texture. They can be glazed or scumbled, and modeling paste can be added to them to achieve a thick impasto. Modern painters like the brilliant, intense colors available in these paints.

Acrylic paints have also suited impatient and inventive artists who like to experiment with new ways of applying paint. They have especially attracted contemporary artists who like to work with areas of flat color, as Kenneth Noland has done in *Trans Flux* (FIG. 10-15). Nevertheless, contemporary Photo-realist painters can create in acrylics as intricate an image as any in the past. Because acrylic can be painted on all kinds of unprimed surfaces, some contemporary Americans like Noland, Helen Frankenthaler (see

FIG 10-16 SAM GILLIAM [American, 1933–], *Carousel Form II.* 1969. Acrylic on canvas, 10 × 75 ft. Washington, D.C. Collection of the artist.

Sam Gilliam experimented with new techniques of applying paint by spreading unprimed, unstretched canvas on the floor and pouring paint directly onto it. The paint soaked in and stained the canvas as he tipped and folded it. It seemed natural to him that canvases that had been so manipulated in the act of painting should not be stretched flat and placed against a wall. Instead, in his work, enormous pieces of canvas were gathered and draped from the ceiling to the floor of the museum gallery. The swooping columns of cloth react upon the viewer standing in the room in a much more dynamic way than if they were on the wall, out of the way. The expressionism of the paint plays hide-and-seek with the folds of the cloth, while the boldly sweeping graceful folds assert themselves over the richness of color and paint.

Lush Spring, p. 108), and Sam Gilliam like to stain the canvas by letting the paint soak into the unprimed material; staining in oil would eventually rot the unprimed canvas. Gilliam, now living in Washington, D.C., stained large canvases and then draped them like curtains, as in his *Carousel Form II* (FIG. 10-16). Gilliam is one of many contemporary artists who frequently manipulate the shape of the canvas.

Watercolor

Artists generally use several other traditional painting vehicles for small-scale work. **Watercolor** is a transparent medium whose vehicle is water, of course, and gum arabic, a thickener derived from the acacia tree in Africa. Watercolor should be painted on good-quality rag paper that will not warp when wet. It is usually "washed" on rather than brushed on, although "dry,"

nearly opaque strokes of color are possible. Since watercolor is inherently transparent, the eye constantly mixes the white of the paper with the color applied to it. The water color artist works from the light of the paper, adjusting the fluidity of the color to render values. With light shining through transparent colors, watercolors are naturally luminous. The watercolor medium demands spontaneity and tolerates few mistakes, although it is possible to blot or sponge or even scrape away errors. It takes a lot of practice not to let the washes run into one another and turn everything muddy. Details can be supplied by a pencil drawing underneath.

Watercolor has been popular with landscapists and topographical artists because the equipment is easy to carry and the sheets dry quickly for transport. The medium lends itself to capturing spontaneous impressions of outdoor light. In the late 1800s Winslow Homer took his watercolor kit to the Adirondack

FIG 10-18 MARK TOBEY [American, 1890–1976], *Serpentine.* 1955. Gouache; graphite; paper; board, 29 3/4 × 39 1/2 in. (76.6 × 100.3 cm). Seattle Art Museum. S.A.M. Silver Anniversary Fund. Photo by Paul Macapia.

woods, where he painted *Guide Carrying a Deer* (FIG. 10-1), and to Quebec in the summer and fall, and to Florida and the West Indies in the winter, where he produced *The Turtle Pound* (FIG. 10-17). His images of isolated woodsmen and boatmen vying with nature may be considered his masterpieces. Watercolor let Homer capture the immediacy, the movement, and the luminous color of sky and water.

Gouache

Gouache is like watercolor but opaque and nonstaining. Because brush strokes of gouache dry fast and do not blend well, they allowed Mark Tobey, in his *Serpentine* (FIG. 10-18), to pile up many strokes of paint without obliterating the gesture of the earlier strokes. The nonglossy gouache also provides a tooth for the sinuous pencil lines. Tobey's calligraphic style of painting enmeshes lines that seem like energetic traces of light moving over the surface. They create a single texture and a one-part composition over the entire surface of the paper.

Gouache has more gum arabic and opaque white pigment in it than does watercolor, and because gouache is opaque, glazing is impossible. Artists often

FIG 10-19 GEORGES BRAQUE [French, 1882–1963], *Musical Shapes (Guitar and Clarinet)*. 1918. Charcoal and gouache, wood-pattern paper, colored paper, and corrugated cardboard pasted on grayish-blue cardboard; 30 × 37 in. (77 × 95 cm). Philadelphia Museum of Art. Louise and Walter Arensberg Collection.

do sketches and other small-scale work in this medium. Since gouache readily builds solid forms, sketches in it can mimic the appearance of a finished oil or acrylic painting.

Collage

When Georges Braque pasted real or imagined materials to the support of his *Musical Shapes (Guitar and Clarinet)* (FIG. 10-19), he was practicing **collage**—one of the most stimulating new techniques of "painting" in the twentieth century. Picasso and Braque developed the collage technique in 1912 and 1913 as a stage in the evolution of Cubism. By pasting onto their canvases pieces of newspaper, colored paper, printed wallpapers, and other materials, Picasso and Braque admitted into the unreal space of Cubism objects from the real world and allusions to everyday life, without breaking away from the flat Cubist relief.

They were also protesting against the pretensions of so-called high art, on the one hand; on the other, they were declaring that ordinary "vulgar" materials could be transformed into art. In a collage the new materials,

whether real or imitation, introduced color and texture and sometimes poetic associations. The combination of painting and drawing with pasted "real" materials confronts the viewer with many fundamental questions about reality and illusion, such as, Are the shapes of pasted material more real than painted shapes, and where do they exist in space?

Mixed Media

The combination of actual materials with paint in a collage is one example of **mixed media.** The combination of tempera and oil paint in a single work is another. Many modern artists practice mixed media when they put together not only different painting media but two different art media in one work. Sometimes it is impossible to say whether their work is a painting, a photograph, or a piece of relief sculpture. The categories of art media are by no means sacred, and their combination can open new avenues of expression for artists.

The artist Robert Rauschenberg pioneered combining painted canvases with actual solid objects, as in his

First Landing Jump (FIG. 10-20), where the objects protrude like sculpture. He called such works combines. In *First Landing Jump* Rauschenberg combined with the oil paint a metal lamp shade, a license plate, a tin can, rags, a highway barrier, a tire, and an electric cord. These are items he probably found on the streets and alleys where he lived—in other words, things he encountered in life. Since Rauschenberg felt at the time the need to incorporate real life into his art, his combine method allowed him to introduce reality into abstract painting.

Rauschenberg did not attempt to express his feelings about these objects, satirize them, or make some moral comment about them. They simply became part of his composition. They create a rich texture and make shapes and lines and value contrasts as well as any painted form. They also create space. Much more

than a traditional relief sculpture, his combine painting comes out into the viewer's space. These objects from the real world assert their presence in the real world alongside the viewer.

Video Art

Since the late 1960s, before the advent of the personal computer, artists have been manipulating the visual images seen on television and recorded on videotape. Nam June Paik has become the almost mythical founder of the video art movement in America ever since he bought a video camera in 1965. The term **video art** encompasses three different possibilities, which frequently appear together. The first possibility is an arrangement or installation of TV monitors in a gallery space, as often created by Paik (see *V-yramid*, Fig. 19-16). The material on the screens may be an essential part of the installation, but the viewer primarily experiences sculptural space and mass.

The second kind of artist's video is videotaped documentaries, interviews, and performances, which range in technical quality from crude home videos to slick social or political exposés suited for commercial television. The impetus behind this kind of video has often been to create something personal, committed, and different from what is normally seen on broadcast television. The rules for filmmaking apply, for the most part, to this kind of video.

The third kind of video art corresponds more closely to traditional principles of painting. Paik and others soon discovered in the 1960s that it was possible to manipulate the video image electronically in a free and creative manner nearly impossible with ordinary film. The magnetic images on videotape can be colored, distorted, fragmented, combined, and abstracted as freely and imaginatively as a painter applies paint to canvas. In *Voice Windows* (Fig. 10-21) Steina Vasulka, another pioneer of video art, illustrated on the screen, with fragments of memories and pieces of words, a story declaimed in an Old Norse dialect. The video images can be appreciated as abstract painting, with the exception that the screen generates rather than reflects light and with the added element of elapsed time as the image evolves.

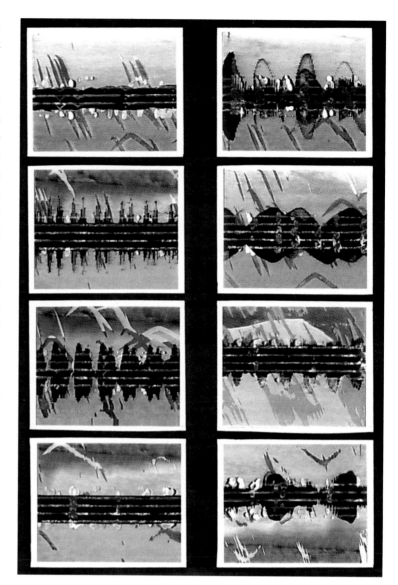

Fig 10-21 Steina Vasulka, [American], *Voice Windows*. 1986. Voice pattern of Joan LaBarbara. In Steina Vasulka, *Voice Windows,* videotape (1987).

Computer Art

The use of computers and other digitized tools for producing visual images is a new and exciting technique for "painting." The vehicle in **computer art** is not a liquid but hundreds of thousands of electronic impulses. Computerized imaging has already revolutionized and conquered graphic design and the advertising industry. Computer-aided design and drafting has also become fundamental to architectural planning. Digitized processes may soon overwhelm photography, television, and filmmaking. They may also soon overpower painting. The use of a computer both challenges and unsettles most artists because its potential is so enormous. In many ways, computer art is both too easy and too much.

Like photography when it was first invented in the nineteenth century, computer art now is still in its

Painting with a computer.

early and formative stages. Technical advances and economic feasibility are proceeding at such a rapid pace, it is hard to discuss anything about computer art that will not soon be out-of-date. Also, it is perhaps too early to tell what direction computer art will take and whether it will develop its own new style and a new aesthetic. Despite its facility to manipulate images and to do enormous amounts of work in an instant, it is hard to characterize the art created or assisted by computer.

At present, the computer can mimic the customary appearance of painting and drawing; it can also offer rapid solutions to complicated design problems. The technical wizardry and the fireworks of the computer are so fascinating, it is easy for an artist to get caught up in and be dazzled by the marvelous new technology that becomes available day after day. Still, many serious artists are not yet sure what unique contribution the computer can make to the visual arts, especially to the tradition of painting.

Aside from its capabilities in photography and video, the computer may be employed simply as a painting tool. Artists, using a keyboard, a mouse, or an electronic tablet, can paint with a computer programmed to translate their commands into lines, colors, values, textures, perspective, and almost every other feature of two-dimensional design. A pressure-sensitive pen can give the artists the feel of a brush, pen, or pencil. Images supplied by a scanner, a video camera, or a CD-ROM can be transferred to the

screen and thoroughly transformed by artists for their own purposes. The algorithms of the computer can replicate subtle light reflections or the texture of tree bark in response to a keystroke or the touch of a button. However, the lack of actual texture and painterly brushwork may provide an impediment to the emotional expressiveness of computer art. Although some computer programs can emulate brush strokes and the thickness of paint, such clever electronics are only copying what oil paint did first and does naturally. A proliferation of software can imitate traditional painting techniques, but a question remains: What new or unique results—other than speed—does the computer contribute to the art of painting?

The digitized image of computer art appears on a video screen or may be replicated on tape, floppy disk, CD-ROM, laser disk, a full-color printout, or a photographic enlargement. The computer itself can only store numbers and do enormously fast mathematical calculations that instantly offer possibilities to the artist for changed colors, repetitions, combinations, enlargements, and so forth. The computer itself supervises complex information; it does not paint. It adds nothing to the digitized image that was not preconceived by the programmer or requested by the artist-operator.

Some imaginative possibilities for computer art have already emerged. With computer technology, artists can more readily transform reality into surrealistic fantasies as Diane Fenster did in her sensitive image *Canto Two/Do Moths Prefer Artificial Light* (FIG. 10-22). By manipulating and colorizing imagery and text that she captured with video equipment, she made them float into one another as in a dream. The computer can also flawlessly manipulate photographic realism into extraordinary images by transforming one image into another—a wall into a face, for example. With the power of a computer, the synthesis of the arts of painting and music that artists have long dreamed about can easily become a reality.

Creative animation also flourishes with a computer, if only because of the speed and facility that the computer affords in contrast to the time and tedium of producing handcrafted animation for motion picture film. Abstract images, designed in a Cubist style of pictorial space, can come alive, as it were, and move through computer animation. In Maureen Nappi and Dean Winkler's *Continuum 1: Initiation* (FIG. 10-23)

Part III: The Visual Arts

FIG 10-22 DIANE FENSTER [American, 1948–], *Canto Two/Do Moths Prefer Artificial Light*. 1994. Iris ink jet print from a digital image. 30 × 40 in. (76.2 × 101.6 cm). Courtesy of the artist.

FIG 10-23 MAUREEN NAPPI [American] and DEAN WINKLER [American], *Continuum 1: Initiation*. 1989. Still image from video animation. © Maureen Nappi/Dean Winkler.

the video screen image explores the changing relationships of Cubist facets in space. However, the single video eye cannot offer the multiple, ambiguous points of view of the classic Cubist artist.

Another stimulating possibility for the computer is interaction. Every work of art has always demanded the viewer's reaction for the art experience to work, but the computer allows the viewer physically to alter the image or at least make selections from seemingly endless programmed choices. The viewer may be invited to change the features of a portrait or to replace them with the viewer's own. Exploring new avenues of perception relates this kind of computer art to Conceptual Art.

As new visual possibilities unleashed by the computer excite the imagination and as powerful hardware and software become generally available to artists, artists and art dealers are developing new ways to market computer art. These new means of communication are unsettling traditional methods of distributing art. Some computer artists are gravitating to the book form to display their work to the public. Computer-generated art might one day be rented on floppy disk, laser disk, or CD-ROM, or transmitted over fiber-optic cable and played at home. Possibilities of mass distribution are breaking down the concept of the high-priced, unique art object marketed by galleries. All in all, it is simply great fun for an artist to be alive in a time of such challenging creative change

Key Terms and Concepts

acrylics
alla prima
cartoons
collage
computer art
easel paintings
egg tempera
encaustic
fresco

gesso
glazes
gouache
ground
impasto
medium
mixed media
murals
oil

pentimento
pigments
scrumbling
support
vehicle
video art
watercolor

PAINTING

Medium	Vehicle	Characteristics
Encaustic	Beeswax	Is applied hot; allows little blending
Fresco	Water	Is applied to wet lime plaster; is permanent; has matte colors
Egg tempera	Egg yolk	Dries at once; allows no blending; is transparent; is permanent
Oil	Linseed oil	Offers flexibility of application; provides a wide range of color and value; is opaque or transparent; dries slowly
Acrylic	Water and plastic resin	Is versatile; dries as fast as water; becomes permanent
Watercolor	Water and gum arabic	Is usually washed on; is transparent
Gouache	Water and gum arabic	Is like watercolor but opaque
Collage		Consists of real or imagined shapes pasted to a support
Mixed media		Comes in two types: a combination of two or more painting media; and a combination of two or more art media
Video art		Results in TV sculpture and documentaries as well as manipulated video images that evolve through time
Computer art		Displays an image that is recorded electronically; offers rapid flexibility, the transformation of one image into another, animation, interaction; is transmitted in various formats—on-screen, tape, floppy disk, laser disk, CD-ROM, printout

PHOTOGRAPHY

Photography has established itself as an expressive and meaningful form of art. Take the example of Dorothea Lange's *Migrant Mother* (FIG. 11-1). In the mid-1930s the federal Farm Service Administration hired Lange and other photographers to document the ravages of the Great Depression on American farm and family life. In her photograph Lange captured a migrant mother and her children, stopping at a roadside camp. Two of the children turn away, seeking comfort and protection from their parent. The mother, perplexed, worried, and holding a newborn in her lap, looks out to the left as she touches the side of her mouth. The language of gestures and facial expressions communicates these feelings as surely as those of any old master painting. Lange made sure that nothing distracts the eye; on the contrary, the tight composition focuses our interest. Lange's sensitive imagination and trained hand were responsible for making the image, just as the imagination and hand of every creative artist make art. Lange's photograph is art because through its style it communicates personal feelings and personal experience.

Photography as Accessible Art

The arts of architecture, sculpture, and painting have been in existence for many thousands of years. The art of photography was invented only about a century and a half ago. From the beginning, when many people considered it an adjunct to painting and printmaking, photography had to struggle to achieve independence as a new form of art. But is photography a form of art at all, or is it merely a mechanical device for recording reality? This question has been debated since photography's invention.

While nineteenth-century artists were still claiming that art is fundamentally an imitation of reality, photography came forward as a technique that records reality on a two-dimensional surface more objectively and faster than painting or drawing. But, according to the same logic, photography seemed too easy to be an art. All one has to do is aim the camera and press the button. The photographer seemed to need no skill, no imagination, no creativity to take a photograph.

When people ask whether a photograph is art or merely reporting and where lies the creative or imaginative part of the process, they are assuming that photography is superficial by nature and that the photographer does not do very much. These questions secretly shelter the prejudice that something has to involve a lot of hard work in order to be any good. Many people assume that, like the product of any wage earner, the artist's work ought to be valued for the time and effort spent on the job.

Of course, the relative ease or difficulty of any medium is irrelevant in questions of art. The symbolic communication of the artist's experience and perceptions can happen in any medium—from a simple pen-

FIG 11-1 DOROTHEA LANGE [American, 1895–1965], *Migrant Mother, Nipomo, California. 1936.* Gelatin-silver print. Courtesy George Eastman House, Rochester, New York.

The Camera Obscura. The Bettmann Archives.

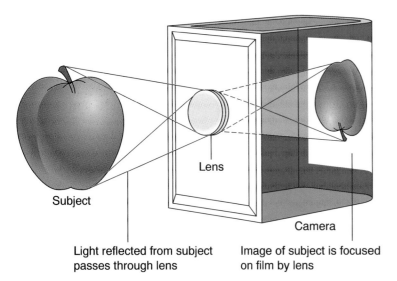

Lens

Subject

Light reflected from subject
passes through lens

Camera

Image of subject is focused
on film by lens

A simple camera diagram.

cil drawing to a complex work of architecture. If art
communicates its significance when the artist and
viewer are on the same wavelength to see, feel, and do
art, it does not matter what sort of material the artist
creates with or how much labor went into the actual
creation of the work.

Nineteenth-Century Photography

The truth is that for a long time photography did
involve a lot of work. For at least the first fifty years of
its history photographers usually made their own film
and did their own developing, right before and right
after exposing the film. If they were photographing
out-of-doors, they had to lug their own chemicals and
equipment around from place to place in order to take
and develop photographs. There was no such thing as
a casual snapshot with factory processing throughout
most of the nineteenth century. The difficulties
involved in taking and creating a photograph made
each photographer a craftsperson, at the same time
that the technical limitations modified the appearance of early photographs.

Photography was invented by several people at the
same time in different places. In January 1839, the
French painter Louis Daguerre announced his photographic process to the French public in Paris. He gave
credit to Joseph Niepce for a major part of his discovery. In England, when W. H. Fox Talbot heard of
Daguerre's announcement, he contacted the Royal
Society in London to discuss his own experiments.
The public in London and Paris eagerly anticipated
demonstrations of the new techniques. Its enthusiasm
indicates that photography was an invention whose
time had come. A middle-class society—founded on
hard facts and mass production—had risen to economic
and political power. It wanted to see a no-nonsense,
accurate reproduction of reality. Photography suited
its taste perfectly.

Neither Daguerre nor Niepce nor Fox Talbot
invented the camera. For centuries it had been known
that light coming through a small hole in a dark room
or a dark box would project an upside-down image of
the outside world on the wall of the box opposite the
hole. The term camera derives from the Italian words
for a dark room, *camera obscura.* Artists had often
used a portable camera obscura, which projected the
image onto a ground glass plate on the top of the box,

Part III: The Visual Arts

Fig 11-2 Louis Daguerre [French, 1789–1851], *Parisian Boulevard.* C. 1838. Bayerische Nationalmuseum, Munich.

to trace the essential lines of an image that they were copying from nature. The camera, in short, was from the start an aid in painting and drawing.

It had also been known for some time that certain chemicals, especially silver salts, react to light and that they can record contrasts of light and dark in a camera obscura. The problem that faced Daguerre and the other inventors of photography was how to stop the chemical reaction on the treated surface. They some-how had to remove the unaffected chemical. Otherwise, exposing a photograph again to light in order to look at it would ruin it.

Daguerre called his invention the **daguerreotype.** It produced a finely detailed image on a metallic sur-face. Since no negatives were involved in the process, each picture was a unique positive. Daguerre original-ly needed twenty to thirty minutes for each exposure. If anything moved during that time the image was blurred. In one of Daguerre's earliest photographs, *Parisian Boulevard* (Fig. 11-2), a great variety of tex-ture and detail was recorded. But only one man having his shoes shined is visible on the city street because he was standing still. Nevertheless, the public was amazed at how much fine detail the camera could reproduce. It was possible to see every paving stone in the side-walk or the texture of every brick in a building. Photography could also record a seemingly infinite range of values—more than any artist ever attempted.

FIG 11-3 [American], *Frederick Douglass.*
1856. Daguerreotype by unidentified
photographer. National Portrait Gallery,
Smithsonian Institution, Washington, D.C.

*A photographer's studio, as seen in an
unidentified movie, C. 1915. The Granger
Collection.*

Some artists declared, prematurely, that painting was
dead. They were soon disillusioned when they came to
realize that the lengthy exposure times meant that the
camera could not record action. Nor could it record
color.

With the use of new chemicals and improved equipment and techniques, the exposure time was soon
shortened to about a half minute. Since it is possible to
hold still that long, photographic portraits finally could
be made. Many people wanted their picture taken, and
photography soon became big business. All over the
world photography studios sprang up to take pictures of
people. Eventually, photography supplanted the traditional artistic activity of portrait painting because the
middle class wanted inexpensive pictures of themselves, just as the aristocracy had obtained expensive
ones for centuries. The United States adopted the
daguerreotype and led the world in its production.

Because the subjects had to collect themselves and
take up sedate poses and sit as though mesmerized
through the long exposure, early photo portraits have
a distinctive, haunting quality about them. At the
time that Frederick Douglass's portrait was taken by
an unknown photographer in 1856 (FIG. 11-3), he
was speaking and writing eloquently against slavery.
To sit for an exposure of long duration, Douglass had
to hold himself rigid, relax his mouth, and remove
any momentary expression from his face. Most of all,
without blinking, he had to stare intently. The technical necessities of the daguerreotype gave him an
expression of serious determination. Furthermore,
nothing in the plain background of this daguerreotype
distracts from the bare revelation of his personality.
An early daguerreotype could not capture a fleeting
instant of passing time, but it could create a striking
presence.

Photographers often made something positive out
of the difficulties of taking portraits. For example, a little later, in the 1860s, Julia Margaret Cameron deliberately used a simple camera that required long exposures and also put the edges out of focus, to make
outstanding portraits of famous writers and artists of
the day. Her portrait of the historian and philosopher
Thomas Carlyle (FIG. 11-4) captures the spirit of the
great Victorian writer perfectly.

Parallel with Daguerre in France, Fox Talbot in
England invented the Talbotype, or **calotype,** process.
The calotype made a negative from which copies

266   Part III: The Visual Arts

Fig 11-4 Julia Margaret Cameron [British, 1815–1879], *Thomas Carlyle.* 1867. Albumen print. George Eastman House, Rochester, New York.

Julia Margaret Cameron entertained many famous poets and writers of her era at her home, where she often cajoled them into sitting for her. Cameron concentrated on the inner spirit of the person and forced her guests to pose until she was satisfied with the result. With regard to "taking the great Carlyle," Cameron wrote, "When I have had such men before my camera my whole soul has endeavored to do its duty towards them in recording faithfully the greatness of the inner as well as the features of the outer man."[1] She experimented with different means to get the effect of simplicity and concentration. She deliberately used poorly made lenses or had lenses specially built so that the image would lack definition and appear softly focused. Her representation of Carlyle fits the leonine, ponderous writer—the image of the man we get from reading his work.

could be printed. The future of photography belonged to a process that could make reproductions from itself. However, Talbot's negatives were made on paper and, because of their texture, fine detail was lacking.

In 1851 an English sculptor, Frederick Scott Archer, invented the **collodion** process. He coated a glass plate with a film of chemicals and placed it in the camera while the plate was still wet. In other words, the plate had to be prepared immediately before taking a picture and had to be developed immediately after the exposure. Nevertheless, because the collodion process was faster, it soon overwhelmed the daguerreotype and calotype.

Despite all the difficulties connected with early photography, photographers traveled all over the world and brought back to the eager public detailed images of inaccessible places like the Holy Land or the Far West. Carleton E. Watkins photographed

FIG 11-5 CARLETON E. WATKINS [American, 1829–1916], *Cathedral Rock, Twenty-Six Hundred Feet, Yosemite, No. 21*. 1866. Albumen print. Metropolitan Museum of Art, New York. The Elisha Whittelsey Fund, 1922.

Cathedral Rock, Twenty-Six Hundred Feet, Yosemite, No. 21 (FIG. 11-5) while on an expedition to survey and document Yosemite. He also arranged to sell prints like this to the public. His photographs revealed the vastness and grandeur of the West to an America eager for expansion. Watkin's spirit also appreciated the cataclysmic forces that tilted and thrust the stratified rock over two thousand feet in the air above the valley floor. He used his camera to reveal to the Bible-reading public the hand of God that controls the awesome forces of nature.

Adventuresome traveling photographers like Watkins had to carry all their equipment—cameras, lenses, glass plates, chemicals, developing tents—across mountains and deserts and onto battlefields.

Artists had often made sketches of faraway places and strange peoples, but their work lacked the credibility of photography. Current events were for the first time realistically documented by the photographers, especially Mathew Brady and Timothy H. O'Sullivan. Under the supervision of Brady, O'Sullivan and over a dozen other men photographed the Civil War from start to finish. Despite the long exposure time, they gave a detailed report of all aspects of the war, including the horrible carnage of the battlefield. Published in *Gardner's Photographic Sketchbook of the War*, these photographs brought the reality of war into ordinary homes. In *A Harvest of Death, Gettysburg, Pennsylvania* (FIG. 11-6) twisted, bloated men are scattered like refuse in the trampled grass as far as the camera could see. Death is the crop of this field. A loss of focus in the distance where a horse and rider stand and watch creates a mood of sorrow and desolation.

After the advent of photography, the public's image of war would never be the same—unless governments chose to censor photographs. Instead of heroic ideal-

FIG 11-6 TIMOTHY H. O'SULLIVAN [American, c. 1840–1882], *A Harvest of Death, Gettysburg, Pennsylvania.* July 1863. Albumen print. Originally printed by Alexander Gardner. New York Public Library, Rare Books and Manuscripts Division. Astor, Lenox, and Tilden Foundations.

FIG 11-7 EADWEARD MUYBRIDGE [American, 1830–1904], *Horse Galloping.* 1884–1887. Collotype print. George Eastman House, Rochester, New York.

Leland Stanford asked Eadweard Muybridge to photograph a horse in order to demonstrate that the horse lifted all four hooves at one point in her gait. Behind the racecourse Muybridge set a backdrop painted with twenty-seven-inch-wide boxes numbered 1 through 18. The moving horse electronically tripped the shutters of twelve cameras operating at a speed of one-thousandth of a second. The sensational pictures revealed facts that the human eye had never observed. The series of photos also revealed the fascinating, graceful fluidity present in the single stride of a galloping horse. In 1883 Muybridge went to the University of Pennsylvania in Philadelphia, where he continued to study animal and human motion in photographs.

ism and athletic adventure, the photographs of Brady's team showed grim reality. The starkness of their images compelled viewers to imagine that they were there at that time. This realization of actuality added a poignancy that no other kind of image could have produced.

In about 1880 dry plates became available. Only then were most photographic materials mass pro-

duced. By then the technology of photography had advanced to the point that exposures could be made in short fractions of a second. For the first time photography could stop action; for the first time cameras could be held in one's hand. Instant photography made under the supervision of Eadweard Muybridge, like *The Horse in Motion* (FIG. 11-7), treated the world to images of humans and animals posed in movements

The first Kodak camera, George Eastman's simple, fixed-focus camera for amateur use, as seen in American magazine advertisements, 1889. The Granger Collection.

FIG 11-8   EDWARD STEICHEN [American, 1879–1973], *Woods Interior.* 1898. Platinum print, 7 7/16 × 6 3/8 in. (18.9 × 16.2 cm). Metropolitan Museum of Art, New York. Alfred Stieglitz Collection, 1933 (33.43.8).

that had never truly been seen before. Also in the 1880s George Eastman first applied photosensitive chemicals to a flexible material that could be wound on a spool. Cameras could thus be loaded with a roll of film and the film processed in factories. Eastman marketed his first Kodak camera in 1888. Anyone and everyone was encouraged to take photographs with the company's slogan, "You press the button, we do the rest."

Photography as Art

As photography became widespread and accessible, some photographers believed they had to raise it to a higher level to make it art. Some tried to imitate the appearance of paintings by arranging artificial compositions of figures that resembled the popular genre paintings of the day. Others deliberately put the film out of focus in order to imitate the brushwork of impressionist paintings, as did Edward Steichen in *Woods Interior* (FIG. 11-8). One of the main stumbling blocks in the nineteenth century to the acceptance of photography as an art was the criticism that since it was so obviously a matter-of-fact and realistic medium, it could not convey a spiritual dimension, assumed to be a necessary component of all great art. To express the spiritual in *Woods Interior*, Steichen borrowed pictorial devices from painting. His dark, softly focused, misty image of woods, low in value contrasts, suggests something mysterious. The vague forms of nature intimate that a presence lies beyond ordinary reality and that the spiritual suffuses this dreamy woodland.

Painters, in turn, adopted some of the techniques of photography. Artists often sketched from photographs when their live model was unavailable. Realist painters in the Victorian period like James Tissot attempted to imitate photography's minute detail and its range of values in their work. Tissot also used photography to pose the figures of his composition *Waiting for the Ferry* (see FIGS. 11-9 and 11-10). The French Impressionist painter Degas, who was an amateur photographer, imitated in his art the tendency of photos to crop reality and to suspend casual action in a moment of time (see *The Dancers*, FIG. 8-16).

In the 1960s Pop Artists incorporated photos into their work and made silk screen stencils from photo

FIG 11-9   JAMES TISSOT [French, 1836–1902], *Waiting for the Ferry*. C. 1878. Christie's, London. Bridgeman/Art Resource, New York.

emulsions. In the 1970s Chuck Close (see *Big Self-Portrait*, FIG. 7-10) and the Photo-realist painters began once again to imitate the tonal contrast and impersonality of photographs. Collage artists like Romare Bearden (see *Black Manhattan*, FIG. 6-1) have continually used photographs as part of their work. The connection between painting and photography has always been a two-way street.

Challenged by photography, modern painters have also reacted against it. Because photography reproduces reality so well, most modern artists no longer cultivate the techniques of reproductive realism. Instead, many have exploited the expressive potential of color and brushwork—realms of art once foreign to photography—and have emphasized nonrealistic elements in painting. The challenge of photography helps explain, in part, the revolutionary appearance of the modern style.

These attempts to compete with painting, indeed the continual dialogue between photography and painting, have caused twentieth-century photographers for the most part to stress the differences between them. They believed that the essence of photography as an art lies in the differences, not in the similarities. Like many artists of their day, early-twentieth-century photographers sought what was essential to their medium as the basis of their art. They sought a pure photography.

FIG 11-10   Photograph. Kathleen Newton and James Tissot with her niece Lilian Hervey and her son Cecil George. With kind permission of Lady Abdy/Christopher Wood.

Fig 11-11 Alfred Stieglitz [American, 1864–1946], *A Portrait (1)*. 1918. Palladio print, 8 × 10 in. (20.3 × 25.4 cm). Collection of the J. Paul Getty Museum, Malibu, California.

More than anyone else, Alfred Stieglitz championed the art of pure photography in America in the early decades of the twentieth century. He led the Photo Secession, an organization of photographers who were committed to the highest standards of art. From 1903 to 1917 he published the journal Camera Work, in which the best photographs of the time were reproduced in high-quality prints. He ran the gallery 291 in New York at 291 Fifth Avenue, where not only new photographers but also Picasso, Matisse, and other modern painters were first introduced to the American public. He also championed the cause of photography with the example of his own strong work. Stieglitz believed that to make a portrait of a person, the artist should detail the individual throughout life by showing various aspects of the individual in a series of photos. A Portrait (1) is one of the first of five hundred photographs Stieglitz took of Georgia O'Keeffe.

In 1921 when Alfred Stieglitz showed *A Portrait (1)* (FIG. 11-11) of the painter Georgia O'Keeffe, who eventually became his wife, the critics were stunned by its artistic merits. As a photographer, Stieglitz strove to make only "perfect" negatives. He felt that the photographers who physically manipulated the photo in order to imitate art produced something fake. Pure photography for Stieglitz meant seeing exactly what he wanted through the viewfinder of the camera. In the darkroom, with few exceptions, he made only contact prints, in which the light-sensitive paper for the print comes in direct contact with the negative with the result that the print is the same size as the negative. Only the contact print, which allows little manipulation, comes close to preserving the range of values of the negative.

Stieglitz's approach has been called **straight photography.** Straight photographers frown upon cropping, or cutting down, the image in order to improve the composition, because the photograph is supposed to represent exactly what the photographer saw through the camera lens. The photographer is supposed to get it right the first time. Straight photographers prefer black-and-white photos that document reality and look like photographs, not paintings.

Photographic Realism

Searching for the essence of their medium, many serious photographers have claimed that its chief characteristic is **realism**—the accurate reproduction of reality. The ability of photographic film to record an incredible amount of detail and an extraordinary range of values at a precise moment in time makes it the perfect instrument for copying reality. Indeed, we enjoy most photographs because they represent an authentic record of the way things were at an exact time. From the daguerreotypes of the battlefields of the Civil War to the news photos of the latest disaster around the globe, we devour photographic images as an unfailing and fascinating source of information. Sam Shere's photograph engraved the explosion of the

Hindenburg zeppelin in 1937 in the popular imagination and made the disaster one of the most remembered catastrophes of the century (see FIG. 11-12). Until photography, no other medium was able to put us so convincingly and so immediately in the shoes of the observer.

Photographs have preserved great events in history as well as the ordinary affairs of daily life. Because they perform these narrative functions so well, photography has preempted from painting the iconographic categories of history painting and of genre in modern times. As an example of genre, Carrie Mae Weems's photograph *Untitled (Man Smoking)* (p. 279), of ordinary people doing ordinary things, is pregnant with possible interpretations about modern life. As for history painting, Margaret Bourke-White's April 1945 photo of the survivors of the death camp at Buchenwald (FIG. 11-13) captures some of the tragedy of that horrible event in human history through the apprehensive expressions of the gaunt prisoners spread out behind the fence. Crowding the fence in anticipation, yet still afraid, they look away from the camera.

Publishing their work in a mass medium like *Life Magazine*, photojournalists have the potential to affect

FIG 11-12 SAM SHERE [American, 1905–], *Explosion of the Hindenburg, Lakehurst, New Jersey.* May 6, 1937. The Bettmann Archive.

FIG 11-13 MARGARET BOURKE-WHITE [American, 1906–1971], *Buchenwald, Germany, April, 1945.* Life Magazine. © Time Warner, Inc.

Margaret Bourke-White epitomized the tireless and aggressive photojournalist who, often at great risk, covers the dramatic events of the times. She was one of the first four photographers on the staff of Life Magazine *when it was founded in 1936. For* Fortune *and* Life *she was a pioneer in the development of the photographic essay. She photographed the Dust Bowl of the 1930s and the effects of the Depression on the rural South. She photographed World War II from the front lines in Italy and was with the American army when it entered the prison camp at Buchenwald. After the war, she covered Ghandi in India and the war in Korea. Without a doubt, she was the most famous photojournalist of her day.*

the conscience of a nation, since their work may convey the moral overtones that the categories of genre and history painting once possessed. Numerous photographs have stirred patriotism or instilled concern for the poor or persuaded the public for or against some cause. In the 1880s Jacob Riis, himself an immigrant to America, set out to document the squalid conditions of poor people in New York City in penetrating photos, many of which were taken with the new technique of flash powder. Following a police search of a tenement, Riis photographed a room he labeled *Five Cents a Spot* (FIG. 11-14). Twelve men and women, each of whom had paid a slum lord five cents, slept in the single room—some on the floor and some in bunks in a small alcove. He captured the overcrowding and squalor even before most of the residents stirred from their sleep. Published in books like his *How the Other Half Lives* (1890) or illustrating his lectures as lantern slides, Riis's crusading photographs aroused public sentiment and did achieve housing reforms.

Since the public expected that the camera always told the truth, any manipulation of the photographic image seemed downright immoral to many of the twentieth century's leading photographers. Seeking to preserve the authenticity they consider to be the essence of their art, some photographers have rigidly required the use of only basic equipment to take photographs and have forbidden any modifications of the photo during the developing of the image in the darkroom. Ansel Adams, who made the nature of the American West his subject (see, for example, *Mount Williamson—Clearing Storm*, FIG. 11-15), was a long-time believer in Alfred Stieglitz's straight photography.

Challenges to Realism

Yet photographs have always been open to the skilled control, or **manipulation,** of photographic techniques and to the arranging, or **fabrication,** of objects in front of the camera. Timothy O'Sullivan may have rearranged the bodies on the Gettysburg battlefield to get a better composition for *A Harvest of Death* (FIG. 11-6). Dorothea Lange may have given directions to the members of the migrant family for *Migrant Mother* (FIG. 11-1). Indeed, the truth of photography has always been relative, since any two photographers could produce quite different images of the same reality.

FIG 11-15 ANSEL ADAMS [American, 1902–1984], *Mount Williamson—Clearing Storm.* 1944. © 1994 by the Trustees of the Ansel Adams Publishing Rights Trust. All rights reserved.

Although Ansel Adams believed in straight photography as opposed to any artificial manipulation of the image, his work did not lack calculation. Adams in fact carefully controlled the exposure and developing of his negative to achieve the subjective effect he wanted. He strove for a great range of gray as well as dramatic light-and-dark contrasts. He adjusted his camera for a sharply focused image from the foremost boulder to the distant clouds. Confronting Mount Williamson, he waited until the sun broke through and streamed down parallel to the diagonal of the mountains. He held the camera so that the mountains in the distance were arranged symmetrically. He chose a low vantage point amid the field of boulders when the angle of light came from somewhat behind them so that their dark bulk would loom before the viewer. Adams produced straight photography with great sophistication.

FIG 11-16 SANDY SKOGLAND [American, 1946–], *Radioactive Cats.* 1980. Cibachrome, 30 × 40 in. (76.2 × 101.6 cm). New York, collection of the artist.

In the late twentieth century more and more photographers challenged the aesthetic of straight photography. Cindy Sherman (see *Untitled*, FIG. 4-3), Sandy Skoglund (see *Radioactive Cats*, FIG. 11-16), and Weems (see *Untitled (Man Smoking)*, p. 279), have made their reputation with photographs of thoroughly staged subjects. Furthermore, retouching and embellishing photographs has always been quite common. Today, through **digital imaging** and the technology of the computer, photographers are capable of rearranging, retouching, distorting, and fabricating images that can pose as flawless reality. Through a computer program, Nancy Burson is capable of altering photographs to create eerie composite images like her wide-eyed "alien" (FIG. 11-17), with its narrow chin and bulbous skull. These examples imply that the realism of photography is only a realism of appearance.

Truly nonobjective photography is another possibility that challenges the notion of photographic realism. To create a kind of abstract photography, many photographers have excerpted and enlarged details of everyday reality—as Georgia O'Keeffe did for decades

FIG 11-17 NANCY BURSON [American, 1948–]. *Untitled*. (89-22), 1989. 24 × 20 inch Polaroid Polacolor ER land print film, 24 × 20 in. © Nancy Burson, 1989. Courtesy of the Jayne H. Baum Gallery, New York.

Nancy Burson has been experimenting with computer-manipulated photography since the mid 1970s. In her untitled work Burson scanned separate images into the computer and seamlessly blended selected parts of them together to create a new being. She exhibits her work as large-scale portraits, taken with a giant Polaroid camera from the video monitor.

The freakish and yet fascinating photograph questions human identity as well as the realism of the photographic medium. The hairless individual that emerges from the black background of her photograph may be either male or female. Burson's mutations offer a provocative glimpse into the future of human evolution. Ironically, she used the latest technology to explore the dark side of the science of genetic engineering.

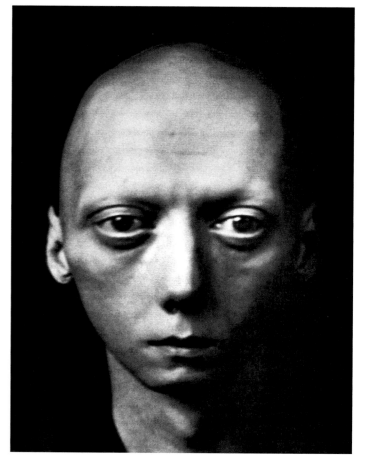

her paintings—so that the viewer appreciates more explicitly the abstract design or pattern of forms latent within the reality. Minor White's photograph *Ritual Branch* (FIG. 11-18) appears at first to be a nonobjective design, but closer inspection reveals that the photographer has achieved this metamorphosis of reality by photographing a dark object through frost on a windowpane. Recall that Alvin Langdon Coburn emphasized the abstract design of a city park in *The Octopus* (FIG. 7-1) by photographing it from an unusual angle.

Creative Possibilities

Even when photography is restricted to the copying of reality, photographers may pursue countless creative possibilities and artistic choices. Before they ever press the button, photographers have to make selections amid a wide range of **technical variables.** For example, different kinds of film are available—high or low light sensitivity, high- or low-contrast, black-and-white or color. **Color photography** is a choice not possible in the early days of photography. Good color in photography is still technically more difficult than black-and-white and photographic color is also not very permanent. Furthermore, art photographers were for a long time prejudiced against color because of its commercial exploitation in garish advertising. They concentrated instead on the subtlety and richness of values in black-and-white photography. Now some contempo-

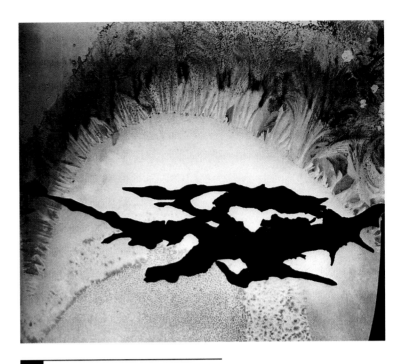

FIG 11-18   MINOR WHITE [American, 1908–1976], *Ritual Branch.* 1958. George Eastman House, Rochester, New York.

rary photographers are eager to display their sensitivity to color in their work, as Joel Meyerowitz did in *Longnook Beach* (FIG. 11-19). Whether the color in a photograph appears to imitate nature—as it does in Meyerowitz's work—or not, the photographer needs an awareness of color theory and a feeling for color relationships as does any other artist.

FIG 11-19   JOEL MEYEROWITZ [American, 1938–], *Longnook Beach.* 1983. Color photograph. Courtesy of the artist.

Text continues on page 280

Chapter 11: Photography

277

Carrie Mae Weems (1953–)

As a child I loved the aroma of coffee. Smelling it drove me nuts cause it reminded me of cocoa, of chocolate, candy. Anyway, my parents rarely drunk coffee. But when they did, I'd stand at the kitchen table begging like a salivating dog for a lick. Momma and daddy would be sitting up, elbows on table, talking, sipping like white folks on t.v., shooing me away with, "Ya don't need no coffee, coffee'll make ya black."

CARRIE MAE WEEMS [American, 1953–], *Untitled*. 1988. Gelatin-silver print, 15 1/2 × 15 1/2 in. (39.4 × 39.4 cm). P.P.O.W. Gallery, New York.

ᴄARRIE MAE WEEMS discovered photography at age twenty-one when her photographer-boyfriend gave her a camera for her birthday. She also saw at that time a copy of the *Black Photographers Annual*, which reproduced photographs of Blacks by Blacks. The images amazed her because for the first time photographs resembled the world of her own experience.

They made her realize the possibility of a professional career as a photographer who focused on Black America. To achieve her goal to document African-American life in the United States, Weems majored not only in art and photography in college and graduate school, but also in folklore, the study of a people's customs, sayings, and myths that are passed on from generation to generation. Weems has a master's degree in folklore from the University of California at Berkeley.

In the 1980s she exhibited her work in not-for-profit galleries around the United States and supported herself with teaching jobs at universities on the West and East Coasts. In the 1990s her career blossomed with considerable media attention, the sponsorship of the P.P.O.W. Gallery in New York City, and a survey of her work that toured the nation.

She clearly belongs to a new generation of photographers who have rejected the aesthetic of straight photography.

Even though her photographs seem documentary in style, Weems has often arranged the objects of her compositions, posed her subjects, and added written and voice-recorded commentary to the photos. Her photographs mounted in exhibitions or printed in book form sometimes appear as a sequence in a narrative. The printed texts and the tape-recorded comments do not exactly explain the photographic images but add another, usually ironic dimension or interpretation to them.

Untitled, the unpretentious and bland still life of a coffeepot and a cup of coffee on a kitchen counter, has printed at the top of it six lines of a childhood recollection aroused by the sight and the smell of coffee. The parents' humor-ous dismissal of the bothersome child in the anecdote transforms the simple coffeepot into an evocative symbol about a Black family's communicating the idea of race to their child. No one, not even Weems as a young girl, believed that drinking coffee would change skin color, but the quip, driving home an awareness of Blackness, communicated to the child an attribute about her race. The text expands the commonplace image, contradicts the ordinary White viewer's response, and forces the viewer to return to the image in a more meaningful way. Curiously, the combination of text and image repeats the way we experience many photographs in newspapers, magazines, and textbooks.

The large square photograph *Untitled*

She'd been pickin em up and layin em down, moving to the next town for a while, needing a rest, some moss under her feet, plus a solid man who enjoyed a good fight with a brave woman. She needed a man who didn't mind her bodacious manner, varied talents, hard laughter, multiple opinions, and her hopes were getting slender.

He had great big eyes like diamonds and his teeth shined just like gold, same reason a lot of women didn't want him, but he satisfied their souls. He needed a woman who didn't mind stepping down from the shade of the veranda, a woman capable of taking up the shaft of a plough and throwing down with him side by side.

They met in the glistening twinkling crystal light of August/September sky. They were both educated, corn-fed-healthy-Mississippi-stock folk. Both loved fried fish, greens, blues, jazz and Carmen Jones. He was an unhardened man of the world. She'd been around the block more than once herself, wasn't a tough cookie, but a full grown woman for sure.

Looking her up, down, sideways he said, "So tell me baby, what do you know about this great big world of ours?" Smiling she said, "Not a damn thang sugar. I don't mind telling you my life's not been sheltered from the cold and I've not always seen the forest or smelled the coffee, played momma to more men than I care to rememeber. Consequently I've made several wrong turns, but with conviction I can tell you I'm nobody's fool. So a better question might be: what can you teach me?"

He wasn't sure, confessing he didn't have a handle on this thing called life either. But he was definitely in a mood for love. Together they were falling for that ole black magic. In that moment it seemed a match made in heaven. They walked, not hand in hand, but rather side by side in the twinkle of August/September sky, looking sidelong at one another, thanking their lucky stars with fingers crossed.

CARRIE MAE WEEMS [American, 1953–], *Untitled (Man Smoking)*. 1988. 27 1/4 × 27 1/4 in. (69.2 × 69.2 cm). P.P.O.W. Gallery, New York.

(Man Smoking) belongs to a series of photographic narratives, the *Kitchen Table Series*, that explores contemporary male-female and mother-daughter relationships. The same wooden table and the same overhead light, appearing in all the photographs, constitute the stage on which the photographer enacts her dramas. Although Weems herself plays the leading role in each of the photographs, the images are not self-portraits, autobiographies, or even personal fantasies. They concern the ambiguity of the decisions that women make in everyday relationships.

Smoking cigarettes and drinking Scotch, the couple in *Man Smoking* are playing cards. It is not known who has to make the next move. Questioning how to play their hand, they eye each other, and the game easily becomes a metaphor for the physical attraction between them. The portrait of Malcolm X on the wall adds a reference to a world outside their game to which the two seem completely oblivious. Weems likes to leave her work open to a variety of opinions and interpretations. The text, which Weems wrote after taking the photograph, was hung alongside the series of photographs in the original exhibition and may or may not apply to that picture.

In her work, Weems usually stays somewhat aloof, like an observant researcher who records the facts. In one series of photographs called *Ain't Jokin* she matter-of-factly visualized racist humor and without comment let the viewer feel the embarrassment of slurs and stereotypes. From her early photographs of her family to her photo-essay of the African-American folk culture of the Sea Islands of South Carolina and Georgia, Weems captures the unique way that African-Americans live in North America. She speaks to Blacks themselves about the drama and the rich humanity of their own culture. She speaks to all races about the nature of the human condition.

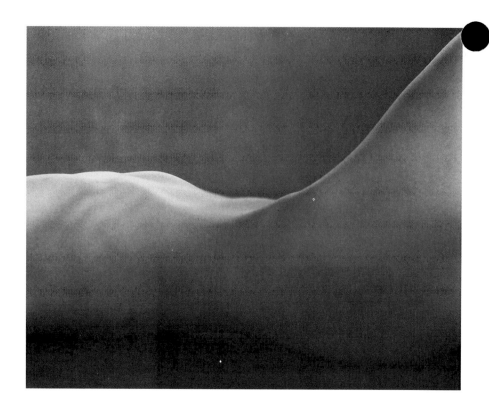

Other technical variables include the many different kinds of cameras on the market, some of which take very different kinds of pictures. The amount of light entering a camera can be controlled by the size of the aperture (f-stop) or the length of time the aperture is open (shutter speed). The size of the aperture affects how much of the subject will be in focus at a given distance from the camera (depth of field). On many cameras the standard lens can be removed and replaced with a wide-angle or telephoto lenses. The same composition looks quite different when taken through one lens or another. Filters can be placed on the lens to change the nature of the light entering the camera and to change the contrasts between light and dark. Flash attachments and artificial lights allow us to see things in new ways or to see things that are not ordinarily visible. All these technical variables influence the appearance of the image that the camera is copying.

Inexpensive cameras offer few of these adjustments. Nevertheless, someone at the factory had to determine what film, what lens, what shutter speed, what aperture the camera was going to have. The manufacturer made most or all of the choices for the photographer. Today many expensive cameras possess a great range of technical possibilities, but operate fully automatically whenever the photographer presses the button because a computer chip has been programmed to make all the choices. The photographer in effect agrees to all these preprogrammed choices whenever she or he decides to use one of these cameras. An automatic camera does not deny creativity, but it does limit the possibilities.

The character of the image can also be changed in the darkroom with variations in the techniques of developing and printing. Photographs are printed on different papers with different finishes. Areas can be highlighted or darkened. The composition can be changed into a new design by cutting off part of the original photograph, or separate photographs can be combined or superimposed to make a new image. The variables of developing and printing explain why original prints made by the photographer-artist are collector's items worth thousands of dollars whereas mass-produced prints of the same image are not. Original photographic prints resemble an original impression from an edition of etchings.

Photography has also initiated the transformation into a digitized format that can be reproduced and manipulated through computer technology, as was

Nancy Burson's photograph in FIG. 11-17. The changes Burson made on the computer from the "reality" of the original image are impossible to detect. A camera can now produce not a chemically altered negative and paper print but a picture encoded in millions of tiny pits on a laser disk that can be viewed on a television monitor. In the twenty-first century, photography, computers, video, and other advanced technology will have merged into even more exciting image-making possibilities for the photographer-artist.

Even with the cheapest camera in hand, the photographer still has to make a number of creative **personal choices.** These choices are probably more important to the art of photography than sophisticated technology; some of the best photographs have been made with rather simple equipment. The photographer first has to select a subject—some potentially meaningful person, place, or thing. Many well-known photographers have devoted their life to the pursuit of a distinct iconography: Ansel Adams championed nature (see *Mount Williamson—Clearing Storm*, FIG. 11-15); Edward Weston, another proponent of straight photography, for many years studied the nude as abstract form (see *Nude*, FIG. 11-20); and Berenice Abbott made portraits of New York City (see *Exchange Place, New York City*, FIG. 11-21) with a large camera that recorded the rich detail of city life. These and many other photographers often create a visual essay about a certain topic, and consequently they publish their series of photographs in book form. Many photographers—like Sandy Skoglund, with *Radioactive Cats* (FIG. 11-16), and Carrie Mae Weems, with *Untitled (Man Smoking)*, have fabricated their subjects, not just for compositional reasons but to express themselves, explore psychic reality, or deliver a particular message through photography.

When something of interest comes along, the photographer has to decide on the distance from the subject: whether he or she wants a long shot or a close-up. The photographer has to decide on the angle from which the subject will be taken. The photographer has to decide how the light will affect the image and whether artificial or natural light should be used. Looking through the viewfinder, the photographer has to examine the entire frame and make sure that the lines, shapes, values, and colors are arranged in a way that reinforces the meaning of the image. Using just

FIG 11-21 BERENICE ABBOTT [American, 1898–1991], *Exchange Place, New York City*. 1934. Berenice Abbott/Commerce Graphics Ltd., Inc.

FIG 11-22 DIANE ARBUS [American, 1923–1971], *A family on their lawn one Sunday in Westchester, New York, 1968.* 1968. Gelatin-silver print, 14 3/4 × 14 3/4 in. (37.5 × 37.5 cm). The Museum of Modern Art, New York. Purchase. Photograph © 1994 The Museum of Modern Art, New York.

the camera and the material in front of it, the photographer has to compose the image with the same principles of consistency and variety and balance that every artist must employ. Photography resembles painting in its use of these principles of design more than in any other way. Whether reproducing reality or manipulating reality, an artistic photograph imposes on reality a significant formal design.

Finally, the photographer has to choose the moment to push the button and snap the picture—the instant when all the technical and personal variables come together to form an image that will mean more than just a reproduction of reality. Some photographers wait for hours in front of their subject until this **photographic moment** arrives. Alfred Stieglitz is said to have once waited three hours in a blinding snowstorm before he pressed the button. Some photographers encourage their subjects to "perform" for them whether

they are professional models or ordinary people. Other photographers constantly shoot film in the hope that one of the images will be the magic moment. Sometimes the moment is pure serendipity. Whatever the case, it takes a sensitive eye to see the moment that will make a good photograph and convey to the viewer a privileged point in time.

In general, having made dozens of technical and personal choices, the photographer makes the ordinary look extraordinary. Few photographers have made the everyday seem stranger than Diane Arbus, who specialized in forthright images of average people, such as *A family on their lawn one Sunday in Westchester, New York* (FIG. 11-22). Photographers like Arbus cause us to stop for a moment and see reality in a new way. They help us to realize the significance latent in the image as we never would have without their intervention.

Contemporary Photography

Many of those who are working in photography today have expanded the medium beyond the traditional privileged moment in time. For example, Barbara Kasten's five-foot-tall photograph *Architectural Site 10, December 22, 1986* (FIG. 11-23) at first glance has about as much reference to a specific time as a colorful Cubist painting. Manipulating camera angle, mirrors, and colored lights, she transformed a rooftop into something extraordinary and virtually outside of time.

Kasten and many other contemporary photographers have rebelled against the fundamental principle of straight photography, prevalent until the 1970s, which said that photography records reality by celebrating a specific time and place. Many photo-artists of the 1980s and 1990s, abandoning the documentary style of straight photography, contend that photographs are "made," not taken. In their own work they fabricate the subject and they manipulate the photographic process. Many very inventive photographs have approached the appearance of painting not only in their freedom of expression but also in their large size. Many in this new generation who "make" photographs dislike being called photographers. They consider themselves primarily artists.

One way or the other, the imposition of form on the flux of visual reality through photography initiates symbolic communication. Photography becomes art when it communicates an awareness of feelings, experience, and personality. The photographer, in creating the image, injects a subjective awareness absent from raw reality. The signs and symbols that convey this subjective message—lines, shapes, values, and colors—are similar to those of the other two-dimensional media. But they most often succeed to the extent that they are dedicated to the special qualities of photography like presence and immediacy.

FIG 11-23 BARBARA KASTEN [American, 1936–], *Architectural Site 10, December 22, 1986*. 1986. Cibachrome print, 60 × 47 in. (152.4 × 119.4 cm). Smithsonian Institution, National Museum of American Art, Washington, D.C. Art Resource, New York.

PHOTOGRAPHY

Nineteenth-century photography	In the nineteenth-century, photography required considerable personal effort. Photography often imitated painting, and painting was influenced by photography.
Straight photography	Straight photography holds that the photographic print should reproduce what the photographer saw through the camera lens when the picture was taken; it claims to document reality.
Fabrication and manipulation	Through fabrication the photographer deliberately constructs or assembles the subject instead of merely documenting existing reality. Through manipulation of photographic techniques and materials, the photographer changes the image from a straight-forward reproduction of reality.
Technical variables	The technical variables of photography include film, camera, lenses, filters, aperture, shutter speed, lights, developing, printing, and the computer.
Personal choices	The personal choices in photography include subject, distance, angle, light, and composition.
Photographic realism	Photography portrays an apparent immediacy whether it is straight or manipulated.
The photographic moment	The photographic moment is the instant when all variables come together.
Photography as art	Photography communicates personal experience through its style, as does any other art.

Key Terms and Concepts

calotype	digital imaging	realism
camera obscura	fabrication	straight photography
collodion	manipulation	technical variables
color photography	personal choices	
daguerreotype	photographic moment	

12 FILM

The Modern Medium

Nothing like film existed before the twentieth century. No other art form in the twentieth century—neither painting nor sculpture nor architecture—commands such attention. None has been so popular. No other art expresses so directly the general culture of a nation, whether in the 1960s, when the film *Easy Rider* appeared (see FIG. 12-1), or in the 1990s. No other art has exerted such a widespread and pervasive

FIG 12-1 DENNIS HOPPER [American, 1936–], Scene from *Easy Rider*. 1969. Photo courtesy Archive Photos.

impact on the century's imagination. Distributed in movie theaters or over media like television, film is everywhere.

Motion picture film, and more recently videotape, serves many functions such as documentation, scien-

FIG 12-2 THOMAS EDISON [American, 1847–1931], *Fred Ott's Sneeze*. 1891. Washington, D.C., Library of Congress.

often driven by market pressures, film seems tainted. In other words, it has been too successful to be art.

Because of film's pervasiveness and success in modern culture, we sometimes experience difficulty in analyzing it. Most of us have been watching film since earliest childhood, and we have grown quite used to it. As with our native language, we have absorbed the vocabulary and grammar of film and use them instinctively. Nevertheless, as with any language, by expanding our vocabulary, we might actually see more. And by making ourselves conscious of the rules of film grammar, we might comprehend more of what we see. Learning the language of film ought to help us better experience and appreciate the artistry of film.

The Nature of Film

Motion pictures became possible at the end of the nineteenth century when the exposure time for photographs became fast enough to stop action and when a flexible film was developed by George Eastman so that it could roll through the machinery of a camera and a projector. The inventors of motion pictures already knew that still images, depicting the successive stages of an action, when rapidly flicked before the eye would produce the illusion of motion. Because of the optical phenomenon known as the persistence of vision, the eye does not see hundreds of discrete still photographs, but the brain retains each image for a fraction of a second so that the eye blurs the succession of still images into continuous movement.

Eadweard Muybridge had mounted his photos of a moving horse (FIG. 11-7) in a revolving wheel of a stroboscope to give the appearance of movement. In 1891 Thomas Edison patented a machine he called a kinetoscope, in which an individual looking through a peephole could view an action photographed by a single camera on a continuous strip of film. Within months of examining Edison's kinetoscope, brothers Auguste and Louis Lumière in France invented a motion picture projector and opened the first movie theater in Paris in December 1895.

The very first motion pictures that demonstrated the new process of course showed things that moved—a couple kissing; a train coming into a station; a man sneezing as in *Fred Ott's Sneeze* (FIG. 12-2), the earliest

tific study, training and general education, reporting of news events, advertising, travelogues, animation, and entertainments of all sorts including sports and musical performances. A filmmaker may transform this kind of film into an art medium. However, the art of filmmaking reveals itself most fully in feature films—narratives that last for at least an hour and a half. They are none other than the movies that have been produced for decades as mass entertainment.

Film's ability to lift its viewers out of humdrum reality and communicate to them another person's experience is tremendous. Yet some people are reluctant to include film among the visual arts because the complexity of making films does not quite fit the traditional categories of art. Moreover, film seems to be too popular, too entertaining, and too democratic. Because it is a multibillion-dollar industry and is most

FIG 12-3 D. W. GRIFFITH [American, 1875–1948], *Birth of a Nation*. 1915. Photo courtesy the Kobal Collection.

Birth of a Nation *paints a broad picture of the South before, during, and after the Civil War through the eyes of two families, one Southern and one Northern, who finally unite in marriage at the picture's end. The most expensive film made until 1915, at $125,000,* Birth of a Nation *had a cast of thousands, big interior sets, and exciting action sequences, as well as an intimate focus on a handful of people. In the battle sequences D. W. Griffith cut from the heroic efforts on one side to the heroic efforts on the other, from long shots of the raging battle to close-ups of individual men, from the living to the dead.*

When the film opened it was condemned by the National Association for the Advancement of Colored People and by liberal politicians for its glorification of the Ku Klux Klan and for its bigotry and racism. Griffith, who wanted Blacks to keep their place, felt that social change was the cause of evil in the world. Although the film was banned in several cities, its huge success indicates that its ignorant and pernicious point of view was shared by a large segment of the American public. A historic, inventive, and dramatic piece of filmmaking, Birth of a Nation *remains an embarrassing reflection of American society as it was in 1915.*

whole film in the possession of the Library of Congress. In short, it has been obvious from the beginning that film specializes in **movement** rather than in the static depiction of things as in still life, landscape, or portraiture. Unlike photography, which has been very successful at reproducing actual, seemingly unrehearsed events, the motion picture medium demands "actors" who know how to move.

And so because of their obvious affinity to actors and acting, films were soon reproducing theatrical productions. The camera gave the viewer the best seat in the house—front row, center. In many of the earliest films, the camera was stationary and never stopped running until the theatrical scene was over. But it was not long before moviemakers realized that not only must the actors move but also the camera can and should move. The camera does not have to sit still. Unlike a member of the theater audience, it can shift to any position, even onto the stage and even behind the scene. Moreover, moviemakers soon realized that a complete film is not constructed from scenes as in a stage play but is based on segments of film shot by the camera.

One of the first persons to exploit the potential of a mobile camera and consequently the potential of a shifting point of view in film was the American director D. W. Griffith, who began making films in New York in 1908. He was the first moviemaker to develop various camera positions and to compose a film by combining the individual pieces of film shot from the changing positions. His 1915 movie *Birth of a Nation* (see FIG. 12-3) was one of the first feature-length films as well as the first blockbuster, earning millions of dollars. In many ways Griffith invented the movies, both the art and the industry.

FIG 12-4   STEVEN SPIELBERG [American, 1947–], *Jurassic Park*. 1993. Industrial Light and Magic, Marin County, California, and Universal. Photo courtesy The Kobal Collection.

A Composite Art

Film is a **composite art form** in the sense that it borrows and combines elements from a number of older art forms. Film resembles theater because it usually has actors and sets and dialogue like any dramatic production. However, unlike a theater production, where the audience goes to see a living performance with all its risks and spontaneity, a film is a recording. Unlike the observer's point of view in a theater, the camera's point of view in a film is not limited to a fixed seat in the audience. The camera can focus now on one part of the dramatic action, now on another, whereas all the actors involved in a theatrical scene remain on a stage and are constantly visible to the audience. Furthermore, by simply juxtaposing the various camera positions recorded on film, the completed movie can rapidly and easily move back and forth between different activities staged at different times and places. A stage play changes scenes, in most cases, as infrequently as it can.

Film is a composite art also because it incorporates the art of photography—in the sense that every image on the motion picture screen is governed by the same principles of design as any good photograph. The big difference between film and photography is, of course, that film images move. The actual movement of lines and shapes in a motion picture adds another element of visual stimulation to be balanced in the composition.

In actual practice, however, the photographic element in film has looked quite different from modern art-photography because film often depicts fantasy. Straight photographers have emphasized the realistic basis of their art in their work, but the movies have always delighted in fantasy—whether historical drama, science fiction, impossible adventure, or outlandishly romantic love stories. Some of the most financially successful movies in the late twentieth century were film fantasies like *Star Wars*, *Batman*, and *Jurassic Park* (see FIG. 12-4).

As a composite art, film often incorporates music, although the music on a typical sound track is not a complete work like that performed at a concert. Music in film is generally subordinate to the action, although in music videos it seems to control the visual imagery. Dramatic productions staged in a theater often have musical interludes, but seldom does the music accom-

Fig 12-5 Walt Disney Company [American], *Beauty and the Beast*. 1991. © The Walt Disney Company.

Fig 12-6 Walt Disney Company [American], cel from *Snow White and the Seven Dwarfs* 1937. © The Walt Disney Company.

pany the action as it does in the movies. Audiences rarely go to the movies to listen to the sound track. Even Walt Disney's *Fantasia*, which includes passages from renowned compositions such as Igor Stravinsky's *The Rite of Spring*, emphasizes the visual element. However, the music in an opening section of Disney's *Beauty and the Beast* (see Fig. 12-5) synthesizes several levels of the action on the screen in a stunning fashion. While Belle sings about her need for romantic adventure and the boredom of provincial life—undercut by visual mayhem on the screen—Gaston sings of his intention to marry Belle, and the chorus of villagers sings about how strange Belle is. The blending of different voices, establishing plot, character, and setting in one song, is almost operatic in its dramatic scope.

Animated feature films like *Fantasia* and *Beauty and the Beast* are a composite art form that also incorporates drawing and painting. Made in the traditional way, an animated feature like *Snow White and the Seven Dwarfs* (see Fig. 12-6), produced in 1937, required close to a million drawings by dozens of artists and took years to complete. Working from storyboards and layouts that sketch out the setting and characters of each small part of the film, background artists draw everything that will appear in a scene except the characters, whose actions the animators draw frame by frame. The animators' drawings are transferred to transparent sheets of celluloid, or cels. Each cel is placed over the background and photographed to create one of the twenty-four frames needed for each second of film.

❼

❻

Today most professional animation is painted through a computer program, which greatly facilitates the production. Through painted animation—both traditional and computer generated—filmmakers have customarily created more vivid characterization, more brilliant color, and more extraordinary flights of fantasy than ordinary film techniques normally allow. For example, even in live action films, computer animation has enabled dinosaurs to stampede in *Jurassic Park* and the silver cyborg to transmogrify itself in *Terminator 2*.

Computer generated imagery appears to be on the verge of revolutionizing all of filmmaking. The new process starts by photographing actors and scenes and backgrounds as raw material that is fed into the computer. There at the computer terminal the filmmaker directs and manipulates the images on the screen with the same freedom enjoyed by a modern artist applying paint to a canvas. The computer can add actors or erase them from the scene; it can change the lighting, transform backgrounds, or create new settings. Images can be combined and manipulated in many ways. Props can be added, moved, or eliminated long after the production phase of the film has ended. Hair-raising stunts, like those in James Cameron's *True Lies* (FIG. 12-7), can be produced with little danger to the actors and actresses and at a much lower cost. With digitized technology, all this film will have the flawless simulation of reality.

Film also resembles the novel and incorporates some of the features of literary fiction. Like a novel, a film can easily develop a story through various times and places. Like a novel, a film can focus now on one character, then on another. Yet film has trouble reproducing the equivalent of a first-person author or all-knowing narrator, a device that is typical of fictional literature. The narrator in a novel can get inside the head of the characters and describe what they are thinking or feeling.

Sometimes in a film a camera angle will establish the point of view of a character, as when the villains are photographed suddenly from above, from Indiana Jones's position on a cliff. The audience may not know exactly what Indiana Jones is thinking, but at least it sees what he sees. In general in the movies, the camera is the main storyteller and has to reveal thoughts and feelings implicitly by the images it captures for the screen.

Film is a composite art form also in the sense that many people collaborate in the making of a typical movie. Painters, sculptors, and printmakers frequently employ assistants, but the assistants usually subordinate their activities to the artist's wishes. Architects depend on numerous contractors and workers to build a building, but they necessarily have to work together to realize the architect's established plans. But in the movie industry many individuals have a strong voice in determining the appearance of a typical film.

A **director,** like Penny Marshall or independent filmmaker John Sayles, plots and supervises the shooting of a film as she or he tries to guide the actors in the interpretation of their roles (see next page). The director is usually credited with the overall responsibility for the outcome of the film as though she or he is the individual author of a novel. The idea that the director functions as the creative artist of a film is known as the **auteur theory** (*auteur* in French means "author"). Most successful films bear the mark of a forceful imag-

Penny Marshall directs Tom Hanks in Big.
Photo courtesy The Kobal Collection.

ination capable of exercising artistic control.

But significant portions of any film are not under the director's immediate control. A producer, for example, arranges for the millions of dollars of financing a movie usually takes. Holding the purse strings, a producer often has a great deal to say about what goes into a film and what the end product should look like. In the 1930s, 1940s, and 1950s, the big film studios in Hollywood tightly controlled every facet of movie production and made most of the big decisions about any film.

The cinematographer oversees the photographic quality of each image on the screen and so gives important directions about the lighting and color. Editors put the pieces of film together, participating in one of the most vital and artistic parts of filmmaking. Someone else chooses a cast of actors, who may or may not cooperate with the director. A scriptwriter prepares a story and dialogue. Professionals design and

Text continues on page 294

John Sayles (1950–)

*J*OHN SAYLES is a rare phenomenon in the movies in the 1990s: a successful independent maker of mass-distributed feature films—one of the few independent filmmakers who survives in the business.

He writes, directs, and occasionally acts in his own films. Because of the multi-million-dollar costs of producing a feature film today, it is extremely rare for the producers who finance films to allow the kind of independence—from choice of actors to final cut—that Sayles insists on having.

Many of the prominent young filmmakers of the 1990s—Spike Lee, for example—are graduates of the topflight film schools in California (the University of California at Los Angeles or the University of Southern California) or New York (New York University). Sayles, however, became a film director through an unusual avenue: that of screenwriter. With sixty thousand dollars that he earned writing screenplays, he made his first film, *The Return of the Secaucus Seven*, in 1980. By 1994 he had written and directed seven films, including the critically acclaimed *Matewan* in 1987, *City of Hope* in 1991, and *Passion Fish* in 1992.

While insisting on his independence, Sayles prefers not to assert his presence on the screen in subjective camera work or idiosyncratic editing. Perhaps because he began his career as a writer, he subordinates all visual effects to the story line. He believes strongly that making a

John Sayles on the set of Matewan. *Photo courtesy The Kobal Collection.*

film is a collaborative adventure and that the director's job is to cajole the army of people working on the film to concentrate on the story. To channel and focus the various talents of the film crew and the cast of actors, Sayles likes to win their cooperation by building a community among them.

A community of people is also the central theme of his films. Sayles likes

to visualize how an action or situation affects a group of people—not through separate stories of individuals but through their interaction. In *City of Hope*—perhaps his best realization of the theme of community—the camera often moves from one set of characters to another while it keeps on filming without a break, so that the audience visually gets the impression that the

*Perhaps because
he began his career
as a writer, John Sayles
subordinates all
visual effects
to the story line.*

JOHN SAYLES [American, 1950–], scene from *Matewan*. 1987. Photo courtesy The Kobal Collection.

lives of all the characters are an unbroken web of relationships. Sayle's films usually do not feature one hero who, in Hollywood fashion, charges in at the end to set things right.

Sayles's movies, which visualize the ambiguity of human affairs, often end inconclusively. He professes a belief in a cyclical sense of time and a feeling of inescapable fate. Rather than a happy ending, his movies conclude with a suggestion that life goes on. In *Matewan,*

the story of a coal miners' strike in the 1920s, a bloody confrontation between the laborers and the bosses settles nothing. Sayles likes to make movies that push beyond the audience's stereotypical expectations and make them ask questions. He forces the audience to work for the answers.

Filmmaking on a low budget puts a number of constraints on the filmmaker. Sayles has learned to do without lavish sets, hundreds of actors, special effects, and complex action sequences with numerous shots, because of their cost. Nevertheless, a low budget does not free the director from the thousands of practical and artistic decisions needed to produce solid images that tell a story. In his dual career as filmmaker and writer, Sayles is very aware that the camera cannot get into a character's head to reveal intimate feelings. But he is also aware that through film, viewers can inhabit other people's bodies and live other people's lives.

Sayles does not direct with a rigid hand. He tries to give his actors some

freedom, balanced with the demands of the visual elements on the screen. He strives not to capture a perfect "take" from an actor when filming any shot but to capture a range of possibilities that he can bring into the editing room. Since parts of any film are normally filmed out of sequence, Sayles is not sure until the shots are fitted together how he might want to interpret a scene. Consequently, he will encourage actors to keep going even if they flub a line, since he may be able to use the other parts of a take. Editing, he feels, is a series of refinements and adjustments, because "no matter how well planned, scenes have a different impact when you start cutting them together."[1]

The movies today are a big business in which corporate financing often makes the most important decisions. Hollywood also produces films to gratify target audiences, while market researchers, testing audience response, often tell directors how to redesign their product for quick profit. In spite of these trends, Sayles and many other filmmakers in and out of the system have the courage and stamina to remain true to their artistic vision.

FIG 12-8 ROBERT ALTMAN [American, 1925–], *The Player.* 1992. A frame from the opening shot. Courtesy Fine Line Cinema.

build sets; other professionals design and make costumes. A gaffer, the chief electrician, achieves the lighting. Experts compose and record music and integrate it with the film. To say the least, even the most talented director depends on the skills of dozens of other people to make a successful film.

The Language of Film

Ever since D. W. Griffith realized that the motion picture camera can and must change its location, the filming done from various positions has become the fundamental building block with which every film is constructed. The basic unit of any film is called the **shot,** which consists of one uninterrupted moving or nonmoving image. A shot is usually one continuous rolling of the camera. It may be only a few frames long or several thousand frames long. It may last for a fraction of a second or for many minutes. In Robert Altman's film *The Player* the opening shot of a fictional Hollywood film company lasts for about eight minutes without a break. To alert the movie audience that a long shot is in progress, a character on screen refers

to Orson Welle's use of such a device in *A Touch of Evil.* The long shot in Altman's film gives the impression that we are eavesdropping through the camera as it continuously moves about.

A longer portion of a film is called a **sequence.** A sequence usually consists of a number of shots that are related to one another by some visual or conceptual coherence. It often resembles a scene in a theatrical production. When we talk about the love scene or the chase scene in a movie, we are probably referring to a sequence. Strange as it may seem, in filmmaking the sequence is subordinate in importance to the shot.

Very little of what appears in any shot is accidental or gratuitous. But since we are so easily swept along by the reality of most films, it is hard for us to realize that everything appearing on the screen at any given moment has been included because of someone's decision. The French, who have been leaders in film criticism, call what is in each frame the **mise-en-scène** (pronounced meez-ahn-sen), which means "put into the scene." This concept helps us analyze a film image by making us realize that all that we see in a shot has been actively and deliberately put there for a reason.

The mise-en-scène includes elements that are similar to those in a theatrical production—the actors, the setting, the lighting, and the costumes. The filmmaker consciously decides who will be in the shot and what part of the set will be included in the frame. Even when the film is made out-of-doors on location, the director has to decide whether he or she wants those trees on the left or on the right of the screen.

Decisions about lighting have to be made. Hollywood and television usually illuminate a set fully with lots of artificial light. More unusual lighting can establish a dramatic mood or it can put a sparkle in the leading lady's eyes. Outdoor filmmaking is bedeviled by the sun's movement through the sky or sudden concealment by clouds while the director spends the day filming two shots that are supposed to be only seconds apart on the screen.

Mise-en-scène also pertains to movement on the screen. This includes the actors' gestures and expressions while standing in place or walking across the screen. Filmmakers have to decide whether the spaceship should fly across the screen from left to right, right to left, or, as in the *Star Wars* movies (FIG. 12-9), appear at the top of the screen and move into the distance. Since the essential element of film is movement, many directors like to see activity in every frame and seldom allow a mise-en-scène that is as static as a still photograph.

Nevertheless, the mise-en-scène of each shot also includes elements that are closely related to the art of photography. These photographic elements are things like lenses, focal length, and depth of field, all of which can dramatically change the appearance of a shot of the same actors in a scene. Camera angle and camera distance have to be decided for each image. In Jane Campion's *The Piano* (FIG. 12-10), close-up shots of hands regularly appear on the screen like a refrain in a work of music. The motion picture photographer also has to unify and balance the composition of every frame with the same principles of design that painters and photographers use, except that the image usually contains real, rather than implied, movement. The cinematographer might film in different projection systems, such as Cinemascope, which require totally different frame ratios for the scene. Moviemakers have had to calculate how the mise-en-scène will look on a wide theater screen *and* on the proportions of a home video screen.

FIG 12-9 GEORGE LUCAS [American, 1944–], *Star Wars*. 1977. Photo courtesy The Kobal Collection.

FIG 12-10 JANE CAMPION [Australian 1954(?)–] *The Piano*. 1993. Photo courtesy The Kobal Collection.

FIG 12-11   ORSON WELLES [American, 1915–1985], shot from *Citizen Kane.* 1941. Photo courtesy The Kobal Collection.

Orson Welles came to Hollywood after gaining fame for his radio dramas, especially his dramatization of an invasion of New Jersey by Martians. His first motion picture, Citizen Kane, *tells the story of the rise and fall of a wealthy newspaper mogul, Charles Foster Kane, who fails to win love and find meaning in his life. The movie opens with the hero's death, then without explanation changes to a strident newsreel biography of Kane. Most of the film is a series of flashbacks prompted by a newsman's search for the real Kane and the meaning of his last word, "Rosebud."*

Citizen Kane, considered by many to be one of the greatest American films ever made, was a disappointment at the box office. For one thing, *it did not have the requisite happy ending. Welles's stylish innovations in camera work, his complex narrative* *techniques, and the tragic mood of the film made unusual demands on the audience in 1941.*

In a frame from Orson Welles's *Citizen Kane* (FIG. 12-11), the youthful and idealistic Charles Foster Kane, played by Welles, commits himself to a "declaration of principles." Kane is costumed in his shirt-sleeves, the image of a hardworking journalist late at night in his plain, cluttered office. His associates and the gas lamp form a solid triangular composition, made emphatic by the unusually low camera angle that causes Kane to dominate the scene. Because of the low angle, we even see the ceiling of the Hollywood set. The actor on the left, Joseph Cotten, holds his head precisely between the lamp and Kane's shirtsleeve. The rhythmic pattern of light and dark patches across the screen is as carefully arranged as the chiaroscuro in any Tenebrist painting in the Baroque style. None of these aspects of the mise-en-scène happened on the screen by accident.

The mise-en-scène of each moment of the film also includes elements that are peculiar to the motion picture camera. The director might speed up the motion—usually for comic effect—or use slow motion to stretch out and savor something that would otherwise happen too quickly for the eye to catch. Slow motion adds grace to the movement of the lovers' embrace or exaggerates the agony of the dying victim of a shooting.

Also, an array of camera movements might be used in any shot. The camera might **pan** by turning on its axis and sweeping horizontally across a scene. Panning across the horizon gave a feeling of wide-open space in

A camera on a track. Steven Spielberg and Harrison Ford discussing a shot for Indiana Jones and The Temple of Doom. *1983. LucasFilms. Photo courtesy The Kobal Collection.*

Part III: The Visual Arts

Fig 12-12 Victor Fleming [American, 1883–1949], crane shot of the railroad station at Atlanta, in *Gone with the Wind*. 1939. Metro Goldwyn-Mayer. Photo courtesy The Kobal Collection.

In this shot Scarlett O'Hara goes to the military hospital in besieged Atlanta, where the doctor refuses her plea to come help deliver Melanie's baby. The shot begins by focusing on her stepping between the wounded and the dying lying outside the train station. The camera, mounted on a crane, gradually moves up and back to reveal more and more of the railroad yard covered with bodies as far as the eye can see. Without saying a word, the camera contrasts the awesome devastation of the war with the self-centeredness of Scarlett. Meanwhile, the "Southern" music on the sound track makes an ironic comment on the once-proud Confederacy. The lengthy shot ends as a tattered Confederate flag, seen very close to the camera, comes into view to the left of the panorama of devastation on the screen.

old cowboy movies. Cameras can **tilt** up and down. Moving up the side of a tall building by tilting the camera emphasizes its height. Another common device is **tracking,** where the camera is pulled on a dolly, normally on small tracks, while it is filming. The tracking camera usually moves along with the actors, who are also in motion. The cinematographer can also smoothly and rapidly change the focal length of the camera's lens so that the camera seems to **zoom** toward something on the screen, although in reality the cam-era has not moved at all. Professional motion picture cameras are now small enough so that they can be **handheld** by an operator who is moving. The slightly jerky shots made by a handheld camera often give a more personal, intimate, or documentarylike appear-ance to the image. At the other extreme, a camera can be born aloft by a **crane,** as it was to film the makeshift hospital at the railway station in *Gone with the Wind* (Fig. 12-12), or perform a complicated series of movements programmed by a computer.

Fig 12-13 George Lucas [American, 1944–], *Star Wars*. 1977. LucasFilms. Photo courtesy The Kobal Collection.

Editing

One of the most distinctive and creative parts of film-making is the construction of a film out of the shots. This essential procedure, lying at the heart of film-making, is called **editing.** Editing means the relating and coordinating of one shot with another. Some people consider editing the essence of film as an art, since it is the one important visual technique that film alone possesses and that no other art form can match. The French call the editing process *montage* (mounting or assembling), which is perhaps a better word because it stresses the positive aspects of connecting the shots. The English word *editing* suggests to us merely the omission of bloopers and unnecessary shots—a negative procedure. However, blunders in filming have usually been discarded before the real editing process begins.

Film editing is primarily a constructive procedure. The director and editors actively choose which parts of the hours of filming finally best fit together. They might even change their mind about what was the best take in the context of the film. Although editing usually takes place after the shooting is over and the actors have gone home, the shooting script usually gives a rough idea of what will be needed from the beginning.

The visual connection or juncture between one shot and another can be made in a number of ways. We are concerned with the visual connection on the screen—not with the physical means of "gluing" one piece of film to another. The image of one shot may grow dim, or **fade** out, the screen turn dark, and then the image of another shot fade in. The speed at which the fade occurs affects the emotional flow of the film, as it can create a quite obvious break between shots. Indeed, it normally creates such a considerable break in the action that it is used infrequently in a typical film. The image of one shot may also merge, or **dissolve,** gradually into the image of another. A dissolve makes the transition to the next shot faster than a fade, but still takes some time to complete. It also is ordinarily saved for special emphasis or special transitions.

Editors in some older films liked to employ a **wipe** to make the juncture between shots. A wipe looks as though a windshield wiper blade, moving across the screen, is removing one image while introducing another. The *Star Wars* movies had a more-than-usual number of wipes to give them the look of an old-fashioned serial (Fig. 12-13). Television sports has played with all sorts of computerized variations on the wipe. The screen might develop a pattern of gradually enlarging diamond shapes that contain the new image while replacing the old image. Or the old image may seem to flip off the screen as though someone were rapidly turning the page of a book to reveal a new page. The computer has also made possible another kind of transition between shots, called **morphing.** In the 1991 Michael Jackson music video *Black or White*, the faces of various people from around the world are quickly transformed one into another.

By far the most common technique of editing is the simple **cut,** where one shot suddenly ends and the next one immediately begins. The cut instantly joins the old and the new image together in the mind's eye. In fact, it mimics the instantaneous sequencing of different thoughts and images that can take place in the human mind. The close resemblance to human consciousness is probably why cutting from shot to shot in a film rarely seems to us abrupt or unnatural. Cutting is as natural as thinking and imagining themselves.

Whatever the means of junction used, editing gives the filmmaker a powerful tool to build a film. More than merely holding the pieces together, it shapes and gives meaning to the whole. To develop the narrative or visual idea, editing functions in a number of ways. Editing may establish purely **visual relationships** between shots. Through editing, the lines, color, light, movement, or any part of the mise-en-scène of one shot is shown to be similar to—or by contrast thoroughly different from—that of the next shot. By stressing the visual relationship between them, editing can relate completely different subjects. A television commercial, for example, might show someone diving into a swimming pool and then cut to a spoon plunging, at the very same angle, into a bowl of breakfast cereal. The cut suggests a connection between healthy activity and eating the cereal. During Clint Eastwood's *In the Line of Fire*, a shot of the would-be assassin entering the door of his storeroom precedes a shot of secret service agents entering the door of the presidential suite of a hotel. The juxtaposition of the two visually similar shots draws a parallel between the careful preparations of each side before a showdown between the two.

Editing may establish a **pace**—a rhythm or a tempo—in a film. To set a pace, editors calculate the shots in a sequence to last on the screen about the same length of time. A series of brief shots tends to correspond to speedier action. Editing or joining a series of longer shots may establish a slower pace. Cuts usually start appearing more frequently in a movie—and shots start getting shorter—whenever the action gets more exciting, as in a chase scene. The editing of the scene of a *Tyrannosaurus rex* attacking a jeep in

THE JEEP PICKS UP SPEED... THE T-REX STARTS TO FALL BACK...

... CLOSE ON GROUP LOOKING RELIEVED!

THE JEEP DRIVES AWAY...

FIG 12-14 STEVEN SPIELBERG [American, 1947–], storyboard for shots of *Tyrannosaurus rex* chasing a jeep, for *Jurassic Park*. 1993.

Jurassic Park, as shown in the storyboard in figure 12-14, sets up a very fast pace. Although the editing may establish a pace only for the sake of consistency in a particular part of a film, the pace will have a psychological effect on the viewer. In television commercials the pace of the editing often reinforces the rhythm of a jingle. Music videos frequently seem to have the same beat going both in the music and in the often frantic pace of the editing.

FIG 12-15 SERGEY EISENSTEIN [Russian, 1898–1948], stills from the "Odessa Steps Sequence," in *The Battleship Potemkin.* 1925. Photo courtesy The Kobal Collection.

Asked to celebrate in film the uprisings of 1905 in Russia that foreshadowed the Revolution of 1917, Sergey Eisenstein decided to concentrate on the mutiny aboard the Potemkin. The first time he saw the steps in Odessa, he realized that they would be the source of the movement of the massacre sequence, even though the event took place in various parts of the city. To film the panic and slaughter on the steps, he used tracking shots, a camera strapped to the waist of a running man, and several cameras filming simultaneously. In this sequence the camera moves, the actors move, the shots jump from one point to another, and the editing creates a rhythm that is intensely felt by the audience. By editing the shots for the maximum psychological impact of their relationships, Eisenstein transformed Soviet propaganda about the solidarity of the masses against capitalism into profound universal drama.

Editing may also establish **spatial relationships.** The moviegoer will believe that two things are in the same place because the editing has connected them. The film may present a shot of the White House, then cut to a man sitting behind a desk. The editing of the film has told the viewer that the man behind the desk is the president of the United States in the White House. In all likelihood, the first shot was filmed in Washington, D.C., and the second shot was filmed three thousand miles away in Hollywood, California.

And editing may establish **temporal relationships.** It can expand or contract time. The Russian film director Sergey Eisenstein, in the famous "Odessa Steps Sequence" from his 1925 film *The Battleship Potemkin* (FIG. 12-15), showed a crowd of people rushing down the steps ahead of the Tsarist soldiers firing at them. Eisenstein dramatized the massacre in shot after shot, quick cut after quick cut, over a period of time that is far longer than the event must have taken in reality. He thus expanded the time of the event.

It is more common to telescope time in editing. For example, an actress in one shot might say, "Let's get away from it all!" Then the film cuts to a second shot, of a jet plane taking off. The film cuts again to a third shot, panning the Eiffel Tower, and a fourth shot, of the actress eating in a restaurant. Through editing, the time it takes to pack, fly across the Atlantic, register in a hotel, and unpack has been condensed to approximately twenty seconds or less. Editing the four shots constructs the journey. It would be absurd for the filmmaker to photograph the entire trip and then, in the editing process, cut out the unwanted parts.

Editing may also establish that different events are happening simultaneously. In one shot, a villain might be threatening innocent victims with death. The film suddenly cuts to a heroine galloping on a white horse. We understand not only that she is racing to save the innocent but also that the two actions are happening at the same time.

Editing, in short, can direct our attention, arouse our emotions, make connections, develop an idea, and further the narrative of a film. Most films do not have a narrator on the sound track telling us the story, but through editing, the camera becomes an omniscient narrator that can go anywhere and see everything. Editing allows the camera to make comments and discoveries for which no dialogue is necessary. If the film cuts from a shot of an actress walking out of a room to a close-up of keys lying on a table, we might imagine that the character has forgotten the keys and is heading for trouble. Many special effects in the movies depend on editing to make them convincing. After a shot of the hero running from his enemy, the film cuts to the hero (this time played by a stuntman) crashing through a glass window, then cuts to another shot of the hero picking himself up from the sidewalk. Editing is often responsible for making the dangerous and daring possible in a film and for making fantasy convincing.

The motion pictures were over thirty years old before **sound** was added to them in the late 1920s. Yet sound has a distinctly cinematic potential and enhances a film in a number of ways. Sound in a movie includes speech, music, sound effects, and even the ambient sound of the location. The manipulation of sound and its relation to the visual images is a vital part of the editing process.

The quality of the sound—whether it is loud or soft, high-pitched or low—affects the emotions of the audience. Sound quality can suggest an ambiance beyond what is actually on the screen. The sound quality of the human voice could suggest that the actress is speaking outdoors in one instance or in a crowded room in another, even though both shots were filmed in the same Hollywood studio.

The sound is usually connected with the image on the screen, but sometimes it is not. Sometimes the sound of the next scene appears before the cut to the next shot is made. Or the music from a dance sequence might continue after a cut has been made to the actress driving away in her car. The source of the sound might be visualized on the screen and in the story's space or come from outside the shot. Many films have actors turn on a radio to provide, realistically, music for the sound track. Aside from film musicals, music on a sound track usually occurs only in certain places, such as love scenes or chase scenes, to heighten an emotion. The kind of music—a symphony or a rock piece—has to fit the character of the entire film.

FIG 12-16 AKIRA KUROSAWA [Japanese, 1910–] *Ran*. 1985. Photo courtesy The Kobal Collection.

Film Style

Since film is a composite art, no one element can distinguish a good from a bad film. Theatrical, literary, photographic, and even musical elements contribute to the overall achievement, or lack of it. The photography in a film may be beautiful, but the acting bad. The acting may be outstanding, but the story trivial. Nevertheless, the visual elements of the mise-en-scène, the shot, and the editing engulf every element in the final analysis. They determine whether the film is a coherent and consistent whole that achieves its desired effect. A mobile and moving camera, visible on screen as edited shots, unfolds the story and develops ideas, while captivating imagery delights the eyes. Throughout the film there is consistency, with variety, about the camera work, the lighting, the color scheme, and most importantly the pacing. No shot is wasted; no shot distracts. Every shot is just the right length and helps build the narrative. To achieve such coherence the director has to impose a design or style from beginning to end. In the hands of directors like Orson Welles, Alfred Hitchcock, and the great Japanese director Akira Kurosawa (FIG. 12-16), the style of the camera work and the style of the editing have a distinctive signature that betrays a unique personality.

Key Terms and Concepts

auteur theory	mise-en-scène	spatial relationships
composite art form	montage	temporal relationships
crane	morphing	tilt
cut	movement	tracking
director	pace	visual relationships
dissolve	pan	wipe
editing	sequence	zoom
fade	shot	
handheld	sound	

13

SCULPTURE

The Nature of Sculpture

The art of sculpture creates solid objects that take up real space. Sculpture has real **mass,** that is to say, solid forms and three-dimensional shapes that have weight. The forms of sculpture project themselves into space, whereas the lines and shapes of painting and drawing can only mimic the real world with two-dimensional illusions of space. Sculpture also shapes space itself. The empty spaces between the masses create **voids** that are an essential part of the experience of sculpture. Sculptural volumes also displace space, and the masses often reach out to take possession of the space around them.

In a real sense, sculptural mass constitutes not just something we see with our eyes, but something we can feel with our body. The experience of sculpture restores for us the primitive feelings we had as an uninhibited infant, crawling on the floor, exploring the fascinating shapes and textures and weights of every new thing we could handle, plus the gaps in between. Sculpture invites us to explore masses and voids once again, to touch solids—if only with our eyes—and find our way between solids in space. Sculpture repeatedly reminds us what it means to be what we essentially are, a body of space. The symbolic forms of sculptural masses and voids communicate their message through the language of our bodily experience in space.

FIG 13-1 HENRY MOORE [British, 1898–1986], *Reclining Figure: Angles.* 1979. Bronze, over–life-sized. Henry Moore Foundation.

Reclining Figure: Angles (FIG. 13-1), the work of the modern British sculptor Henry Moore, clearly demonstrates the equal importance of the solid masses and empty voids that constitute the sculptural experience. The reclining female figure was Moore's favorite theme throughout his long career because he liked the naturally swelling masses of the female form. He deliberately exaggerated the knees, hips, and shoulders of his figure so that we recognize without fail the projection of the masses in space—big, bulky masses that jut out into space at differing angles. Equally important are the cavities that he created between and under the legs and arms and the great void between the torso and the knees. The visual relationship between the masses and voids of *Reclining Figure* shifts and changes as we move around the figure. Moore's sculpture captures and proclaims our fundamental awareness of mass and volume in space. His sculptural forms approach the naturalness of time-worn rocks and caverns. It seems fitting to compare his figure to a landscape with mountains and valleys. Moore was also impressed by the grandiloquent sculpture from the Athenian Parthenon in the British Museum in London (see *Three Goddesses*, FIG. 2-9).

The Comparison of the Arts

Because essential differences exist between painting and sculpture, artists and writers for centuries have debated which medium is better. The discussion is called the Paragone, or the Comparison of the Arts. Of course, no one can possibly resolve such a pretentious question. Those who ask the question are usually prejudiced toward one or the other medium and have their answer ready. In the Renaissance Leonardo da Vinci declared that painting was superior to sculpture because it can reproduce all that sculpture can and more.[1] Michelangelo, who practiced both painting and sculpture, thought painting was subordinate to sculpture because painting is essentially modeling into three-dimensional form—a sculptural activity.[2] The Baroque sculptor Bernini contended that painting was better than sculpture because it is more difficult to create mass and three-dimensional space by the two-dimensional illusions of painting.[3]

Most of the time, the argument of the Paragone concerned which medium was better at imitating nature—an issue that does not trouble most of us any more. Even in terms of imitation, one can only point out the differences between the two media. Sculpture requires less of an illusion of reality than painting because sculpture itself is actually present in real space—sculpture creates a duplicate of reality that shares the space we physically inhabit. In contrast to traditional painting, which has a fixed point of view, sculptural reality can be designed and usually can be studied from many different angles.

The Visual Elements in Sculpture

The human eye tends to follow lines created by the axis or the thrust of three-dimensional masses. In Henry Moore's *Reclining Figure: Angles* (FIG. 13-1) the thrust of limbs and the projection of all masses generate direction and movement into space. As an art that often concentrates on the human body, sculpture places special importance on the lines of contrapposto—the counterthrusts resulting from, for example, the weight shift of the *Spearbearer* (FIG. 2-8) or the torsions of Michelangelo's figures (see *Awakening Slave*, p. 184).

Lines are also formed by the edges and grooves of sculpture, especially in the folds of drapery. Lines of cloth stretched tightly over prominent projections like knees may reveal the underlying masses and accentuate their roundness. Between the projections there may appear lines of tension as the masses pull against the cloth. Drapery folds may also accentuate masses by flowing around them in curved lines and, in effect, modeling the masses.

Although in deploying drapery the sculptor may be trying to imitate the behavior of a certain kind of material that falls and wrinkles in a certain way, the movement of the folds might also betray the distinct character of the sculptor's personal style. This is because many sculptors take up and maintain a distinct manner of creating folds and creases no matter what the natural material might be. The German sculptor Tilman Riemenschneider in his statue *The Virgin with the Christ Child* (FIG. 13-2) employed drapery that breaks at right angles and folds in sharp creases—not so much like any ordinary wearable cloth but like heavy aluminum foil. These distinctive folds become the signature of his hand. In this statue, the slashes and jagged breaks of the drapery folds contrast with the oval configurations of Mary and the perky Christ child. Whether accentuating mass, imitating

FIG 13-3 JUAN MARTÍNEZ MONTAÑÉS [Spanish, 1568–1649], Saint John the Baptist. C. 1630. Painted wood, 61 in. (154.9 cm) high. Metropolitan Museum of Art, New York.

FIG 13-2 HANS TILMAN RIEMENSCHNEIDER [German, C. 1460–1531], *Madonna and Child.* C. 1490. Lindenwood, 14 1/2 in. (37 cm) high. Museum of Fine Arts, Boston. Gift in memory of Felix Warburg by his wife, Freida Schiff Warburg.

actual material, or following a personal manner, it is always the sculptor's job to decide how to "fold" the drapery and fabricate lines. Drapery does not automatically fall into place.

It was long assumed that sculpture lacked color. For many centuries sculptors confined themselves to the pure white of marble or the several colors of **bronze,** which is an alloy of copper and tin. When people in the Renaissance rediscovered the sculpture of Greece and Rome, they saw no paint on it. Dedicated to the emulation of antiquity, they concluded that true sculpture was without color and that color would detract from the beauty of pure sculptural forms. Color is the element most often mentioned by them as missing from sculpture as a reproduction of reality.

But they were mistaken: sculpture in ancient times did not lack color, nor does color detract from sculpture. The Greeks normally painted their sculpture, and statues in the Middle Ages were also frequently painted. Sculpture from around the world—masks from North America, Africa, and Japan, for example—was customarily painted. Color certainly stimulates our awareness of the physical actuality of sculpture, a phenomenon demonstrated clearly in Juan Martínez Montañés's *Saint John the Baptist* (FIG. 13-3). Narrowing the gap between art and life, color attracts the eye and forces further examination of the sculptor's transformation of reality. Some modern sculpture is once again painted in full color, for example, Viola Frey's *Untitled (Prone Man)* (see FIG. 13-19) and Duane

FIG 13-4 RICHARD SERRA [American, 1939–], *Tilted Arc*. 1981. Hot-rolled steel, 12 × 120 ft. (3.7 × 36.6 m). Formerly New York, Federal Plaza. Courtesy Art on File.

The General Services Administration of the federal government, under its Art-in-Architecture Program, commissioned Tilted Arc *from Richard Serra specifically for the plaza in front of the Javits Federal Building in lower Manhattan. Serra erected there a thick, single, curved slab of steel, twice human scale.* Tilted Arc *leaned ominously to one side and created a wall that bisected the plaza and deliberately contradicted the plaza's curved design. The threatening intrusion of the piece called attention to the forceful experience of its leaning and curved form in space. The office workers in the federal building did not like the piece, and they petitioned to have it removed. The storm of controversy that raged around its removal raised numerous artistic and legal issues, especially since the removal of a work designed for a specific site destroys its meaning. Many in the arts community claimed that an artist has a right to the preservation of his or her work even though it is owned by someone else. Serra filed suit, claiming that mutilation of an artist's work violates freedom of speech. The incident raised the larger question of whether the taxpaying public, which commissions art, has a right to "censor" a work it does not like. Even though Serra lost his lawsuit and* Tilted Arc *was put in storage, the questions surrounding it have not been given final answers.*

FIG 13-5 EDGAR DEGAS [French, 1834–1917], *Dancer Looking at the Sole of Her Right Foot*. 1896–1911. Bronze, 18 in. (45.7 cm) high.

Hanson's *Woman with Dog* (see FIG. 13-23). Although it has taken some time for the modern world to overcome its prejudice against painted sculpture, color is now free to add its space-creating potential and its sensuous appeal.

In sculpture the design principle of balance takes on a special significance. Since sculpture often consists of weighty solids that are influenced by gravity, we intuitively have a sense of a work's physical balance and stability—or lack of it: Richard Serra often creates works, like *Tilted Arc* (FIG. 13-4), that seem to be in danger of falling. In traditional figural sculpture we instinctively understand how the symmetrical human body achieves balance when any of the body's masses are displaced. The French Impressionist painter Edgar Degas, late in his career, modeled figures of dancers in wax, conceiving fully three-dimensional forms, twisting and thrusting out into space in several directions. As in his paintings of dancers, Degas chose not some classic pose of a ballerina but an unguarded, potentially awkward moment. In *Dancer Looking at the Sole of Her Right Foot* (FIG. 13-5), to balance her weight and the thrust of her projecting limbs, the figure throws

FIG 13-6 [Greek], caryatids, Porch of the Maidens, Erechtheion. 421–405 B.C. Acropolis, Athens.

her leg, hip, torso, and head into a continuous curve so that the foot on the floor lies under the center of gravity. (The poor model had to hold this pose for Degas!) Out of a spontaneous, mundane action springs a new, sophisticated configuration of the poised and balanced nude figure.

A Public Art

Because sculpture is often made of metal or stone, it can be placed out of doors. Throughout history, sculpture has often been found on the facade of a building or in the open space before a building. In these contexts it plays a public role, similar to that played by architecture, because sculpture's exposed presence makes a public statement. As a consequence, institutions in communities have called on sculpture to fulfill the same task time and again: namely, to make tangible the gods and goddesses, and heroes and heroines of the society.

Examples of sculpture in this public role are not hard to find. The **pediments,** the triangular gables at either end of the Parthenon in Athens, had splendid sculptural groups of Athena and other gods and goddesses (see *Three Goddesses,* FIG. 2-9) that told the essential myths of the foundation of the city. Other statues of the deities and legendary figures cherished

by the city were located in the open space around the temple. Nearby, also on the Athenian Acropolis, or upper part of the city, was located the Porch of The Maidens (FIG. 13-6). This structure featured a group of **caryatids**—female statues that actually perform an architectural function, supporting a horizontal part of the building. Graceful and reserved, the six maidens do not express the strain of their burden. Only the vertical folds of their gowns, like the fluting of a column, emphasize their supporting role.

When large-scale sculpture returned to Europe after the fall of Rome, teams of sculptors in the Christian Middle Ages carved dozens of statues of saints and the sacred ancestors of the community for the porches of Gothic cathedrals. In the Middle Ages and the Renaissance, countless tombs with figural sculpture, often placed inside the church, celebrated the memory of noteworthy individuals. The tradition of erecting public monuments and memorials in sculpture is a long one. Painting lacks this public dimension, which is a mainstay of sculpture, although mural painting comes close to it. Nevertheless, sculpture plays the public role better.

Indeed, outdoor, public sculpture is thriving in the contemporary art world. Throughout the United States and many other countries it is not hard to find large-scale outdoor pieces—some of them of high

FIG 13-7 MAYA YING LIN [American, 1960–], *Vietnam Veterans Memorial.* 1981–1983. Marble, each wing 246 ft. (75 m) long. Washington, D.C. Photo courtesy Art on File.

quality—situated in or on public buildings or in the open spaces of cities. Washington, D.C., the nation's capital, is dotted with sculpture memorializing the nation's heroes and heroines. For some years Maya Ying Lin's *Vietnam Veterans Memorial* (FIG. 13-7) has been the most popular attraction in Washington. The stark V-shaped black marble slab, half sunk into the earth and inscribed with the names of the dead, exercises a strange power over visitors. Federal, state, and local governments often allocate a percentage of the cost of a new building toward art, including a prominent piece of sculpture. This was the case for Richard Serra's ill-fated *Tilted Arc* (FIG. 13-4), commissioned for a federal office building in New York City.

Imagery

Considering the nature of sculptural mass and the commemorative role that sculpture often has to play, it should come as no surprise that the favorite iconography of sculptors has been the human figure. Landscape and still life are generally absent from sculpture, although they are frequent subjects for painters. The predominance of the human subject makes sense. If sculpture is the arrangement of solid and voids in space to duplicate the experience of our body, then the figure, and often the nude figure, is logically the essential expression of sculptural form. The nude human figure has proved especially suitable to

sculpture because it offers a great range of readily communicated expression through the configuration, tension, and movement of its masses and voids.

Embodying the deities and legendary figures of a society, the human figure in sculpture has served religion well. Greek and Roman sculptors carved their gods and goddesses in human form. Indian, Chinese, and Japanese sculptors for a long period of time have made statues of Buddha, including the enormous bronze *Amida Butsa, the Great Buddha* (FIG. 13-8) at Kamakura, Japan. This Buddha sits in a restful position meditating in order to free himself from earthly desires and to achieve perfect peace and happiness, or *nirvana*. The figure slumps forward, completely at rest, and the curved flow of his robe reinforces the expression of tranquil relaxation. For centuries Christians carved statues of Christ and the saints for veneration and to inspire the faithful. Even in prehistoric times sculptors represented the human figure in keeping with their beliefs. Although the *Venus of Willendorf* (FIG. 13-9) does not, as its name implies, represent the Greek goddess Venus or probably any deity, it must have embodied the beliefs of the community.

Sculptors sometimes depict animals other than the human animal. Many cultures around the world have expressed the natural powers of bulls, birds, and lions in sculpture. Horses have been very common subjects, especially in the days when the horse was the major means of transportation. Many older cities in Europe

FIG 13-8 [Japanese], *Amida Butsa, the Great Buddha*. Kamakura period, A.D. 1252. Bronze, 37 1/3 ft. (11.4 m) high. Created under the patronage of samurai Yoritomo. Kotoku-in, Japan. Werner Forman/Art Resource, New York.

FIG 13-9 *Venus of Willendorf*, frontal view. Twenty-fifth millenium B.C. Limestone, 4 1/2 in. (11.4 cm) high. Naturhistorisches Museum, Vienna. Erick Lessing/Art Resource, New York.

This very small piece of sculpture from the Stone Age is thousands of years older than the splendid cave paintings discovered in Spain and France. Those cave paintings represent animals almost exclusively, whereas the earliest European sculpture represents the female human figure more than any other subject. The paintings are remarkably true to nature, but the sculpture distorts physical features for symbolic purposes. The sculptor inflated the breasts, hips, and abdomen of the figure—the areas of fertility, sexuality, and maternity. A blob of a faceless head, wearing a stylized cap of hair, looks down on these features. The arms, folded over the breasts, are barely incised on the torso. The legs taper toward the missing, inconsequential feet. Only the swelling of rounded masses seem to have meant anything to the sculptor, who may have felt that the shaped stone had the power to ensure the changes due to pregnancy in female members of the tribe.

FIG 13-10 ÉTIENNE-MAURICE FALCONET [French, 1716–1791], *Monument to Peter the Great*. 1782. Bronze. Head modeled by Falconet's associate Marie-Ann Collot. St. Petersburg, Russia. Giraudon/Art Resource, New York.

or America feature an **equestrian monument,** which is a statue of a horse ridden by some famous hero or heroine who led the nation to victory.

In an equestrian monument, the sculptor has to decide the pose and expression of the horse as well as those of the rider. The sculptor has to determine whether the horse is moving or standing, and if the horse exhibits a certain gait, how to balance the weight of the horse and the rider on three or perhaps only two legs. Leonardo da Vinci was the first Renaissance artist to design an equestrian monument in which the horse rears up on its hind legs, although the piece was never executed. The eighteenth-century French sculptor Étienne-Maurice Falconet did com-

plete an equestrian statute of Peter I on his rearing horse, called *Monument to Peter the Great* (FIG. 13-10) —a very famous statue in Russia. Falconet imagined that the emperor has just charged up a rocky prominence and, as his horse rears up dramatically, raises his hand over his people to assure them of his protection. The wild pose of the horse and the relaxed pose of the rider give the statue energy and authority. To stabilize and balance the work on the horse's two hind legs, Falconet gave the horse an enormous tail that makes contact with the base to form, in effect, a tripod.

Portrait **busts,** which show only the head and the shoulders or chest, have always been popular, even though it must be rather difficult to capture the likeness of someone in a hard, white material like marble. The famous Baroque sculptor Gianlorenzo Bernini once remarked that a face that has lost all its color is hard to recognize. Consequently, Bernini did not hesitate to manipulate the flesh of his portraits in marble to produce a fluid surface so that it would catch some light and create some shadow and thus *appear* to come alive. Bernini said that a person who sits still for a long time loses the traits that make the person an individual. To capture a likeness of cardinal Scipione Borghese in stone (see FIG. 13-11A), Bernini had the cardinal move around and talk, while Bernini made sketches of him (see FIG. 13-11B). His portrait of Cardinal Borghese can truly be called a speaking likeness.

Whereas portraits attempt to reproduce the characteristics of an actual person, **masks** that cover the face or head allow someone to impersonate a totally different persona—perhaps even that of a spirit or a monster. Masks are affiliated with the worlds of theater and religious ritual, where they are worn in a performance. Chinese and Japanese and Greek and Roman theater employed masks. Africans and Native North Americans have extensive traditions of mask making closely tied with life's rituals. *Bird Mask* (FIG. 13-12) represents the fearful bird spirits that guard the Man-Eater at the North End of the World. Wearing the mask in a ceremony, a person assumes the spirit of someone else. Masks hide the identity of the wearer and imbue the wearer with the powers of another. In general, then, mask makers are concerned not with the imitation of reality but with the expression of the forces within the adopted persona.

Part III: The Visual Arts

FIG 13-11A   GIANLORENZO BERNINI [Italian, 1598–1680], *Cardinal Scipione Borghese.* 1632. Marble. Galleria Borghese, Rome. Scala/Art Resource, New York.

FIG 13-12   [Kwakiutl], *Bird Mask.* 1938. Wood, carved and painted, 47 in. (119.4 cm) long. Denver Art Museum.

Bird Mask *was worn in the Hamatsa society's winter ceremonial dances of the Kwakiutl people living on the northwest coast of North America, in British Columbia. Initiates into the Hamatsa society had to confront guardian bird spirits. The dance reenacted the killing of the Man-Eater and the revival of dead tribespeople. The Man-Eater symbolized the mouth of a river that annually devoured the salmon.*

This single mask contains four bird spirits pointing in three different directions. The beaks project far from the face and the lower part is movable to make the bird spirits more frightening. The dancer could manipulate one or all the beaks by strings. The painting accentuates the shapes of the mask. Red lines emphasize the lines of the mouth and the flair of the nostrils. Black and white lines accent the curves of the beak. Within the confines of a traditional style and iconography, the artist has displayed a sensitivity to mass and void, line and color.

FIG 13-11B   GIANLORENZO BERNINI [Italian, 1598–1680], *Cardinal Scipione Borghese.* 1632. Chalk. Morgan Library, New York.

FIG 13-13   DESIDERIO DA SETTIGNANO [Italian, 1428–1464], *Saint Jerome in the Desert*. C. 1460. Marble relief, 16 15/16 × 21 5/8 in. (43 x 54.9 cm). National Gallery of Art, Washington, D.C.

Types of Sculpture

Reclining Figure: Angles (FIG. 13-1), by Henry Moore, is sculpted fully **in-the-round.** In other words, it is freestanding and finished both back and front so that a person could walk all around it to observe it. An amazing thing about Moore's *Reclining Figure* is that as one examines it from different points of view, the masses and voids easily shift into new and revealing relationships. Perhaps that is why Moore subtitled the work *Angles*. Although sculpture is often made in-the-round, not every such piece looks good from every point of view. Usually, when figures are carved for niches in a wall, they are executed in-the-round but not designed to be seen from the back.

Desiderio da Settignano's *Saint Jerome in the Desert* (FIG. 13-13) illustrates another kind of sculpture, called **relief,** in which the work projects from a background. Viewers usually cannot walk around relief sculpture, but if they did, they would not see anything in the back, since a sculptor does not design or finish that side. The surface of almost any relief does not extend physically very far into space, although the relief itself can be described as low or high. Low relief, often referred to by the French term *bas relief* (pronounced bah relief), and high relief are thoroughly relative terms. The surface of a very small piece of relief sculpture that protrudes two inches from the surface might be called high relief, whereas a very large relief sculpture that protrudes only two inches from the surface might be considered low relief. Nevertheless, in all relief sculpture, masses still physically swell and cavities move back in real space—exhibiting the sculptor's sensitivity to three-dimensional form.

Desiderio treated the marble slab of his relief *Saint Jerome* like a canvas on which he depicted a landscape and a little story. In the center of the composition, St. Jerome, carved in low relief, is kneeling in rapt adoration of the crucifix. Behind him the lion who became his mascot chases away a very frightened intruder. Although the figure of St. Jerome protrudes somewhat from the surface, the lion and the fleeing man are barely raised, as an indication that they lie deeper in space. Trees diminish in size into the distance, and clouds in the sky are suggested merely by random scratches in the marble. The delicacy of the low relief carving reflects the delicacy of Desiderio's overall style.

Relief sculpture like *Saint Jerome* resembles painting in its use of pictorial effects like perspective, in its openness to different kinds of iconography like landscape, and in its capability to illustrate a narrative.

These features come about because reliefs construct a composition visualized from a single point of view, as do two-dimensional works. Overlapping and diminishing size in relief sculpture may once again give an illusion of space. And relief sculpture may also give the sensation of recession in space by variations in depth, as *Saint Jerome* does. The device works because a decrease in depth produces less contrast of light and dark and thus simulates the decreased chiaroscuro of atmospheric perspective in painting and drawing.

Other variations on the relief method are possible. The ancient Egyptians, for example, liked a distinct form of low relief, illustrated in *Portrait of Akhenaten* (FIG. 13-14), in which the carving sinks the figure into the slab instead of removing the background. The Egyptian method emphasizes the outline of the figure by, in effect, doubling it. Caught in a raking light, the depression in *Portrait of Akhenaten* causes a dark outline around the head cloth that the king wears and also a highlight around the contour of his face. Recessing the portrait only a few centimeters into the stone, the sculptor still built forms by swelling masses (the head cloth, the bulbous chin, and the thick lips) and sinking concavities (the hollow cheeks, for example).

Unlike the gradually swelling reliefs of the Renaissance and of Egyptian sculptors, most of the reliefs carved by Mayan artists are flat along their outer surface. One example produced at the end of the classical Mayan period, a relief from the Pyramid of the Feathered Serpent (see FIG. 13-15) at Xochicalco (pronounced Show-chee-*cal*-co), near Cuernavaca in Mexico, portrays an enormous serpent god with squatting noblemen framed in the serpent's undulations.

FIG 13-14   [Egyptian], *Portrait of Akhenaten.* C. 1360 B.C. Limestone relief, 13 11/16 × 9 3/16 in. (34.8 × 23.3 cm). Metropolitan Museum of Art, New York.

This relief stands straight out from the surface like the raised letters on typewriter keys. It thus has two flat surfaces—the recessed background and the basically flat upper surface of the serpent and human figures. Although the Mayan relief stands out starkly, aided by strong light-and-dark contrasts, it still respects the flat surface of the wall. Instead of dissolving the wall in a pictorial illusion, this kind of bold relief strengthens the appearance of the wall's thickness.

FIG 13-15   [Mayan], relief from Pyramid of the Feathered Serpent. After 800. Xochicalco, Mexico. Photo by James Prigoff.

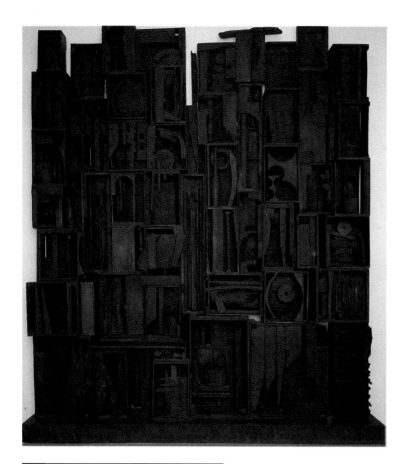

FIG 13-16 LOUISE NEVELSON [American, 1900–1988], *Sky Cathedral*. 1958. Wood construction painted black, 135 × 120 × 18 in. (343 × 305 × 46 cm). Museum of Modern Art, New York. Gift of Mr. and Mrs. Ben Mildwoff.

Louise Nevelson collected old pieces of wood—rejected fragments of urban life such as shafts of columns, chair and table legs, and bits of decorative molding—which she most often painted a dull black so that the various found parts would be brought together into a unity and the formal properties of the piece would be heightened. In Sky Cathedral *she intuitively arranged the found pieces—vertically, for the most part— in boxes stacked one on top of the other like the spires of a cathedral. The solid shapes in each box both stand out from the far surface and sink into the shadowy space of the box. The paradoxes of utilitarian objects and an intuitive design, of regularity and irregularity in the design itself, or flatness and a rich array of masses and dark voids make Nevelson's work appear mysterious—like the indecipherable hieroglyphs on the walls of an ancient ruin.*

Inspired by reliefs on Mayan and Aztec architecture, Louise Nevelson constructed numerous reliefs that appear to be both raised from the back and recessed into the front surface. Stacking many boxes of various dimensions in her work *Sky Cathedral* (FIG. 13-16), Nevelson also created a flat wall. In other words, the front plane of her relief is very pronounced along with the murky space behind it. Her relief both projects from the back plane and sinks away from the front plane.

Another way of categorizing sculpture is to ask whether the artist adds to the material or subtracts from the material when making the sculpture. Leon Battista Alberti first made this distinction in his book *De statua (On Sculpture)* about 1435. Taking lumps of clay and forming them into a head is an example of **additive** sculpture. Taking a block of stone and eliminating part of it with a chisel is an example of a **subtractive** process. Both processes are essential and traditional forms of the art of sculpture, although some sculptors have preferred one method over the other. Michelangelo insisted that the subtractive process defined the essential activity of a sculptor. In his mind, the additive process duplicated the activity of a painter.

Making the distinction between additive and subtractive processes often suggests that a different mental outlook governs each process and that the results of the additive process ought to look different from the results of the subtractive. But the consequences of the distinction are hard to demonstrate in practice. In fact, many subtractive statues are based on additive models that the sculptor executed beforehand, perhaps in clay. A sculptor's small "sketch" in clay or wax is called a **maquette.** Henry Moore usually made small clay models of his large-scale stone works so that he could readily turn the maquettes in his hands and carefully examine their forms from every angle. In other words, the important first moments of his artistic inspiration involved the process opposite that of the finished product.

Part III: The Visual Arts

Traditional Materials and Techniques

Since sculptors constantly translate their work from one material to another with little change, it would be hard to maintain that one kind of sculptural material produces styles essentially different from those possible with the others. Even the influential early-twentieth-century sculptor Constantin Brancusi, who told his generation to respect the nature of the material, often translated his own pieces—like *Mademoiselle Pogany*, FIG. 18-30—from stone to bronze with little change. The rallying cry "Truth to the nature of the material" meant in practice that sculptors should bring out the stoniness of stone and the woodenness of wood and should not imitate foreign substances like silk or puffy clouds as Bernini did in his *Ecstasy of St. Teresa* (FIG. 5-13).

Nevertheless, materials and techniques sometimes do make a difference in the appearance of sculpture. Since different materials require different techniques, some visual effects are possible, or at least easier, in one material or another. Louise Nevelson could never have invented her painted wooden boxes in *Sky Cathedral* (FIG. 13-16) if she had been confined to stone carving. The lumpiness of Rodin's figures, like his *The Thinker* (FIG. 18-9), initially modeled in clay and in plaster, distinguishes them from the chiseled marbles of Michelangelo despite Rodin's affinity for Michelangelo's style.

Modeling, or shaping forms with clay or wax, is an old technique found in most ancient civilizations. Peruvian potters of the classical period, about A.D. 250 to A.D. 750, often made vessels of clay in human form, as in *Portrait Jar* (FIG. 13-17), or in animal form or in a combination of both. They cleverly amalgamated the swelling of the vessel with the masses of natural forms. Soft and pliable, clay, wax, or modern plastic equivalents are easy to manipulate compared with stone. Clay and wax can be pinched, squeezed, kneaded with the hand, or shaped with tools. Extra

FIG 13-17 [Peruvian, Moche], Portrait vessel, three-quarter view, from the north coast of South America. C. 100 B.C.–A.D. 500. Ceramic, 10 1/4 in. (26 cm) high. Art Institute of Chicago. Buckingham Fund (1955.2338). Photo by Robert Hashimoto.

FIG 13-18 LUCA DELLA ROBBIA {Florentine, 1399(or 1400)–1482], *Madonna and Child*. Enameled terra cotta. Detroit Institute of Arts.

lumps or rolls of the material are added as the work progresses. An armature, a skeletal bracing within the clay or wax, is frequently needed to support the soft and malleable material before it hardens. Since mistakes can be corrected, modeling materials provide the sculptor with the closest thing to a three-dimensional sketching medium.

Forms in clay can be made hard and permanent by firing the clay in a kiln. The result is known by the Italian words **terra cotta** (baked earth). The unpainted orangish flowerpots sold in nurseries are made of terra cotta. In the Renaissance, three generations of the della Robbia family from Florence became well-known for their charming and pious religious work in terra cotta. In *Madonna and Child* (FIG. 13-18) Luca della Robbia applied to the clay colored **glazes,** which are glasslike coatings that are baked right onto the clay.

Kiln-fired works of any kind, whether sculpture or pottery, may be called **ceramics.** Because of its malleability and the permanent bright colors possible with glazes, ceramic sculptures again became popular in the 1980s. Viola Frey and a number of West Coast sculptors have modeled in their preferred medium of clay, even though they work on the scale of life. Their imagery and techniques often derive from popular culture, or effect the deliberately simple look of a modern amateur artist. Frey's bulky *Untitled (Prone Man)* (FIG. 13-19), with a large head, seems like a slumbering giant. Animation comes from the garish color liberally laid on the figure with dabs and crude lines that usually accentuate the swelling masses.

FIG 13-19 Viola Frey [American, 1933–], *Untitled (Prone Man)*. 1987. Glazed ceramic, 19 1/2 × 41 × 99 in. (49.5 × 104.1 × 251.5 cm). Photo by Jacques Gael Cressaty, courtesy Rena Bransten Gallery, San Francisco.

Carving, or cutting, wood or stone with hammer and chisel is also an old technique. Sculptors' tools include punches, flat and claw-toothed chisels, saws, drills, abrasives, and today all kinds of power tools including lasers. In addition to various kinds of wood and stone, sculptors also used to carve ivory—a material that can no longer be traded legally in most countries around the world. Stone sculptors have long preferred marble, a metamorphic rock that is hard yet pliable enough for subtle carving.

The ancient Egyptians, who were greatly concerned with permanence, often carved in harder igneous stones like granite or basalt and therefore developed a style of large, simple forms and smooth, polished surfaces. Actually, the connection between Egyptian material and Egyptian style must be a chicken-and-egg problem because it is impossible to determine which came first, the material or the style that preferred the material. Whether carved from hard basalt or from soft limestone like *Hatshepsut Enthroned* (FIG. 13-20), almost all Egyptian statues seem to have the same rigid style.

Queen Hatshepsut, assuming the centuries-old image of the pharaoh of Egypt, sits bolt upright, her hands flat on her thighs. The uncarved part of the block of stone becomes her throne. Every mass of the throne and figure lies at right angles to every other. Her legs and arms have been generalized into cylindrical forms. Her torso, however, subtly narrows at the waist; the chest softens to suggest breasts; and her face with its small features and narrow chin has a feline look about it. If not an exact likeness of Hatshepsut, the sculpture is, in the face and torso, an attempted characterization of an individual.

FIG 13-20 [Egyptian], *Hatshepsut Enthroned,* from Deir el Bahri, Temple of Hatshepsut, Thebes. Eighteenth Dynasty (c. 1503–1482 B.C.). Indurated limestone, painted, about 77 in. (195.6 cm) high. Metropolitan Museum of Art, New York. Rogers Fund and Contribution from Edward S. Harkness, 1929 (29.3.2).

FIG 13-21 AUGUSTE RODIN [French, 1840–1917], *Balzac.* 1897. Bronze. Museum of Modern Art, New York.

When Auguste Rodin's statue Balzac was rejected by the French literary society that commissioned it, he kept the work for himself. At his death in 1917, Rodin left the original plaster version to the French state. Under the care of the Musée Rodin in Paris, twelve bronze castings of Balzac were made—the first in 1930—by the foundry of Alexis Rudier, who had worked with Rodin since 1902. No other work of his satisfied Rodin as much or summed up so profoundly what he believed in as an artist. Rodin imagined the writer Honoré de Balzac wrapped in a voluminous dressing gown striding across his room in the throes of inspiration. Imperious yet almost shapeless, the powerful figure thrusts up and back from his tall pedestal. By exaggerating the masses and voids, Rodin captured the genius of the writer rather than his appearance.

Casting in a permanent material like bronze goes back several millennia. The process of casting requires molds into which the molten metal can be poured. The molds themselves are usually formed around a clay model or plaster model as was Auguste Rodin's *Balzac* (FIG. 13-21). In short, most bronze statues begin with modeling in clay or plaster. Bronze may be polished to a mirrorlike surface or allowed to tarnish. When it is exposed to certain chemicals or to the weather, it oxidizes and forms a brown or greenish **patina.** This thin film is usually desired and actually protects the bronze from further oxidation.

Since a large amount of solid bronze can get heavy and expensive, a large-sized bronze statue will have a hollow center. Rodin's statue of the great French writer Honoré de Balzac is hollow because it was cast in bronze by what is known as the **lost wax process** (*cire perdue* in French). The secret of this process is to create two molds, an inner core and an outer shell, kept apart by a suitable thickness of wax. When the molds are heated, the wax melts, runs out the bottom, and leaves a gap between the outer shell and the inner core. Molten bronze poured in through a hole at the top replaces the wax between the two molds and fills the gap. The idea of the lost wax process is simple; however, the execution is quite difficult and requires the collaboration of a team of craftspeople, as does most bronze casting. Therefore, large-scale metalworks are often cast in pieces, which are then welded together.

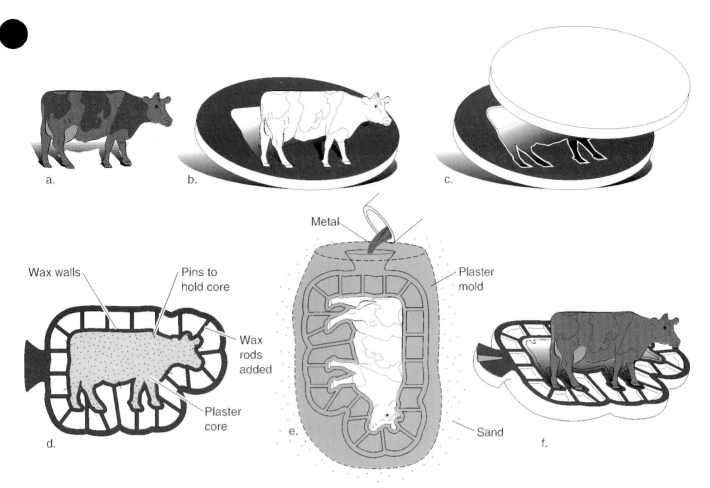

a.

b.

c.

Wax walls — Pins to hold core

Wax rods added

Plaster core

d.

Metal

Plaster mold

Sand

e.

f.

The Stages of Lost Wax Casting

a. The artist models the sculpture in clay or other materials.
b. The sculptor and his assistants make a latex rubber mold of the original clay sculpture. Cut in half, this negative mold, which has received an accurate impression of the clay original, can be reused for several more castings.
c. After removing the original sculpture from it, the artist coats the inside of the latex molds with a layer of wax—as thin as possible. After joining the two halves, workers fill the hollow with a core of liquid fireclay. The fireclay will become rigid and heat-resistant and will be crumbled away after the casting in metal.
d. After the rubber molds have been removed, metal pins are inserted through the wax into the core to hold the hardened core in place during the casting. Workers then construct a circulatory system around the wax model. Main arteries and their extensions will carry the metal to all parts of the piece; other vents permit air to escape.
e. The foundry team covers the wax model and also the circulatory system with more fireclay to create an outer mold. When the mold is heated in a kiln, the wax melts away and is lost. Into the gap created by the lost wax, foundry workers pour the molten metal which fills all the channels and the empty space around the inner core.
f. When the metal has cooled, the circulatory system and the figure are removed from the outer mold. The channels are cut away, the inner core is broken and removed through a small hole, and the surface of the piece is repaired and finished with hand tools.

New Trends

New Materials

In the twentieth century, sculptors work with new metals, plastics, or any other material that suits their imagination. The new materials open up new possibilities of style and give rise to work that is thinner, more delicate or rugged, more transparent, stronger or larger in scale, or more pliable than work in traditional materials. Mostly, the new materials open up new possibilities of self-expression. Some sculptors feel that these new materials, because they belong to contemporary society, better reflect the modern age of technology and rapid change than do traditional marble or bronze. But in modern times even the most commonplace materials may be transformed by the sculptor.

In the late 1960s Eva Hesse turned to fiberglass, a polymer of polyester resin, which allowed her to shape

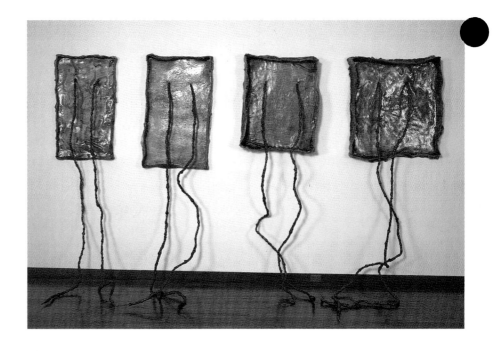

FIG 13-22   Eva Hesse [American, 1936–1970], *Untitled*. 1970. Fiberglass over wire mesh, latex over cloth and wire, 4 units, each unit approximately 40 × 30 in. (101.6 × 76.2 cm). Des Moines Art Center, purchased with funds from the Coffin Fine Arts Trust, Nathan Emory Coffin Collection. 1988.6 Photo by Ray Andrews.

FIG 13-23   Duane Hanson [American, 1925–], *Woman with Dog*. 1977. Polyvinyl, polychromed in oil, life-sized. Whitney Museum of American Art, New York.

the shallow boxes of her work *Untitled* ("Wall Piece") (FIG. 13-22) freely in a permanent fashion. Trained as a painter, Hesse had a short-but-influential five-year career as a sculptor. Most of her works are wall hangings or elaborate collages to be viewed from the front. In "Wall Piece", the luminous windows or trays of fiberglass allowed a permanent record of her self-expression. In contrast, two rubbery latex cords dangle to the floor from each box in a haphazard fashion determined by whoever installs the piece. Hesse often said the contrast of extremes suited her personality.

The contemporary sculptor Duane Hanson produces sculpture by the traditional casting process, but the material he used for *Woman with Dog* (FIG. 13-23) was polyvinyl plastic, not bronze. (However, Hanson has returned to bronze because of the toxicity of vinyl.) Hanson formed the mold of his *Woman* from plaster casts of a living human being; then, into the plaster molds he poured the modern material in liquid form. In addition to the painted plastic material of the figure's body, the work includes natural hair, clothing, shoes, and props taken from the real world. Beyond the startling realism of the material, Hanson is just as

FIG 13-24 MARK DI SUVERO [American, 1933–], *Are Years What? (for Marianne Moore).* 1967. Steel painted orange, 40 × 40 × 30 ft. (12.2 × 12.2 × 9.1 m). Storm King Art Center, New York.

concerned with the meaningful arrangement of masses and voids in space as are sculptors using traditional materials.

Artists sometimes simply find objects that are already made and combine them, rather than shaping raw material into sculptural form. This sort of work has been called **found object sculpture.** This concept implies an element of chance in the discovery of a ready-made item, at the same time that it asserts that the artist's appropriation of the item transforms it into art. Marcel Duchamp started the trend of found sculpture with work such as *Fountain* (FIG. 1-21). The sculptor Louise Nevelson included pieces of ordinary building materials and other common items in her high reliefs of stacked boxes in *Sky Cathedral* (FIG. 13-16). The pieces she "found" were cut and assembled and transformed when they were incorporated into her abstract compositions. The usual word for her kind of construction is **assemblage** (pronounced like *collage*).

Nevelson's work makes it clear that clay is not the only material that can be added to and built up to form a piece of sculpture. All sorts of material can be put together into sculpture. Mark di Suvero assembled his sculpture *Are Years What? (for Marianne Moore)* (FIG. 13-24) with gigantic steel I-beams, the essential structural supports of modern urban industrial society. Instead of forming the horizontals and verticals of buildings and bridges, these beams intersect along mostly diagonal lines in di Suvero's work. The composition of the lines and their intersections change as the viewer moves around the piece. The beams touch the ground like the long legs of a spider so that the space between them is left open for exploration. A beam folded in an acute angle, suspended from a cable attached to a mock crane, sways and twists in the wind. *Are Years What?* makes heavy steel beams delicate and light. Modern sculptors like di Suvero or Nevelson are as likely to have a welding torch, glue, or hammer and nails in their hands as a hammer and chisel. Many, if not most, contemporary sculptors assemble and construct their work.

FIG 13-25 JUDY PFAFF [American, 1946–], *3-D*. 1983. Mixed media environment. Installation at Holy Solomon Gallery, New York.

FIG 13-26 ALEXANDER CALDER [American, 1898–1976], *Lobster Trap and Fish Tail*. 1939. Hanging mobile—painted steel wire and sheet aluminum; about 102 in. (259.1 cm) high × 114 in. (289.6 cm) in diameter. Museum of Modern Art, New York. Commissioned by Advisory Committee for museum stairwell.

Mixed Media

Artists around the globe are experimenting with new forms of sculpture, combining materials in works of mixed media. Modern artists love to break down the boundaries between one art form and another and combine them, blurring even the distinction between architecture and sculpture. Some sculptors transform the whole of an interior space to create an **environment** into which the viewer enters and moves and which then surrounds the viewer on all sides. In Judy Pfaff's environment *3-D* (FIG. 13-25), installed in the Holly Solomon Gallery in New York in 1983, actual colored planes, cylindrical masses, and wirelike lines protruding from the floor, walls, and ceiling crisscross within the space. Viewers move through the environment as though they had shrunk and entered the world of a very expressive abstract painting. Pfaff's *3-D*, Petah Coyne's *Untitled #465A* (p. 324), and a number of other contemporary works of sculpture are so large and complex that they arrive in pieces that must be assembled and situated within the gallery space. Thus, sculptors have coined the generic term **installation** to describe them.

New Techniques

At the same time that new materials are leading to new kinds of sculpture, new techniques are devised for materials both old and new. Sculptors have constructed **kinetic sculpture**—work that actually moves because of wind or water or is powered by an electric motor. Alexander Calder made kinetic sculpture popular in the form of works he called **mobiles,** like his intriguing and fanciful *Lobster Trap and Fish Tail* (FIG. 13-26). Balanced on wires suspended from the ceiling, the shaped vanes of aluminum in this work catch any breeze and change relationships as they dance about each other in space. Although some of Calder's shapes clearly resemble fins, fish, and a lobster pot, the pivoting movement of the thin planes attached to rods suggests the delicate balance of tightrope walkers in the circus more than floating marine life. The open-wire cage balances all the triangular vanes, and each vane balances the remaining vanes. The pivoting movement of the pieces sets up numerous random relationships among them so that Calder's mobile has more than just continuous predictable movement.

FIG 13-27 MICHAEL HEIZER [American, 1944–], *Double Negative.* 1969. 30 × 1,500 × 50 ft. (9.1 × 457.2 × 15.2 m). Mormon Mesa, Nevada. Photo by Tom Vinetz.

Disparaging the overcrowded museums and galleries of America's cities, Michael Heizer chose the peaceful and untouched open space of the western desert for his work. Heizer began making earthworks in the desert in the late 1960s, as did his friends Walter De Maria, Robert Smithson, and Nancy Holt. For Double Negative Heizer gouged out two enormous trenches facing each other across a depression in the rock. The material for his sculpture is the earth itself, the very space in which the work is located. Expanding the principles of Naum Gabo's sculpture, Double Negative is pure void; the excavated material forms no shape or mass. Unlike Gabo's Constructed Head No. 2 (FIG. 6-9), this piece has no man-made planes to define the voids. Heizer's voids are one with the very setting of his piece. They echo and attract one another across the gap.

Double Negative seems like a mysterious ruin, an enigmatic trace of a lost civilization—perhaps for good reason: Heizer's father was an archaeologist. The work has been criticized, however, for destroying the peace and pristine nature of the environment with a manufactured scar. And paradoxically, despite his depreciation of the commercialization of art, Heizer's project received financial backing from the Dawn Gallery in New York. The contradictions only make Double Negative seem even more relevant to modern life.

Some sculptors make earth sculpture, or **earthworks,** by using outdoor nature as their material and by shaping earth and rocks, often in remote places. When Michael Heizer constructed *Double Negative* (FIG. 13-27) in Nevada, his tools were bulldozers and power shovels. Earthworks are created at the site, not in the studio, and often take into account the environmental conditions of the site. They sometimes make points about the environmental crisis and about the relationship between the earth and humankind.

Sometimes sculptors and other artists become performers who put themselves and their creative activity on display before an audience as a form of **performance art.** In 1969 two London art students, Gilbert

Text continues on page 326

Petah Coyne (1953–)

ETAH COYNE has developed a personal style of sculpture in which she suspends large-scale masses of organic materials like tree branches, hay, and mud from the ceiling of a gallery or museum, as in her work *Untitled #465A*.

Working intuitively on each piece, without preliminary drawings or clay models, she ties, wraps, and binds the material together with clay and mud. Branches and twigs often project from the mass like tentacles. Her works challenge our expectations of sculpture because they are made from impermanent material, which in fact will disintegrate and rot, and also because the bulbous masses defy gravity. Instead of resting securely on the floor like ordinary sculpture, they are suspended in midair. The atmosphere seems to be sustaining their growth at the same time that it eats away at their substance.

A number of sculptors besides Coyne have employed organic materials for the sake of their visual appearance as well as to stress that art is a process of creative seeing and making and not merely objects made from culturally consecrated materials. The nature of the material asserts itself in Coyne's organic work and remains untransformed. The materials suggest to the sculpture a natural form of growth. They also make a statement about our environment, which because of human pollution is causing the death and destruction of nature. Coyne herself refers to each of her

PETAH COYNE [American, 1953–], *Untitled #465A*. 1987. Barbed wire, steel, chicken wire, cable, wire, mud, wood, hay, cloth, clay, polymer, tar, paint. Installation at Whitney Museum of American Art at Equitable Center, New York. Photo courtesy Jack Shainman Gallery, New York.

pieces as a female personage. When Coyne first began making hanging masses covered with mud and cloth, she was working with cancer victims and AIDS patients. The bulbous protuberances suggested to her the growth and rot of tumors. Her symbolism is both personal and contemporary.

Although Coyne attended Kent State University and the Art Institute of Cincinnati, she came to her style by taking advantage of a number of chance

*Her works challenge
our expectations of sculpture.
They also stress that art is
a process of creative seeing
and making and not merely
objects from culturally
consecrated materials.*

PETAH COYNE [American, 1953–], *Untitled #763*, 1993. Mixed media. 66 × 46 × 44 in. (168 × 117 × 112 cm). Jack Shainman Gallery, New York.

occurrences. In 1978 she heard a lecture in Akron by several prominent sculptors, that provoked her move to New York to become a professional sculptor. In New York she lived in Chinatown, where the local markets all dangled plucked chickens and displayed raw fish in their windows. Intrigued by their appearance, Coyne began to hang fish in her apartment. She coated some with mud or plastic paint, and wrapped others like ancient mummies. Of course, they began to grow putrid and smell. In the process of installing her absurd sculpture, she remembered that the fish was an ancient symbol of Christianity, and realized that her attempt to preserve the fish from death resembled the care given for terminally ill cancer and AIDS patients. The frightening realizations of her imagination suddenly made her sculpture extremely relevant to modern life. Finally, on a trip to Florida, she discovered a rich array of exotic materials for sculpture in a swampy nature preserve. She sent several crates of twigs, branches, and mud back to New York, where they appeared in her mature work.

Like many a young artist, Coyne first drew the critic's attention through her participation in group shows. With recognition, she was asked to install her work in a gallery where about a dozen pieces developed a visual theme. At the Whitney Museum of Art at Equitable Center in New York in 1987, she installed an unlucky thirteen of her biomorphic personages, including *Untitled #465A*. Each personage had a strange presence and a different character. Aggressive and threatening, yet also fragile, they aroused visceral feelings. To increase their menace Coyne wrapped these excrescences in barbed wire. Twisting and writhing, the massive tumors grow up or down from their stem. They are symbols of death and of life, for they also resemble cocoons.

In 1994 Coyne turned away from her dark and brooding "personages" to white wax-encrusted pieces she calls "girls." Her new work, like *#763*, also hangs from the ceiling, on chains covered in white satin. Many of the new pieces resemble chandeliers, and also dresses, wedding cakes, and hats. Nevertheless, her sculpture is still grown organically in a process similar to that of her previous work in perishable materials. As many as 90 layers of translucent white wax cover an armature of wire mesh. Some of the melted wax comes from the lighting of dozens of candles inserted into the armature—like the popular Catholic ritual of lighting candles in church as prayers for family and friends. Coyne believes that the white wax symbolizes tears. These enchanted creatures from some fairy tale are weighty, yet seem fragile and vulnerable. This brighter, more optimistic work was a bold move in a surprising new direction for the sculptor.

FIG 13-28 GILBERT [British, 1943–], and GEORGE [British, 1942–], *The Singing Sculpture: We Dream Our Dreams Away,* installation view. 1991 re-creation of performance originally staged in 1971. Sonnabend Gallery, New York. Photo by Jon and Anne Abbott.

bought and sold. Their performance stimulates new perceptions about experiencing art and about the relationship between artists and their work. Performance art emphasizes the process of creating art and the imaginative attitudes that make art possible.

Performance art, to be sure, can make the borderline between the visual arts and theater very fuzzy. At the beginning of the twentieth century the Futurists, Dadaists, and Surrealists, in cabarets, in galleries, and in the streets, staged numerous performances combining nonsense declamations, bizarre costumes, and absurd activity. They strove to shock the insensate public into a heightened awareness of art. Their artistic revolts sometimes protested political events, and they sometimes protested the artistic establishment, since, by its nature, performance art is ephemeral and does not create an object that can be sold to a collector or hung in a museum. Performance art grew quite popular in the post-World War II years as younger artists again attempted to shock the public and also, paradoxically, eliminate the distance between the artist and the artist's public. Shocking or not, performance art almost always provides a feast for the eyes and delights several senses at once as it tries to turn life into art. In general, performance art aims at communicating an increased understanding of art through the making, thinking, and imagining of the art process itself.

In the 1940s and 1950s the musician John Cage, the dancer Merce Cunningham, and the young painter Robert Rauschenberg staged performances at Black Mountain College, North Carolina, an institution famous for its experimental approach to art teaching. In 1959 Allan Kaprow, who had studied with Cage, invited an audience to participate in *Eighteen Happenings in Six Parts,* held in the Reuben Gallery in New York (see FIG. 13-29). The performers, reciting fragmentary speeches, moved amid the audience sitting in three separate "rooms" created by plastic sheets. Meanwhile, painters painted, musicians played, and slides were shown—all simultaneously. Kaprow's eighteen carefully orchestrated events provided a total immersion in art. Similar **happenings,** or loosely staged public events of all descriptions, were organized by other artists in the 1960s, and the term *happening* entered the popular vocabulary of Americans. In the 1970s and 1980s performance art went commercial. Robert Wilson's *Einstein on the*

and George, declared that they were "living sculpture" as they performed their work *The Singing Sculpture: We Dream Our Dreams Away* (see FIG. 13-28). Properly dressed in suit and tie, they painted their faces gold and stood on a small table for about six minutes while a tape recorder played the song "Under the Arches." They moved slowly and stiffly like robots. If artists have the freedom to transform any material into art, Gilbert and George took the final step of transforming themselves into art. By doing so, they completely severed the barrier between the artist and the artist's work so that they could communicate directly with their audience. Like Conceptual artists, they challenged conventional notions about art as a commodity to be

FIG 13-29   ALLAN KAPROW [American, 1927–], *Part Four, Room 1: The Orchestra,* in *Eighteen Happenings in Six Parts.* 1959. Performed by Shirley Prendergast, Rosalyn Montague, Allan Kaprow, and Lucas Samaras at the Reuben Gallery, New York. Courtesy of the artist. Photo by Scott Hyde.

Beach, 1976, a work of operatic scope, has become an international success. Laurie Anderson's *United States* (FIG. 13-30), a four-part piece performed in the early 1980s, included the high-tech projection of drawings and images from the movies and television, plus songs and stories and constant comments on the process of perception by the artist. The five-hour performance rivaled the spectacle of a rock concert.

Because these experiments have a three-dimensional quality or at least exist in the real space of the viewer, they can be classified, albeit quite loosely, under the traditional heading of *sculpture.* Thus, in the late twentieth century, sculpture has become a most daring and exciting art.

FIG 13-30 LAURIE ANDERSON [American, 1947–], *United States.* 1980. Presented by the Kitchen at the Orpheum Theater, New York. Photo by Ebet Roberts.

SCULPTURE

The nature of sculpture	Sculpture consists of masses and voids in real space.
The visual elements	The thrust of masses, the lines of drapery, and color accentuate masses in space.
A public art	Sculpture is often connected with architecture. Sculpture often illustrates a community's values.
Common iconography	The human figure, animals, portrait busts, and masks are all found in sculpture.
Types of sculpture	The types of sculpture include in-the-round and relief; additive and subtractive.
Traditional techniques	Traditional sculpting techniques include modeling, carving, and casting.
New techniques	New sculpting techniques include assemblage, installation, environment, kinetic, earthworks, performance, happenings.

Key Terms and Concepts

additive
armature
assemblage
bronze
busts
carving
caryatids
casting
ceramics
earthworks
environment

equestrian monument
found object sculpture
glazes
happenings
installation
in-the-round
kinetic sculpture
lost wax process
maquette
masks
mass

mobiles
modeling
patina
pediments
performance art
relief
subtractive
terra cotta
voids

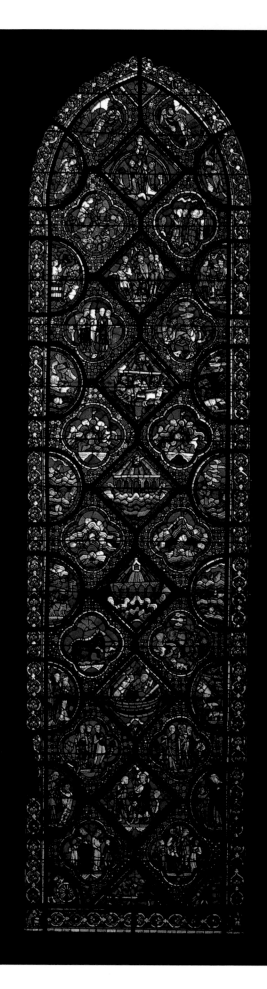

14 APPLICATIONS OF DESIGN:
Crafts, Industrial Design,
Graphic Design, and Computer-Aided Design

Crafts

In the pursuit of more adequate food and clothing, prehistoric people everywhere began to make weapons and tools, sew skins and weave fibers for clothing, make baskets for transporting goods, and shape clay pots for cooking and storage. Every implement they needed to support life, they made by hand. Ordinarily, certain people in the community developed these activities into **crafts,** or special skills for making this kind of practical object. The word *craft* derives from the German word for power, *Kraft*, because the maker of useful items exercised a kind of magic power over nature. Over the years, as our basic tools and utensils have become mass-produced by machines, the word *craft* has evolved into a term charged with several new layers of meaning. To see the different levels of meaning, we can examine the craft of glassmaking throughout the ages.

Glassmaking

Medieval Stained Glass. To begin to understand what the modern world means by craft, we should try to visualize the production of "art" in the Middle Ages. As soon as the workers building Chartres Cathedral had vaulted a part of the nave, another team of workers began installing the stained glass windows. Within about thirty-five years all 164 windows in the church had been filled with deeply colored glass. In modern times Chartres is unique because, of all the great medieval cathedrals in France, it is the only one whose original windows remain intact. No discordant

FIG 14-1 [Medieval French], *The Noah Window*. C. 1210–1220. Stained glass. Chartres Catherdral, north aisle of the nave. Photo by Sonia Halliday.

style of window from another age or, worse, clear glass spoils the effect of the ensemble of glowing colored walls. The glass at Chartres, famous for its deep red and its celestial blue, transports the architecture into the sublime and makes it a vision of the heavenly city.

The king of France and the local aristocracy paid for some of the windows, as did many of the **guilds** (associations of workers) who identified themselves by incorporating scenes of their occupation in the windows. The carpenters, cart builders, and barrel makers probably paid for *The Noah Window* (FIG. 14-1), one of the first to be installed. To complete so many windows in such a short time, craftspeople came from different parts of France and no doubt coordinated their efforts in a common workyard. Six master designers seem to have been at Charters at one time, each with about four or five assistants to cut and assemble the glass.

The design for each window was drawn on a large wooden table over which the pieces of glass were cut and fitted together like a mosaic into H-shaped borders of lead. The thick, dark borders—called, appropriately, leading—kept the colors separate so that, without interference, they retained their brilliance. Manufactured by hand on the site, the glass had numerous imperfections and impurities and an uneven surface—all of which increased the refraction of the light and the richness of the color. This glass is called pot metal because metal oxides like cobalt, copper, or gold, permeating the molten glass, fused with it to give it color. Details like facial features and drapery folds were painted with similar oxides onto the glass, which was then refired so that the paint fused with the glass.

For nearly two centuries Western civilization has looked back with nostalgia on the Middle Ages as a golden age for crafts and has romanticized the medieval craftspeople. Westerners imagine that the craftspeople at Chartres created with their own hands a product of great beauty in the service of their Creator out of the simple sand of the earth. They like to believe that these skilled workers had a close familiarity with the materials they handled and an intimate knowledge of all the techniques of glassmaking. The craftspeople, it seems, directed the whole of the creative process from the initial conception to the final touches and had the skills in their hands to shape an object out of raw materials into a finished product. Westerners want to believe that medieval craftspeople, respected for their skills, lived meaningful lives as they practiced their craft in total harmony with their culture. They admire the talents and skills those artisans possessed to achieve artistic results with basic materials, "primitive" tools, and little modern science.

Tiffany Glass.   In the late nineteenth century, during a surging revival of the use of stained glass in Europe and America, Louis Comfort Tiffany in New York experimented with glass to achieve the translucency and richness of medieval stained glass. An early commission, *Flower, Fish, and Fruit* (FIG. 14-2), decorated the transom of the dining room of a private home in Baltimore. Tiffany—and the painter John La Farge—invented an opalescent glass that was only partially translucent and could therefore imitate the imperfection of medieval glass with its supple texture and variegated surface. Tiffany insisted that details in a window come only from the color of the glass, not from painting on the glass, and that the leading should surround only the shape of each object.

Like the medieval craftspeople at Chartres, Tiffany trained apprentices and controlled the manufacture and design of each window from the production of the pot metal to the installation of the panel in the client's home or church. However, Tiffany did not manufacture all his raw materials, he employed some modern machinery, and he ran his studio and shops like a modern business with workers who specialized in only certain aspects of the operation. A similar factorylike atmosphere may in fact have been more true of a medieval workshop than our Romantic notions allow. An energetic promoter of the superiority of his glass, Tiffany frequently had to conform to clients' less-than-avant-garde tastes for sentimental imagery. Moreover,

independent designers outside the firm sometimes supplied the imagery for windows, which the Tiffany Company then produced.

Another big difference between Tiffany's stained glass artistry and medieval practice resides not in style and technology but in purpose. Tiffany glass was a luxury item crafted for the well-to-do. It was created in an age when industrial techniques of mass manufacture could produce endless quantities of cheap and perfectly flawless clear glass—something people in the Middle Ages could not dream of doing. For those who could afford a more personal look and who cultivated a fashionable nostalgia for medieval handiwork, Tiffany's craft was a revolt against the uniformity, impersonality, and tastelessness of modern mass-manufactured goods. Positively speaking, Tiffany glass was also a promotion for integrity, self-expression, and individuality. Medieval craft objects never carried such a heavy burden of connotations when they were first made. The comparison between the Chartres window and the Tiffany window already begins to demonstrate that craft work can have very different meanings from age to age.

Another significance for traditional craft skills like glassmaking developed in just the late twentieth century. Some craft objects are now made, exhibited, sold, and collected predominantly as works of art. Although people now consider the Chartres and Tiffany windows to be works of art, they were also manufactured to serve practical functions, such as keeping out the weather or letting light into a room. The glass sculpture *Blue/Green Crossed Forms* (FIG. 14-3), by Harvey K. Littleton, could never serve a practical function as either a vessel or a window. Littleton's skillful shaping of glass only makes sense as art. In many ways Littleton acted like a sculptor whose medium was glass.

Glass as a sculptural material can be opaque, as well as absolutely transparent so that one can see clearly deep inside a mass many inches thick. A transparent mass might possess as well a series of colored layers. Another accomplishment of glass is that it transports light and contains light as though it were itself a source of light. Since glass is initially worked in a molten state, it frequently retains the appearance of a frozen liquid as in Littleton's *Crossed Forms*. Glass can have a perfectly rounded, polished surface, or it can have a perfectly straight, razor-sharp edge. Glassmakers can blow hot, liquid glass into a bubble

FIG 14-2 LOUIS COMFORT TIFFANY [American, 1848–1933], *Flower, Fish, and Fruit.* 1885. Stained glass. Baltimore Museum of Art.

FIG 14-3 HARVEY K. LITTLETON [American, 1922–], *Blue/Green Crossed Forms.* 1984. Glass sculpture, 13 × 13 × 13 in. (33 × 33 × 33 cm). Heller Gallery, New York. Photo by John Littleton.

In 1962 Harvey K. Littleton demonstrated in a workshop at the Toledo Museum of Art that individual artists could have their own furnace in a studio so that they could work hot glass themselves. In this way they could be directly involved in the creative process and realize individual works of art. Previously, artists had submitted designs to the glass industry for manufacture. Littleton, the father of the studio glass movement, caused a revolution in glassmaking that still continues to grow.

Glass blowing. Photo by Erich Hartmann, Magnum.

and spin it into shape or press hot glass into a mold. They can etch cold glass with acid, cut it with grinding tools, or blast it with a thin stream of sand to produce a rough texture. Above all, the glassmaker's primary "tools" are heat and gravity, which, for example, caused Littleton's *Crossed Forms* to slump into their curved shapes.

Glass is a difficult medium to work in and takes considerable skill. However, modern craft-artists like Littleton are not just concerned with reviving and mastering traditional materials and techniques, they are more concerned with expressing themselves and creating art, just like colleagues in painting or sculpture. Many craft-artists have abandoned even the appearance of a practical function for their craft object. Many contemporary craft-artists, who practice so-called **studio craft,** consider glass, clay, wood, fiber, or metal to be simply the means to an end—namely, art. Most craft-artists today have received the same kind of training in the same art schools and university art departments as painters or sculptors. They create unique and original works of art that are sold in galleries and collected by individuals or museums just like painting or sculpture.

The Nature of Craft

The ethereal stained glass of Chartres, the luxury glass of Tiffany, and the studio craft of Littleton demonstrate that the term *craft* cannot simply be defined as the making of objects that are useful, as opposed to the creation of nonfunctional art objects made for their own sake. Recall that some people have answered the question "What is art?" by distinguishing the fine arts from the so-called applied arts or crafts. This distinction presumes that the fine arts of painting, sculpture, and architecture do not serve a utilitarian purpose, whereas the applied arts do. But the fine arts themselves serve many practical purposes, from relaying religious messages and serving ritual needs to allowing a therapeutic release of personal emotions. The nature of architecture, whose purpose is to enclose space for living and working, is clearly utilitarian. Moreover, compared with many traditional museum pieces, the objects we now designate as crafts may just as readily and just as deeply express through their forms the personality and culture of the person who made them. (See Shaker side chair, FIG. 1-18.) The so-called crafts also give aesthetic pleasure and speak the symbolic language of art if the viewer's imagination is open to the experience.

The distinction between the fine arts and crafts arose in the Renaissance among artists who wanted to improve their social status by insisting that they were not mere laborers who worked with their hands but intellectuals who employed their mind and imagination. Despite the esteem in which some Greek painters and sculptors were held, even the ancient world considered most artists manual laborers, low on the social scale. Renaissance artists wanted to be seen as free people—free from guild restrictions and free from the grind of repetitious or mechanical production. The distinction between art and craft helped Michelangelo and other Renaissance artists claim that they were inspired geniuses, independent and not restricted by the traditions of handwork. No other culture or period but the Renaissance and the centuries that followed it so isolated the fine arts from other activities.

In the twentieth century, the major differences between the fine arts and crafts are frequently economic. In the current art world, crafts are normally given less exhibition space, less critical attention, and much lower prices. Despite these disadvantages, craft work attracts many people because it has become an alternative way of life for individuals seeking self-expression and self-fulfillment. Instead of working for an industry or business as a small, mindless cog in a giant mechanism, the modern craftsperson imagines, designs, and creates things with her or his own hands. Shaping the forms of an object in the process of creation, the craftsperson works according to the rhythms of her or his own talent, imagination, and enthusiasm. Craft work becomes a satisfying way of life protesting the alienation of mass culture. It asserts the worth of the individual through personalized production of often familiar, comforting items.

In short, people practice at least four types of craft work, each of which gives a somewhat different meaning to the word *craft*. The four types are (1) the employment of an original handicraft skill to create a useful item out of raw material; (2) the revival of original handicraft skills in modern times as a rejection of mass manufacture and an assertion of personal integrity; (3) the use of traditional craft materials specifically as an art medium; and (4) the production of luxury goods, whenever the preciousness of the materials, the skilled artisanship, or the artistic quality make the object rare and desirable for collection and display. These four types constantly overlap in actual practice and appear in all the traditional craft materials such as fibers, metals, and clay.

Fiber Arts

A great variety of crafts have been designated **fiber arts** because they involve sewing, weaving, or joining in numerous ways all sorts of fibrous materials. Since prehistoric times human beings have woven fibers to manufacture clothing, blankets, carpets, and containers. In addition, fibers can be entwined to make ropes.

Basket Weaving. In the beginning of civilized existence, when all goods were handcrafted, **basketry** achieved a high level of technical skill in the production of useful and beautiful forms. People made baskets for storage and transportation of goods even before they made pottery, which presupposes a sedentary existence. In creating a basket, organic materials from the weaver's own environment were used. Unlike most workers today, the handworker, who had to understand the entire process of production, cared for and worked with nature and the seasons. In the process of twining, plating, or coiling the vegetable materials from the center out, the weaver gave shape to the

FIG 14-4 DATSOLALEE [Washo, Native American, 1831–1926], *Washo Bowl.* Coiled mountain willow, bracken fern root, and redbud bark, 12 1/4 in. (31.1 cm) high × 16 1/4 in. (41.3 cm) in diameter. Philbrook Art Center, Tulsa. Clark Field Collection.

three-dimensional form already present in his or her imagination. In early societies such specialized crafts often proceeded like a religious ritual. Women typically wove baskets, and they continued to be the primary practitioners of most crafts as long as the crafts remained centered in the family.

Early in the twentieth century several Native American women in the western United States still practiced the ancient art of basket weaving. Centuries-old tradition had passed on to them the technical skills, the appreciation of proportion, and the ability to integrate form and decoration. The bowl-shaped basket of figure 14-4 is an example of the work of Datsolalee of the Washo tribe in Nevada. Datsolalee built the basket with a very tight and uniform weave. From a narrow base the basket swells in a fully rounded curve toward a narrow opening that reflects the diameter of the base. Four groups of three vertical stripes decorate the piece. The stripes with their featherlike design bend away from one another in harmony with the expanding shape of the basket. The decoration enhances the monumental appearance of the small container.

Fig 14-5 [Medieval French], *Bayeux Tapestry*, detail. 1070–1080. Linen and wool embroidery, about 1 2/3 × 230 ft. (0.5 × 70 m). Musée de la Tapisserie, Bayeux, France. Giraudon/Art Resource, New York.

Datsolalee's baskets were immediately sold to collectors who appreciated their artistic merits—they never served a useful function. But she did not consider her baskets a form of art because her culture had no distinction between art and handicraft or any other form of visual expression. Perhaps as a consequence of her approach to craft, she easily possessed the integration of life and art that many craftspeople in modern times have sought in the revival of older crafts.

Needlework. Traditionally, women also practiced the craft of **embroidery,** the decoration of cloth with needlework designs. Throughout history queens and princesses were known for their skill in the crafts employing needle and thread. According to legend, Queen Matilda, the wife of William the Conqueror, embroidered the famous *Bayeux Tapestry* (see Fig. 14-5) with the events of the Battle of Hastings and the Norman conquest of Britain in 1066. The *Bayeux Tapestry* is not a woven tapestry, with the design created by interlacing differently colored threads, but a strip of linen 230 feet long embroidered with colored wool cutouts that have been stitched onto it. Along the continuous strip the "tapestry" narrates events that happened only a few years earlier. An important source of historical information about the period, the scenes are full of accurate detail and lively movement despite the absence of modeling and perspective. The unity of style throughout the entire length of the *Bayeux Tapestry* indicates that it is the work of a single designer, whoever that might have been.

In the 1970s the American painter Judy Chicago resolved to make contemporary art using techniques long associated with women and with explicitly feminine imagery. One result of her determination was *The Birth Project*, a series of needlework images of childbirth. From the start she intended childbirth to symbolize creation itself, but she was soon amazed that childbirth—one of the basic facts of life, one of the most awe-inspiring and joyful experiences in life—had almost never been illustrated in art. *The Crowning NP 4* (FIG. 14-6) illustrates the moment when the child's head first appears in the birth canal. The woman, who holds her legs, demonstrates powerful muscular movements to bear the child. The symmetrical design includes the fallopian tubes and the nurturing breasts. Lines of force radiating from the woman generate energy and life throughout the universe.

Feminist art in every sense, *The Birth Project* also created an unusual participatory form of art. The artist consulted with hundreds of women about their experience of childbirth as she developed imagery for the series. The work, done by dozens of needleworkers in collaboration with the artist, become the property of the nonprofit corporation Through the Flower, which maintains and exhibits it around the United States. In many ways *The Birth Project* opened the art world to a fresh breeze.

American women needleworkers had practiced a communitywide craft generations earlier in the eighteenth and nineteenth centuries: namely, quilting. A **quilt** in fact has become a popular modern metaphor for personal expression in the service of a common good. When women in a community came together for a quilting bee, the completing of a quilt was a social event and a cause for celebration. The top of a patchwork quilt was made either by appliqué, which involves sewing cutout patches to a white backing, or by the piecework method, which involves sewing straight-edged geometric shapes to one another to form a pattern. At first quilt makers cut material salvaged from discarded goods, but by 1800 they generally purchased a special selection of colored and printed materials just for their quilt.

FIG 14-6 JUDY CHICAGO [American, 1939–], *The Crowning NP 4,* from *The Birth Project.* 1984. Needlepoint, 40 1/2 × 60 in. (102.9 × 152.4 cm). Executed by Frannie Yablonsky. © Judy Chicago. Photo © Michele Maier.

Over a five-year period, from 1980 to 1985, Judy Chicago created a whole series of designs or patterns for The Birth Project, *which she then gave to volunteer needleworkers all over the United States and Canada. The craftswomen interpreted the designs in embroidery, quilting, needlepoint, crocheting, and knitting according to the directions and with the materials supplied by Chicago. The Crowning NP 4 was executed by Frannie Yablonsky of Somerville, New Jersey, in a rich texture with a variety of stitches that try to match the feeling of the design.*

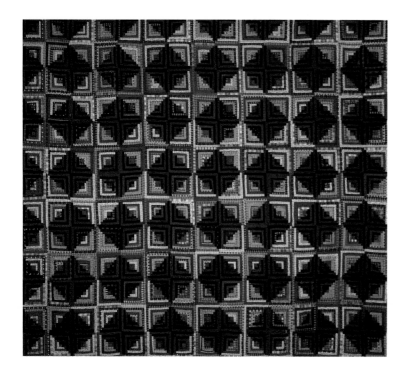

The pieced method, usually reserved for everyday blankets, often produced the most astonishing abstract designs in lively colors. Patterns, some of them handed down and spread around, were given popular names like Courthouse Steps, Log Cabin, or Crazy. The Log Cabin quilt of figure 14-7 was pieced together from rectangular patches of different colors and designs sewn around identical squares. The quilt maker, with a keen eye for value and color contrast, put together a

coverlet full of shifting spatial illusions created through alternating light-dark variations of color. Her quilt delights the eyes at the same time that it provides the security of a warm bedcover.

Tapestry. In contrast to blankets or clothing produced for everyday use, **tapestries** are fabric wall coverings for the well-to-do. Tapestries woven into pictorial designs have been treasured as works of art for centuries. The *Unicorn Tapestries* including *The Unicorn Leaps the Stream* (FIG. 14-8), at the Cloisters, the branch of the Metropolitan Museum in New York devoted to medieval art, is a prized example of the art of tapestry weaving. Between strong, tightly twisted vertical threads of undyed wool (the warp), craftspeople, working from the back, wove finer horizontal threads of brilliantly colored wool (the weft). They also employed silk and metallic thread to complete the highlights of the image.

Modern Fiber Art. Since the 1950s a number of artists sympathetic to the traditions of fiber work have explored ways to make fiber a vehicle for self-expression by moving the craft in the direction of sculpture. Modern fiber art has evolved into a major means of artistic expression. The wall hangings of fiber artists do not simply imitate two-dimensional paintings like many older tapestries, but emphasize the texture of the material and the three-dimensional relief of the fibers. Many modern works of fiber art, which were never woven on a loom, are suspended or draped from a wall or a ceiling, stuffed and fitted over an internal support, or flopped on the floor. These fiber works have acquired sculptural mass and movement through space while maintaining some of the traditional techniques of fiber handicraft and only a symbolic reference to their original function.

In her work called *High Rise* (FIG. 14-9) Claire Zeisler, a pioneer of fiber art in America, braided thick ropes that hang from the ceiling and spill out on the floor. The bright red thread wrapped around the braiding belies the muscularity of the rope. The rope, swelling as it descends from the ceiling, changes into thousands of carefully combed strands, then cascades across the floor in fluid disarray. It is possible to follow the linear movement of the strands descending from order into disorder, or in the other direction, rising up out of chaos into order, as the title implies. *High Rise* creates a powerful and energetic three-dimensional sculptural presence in the room.

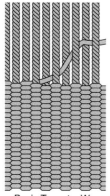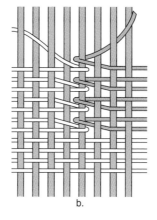

a. Basic Tapestry Weave
and Formation of Ribs

b.

FIG 14-8 [Medieval (French?)], *The Unicorn Leaps the Steam,* from the *Unicorn Tapesties.* C. 1500. Wool, silk, silver thread, about 145 in. (368.3 cm) high. Cloisters, Metropolitan Museum of Art, New York.

The Unicorn Leaps the Steam *is one in a series of seven tapestries that tell the story of the hunt of the unicorn. The unicorn, a fabulous horselike creature, has on his head a single white horn, which is capable of repelling poison. In medieval thought, the story of this creature is an allegory of Christ and the Virgin Mary. In the tapestry shown here, the third of the series, the unicorn narrowly escapes the dogs and spears of the hunters by leaping across a stream. The ten hunters and as many dogs pursue the unicorn in a landscape dominated by a steadfast oak tree and strewn with hawthorn, pomegranate, daisy, primrose, and iris—all of which have symbolic meaning. Unable to capture the unicorn by force, the hunters trick him and he is tamed into submission by a maiden. Although he is killed and brought back to the castle, the last tapestry shows the unicorn happily alive in a flowery meadow.*

FIG 14-9 CLAIRE ZEISLER [American, 1903–], *High Rise.* 1983–1984. Hemp, synthetic fiber, thread. Milwaukee Art Museum.

Chapter 14: Applications of Design

FIG 14-10 [Egyptian], pectoral with solar and lunar emblems. C. 1340 B.C. Gold, silver inlaid with carnelian, lapis lazuli, calcite, obsidian (?), turquoise, and red, blue, green, black, and white glass, 5 7/8 × 5 11/16 in. (14.9 × 14.4 cm). Egyptian Museum, Cairo.

Metalwork

Through the centuries, craftspeople skilled in working with metals have produced useful objects of great artistic merit such as horse bridles, ceremonial swords, weather vanes, grillwork, vessels, and countless other items. **Metalwork** has also long been associated with the making of luxury goods like jewelry. The rarity of gold, silver, and precious stones as well as their color and radiance have made jewelry a pleasure-filled extravagance for most people. Although these goods may serve a practical function as elements of dress and decoration for the human body, their sumptuousness and costliness place the jewelry making craft far beyond the common meaning of the word *functional*.

Nevertheless, throughout history jewelry has had many functions other than providing a superfluous ornament and expressing personal vanity. Jewelry has been made and worn to mark important stages in a person's life like birth, marriage (wedding rings), and death. In the ages before democratic societies, it expressed social rank and upper-class status. It also indicated that the owner possessed wealth and therefore power. In times when currencies were nonexistent or unstable, jewelry was a guaranteed security, a form of capital investment.

The ancient Egyptians spent lavishly for jewelry, and a pectoral, or chest ornament, in Cairo's Egyptian Museum (see FIG. 14-10) is a splendid example of their skill. It was found wrapped in the cloths covering the mummy of King Tutankhamen of Egypt (c. 1370–1352 B.C.) in 1923. The discovery of King Tut's tomb—the only tomb of an Egyptian pharaoh uncovered in modern times that had not already been robbed of its treasure—produced sensational headlines around the world. The splendid jeweled chest ornament, less than six inches across, was more than a lavish display of the wealth of the pharaoh. Its design has religious symbolism that transformed it into a talisman appropriate to be buried with the king.

The pectoral represents the moon and the sun. The Egyptians revered the sun as the creator and ruler of the world and the renewer of life and of external existence. The sun appears in the form of both a falcon and a scarab (a beetle). The royal jeweler cleverly made a composite animal from the body of the insect and the wings of the bird. The wings and tail of the falcon as well as other parts of the pectoral were made in the **cloissoné** technique by setting colored glass and

340   Part III: The Visual Arts

semiprecious stones within borders of gold. At the top, the left eye of the god Horus, the crescent, and the silver circular disk stand for the moon. The fringe dangling at the bottom represents lotus and papyrus flowers and poppy buds. Interred with his jewelry, Tutankhamen was protected and equipped for the afterlife in royal splendor.

Royal courts in Europe sometimes maintained their own workshops where luxury goods were created for the palace. Some of the most splendid and sumptuous examples of jewelry and goldsmith work are the Easter eggs that were produced by the firm of Peter Carl Fabergé in imperial St. Petersburg. Ironically, Fabergé eggs derive from a centuries-old folk tradition of decorating eggs at Easter as a natural symbol of new life in the warmth of spring. The upper part of the Renaissance-style Fabergé egg in figure 14-11, covered with a delicate trellis design, has a lid that opens to reveal another surprise gift of jewelry inside. The body of the egg is made of milk white chalcedony, a quartz. A red ruby and four diamonds form a flower at each intersection of the gold and enamel bands of the trellis. The date on top is written in diamonds. Floral motifs in red, green, and blue translucent enamel alternate with opaque white enamel around the egg. Not just the cost of the materials but the precision, delicacy, and handsome classical balance of the gold, enamel, and jewelry work make this Fabergé Easter egg a priceless treasure.

Ceramics

Pottery is one of the oldest crafts, synonymous with civilization itself. It grew out of the essential human need to store and carry food and drink. At the same time pottery has been for centuries a collector's item, a precious and treasured object, a symbol of status and wealth, and a piece of admired beauty. It epitomizes the paradoxical power of craft to transform the mud of the earth into something rare and beautiful.

Pottery is made of clay (chiefly pulverized granite and gneiss), sand, and other materials, which, when wet, can both retain their shape and be molded by the human imagination into a thousand forms. When the dried clay is fired in open flames or in a kiln, it is baked to permanent hardness because the particles within it begin to melt and run into one another above 1200 degrees Fahrenheit (650 degrees centigrade). Fired at

FIG 14-11 PETER CARL FABERGÉ [Russian, 1846–1920), Renaissance egg. 1894. Gold, chalcedony, rubies, diamonds, enamel, 5 1/4 in. (13.3 cm) wide. Forbes Magazine Collection, New York.

From 1886 to 1916 the talented craftspeople of the Fabergé company produced fifty-three Easter eggs for the Russian imperial family. A number of other, only slightly less sumptuous Easter eggs were made for the very wealthy. The imperial eggs were presented by the Russian tsar—first Alexander III, then Nicolas II—each year to his wife and mother as Easter presents. The Renaissance egg, given to Tsarina Maria Feodorovna in 1894, was designed by Michael Perchin, who created all the imperial Fabergé eggs until 1903. The five-inch Renaissance egg, unlike most Fabergé eggs, rests on its side.

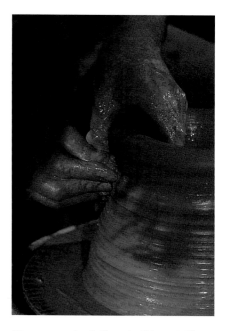

The pottery wheel. Photo by Wayne Miller, Magnum.

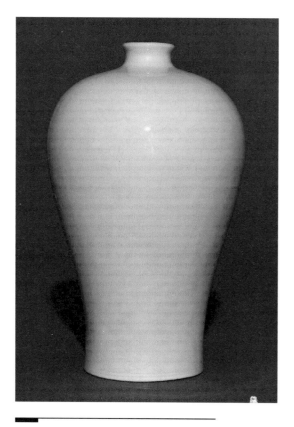

Fig 14-12 [Chinese, Jiangxi Province], *Meiping (Prunus) (Vase with Cloud Collar and Peony Sprays).* Ming dynasty, reign of Yung-lo, 1402–1424. Porcelain with incised decoration and white glaze, 12 5/8 in. (32.1 cm) high. Cleveland Museum of Art. Severance and Greta Milikin Collection. (64.167).

a low heat, the clay remains grainy and porous and is called **earthenware.** Increased heat produces smoother and harder **stoneware** because more of the particles melt into one another. At the highest temperatures the particles melt and fuse completely, producing creamy white **porcelain**—provided that the clay is highly refined and properly mixed with the white clay kaolin.

Traditionally, almost all pottery was molded by hand, and the essential form of a pot remains the shape of the cupped hands. In the simplest procedure for making clayware, potters stick their thumbs into a lump of clay and, between their thumb and fingers, squeeze the clay up into containing walls. Another very old procedure is to coil a rope of clay around and around to build up the walls of the pot, then beat the walls against a smooth stone held against the inside. Still another procedure is to assemble a piece from slabs of clay. The most common procedure is to "throw" the clay on a flat, rotating wheel, and as the wheel turns, run the clay between wet hands that raise and shape the forms of the pot.

Most pottery is circular in its horizontal circumference—unless it is assembled from slabs. The endless creative variations of pottery usually lie in the vertical elevation—the generally convex swelling of the form. Almost all pottery is made to stand erect on the ground like a human being, and for centuries potters have spoken in anthropomorphic terms about the body of a pot, its lip, neck, shoulder, belly, and foot.

To make a pot impervious to liquids and to enhance its appearance, potters frequently apply a **glaze**—a hard, glasslike coating. The countless recipes for glaze include coloring pigments (if desired) and some form of silica, which will liquefy in the kiln and coat all parts of the pot to which the glaze was applied with a thin layer of glass. The chemical relationship of the glaze to the clay, the humidity of the air, and the time for the firing and cooling process can all make some differences in the color and texture of the glaze.

During the Ming dynasty in China (1368–1644), an imperial kiln was established at Ching-Te-Chen, where thousands of the best Chinese porcelains were produced for six centuries. Some of the finest white porcelains were made during the reign of Yung-lo in the early 1400s. A delicate curvilinear floral motif was incised on the vase in figure 14-12 before it was glazed. The thick transparent glaze tints the vase slightly, and mysteriously hides the decoration underneath it. The broad, slightly concave foot of the vase gathers together the forces of the earth around it, then it gradually rises and swells in a broad, bulbous upper body. The shoulder rapidly folds over the interior toward a narrow, high lip. Vases such as this were appreciated by the Chinese for the skill of the worker and for the subtle variations that resulted from hand throwing on the potter's wheel. They contemplated in the vase, as do we, the very meaning of swelling and closure.

On the rugged peninsula of Korea, the ceramic workshops of the court and monasteries often imitated the styles of Chinese pottery. But the Korean peasant rice bowl in figure 14-13 displays something lacking in the Chinese Ming vase—a feeling for clay as clay. Even though the shape of the rice bowl is irregular, the surface is coarse, and the glazing is pitted, the anonymous potter stayed in close touch with the medium. From a small base the sturdy sides of the bowl flare to a slightly curved lip. Korean potters had a taste for plain, undecorated ware so that nothing would get in the way of appreciating the shape of the pieces. The upper half of the rice bowl was dipped in a white slip of liquid white clay, which also coated the inside of the bowl. Over years of use, liquids easily penetrated the cracks and pinholes in the glaze and stained the white slip. The signs of use in the bowl give added delight to its frugal and humble appearance.

The Japanese cultivated a similar style of "peasant" pottery in conjunction with their sophisticated and ritualized tea ceremony. The aristocracy and upper middle class deliberately chose to use at this ceremony a directly modeled peasant style of pottery like that of the Raku *tea bowl* in figure 14-14. The Japanese also appreciated the bowl for its simplicity and its rough irregularity, for the evidence of hand artisanship visible in the dimples and bulges, and for the lack of symmetry, the uneven glaze, and the pitted surface. The clay was usually mixed with ground-up flint so that when it was rapidly fired the clay body would "open up" to display evidence of the firing. Cupping the bowl in the palms of the hand, the user could feel the weight of the ceramic and could feel the hand of the artist in the very surface of the piece. The Japanese self-conscious and cultivated taste for irregularity in Raku teaware became an art of profound dignity under the influence of Zen Buddhism, which stressed simplicity and challenged formality.

FIG 14-13 [Korean], Punch'ong ware bowl. Yi dynasty, fifteenth to sixteenth centuries. Glazed stoneware partially covered with white slip, 3 3/4 × 7 1/8 in. (9.5 × 18.1 cm). Brooklyn Museum of Art.

FIG 14-14 HONAMI KŌETSU [Japanese, 1558–1637], tea bowl. Raku stoneware. Freer Gallery of Art, Washington, D.C.

FIG 14-15 Peter Voulkos [American, 1924–], *Untitled Stack Pot.* 1964. Stoneware sculpture, 10 5/8 × 29 15/16 in. (27 × 76 cm). Detroit Institute of Arts. Purchase of Founders Society; Miscellaneous Memorials Fund.

The ceramist Peter Voulkos was encouraged to change clay into a vehicle for self-expression by the freedom of Japanese teaware, by its evidence of the maker's hand, and by its incorporation of random accidents. In 1954 Voulkos had just witnessed Abstract Expressionist painters Franz Kline and Willem de Kooning at work in New York City before he went to head the department of ceramics at the Otis Art Institute in Los Angeles. Later, he moved to the University of California at Berkeley.

Although the Japanese revere pottery as a form of art, many American potters, inspired by the words and examples of the British potter Bernard Leach (1887–1979), have considered themselves primarily professional craftspeople. Having mastered the techniques of pottery making, they developed the handcrafting of vessels of clay into a wholesome way of life. The meaning of their craft and of their lifestyle was upset in the mid-1950s when several ceramists ignored traditional techniques and contradicted clay's symbolism as a material for a functional vessel. They used clay instead to make expressive ceramic sculpture. Peter Voulkos's *Untitled Stack Pot* (FIG. 14-15) looks like it may have originally been thrown on the potter's wheel but then was reassembled, ripped open, pierced, and painted in an emotional struggle between the clay and the potter. Voulkos negated the pot's pretensions toward a function. He manipulated clay with the bold freedom of a contemporary Abstract Expressionist painter. The expressionist potter and the Expressionist painter both leave evident traces of their creative activity in their medium.

The Impact of the Industrial Revolution on Crafts

At the same time that Josiah Wedgewood in eighteenth-century England produced handcrafted luxury ceramics for the upscale market, in another division of his organization he mass-produced "useful ware" like the tureen in figure 14-16. This division specialized in manufacturing a creamy white earthenware that had the appearance of porcelain but was cast by repeatedly pouring liquid clay into molds. Wedgewood touted the elegance, simplicity, and uniformity of his useful ware coated with an even, clear glaze and painted with a simple design that was mechanically transferred to the ceramic. Aggressively marketed as queen's ware because sets of it had been sold to the British royal family and Catherine the Great of Russia, the earthenware was easily and quickly manufactured and the product was of reliable quality and cheap. Its salability became as important as, perhaps more important than, its artistic style.

Wedgwood, in short, "invented" the modern mass production of ceramics and became a pioneer of the industrial revolution. He built a factory filled with machines that turned out a high volume of his prodcts. More important, the different activities necessary for the manufacture of his useful ware were separated among distinct groups of workers for the sake of efficiency. This division of labor meant that no craftsperson ever worked on an object from beginning to end or had any control over its form. Although Wedgwood employed several designers at his factory, as well as outside artists, their activities were usually separated from the actual manufacturing process, over which they had no control.

The success of Wedgwood's inexpensive cream earthenware stimulated the modern divorce between design, materials, and manufacture. Small-scale mass production, the division of labor, and the separation of the designer from production had each existed to some extent before Wedgwood, but the efficiency and thoroughness of his operation and the aggressive marketing of his products were new.

FIG 14-16   JOSIAH WEDGWOOD [English, 1730–1795], queen's ware dinner set, Green Water Leaf pattern. C. 1790. Wedgwood Museum, Barlaston, Staffordshire, England.

Arts and Crafts Movement

The modern revival of crafts as a form of art and as a way of life began in the late nineteenth century, not to rectify Renaissance theory about fine art and applied arts or to challenge the status of the fine artist, but to protest the dismal quality of mass-manufactured products. In nineteenth-century England the writer John Ruskin and the painter William Morris, who both called for the return to handcrafted work, started the **Arts and Crafts movement** in response to the ugliness of manufactured goods. Many machine-made products at that time tried to imitate something other than what they were or tried to camouflage what they were in florid, extraneous designs. Ruskin and Morris could not imagine that machine-made products might have artistic value in any form.

To remedy the poor state of industrial design, Ruskin and Morris insisted that the designer should also be the one who makes the product, so that the object reflects an individual's humanity. Handmade work, they believed, would not have the exact finish and precision of a machine-made item and thus would reveal the personality and skill of the maker. And since the designer would understand the entire process of making, the craftsperson would take delight in the possibilities of the material and exploit the genuine nature of the material. There would be no more false imitations.

FIG 14-17   WILLIAM MORRIS [England, 1834–1896], *Trellis* wallpaper. 1862. William Morris Gallery, Walthamstow, London.

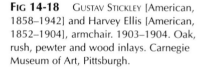

FIG 14-18   GUSTAV STICKLEY [American, 1858–1942] and Harvey Ellis [American, 1852–1904], armchair. 1903–1904. Oak, rush, pewter and wood inlays. Carnegie Museum of Art, Pittsburgh.

In 1861, several years before Louis Comfort Tiffany set up shop in New York, Morris established in England the design firm Fine Art Workmen, soon called Morris and Company, in order to bring the qualities of handcrafted work to commercial products for the household. His *Trellis* pattern (FIG. 14-17) was the first of the famous wallpapers designed by his company. Hand printed from twelve different blocks, his simplified pattern of straight-lined trellis and curving vine is offset by the sprightly activity of birds. Straightforward and based on nature, the *Trellis* paper may have given a small room an airy appearance as though it were the interior of a garden bower. Morris's wallpapers set a high standard of quality and were affordable for the general public. Unfortunately, handcrafted items usually cost more than mass-produced goods, making it difficult to bring good personalized design to the general public.

The British Arts and Crafts movement soon spread to America, where craftsmen and craftswomen were not so reluctant as Ruskin and Morris to industrialize and massmarket handcrafted goods. In the opening

FIG 14-19   WENDELL CASTLE [American, 1932–], *Desk.* 1967. Mahogany and cherry laminated to plywood; gesso, silver leaf, 40 1/2 × 89 × 62 1/2 in. (102.9 × 226.1 × 158.8 cm). Charles A. Wustum Museum of Fine Arts, Racine, Wisconsin. Gift of S.C. Johnson Wax.

To build this desk, Wendell Castle first glued together a number of boards that had been cut so that when stacked, they would resemble the final piece. The first person to apply the procedure to furniture, he calls his method "stacked lamination." To begin shaping the rough mass of wood, he first worked over the piece with a chain saw. Castle then smoothed the surface with an assortment of power tools as well as old-fashioned chisels and sandpaper. Noted for his exquisite craftsmanship, Castle does not care what tools he uses as long as he can push wood beyond the ordinary.

years of the twentieth century, Gustave Stickley ran his Craftsman Workshops as a business where Harvey Ellis designed the armchair in figure 14-18. Stickley sought to restore simple, clean lines to furniture so that the material would express itself naturally. Except for Ellis's abstract floral design on the central back slat, Stickley avoided extraneous ornament and let the lines and proportions of the chair speak for themselves. The Craftsman Workshops built simple, massive furniture meant to last, by assembling each piece with old-fashioned mortise-and-tenon joints instead of screws and nails. While promoting his furniture as art that was hand wrought by a craftsperson, Stickley "mass-produced" artistic goods that the general public could afford. He characterized his work as the mission style because in the home it would fulfill a moral mission to educate the American family in good proportions and honest construction and thus influence their life toward goodness and truth.

Art Furniture

The flowering of art furniture in the late twentieth century has kept alive the idea of the individual craftsperson, who now often approaches furniture design as a form of art. Since the 1960s, Wendell Castle, perhaps America's most famous woodworker, has deliberately turned his back on traditional furniture design in order to clear his mind of preconceived notions and to make something original. His desk in figure 14-19 seems more like an organic growth in which the rootlike legs have sprouted a top, than the standard desk assembled with a rectangular top, side pieces, and four screwed-on legs. Castle's desk in fact rests on only three points, two of which are far to the left of the top. More than building a piece of furniture, Castle sought to create a piece of sculpture in which he delighted in the curved lines, swelling masses, and color contrasts as a means of personal expression.

FIG 14-20 FRANK GEHRY [American, 1929–], armchair. 1990. Wood (maple plywood). KnollStudio. New York.

In the 1990s, the furniture company KnollStudio commissioned the California architect Frank Gehry to design lightweight chairs made out of ordinary wood, which could be mass manufactured at a competitive price. Gehry created his unusual chairs (FIG. 14-20) out of thin wooden slats that look like enlarged Popsicle sticks, which are bent, then woven and glued together. No nails, screws, or staples secure the joints. Each slat consists of seven one-thirty-second-inch veneers of maple laminated together into the required shape. Consequently, the very lightweight chairs use very little wood. Weaving the curved wooden slats creates an integrated structure that supports itself on unusually thin members. Because the structural support is achieved through interwoven S-curves, the light strips of wood remain springy; they flex and adapt themselves to the shape of the body. Although Gehry's innovative and comfortable chairs use a traditional material and the design is reduced to its essential structure, the chairs have a far-from-functional look about them.

Industrial Design

The Arts and Crafts movement was not likely to push back the tide of mass manufacture initiated by Josiah Wedgwood and other pioneers of the industrial revolution. The newly enfranchised middle class demanded their share of the relatively inexpensive consumer goods now available. These goods were produced in factories where workers, who might have been engaged in handicrafts at home, now performed monotonous, grinding labor. Although a good number of early machine-produced goods often tried to imitate the styles of earlier periods in history, many developed a bland styleless style designed mostly by engineers for manufacturing efficiency.

It was the rapidly increasing demand for consumer goods for the home starting in the 1920s that gave rise to the art of **industrial design.** An industrial designer creates for the manufacturer's product a style that will increase its usefulness and efficiency and, most important, increase its appeal to the consumer. Industrial designers compose their work with the same visual elements and principles of design used by every artist, but, unlike most artists or craftspersons, they do not usually get their hands dirty making something. Although designers may help set up the means of production, they usually leave the actual manufacture of the object to someone else.

A designer or, more likely, a team of designers has shaped and styled all the machine-made vehicles, appliances, communications equipment, furniture, tools, toys, and utensils that we constantly use. The possession of an increasing amount of stylish consumer goods and the status they afford has been a passion with the American public for generations. With countless mass-manufactured goods filling the homes and businesses of people around the world, industrial designers have now become a powerful influence on our daily visual experience. Perhaps industrial designers create a contemporary visual style more pervasive than the so-called fine artist or craftsperson could ever hope to achieve.

As they did in Wedgwood's day, industrial designers still keep themselves apart from the actual manufacturing of mass-produced goods. The separation between design and production is what fundamentally distinguished their work from craft work. But the separation does not necessarily result in bad design,

Contemporary telephone, AT&T VideoPhone
2500. Courtesy AT&T.

Early-twentieth-century telephone.
Bettmann Archive.

because in the twentieth century, industrial designers
have grown much more aware of the processes of production. They also try to respect the inherent nature
of the materials and the materials' potential for expression within a machine-made product.

Although machines can repeatedly manufacture
goods with far greater accuracy and precision than the
human hand, the judgment, skill, and imagination of
designers still gives shape to each product. Their
inventiveness often challenges the impersonality of
the machine or exploits the machine's precision. The
common paper-thin aluminum Coke can (FIG. 14-21),
for example, has an attractive simplicity and precision.
Earlier metalworkers would have admired not only its
balanced design but also its accuracy and perfection,
which can be repeated over and over again.

Whereas the significance of the lines, shapes, and
colors in works of art are normally judged by their
visual relationships to one another, somewhat different "rules" are used to judge the visual elements of
mass-produced products. When people talk about the
good or bad design of an automobile, an airplane, or a
toaster—products of industrial design—they are not
merely referring to the painted stripes or the chrome
trim of the item. They are commenting on all the visual elements of the item and whether they work well
within that product. They are also referring to the
inventiveness of the forms and the enhancement of
the materials used through the design.

FIG 14-21   Coca-Cola can from China.
Courtesy Coca-Cola China, Limited.

Purely visual concerns are not enough to determine whether the shapes of an industrial product are
part of a good design. Industrial designers have to consider other important design elements not usually
found in traditional works of art. The visual elements
must satisfy the functional needs of the product and
enable it to work well. The shapes must also be suited
to efficient and low-cost manufacture by machines.
Finally, the design must be eye-catching and yet not

FIG 14-22   Ford Model T. 1908.
Photo: Bettmann

FIG 14-23   Lincoln Zephyr. 1936.
Photo: Bettmann

FIG 14-24   Cadillac Eldorado Brougham.
1955. Photo: Bettmann

too innovative, so that it will give the product an identity that appeals to the mass market.

The evolution of the visual appearance of one product, the American automobile, illustrates the complex nature of industrial design. Henry Ford created a revolution when he mass-produced the Model T at the beginning of the twentieth century (see FIG. 14-22). Before that cars were handcrafted. Ford's introduction of standardized parts, assembled by people working at a moving assembly line, meant a high volume of production. The same factors meant low cost to the consumer, since the constancy of the standardized parts reduced costs. For years Ford refused to change the Model T's design, until he was forced to do so by the increased sales of other manufacturers who had introduced new styles of body design to entice buyers.

The introduction of new styling soon became a yearly event calculated to make an old style obsolete—a policy called planned obsolescence—and to force new sales. Design became an important issue in marketing the product. Streamlining was introduced to automobiles in the 1930s (FIG. 14-23). Lights were absorbed into the fenders, and fenders took on teardrop shapes and began to merge into the body. The shape of the hood became united with the passenger compartment.

In the 1950s styling became a futuristic Buck Rogers fantasy (FIG. 14-24). Cars of enormous size and weight had bullet noses, tail fins, and simulated jet exhausts. These symbols of speed and advanced science increased the appeal of the cars to consumers, but they did little to further the effective functioning of the machine.

In the late twentieth century, auto design has been influenced by the desire for fuel efficiency, by the cost and conservation of raw materials, by adaptations to robot manufacture, as well as by aerodynamics. Masses, shapes, and lines have become fewer, smaller, simpler, more rounded, and cleaner. Many consumers now look to see that lightness, energy efficiency, and concern for the environment are incorporated in any product's design.

The design of the automobile has its own history of styles that express the age in which they were created. In many ways they reflect the taste of the time and the

Text continues on page 354

Part III: The Visual Arts

Gerald Hirshberg (1939–)

*W*HEN automobile designer Gerald Hirshberg sent his plans for the Nissan Infiniti J30 to the parent company in Japan, Japanese officials were displeased with the front end of the car. Hirshberg and his design team were surprised but soon realized that like other Westerners, they imagine a car by its side view.

In contrast, the Japanese read personality and expression into the front, or "face," of a car. The Japanese found the headlights (the "eyes") of the new Infiniti sleepy; they found the grille (the "mouth") angry. Hirshberg compromised and redesigned the headlights and the grille for wider, more expressive eyes and a smaller, less angry mouth. Before their collaboration with the Japanese, the American designers had never imagined the kind of criticism that came from another cultural perspective. Working for a Japanese firm continually gives Hirsberg new insights into product design.

Since 1980 Hirshberg has been the chief American director of Nissan Design International (NDI) in San Diego. Nissan created this subsidiary and hired Hirshberg to design Nissan cars for the American taste. NDI is one of about twenty design studios that domestic and foreign automakers have set up in southern California, where the automobile culture leads the United States. Nissan, which had a reputation for boxy and stodgy cars, established an

GERALD HIRSHBERG [American, 1939–] and Nissan Design International, Infiniti J30. 1993. Courtesy Nissan Design International, Inc.

innovative and experimental design center to bridge the two cultures. Its experiment paid off. Half the Nissans sold in the United States were designed in San Diego, and NDI has seen more of its cars go into production than have

any of the other California design subsidiaries.

Car designers in the past have typically imagined dream cars and then turned their designs over to engineers for factory production, where they were

Continued on next page

Hirshberg and his team approach design with thought and analysis. They request all the technical data for a new model ahead of time, because Hirshberg believes that obstacles are the primary motivation for creativity.

Gerald Hirshberg

drastically changed. Hirshberg wants instead to get engineers involved in the aesthetic aspect of automobile design and designers in its functional aspects. He wants the two groups to explore problems together. At NDI everyone participates in a project; everyone gets a hearing and is listened to. Not only the three dozen designers and engineers enter into the criticism of the projected design; Hirshberg insists that even secretaries, administration people, and maintenance staff make direct comments.

Hirshberg has also insisted that NDI be allowed to design other products for outside clients, as well as Nissan cars. This outside work, which amounts to less than 10 percent of the organization's business, offers the team fresh perspectives for car design. The commission to design a one-hundred-foot yacht made the NDI design team more sensitive to issues of form that had not been thought of before. Hirshberg believes that designers need an occasional break. They need to distance themselves from auto design to be cre-

ative, to imagine something new, and to turn out the unexpected.

Hirshberg also firmly believes that automobile design is not just a matter of restyling headlights or door handles. To create a new car, his designers do not immediately start drawing cars. They sit and think about the product, ask questions about its functions, and approach its design with thought and analysis. They request all the technical data for a new model ahead of time, because

Hirshberg believes that obstacles are the primary motivation for creativity. Before developing the Quest minivan, which won an award for its design, Hirshberg and his staff spent several weeks driving the minivans of the competition. They noted how owners used the vehicle. Because a minivan is primarily a utility vehicle, the NDI team designed the interior first, then used it to guide their shaping of the exterior. Instead of a pointy-nosed design that

GERALD HIRSHBERG [American, 1939–] and Nissan Design International, Nissan Quest minivan. 1993. Courtesy Nissan Design International, Inc.

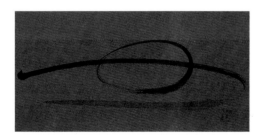

Doug Wilson's sketch for the Infiniti J30.

tries to give a van the look of a racing car, the Quest received a flexible boxy styling that grew out of its function.

While working on a project, Hirshberg and his team develop a "mind map" to set out some of its goals. They spread out the images and words of their design on a twenty-foot board.

Eventually they unify the multiple perspectives before them into a simplified shape. The Nissian design team usually does not take the time to make elaborate illustrations of a new car. It often works with its rougher initial sketches, which have a tension and spontaneity that precise renderings lack. For example, designer Doug Wilson's sketch of an egg crossed by an arched line became the organizing principle for the rear slope of the Infiniti J30. Hirshberg then looked for ways to express what Wilson had drawn—a concept opposed to the popular sloping wedge shape of many automobiles.

At thirteen years of age Hirshberg knew he wanted to be an industrial designer. He was attracted by the diversity built into a profession where designers had to learn as much as they could about a new field and then express themselves through it. Hirshberg was thought of as an artist when he majored in mechanical engineering at Ohio State and was thought of as an engineer when he studied industrial design at Cleveland Institute of Art. He worked for General Motors for sixteen years before joining Nissan. Hirshberg is learning to speak Japanese, but he feels that his intimate acquaintance with a foreign culture has been more of a path to self-knowledge than an education in that culture. Time and again he has had to throw out his own preconceptions, which were only an impendiment to creativity.

Hirshberg likes to maintain a healthy diversity among the designers at NDI so that the team has more than one perspective. Hirshberg feels that there is a greater likelihood for creativity through unexpected juxtapositions when different points of view rub against each other. People then take risks. The designers and engineers he hires for NDI share only two things in common, passion and talent. Those two words fit Hirshberg perfectly.

FIG 14-26 Sony Handycam Camcorder.
Courtesy of Sony Electronics, Inc.

FIG 14-25 MARCEL BREUER [American, 1902–1981], Cesca side chair. 1928. Chrome-plated tubular steel, wood, and cane; 13 1/2 × 17 1/2 × 18 3/4 in. (80 × 44.5 × 47.6 cm). Possibly an adaptation of a design by Mart Stam. Museum of Modern Art, New York. Purchase of museum. Photo © 1994 The Museum of Modern Art, New York.

values of the population. The 1950s Cadillac symbolizes the post-World War II boom years of American consumerism, for example, and the subsequent downsizing of cars reflects the energy and environmental crises of more recent times. The example of the automobile suggests that industrial design goes beyond visual appearances alone and that, unlike the fine arts, it includes distinctive considerations such as ease of production, marketing potential, and function.

Many designers have claimed that good design results when the form of the product follows from its function. They want to see a design that does not disguise what the product was built for, how it operates, how it was constructed, and the material from which it was made. Throughout most of the twentieth century a straight-edged, plain, and simple look—influ-

enced to some extent by modern art movements—has been identified as the modern style that results from machine manufacture. Only in the late twentieth century have designers realized and admitted that the modern machine-made look is not necessarily functional and is a stylistic choice that an individual designer is free to make or not make.

The functional look is often associated with the Bauhaus, even though the German art school produced only a few viable examples of industrial design. In the mid-1920s Walter Gropius, the director of the school, declared that the workshops of the Bauhaus would henceforth be laboratories to develop prototypes for massproduction by industry. The Bauhaus would train students in the technology of materials as well as in the elements of artistic design.

One member of the Bauhaus faculty, Marcel Breuer, designed extremely innovative chairs that eventually went into limited production and were widely imitated. Employing chrome-plated tubular steel—like that used for bicycle handles—Breuer created a revolutionary chair with an S-curved frame, in which the seat and back were thrust away from the two front legs, their only support (FIG. 14-25). Breuer thought that all his tubular steel furniture had a modern, styleless style, since the design resulted only from the quality of the material and the simplified structure. The bent tubing makes the chair lightweight and springy, and the aggressively simple design is transparent and mass-

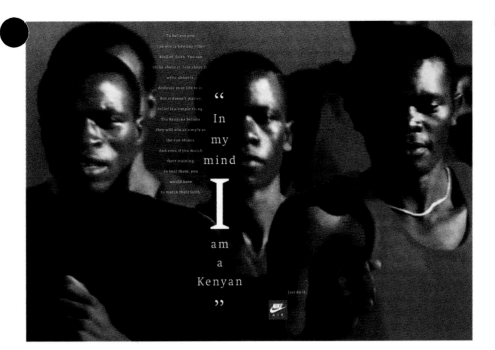

less. Chrome furniture never found much place in the home furnishing market, but it became fashionable for the office, where the note of avant-garde taste and modernity made it a status symbol.

The modern simple-and-plain design of most contemporary electrical equipment—computers, videocassette players, telephone answering machines, and many other such items—often takes exception to the rule that form follows function. The complex internal functioning of most of this equipment is seldom expressed in the external design of the product. Since the operation of most electrical equipment lies far beyond the average person's comprehension, expressing its inner workings would probably only confuse and dismay most consumers. Most designers for years have simply housed such high-tech equipment in a sleek but plain black box. The best that many product designers have achieved is to make the external controls arrayed by the electronic engineers easy to find and easy to use.

Still, it is possible to achieve good design in consumer electronic equipment. The Sony Handycam Camcorder (FIG. 14-26) displays a very efficient design in which the rubberized housing curves around the lens, leaving little empty and unnecessary space inside. Created with the traveler in mind, the curved design fits comfortably in the palm of the hand. Moreover,

since the video camera weighs only one pound five ounces, its lightness is very appealing. The controls, connected with the feature that they govern, remain within easy reach. To produce something so efficient and agreeable to the consumer, the designers and engineers did not skimp on features and company quality.

Graphic Design

To sustain the mass production of goods, manufacturers must continually advertise their products to the public to stimulate sales (see FIG. 14-27). Advertising enables the consumer to identify a product at the point of sale; it informs the consumer about the product; it persuades the consumer to want a particular brand of the product. Advertising can attribute something unique like a special status to the possession of a particular brand. Advertising can create an atmosphere, a fantasy, that transports the viewer to new experiences. Some would say that advertising can create the very need to have any product. Advertising can also identify and promote services. Medical, legal, financial, and charitable institutions as well as government and political parties buy advertising to inform the public about issues and promote the personal services they offer.

ROMAN

The quick brown fox jumped over the lazy dog.

12-point Goudy

SANS SERIF

The quick brown fox jumped over the lazy dog.

12-point Futura

ITALIC

The quick brown fox jumped over the lazy dog.

12-point Palatino italic

SCRIPT

The quick brown fox jumped over the lazy dog.

12-point Shelley Allegro script

Classes of type.

The Times-Picayune

The Miami Herald

The Atlanta Journal

FIG 14-28 *Blackletter nameplates.*

Advertising is probably the most common form of **graphic design.** Graphic design encompasses all printed and visual images that communicate messages—messages that identify, inform, and persuade. The messages of graphic design may appear in a variety of media from traditional printed publications to film and television. Graphic designers are also responsible for the arrangement of museum exhibits and the exhibition of commercial products. They design packaging and displays of all sorts as well as informational systems.

To perform its task, graphic design should be attractive in the sense that it catches the attention of the audience, and at the same time it should be accessible in the sense that the audience gets the message. All art is a form of communication between a sender and a receiver through a medium, but in graphic design not only does the medium very often involve words, the message is normally directed to a mass audience. Graphic designers generally use a simple vocabulary that the average person can understand, and like architects they take a considerable amount of direction from the client. Even in today's market, where advertisers are targeting special groups of people and are more responsive to age, ethnic group, and socioeconomics, the messages of the graphic designer are made to be understood.

Typography

The root meaning of the word *graphic* (*graphein* in Greek) refers to writing, and one of graphic design's major tasks is to create the visual appearance of words and numbers, or **typography.** In printing, designers normally work with four general styles of letters or type: script, italic, roman, and sans serif.

Script looks like handwriting because the fluid letters slant and are connected. Italic type, *which conveys an emphatic impression*, also slants, but the letters are not connected nor do they appear as fluid. Roman type resembles the elegant letters carved in ancient Roman inscriptions. The main strokes of each roman letter end in a distinctive finishing stroke called a serif. The bolder, modern-looking sans serif letters do not have these finishing strokes (*sans* in French means "without"). Another possibility, the solemn Old English, or black letter, type, resembles the lettering used in the European Middle Ages. Because of its serious and traditional character, black letter is still used

FIG 14-29   HERB LUBALIN [American, 1918–1981]. Typography. Courtesy Rhoda Sparber Lubalin.

to print the nameplate of many newspapers (FIG. 14-28). Each style of lettering comes in hundreds of individual variations in the formation, size, and weight of the letters. A certain style and size of lettering is called a **typeface.** In addition to legibility and emphasis, a creative designer like Herb Lubalin is capable of expressing visual meaning in the spacing, expansion, contraction, elongation, or thickness of the type, as illustrated by the examples of his work in figure 14-29.

Graphic designers also fashion all kinds of signs, some of which may convey their messages in images alone. Such signs, called **pictographs,** use visual images to represent a word or an idea. A red cross in most countries around the world signifies medical and relief organizations. A highway sign with a curving black arrow on a diamond-shaped yellow background clearly alerts a driver to an upcoming curve in the road. A diagonal red bar through a cigarette conveys perhaps a stronger message not to smoke than do the words No Smoking. Utilizing a number of these well-known symbols, the U.S. Department of Transportation developed a consistent system of pictographs for use in transportation terminals throughout the United States (see FIG. 14-30). In a sign system like this, designers often strive for clarity and an appealing cohesiveness by designing all the pictographs on the same sort of grid. The clarity and consistency of signs throughout an airport, office building, or hospital are welcome to a visitor and project an image of concern and competence.

FIG 14-30   ROGER COOK AND DON SHAOSKY, Cook and Shanosky Associates, Inc. U.S. Department of Transportation Symbol Signs System. 1974.

FIG 14-31 Kodak Gold Plus 100 film box. Reprinted courtesy Eastman Kodak Company.

FIG 14-32 Saturn logo. Registered trademark of Saturn Corporation. Used with permission.

Product Packaging

Product packaging, usually a three-dimensional design problem, is calculated not only to inform the viewer but to create a favorable image and a distinctive identity for the product that the consumer can readily pick out on the shelf. Most people around the world recognize Kodak film by the distinctive yellow of its box and the lowercase roman type of its name (FIG. 14-31). Most people around the world recognize a Coca-Cola soft drink by the florid script of its name set against a bright red background (see FIG. 14-21). A sophisticated

packaging design can also symbolize quality, prestige, or status for the manufacturer. Many corporations strive to design for themselves a distinctive trademark, whether through typography or through a symbolic logo or through both. The Saturn logo (FIG. 14-32) combines dynamic references to speed, soaring and movement, the planet Saturn, and condensation trails in the sky, with type similar to that used by the National Aeronautics and Space Agency for its acronym, NASA. The designers of the logo were inspired by the Saturn space program launched by NASA in the early 1960s, which represented to them a powerful vision and determination in conquering new frontiers.

Print Media and Computer Graphics

Graphic designers also design book jackets, recording covers, and magazine covers (FIG. 14-33) and create the page layouts for books, magazines, and brochures. For these tasks they must choose the size and style of type; arrange the columns of print; and integrate, balance, and harmonize headings, text, borders, and images on each page and on a series of pages. The designer usually tries to create an overall format or a consistent style for an entire publication so that the publication will have cohesion and personality and so that the design will captivate and guide the reader through the publication as well.

The kind of work that graphic designers do in the print media is illustrated in an unusual magazine advertisement for Hershey's Bar-None candy bar (FIG. 14-34). For the words in the nearly borderless background of the ad, the designer Carlos Caicedo chose a roman type with an almost arbitrary mix of capital and lowercase letters. He deliberately scrambled the size and weight and placement of the letters for a very unconventional effect. He printed the letters in a bright red against a dark green and slightly out of register so that they stand out and attract attention. The blue sans serif name of the product matches the discordant blue of the textured paper on which it rests. Subtle cast shadows emphasize the three-dimensional reality of the candy bar. Caicedo created his design— one of a series with different typefaces and colors—on a Macintosh computer.

For decades the cover of Time Magazine *has usually featured the portrait of a political leader surrounded by a red border. To promote the featured essay on evil, the cover designers of the June 10, 1991, issue took the bold step of illustrating only the word* evil *in a tall roman lowercase type against a dark gray background. The roman letters vary the traditional bold roman type of the magazine's name. The dark background and especially the lack of contrast with the word* evil *are enough to create a sinister aura.*

Chapter 14: Applications of Design

"Gabbing with Gabby" :30
(Open to white satin sheets, on which appear the words "Gabbing with Gabby" in purple script)
SFX: Background music, typical daytime soap music, lots of strings.
Announcer (VO): It's Gabbing with Gabby, Gabrielle Reese, model and volleyball star.
(Cut to Gabrielle Reese lying on satin sheets, posing and twisting while cameras click and flash)
Gabrielle: Being a model, I get asked for lots of tips.
SFX: Cameras clicking and flashing
(Close up of Reese's face)
Gabrielle: For one, always wear smudge-proof mascara.
(Cut to Reese jumping up, hitting volleyball and wiping sweat from brow. Cut back to close up of Reese's face, now hanging upside down from side of bed.)
Gabrielle: Watch your weight!
(Cut to her face covered with sweat, the sound of weights clanging, shot of her lifting weights. Cut to Reese sitting on white draped couch, head on hands.)
Gabrielle: Take things one step at a time.
(Cut to Reese running by from left to right, close up of her feet, pull back to full view. Cut to Reese on bed, now with legs and hips up over her head, with a telephone lying next to her)
Gabrielle: Be aggressive. Boys like it when you make the first call.
(Cut to Reese on tennis court, swinging aggressively, missing the ball, shouting: "What?! That was OUT!" Cut to Reese against white background, close up of Reese's smiling face)
Gabrielle: Be friendly, a winning personality can take you far in life.
(Cut to Reese jumping up and spiking volleyball over net)
Gabrielle (VO): Okay, I'm warmed up. How about basketball?
Music
Super: Just Do It

FIG 14-35   WEIDEN & KENNEDY, Advertising Agency. "Gabbing with Gabby," television commercial, Nike "Just Do It" campaign. © 1994 Nike, Inc. Reprinted with Permission.

Since advertisements for products, services, and political ideas appear in a variety of formats, an advertiser will often develop the same message or concept, like Nike's "Just Do It" campaign, in both electronic and print media at the same time (see FIGS. 14-27 and 14-35). Television advertisers frequently spare no expense on a dazzling array of film techniques—including camera work, production values, and editing—to persuade the consumer to think favorably of the product and to want it. The computer's easy ability to manipulate and to make words and images move also appears more and more on television ads and in the animated lead-ins that graphic designers have created for almost every new television show (FIG. 14-36) or channel identification.

To manipulate images and text all at once, the electronic computer has assumed a major role in the design profession. With the advent of powerful yet relatively inexpensive hardware along with sophisticated desktop software, amateur and professional communicators have at their fingertips all the common tools of the graphic designer. To produce the pages of a company report like those in figure 14-37 on a computer, a designer can easily edit, manipulate, and print in a multitude of typefaces and colors the text that was written and edited through a word processing program. The designer can also illustrate or enhance the text with designs and images stored in the computer. Full-color photographs can be added to the computer by means of a scanner or a video camera. Computer programs can create charts, maps, and other illustrations. The computer allows the communicator to arrange and harmonize text and visuals in a total design on the page. It telescopes all these functions into one, and is the perfect sketch pad because alterations of any or all the design elements are easy and rapid and instantly have a finished appearance. But even though the computer allows a graphic designer great versatility, flexibility, and speed in designing layouts, only a trained eye and a creative imagination can create the bold dignity and harmony of a two-page spread like that in figure 14-37.

FIG 14-36   WCCO-TV "Twins Time." March, 1994. Animated television promotion created on a Quantel Harriet computer, using Vertigo 3-D software. Designer/Animator: Yancy Lindquist. Writer/producer: Mark Foreman.

FIG 14-37   Frankfurt Balkind Partners (New York), design firm. Adobe Systems, Inc. 1992 Annual Report. Courtesy Adobe Systems, Inc.

FIG 14-38 RAND MILLER AND ROBYN MILLER,
CYAN, INC. [American 1960– and 1968–],
Myst. CD-ROM adventure game. Courtesy
Brøderbund Software, Inc. Novato,
California.

*Myst is a surrealistic adventure game,
based on a complex storyline. It
begins when you stumble upon an
old battered book, pick it up and find
yourself transported to an alternative
reality. The game invites you to
explore a number of fantastic worlds,
and in doing so to untangle the
mystery of what happened to the
people who once lived there.*

*These two images from the game
illustrate how a player moves through
these worlds, discovering intriguing
artifacts and clues, such as this model
ship floating in a fountain.*

*Myst features three-dimensional
realistic graphics, a non-linear
storyline, an original soundtrack,
sound effects, and full-motion video
and animation.*

Through the power and speed of a modern desk-top
computer, a designer can create work that is genuinely **multimedia.** Multimedia requires high-powered
hardware equipped with a sound card, a CD-rom
drive, and sufficient speed and capacity to combine
text, graphics, sound, animation, and full-motion
video. Multimedia work has already flourished in commercial presentations, educational programs, and
games, such as the visually stunning adventure game,
Myst (FIG. 14-38). A great advantage of computer-
generated multimedia is that it can be interactive. Not
just a passive video presentation, multimedia can
engage the viewer who must participate by selecting
the pace and the direction of the message.

Posters

Posters and billboards challenge graphic designers to
communicate effectively in a large-scale, public format. Since they must catch the attention of the
passerby, posters and billboards have for a long time
emphasized a visual simplicity and directness. The
artistry of posters has made them collector's items
since they first appeared in the late 1800s. At the end
of the nineteenth century, following new developments in color lithography, the French painter Henri
Toulouse-Lautrec brought the poster to a new level of
art and effective advertising. In his poster advertising
the Moulin Rouge (FIG. 14-39), the text in a rounded
sans serif remains simple and integrated with the total
composition. Toulouse-Lautrec also simplified the
imagery and boldly manipulated space in the manner
of Japanese printmakers. Four simple flat colors and
the strong outline of each form make a striking and
original design.

Although the dominance of commercial posters in
American advertising has been overtaken by magazine
and television ads, the poster more than ever appeals
to collectors of the art of graphic design. Consequently,
in addition to announcing an ad campaign, a well-
designed poster may simply lend prestige to an advertiser who sponsors it as an art form. The imaginative
works of Julius Friedman, for example, are preserved
and displayed long after the event they announce.
Friedman, who has designed over 250 posters, realizes
that a good poster needs an arresting image that will
make an impression. His *Louisville Ballet* poster (FIG.
14-40) captures attention by the stark simplicity of its
axial design, its striking pink-and-black contrast, and

FIG 14-39 HENRI TOULOUSE-LAUTREC [French, 1864–1901], *Moulin Rouge (La Goulue)* poster. 1891. Color litograph, 75 3/16 × 46 1/16 in. (191 × 117 cm). Art Institute of Chicago.

In 1891 the manager of the Moulin Rouge nightclub in Paris commissioned a new poster from the painter Henri Toulouse-Lautrec. When three thousand copies of his very large lithograph appeared on the street, Toulouse-Lautrec became the talk of Paris. The artist featured the dancer La Goulue (Louise Weber) in the very center of the poster, where she performs her notorious high kicks. Her shadowy, grimacing dance partner (Valentin-le-Désossé) looms close to the surface in the foreground. The audience have become black silhouettes in the background. Three yellow globes of a gas lamp appear on the left. Proud of his poster, the artist submitted it to two art exhibitions.

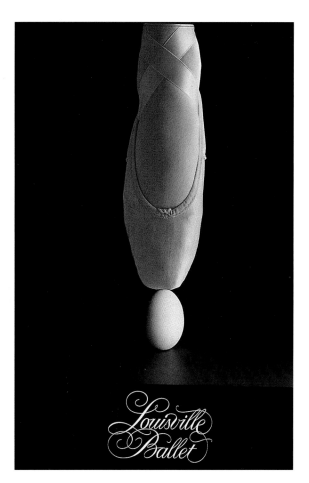

FIG 14-40 JULIUS FRIEDMAN [American, 1943–], *Louisville Ballet* poster. 22 × 35 in. (55.5 × 89 cm). Courtesy Julius Friedman, Louisville, KY.

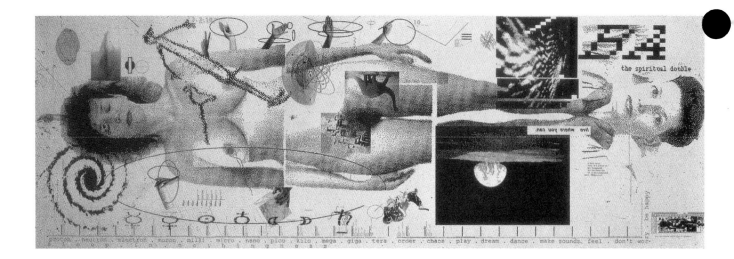

Fig 14-41 April Greiman [American, 1948–], *Does It Make Sense?* poster. 1986. Courtesy April Greiman Associates.

the surreal impression of a dancer standing on an egg. The airborne lightness and delicacy implied in the image is reinforced by the florid script of the minimal text, Louisville Ballet.

April Greiman, who has pioneered the use of computers in graphic design, printed a poster for *Design Quarterly*, titled *Does It Make Sense?* (Fig. 14-41), entirely on her Macintosh computer. The six-foot-long poster was folded and mailed as an issue of the magazine. To create it, images from a video camera were digitized and translated into tiny dots (pixels), which were then edited by the MacPaint program. The text was printed on the screen in various typefaces and arranged in the composition as it evolved. Lines were produced with the computer's MacDraw tool. The Macintosh computer could segment the finished design into parts so that Gremain could print her original poster on about two dozen pieces of ordinary 8½-by-11-inch bond paper, which were then fitted together like mosaic tiles. Her poster preserves the feel

of the computer and the emerging world of electronic vision it explores.

Whether creating a sign, a poster, a magazine ad, or the page layout for this textbook, graphic designers utilize the same visual elements and principles of design as every artist. They adjust the visual elements on the paper or video screen to establish a dominance or focus to the message, consistency and variety among the formal elements, and balance within the total design. In applying these principles, they organize words and images to attract and inform the audience and to persuade it, not about their own personality but about the company, the product, or the service. Like the products of industrial design, the messages of graphic design are everywhere, calling for our attention and shaping our attitudes and way of life. Through their widespread and pervasive work, creative designers bring artistic values out of the museums and into daily experience.

CRAFTS

Four types of craft work exist:
1. The practice of original handicraft skills to make useful items.
   Examples: Basketry, pottery, quiltmaking
2. The revival of original handicraft skills to oppose mass manufacture and to reassert personal integrity.
   Examples: Morris, Stickley
3. The use of traditional craft media as art media.
   Examples: Castle, Littleton, Voulkos, Zeisler
4. The production of luxury goods because of their fine materials, skillful execution, or design.
   Examples: Fabergé egg, Tutankhamen's pectoral

INDUSTRIAL DESIGN

Industrial design is the creation of mass-produced objects, manufactured largely by machines, by someone who is normally not involved in the actual manufacture of the object.

Industrial design has four main characteristics:
1. It uses the same visual elements and principles of design as every artwork.
2. It fulfills and enhances the functional needs of a product.
3. It is suited to manufacture by machines.
4. It creates an appeal for the mass market.

GRAPHIC DESIGN

Graphic design is the creation of printed and visual messages.

Its purpose is to inform and persuade a mass audience.

The major kinds of graphic design are typography, signs, publishing layouts, advertising, film and TV production, packaging, exhibitions.

Key Terms and Concepts

Arts and Crafts movement
basketry
colissoné
crafts
earthenware
embroidery
fiber arts
glaze

graphic design
guilds
industrial design
metalwork
multimedia
pictographs
porcelain
pottery

quilt
stoneware
studio craft
tapestries
typeface
typography

15

ARCHITECTURE

An Architectural Experience: Chartres Cathedral

Imagine what it is like to experience a great building like Chartres Cathedral (FIG. 15-1). From a distance, we see the impressive bulk of the stone building with its spires and pinnacles rising above the rooftops of the city. Up close, the asymmetry of the two spires flanking the front entrance presents a puzzling but picturesque outline against the sky. The spire on the right appears simple, massive, and clear-cut, even stodgy by comparison with its counterpart. The spire on the left, rebuilt later in a newer, more up-to-date style, has taller and more slender members and is more open and delicate.

The narrowing depth of the three front porches funnels us inside the church. On the left and right of the porch we notice statues as thin as the columns. Once through the door we are thrilled by the depth, breadth, and height of the cathedral. At the same time we are immersed in its cool darkness. A colored fog seems to fill the space; the gray stones of the walls seem faint. The most striking sights are the large windows filled with glass glowing red and blue.

After we have adjusted to the dim light and the soaring space, the repetition of the arches down the center of the building impels us to move forward. As we advance along this avenue lined with thick clusters of columns, our eye turns to follow their thin lines up the wall. They thrust up between the windows and then, spreading like a fan, cross the ceiling. As we walk, we sense the worn stones beneath our feet, the texture and color of eight-hundred-year-old stone walls. Footsteps and voices reverberate within the

Chartres, France, West facade. Giraudon/Art Resource, New York.

stone vaults. All our senses are heightened.

Halfway through the church, spaces similar in their proportions to the main body of the building open to the left and right and interrupt our progress forward. This crossing of east-west and north-south directions is marked with thicker supports at the corners and a square vault overhead. We pause to look around and appreciate the extent of the symmetry in all four directions. We notice particularly the great circular rose windows—shaped like the blossoms of a rose—in three of the arms.

Eventually we are forced to choose an aisle to the side of the main altar. The aisle proceeds forward, then moves us around the altar. In this far, east end of the church, external walls radiate out into small chapels. Before starting our return journey, we stop to delight at the way the building itself has guided our pilgrimage through it.

Inside the church are many more places to explore and many more observations to make. But perhaps at one point we are persuaded to leave the building through a side door. Outside we are surprised to see, extending beyond the building, porches more elaborate than those between the front towers. More lifelike and animated sculpture fills the space around us. Stepping down from the church, we notice heavy piles of stone that protrude from the building and almost engulf the windows between them. They impress us

FIG 15-1 [French], Chartres Cathedral, interior looking east. Begun in 1194. Chartres, France. Scala/Art Resource.

Chartres, France, panoramic view.
Giraudon/Art Resource, New York.

with their sturdy mass. These buttresses rise above the outer walls of the building and support arches that reach out like arms to apply pressure against the walls of the tall central nave. We sense power and dynamic forces in the masses and lines of the exterior.

Even without knowing the history of the building and the culture associated with it, we could spend hours exploring the architecture. The simplest pilgrims in the Middle Ages had the same experience. Although the pilgrims were probably unable to articulate it, their experience of the beautiful cathedral building may have been made more intense by the contrast with their ordinary surroundings.

The Experience of Architecture

Our imaginary pilgrimage through Chartres discloses that architecture shapes our experience like no other art form. Architecture physically causes us to live in a certain way and makes it difficult, if not impossible, to live in other ways. In a building like Chartres, hundreds of people can assemble in an open space that seems like a world of its own. In the narrow corridors inside a modern office building, even a few people moving about may feel claustrophobic. We may feel cramped in an interior space, or exhilarated with an extensive open area around us. Solid walls and supports give us shelter and security, or they obstruct, confine, and confuse movement. Stairs are either convenient or inconvenient. The lighting and ventilation make it a pleasure to pursue the intended activities within a building, or they make those activities almost impossible. On the exterior the masses and height of the architecture may make a forbidding presence, or the architecture, growing up with its surroundings, may welcome the visitor. Space, masses, movement, light, and many other architectural properties that mold our experience influence our judgment of a building.

The forms of architecture compel us to view architecture differently than we view other kinds of art. Painting is two-dimensional; it is best viewed from an angle perpendicular to the picture plane. Since sculpture is three-dimensional, we may be able to walk around it and view it from different angles. We can walk around architecture to examine it, but we can also get inside it to perceive it. We experience architecture by spending time within it. Not only are architectural forms on a larger scale than sculptural masses, they wrap around us and shelter us. Architecture separates a space apart from the endless space of nature and creates an environment for our activity.

The experience of architecture differs from the experience of painting and sculpture because architecture takes an amount of time to observe. Although all art takes time to appreciate, we can usually absorb the whole of a painting and most statues from one spot in one brief or lengthy moment of time. But architecture has to unfold itself over time, the way music needs to be played for its forms to develop in time. Architecture discloses itself in time because we can seldom see the whole building from one spot; we have to move around and through the building to experience it.

One might compare experiencing architecture to watching a movie. Like our tour of Chartres Cathedral, the movie might start with a panoramic establishing shot of the whole building in its context, then move in for a closer look. Suddenly the film cuts to some detail, dwells on some aspect, or moves in a rapid rhythm from image to image. Or the film moves slowly from room to room to explain how the sequence of spaces unfolds. Both the film and the building have to reveal themselves gradually to a probing, shifting eye. But even a film cannot give an awareness of masses looming in our presence or a truly three-dimensional experience of space or the feeling of being surrounded and covered all over.

The body of Chartres Cathedral is divided into a central space called a **nave** with subsidiary spaces called **aisles** running either side of the nave. The square or rectangular subsections of the plan indicate **bays.** Since the nave is taller than the aisles, windows placed in the nave above the aisles can bring light to the center of the church. This upper part of the nave is called the **clerestory.** About halfway down the church, something like a second nave crosses the first at right angles. It is called the **transept.** The nave and aisles continue beyond the transept, but the central space beyond the **crossing** is called the **choir** because this is where the monks stood and sang their office each day. In medieval times this area was actually screened off from the rest of the church. Pilgrims and tourists can walk around the choir by means of the semicircular aisle surrounding it, called an **ambulatory,** from which they may visit the chapels radiating around the east end of the church. A semicircular extension of the interior space, as in one of the chapels, is called an **apse.**

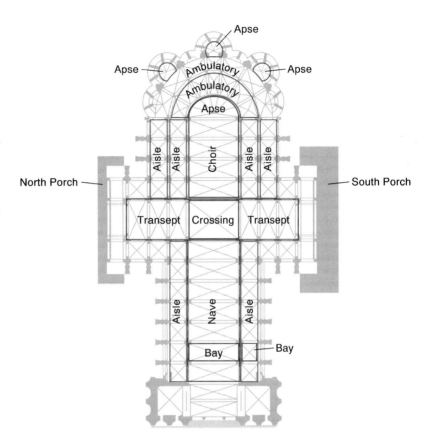

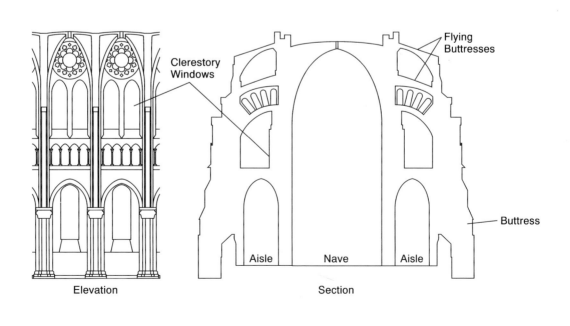

FIG 15-2 [Tallensi], a compound at Tongo. 1969. Ghana, Africa. Diagram from *Architecture in Northern Ghana* by Labelle Prussin. © 1969 The Regents of the University of California. Photo by Dennis Stock, Magnum.

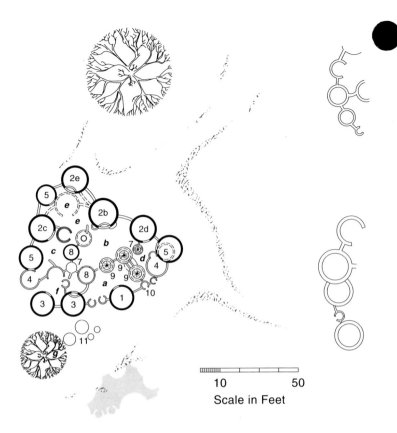

Among the Tallensi people in northern Ghana, building technology is extremely well suited to the available materials, the semiarid climate, and the way of life of the people. Male relatives and friends build the walls of circular sleeping rooms and granaries by applying layer upon layer of wet mud balls; the women finish the surfaces and decorate the tapering walls with incised patterns. Extended families live in compounds that are vaguely circular like the circular huts themselves. Since most of daily life takes place in the courtyards and other open areas of the compound, the entire compound shapes spaces for living. The layout of the compound effectively diagrams family relationships. When family relationships change, parts of the architecture are demolished, altered, and added to.

The parts of the compound in this illustration are labeled as follows: a, subcompound for the animals; b, senior wife's courtyard; c, second wife's courtyard; d, brother's wife's courtyard; e, son's wife's courtyard; f, unmarried sons courtyard; g, shade tree and sitting area; 1, compound founder's (present owner's father's) room, containing his possessions; 2b–e, wives' rooms; 3, unmarried sons' rooms; 4, dry season kitchens; 5, wet season kitchens; 6, bathing enclosure; 7, millet granaries; 8, millet-grinding rooms; 9, sheep and goats; 10, chicken roosts; 11, ancestral shrines.

Architecture as a Social Art

Many of us may never experience Chartres Cathedral, and yet architecture remains a very familiar branch of the visual arts, because everyone spends a good part of every day living in some form of architecture. Architecture is also perhaps the only essential art form, since we must have buildings to live comfortably, safely, and efficiently. We may ignore any painting on a wall or any statue on a pedestal, but we cannot get along without architecture. Unlike much painting and sculpture, architecture has to be practical and serve a purpose. It is hard to imagine an example of architecture ever being built solely as a work of art, without any function. Furthermore, we normally judge the quality of a building, at least in part, on the sturdiness of its construction—something we seldom look for in paintings and drawings.

Some critics have distinguished between Architecture with a capital A and ordinary buildings that merely provide human shelter. They define architecture as a special form of building that affords a privileged aesthetic experience similar to that of other kinds of "fine" art. However, the distinction between high-minded Architecture and ordinary buildings is hard to maintain because it is impossible to demonstrate that a distinct class of structure provides the architectural experience exclusively. Structures of all kinds and shapes may embody the architectural experience—some more, some less—provided our imagination is open to it.

For instance, the Tallensi people in northern Ghana, like many other people south of the Sahara in Africa, tend to build simple rounded mud structures with thatched conical roofs (see FIG. 15-2). Although their technology is simple and basic, they sculpt their dwelling spaces around them like a sensitive potter working with clay. More than most people, they express in the spaces they create the essence of their way of life.

In short, all kinds of buildings can speak to us and symbolize the same kind of personal, feeling-filled awareness that the other forms of art express through their iconography and style. Architecture communicates its own personalized experience of shelter and the personal experience of living in space through a language of forms, materials, and techniques that architects have developed and are continuing to expand.

Sometimes a building may stand out as the personal expression of an individual great architect. Just as often a building communicates the ideas and aspirations of the society for which it was built. Even though we do not know the names of the architects, the ruins of the metropolis of Teotihuacán (pronounced Tay-oh-tea-wha-cahn) (FIG. 15-3) in central Mexico speak volumes about the culture of the ancient people who lived there about 100 B.C.. to A.D. 500. And the skyscrapers of a big city like Chicago (FIG. 15-4) symbolize a modern society built on technology, even though we do know the name of each architect of each modern building.

The center of an empire in central Mexico, Teotihuacán had a population of about two hundred thousand. The city was set out in a gridlike pattern and covered eight square miles. The three-mile-long

FIG 15-3   Pyramid of the Sun, with Pyramids of the Ciudadela in foreground. C. 100 B.C.—A.D. 500. Teotihuacán, Mexico. Werner Forman/Art Resource, New York.

FIG 15-4   Chicago skyline. Photo © Mark Segal, Tony Stone.

FIG 15-5 Round Tower. C. 7000 B.C. Jericho, Jordan.

Over the centuries, new generations at Jericho built their dwellings on the ruins of the peoples that went before them, creating a tell, or mound, that rose over fifty feet above the valley floor. In the 1950s archaeologists led by Kathleen Kenyon probed through the site to the bedrock, uncovering the successive layers of civilization. At some of the lowest, earliest levels, the people built round, single-room houses of oblong bricks. From a small porch, narrow steps led down to the slightly sunken floor of the house. The houses were spread over an area of ten acres and were surrounded by massive walls at least twenty feet high. Flanking the wall was an even taller stone tower with an interior staircase that gave access to the top of the wall. In defense of their water, the people of Jericho organized into a community and built the first monumental architecuture.

Avenue of the Dead ran north-south through the heart of the city and terminated in the Pyramid of the Moon. More than seventy five temples, situated on the flat tops of pyramid mounds, lined the Avenue— including the largest building in the city, the Pyramid of the Sun, 230 feet high. Since the inhabitants of the empire believed that Teotihuacán was the birthplace of the sun and the moon, the city became an important religious center. The scale and regularity of the architectural remains indicate the religious fervor of the people and point to a strong authority and an organized workforce that lasted for centuries in the Valley of Mexico.

The skyline of America's third largest city, its towers rising above the water, presents a dramatic image of the financial and technological vitality of the country. The towers serve the needs of banking, management, communications, commerce, and government—the complex nervous system of modern life. To function, the buildings themselves demand complex public services—transportation, utilities, and electronic communications. Coupled with the technology that makes tall buildings possible, the skyline symbolizes at a glance the dynamism of modern life.

Both the pyramids and the skyscrapers are the products of the best technology of the time, but they express the completely different concerns, functions, and purposes of completely different cultures.

Perhaps there was a time when no one built anything and perhaps there are even now tribes in the world that do not build anything, but once men and women start to create shelters, architecture provides a powerful record or expression of their civilization. Consider, for example, how people sheltered themselves in the city of Jericho (see FIG. 15-5), very likely the oldest town in the world. Located at an oasis in the Jordan River Valley only nine miles from the Dead Sea, Jericho is one of the earliest places where nomadic men and women, because they invented agriculture and discovered irrigation, settled, and made permanent architecture.

Vitruvius

The distinctive character of architecture was long ago recognized by the Roman architect Vitruvius, who, in the late first century B.C. wrote a book called *About Architecture*. His was the only architectural treatise

Some of the most remarkable achievements in architecture in the nineteenth century were made by engineers who designed thoroughly utilitarian structures like factory buildings, railway bridges, railway terminals, market halls, and shopping arcades with glass-covered vaults constructed of prefabricated iron parts. The Crystal Palace set the standards for a series of spectacular iron-and-glass exhibition structures in the late nineteenth century. For such new building types, the weight of architectural tradition did not impede the inventiveness of the structural engineer. Joseph Paxton had experience with building hothouses when he was called upon at the last moment to design the Crystal Palace. Not only was the entire building sheathed in glass but its modular parts were mass-produced and shipped to the site. Once underway, the Crystal Palace took only four months to construct. Framing an enclosed world, the thin structural members dissolved in the light. The heat radiated by the sun—a greenhouse effect—plagued the Crystal Palace, as it does every glass building.

from ancient times that survived the fall of the Roman Empire. His ideas were revived and revered in the Renaissance, and for centuries they have formed the basis for the discussion of architecture in the West, even when they have been rejected.

Vitruvius wrote that architecture has three characteristics: *firmitas, utilitas,* and *venustas.* The words mean, respectively, "firmness," "utility," and "the pleasures of Venus." In plainer English, Vitruvius probably meant something like solid construction, suitability, and beauty. His words refer to building materials and techniques, appropriateness or practicality, and the artistic expression of architecture.

Everyone agrees with his first principle, that a building should be well built. Vitruvius wrote at length in his book on such fundamental things as bricks, concrete, and stone and the proper methods of building walls. "Durability will be assured," he wrote, "when foundations are carried down to the solid ground and materials are wisely and liberally selected."[1] In modern buildings, we too want the walls to stand on solid foundations, and we want the plumbing to work. An architect has to be concerned with the available mate-rials, with construction techniques, and with the principles of engineering that make things work.

Some modern architects and engineers are concerned *only* with technology, and they even claim that technology determines the very appearance of a building. Vitruvius's suitability and beauty take a back seat to solid construction. After all, building techniques and available materials leave open only certain possibilities for the shape of a building. For example, the discovery of new techniques of lightweight stone vaulting made possible the great cathedrals of the Middle Ages like Chartres. In the distant past, stone walls had to be thick and massive in order to sustain a large roof or numerous stories. In the present, iron or steel beams can be assembled into the skeleton of a building and leave open large amounts of interior space—an achievement demonstrated at an early date in Joseph Paxton's *Crystal Palace* (FIG. 15-6).

Technical developments do effect changes in architectural style, and they stimulate creativity—a point especially obvious in the twentieth century, when modern technology and new materials have had profound consequences in our architecture. In fact, most

FIG 15-7   [Greek], Temple of Athena Nike. 427–424 B.C. Acropolis, Athens. Scala/Art Resource, New York.

architects today are trained primarily not as artists but as engineers who must master a complex technology. Nevertheless, the whole story of architecture cannot be reduced to technology and construction techniques, since the needs of the society and the imagination of the architect also significantly influence the medium.

Architects have argued much more over Vitruvius's two characteristics suitability and beauty. Vitruvius understood suitability to mean, on the one hand, that certain styles and building types were proper for certain uses. According to Vitruvius, male gods like Mars should have a virile style of temple; delicate divinities like Venus should properly have a feminine style of temple. The Temple of Athena Nike (FIG. 15-7) in Athens is one of the earliest temples built in a feminine style on the Greek mainland. Although the nearby Parthenon (FIG. 16-14) is dedicated to the same goddess, its style is masculine. Perhaps the Greeks felt that the celebration of Nike, which in Greek means Victory, was more delicate and fragile. The small scale, slender columns, and precise carving of the Nike temple convey that feeling.

On the other hand, Vitruvius also understood that suitability will be assured when the arrangement of the rooms is "faultless and presents no hindrance to use."[2] Houses in town should have one form of building, he wrote, and farmhouses in the country another because they each have different functions to perform. He proposed, in short, that different building types were suitable for different purposes.

Many leading architects of the modern age seem to have agreed with Vitruvius when he said that the shapes of a building (its form) depend upon the practical demands made of the building (its function). The first person to use the catchphrase Form follows function was the nineteenth-century American sculptor Horatio Greenough, who found exceptional beauty in the sleek, functional lines of the clipper ship. At the end of the century, the Chicago architect Louis Sullivan developed the maxim into a theory of architecture. In his work Sullivan sought to combat the rampant, meaningless revivalism of past styles in architecture and to develop a new organic style that would grow out of the structure and functions of the building. He put his principles into practice in one of the first "skyscrapers" to take advantage of steel-frame construction, the *Guaranty Building* (FIG. 15-8) in Buffalo.

Part III: The Visual Arts

Form follows function was adopted as the rallying cry of many modernist architects of the mid-twentieth century who wanted to strip architecture of all ornament and build only with spare, sharp-edged, machine-made forms. They wanted the structure and the materials to reveal how the building was put together and how it operated. With its efficient, industrial-style forms, this pure and rationalized architecture, they thought, would lead humankind to a bright tomorrow. Surprisingly, the fundamental intellectual ideals supporting modern functionalism in architecture were idealistic and utopian.

Lastly, Vitruvius and hundreds of others following him have declared that architecture should have beauty. Many architects still seem to think that beauty involves pretty, ornamental details, like columns or potted plants, added at the last minute. By *venustas*, Vitruvius meant that architecture should have more than some decorative elements attached to it or a pretty coat of paint to distract the eye. He felt that the whole of the building, including the details, should give pleasure because of the harmony built into the entire work. Beauty is assured, he wrote, "when its members are in due proportion according to correct principles of symmetry [harmony]."[3]

Proportions

Vitruvius and other classical and Renaissance architects believed that the beauty of architecture lay primarily in the proportions of a building. By proportions they meant the correspondence and relationship of one dimension to another. All parts of the building were to relate to one another and to the whole. A certain system governs the relationships of height to width to depth of rooms, walls, and all solids and voids throughout the entire building.

Vitruvius declared that "there is nothing to which an architect should devote more thought than to the exact proportions of his building with reference to a certain part selected as the standard."[4] The proportions that Vitruvius and many other architects envisaged were ratios of simple, small whole numbers like 1:1, 1:2, or 3:4. Selecting the width of one room in a proposed building as the standard, an architect might design that room as a square (1:1), for example, and the room next to it as a rectangle twice as long (1:2).

FIG 15-8 DANKMAR ADLER [American, 1844–1900] and Louis Sullivan [American, 1856–1924], *Guaranty Building*. 1895. Buffalo. Photo by Patricia Layman Bazelon.

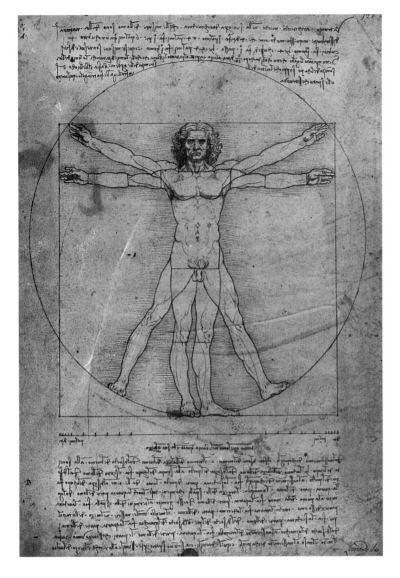

These proportions reproduced the harmony and symmetry found in music and in the human body. Vitruvius wrote that just as small whole number ratios govern the proportions of the human body, they ought also to govern the relationships among the parts of a building. To prove his point he demonstrated how the "perfect" geometrical figures, the square and the circle, can be derived from the body, using the navel as the natural center:

> For if a man be placed flat on his back, with his hands and feet extended, and a pair of compasses centered at his navel, the fingers and toes of his two hands and feet will touch the circumference of a circle described therefrom. And just as the human body yields a circular outline, so too a square figure may be found from it. For if we measure the distance from the soles of the feet to the top of the head, and then apply that measure to the outstretched arms, the breadth will be found to be the same as the height, as in the case of plane surfaces which are perfectly square.[5]

Leonardo da Vinci illustrated this analogy in the drawing *Proportions of the Human Figure (after Vitruvius)* (FIG. 15-9).

Vitruvius's belief that the square and the circle can be generated from the human body betrays his belief that human beings are the most important things in the universe. Since these forms—the square and the circle—are the essence of symmetry, uniformity, and harmony, which are the principles that govern the universe, the Vitruvian Man graphically illustrates the Greek saying that man is the measure of all things.

The urge to achieve harmonic beauty through proportions has a long history in architecture. The Greek architects Iktinos and Kallikrates, long before Vitruvius, designed the Parthenon (FIG. 16-14) in ancient Athens using the ratio 4:9 for several essential dimensions. And the Roman Pantheon (FIGS. 16-17 and 16-18), several generations after Vitruvius, conforms to a perfect circle and sphere. In the Renaissance, Brunelleschi, Alberti, Bramante, and Palladio revived Vitruvius's understanding of architectural beauty when they designed proportional buildings. The modern French architect Le Corbusier in the 1930s once again devised a system of proportions, this time based on the golden section. He called it the **modulor,** or the module of gold (FIG. 15-10).

Although the ear naturally intuits the harmonies of music, the eye has not been constructed to perceive

FIG 15-9   LEONARDO DA VINCI [Italian, 1452–1519, *Proportions of the Human Figure (after Vitruvius).* C. 1485–1490. Pen, 13 1/2 × 8 3/4 in. (34.3 × 22.2 cm). Venice, Galleria dell' Accademia. Alinari/Art Resource, New York.

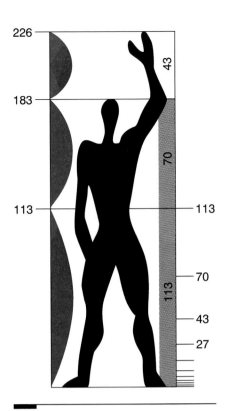

FIG 15-10 LE CORBUSIER (Charles-Édouard Jeanneret) [French, 1887–1965], modulor figure.

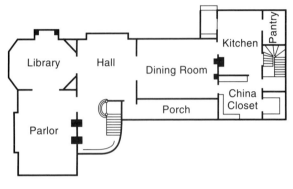

FIG 15-11 H. H. RICHARDSON [American, 1838–1886], Stoughton House. 1882–1883. 90 Brattle Street, Cambridge, Massachusetts. Library of Boston Athenaeum.

numerical relationships immediately in physical dimensions. But if we are not aware of the proportional system in a building, how can the structure's proportions affect our judgment and how then can we experience its beauty? These objections would not have mattered to Vitruvius because to him a building with systematic proportions is inherently beautiful. Proportionality is an intellectual idea, not a matter of perceptions. Even in music, we do not have to know the exact relationship of a chord to appreciate its harmony. Whatever our level of awareness, architecture designed with a system of proportions usually produces spaces and masses that are elegant, integrated one with another, and pleasant to the eye.

With or without a system of proportions, the stability of buildings encourages balance and symmetry in their construction. The main door in most buildings lies in the center—a logical and easy place to find it—where it may become a focus. However, many excellent buildings, despite Vitruvius, are asymmetrical in design. H. H. Richardson gave the facade of Stough-ton House (FIG. 15-11) in Cambridge, Massachusetts, a very agreeable irregularity and diversity in keeping with the structure's asymmetrical L-shaped room arrangement. The rooms on the interior, in a variety of sizes and shapes, are loosely and conveniently organized around a spacious hall. The parlor, protruding on the left, ends in a gable on the exterior; a round stair tower bulges from the angle of the L; and the entrance porch penetrates into the house. Richardson surrounded the house with a skin of dark olive-green shingles, thereby eliminating almost all ornament or surface articulation so that the masses and void stand out all the more. This massive, sturdy-looking Shingle Style grew quite popular in the eastern United States in the 1880s, and Stoughton House is one of its finest extant examples.

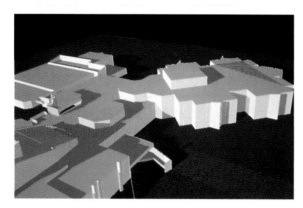

Architectural plan for a high school building, made using ARRIS software.

A three-dimensional model.

A Three-dimensional interior perspective. All drawings courtesy ATS&R, Architects and Engineers, Minneapolis, MN.

Computer-Aided Planning

In preparation for construction, architects may not employ Vitruvian proportions but they generally devise a comprehensive **plan**—a horizontal diagram of the parts of a building—in addition to three-dimensional views of the proposed building. By means of a plan, like the one of Chartres Cathedral on page 369, an architect arranges the spaces and other parts of a building over a horizontal area.

Since the 1980s, practicing architects are just as likely to design supports and spaces through sophisticated computerized graphic design programs. Many architects have thrown away their pencils and drafting tables and instead, from the beginning, roughly sketch out a two-dimensional or three-dimensional design on the computer. While the architect designs the building, computer-aided design and drafting (CADD) programs can calculate the laws of physics and the nature of the materials and can take into account the local building codes and the foreseeable stresses on any structure. Modifications in the design can be made easily and rapidly. Computer programs can test the design for the adequacy of the lighting, ventilation, and heating. The computer can then send the detailed information to a printer or plotter, which automatically produces the drawings needed by the suppliers and construction teams. From enormous databases the computer can select materials and fixtures and at the same time prepare cost estimates. The computer program can also depict the building from any angle or even allow the client to take a video walk through or flight over the proposed building. More and more, clients themselves are requesting that architects submit their proposals in a computerized format.

Traditional Materials and Construction Techniques

Many of the building materials that Vitruvius discussed in the first century B.C.—such as wood, brick, stone, cement—are still in common use today. Modern builders also employ several new materials, like reinforced concrete and steel, and a host of new methods of construction.

Solid Wall Construction

Technically speaking, it is not very difficult to build a human shelter, provided the structure is small and the space uncomplicated. Four walls erected with bricks or stone blocks, and a roof laid across the walls will suffice. In the resulting **solid wall construction** technique, the solid mass of the wall holds itself up and supports the roof or an upper floor. This technique can also be referred to as a shell system of architecture. It might be used even today to build a small shop with cinder block walls on which rest thin steel or wooden **trusses** supporting a roof. Taking advantage of the stability and strength of the triangle, which cannot easily be pushed or pulled out of shape, the rigid and lightweight framework of a truss can span considerable space.

Problems with solid wall construction arise when the builder wants to put holes in the walls for windows and doors or when the walls are asked to support more than a few stories. Doors and windows rob a solid wall of its basic strength, and the added weight of tall elevations requires walls at ground level that would be prohibitively thick.

Post-and-Lintel System

To cover space and to avoid overly thick walls, another simple construction method entails placing a beam across two uprights. In this technique a solid wall is replaced, as it were, by the open structure of posts and beams. This is called the **post-and-beam system** or the **post-and-lintel system.**

Uprights of any kind will support beams over the interior of buildings to create large rooms. The span covered by a beam depends on the material. A sturdy wooden beam can cross some distance because wood is naturally elastic and can absorb a considerable amount of bending and stretching under its load before it becomes permanently deformed and snaps. Although a stone lintel might not rot or catch fire like wood, it is more likely to crack when it is stretched across two posts. Consequently, a stone lintel has to be shorter.

When a beam of stone or any other material rests on two upright posts and bends under its load, the top

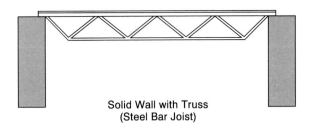

Solid Wall with Truss
(Steel Bar Joist)

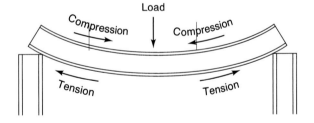

Post and Lintel

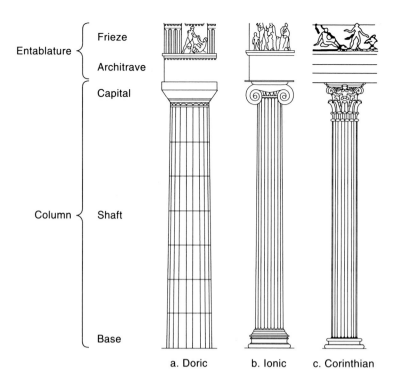

Entablature { Frieze, Architrave

Column { Capital, Shaft, Base

a. Doric   b. Ionic   c. Corinthian

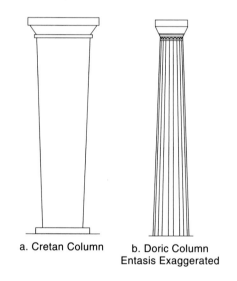

a. Cretan Column

b. Doric Column
Entasis Exaggerated

part of the beam is pushed together and compressed, and the bottom part is in tension because it is being stretched and pulled apart. Since stone has great compressive strength but weak tensile strength, stone lintels have obvious limitations as building elements.

The Classical Orders

Despite stone's weak tensile strength, the ancient Greeks made their famous temples with close-fitting blocks of stone in the post-and-lintel system. The Greeks and Romans had three basic systems for the design of the posts and lintels—three systems that have become perennial motifs in Western architecture. These basic systems are called the Doric, Ionic, and Corinthian orders.

In the terminology of classical architecture, the orders encompass the columns and the **entablature,** which is the horizontal part of the building above the vertical columns. The shaft of every column tapers toward the top, but the Greeks generally modified the straight line of this tapering into a subtle curve, called **entasis.** With entasis, the shaft bulges out slightly, with the greatest deviation from the straight tapering about a third of the way up. Entasis makes a column seem elastic, as though it is flexing under the weight it carries. Columns without entasis seem by contrast too rigid, unyielding, and brittle.

Since the **Doric order** was designed as the most solid and hefty of the three classical orders, the Greeks thought of it as masculine. The tapered shaft of the Greek Doric column, fluted with vertical, concave grooves, rests right on the platform without a base. The column terminates in a simple cushionlike **capital,** which makes a nice transition between the vertical lines of the shaft and the horizontal lines of the entablature. A Doric entablature is carved with **triglyphs** (three vertical cuts) and **metopes** (nearly square relief panels).

The **Ionic order** is more decorated than the Doric. It is taller and has more elegant proportions, including a thinner entablature without triglyphs and metopes. Sometimes the Greeks placed a continuous band of relief sculpture in the entablature, called a **frieze.** The Greeks thought of the Ionic as feminine (see the Temple of Athena Nike, FIG. 15-7). The Ionic column has a base to form a transition between horizontal and vertical, and the Ionic capital has four distinctive volutes, or scrolls.

Part III: The Visual Arts

FIG 15-12   HENRY BACON [American, 1866–1924], Lincoln Memorial. Completed 1917. Washington, D.C. SEF/Art Resource, New York.

FIG 15-13   JOHN RUSSELL POPE [American, 1874–1937], Jefferson Memorial. 1938–1943. Washington, D.C. Photo: Spencer Grant Liason International.

The **Corinthian order** is a larger, more elaborate version of the Ionic and has somewhat different proportions too. Its capital has a big, basketlike arrangement of acanthus leaves. The Romans made more use of the majestic Corinthian order than did the Greeks.

The Greek Doric, Ironic, and Corinthian orders can be found all over the United States. Because Greece was the home of democracy and because Rome once had a republican form of government, classical architecture expressed the ideals of America. During the neoclassical period, approximately 1775 to 1825, and well into the twentieth century, it was common to give government buildings a classical look by employing the orders. The architecture of Washington, D.C., offers some splendid examples: the solemn Doric of the Lincoln Memorial (FIG. 15-12), the festive Ionic of the Jefferson Memorial (FIG. 15-13), and the imposing Corinthian of the Supreme Court Building (FIG. 15-14).

Designed by Henry Bacon in imitation of a Greek temple, the Lincoln Memorial houses a giant statue of President Lincoln, by Daniel Chester French. However, the Lincoln Memorial does not have a short end with a triangular gable like the front of a Greek temple; in fact, the entrance to the chamber is in the middle of the long side instead of the short side. Above the Doric columns, Bacon set a narrow Ionic frieze of floral swags instead of the triglyphs and metopes expected of the Doric order. And in place of a pitched, gabled roof, the architect substituted a

FIG 15-14   CASS GILBERT [American, 1859–1934], Supreme Court Building. 1932–1935. Washington, D.C. SEF/Art Resource, New York.

blocklike attic, also decorated with swags. The abstraction of the attic's form is perhaps the only concession to the twentieth century in this severe and impressive building.

The Jefferson Memorial, designed by John Russell Pope and built in 1938–43, imitates the combination of temple porch and domed rotunda made famous in the Roman Pantheon and in Jefferson's own architecture for the University of Virginia (see FIG. 17-38).

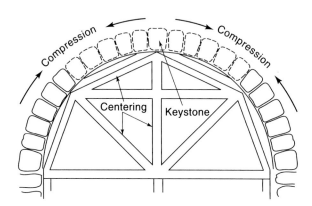

Pope employed the Ionic order not only in the porch but also in the "ambulatory" around the periphery of the rotunda. Instead of resting on thick walls, the dome swells above an open Ionic colonnade. What the building thus loses in apparent strength in the absence of external walls, it gains in grace and openness, a perfect fit for its picturesque setting above the tidal basin in the midst of cherry blossoms.

Also in the 1930s, Cass Gilbert designed the Supreme Court Building to have a noble and stately porch of eight Corinthian columns set on top of a broad and tall flight of steps. Its use of the classical order fulfills splendidly the popular ideal of Roman grandeur.

Arches and Vaults

Since stone beams have to be short, columns cannot be very far apart. With stone lintels, a considerable amount of floor space is taken up by the numerous heavy columns needed to support the stone. Stone **arches,** however, can span wider spaces. Arches are made from wedge-shaped stones placed, usually, in a semicircle so that they press against one another. Since stone has great compressive strength, the pressure of one stone on the other can hold up an arch spanning a considerable distance and supporting considerable weight.

Arches are built over wooden scaffolding, or centering, which is dismantled once the structure is completed. The top stone, or **keystone,** is probably the last stone put in place before the centering is removed. However, all the stones, not just the keystone, maintain the arch because their weight wedges them against one another. They cannot open up or pull apart as long as they are buttressed at the sides to counter the pressure that an arch exerts to the sides. The buttressing might be additional heavy masonry, the sides of a valley, or, more often, another arch.

The Romans made good use of arches to build large bridges, and the adaptability of the arch allowed them to build extensive aqueducts to bring water over considerable distances to urban populations. In many ways, the arch made the cities of the Roman Empire possible. The Roman aqueduct at Segovia (FIG. 15-15) stretches nearly nine hundred yards across a valley to bring fresh water to the hilltop town. The water channel, carried one hundred feet above the lowest point of

Fig 15-15 [Roman], aqueduct. C. A.D.100. Segovia, Spain. Adam Lubroth/Art Resource, New York.

the valley, rests on top of a series of 128 arches. The Romans built the aqueduct with big, rough-cut, almost square blocks of stone as an expression of the sturdiness of their construction.

Semicircular arches can be expanded through space in one direction to form a semicylindrical roof called a **barrel vault** or a **tunnel vault.** The three enormous tunnel vaults of the Basilica of Constantine (Fig. 15-16) on the Roman Forum still command respect. Tunnel vaults, like arches, also need buttressing at the sides to support their lateral pressure. If two tunnel vaults intersect, a **groin vault,** or **cross vault,** results. Cross vaulting opens up the floor space underneath it because now the weight of the vault rests only on the

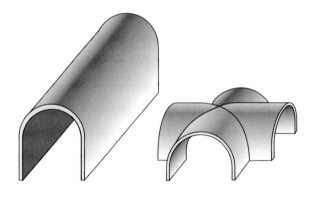

a. Barrel Vault   b. Groin Vault

Fig 15-16 [Roman], Basilica of Constantine. Begun by Maxentius in 307–312, completed by Constantine after 312. Rome. Scala/Art Resource, New York.

All that remains of this magnificent building of ancient Rome is these three enormous barrel vaults that once formed the north side or aisle of the basilica. Their walls served as the supports for the cross vaults that covered the central hall 115 feet above the floor. Most basilican plans separate the nave from the side aisles by an arcade or colonnade. The large side barrel vaults, set perpendicular to the central hall, do not. The space flows continuously east-west and north-south throughout the building.

FIG 15-17 [Mayan], The Great Arch, at the entrance of the causeway to Uxmal. 700–900. Kabah, Yucatán, Mexico. Erich Lessing/Art Resource, New York.

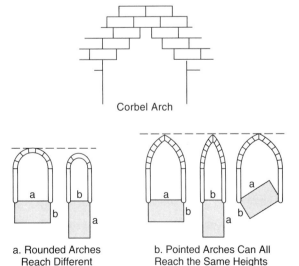

Corbel Arch

a. Rounded Arches Reach Different Heights

b. Pointed Arches Can All Reach the Same Heights

four corners. Lofty cross vaults once covered the central hall of the Basilica of Constantine where its vast interior space flowed uninterruptedly into the barrel-vaulted aisles.

When the peoples of Central America and South America built extensive cities, temples, and roads through all the centuries before Columbus, they never took advantage of the arch. Their architects achieved a similar, though narrow, penetration of a wall with the so-called **corbel arch** (see FIG. 15-17), which, despite the name, is not a true arch. In a corbel arch each stone protrudes slightly beyond the stone beneath it until the sides of the "arch" meet. In Central America, the Mayans extended the corbel arch along one axis into corbel vaults: the stone temple sitting on top of the steep Mayan pyramid at Tikal (FIG. 17-10) has lofty but relatively narrow inner chambers covered with corbel vaults.

Architects in the Middle Ages preferred to use pointed arches because they may rise much higher than semicircular arches and they also exert somewhat less lateral pressure. The height of a semicircular arch is determined by the span between the posts from which the arch springs. Since the span is equal to the diameter of the semicircle of the arch, the height of the arch has to be the radius of the semicircle. In contrast, the height of a pointed arch bears no relationship to the span underneath, and the "angle" of the point may vary.

Whether they span the short side of a rectangular bay or the long side or the diagonal, all the pointed arches of that bay can reach the same height. Semicircular arches over those three different spans would attain three different heights. Gothic architects, taking advantage of the increased height of the pointed arch, drove stained glass windows way up into the top of the vaults (see Chartres Cathedral, FIG. 15-1), to nearly the same level as the apex of the vault.

A pointed arch works basically the same way as a circular arch. Although the first few stones at the bottom of a tall pointed arch practically rest on one another, eventually the upper stones wedge themselves together like the stones of any other arch. Gothic architects never failed to secure pointed arches at the sides with buttressing to counter lateral pressure. The pointed arches in a Gothic vault form ribs—a framework upon which have been set lighter stones that create a webbing between the ribs. When all the stones of the vault are in place and have bonded, the ribs might no longer be necessary to support the vault, although visually they appear to do so. Ribs in Gothic cathedrals have been damaged and fallen while the vault stood firm.

Domes

If a round arch is rotated through space 360 degrees, a hemispherical **dome** results. A dome, therefore, operates according to structural principles similar to those of an arch, since the stones in a dome compress one another for support. A dome is even more stable than an arch because the stones are being compressed from all four sides and so cannot buckle. The horizontal layers of stone at any of the upper levels encircle the dome like hoops surrounding a barrel. The compression of these stones inward against one another prevents warping and wobbling. At the lower horizontal levels of the dome, the circles of stone are in tension as they resist the pressure to expand and move out. Many domes also have something like a steel chain tied around their lower circumference to help prevent this expansion. Because of the advantageous dynamics of a dome, its material can be much thinner than that of an arch with a comparable span.

A contemporary architectural writer calls the dome "the king of all roofs, . . . the greatest architectural and structural achievement of mankind in over 2,000 years of spiritual and technological development."[6] Ancient writers thought the dome imitated the shape of the heavens, and even today its endless and perfect circular shape shelters church goers or sports fans like a friendly sky. The most famous and most ambitious dome that the Romans built, the dome of the *Pantheon* (FIGS. 16-17 and 16-18), Emperor Hadrian's temple to all the gods, set a standard that has seldom been surpassed. In Renaissance Italy, domes became the dominant feature of churches, whereas in the United

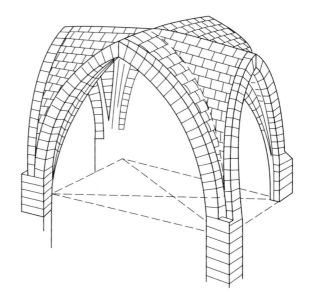

Gothic Ribbed Vault

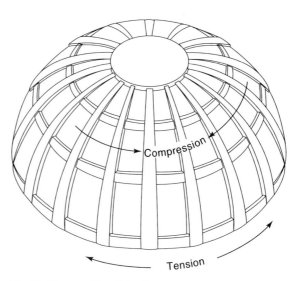

The Meridians and Parallels of a Dome

FIG 15-18 Anthemius of Tralles [Byzantine, sixth century A.D.] and Isidorus of Miletus [Byzantine, sixth century A.D.], Hagia Sophia. 532–537. Constantinople (now Istanbul, Turkey). Erich Lessing/Art Resource, New York.

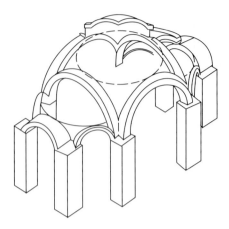

Dome on Pendentives at Hagia Sophia

pendentives. The curving surfaces of pendentives make a smooth transition between the rectangular arrangement of the four pillars below and the circle of the dome's base above.

Originally Anthemius designed a shallow dome, ninety feet in diameter but only about twenty five feet high. Furthermore, he pierced the lower circumference of the dome with forty windows so that when light shone through them, it effectively cut the dome off from the structure below. The dome even today seems to float miraculously over the church as though suspended from above. Unfortunately, earthquakes caused parts of Anthemius's daring architecture to collapse and the dome was later rebuilt in a hemispherical fashion.

Modern Architectural Techniques

During the nineteenth and twentieth centuries new building techniques as well as new construction materials have energized architects to create many exciting and very different new buildings. The new techniques and materials have changed the very shape of architecture because they are better suited to the new needs of modern society. A new material like steel and a new technology like reinforced concrete allow structures that are relatively lighter in weight and very much stronger than traditional building materials. They have both high compressive and high tensile strength. They allow large areas like factory floors to be spanned.

States, domes are commonly the distinctive feature of state capitol buildings as well as of the Federal Capitol Building in Washington, D.C.

In 532 Anthemius of Tralles, assisted by Isidorus of Miletus, designed for the Byzantine emperor Justinian perhaps the most splendid dome of all times for the church of Hagia Sophia (FIG. 15-18) in Constantinople (now Istanbul, Turkey). Instead of resting a hemispherical dome on the solid support of a thick cylindrical wall, as in the Roman Pantheon, the Byzantine architect set his shallow dome at the apex of four giant arches that rose from four large pillars within the church. The curving triangular areas underneath the dome and between the arches are called

FIG 15-19 Curtain wall office tower under construction. Photo by Alena Vikova, Tony Stone.

15-20 PHILIP JOHNSON [American, 1906–] and JOHN BURGEE [American, 1933–], Pennzoil Plaza. 1970–1976. Houston.

Steel Cage and Curtain Wall Construction

Tall structures like office towers can be erected using **steel cage construction,** with a skeleton of steel girders, instead of thick exterior walls to support the building. Since the outside walls of a steel cage building do not support the building, they can be covered with any material—brick, stone, glass, bronze, or plastic—to keep out the heat or the cold, the wind or the rain. These walls are hung on the frame like a curtain, hence the name **curtain walls** (see FIG. 15-19).

Steel cage and curtain wall construction can be seen in Philip Johnson and John Burgee's black-glass, prism-shaped towers that cleverly confront one another at Pennzoil Plaza (FIG. 15-20) in Houston. Office towers all over the world are the landmarks of a prosperous urban life dominated by big corporations and large government bureaucracies. Soaring dramatically,

they literally scrape the sky when their top is hidden in the clouds on a stormy day. Many of these high-rising towers have a similar appearance of straight lines, boxlike shapes, and rectangular panels of plate glass. With their tall and relatively thin supports, these giant-sized pieces of architecture paradoxically afford little experience of solid mass, since the thin curtain walls merely confine volumes.

Steel cage and curtain wall architecture—in many ways the product of the belief that technology alone should determine the appearance of the architecture—seems stripped to the bare essentials, and many recent architects have reacted against it. Nevertheless, architects like Johnson and Burgee, with a good feeling for design and for proportions, or for the expression of structure and materials, have created many impos-

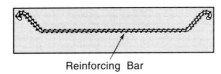

Reinforcing Bar

FIG 15-21 EERO SAARINEN [American, 1910–1961], Trans World Airlines Terminal Building. 1962. Kennedy Airport, New York. Photo by Ezra Stoller, © Esto.

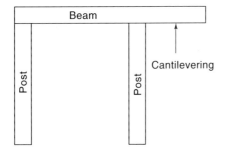

ing glass towers. But too often the construction of such buildings is determined more by expediency, economics, and zoning laws, resulting in a plethora of sterile and monotonous glass boxes.

Reinforced Concrete

Reinforced concrete has become a versatile new building material in the twentieth century. Concrete, such as the ancient Romans used, has great compressive strength, but it easily cracks because it lacks tensile strength. Embedding steel rods in a concrete beam and tying the ends of the rods to the vertical supports gives the concrete beam tensile strength. Fireproof reinforced concrete can replace steel beams to erect rather lofty office towers. Concrete also can be molded into any shape or form. This flexibility allows architects to express themselves or symbolize natural forms with nearly the same freedom as sculptors modeling clay. The soaring shapes of Eero Saarinen's Trans World Airlines Terminal Building (FIG. 15-21) in New York dramatically express the feeling of flight and demonstrate the strength and malleability of reinforced concrete.

Cantilevering

The strength of reinforced concrete (and of steel beams) makes it possible for the upper floors of a building to extend out beyond the first floor. This technique is called **cantilevering.** In one form of cantilevering, vertical pillars are placed at a short distance in from the ends of a beam so that a part of the beam hangs out beyond the pillars. In this way, relatively little of the beam is actually cantilevered.

Frank Lloyd Wright, a great architect of the twentieth century, realized that cantilevering allowed the construction of a treelike building. Since Wright felt that the tall office tower ought to resemble the forms of nature, for the Johnson Wax research laboratory (FIG. 15-22) he designed a building with a stable central core like a tree trunk and cantilevered branches balancing one another around the core.

*In imitation of the structure of a tree,
Frank Lloyd Wright built the fifteen-
story Johnson Wax laboratory building
with a core of reinforced concrete,
which holds all utilities, and floors
that cantilever out from the core. The
floors alternate in size. The upper
floor in each pair has private offices
and acts like a balcony overlooking
the floor below. Instead of
accentuating the vertical lines of the
tower on the exterior, Wright
accentuated the horizontal, with brick
bands that correspond only to the
larger alternate floors. Instead of using
sharp corners, Wright curved the glass
around the corners. And instead of
installing plate glass, Wright inserted a
curtain of glass tubing. His ingenuity
created a structure that is as simple as
it is unique.*

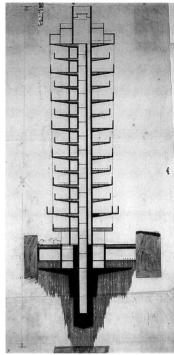

*Section of the Johnson Wax Tower,
© 1948, 1988, The Frank Lloyd
Wright Foundation.*

Suspension

For centuries the pre-Colombian peoples of America crossed precipitous ravines with bridges that were suspended from fiber ropes attached to the cliffs at either end. In modern times the suspension of roadways from very strong steel cables has enabled the erection of enormous rail and auto bridges, including the Brooklyn Bridge (FIG. 15-23); these **suspension bridges** are some of our most spectacular feats of engineering. A number of architects have also designed buildings in which roofs or floors are likewise suspended on steel cables.

FIG 15-23 JOHN ROEBLING [American,
1806–1869] and WASHINGTON ROEBLING
[American, 1837–1926], Brooklyn Bridge.
1865–1883. East River, New York. Museum
of the City of New York.

Urban Environment

Contemporary architects have become increasingly aware that the practice of architecture involves more than erecting individual, isolated structures. No matter how beautiful or grand they are, buildings cannot ignore their surroundings and the context in which they operate. The architects and builders of our cities now realize that they have created an **urban environment** (FIG. 15-24)—a human-made landscape of buildings, roads, open spaces, and facilities that have been built over the natural landscape. The words *urban environment* signify all our visible physical surroundings in a city, not just the air quality. The architecture of the people-built urban environment affects our way of life much more than does any individual building.

Every building is connected to its environment and forms a part of it. A building in the twentieth century needs electricity, fuel, water, and sewage from the local community. Buildings attract people, and the flow of people means that for every new building, the community is concerned about transportation, parking, safety, food distribution, the rights of other people to light, air, and freedom of movement. Urban areas pass building codes and zoning regulations to make sure that architects take these elements into consideration for the greater good.

Communities take a broad view of the relationship of one building to another, since they have to deal with problems of transportation between homes, shops, jobs, and schools, with problems of safety, of natural resources and advantages, of open spaces, and of livability. Most communities try to put these needs on a rational basis and engage in **urban planning** to control and direct growth. After decades of unregulated growth, America is realizing that suburban planning is needed also. Although few people ever have the opportunity to choose an architect for a new office tower, every citizen is affected by the physical development of the urban community, even those who do not live inside a city's limits. The distinctions between urban and suburban, even between urban and rural, have largely broken down, and the vitality of urban life influences the nation.

Cities are still quite important to American life. Most cities are transportation hubs; some cities specialize in certain industries and kinds of commerce; all cities have become management and media centers and the heart of cultural life. Typically, cities developed a downtown (see Fig. 15-25)—a focus of urban life—where shops and leisure time activities flourished. The critical mass of people found only in cities allows urban areas to develop hospitals, museums, theaters, libraries, sports arenas, and parks that provide some breathing space in the midst of a concrete and asphalt landscape.

The Automobile and American Cities

To understand how the built environment in any urban area is an interconnected web of relationships, consider how the introduction of just one new element—the automobile—has shaped American cities during the twentieth century. The automobile has gone from a convenience and a source of independence to a necessity in modern life. In the process it has profoundly changed the urban environment.

When automobile use became widespread, old roads had to be paved and widened to accommodate the increased traffic. Mass transportation facilities in many cities were generally neglected in favor of the auto. Highways between cities became the major means of transportation—the passenger train has nearly vanished. Even rural areas are now crisscrossed with highways that connect them with urban centers. The expressway system has often cut right through urban neighborhoods and divided cities as the railroad tracks once did. Urban streets have become congested with parked cars, and a parking lot or a parking garage often must accompany a new building in any city. Old, narrow streets in many downtown areas make it difficult to travel them by automobile, leading to the neglect of those areas.

The automobile has allowed people to move farther from work and away from means of mass transportation. In every city from New York to Los Angeles, suburbs have spread out from the urban center because of the automobile, with the result that today half the population lives in suburban developments. Many people in fact no longer go downtown for work, for shopping, or for entertainment because these activities have themselves moved out into the suburbs, away from downtown. Downtown areas tend to contain

Fig 15-26   Market Street, Mall of America, Bloomington, Minnesota. Photo by Bob Purcell.

mostly bank buildings, government buildings, and convention hotels. They are often dangerously deserted at night. Instead, Americans congregate at the environmentally controlled shopping malls that have sprung up in the suburbs (see Fig. 15-26). In many areas, malls, with their restaurants, theaters, and recreational activities, have become the new hub of social interaction. In the suburbs, thoroughfares that were once country lanes have developed into garish commercial strips that cater to the automobile trade. Vast areas of the earth have been covered with the dead space of parking lots. The whole of suburban sprawl has used up resources, not always in the most efficient manner.

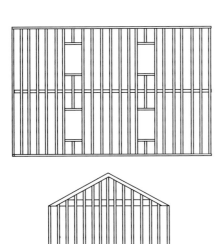

Suburban homes. Photo by Mark Richards.

Suburban American Housing

The automobile is not the only reason for the enormous expansion of suburbs in the United States in the twentieth century. Americans also like the independence of owning their own home. Whether they got the idea from the tradition of the English country estate or from the family farmhouse that once punctuated their own vast agricultural land, the American dream has focused on owning a private house that is surrounded by at least a few feet of grass. A house will probably be the biggest purchase they ever make in their life and the only piece of architecture they will ever own.

Individual architect-designed homes are generally expensive, and most homes, even though they are built singly on the site, are economically focused on the mass market. Therefore, most of the private houses in the suburbs were not designed by architects. They may have been designed by building supply companies or individual builders who have limited resources and who may be familiar only with traditional designs and materials. Prefabricated and mobile homes are also a big part of the housing industry.

The shapes and fixtures of most houses are also limited by the materials available at local building supply houses. Partly for economic reasons, at any one time only a few common housing types seem to be possible, like the Cape Cod, the split-level, the ranch, and the Georgian or colonial (FIG. 15-27). What the great majority of Americans seem to want in a house is something traditional and comfortable. Therefore, the design of the typical suburban house tends to resemble something out of the past—colonial, for example—or perhaps some regional style. Although they often lack imagination, traditional or local types give the homeowner a sense of belonging.

Many home builders use the **balloon frame** technique that was invented in the United States in the early 1800s. The walls of a balloon-framed house are constructed with two-by-fours and then covered with veneers both inside and out. Balloon frame construction has made possible the rapid and easy expansion of suburban housing.

Balloon frame construction. Adapted from William D. Bell's Carpentry Made Easy, 1858.

a.

b.

c.

d.

FIG 15-27   Common suburban housing
types. (a) Cape Cod, (b) split level, (c) ranch,
(d) colonial. Photos by Richard Anderson.

For decades, suburban developments in America
have taken a tract of land; traced on it a system of
wide, curving streets, usually serviced by one main
artery; and then subdivided the remaining land into
small, homogeneous plots. Set back from the street,
repetitious houses on these plots are typically designed
by formulas worked out by the developers, builders,
and financial institutions. This kind of suburban subdivision generally lacks any sense of identity or sense
of community.

FIG 15-28 ROBERT DAVIS [American], developer; Andres Duany [American] and Elizabeth Plater-Zyberk [American], architects; Seaside, Florida. Begun c. 1980. Duany and Plater-Zyberk are both photographers and designers of the master plan of Seaside.

The building code of Seaside specifies that the houses must be constructed of wood. They must have specific roof pitches and windows that are square or rectangular in a vertical direction. There are no picture windows or plate glass patio doors in Seaside. Houses on many streets must have front porches, just as they have traditionally had in the South. The porch helps extend the house into the public sphere. Street and alleys must have picket fences. Building materials must be those generally available before 1940—no synthetics or imitations allowed. The architects who designed Seaside, Andres Duany and Elizabeth Plater-Zyberk, have not built a single house in the town, since they want different architects and builders to develop over the years a great variety of house designs.

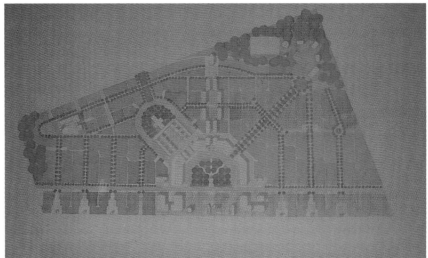

At Seaside, Florida (FIG. 15-28), a new attempt to establish suburban housing has had great success. The developer Robert Davis has tried to imitate an old-fashioned small town of the kind already existing in the region (the Florida Panhandle and southern Alabama). Seaside was deliberately placed straddling the main highway along the Gulf coast so that an active commercial center would develop there as it has in many towns. Seaside's streets radiate from this town center in a regular, straight-line pattern. Most streets are kept narrow and houses are set close to the street so that roadways become shared places for people on foot to interact, rather than throughfares to drive through. A building code makes sure the houses resemble the common architecture of the American Southeast before 1940, since this style has the best chance of being compatible with its environment. Rather than instantly dropping on the land an isolated, anonymous, and exclusive subdivision with a name like Hilldale, the developers have encouraged Seaside to grow organically like a small town—a place that people can identify with, a place that people can say they come from.

Text continues on page 398

Richard Fernau (1946–) and Laura Hartman (1953–)

$\mathcal{F}$ ROM THEIR OFFICES in Berkeley, California, the small architectural firm of Richard Fernau and Laura Hartman has designated residential, commercial, and institutional buildings throughout the San Francisco Bay Area.

Through the publication of their work in magazine features, they have received national and international attention and obtained other commissions in Colorado, New York, London and Frankfurt. Since their California architecture springs from the local tradition of building in the Bay area, Fernau and Hartman have been labeled regionalists—a term they sometimes dispute.

Regionalism, to Fernau and Hartman, does not mean imitating a historical style from San Francisco's past but involves adopting the character and the attitude of mind of the building tradition of a particular place, whether San Francisco or London. For many years in the late nineteenth and early twentieth centuries, architects of the San Francisco Bay Area were known for their inventiveness. San Francisco architects like Bernard Maybeck and Julia Morgan combined an eclectic and surprising variety of past styles, had sympathy toward local materials (wood and stone especially), and incorporated the

Continued on next page.

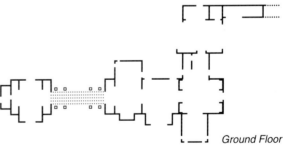

Ground Floor

RICHARD FERNAU [American, 1946–] and LAURA HARTMAN [American, 1953–   ] Berggruen House. 1986–1988. Napa Valley, California. Photo by Christopher Irion.

Fernau and Hartman's structures often appear deceivingly simple because they are not calculated to proclaim the ego of a self-centered architectural genius.

dramatic Bay Area landscape into the planning of the architecture. This was the native language of architecture that was generally spoken in the region. Fernau and Hartman have revived that inventive attitude by combining old and new materials and letting the site guide the building's composition.

So far their buildings have been modest in size, and their structures often appear deceivingly simple because they are not calculated to proclaim the ego of a self-centered architectural genius. Their work, like the Berggruen House, comes across instead as fresh and delightful. Fernau and Hartman designed the Berggruen House for two painters who needed living and working space on property in the rural Napa Valley. Lying in the midst of extensive vineyards, the property contained workers' shacks that the painters had converted into a home. The ramshackle arrangement of the old buildings inspired the casual layout of the new construction. The architects set one of their clients' studios in a towerlike construction among the treetops. In general, the Berggruen House gives the appearance of a cabin nestled in the woods and built haphazardly over a long period of time. Triangular gables and

single-sloping shed roofs cover different parts of the house as though these parts were added at different periods. Corrugated galvanized metal covers the many bays that project from the house, and the wooden parts are painted in vivid colors.

When Fernau and Hartman were asked to design a student center for the University of California at Santa Cruz, the building was planned for the middle of a meadow, the only unbuilt open space on the campus. Fernau and Hartman decided to place the student center buildings instead at the edge of the forest so that the meadow would remain unspoiled. By composing the buildings in an L-shape, they in effect made the meadow part of the courtyard of the south-facing (sun-facing) terraces overlooking the meadow. The courtyard

has become a favorite student gathering space. Old farm buildings still in existence on the modern campus provided some of the inspiration for the architecture of the student center. The asymmetrical main block has gabled wings configured in a U-shape, some of it clad in unpainted shingles. The architects deliberately contrasted different materials throughout the buildings in order to call attention to the character of the materials. Because they often choose materials that will weather and change over time, they essentially plan for the aging of the building.

Both partners participate in the design of each project, and both of them like to stay directly involved with each project. The firm of Fernau and Hartman includes several other architects, one of whom works on each spe-

Richard Fernau [American, 1946–] and Laura Hartman [American, 1953–], student center, University of California at Santa Cruz. 1985–1989. California. Photos by Richard Barnes

cific project with the two partners. The architects begin by holding extensive discussions with the clients in order to ascertain their needs and wishes. The partners visit the site, not with preconceived plans but in a search for inspiration and ideas from the land itself. The intense design process that follows goes through three stages that are rather typical of architectural development everywhere. After a lot of brainstorming that yields an idea or variety of ideas, the architects first draw up schematics, which are sketches and rough plans and elevations of the project. They also construct a very crude and changeable model out of cardboard, scraps, and erasers to get a three-dimensional feel for the building. If the client approves, the client signs a letter of agreement.

In the second stage, called design development, the agreed-upon idea is elaborated in more specific drawings and in a more substantial model made of basswood and painted board. (Fernau and Hartman do not yet use computers as a design aid.) The project is staked out on the site and local building codes are checked.

The third and final stage results in working drawings that are basically legal documents between architect and client and are incorporated in the contract. Throughout the process an estimator assesses the cost of construction for the architects and client, who then submit the detailed project to builders for bids. For their work, the architects receive a set percentage of the building's cost to the client.

Like almost every architect, Fernau and Hartman dream of large-scale public

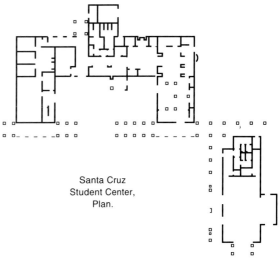

Santa Cruz
Student Center,
Plan.

projects that will challenge their imagination and make their reputation. Growing into a larger firm will also challenge their personal and spontaneous approach to architectural design and the direct participation of the partners in every stage of a project's development.

Historic Preservation

Most people like to see in architecture evidence of a sense of belonging and the roots from which they came. These desires can also be satisfied in part when the urban environment includes the visible presence of the location's past. The retention of historic buildings helps give a region some character and identity. Therefore, a vital part of urban planning is to preserve what is good and meaningful from the architectural history of the area. Making sure that a region can find its roots through its building history is called **historic preservation.**

Historic preservation in the United States at first entailed the saving of historic landmarks, like Jefferson's Monticello and Washington's Mount Vernon, or sites of famous battles, like Fort Sumter, because of their association with historic people or events. A new kind of historic preservation happened at Williamsburg, Virginia, starting in the 1920s: at Colonial Williamsburg the entire town was preserved, reconstructed, and maintained like an open-air museum to give an idealized picture of what life was like in colonial days.

In addition to creating "museums" like these, historic preservation can help revitalize whole neighborhoods and restore community life to a viable residential area. Charleston, South Carolina (FIG. 15-29), and Madison, Indiana, are two examples of many preservation success stories of this kind. Maintaining and preserving the integrity of a neighborhood usually makes better sense than tearing it down through urban renewal and then waiting for new development to happen.

On a smaller scale, historic preservation often engages in **adaptive reuse** by finding new functions for an old building compatible with the building and its surroundings. Abandoned railroad stations around the United States have been turned into restaurants and specialty shopping malls. Boston has converted Quincy Market (FIG. 15-30) and New York City the Fulton Fish Market into a restaurant and shopping arcade. In this way, preservation has brought people back into the urban area and in some cases has been the focus of economic development in the area. Historic preservation not only maintains precious bits of American architectural history, it also preserves the character and feel of a city. The restoration of an important old building can act as an anchor to stabilize a changing community. Historic preservation often upgrades property values in an area and increases economic prosperity through tourism. It has begun preserving America's ethnic and multicultural heritage as well. The National Park Service is attempting to preserve Auburn Avenue in Atlanta—the site of the birthplace of Martin Luther King, Jr. and the longtime center of the African-American business and social community in the city. Historic preservation has challenged the ingenuity of architects to seek new solutions for buildings while respecting tradition, respecting people, and respecting the urban environment.

FIG 15-30 ALEXANDER PARRIS [American] Quincy Market, Boston. 1824–1826. Restored in 1976 by Benjamin Thompson and Associates, Cambridge. Photo by Costa Manos, Magnum Photos.

Key Terms and Concepts

aisles	Corinthian order	modulor
adaptive reuse	crossing	nave
ambulatory	cross vault	plan
apse	curtain walls	post-and-lintel
arches	dome	reinforced concrete
balloon frame	Doric order	steel cage construction
barrel vault	entablature	suspension bridge
bays	entasis	transept
cantilevering	firmitas	triglyph
capital	frieze	truss
centering	groin vault	tunnel vault
choir	Ionic order	utilitas
clerestory	keystone	venustas
corbel arch	metope	

SUMMATION BOX

ARCHITECTURE

The nature of architecture	Architecture shapes living experience.
	The experience of architecture unfolds in time.
	Architecture is the functional art.
	Architecture expresses the way a society lives.

VITRUVIUS

Vitruvius's Principle	**Modern Equivalent**
Solid construction (firmitas) requires the correct materials and the correct method of building.	Architecture is engineering.
Suitability (utilitas) depends on the correct use of architectural orders and the proper building type.	Form follows function.
Beauty (venustas) comes from symmetry and proportions.	Beauty involves the symmetrical or asymmetrical planning of the experience of space.

THE PRACTICE OF ARCHITECTURE

Construction techniques	Architectural construction techniques include solid wall, truss, post and lintel, arch, barrel vault, cross vault, corbel arch, corbel vault, suspension, dome, steel cage, reinforced concrete, and cantilevering.
Urban environment	The urban environment is a built environment.
	The automobile has profoundly changed the nature of American cities and suburbs.
	Suburban housing has followed conventional design.
Historic preservation	Historic preservation is preserving the roots and character of a locality through its historic buildings.
	Three types of historic preservation are saving historic houses or sites as museums, finding new uses for old buildings, and revitalizing neighborhoods.

CRITICAL ANALYSIS III

When Mary Cassatt began an oil painting like *Summertime: Woman and Child in a Rowboat*, she sketched the contours of the main forms with a color diluted in turpentine. Painted contour lines around the two women are still highly visible in *Summertime*, although most of them were added later to strengthen the original sketch. We can get a better idea of the procedure that she used in painting by examining an unfinished work, *Young Woman Picking Fruit*. In both pieces, after sketching the essential contours, Cassatt then probably roughly laid in the basic colors of the figures, including their flesh areas. Rather than filling in the contour with a smooth layer of paint, at this stage she often thinly scrubbed or rubbed the opaque paint with her brush across the texture of the oatmeal-colored canvas to create a fuzzy blur of colors. Other strokes of opaque paint were scumbled across the canvas. Cassatt then usually let these roughed-in colors dry.

In general, she seems to have preferred to paint with thick-bristled hogs-hair bushes that leave their traces in the

Mary Cassatt [American, 1845–1926], *Summertime:* Woman and Child in a Rowboat. 1894. Oil on canvas, 42 × 30 in. (106.7 × 76.2 cm). Terra Museum of American Art, Chicago.

Mary Cassatt [American, 1845–1926], *Young Woman Picking Fruit.* sketch for a mural. 1892. Oil on canvas, 23 5/8 × 28 3/4 in. (60 × 73 cm). Sotheby's Transparency Library.

paint. At first glance, *Summertime* looks like a mosaic of different colored bush strokes set side by side. On closer inspection, it becomes clear that Cassatt built up her painting with successive layers of paint. Sometimes a brush wet with paint was scumbled over the dry paint underneath. Sometimes a brush wet with one color was dragged through an area of another wet color. This wet-into-wet technique achieves a rich fusion of the two colors without actually blending them. Sometimes Cassatt took a completely dry bristle brush and dragged it over wet colors to soften and blur them. Her varied yet decisive brushwork captures atmosphere, light, and movement.

The unfinished painting *Young Woman Picking Fruit* was a sketch for *Modern Women*, the only mural Cassatt ever painted. Since the face is finished more than any other part, Cassatt probably painted the sketch to study the difficult foreshortening of the head. The mural, which stretched fifty-eight feet across, illustrated modern women and their progress in modern times. Painted in Paris, it was commissioned in 1893 for the Woman's Building of the World's Columbian Exposition in Chicago. Although it was placed about forty feet above the viewer, the large scale of Cassatt's figures and broad areas of color ought to have carried into the room. Unfortunately, the painting was not preserved when it was taken down after the fair.

Like many artists Cassatt had skill in more than one artist's medium. In addition to painting, she was accomplished at drawing and printmaking. Although she was required to draw exclusively for a year and a half as a student at the Pennsylvania Academy of Fine Arts in Philadelphia, she preferred painting as the highest form of art. Consequently, pastel chalks, which resemble paint, became her favorite drawing medium. From her earliest association with the Impressionists she exhibited paintings, pastels, and prints that reproduced nearly the same compositions.

The pastel-and-charcoal drawing *At the Window* resembles in many ways the slightly later drypoint print *Baby's Back* (FIG. 9-12), although the composition of *Baby's Back* is reversed, of course, because of the printing process, and the window theme disappears in the print. While retaining her own feeling for the intimacy of the subject, Cassatt adopted the pastel techniques of Edgar Degas. Like Degas (see FIG. 8-16), Cassatt found ways to fix the preliminary layers of pas-

Mary Cassatt [American, 1845–1926], *At the Window*. 1889. Pastel and charcoal on gray paper, 29 3/4 × 24 1/2 in. (75.6 × 62.2 cm). Musée d'Orsay, Paris. © RMN-ADAGP. Photo © RMN-ADAGP.

tel, and in *At the Window* the charcoal lines too, so that she could draw on top of them vigorous strokes of very different color. Intermeshed warm and cool colors, mixed optically by the eye, enliven the somber gray tone of the whole drawing.

Cassatt once declared that it was the discipline of printmaking that taught her how to draw. Her intaglio print *Baby's Back* demonstrates her point. The unforgiving scratches of the drypoint needle in the copper plate demanded of her a precise eye and an exacting line.

As a printmaker, Cassatt is most famous for her two dozen full-color works. Here too she took a painterly approach. Her print *Feeding the Ducks* bears an obvious resemblance to her oil painting *Summertime*. Indeed, its composition resembles even more closely several oil sketches—now in Washington and Los Angeles—for that piece. Only months before creating these paintings and prints, Cassatt had moved her

Mary Cassatt [American, 1845–1926], *Feeding the Ducks*. C. 1895.
Drypoint, soft ground etching, and aquatint, 11 5/8 × 15 1/2 in. (29.5
× 39.3 cm). Allen Memorial Art Museum, Oberlin College, Ohio; R. T.
Miller Jr. Fund, 1957.

intaglio press from Paris to a pavilion overlooking a little lake on the property of her summer home at Mesnil-Beaufresne, France. She could look out on the scene as she was making her print.

Cassatt began *Feeding the Ducks* by first delineating in drypoint the contours of the boat, the figures, and the ducks. At this point Cassatt printed one impression of her work thus far to get a better idea of what her design looked like— such a trial impression is known as an *artist's proof*. She continued to do additional drypoint work on the plate, giving more detail to the dresses and the ducks. At the third stage, or *state*, in the development of her plate, she added aquatint to the area of the boat.

To supply color to the print, Cassatt etched two more copper plates with aquatint; she probably used the soft ground method to transfer the design by tracing it onto the second and third plates. On these plates she created different values

of green in the water by stopping out the distant water and the nearby ripples with varnish brushed freely on the plate before it was returned to the acid bath. She made the polka dots on the woman's blue skirt with drops of stopping-out varnish applied to the plate. Like the Japanese ukiyo-e printmakers she admired, Cassatt brushed the individual colored inks onto each plate, then hand wiped the plates to force the ink into the grooves. Pinholes in the same location on each plate kept the colors exactly registered. As the third plate lay on the bed of the printing press, Cassatt painted several monotype touches on the plate—the reflections under the boat and the purple duck—just before the impression was made. Since she varied the monotype work and the inking of the plates with each printing, the coloring of each impression of *Feeding the Ducks* varies. Only ten impressions of the print are known.

A History of
World Art

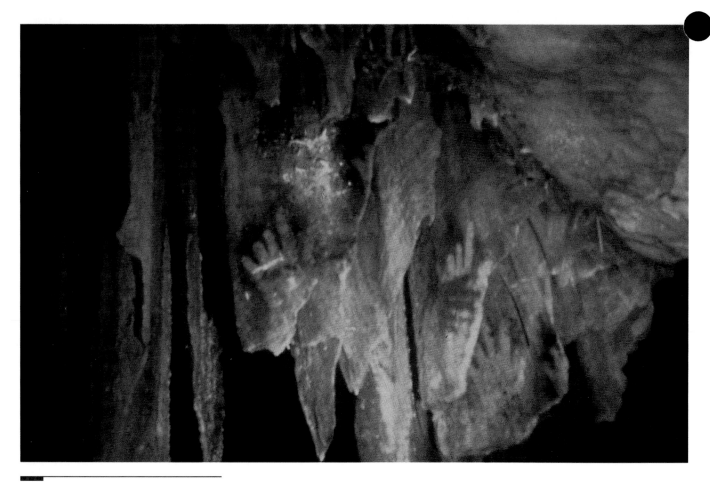

FIG 16-1   Handprints, Cosquer Cave. Old Stone Age, 25,000 B.C. Cape Morgiou, France. Sygma.

FIG 16-2   Ibex engraved over two horses, Cosquer Cave. Old Stone Age, 17,000–16,000 B.C. Cape Morgiou, France. Sygma.

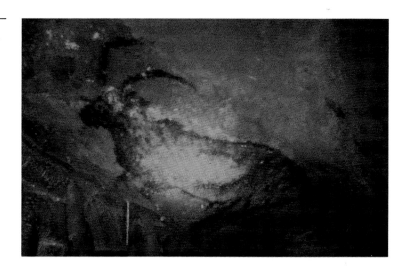

16 ART OF THE ANCIENT AND MEDIEVAL WORLDS

Old Stone Age Art

In 1991 a French diver named Henri Cosquer (pronounced Kos-kay) explored an underwater cave along the Mediterranean coast near Marseilles, France. The entrance to the cave had been concealed when the glaciers melted and the sea level rose at the end of the last ice age, about 10,000 B.C. After swimming through a 450-foot-long submerged tunnel, Cosquer entered a large air-filled cavern or grotto, part of which now lay above sea level. He discovered there dozens of drawings of animals painted on and incised (scratched) into the cave wall in addition to dozens of hands "printed" on the wall by tracing their outlines in paint (FIG. 16-1).

A few months later, a research team from the French Ministry of Culture swam into the Cosquer Cave and confirmed that its art came from the Paleolithic period—the Old Stone Age. Indeed, the scientists determined through the technique of radiocarbon dating that many of the hand-stencil paintings might have been produced about 25,000 B.C., making them among the oldest works of art in the world. The approximately one hundred paintings and incised drawings of horses, ibex, and other animals date from a later period, about 17,000 to 16,000 B.C.

Cosquer had discovered new prehistoric art that was created earlier than the famous paintings at Lascaux (see FIG. 2-12) in southwest France. Although scientific tools can date a cave painting to within a decade of its creation, no one knows for sure why the art was made. Because some of the Cosquer Cave drawings have been cut on top of animals that

already existed on the wall (FIG. 16-2), as though the early art had already served its function, the hands and animals have been interpreted as part of a magical or religious ritual to ensure fertility or success in hunting. Certainly, the deceptively simple pictures required a considerable amount of careful observation and previous practice on the part of the primitive artist. Through the magic of artistic representation, the people could exercise some control over the forces of nature. Still unanswered are the questions: Why is there an eight-thousand-year gap between the first period of cave painting and the second? What happened to these people and their talent when the ice age ended and the herds moved away?

Text continues on page 410

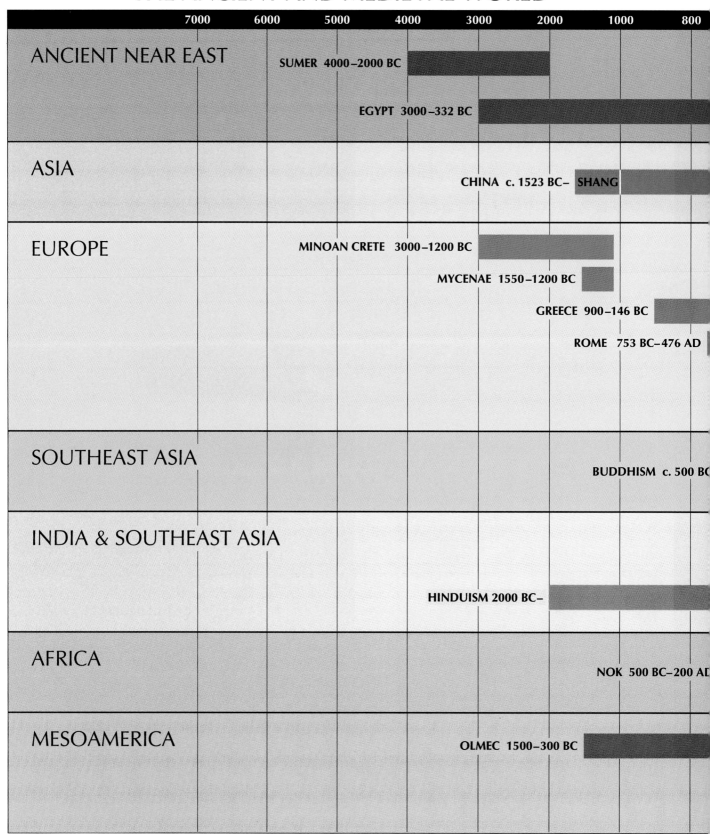

	7000	6000	5000	4000	3000	2000	1000	800
ANCIENT NEAR EAST				SUMER 4000–2000 BC				
					EGYPT 3000–332 BC			
ASIA					CHINA c. 1523 BC– SHANG			
EUROPE			MINOAN CRETE 3000–1200 BC			MYCENAE 1550–1200 BC	GREECE 900–146 BC	ROME 753 BC–476 AD
SOUTHEAST ASIA							BUDDHISM c. 500 BC	
INDIA & SOUTHEAST ASIA						HINDUISM 2000 BC–		
AFRICA							NOK 500 BC–200 AD	
MESOAMERICA					OLMEC 1500–300 BC			

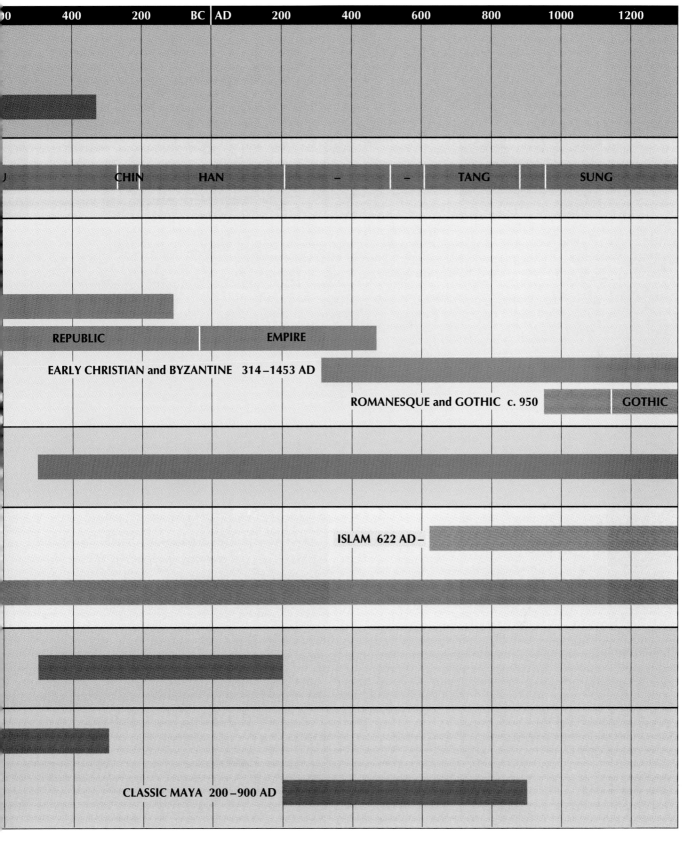

	400	200	BC	AD	200	400	600	800	1000	1200

CHIN HAN – – TANG SUNG

REPUBLIC EMPIRE

EARLY CHRISTIAN and BYZANTINE 314–1453 AD

ROMANESQUE and GOTHIC c. 950 GOTHIC

ISLAM 622 AD –

CLASSIC MAYA 200–900 AD

Fig 16-3   Venus from Dolní Vestonice. Paleolithic period, c. 25,000 B.C. Baked clay, 4 5/16 in. (11 cm) high. Czech Republic, Moravian National Museum. Photo © 1989 by Ira Block.

Archaeologists have also discovered dozens of small-scale female figures like the limestone Venus of Willendorf (FIG.13-9). It has long since been conceded that the figures do not represent a goddess like the ancient Greek Venus or an ideal of feminine beauty. These Stone Age figures more likely had a magical function in primitive society, where they helped ensure fertility. A group of similar clay "Venus" figurines has been discovered at Dolní Vestonice, about twenty miles south of Brno in the Czech Republic. Most of the Czech figures, which date from about 25,000 B.C., are broken like the one in FIG. 16-3 with a fracture in its right hip and thigh. From the nature of the fractures researchers have recently speculated that the figurines were created to be tossed into a fire. The artist, it seems, only partially or imperfectly dried the clay figure so that it would explode with a bang in the flames. The fragmentation of the ceramic figures very likely served some ritual or divination purpose. It is peculiar that these people were making fire-hardened ceramic figures for magical reasons, thousands of years before the first examples of useful pottery appeared.

Sumerian Art

About 8000 B.C. the human race discovered the benefits of agriculture. This great change from hunting and gathering food meant that groups of people settled permanently in fertile river valleys where they built homes and defenses like the Round Tower of Jericho (see FIG. 15-5) to protect their farms. Thousands of years ago human beings also moved into the fertile plains of southern Iraq, where they harnessed the waters of the Tigris and Euphrates Rivers for farming. We know these people as the Sumerians, who invented an early form of writing called **cuneiform** as a means of controlling their extensive commerce.

The Sumerians in the fourth and third millennium B.C. built a thriving civilization of great walled cities in Mesopotamia, the land between the two rivers. The plains they lived on lacked stone and timber, so they built their walls of mud brick. In the center of each city rose a mountainous **ziggurat,** an enormous mass of mud brick faced with kiln-hardened burnt brick set in

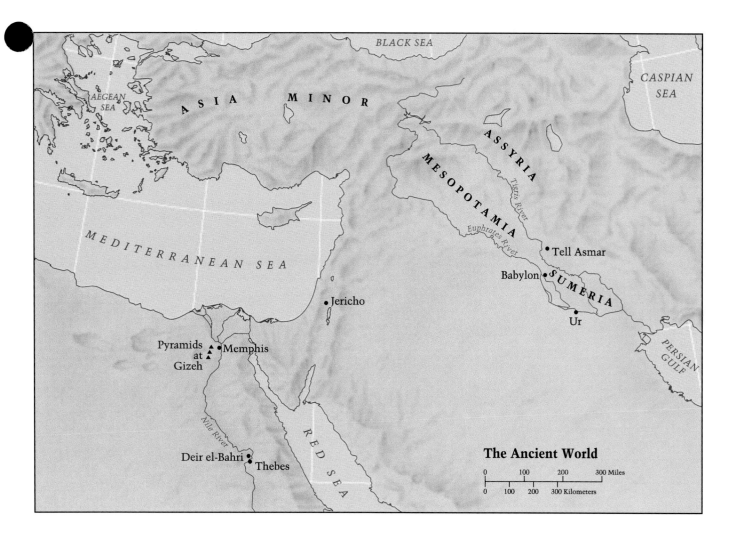

bitumen. The land belonged to the god, and the people turned to the god they worshiped atop the ziggurat to protect them from calamity. The great ziggurat of Ur (FIG. 16-4) was built in the Third Dynasty of Ur (the Neo-Sumerians) by Ur-Nammu, whose stamp appears on every brick. The walls and buttresses of the restored ziggurat at Ur slope inward to sustain the enormous mass that rises in three stages to the temple at the top. Three flights of stairs lead straight to the temple. The author of Genesis 11:1–9 in the Hebrew Bible surely was thinking of such a ziggurat when describing the folly of reaching the heavens in the Tower of Babel.

FIG 16-4 [Sumerian], ziggurat, northeastern facade with restored stairs. C. 2100 B.C. Ur, Iraq. Robert Harding Picture Library.

FIG 16-5 [Sumerian], statuettes from the Abu Temple, Tell Asmar. C. 2700–2600 B.C. Marble with shell and black limestone inlay. Male figure 28 in. (72 cm) high, female figure 23 in. (59 cm) high. Iraq Museum, Baghdad. Erich Lessing/Art Resource, New York.

The Sumerians depicted their gods and goddesses in human form although usually on a slightly larger scale. Among a group of small limestone figures found at the Abu Temple, Tell Asmar (FIG. 16-5), the tallest figure may be the god Abu or it may be a priest. The other, smaller figures represent worshipers. All of them clasp their hands across their chest. Broad shouldered and stiff legged, they wear rounded skirts, many of which terminate in featherlike fringes. Most of the men wear full, curly beards. The most distinctive feature of these Sumerian statues is their large, bug-proportioned eyes, exaggerated by the colored shells set in them. Their fixed stare probably symbolized religious awe and constant vigilance in the presence of the all-powerful deity.

Egyptian Art

About the same time that civilization arose in the valley of the Tigris and Euphrates rivers in southern Iraq, the Egyptian civilization established itself in the valley of the Nile River in northeastern Africa. As the Nile River flows north, it transforms the African desert into the fertile land of Egypt. By 3000 B.C. the narrow strip of land along the river had been unified under a powerful pharaoh, King Menes. Isolated and relatively safe from invaders, Egypt enjoyed a continuous culture for approximately the next three thousand years.

Constancy characterized life along the Nile not only because of the long periods of political stability but also because of the regularity of the river itself. Without fail, each spring the river would inundate the land and deposit rich silt to fertilize the fields. Change from one generation to the next was negligible. Life seemed to stretch endlessly into the future as it did into the past. Perhaps as a consequence of their steady existence, the Egyptians tended to think of life after death as a repetition of life along the Nile. Wealthy Egyptians arranged to have their bodies embalmed and mummified so that their spiritual alternate, the *ka*, could inhabit their bodies after death. And on the chance that the mummy did not survive, statues that substituted for the embalmed body were placed in the tomb and in the temples of the tomb complex.

FIG 16-6 [Egyptian], Great Pyramids of Giza. Cheops Pyramid, c. 2530 B.C.; Chephren Pyramid, C. 2500 B.C. Giza, Egypt. Photo © Hugh Sitton, Tony Stone.

Most of the art of ancient Egypt that we now possess comes from tombs. One form of Egyptian tomb architecture, the **pyramid,** is the obvious expression of the permanence and stability that Egyptian culture sought in the afterlife. Of the eighty-some pyramids that we know of, the most famous are the three at Giza (FIG. 16-6), across the Nile River from Cairo. These giant pyramids bear witness to the strong religious beliefs of the ancient Egyptians and to the power and wealth of the pharaohs that enabled their construction. The simple, stable pyramid shape epitomizes permanence, and the pyramids themselves needed an army of laborers to quarry and transport the stones and haul them up ramps to their place. The largest of the three pyramids, the Great Pyramid of Cheops, con-

tains over two million blocks of stone. An average stone weighs five thousand pounds. This human-made stone mountain covers thirteen acres and was 481 feet high when all its stones were in place. The second largest pyramid, the Pyramid of Chephren, was 471 feet high, only ten feet lower. The sophistication of the builders is remarkable. Erected on a completely level site, each side of the Great Pyramid was about 755 feet long, within a tolerance of a few inches. Each side is oriented exactly north-south and east-west. Never has humankind so striven to secure such a permanent site for the dead.

The same feeling for rigid geometric simplicity and massiveness characterizes the style of ancient Egyptian sculpture. In a remarkable group now in the Boston

FIG 16-7 [Egyptian] King Mycerinus and Queen Kha-merer, Valley Temple of Mycerinus, Giza. Fourth Dynasty, 2548–2530 B.C. Greywacke, 54 1/2 in. (138.4 cm) high. Museum expedition. Museum of Fine Arts, Boston.

Museum of Fine Arts (FIG. 16-7), Mycerinus, the builder of the third pyramid at Giza, stands alongside Queen Kha-merer. The strength and solidity of the sculpture, in fact and in appearance, is ensured by the presence of some of the original block of stone behind and between the figures and at their feet. They both stand stiffly erect and frontal, and both place the left leg forward, as does almost every standing Egyptian figure. Mycerinus holds his clenched hands at his side, and Queen Kha-merer bends her left arm at a right angle to touch him while her right arm embraces him around the waist. It has been suggested that the embrace signifies that she is conferring legitimacy and power on her husband because the Egyptians traced descent through the female line. The limbs and tightly wrapped clothing of the figures reveal almost no details, and essential elements of the anatomy like the legs and chest seem swollen to exaggerate mass. Yet within those masses the Egyptian sculptor exhibited a subtle sensitivity to the differences between male and female anatomy and even displayed some character on the face. The Egyptian style gives the figures serenity and strength.

The ancient Egyptians also painted the walls of their tombs, especially the corridorlike tombs cut into the rock along the west bank of the Nile near ancient Thebes in the so-called Valley of the Kings. In a small portion of the 344-foot-long tomb of Haremhab (FIG. 16-8), we see the king standing before the god Hathor on the left and again before the hawk-headed god Harsiese on the right. As discussed in chapter 4,

FIG 16-8 [Egyptian], Haremhab with Hathor and Harsiese, tomb of Haremhab, No. 57, Valley of the Kings, Egypt. Eighteenth Dynasty, 1319–1307 B.C. Robert Harding Picture Library, London.

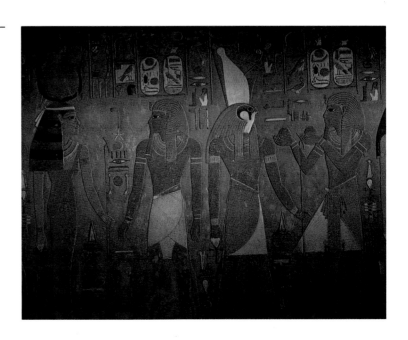

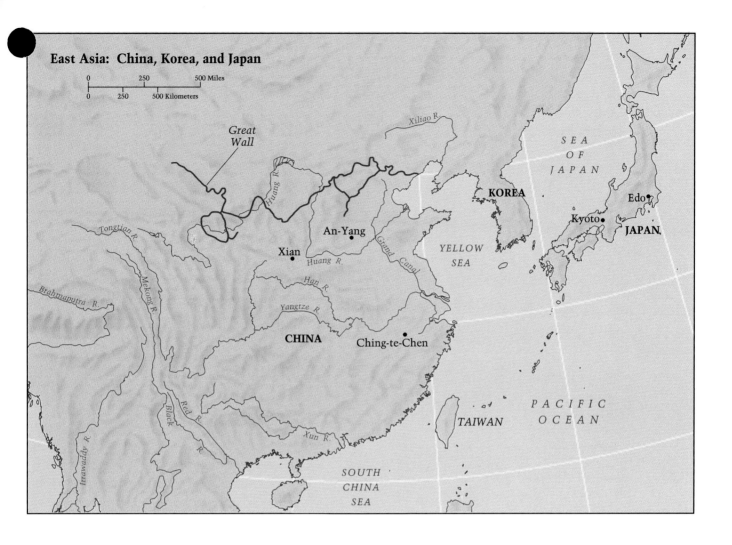

East Asia: China, Korea, and Japan

Egyptian artists employed conventions of representation of the human figure in their art. Rather than imitating their perceptions of reality, they made diagrams of reality to illustrate information about the subject. They combined the most characteristic and thus the most constant aspects of a figure. They did not use foreshortening or single-point perspective either—the figures stand on a horizontal baseline. The picture surface remains intact because the figures are as flat as the adjacent **hieroglyphics**—pictures and symbols that constitute their system of writing. In addition to black and white, Egyptian artists generally used the four psychological primaries: red, yellow, blue, and green. The unmixed color was applied flatly, without modeling, within a precise outline. Another of their conventions required that males be usually dark skinned and females light skinned. Egyptian conventions were relaxed only for some representations of workers and subordinates.

Early Chinese Art

A few centuries after the building of the pyramids in Egypt and the ziggurats in Sumer, historic civilization began in China in the valley of the Huang He (Yellow River). Unlike unified Egypt, China for a long time was divided into many small states, until the creation of the Shang dynasty about 1750 B.C. After that date, the history of China and its art would be closely associated with the series of dynasties that ruled China until the twentieth century. One of the great civilizations of ancient and modern times, China has to its credit the invention of gunpowder, paper, and silk, and developed one of the earliest systems of writing. It is the invention of writing that the Chinese treasure the most and equate with civilization itself. Chinese writing is **ideographic writing,** with thousands of symbols and characters standing for objects or concepts. From the start it was an art form—we call it calligraphy (see

FIG 16-9 [Chinese], ritual vessel *(yu)*. Late Shang dynasty, second or first century B.C. Bronze, 14 3/8 in. (36.5 cm) high. Freer Gallery of Art, Washington, D.C.

Chao Meng-fu's *Spring Poem*, FIG. 4-14)—closely related to the art of painting.

Not much remains of the architecture or painting of early China, but hundreds of splendid bronze vessels exist from the Shang dynasty (c. 1750–1045 B.C.) and the early Chou dynasty (1045–256 B.C.). During that time, for over a thousand years, Chinese craftspeople excelled at casting these richly decorated vessels that the aristocracy employed in ritual offerings of food and wine to the spirits of their ancestors. Because of their quasi-sacred character and their artistic achievement, these bronzes have been treasured by Chinese collectors for centuries. In the twentieth century in excavations at Anyang in the Yellow River basin in northern China, many more bronze vessels have been discovered in tombs, where they acquired their green or blue patina. It was the custom in China, as it was in ancient Egypt, to bury with the dead their finest earthly possessions—their clothing, jewelry, carriages, and in Shang China even human sacrifices—as well as the ritual bronze vessels.

The Shang and Chou bronzes come in all sizes, from a few inches to a few feet high, and in all shapes, from cooking tripods to bowls and pitchers like the *yu* (a covered wine jar) in the Freer Gallery of Art in Washington, D.C. (FIG. 16-9). The vessels were cast

FIG 16-10 [Chilkat Tlingit], blanket. Nineteenth century. Mountain goat wool and cedar bark, 69 × 34 in. (175 × 86 cm). Courtesy of the Southwest Museum, Los Angeles. Photo #CT.37.

Fig 16-11 [Minoan], view of the interior of the palace at Knossos, Crete, Greece. 1600–1400 B.C. Michos Tzovaras, Art Resource, New York.

in separate pieces with a precision that is still remarkable—for instance, the walls of every incision are straight perpendicular cuts. Each channel is a perfect groove. The linear designs that curve and spiral in bands around the vessels are based on animal motifs like the tiger, water buffalo, or elephant that have been abstracted, combined, and stylized almost beyond recognition. A favorite device was to split the eyes, mouth, and tail of an animal in two and spread the two sides out in mirror fashion, as though someone could see the two side views from the front. The complex design of small and large squared spirals covers the whole surface. Small and large forms alternate dynamically across the surface like a theme and variations in music.

It is quite possible that Chinese craftspeople adapted their animal motifs from the nomadic peoples of the steppes and forest of Siberia. These northern neighbors of the Chinese are also remotely related to the native people of Alaska, British Columbia, and even Central America, with whom they may have had some contact across the Bering Strait. Because of these links, the style of the Chinese bronzes resembles the more recent art of the indigenous cultures of the northwest coast of North America. The blanket in FIG. 16-10, woven of cedar bark and mountain goat wool, had seen several generations of use by the Chilkat Tlingit of southern Alaska before it was pur-

chased by the Southwest Museum in Los Angeles. The design consists of abstracted animal motifs spread out in bilateral symmetry as on the Chinese bronze yu.

Minoan Art

The Egyptians were not the only ancient culture in the Mediterranean region. In the second millennium B.C., a separate culture flourished on the island of Crete. It has been called Minoan after a legendary ruler of that island, King Minos. The Minoans were seafarers whose island was strategically placed for trade through which they spread their influence to the islands of the Aegean Sea and to the European mainland. Like the cities of Egypt, protected by the desert, the cities of Crete did not have defensive walls, because they were protected by the sea.

Around 1600 B.C. a new palace was built at Knossos on the island of Crete. The large and comfortable residence, constructed around a large courtyard, contained rows of storerooms, suites of living quarters, reception rooms, and in the northwest corner a small arena with theaterlike steps on two sides to serve as seats. The palace was built two and three stories high in places. Stairs went around light wells that brought illumination and ventilation to the lower floors. The reconstruction in figure 16-11 shows that the Minoans employed a column that, strangely, tapered downward.

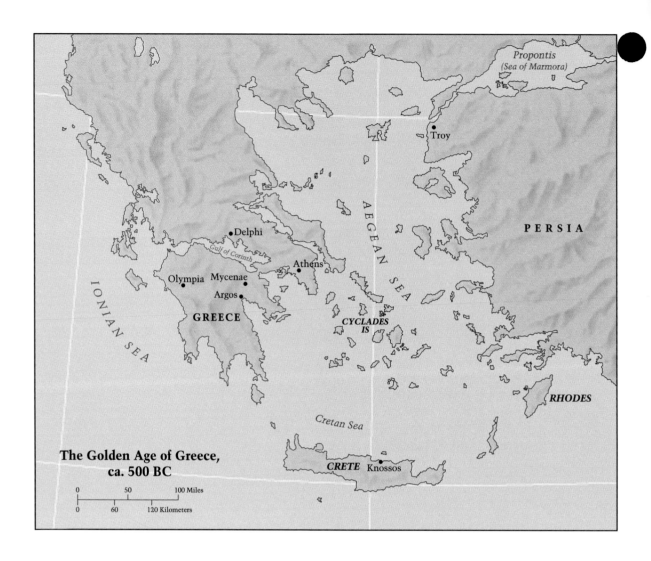

The Golden Age of Greece,
ca. 500 BC

0   50   100 Miles

0 60 120 Kilometers

The palace at Knossos even had plumbing—terra cotta pipes in the floor that drained the complex. The complicated plan of the palace may have given rise to the Greek legend that Minos had the monstrous Minotaur kept in an enormous labyrinth.

Many of the walls of the palace at Knossos were painted with colorful frescoes like *Bull Leaping* (FIG. 16-12), reconstructed from fragments found in the palace. Instead of being trampled by the charging bull, a dark-skinned young man in the fresco seems to be tumbling over its back while a fair-skinned young girl on the right waits to catch the acrobat. Another girl on the left grabs the horns of the bull to begin her dangerous performance over the bull's back. The artist made bull leaping appear to be a death-defying stunt rather than the solemn mortal ritual it might have been. All the curved lines of the painting convey

buoyancy and liveliness. Even the curved lines of the border pulsate around the fresco with vital energy. Whether or not the bull had religious meaning for the Minoans, we enjoy this fresco for its dynamic design.

When the Minoan culture of Crete was devastated by an earthquake about 1400 B.C., the people living on the Greek mainland asserted their power. They are called Mycenaeans after one of their heavily fortified cities, Mycenae. From these cities sailed the warriors who attacked the stronghold of Troy on the Bosporus Strait and who were later immortalized by the poet Homer in his epic poems *The Iliad* and *Odyssey*. The Mycenaeans built their thick walls of roughly cut blocks of stone so large that later Greeks imagined the walls had been constructed by the mythical one-eyed giants called Cyclopes. The Lion Gate (FIG. 16-13) formed an impressive entrance into the citadel of

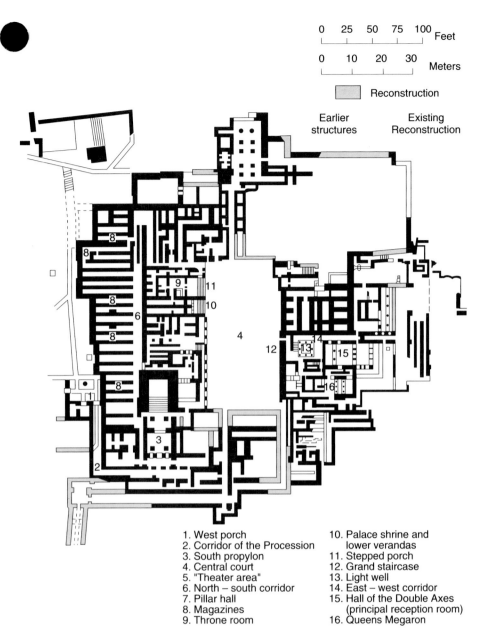

Plan of the palace at Knossos, Crete

0 25 50 75 100 Feet

0 10 20 30 Meters

Reconstruction

Earlier structures

Existing Reconstruction

1. West porch
2. Corridor of the Procession
3. South propylon
4. Central court
5. "Theater area"
6. North – south corridor
7. Pillar hall
8. Magazines
9. Throne room
10. Palace shrine and lower verandas
11. Stepped porch
12. Grand staircase
13. Light well
14. East – west corridor
15. Hall of the Double Axes (principal reception room)
16. Queens Megaron

FIG 16-12 [Minoan], *Bull Leaping,* from the palace at Knossos. C. 1500 B.C. Fresco, 32 in. (81.3 cm) high. Archeological Museum, Hērákleion. Photo: Ancient Art and Architecture.

FIG 16-13 [Mycenaean], Lion Gate.
C. 1300 B.C. Limestone, relief panel about
114 in. (289.6 cm) high. Mycenae, Greece.
SEF/Art Resource, New York.

Mycenae. The gate itself is capped with an enormous lintel, and above it the blocks rise to form a corbel arch, which relieves some of the pressure on the lintel. In the triangular space under the arch the Mycenaeans carved a relief of two lions who have placed their front paws on an altar at the base of a Minoan column. Their heads, made from separate stones, have fallen. The lion relief acts as a gigantic heraldic device of fearsome power at the approach to the city, just as the brutally simple and massive architecture conveys strength and dignity.

The massive fortifications of Mycenae did not protect the city for very long: within a few generations Mycenae was sacked and burned. Mycenaean civilization on the Greek mainland collapsed by 1100 B.C., perhaps under the weight of invasions from the north. A "dark age" ensued, but by the fifth century B.C. the people of Greece again came to dominate the Mediterranean world.

Greek Art

In the fifth century B.C. the rocky peninsula of Greece and the Greek islands of the Aegean Sea were peopled by independent city-states, although the city of Athens soon overshadowed them in almost every respect. Athens was home to some of the most famous philosophers, scientists, historians, playwrights, poets, and artists of ancient times. The Athenians invented a democratic form of government and amassed an intellectual heritage of which Westerners are still the proud heirs. In this golden age, Athens spared no expense to make its civic and religious center the showplace of the Greek world and the expression of its high culture.

The center of the city of Athens was a citadel called the Acropolis, and the major building on the Acropolis was the Parthenon (FIG. 16-14), the temple dedicated to the patroness of Athens, the virgin goddess Athena. Despite its ruined condition, the Parthenon has long been considered one of the most beautiful buildings in the world. Behind the porch that ran around all four sides of the building, the Parthenon contained one small storeroom and one large room whose single purpose was to house a giant statue of Athena. An altar for religious sacrifice was located outside the building; Greek religion demand-

FIG 16-14   IKTINOS [Greek, fifth century B.C.], and Kallicrates [Greek, fifth century B.C.], Parthenon. 448–432 B.C. Athens, Acropolis. Erich Lessing/Art Resource, New York.

ed relatively little communal worship. The famous Greek sculptor Phidias carved the overpowering idol of Athena of ivory and gold and also supervised the carving of much of the sculpture placed on the building itself. Except for the statue of Athena, the interior structure of the Parthenon was ordinary and of little significance. The shaping and elaboration of the exterior was much more important to the Greeks.

The basic design of the Parthenon is similar to that of other Greek temples built in the Doric order, although the Parthenon has eight columns across the front instead of the usual six, making it broader than others. Other temples also had a large room for the statue of the god or goddess, porches, and a pitched roof forming gables at the ends. What does make the Parthenon different is the so-called refinements that brought this building to a kind of perfection.

The Acropolis. Photo: Scala/Art Resource.

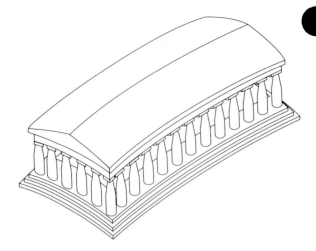

Parthenon refinements

Metopes: Battles of Greeks and Amazons
Pediment: Disputte of Athena and Poseidon

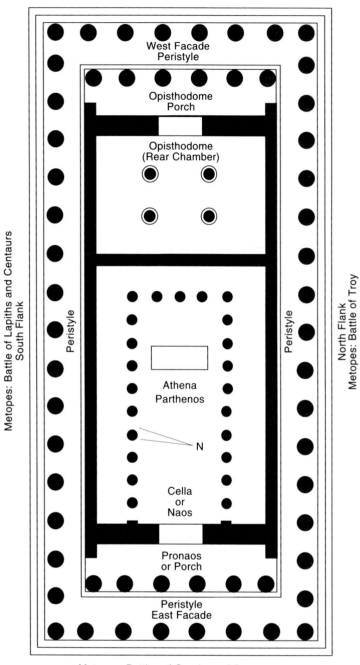

West Facade
Peristyle

Opisthodome
Porch

Opisthodome
(Rear Chamber)

Metopes: Battle of Lapiths and Centaurs
South Flank

Peristyle

Peristyle

North Flank
Metopes: Battle of Troy

Athena
Parthenos

N

Cella
or
Naos

Pronaos
or Porch

Peristyle
East Facade

Metopes: Battles of Greeks and Amazons
Pediment: Disputte of Athena and Poseidon

Plan of the Parthenon, Athens

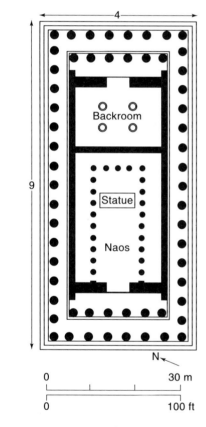

4

9

Backroom

Statue

Naos

N

0   30 m
0   100 ft

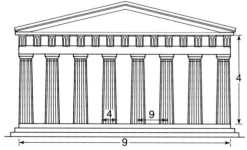

4

4

9

9

Parthenon proportions

Iktinos and Kallicrates, the architects of the Parthenon, believed they could perfect the design of their temple if harsh straight lines were avoided. In fact, every line in the building curves slightly. The platform on which the temple sits curves upward gradually toward the middle of each side. It deviates from the true horizontal 4 5/16 inches in the middle of the long side and 2 3/8 inches on the short side. The platform is in fact a rectangular section of a very large sphere. The same sort of curvature appears in the entablature, the horizontal part placed on top of the columns. The columns themselves have a refined *entasis*—a slight bulge in the tapering about a third of the way up the shaft. (Some earlier temples employed an exaggerated entasis.) The columns furthermore do not stand exactly perpendicular. They all lean in slightly toward the center of the building. Finally, the four corner columns are thicker than the others, and they are placed closer to their neighboring columns to make them appear stronger and more stable—isolated as they are against the light of the sky. All these curves and deviations from a rigid scheme make the Parthenon appear elastic and alive, like a human body flexing in the performance of a task.

The architects also believed that, to harmonize the work, to make it "beautiful," the building should embody in its dimensions a system of proportions with the relationships of small whole numbers. In fact, the ratio 4:9 can be found in several important places in the building. The width-to-length ratio of the entire building is 4:9. The ratio between the height of the order (the column and the entablature) and the width of the building is 4:9, and the distance between the central axes of two columns is related to the diameter of the column in the ratio 4:9.

The ancient Greeks knew that these mathematically determined ratios did not necessarily add to the structural stability of the building. Many Greeks believed, nevertheless, that for the building to be harmonious and beautiful, worthy of the great goddess, such simple ratios must determine its dimensions. Only numerical relationships could achieve perfection because numbers had a universal validity. In fact, simple number relationships seemed to be one of the basic laws governing the universe.

The Greek sculptor Polyclitus, from the city of Argos, demonstrated that numerical relationships also produced the perfect or ideal human being when he

FIG 16-15 POLYCLITUS [Greek, fifth century B.C.), *Spearbearer (Doryphoros)*. Roman marble copy after the bronze original of c. 450–440 B.C. Minneapolis Institute of Arts.

made his statue *Spearbearer* (see FIG. 16-15) around 450 B.C. He was so convinced of his achievement that he wrote a book of rules, the *Canon*, about the correct proportions to be used. Unfortunately, his book no longer exists, but we know that it discussed human proportions in terms of ratios. The height of every normative male statue was to be eight times the length of the head; the fingers were to be in proportion to the palm of the hand, the palm of the hand in proportion to the forearm, and so forth.

The original bronze *Spearbearer* no longer exists. Fortunately, quite a few copies were made of it in ancient times so that we have a rough idea what it looked like. Marble copies need some extra support, like the tree trunk against the ankles in figure 16-15,

Text continues on page 426

Phidias (Active c. 470–430 B.C.)

*A*FTER DEFEATING the Persians in 479 B.C., many of the cities of Greece paid Athens a regular assessment to maintain a strong navy against a renewed Persian threat. By midcentury Athens had grown powerful and wealthy.

Pericles, the leader of the Athenian democracy, then decided to spend a portion of his city's wealth on the rebuilding of Athens's temples, which the Persians had destroyed. Pericles maintained that the allies would share in the fame and glory that future generations would give Athens for the grandeur and beauty of its monuments. The new temples would also symbolize Athens's power and prestige and be a fitting memorial to the Greeks' triumph over the "barbarians." Pericles appointed the sculptor Phidias as the director and overseer of all the projects. The sculptor was to answer immediately to Pericles.

The major monument of Pericles's program for Athens was the new temple to the patron goddess Athena, the Parthenon. In addition to the perfection of its architecture, the lavish amount of sculpture that adorned the building helped the Parthenon to stand out from all other Greek temples. In the brief fifteen years of the temple's construction, Phidias could not possibly have carved all the sculpture; in fact, artists from different parts of Greece

must have been pressed into service. While Phidias supervised and directed all these sculptors, he concerned himself mainly with the creation of the gigantic statue of Athena located inside the temple.

The costly statue of Athena has long since vanished, but pieces of the statues and reliefs that were located in other places on the temple remain: in the pediments (the triangular gables at each end of the building), in the metopes (the squarish blocks above the columns), and in a frieze (continuous relief carving) located high up under the porch. Phidias developed the iconographic program that unifies all the sculpture, and he developed the extraordinary style that he imposed on the many carvers of the

School of Phidias [Greek, fifth century B.C.], A lapith triumphing over a wounded centaur. (South metope XXVII). 447–438 B.C. Marble, 56 in. (142 cm) high. British Museum, London. Art Resource, New York.

pediment sculpture. They were able to combine large-scale masses with the sensuous, supple flesh and gossamer, wind-blown clothing of the gods and goddesses (see his *Three Goddesses*, FIG. 2-9).

The focus of the iconographic program of the Parthenon sculpture—especially in the pediments—is the relationship between Athens and its patroness Athena. The metopes on all four sides of the temple illustrated legendary or mythological conflicts in the history of

Phidias developed the extraordinary style that he imposed on the carvers of the pediment sculpture. Under his direction, they were able to combine large-scale masses with the sensuous, supple flesh of the gods and goddesses.

School of Phidias [Greek, fifth century B.C.], Horsemen. 442–438 B.C. Marble, about 43 in. (109 cm) high. From Parthenon frieze. Acropolis Museum, Athens, Greece. Scalla/Art Resource, New York.

Greece: on the short east end, the battle between the gods and the giants that initiated the reign of the Olympian gods; on the west, the battle between the Greeks and the Amazons (female warriors who came from the east like the Persians and once attacked Athens); on the longer north side, the Trojan War (another east-west conflict); and on the south, the battle between the Lapiths and the Centaurs. Only a group of these Lapith and Centaur metopes from the south flank have been well preserved. Since Centaurs were half-animal and half-human, they symbolized for the Greeks the animal side of human nature, easily succumbing to unbridled emotions. The battle symbolizes the conflict between rational control and lower instincts.

The frieze, located under the porch on the upper wall of the building, is quite an unusual feature in the Parthenon program and in any Greek temple like the Parthenon. It illustrates the Panathenaic Procession, the religious procession in honor of Athena that took place every four years in Athens. Instead of recounting the deeds of gods or goddesses, legendary heroes or heroines, the frieze extols the religious piety of mere mortals like the Athenians themselves who accept their fate and fulfill their duty. The immortal Greek gods and goddesses in Greek art were seldom depicted as so noble or so serious.

The centerpiece of Phidias's program was the statue of Athena, raised on a base inside the temple and towering forty feet above the floor. Athena's flesh was carved in ivory; her robes formed from sheets of gold, thick enough to support themselves. The statue was in effect part of the city treasury. Afterwards, Phidias also made a colossal ivory-and-gold statue of Zeus for the god's temple at Olympia. Phidias's conception of the gods and goddesses made them so vivid in the Greek imagination that one ancient writer said that their beauty "added something to traditional religion."[1] The majestic sculpture of Phidias became a prototype or standard for the representation of divinity in the Western world.

FIG 16-16   Euthymides [Greek, sixth to fifth century B.C.], *Revelers*. C. 510–500 B.C. Red figure vase painting, about 24 in. (61 cm) high. Staatliche Antikensammlungen und Glyptothek, Munich. Photo: Studio Koppermann.

to sustain the solid stone torso. Even the best marble copies probably lack the delicacy and precision of the bronze original. Compare the crispness of detail and the subtle modulation of the masses in the Riace Bronze Warrior (FIG. 4-18) with the copied marble *Spearbearer*.

In his statue Polyclitus depicted a young man in the prime of life and in the nude. The spearbearer is perhaps taking a step, but otherwise he is not doing anything special. The shifting of weight caused by taking a step sets up within a figure a series of balanced contrasts between relaxed and tensed muscles and contrasts in the directions of the limbs. He once carried a spear in his right hand—a reminder that Greek society specially rewarded athletic achievement and heroism on the battlefield. These two important objectives in Greek life are implicit in the meaning of *Spearbearer*. Furthermore, in both their literature and their art, the Greeks depicted their gods and goddesses in human

form. This similarity lent to humankind a certain divine dignity, whereas a person's fate (death) gave to a human being a nobility and seriousness absent from the immortal deities.

The young man in *Spearbearer* appears well built and athletic, yet a certain chunkiness or blockiness about his anatomy shows that Polyclitus created his figure not so much from copying a model but from his system of measurements. The lines separating chest from abdomen and abdomen from thigh and so forth are quite precise, perhaps overly precise. Furthermore, the major blocks like the chest and thigh are rather smooth and almost abstracted into solid geometric forms. Few tendons or individual muscles are shown. There are no dimples or ridges, no deviations from the norm or other individuating differences—just the essentials. All these elements indicate that *Spearbearer* is the representation not of an individual but of an ideal. The figure represents not any man as he is (a fact), but man as he ought to be (a necessity).

The art of fifth-century Greece has been called classical. The word *classic* means not only something outstanding and of lasting significance, but also something that establishes norms or rules for others to follow, as Polyclitus did. Not all Greek art shared the same classical style as that of the fifth century. Greek classical art evolved from earlier forms now called archaic, and the following Hellenistic period experimented with new variations on the Greek style. Nevertheless, later generations throughout the history of Western art have believed that Greek art achieved a high point of perfection and harmony that set standards for their age too.

Several Greek painters, such as Polygnotus and Apelles, seem to have had even higher reputations than the sculptors. Unfortunately, not one piece of the work of these painters survives. To catch a glimpse of what Greek painting looked like, we have to examine the imitations of it made at a later date by the Romans or examine the small pictures baked onto the pottery that contemporary Greek craftspeople manufactured.

Among the many fine examples of Greek vase painting available is *Revelers* (FIG. 16-16). This illustration of a drunken revel on an *amphora* (a wine storage jar), by the artist Euthymides, displays many of the characteristics of Greek painting. (Euthymides, active about 500 B.C., lived two generations earlier than Phidias.) The humorous subject, appropriate to a wine ug, shows that the Greeks recognized the existence of irrational, drunken behavior. It is no accident that male nudes are again the subject, since a statuesque conception pervades the appearance of these tipsy revelers. They fill the surface as they stumble across the lower edge of the frame, which also serves as the ground line. There is no background, no space around the figures—only the space created by the men themselves. Euthymides conveyed their twisting and bulky forms merely by an outline drawing. Few details appear inside the outline, no modeling in light and dark rounds out their bodies. Whether large-scale painting in fifth-century Athens looked like Euthymides's work is almost impossible to say, but it is likely that Greek painting concentrated, as did Euthymides, on the human figure imagined as a statue.

These examples of Greek art tell us several important things about their culture. Greek artists illustrat-ed the belief of their society that man is the measure of all things. The human form dominates their art. By this maxim the Greeks also meant that human reason should dominate life and that human beings should control nature. Building a structure or carving a statute, reason controls even physical reality by creating ideals that establish norms. Greek art thus mirrors the minds of the greatest Greek thinkers such as Plato, who in his philosophy examined the meaning of ideals like goodness, truth, and beauty.

Roman Art

The Romans, who eventually absorbed much of Greek culture, were an active people whose military power took Rome from a small city to a mighty republic (see map, below). Then, in the first five centuries of the Christian era, Rome extended its control over a vast

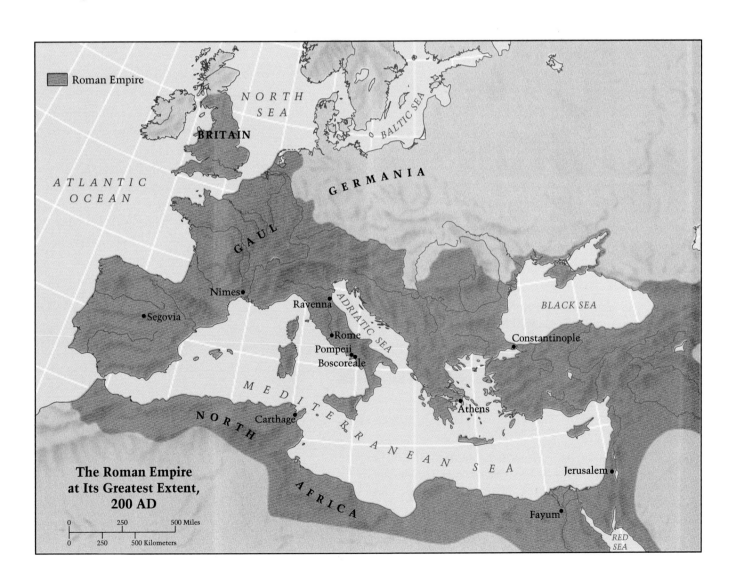

The Roman Empire at Its Greatest Extent, 200 AD

FIG 16-17 [Roman], Pantheon, exterior.
C. 118–125. Rome. Vanni/Art Resource,
New York.

FIG 16-18 [Roman], Pantheon, interior
with partial view of the dome. C. 118–125.
Rome, Italy. Painting by Giovanni Paolo
Pannini, *The Interior of the Pantheon, Rome*.
National Gallery of Art, Washington, D.C.
Samuel H. Kress Collection, © 1994 Board
of Trustees.

empire in which Roman law and practical sense built
great cities as well as the roads, bridges, aqueducts,
markets, and large government buildings to serve
them. (See FIGS. 15-15 and 15-16.) The very ruins of
their empire teach us how great it was. Although they
borrowed heavily from Greek art, the Romans developed new forms of art and architecture to serve their
needs.

The arch and the dome, concrete and bricks served
the Romans' need to cover large spaces better than did
the precisely cut blocks of rare marble used in the
Parthenon. The Pantheon (FIGS. 16-17 and 16-18),
still standing as it was originally built, demonstrates
the amazing structures the Romans could erect with
these ordinary materials. The Emperor Hadrian built
the Pantheon in A.D. 125 as a temple to all the planetary gods and as his audience hall. In the Greek
Parthenon the architectural achievement is best seen
from the outside of the building; in the Roman
Pantheon it is best understood inside the building.

The visitor enters the Pantheon through what
looks like the porch of a Greek temple, incongruously
connected to a large **rotunda** (a circular building or
room). In ancient times, adjacent construction close
to the building made it impossible to walk around the
Pantheon to examine the exterior of the rotunda. The
only door into the building opens onto an enormous
cylinder of space that is capped with a hemispherical
dome 142 feet in diameter—the largest dome in antiquity. If the full circle of the shape of the dome were

428 Part IV: A History of World Art

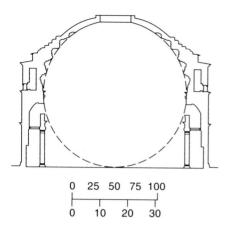

0 25 50 75 100
|—|———|———|———|
0 10 20 30

Section of the Pantheon, Rome

FIG 16-19   [Roman], portrait head of
Emperor Caracalla (211–217). C. third
century. Marble, 14 1/4 in. (36.2 cm) high.
Said to be from Italy. Metropolitan Museum
of Art, New York. Samuel D. Lee Fund, 1940
(40.11.1a).

inscribed within the building, its lowest point would
be tangent to the floor. In other words, the height of
the dome above the floor and the diameter of the
rotunda are the same.

Although the rotunda is quite thick to withstand
the weight and pressures of the dome, it is actually
built of concrete and bricks in a system of arches that
allows it to be penetrated with rooms that lie behind a
screen of columns. These openings along the circumference of the rotunda remove from the interior any
feeling of confinement. The dome is made not of cut
stones but of solid concrete shaped on the interior into
a pattern of **coffers** (sunken squares) that gives the
appearance of ribs.

On the exterior, the lower part of the dome
descends in steps that thicken the base of the dome
against the pressures to pull itself apart. Right at the
apex of the dome, where the keystone of an arch
would be located, is an opening or **oculus** (Latin for
eye). Since the opening is circular, the compression of
its solid ring of material makes a keystone unnecessary.
Drains in the floor remove the rainwater that enters
through this opening. The only window in the
Pantheon is the oculus, which nevertheless suffuses
the interior with more than enough light and also projects a disk of sunlight that jiggles perceptibly as it
moves across the walls. Open to the sky and built in
the shape that the ancients imagined the dome of the
universe, the Pantheon functions like a planetarium
demonstrating the rotation of the earth. The experience of vast space contained within the building is like
no other in the world.

When it came to creating sculpture, the Romans
depended heavily on Greek models for inspiration.
The Romans collected Greek art avidly, made copies
of it frequently, and imitated Greek classicism extensively in their own work. Only in one respect—in portraiture—did the Romans display outstanding sculptural originality. Roman sculptors created some of the
most lifelike and expressive heads ever carved. For
example, the head of the Roman emperor Caracalla
(FIG. 16-19) conveys the vivid impression of a mean
and fierce individual. Caracalla glares out from under
knotted eyebrows; his mouth turns down in a sneer.
History books confirm that our impression is correct:
Caracalla killed his brother to get the throne. After
that, he spent most of his short reign fighting the barbarians on the far borders of the empire.

We might have expected the sculptor to have flat-
tered the emperor by making him more handsome. We
cannot imagine that the sculptor did not know how to
portray the emperor favorably and that the artist just
imitated what was seen. But the mean and aggressive
look—if indeed it represented what the emperor really looked like—apparently pleased the ruler; after all,
Caracalla must have approved this official image. If
the emperor wanted everyone to see him as alert and

Chapter 16: Art of the Ancient and Medieval Worlds

FIG 16-20 [Roman], *The Punishment of Ixion*. C. A.D. 79. Fresco, about 30 in. (76.2 cm) high. House of the Vettii, Pompeii. Art Resource, New York.

ruthless, the image was good propaganda. Although we cannot be sure how accurate the portrait is, compared with the smooth and expressionless head of a Greek ideal statue, it invites us to interpret an individual's character.

The Roman writer Pliny the Elder, when he listed the famous painters of Roman times, included some women such as Iaia of Kyzikos, who painted portraits on ivory in Rome in the early first century B.C. Iaia had such facility and talent "that her prices far exceeded those of the most celebrated painters of her day."[2]

As in ancient Greece, most Roman painting, including the work of Iaia, has been destroyed by time. Fortunately, the Fayum Oasis in the deserts of Roman Egypt has preserved a number of examples of Roman painting—small portraits painted in encaustic on wooden panels that were once buried with the mummy cases of ordinary people. One painting from the second century of the Roman Empire, *Portrait of a Man* (FIG. 10-4), portrays a sensitive-looking young fellow with a distinctive hairstyle and beard whose wide-open brown eyes gaze thoughtfully at us and whose bow-shaped mouth seems ready to speak. Separate brush strokes of light and dark color round out the features of his face and make him come alive. The Roman artist was capable of creating a portrait of a distinct individual—a person we could imagine meeting.

A more considerable amount of Roman painting has been unearthed under the ruins of Rome and under the ash laid down by the eruption of Mount Vesuvius over Pompeii in A.D. 79. Most of these paintings from Pompeii, like *The Punishment of Ixion* (FIG. 16-20), are murals that once decorated the walls of the homes of the well-to-do. In the painting, perhaps a copy of a Greek painting, Ixion's punishment on a wheel is relegated to a partial view on the left. The nude figure of the god Mercury (in the contrapposto stance of the *Spearbearer*) and the reclining figure of the goddess Hera pose like their statues. Just as solid massive statues take up real space, the figure of these deities take up the space within the frame. Like the Greeks, this painter imagined that the artist's task was to reproduce the illusion of three-dimensional sculpture. The Romans, the conquerors of the Greek peninsula, were conquered by Greek culture.

FIG 16-21 [Chinese], bodyguards of the
First Emperor of China. Qin dynasty,
221–206 B.C. Painted ceramic, 72 in. high
(182.9 cm), Xi'an, Shensi Province, China. ©
Julian Calder, Tony Stone.

Art of the Chinese Empire

When the legions of the city of Rome had captured
the whole of the Italian peninsula and had begun
forming an empire in the West, in the East, Qin Shi
Huangdi (the Chinese words mean the First Emperor
of China) united China in 221 B.C. (see map. on p. 415).
The First Emperor of China built the Great Wall to
protect his empire from nomads of the Asian steppes.
To defend the Wall he conscripted an enormous army.
He also spent more than three decades building an
elaborate tomb complex with forced labor. The emper-
or was buried near the city of Xi'an under a fifteen-story
earth mound, which remains largely unexcavated.

In 1974 some farmers digging a well discovered a
subterranean area, less than a mile to the east of the
tomb-mound, which contains a huge army of approximately seven thousand life-sized soldiers, one hundred
chariots, and four hundred horses (see FIG. 16-21).
The horses and soldiers were made of clay pieces molded or modeled by hand and then joined together.
Excavations revealed row upon row of soldiers, still on
guard after more than two thousand years. Once
brightly painted, they were in a sense stand-ins for the
living sacrifices that were made in earlier Chinese
royal burials.

No two soldiers look exactly alike. The artists used
a fine clay for the faces, individualizing them with various types of features, styles of facial hair, and kinds of
expression. Perhaps these faces imitated those of actual soldiers in the imperial guard. Obsessed with security and eager to perpetuate his life, the emperor
ordered this ceramic army to guard forever his tomb
and the approach to the capital of his new empire.

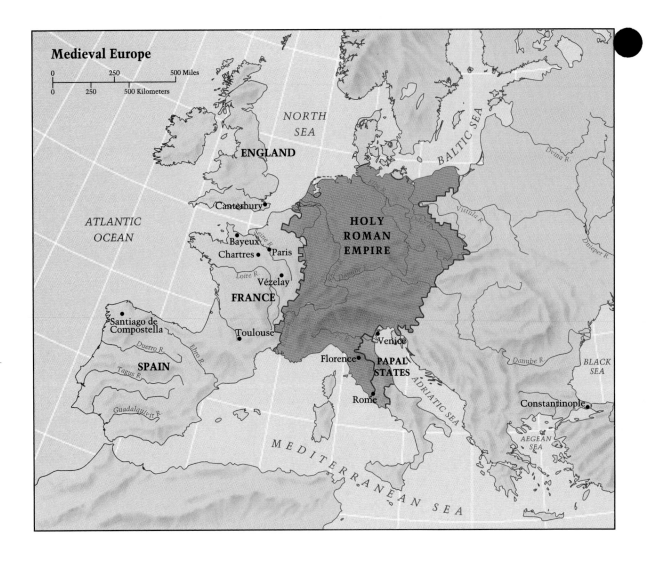

The Medieval World

In the West, the period after the fall of the Roman empire has been called the Middle Ages because it was seen as a mere gap between Rome and the revival of classical culture in the Renaissance in the fifteenth century. But even before the Roman empire fell apart, forces were at work building the foundations of vigorous new cultures. New peoples migrated into the Mediterranean world—the Greeks and Romans called them Barbarians. Several major religions of the present world began their territorial expansion at this time. First Christianity and then Islam spread through Asia, Europe, and Africa. Buddhism worked its way east through Asia during the period. Each religion brought with it a new imagination and a new view of life that transformed the art and architecture of the world.

Early Christian and Byzantine Art

In A.D. 330 the Roman emperor Constantine established a new capital of the Rome Empire in the East at Byzantium on the Bosporus Strait separating Europe and Asia. He changed its name to Constantinople; the city is now known as Istanbul. Constantine had recognized Christianity as an official religion of the empire, and he and his family sponsored magnificent church buildings for Christian worship—buildings like old St. Peter's at Rome and the church of the Resurrection in Jerusalem. After years of persecution, Christianity now came out in the open and soon became the dominant force in the declining, battered empire. People throughout the Roman Empire found meaning in Christianity as life around them grew more uncertain. As the Roman Empire decayed, as barbarians sacked Rome itself in 410—in short, as the reali-

FIG 16-22 [Early Christian], Sant' Apollinare in Classe, interior. C. 533–549. Ravenna, Italy. Scala/Art Resource, New York.

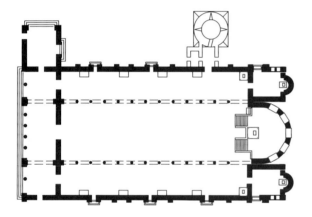

Plan of Sant' Apollinaire in Classe, Ravenna, Italy.

ties of this world crumbled away—Christianity gave people hope in a future life. This new attitude to nature and spirit gave rise to new forms of art.

At Constantinople a Christian-Roman empire survived the fall of western Rome for another thousand years. In the sixth century, the Byzantine emperor Justinian I built the splendid church of Hagia Sophia in his capital city (see FIG. 15-18). Justinian even won back the Italian peninsula from the barbarian people who ruled the remains of the western Roman Empire. The Byzantine Empire controlled Italy through the city of Ravenna, a few miles below Venice on the Adriatic coast. That city still contains some of the best

preserved examples of art and architecture from those early years of Christian Byzantine rule.

The earliest Christians during the years of persecution had generally worshiped in private houses. When congregations became larger after Constantine, Christians adopted for their churches an all-purpose Roman building type called the **basilica.** The basilica filled their needs because it is fundamentally a large covered hall. Its big interior space provided room for the entire Christian congregation that came together every Sunday to hear scripture, listen to sermons, and participate as a group in the liturgy.

Sant' Apollinare in Classe (FIG. 16-22), in Ravenna, Italy, illustrates a typical early Christian basilica. The long space within the building is covered by wooden roofs and subdivided by two **arcades.** In the arcades the arches rest on top of the columns—a combination that was rare in Roman architecture. The repetition of columns and arches creates something like a covered street leading to the altar. Sant' Apollinare already possesses some of the essential features of church planning that are later present at Chartres Cathedral (FIG. 15-1). It has a nave, aisles, and an apse that terminates the nave. The clerestory windows above the nave arcades throw light into the center of the church. The simple plan of Sant' Apollinare became the standard design for a Christian church in the West.

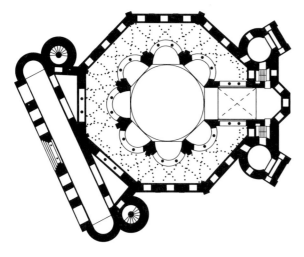

Plan of San Vitale, Ravenna, Italy

San Vitale (Fig. 16-23), a smaller, more intriguing building also in Ravenna, resembles the more complicated kind of church built at Constantinople under the Byzantine emperor Justinian. Unlike the rectangular basilican shape of Sant' Apollinare, San Vitale's is octagonal. The tall central space has clerestory windows and is covered by a dome. Dome-covered churches became more popular in eastern Christianity, whereas the basilican type dominated in the West. An ambulatory, a circular aisle that allows the circulation of people around most of the church, surrounds the central space. The upper part of the outer octagon is known as a **gallery**—an area over the ambulatory reserved for less distinguished participants in the liturgy. A tall and deep **chancel,** or altar area, breaks the ring of the ambulatory and gallery around the central core. Apses between most of the **piers,** or wedge-shaped upright supports, billow out from the central octagon into the ambulatory and gallery, nicely meshing and interlocking the inner and outer spaces of the interior of the church.

The interwoven spaces of the interior of San Vitale take a bit of time for the visitor to figure out. The shape of the interior is also made unclear because the surfaces are covered with **mosaics** (pictures made from small colored pieces of glass or stone) and veneers (thin slices) of colored marble. The color and the reflections from these surfaces take away any impression of solid structure in the building. Even the capitals of the columns are carved with a lacelike pattern of circles and floral motifs, undercutting the solid appearance of the stone. The carving of the capitals, the mosaics, and the colored veneers dematerialize and mystify the interior and help make it a sacred space.

The chancel walls of San Vitale hold some of the most famous mosaics in the world: *Justinian and Attendants* (FIG. 16-24) and *Theodora and Attendants* (FIG. 16-25). The two mosaics show Emperor Justinian and his wife Theodora, who probably never came to Ravenna, surrounded by their court as though they are making the offerings of bread and wine for the liturgy. They both wear halos as an indication of the spiritual importance of the Byzantine emperor, who considered himself the direct representative of the divine on earth. In fact, almost everybody and everything in the mosaics is spiritualized by the style of representation. There is very little indication of space around or behind the emperor. The gold background, rich and reflective, naturally symbolizes the measureless heavens. Everybody's feet are spread flat out, giving the impression that the figures are levitating. Dark lines represent the folds in their garments, but the garments do not seem to wrap around solid bodies. The symmetrical facial features of classical art have turned into a stereotyped stare that seems to look beyond the viewer into the next world. Throughout the mosaics representation of the realities of this world has given way to representation of a spiritualized existence. The style of the mosaics reflects the change in values brought on by Christianity.

FIG 16-24 [Byzantine], *Justinian and Attendants,* mosaic from the north wall of the chancel of San Vitale. C. 547. Ravenna, Italy. Scala/Art Resource, New York.

FIG 16-25 [Byzantine], *Theodora and Attendants,* mosaic from the south wall of the chancel of San Vitale. C. 547. Ravenna, Italy. Scala/Art Resource, New York.

FIG 16-26 [Chinese, Northern Wei Dynasty], *Standing Buddha,* 477. Gilt bronze, height: 55 1/4, width × 19 1/2 in. (140.2 × 48.9 cm). The Metropolitan Museum of Art, New York. John Stewart Kennedy Fund, 1926 (26.123)

Buddhist Art

Although Buddha (c. 563–c. 483 B.C.) lived five hundred years before the birth of Christ, the first images of Buddha in art appeared in the Christian era. Born in Nepal on the northern border of India, Buddha guided his followers on an ethical path that led them to peace of mind, to wisdom, and to enlightenment. Buddha taught that the only way to escape the troubles of the world was through detachment, meditation, and good works. In this way one could break the cycle of death and rebirth to achieve perfect peace and happiness, or *nirvana.* Buddhism spread rapidly through India and from there to China and Japan and to all of southeast Asia, subsuming, as it went, many local religious traditions.

For centuries Buddha was not shown in human form, but was symbolized by things like his footprints or the tree under which he achieved enlightenment. The nearly life-size gilt bronze *Standing Buddha,* from China (FIG. 16-26), illustrates Maitreya, the Buddha of the Future, or the Buddha yet to come. He stands front and square on a lotus covered platform, spreads out his arms, and raises one hand as if to speak or perhaps to bless. His gesture unfurls his robe like the wings of a beatific angel. His eyes lowered, Buddha smiles serenely, mysteriously, charmingly. His monk's robe clings to him like wet cloth and reveals the smooth modeling of the body underneath. The double pleated folds of his robe fall in loops down his torso and descend in V-shaped folds between his legs and end in swirls at the hem. Because of these curving and concentric lines, his golden body appears to radiate his glory.

The most typical Buddhist monument in India is the **stupa,** a large hemispherical solid mass that may have originally contained relics of the Buddha. A stupa also symbolizes the World Mountain. The Great Stupa (FIG. 16-27) at Sanchi, India, has four gateways—facing north, east, south, and west—that penetrate a high railing. The pilgrim entering the gate would follow counterclockwise the Path of Life by walking the route marked by the railing around the stupa. The bricks that cover the mound of rubble and earth underneath the stupa were once coated with white stucco and gilded. The three umbrellas at the top of the stupa symbolize Buddha, Buddha's Law, and Order—the three aspects of Buddhism. The stupa is a structure to be experienced from the outside, rather than an architecutural construction that encloses interior space.

FIG 16-27 [Buddhist], The Great Stupa. Completed first century. Sanchi, India. © AAAUM.

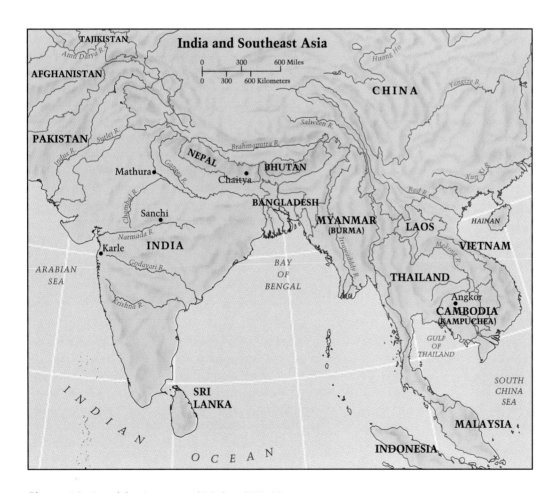

Chapter 16: Art of the Ancient and Medieval Worlds

437

FIG 16-28 [French Romanesque], St. Sernin, exterior. C. 1080–1120. Toulouse, France. Photo: © ND–Viollet.

FIG 16-29 [French Romanesque], St. Sernin, view of central nave. C. 1080–1120. Toulouse, France. Scala/Art Resource, New York.

Romanesque Art

In western Europe, Christianity survived the fall of the Roman Empire and the decline of civilization that followed. In fact, for centuries after the fall of Rome the Christian church in the West took charge of many essential aspects of social life such as education, social welfare for the poor and sick, and the establishment of law and order. As Christian missionaries and monks spread the faith among the barbarians, they brought new territories in Europe under cultivation. In the Middle Ages, the church created a new society of the invading peoples and the remains of Rome—a society in which Christian spiritualism pervaded every aspect of European life. Medieval life centered around the church and the estates of the feudal lords. When people traveled across Europe, they often did so for religious reasons in pilgrimages or in crusades to the Holy Land. Gradually, commerce returned and cities slowly came back to life while the reinvigorated arts flourished in towns, at court, and in monasteries.

During the Middle Ages, the pilgrimage was a popular form of devotion. Chaucer's *Canterbury Tales* are told by pilgrims on their way to the shrine of St. Thomas à Becket in Canterbury, England. Even more pilgrims traveled to the Holy Land, when they could, to the shrines of Peter and Paul and other early martyrs in Rome, and to Santiago de Compostela in northwestern Spain, where the apostle Saint James was buried. Monasteries in France and Spain along the routes to Santiago de Compostela built hostels for the pilgrims about every twenty miles, and at strategic sites large churches rose up to accommodate the flow of travelers. During the eleventh century, the first century of the new millennium, several of these pilgrimage churches developed a similar style of architecture and sculpture that we now call Romanesque because of its similarity to aspects of Roman architecture. No doubt the solid walls and sturdy round arches of Roman buildings were on the mind of the medieval builders of these churches, who nevertheless developed a distinct style.

Dedicated to St. Sernin, the Romanesque pilgrimage church at Toulouse in southern France (FIGS. 16-28 and 16-29) lies on the road to Santiago de Compostela in Spain. On the ground, St. Sernin follows the traditional plan for a Christian basilica. It has a nave with two aisles on either side of it, and, about halfway down the church, a transept with its own aisles crosses the nave at right angles. Beyond the transept lies the choir, where the monks sang their prayer, and an ambulatory that runs around the choir. The ambulatory allowed pilgrims to walk around the choir and visit the altars and the miracle-working relics in the chapels off the transept and in the chapels around the east end of the church.

The Romanesque architecture of St. Sernin affords ample and grand spaces intelligently organized for the use of many people. All parts, both in the plan and in the physical masses of the building, tend to be block-like in shape, and the eye can easily separate the parts one from another. The thick walls also give a sense of security. In fact, the monastery of St. Sernin used to be fortified. Thick round arches cross the nave, and between the arches, the nave is covered by a stone barrel vault. The stone vaulting fireproofed the church, and, like tiles in a shower stall, made ordinary voices sound wonderful. The vaults amplified the sound and created a long reverberation time perfectly suited for the wavelike melodies of the monks' Gregorian chant.

A barrel vault needs almost continuous buttressing along its sides to support it. Therefore, the unknown architect of St. Sernin was unwilling to break open the nave vault or walls for clerestory windows to illuminate the nave. Instead, a gallery was built over the aisle so that arches in the vaulting of the gallery could buttress the nave vaults. Only the clerestory windows in the east end and the light filtering through the gallery from the windows in the outside wall light up the somber nave.

Romanesque churches were also embellished with sculpture—not freestanding statues but carving virtually incorporated into the architecture. Romanesque sculpture appeared in the capitals of the columns of the nave, and large-scale sculpture surrounded the doors of more than a few Romanesque buildings. It was as if medieval sculpture grew out of the architectural decoration.

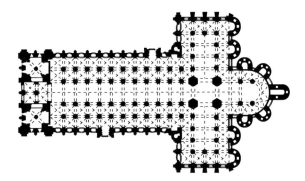

Plan of St. Sernin, Toulouse, France

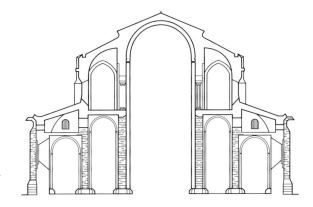

Section of St. Sernin, Toulouse, France

FIG 16-30 [French Romanesque], *The Ascension of Christ and the Mission of the Apostles,* from the narthex portal of La Madeleine. 1120–1132. Vézelay, France. Scala/Art Resource, New York.

The style of the biblical figures at Vézelay corresponds to their spiritual reality. The laws of nature do not apply to their representation. The pencil-thin human figures in the tympanum dangle like marionettes on strings, and the zigzag figure of Christ seems to jolt them with spiritual energy. Their highly charged clothing swirls about them, and the many folds of their garments make elaborate patterns of lines that abstract them further from reality. The Vézelay relief vividly expresses the religious enthusiasm that fired the medieval crusaders.

Islamic Art

Militant European crusaders traveled to the Near East because the Holy Land was in the possession of Islamic rulers. Although their dream of rescuing the Holy Land was short-lived, European contact with the more-advanced Islamic civilization to the south and east of Europe stimulated the growth of medieval civilization in many ways.

Islam is the religion preached by the prophet Muhammad from Mecca, his birthplace in Saudi Arabia. Within a hundred years of Muhammad's death in 632, his Islamic followers conquered most of the Near East, North Africa, and Spain. Areas of the Islamic world soon developed into wealthy and thriving monarchies while western Europe was struggling to recover from the collapse of the Roman Empire.

The most distinctive kind of Islamic architecture is the **mosque** (from the Arabic word *masjid,* which means "a place of kneeling"). Like a Christian church it is a place for worship, prayer, scripture reading, and preaching. A fine example of an early mosque survives in the Spanish city of Córdoba, once the center of Islamic civilization in Spain (see FIG. 16-31). The high walls of the Great Mosque of Córdoba enclose on the north a rectangular courtyard. Built into the wall at the entrance is a **minaret,** a tower from which the muezzin (Muslim crier) chants a call to prayer five times a day.

Enlarged several times over the course of two hundred years, the covered sanctuary of the Great Mosque at Córdoba contains along the south wall a **mihrab,** a niche that points to Mecca. Worshipers must face Mecca during prayer. The original wooden roof of the sanctuary was sustained by eighteen arcades formed

The Romanesque sculpture *The Ascension of Christ and the Mission of the Apostles* (FIG. 16-30 and 4-10) comes from the church of La Madeleine at Vézelay in France. At this church, crusaders were urged at various times to conquer the Holy Land to make it safe for Christian pilgrims. Over the inner door, a carved semicircle of stone, called a **tympanum,** reflects the spirit of the Crusades. In the center of the tympanum, Christ ascends into the heavens after his Resurrection and commands the apostles beneath him to go forth and preach the gospel to all nations. The iconographic message clearly spoke to any would-be crusader. In the horizontal lintel below Christ and the apostles, the sculptor depicted the fabulous people who in the Middle Ages were believed to be living in far-off places. Some have pig snouts, others have elephant ears.

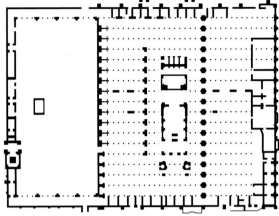

Plan of the Great Mosque at Córdoba, Spain

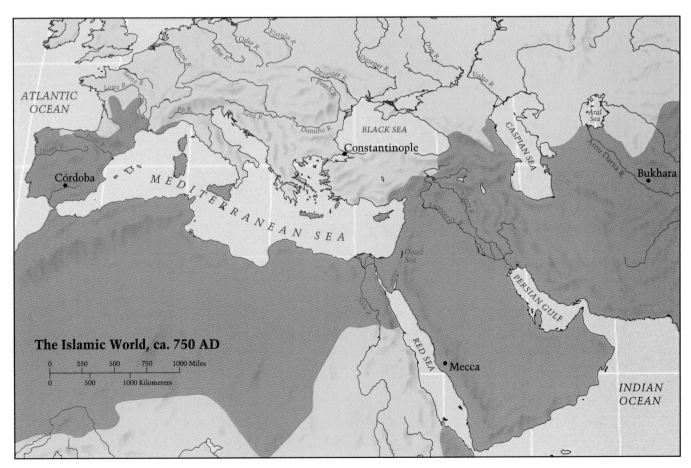

ATLANTIC
OCEAN

BLACK SEA

Constantinople

CASPIAN SEA

Aral Sea

Bukhara

Córdoba

M E D I T E R R A N E A N   S E A

Dead Sea

PERSIAN GULF

The Islamic World, ca. 750 AD

| 0 | 250 | 500 | 750 | 1000 Miles |

| 0 | 500 | 1000 Kilometers |

RED SEA

Mecca

INDIAN OCEAN

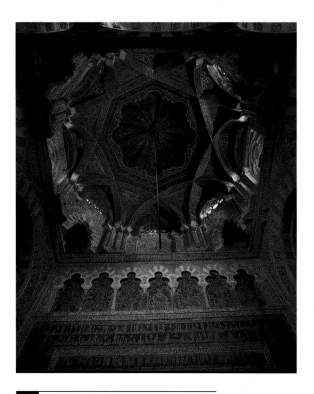

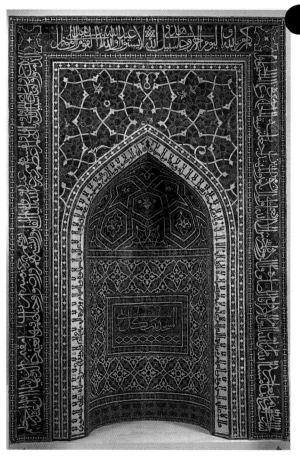

FIG 16-32   [Islamic], Great Mosque, dome
over the bay in front of the mihrab.
786–988. Córdoba, Spain. Werner
Forman/Art Resource, New York.

FIG 16-33   [Islamic], Mihrab. 14th
century. C. 1354. Composite body, glazed,
sawed to shape and assembled in mosaic,
11 ft., 3 in. (342.9 cm) high. Metropolitan
Museum of Art, New York. Harris Brisbane
Dick Fund, 1939. (39.20)

with a remarkable series of arches. To raise the height
of the roof of the sanctuary, pillars were constructed on
top of the small columns to support semicircular arches
under the roof. To stabilize these lofty arches, horseshoe-
shaped arches were inserted below to brace the pillars.
All the arches, decorated in stripes of alternating brick
and stone, seem to billow up from the slender columns
and keep the extensive interior light and airy in
appearance.

    In front of the mihrab of the Great Mosque lies a
square bay covered with a remarkable dome (FIG.
16-32). The scalloped dome in the center of the ceiling seems to rest on an octagon created by intersecting
ribs springing from the side walls of the clerestory.
Each semicircular rib, rising from a slender column,
skips the nearby vertical support and crosses over to
the next set of columns. The result is a star shape
interwoven with the octagon of the clerestory. Rather
than leading to a new way of building, the sophisticated structure of the dome at Córdoba remained a dazzling architectural fantasy.

    The dome is covered with gold mosaic, lavishly
decorated with plant motifs. Since the Koran forbids

the representation of human beings and animals,
Islamic religious art never developed a tradition of
painting and sculpture that illustrated the characters
and stories of its scripture, as did Christianity in the
West and Buddhism in the East. Instead, Islamic
craftspeople often made the beautiful calligraphy of
the Arabic text of the Koran itself part of the decoration of sacred architecture, as they did in the mihrab
from Iran that is now in the Metropolitan Museum of
Art in New York (FIG.16-33). Composed of red, white,
and for the most part blue glazed ceramic tiles, this
pointed niche, has a border of ornate calligraphy. The
unequaled decoration in the borders and other areas
filled with interwoven plant and floral motifs almost
conceals the architectural structure of the mihrab.

FIG 16-34 [French Gothic], Notre Dame Cathedral, exterior. Begun 1163. Paris. © Chad Ehlers, Tony Stone.

Gothic Art

At the end of the twelfth century in western Europe, a new medieval style arose called Gothic. The name was given by architects of the classical Renaissance who despised Gothic architecture and thought it had been invented by the Goths, one of the barbarian tribes that had ravaged the Roman Empire. People living in the thirteenth century simply called the new style modern. The Gothic style manifests itself best in the great cathedrals that rose heavenward in the cities of France and throughout most of Europe between 1150 and 1500 (see map on p. 432).

The revitalized cities of Europe now possessed increased wealth to afford the cathedral's construction and had sufficient numbers of skilled craftspeople, organized into guilds, to carry them out. The vertical thrust of these buildings clearly expresses the religious aspirations of the age when almost all of western Europe was Christian. The carefully articulated and balanced elements of the Gothic cathedral, which symbolized the heavenly city, seem to sum up the medieval Christian concept of the universe just like the medieval philosophical system of Scholasticism, which was attempting to establish a compendium of all knowledge.

The Cathedral of Chartres (FIG. 15-1) was one of the first and one of the most famous cathedrals in the Gothic style. The equally famous Cathedral of Notre Dame in Paris (FIGS. 16-34 and 16-35) also has high, soaring, pointed arches supporting thin, tentlike cross vaults in the ceiling. Notre Dame still retains an old-

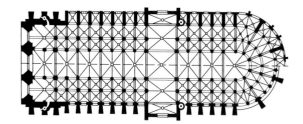

Plan of Notre Dame, Paris

fashioned gallery above the inner aisle, like the Romanesque church of St. Sernin, but the introduction of flying buttresses allowed Notre Dame's clerestory windows to expand above the gallery between walls that now seem light and thin compared with the heavy walls of the Romanesque style.

The architects at Notre Dame quickly took advantage of the new lightweight Gothic vaulting technique and abandoned the heavy Romanesque style and its emphasis on mass. All ribs in the vaulting now reach approximately the same height because their arches are pointed. The pointed arches and the thin, light rib vaulting of the Gothic style allowed the architects of Notre Dame to open up the walls of the building as much as possible to stained glass windows, because the walls no longer supported the vaults. The system of ribs and massive external buttressing does most of the work of supporting the vaults.

On the exterior of the church, the architecture displays all the muscles and bones of the structure. Heavy masonry **buttresses**—masses of stone set perpendicular to the walls—stabilize internal forces. Arcing over the roof of the aisles, **flying buttresses** between the upper walls and the external buttresses counter the thrust of the clerestory vaults.

On the interior, the Gothic architect created a vision of the biblical heavenly Jerusalem out of the spider's web of thin supports and tentlike stones and the brilliant jewellike color of the glass that once filled the windows.

Medieval sculptors surrounded the front doors of Notre Dame and Chartres with statues that began to work free of the architecture. In the elaborate porches at the ends of the transept at Chartres, a later generation of sculptors set the figures entirely free from the architectural supports around the doors. Compared with the ecstatic figure of Christ over the door at Vézelay (FIG. 16-30), the so-called *Beau Dieu* (*Handsome God*) at Chartres (FIG. 16-36) has swollen to more normal proportions. In fact he possesses somewhat classical features. This figure of Christ, attached to the central doorpost (or *trumeau* in French) of the south porch at Chartres, holds his gospel message in one hand and blesses those entering the church with the other. His calm and serene expression is accentuated by the severe and austerely beautiful vertical lines of the drapery folds that fall down the figure. His seren-

FIG 16-36 [French Gothic], *Beau Dieu,* from the porch of the south transept, trumeau of the central portal, Chartres Cathedral. C. 1220–1240. Chartres, France. Giraudon/Art Resource, New York.

FIG 16-37 {English], *The Annunciation,* manuscript illumination from a Psalter. C. 1250. Walters Art Gallery, Baltimore.

ity resembles to some extent that of the Chinese *Standing Buddha* (FIG. 16-26).

While craftspeople designed the large, colorful stained glass windows for the Gothic cathedrals of Europe (see *The Noah Windows,* FIG. 14-1), other artists painted on a small scale illustrations and decorations in sacred books. Throughout the Middle Ages this practice, called **illumination,** had been carried out by monks in monasteries, but by the thirteenth century ordinary laypeople started to paint miniature pictures in prayer books that were increasingly paid for by the wealthy for their own use. The English miniature *The Annunciation* (FIG. 16-37) in the Walters Art Gallery in Baltimore, comes from a Psalter, a prayer

book that contains the Book of Psalms from the Bible. The decorative background is actually polished gold leaf applied to the vellum.

While the angel Gabriel greets Mary with the words "Hail Mary full of grace" (written in Latin on the scroll that flies from the angel's hand), Mary raises her right hand in astonishment. The elongated figures both sway gracefully, and the artist attempted to depict the natural flow of their robes. The subjects stand under a triple arch into which the angel's wings neatly fit, but incongruously Gabriel stands in front of the border. The flat decorative areas, the inconsistent space, and the elegantly insubstantial figures emphasize the spiritual significance of the event.

Text continues on page 448

The Architect in the Middle Ages

*A*LTHOUGH the names of the architects who first designed Chartres Cathedral and the Cathedral of Paris have been lost, we know the names of thousands of architects who designed many of the castles and cathedrals of the Middle Ages.

Like any modern architect, architects in the Middle Ages were responsible for planning the spaces, ensuring adequate foundations, determining the height and width of columns and walls, designing vaulting and windows, and overseeing the construction. Unlike a university-trained modern architect, architects in the Middle Ages had actual building experience cutting stones and laying them in walls or arches. They received both practical and theoretical training.

More than likely a medieval architect had a father or at least a cousin who was an architect, since professions tended to be passed down in families through generations. Very likely a member of the gentry, a young architect-to-be might receive instruction in reading and writing Latin and his native tongue. At the age of thirteen he was apprenticed to a master craftsman for up to seven years in order to learn the trade. Apprenticeship was a contractual obligation and the apprentice sometimes paid the master for the privilege of working for him. Through hard labor, the apprentice learned the basic manual skills of the

The Architect in the MIddle Ages, as pictured in a manuscript illumination. The British Library, London.

building trade—how to cut and dress stone, how to mix cement, how to join stones together. Eventually, the apprentice would also learn the secrets of the building profession—how to build straight or perpendicular walls or how to plan a series of spaces according to correct proportions. These trade secrets were guarded by medieval builders with the same jealousy that modern industrial firms have to protect the technology of production.

At the end of his apprenticeship, the future architect became a journeyman because he could now receive a day's wage for his work (*jour* in French means

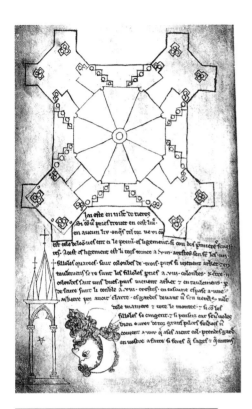

Villard de Honnecourt [French, c. 1225–c. 1250], page from a notebook. C. 1240. Bibliothèque Nationale, Paris. Giraudon/Art Resource, New York.

"day"). He also might spend a year traveling across the country or even to foreign lands to see and learn all he could about architecture—in Germany this year was called the *Wanderjahr*, "travel year." Most medieval builders remained journeymen, moving from place to place, from job to job. But if an ambitious journeyman inherited wealth or married into wealth, he might set up his own shop as a master. In some countries, the architect had to successfully produce a specified "masterpiece" to become a recognized master.

A master who sought to design new buildings would of course consult with his clients, listen to their wishes, and assess their finances. The bishop who wanted a new cathedral probably gave him general directives such as, Make the new church bigger and better than the old church; Make it the finest in France, or Make it resplendent in the latest style. Other clergymen might remind the architect of the sacred symbolism of the church and the scriptural texts that were appropriate. The architect then set about drawing plans. Because of their temporary nature and because of trade secrecy, only a few architectural drawings from the late Middle Ages have survived, the most significant exception being the notebook of Villard de Honnecourt of about 1240. The architect also made templates for the stone carvers to use when cutting the profiles of blocks of stone that were to be stacked and formed into clusters of columns.

The design of each profile as well as the larger dimensions of every space, such as the height and width of the nave, were probably determined by geometry. In addition to the square, a favorite geometrical configuration of the Middle Ages was undoubtedly the triangle. The medieval architect knew enough Euclidian geometry to arrange proportions based on the ratio between the height and the side of an equilateral triangle, between the height and the hypotenuse of a right triangle, between the side and the diagonal of a square, or between the sides of the golden rectangle.

A medieval preacher once complained about architects who, carrying a measuring stick and wearing gloves, gave orders and did no physical labor themselves. The preacher also protested that these chief masters were paid two, three, or four times the wage of a journeyman. Architects, in addition, got free meals at the prestigious high table in the monastery dining hall. But in reality they had worked hard to acquire a firsthand acquaintance with the building trade. They also had specialized knowledge of the building techniques and principles of design that enabled them for several centuries to experiment boldly with ever more lofty, glass-filled Gothic cathedrals.

Construction of a Gothic Cathedral. Austrian National Library, Vienna.

FIG 16-38 [Khmer], view of the temple complex near Siĕmréab, including Vishnu temple of Angkor Wat. 1113–1150. Cambodia (Kampuchea). SEF/Art Resource, New York.

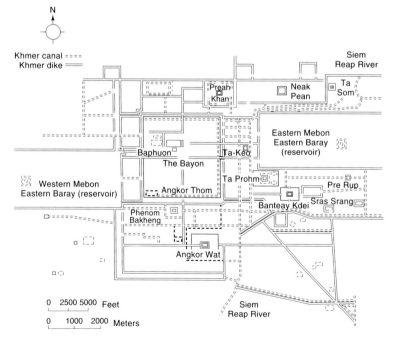

Overall Plan of Angkor Site, Cambodia, during the Twelfth and Thirteenth Centuries.

Hindu Art in Southeast Asia

Half a world away in Cambodia (Kampuchea), the Khmer people ruled a kingdom second only to that of China in East Asia (see map on p. 437). Their capital at Angkor (which means "city" or "capital") (FIG. 16-38), stretching fifteen miles east to west and five miles north to south, supported a population of a million people through an extensive system of reservoirs and canals. Each of the successful kings of Cambodia since the ninth century enlarged and improved the irrigation system that allowed three crops of rice a year on the fertile soil. Each king also had the duty to build at Angkor a temple to the Hindu gods, which would also be a monument to his own glory as god-king. Although the houses and palaces of Angkor were made of wood that has long since gone back to the soil, the seventy-two stone monuments that rise up from the flat floodplain with its network of canals still attest to the magnificence of Angkor.

Only a few years before the citizens of Paris and Chartres built their cathedrals, Cambodia's King Suryavarman II, who ruled until 1150, built the enormous temple of Angkor Wat. Of all the temples of Angkor, Angkor Wat is the largest, the most beautiful, and the best preserved. Dedicated to the Hindu god Vishnu, the enormous splendor of Angkor Wat repreents the Hindu view of the universe. (Hinduism, a major religion of India and southeast Asia, developed gradually over thousands of years.)

The five main towers are the peaks of Mount Meru, home of the gods and center of the universe, and the outer wall represents the mountains at the edge of the world. These walls, a half mile in circumference, contain corbel vaulted galleries where the myths of Vishnu, Krishna, and Rama are carved in low relief. Up stair ramps aligned with the cardinal directions, terraces rise to the five main towers, which are connected by a rectangular grid of galleries. The central tower reaches a height of 215 feet. Soon after the Kingdom of Siam sacked a declining Angkor in 1431, the city disappeared in the Cambodian jungle until its rediscovery in the late nineteenth century.

Just as the porches of French cathedrals are filled with sculpture, so is almost every square foot of the magnificent stone temple-mountain covered with reliefs depicting such scenes as the Hindu myth of creation, Churning of the Sea of Milk (FIG. 16-39). This 160-foot-long, very low relief in one of the galleries shows an incarnation of Vishnu when he gained the cooperation of the gods and demons to agitate the Sea of Milk with a serpent. By churning the Sea of Milk, Vishnu obtained the Dew of Immortality for the gods and other benefits for humankind. Vishnu appears in the center portion of the relief holding, with a pair of additional arms, his attributes—a club and a discus—while he directs the numerous figures holding the serpent churning the sea. Vishnu also manifested himself on earth in the form of a tortoise, depicted below his figure. The small figures flying through the air were born of the foam and symbolize the god-king's beneficence.

The Cambodian sculptors delighted in lively and active poses that make the figures look as though they are in the middle of a ritual dance. Their identical and repeated movements are not static but appear to interlock in a curvilinear rhythmic design. Walking along the gallery of Angkor Wat, visitors had to let the low relief unfold as they moved. Unfortunately, Angkor Wat was the scene of fighting in a war that devastated Cambodia in the 1970s. The temple and the relief need immediate help to preserve them.

FIG 16-39 [Khmer], Churning of the Sea of Milk, from Angkor Wat, near Siĕmréab, view of the temples. 1113–1150. Cambodia (Kampuchea). Robert Harding Picture Library.

Key Terms and Concepts

arcades	hieroglyphics	piers
basilica	ideographic writing	pyramid
buttresses	illumination	rotunda
chancel	mihrab	stupa
coffers	minaret	tympanum
cuneiform	mosaics	ziggurat
flying buttresses	mosque	
gallery	oculus	

17

EXPANDING HORIZONS OF WORLD ART: 1300 TO 1850

Early Renaissance Art

As the thirteenth and fourteenth centuries advanced, European cities, with their independent merchants and craftspeople, continued to prosper and grow. They eventually bypassed feudal manors and monasteries in importance. Town life flourished especially in Italy, where, by the fifteenth century, a number of thoughtful people came to believe that a new age had arrived. When the intellectuals of this new age discovered and studied ancient Latin and Greek manuscripts, they grew confident that their generation could emulate the achievements of Roman art and architecture. They were especially proud of their own accomplishments in literature and in the fine arts. Their artists were at the forefront of those who were rediscovering the world around them and finding the means to record their observations. They began to call this renewal of ancient thought and this return to a more correct ancient style the Renaissance, or rebirth (the Latin word *renasceri* means "to be born again").

In painting, the Italian Renaissance in many ways began as early as 1300 with the Florentine artist Giotto. Although Giotto still lived in the medieval world, his artistic accomplishments look forward to key aspects of the Renaissance style. Not in Florence, but in the city of Padua, inside a small building known as the Arena Chapel (FIG. 17-1), Giotto painted his best-known work.

The Arena Chapel has few windows and very plain walls, an architecture that seems to have been designed for murals. Its style contrasts with the French medieval practice of transforming as much of the wall space of a church as possible into light-filled stained glass. An Italian banker named Enrico Scrovegni paid for the Arena Chapel and its murals in order to atone for his father's sinfully attained money and to win his own eternal salvation. Pointing to the example of Scrovegni's commission and to that of many other wealthy individuals during the Renaissance, some Marxist historians have contended that the development of capitalism produced the Renaissance. By contrast, it is presumed that all classes of people—workers, clergy, kings, and queens—paid for the medieval Chartres Cathedral and its decoration.

Giotto covered the interior of the Arena Chapel in the fresco technique with a mural that narrates on its three levels the life and death of Christ. One of the scenes he painted is *Lamentation* (FIG. 17-2), depicting a moment of mourning in between Christ's death and burial. As discussed in chapter 4, Giotto used the lines of the composition to concentrate on the human drama—the embrace of mother and son—so that their example of emotion and suffering will motivate us to imitate Christ and Mary. Two of the mourners around the body of Christ have their back to us to contem-

plate Christ as we do. The mother, now searching his face for answers, holds her child once again as she did in his infancy. She is about to embrace him one last time, but Giotto sustains the drama by keeping them a suspenseful inch apart. The bystanders, for the most part, also restrain their grief and thereby make us feel the tragedy all the more.

Modeling them in light and dark, Giotto painted weighty, bulky figures that take up real space and sink like rocks to the bottom of the composition. Giotto was a pioneer in the use of chiaroscuro as well as in the depiction of human emotion and expression on figures. He was no expert in anatomy, but it is obvious that he wanted his figures to have the gravity and grandeur consistent with the deep emotions they feel. Giotto likely had in his imagination the statuelike figures of ancient Roman painting (see *The Punishment of Ixion*, FIG. 16-20) or actual Roman sculpture. In the Arena Chapel, he created nothing short of a revolution in art, when we compare his work with the weightless and ethereal figures in the mosaics at Ravenna (FIG. 16-23) and the relief at Vézelay (FIG. 16-30).

The importance of Giotto's discovering for painting the statuelike human figure can be seen in the work of Masaccio, an artist who lived one hundred years later. On the walls of a Florentine chapel belonging to the Brancacci family, Masaccio depicted in fresco *The Tribute Money* (FIG. 17-3). It seems that *The*

Tribute Money was initially commissioned to encourage all Florentines to pay a new tax that was imposed on them in 1425. In the painting, the artist told the gospel story of Peter and the tax man in an old-fashioned way—often called **continuous narrative**—by spreading three events from the narrative across a single landscape. The story begins with the main group in the center, where Christ instructs the apostle Peter to pay a tax after a tax collector has approached them for it. On the left St. Peter miraculously finds the money in the mouth of a fish, and on the right he reluctantly pays the tax.

The three incidents take place in a unified landscape. To render the buildings on the right in space, Masaccio utilized the new system of perspective projection that his friend, the architect Brunelleschi, had just invented. On the left the trees diminish in size as they go back in space, like telephone poles along a roadway. The treeless hills seem far way not only because they are small in size but also because they are enveloped in atmosphere; compare them with Giotto's conventionalized hill in *Lamentation*.

But Masaccio captured a three-dimensional feeling best by painting grand, simple, solid figures whose bulk fills up and creates space. Like Giotto's figures in his *Lamentation*, Masaccio's in *The Tribute Money* develop space by encircling the figure of Christ. One of them, the tax man, even has his back toward us and faces in, as do two of Giotto's figures. Masaccio had a better understanding of anatomy than Giotto and also a better understanding of how natural light falls consistently across rounded objects from a single source. The light source in Masaccio's fresco in fact lies on the right where a window in the chapel is located. The figures, therefore, cast shadows on the ground toward the left. In sum, Masaccio expanded upon Giotto's lesson that human figures attain dignity and grandeur when treated as painted sculpture.

EXPANDING HORIZONS OF WORLD ART

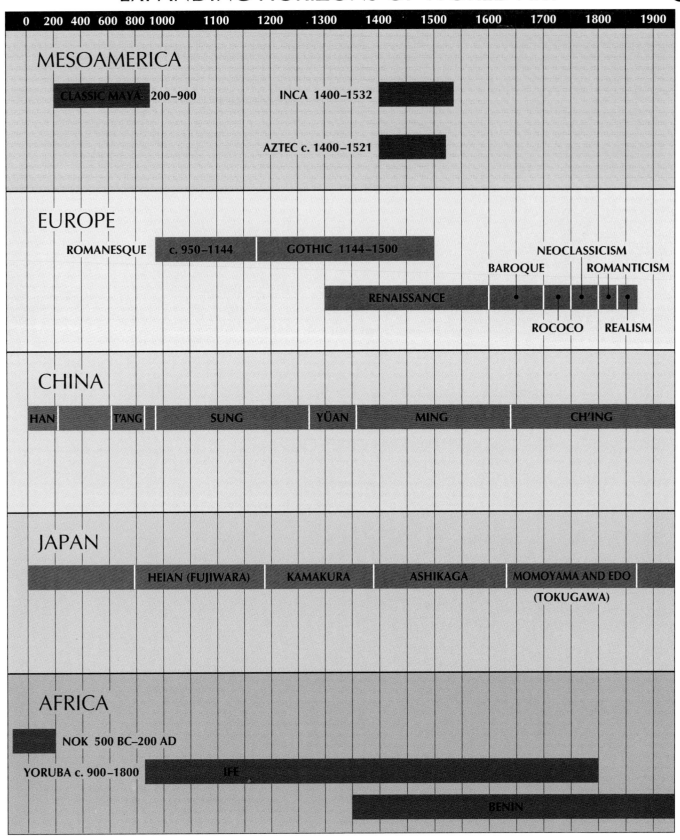

| 0 | 200 | 400 | 600 | 800 | 1000 | 1100 | 1200 | 1300 | 1400 | 1500 | 1600 | 1700 | 1800 | 1900 |

MESOAMERICA

CLASSIC MAYA 200–900

INCA 1400–1532

AZTEC c. 1400–1521

EUROPE

ROMANESQUE c. 950–1144

GOTHIC 1144–1500

RENAISSANCE

BAROQUE

NEOCLASSICISM

ROMANTICISM

ROCOCO

REALISM

CHINA

HAN   T'ANG   SUNG   YÜAN   MING   CH'ING

JAPAN

HEIAN (FUJIWARA)   KAMAKURA   ASHIKAGA   MOMOYAMA AND EDO (TOKUGAWA)

AFRICA

NOK 500 BC–200 AD

YORUBA c. 900–1800   IFE

BENIN

Eastern Landscape Art

Despite Masaccio's considerable achievement in rendering space and atmosphere in *The Tribute Money* (FIG. 17-3), his landscape remains a background subordinate to the main interest in the biblical narrative. It will be several more generations before European artists begin to concentrate on nature itself as their primary focus—as some Roman painters seem to have already done in ancient times. But by this time, the fifteenth century, artists in China have behind them a centuries-old tradition of landscape painting. And Asian artists will concentrate on landscape painting for centuries to come.

The classic Chinese landscape *A Solitary Temple Amid Clearing Peaks* (see also FIG. 2-30) was painted by the artist Li Ch'êng—one of the many great names of Chinese landscape painting, which flourished during the early Sung dynasty in the tenth century. The Chinese always looked back on that period as an exemplary high point of their landscape painting tradition. In Chinese Taoism and Ch 'an Buddhism, human beings are considered to be a part of nature. Through the contemplation of landscape, viewers try to put themselves in tune with nature and seek there consolation for the return to life.

Although Chinese landscape artists studied nature carefully, observing the changing seasons and the alteration of light from morning to evening, they also tried to distill in what they depicted the essence of trees, rocks, hills, or clouds. As in Li Ch'êng's landscape, the viewer was offered a journey to wander through the land and contemplate fresh scenes of nature at every turn. Because the restrictions of a single point of view would hinder such a journey, the Chinese artist deliberately avoided perspective and shadows that fell from a single source of light—two of the high points of Masaccio's historic achievement in painting. Sensitive to subtle changes of light in atmosphere, the Chinese developed, like Masaccio, aerial perspective.

We understand Masaccio's conquest of perspective and light in nature as part of a Renaissance scientific victory over nature, even though the subject of *The Tribute Money* is biblical. The Chinese, however, saw nature as spirit. They felt that the artist who could use painting to reveal the truth that lay beneath the sur-

Attributed to LI CH'ÊNG [Chinese, 919–967], *A Solitary Temple Amid Clearing Peaks* (Ch'ing-luan hsiaossu). Northern Sung dynasty (960–1127). Hanging scroll, ink and color on silk, 44 × 22 in. (111.8 × 56 cm). Kansas City, Missouri. Nelson-Atkins Museum of Art, Purchase of Nelson Trust.

face appearances of nature must be very much in tune with the divine spirit of the universe. In her or his art the painter would pass on that spiritual experience to the viewer. The Chinese also believed that the landscape artist could find moral law and order in nature just as it exists in the heavens and in humankind.

The Chinese in addition developed a tradition of scholars and poets who painted landscapes. These people avoided associating with professional artists, and they avoided the style of those who worked for the court. Their aim was no longer to evoke in the viewer the same feeling experienced by wandering in an actual landscape, but to express their own mood and personality at the time of painting. Their brushwork especially reveals their personal character.

Of the Four Great Masters of the Yüan dynasty, who founded a new school of "literary" painting in the early fourteenth century, Ni Tsan was the most famous. A poet in paint, he always considered himself

an amateur, rather than a professional painter. His landscape *The Jung-hsi Studio* (FIG. 17-4), with its collectors' stamps and commentary written right on the picture's surface, is a good example of his style.

Ni Tsan depicted only a few bare trees growing out of the rocks in the foreground and several hills on the other side of the water. He built a tension between them by their ambiguous spatial relationship to each other. His austere landscapes are always devoid of the human figure. For the most part he outlined rocks and mountains with long, thin, very dry brush strokes that appear gray on the paper. In contrast, Ni Tsan also set down dashes of paint for the sparse leaves in the trees. He kept a good part of the paper empty as though he were saving precious ink, as a Chinese commentator once observed. The distinct style of Ni Tsan's landscapes suggests very delicate and very personal emotions.

Northern Renaissance Art

At approximately the same time that Masaccio in Italy was painting *The Tribute Money* (FIG. 17-3), a very talented artist named Jan van Eyck, living in Flanders in the north of Europe, was developing a different approach to the depiction of reality. Van Eyck based his approach on precise observation of nature rather than on general rules like perspective and the imitation of Roman sculpture. His personal style of exacting realism is revealed in his portrait of Giovanni Arnolfini and Giovanna Cenani, frequently called *The Arnolfini Wedding* (FIG. 17-5). The couple are standing in their bedroom and seem to be exchanging marriage vows. In a real sense van Eyck's portrait was meant to certify their wedding. The artist, a witness to their vows, signed his name apparently on the back wall of the room, and he also indicated his presence by including his own reflection in the mirror.

Marriages at that time did not have to take place in a church, and the prominent bed in the painting of course refers to the necessary consummation of the marriage. Although it is unlikely that Cenani was already pregnant at the time of her marriage, her large belly, a fashion of the day exaggerated by the folds of her dress, certainly was meant to forecast a fruitful union. A number of other, seemingly everyday items in the room are in fact symbols of the religious dimensions of marriage, one of the Seven Sacraments of the church. The dog at the couple's feet represents fidelity. The figure of St. Margaret, the patron saint of childbirth, is carved into the bedpost. The convex mirror resembles the all-seeing eye of God. The single candle burning in the chandelier symbolizes the presence of Christ, the light of the world. The couple have removed their shoes as Moses did when he witnessed God's presence in the burning bush. Even as van Eyck respected the material reality of ordinary things in his meticulous depiction of them, he saw these objects themselves as the handiwork of God, full of spiritual meaning.

Van Eyck had not yet learned about the Italian discovery of perspective, and he did not understand anatomy as well as his Italian contemporaries. But he surpassed them easily when it came to rendering the surface appearance of things in great detail—an achievement made possible with the discovery of oil painting. His works are totally different from the broadly painted frescoes of Giotto and Masaccio owing to the different techniques required for painting panels. Part of van Eyck's success in rendering reality came not just from using tiny paintbrushes but from observing how light reflects from different textures like fur or wood or brass. He found in the new medium of oil paint the means to record these reflections on every different surface. Throughout *The Arnolfini Wedding*, light suffuses into the room and casts soft shadows just as it would in an actual interior space.

FIG 17-5 JAN VAN EYCK [Flemish, before 1395–1441], *The Arnolfini Wedding*. 1434. Oil and tempera on wood, 32 1/4 × 23 1/2 in. (81.9 × 59.7 cm). National Gallery, London. Bridgeman/Art Resource, New York.

Italian Renaissance Architecture and Sculpture

In architecture, the Renaissance in Italy began in the early fifteenth century with Filippo Brunelleschi, the architect who taught Masaccio the new science of perspective. The people of Florence boasted that their adopted son Brunelleschi was the first architect to turn away from the barbarism of the Gothic style and to introduce the good principles of the ancients. He amazed them with his technology and engineering skills when he erected over the cathedral of Florence a

FIG 17-6 FILIPPO BRUNELLESCHI [Italian, 1377–1446], Florence Cathedral, view of the dome. 1420–1436. Photo by George Tatge. Alinari/Art Resource, New York.

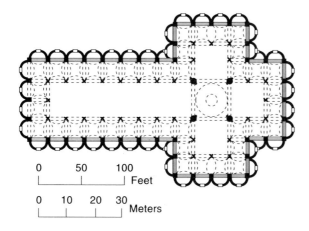

Plan of Santo Spirito

dome nearly as wide as that of the Pantheon's in Rome (FIG. 17-6). Although he gave the dome a Gothic, pointed profile, Brunelleschi placed it on the walls of the cathedral, and solved the structural problems of this configuration by building the dome out of two lightweight inner and outer shells. After his success, double-shelled domes became standard for most large-sized buildings.

When Brunelleschi examined the architecture of ancient Rome to find models for his new architecture, he included structures, like Sant' Apollinare (FIG. 16-22), built by the early Christians during the last years of the Roman Empire. To him, these buildings had the advantage of being both Roman and Christian. Also, classical architecture meant more to Brunelleschi than a return to rounded arches and correctly used columns. He realized that ancient builders achieved perfection by arranging the architectural spaces according to a system of proportions. He must have felt that a Christian house of God, more than any other type of building, ought to repeat through numerical ratios the same principles that harmonize the universe and reflect the perfection of the Divine Architect.

When Brunelleschi designed the church of Santo Spirito in Florence in 1436 (FIG. 17-7), he made the crossing—the bay where the transept "crosses" the nave—a square with, of course, a "perfect" ratio of 1:1. This crossing bay became the **module** out of which the rest of the church was shaped. For example, the choir and each arm of the transept repeat the module of the crossing. Brunelleschi made the nave exactly two times as high as it is wide and four times the module in length. Each bay of the aisle is half the length or one-quarter the area of the module, and apses that project from each bay of the aisles are one-half the length of an aisle bay. Brunelleschi intended to run the aisle around the entire church—around the transept and choir and even across the front. If the church had been built as he conceived it, it would have had a kind of symmetry. A spectator standing in the center of the crossing and looking in all four directions would have gotten the same perspective view in each direction. However, Brunelleschi died before the church was completed, and this part of his plan was not carried out.

One outstanding sculptor of the early years of the Renaissance in Florence went by the name of Donatello. The exact circumstances surrounding Donatello's casting the bronze statue *David* (FIG. 17-8)

FIG 17-7   FILIPPO BRUNELLESCHI [Italian, 1377–1446], Santo Spirito, interior. Begun 1436. Florence. Scala/Art Resource, New York.

remain a mystery, although in general the small city of Florence sometimes considered itself a David against enemies that were the size of Goliath. Donatello made David nude in imitation of classical sculpture, yet his David wears boots and a broad-brimmed hat. Donatello also invented his own version of idealism. Unlike the more mature and chunky Greek figure in *Spearbearer* (FIG. 16-15), Donatello's David is a boy with soft flesh and an undefined physique. The pose is different too, most noticeably in the rather medieval thrust of the hips, the outward thrust of the elbow, and the turn of the head. Whereas Polyclitus seems to have been studying the mechanics of the body in the pose of the Spearbearer as well as the body's balance in motion, Donatello used the pose of David to express a psychological content. David looks down toward the head of Goliath at his feet and yet seems to be actually contemplating his own flesh and his newly discovered powers.

FIG 17-8   DONATELLO [Italian, 1386?–1466], *David*. C. 1428–1432. Bronze, 62 1/4 in. (158.1 cm) high. Museo Nazionale del Bargello, Florence. Erich Lessing/Art Resource, New York.

Chapter 17: Expanding Horizons of World Art: 1300 to 1850

Fig 17-9   Sandro Botticelli [Italian, 1445–1510], *The Birth of Venus*. C. 1482. Tempera on canvas, about 68 × 109 in. (172.7 × 276.9 cm). Uffizi Gallery, Florence. Erich Lessing/Art Resource, New York.

Late-Fifteenth-Century Painting: Botticelli

In the second half of the fifteenth century, Sandro Botticelli, one of the leading painters of Florence, embarked on a personal stylistic journey that in many ways ran counter to the mainstream. His *The Birth of Venus* (FIG. 17-9), painted for the Medici family, the wealthy and powerful rulers of Florence, illustrates the pagan myth of the birth of the goddess Venus from the sea. In Botticelli's work, her already full-grown figure is perched on the edge of a seashell and blown by zephyrs (winds from the west) to her island of Cyprus on the right, where a spirit or a nymph flies through the air to clothe her with a flowered red robe. The representation of pagan mythology and the nude figure shows not so much the secularization of art in the Renaissance as the sophistication of the aristocratic society for which it was painted. By the end of the fifteenth century the Medici and their courtiers were giving elaborate and often arcane interpretations to pagan mythology—interpretations based on Christian allegory and a revival of Platonic philosophy. In general, according to their interpretation, Venus in Botticelli's painting represents not the Greek goddess of love and passion but the inspiration of Divine Beauty into the mind of the artist and the viewer.

Botticelli derived the pose of his Venus from an ancient statue that was part of the Medici collection and represented the *Venus pudica*, or "modest Venus," who covers herself with her hands. Beyond that reference, he went out of his way to deny the ponderousness of classical sculpture by ignoring many of the achievements of Giotto and Masaccio in Florentine painting. Only lightly modeled by a light source from the right, his Venus stands off-balance, moving light as a feather in a breeze toward the right. Instead of her solid mass, Botticelli emphasized her willowy outline and the undulating curves of her hair—echoed in the contours of the cloak. Throughout the painting, curved lines play across the surface. Botticelli of course knew about perspective, but he made the sea virtually a flat background with a pattern of stylized V-shaped waves. The total effect of his sharp-focused style creates an unreal world and a beautiful dream.

Olmec, Mayan, and Aztec Art

The Spanish explorers have epitomized for many historians the adventurous spirit of the Renaissance. A decade after Botticelli painted *The Birth of Venus* (FIG. 17-9), Christopher Columbus reached America for the first time. The Spanish, who came in search of gold and the fabled countries of the East, found a rich culture that Europeans never knew existed. They discovered the flourishing cities of the Aztecs who had recently come to power in Mesoamerica, as well as the cities of the Inca in South America. Tragically, the Europeans, who could not comprehend what they discovered, did not appreciate the art of the people they so quickly conquered by means of their superior weapons and contagious diseases.

The Spanish conquerors were not aware that great civilizations had flourished in North and South America in the past. They did not see the abandoned massive sculpture of the Olmec (see Las Limas sculpture, FIG. 4-24) or the deserted cities and pyramids of the Maya, which largely remained covered with jungle growth until the twentieth century. In the third century, alongside the empire of Teotihuacán near Mexico City (FIG. 15-3), the Maya in Guatemala had also built extensive cities dominated by steep temple-pyramids and broad, open plazas. Erected many centuries later than the pyramids of Egypt and the ziggurats of Sumer, the Mayan pyramids manifest the same urge to build a mountain stairway to the sky and the gods. The Maya also developed writing in the form of hieroglyphics and a sophisticated arithmetic by means of which they kept a complex but very accurate calendar.

The Mayan city of Tikal once spread over an area of about seventy-five square miles. Causeways connected the ritual centers where massive stone temples, tombs, and pyramids rise above the city. The most impressive complex at Tikal is the Great Plaza, where the two largest pyramids face one another across an open court. At the top of one pyramid sits the Temple of the Giant Jaguar (FIG. 17-10), a structure that imitates in stone the shape of the Mayan thatched house. Inside, three corbel vaults run the length of the temple. For unknown reasons the Maya abandoned Tikal about 900.

FIG 17-10 [Mayan], Temple I (Temple of the Giant Jaguar and Great Plaza). C. 700. Tikal, El Péten, Guatemala. D. Donne Bryant/Art Resource, New York.

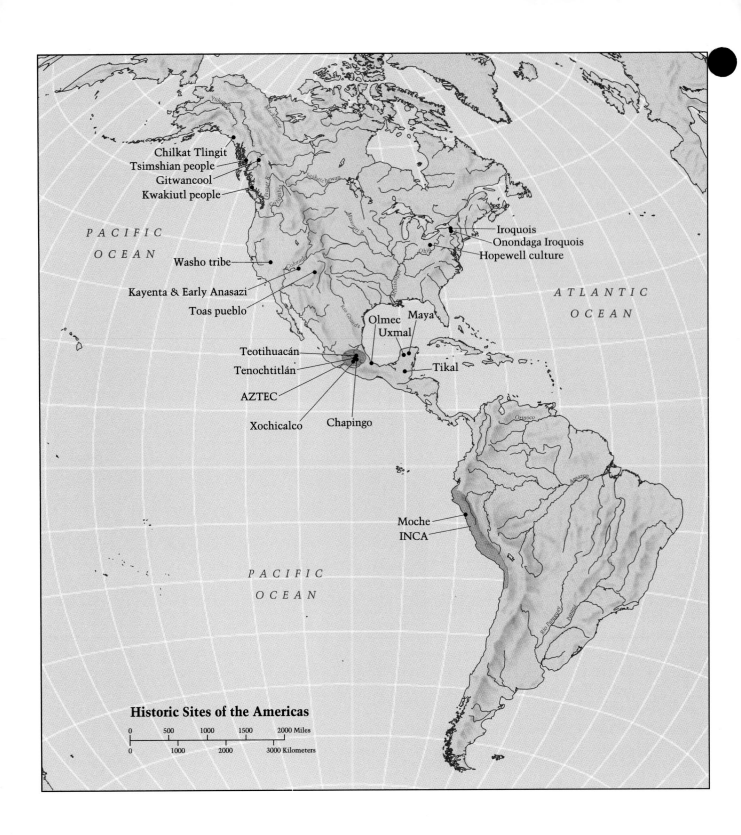

PACIFIC
OCEAN

Chilkat Tlingit
Tsimshian people
Gitwancool
Kwakiutl people

Washo tribe

Kayenta & Early Anasazi

Toas pueblo

Teotihuacán
Tenochtitlán

AZTEC

Xochicalco   Chapingo

Olmec   Maya
Uxmal

Tikal

Iroquois
Onondaga Iroquois
Hopewell culture

ATLANTIC
OCEAN

Moche
INCA

PACIFIC
OCEAN

Historic Sites of the Americas

| 0 | 500 | 1000 | 1500 | 2000 Miles |

| 0 | 1000 | 2000 | 3000 Kilometers |

FIG 17-11 [Aztec], *Coatlicue (Lady of the Skirt of Serpents)*. Fifteenth century. Andesite, about 101 in. (257 cm) high. Museo Nacional de Antropología, Mexico City. Werner Forman/Art Resource, New York.

In 1519, twenty-seven years after Columbus landed at San Salvador in the Bahamas, the Spanish conquistador Hernando Cortés entered the flourishing Aztec capital Tenochtitlán (pronounced Tehn-oak-teet-*lan*) (now Mexico City) in astonishment. Although Cortés and his men greatly admired the city with its canals, markets, and magnificent pyramids and temples, they were horrified by the blood that covered the walls and floors of the Aztec sanctuaries. Fierce and ruthless warriors, the Aztecs practiced human sacrifice to placate their gods and to keep their conquered victims in submission. In their ritual sacrifice, the victims probably had to face the awesome statute of *Coatlicue* (pronounced kwah-*tlee*-kwey) (*Lady of the Skirt of Serpents*), (FIG. 17-11). A massive freestanding statue over eight feet tall, every inch of it is designed to strike terror. In place of her head, two serpent heads, their fangs bared, face each other. She wears a necklace of severed hands and excised hearts. Her skirt is woven with snakes. Leaning forward, she stands on enormous clawed feet with which she tears human flesh. The details of the sculpture are carved in relief on the statute's enormous masses, which by themselves have an overpowering effect.

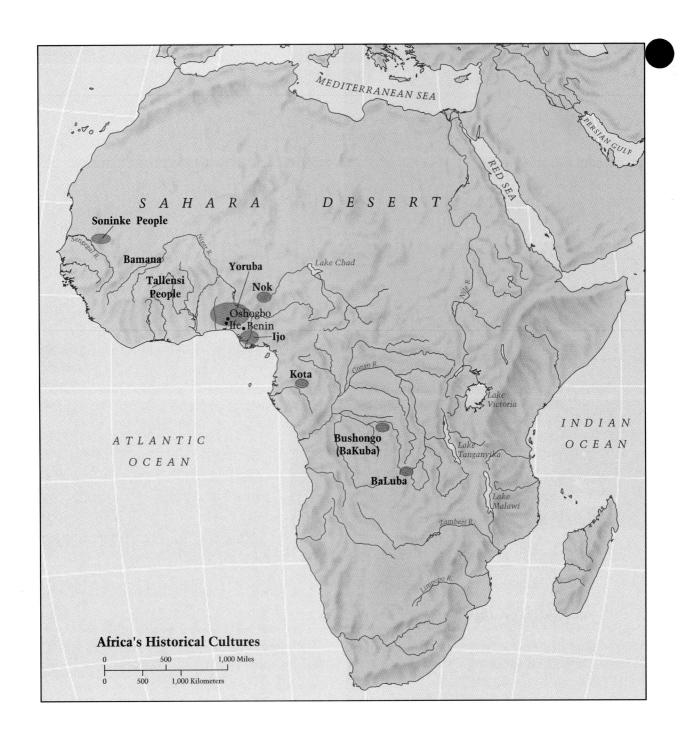

Africa's Historical Cultures

0   500   1,000 Miles

0   500   1,000 Kilometers

West African Art

Five years before Columbus reached America, Portuguese explorers discovered the kingdom of Benin flourishing on the coast of West Africa. When other Europeans later visited the capital city Benin (now located in Nigeria), they saw a wealth of exceptionally well crafted bronze sculpture produced for the court of the Oba, the god-king of Benin. The Beninese admitted that they had been taught the skills of bronze casting from Ife, another sacred city about one hundred miles to the northwest. It was only in the twentieth century that excavators unearthed in Ife itself about thirty bronze heads, like the one in figure 17-12, which are probably portraits of ancestors of the god-king of Ife, the Oni.

More recent African sculptors have generally avoided lifelikeness in art, but at Ife hundreds of years ago it was the rule. The full facial features of the bronze heads are consistently smooth and rounded to perfection. The small holes across the heads indicate that facial hair and probably a wig were once attached to the heads—a practice common in African art.

These striking and sensitive idealized masterpieces parallel the classical art of Europe both in antiquity and in the Renaissance. They were cast flawlessly by means of the lost wax process. Their perfected naturalism and cool demeanor remind us of the emotionally reserved classicism of classical Greek art, although the line of the mouth is a little lower on the face. However, the African artists could not have come in direct contact with European art or learned the sophisticated technology of bronze casting from European artists. Their discoveries seem to be indigenous.

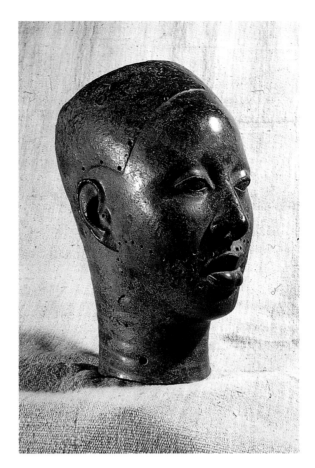

Fig 17-12 [Ife, Nigerian, African], *Seated Man of Tada,* head only. Late thirteenth to fourteenth century, Tada, Nupeland. Tsoede bronze, 11 1/2 in. (29.2 cm) high. National Museum, Lagos, Nigeria. Photo © Dirk Bakker.

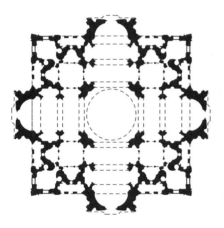

FIG 17-13   CHRISTOFORO FOPPA CARADOSSO [Italian, c. 1452–c. 1526], medal showing Bramante's design for St. Peter's. 1506. Giraudon/Art Resource, New York.

Bramante's Plan for St. Peter's

Italian High Renaissance Art

In the opening years of the sixteenth century, a number of artists, trained in the Florentine style, began to work for the Catholic Church in Rome. They came to Rome during the reign of Pope Julius II (1503–1513), who had great ambitions to make the papacy the dominant power in all Italy. This warrior pope nearly succeeded in doing it. His ambitions as a patron of the arts matched his political aspirations. For example, Julius commissioned Michelangelo to build for him a three-story tomb covered with some forty pieces of sculpture and then had the sculptor paint the Sistine ceiling. In a suite of rooms in the Vatican apartments, Julius had the artist Raphael paint large murals illustrating learned themes that appealed to Renaissance humanists like the pope.

For his most ambitious scheme, the pope tore down the venerable basilica of St. Peter, built by Emperor Constantine in the fourth century, and asked the architect Bramante to erect a new church of magnificent dimensions in its place (see FIG. 17-13). It was said that Bramante proposed to place a solid dome like that of the Pantheon (FIG. 16-17) on top of four intersecting barrel vaults on the scale of those of the Basilica of Constantine (FIG. 15-16). The new St. Peter's, with its complex interior configuration of circle, square, and cross shapes, was to have a perfectly symmetrical **central plan.** The plan was in reality an impossible scheme—the four piers in the center were not strong enough to hold the weight of such a solid dome. Before his death in 1514 Bramante built only the four piers of St. Peter's.

One reason for fixing on this period as the high point of the Renaissance is that at no other time during the Renaissance did so many artists of such talent plan and achieve works of such scale and merit. Some have speculated that the very instability and challenges of the Roman papacy under Julius brought out the best work of these great talents. The term *High Renaissance* also implies that during this period, the first two decades of the sixteenth century, the Renaissance style reached a point of perfection. It was as though all the previous experiments in anatomy, perspective, figure movement, and the imitation of antiquity came together to produce a balanced and harmonious style that resembles the high classical period of fifth-century Greece. Used in this sense, the term implies that the Renaissance style, like a human

FIG 17-14 LEONARDO DA VINCI [Italian, 1452–1519], *The Last Super*. 1495–1498. Santa Maria delle Grazie, Milan. Scala/Art Resource, New York.

being, had a birth, growth, maturity, and then decline. This analogy makes a certain kind of sense, but it also suggests that the ongoing development of a style follows a regular life-cycle—as though one could predict the results ahead of time. Even if such a biological analogy is apt, who can say that the period of maturity is always better—"higher"—than that of youth?

The Last Supper of Leonardo da Vinci (FIG. 17-14) is often considered the first work of the High Renaissance because in this late-fifteenth-century painting Leonardo achieved perfect harmony. He not only balanced the elements of his composition in rigid symmetry, he also intensified the emotional content. He packaged an intense drama within the strict organization of a design that includes a single-point perspective with its vanishing point at the head of Christ. Because of the pressure of the confined emotion, the drama, like compressed gunpowder, explodes with all the more force to the left and right of Christ's serenely stable figure.

In *The Last Supper* Leonardo illustrated the eucharistic meal as well as the moment after Christ says that one of his disciples will betray him. The figure of Christ, in the center of the composition, remains calm and resigned whereas all twelve apostles are agitated and visibly disturbed by the accusation. Each apostle exhibits a different emotional reaction to Christ's words. The apostles are nevertheless distributed symmetrically about Christ—six appear on one side and six appear on the other. In its balanced control of tension, the painting defines the High Renaissance style: the emotional storm is confined within strict symmetry whereas the figures move and emote with ease and naturalness and with the nobility and grace of classical sculpture.

FIG 17-15 LEONARDO DA VINCI [Italian, 1452–1519], *Mona Lisa*. C. 1503–1506. Oil on wood, about 30 × 21 in. (76.2 × 53.3 cm). Louvre, Paris. Scala/Art Resource, New York.

Ease and grace characterize another famous work by Leonardo, *Mona Lisa* (FIG. 17-15). *Mona Lisa* is a portrait of an actual woman, but Leonardo so perfected her portrayal, and her image has become so popular, that she seems more like a religious icon, a goddess, or a saint. She is seated in an armchair on a terrace that

Text continues on page 470

Chapter 17: Expanding Horizons of World Art: 1300 to 1850

Leonardo da Vinci (1452–1519)

ONSIDERED by many people to be a universal genius, Leonardo da Vinci was in many ways a typical Renaissance artist.

Like every artist of that period, Leonardo served an apprenticeship, starting in his early teens, probably to a sculptor and painter named Verrocchio. As an apprentice Leonardo learned all about the materials and techniques of painting and sculpture, for artists in the Renaissance had to grind their own colors, make their own brushes, and prepare their own panels.

The general public in the early Renaissance considered artists to be no different from any other craftspeople who worked with their hands, especially since they had their workshops alongside the shops of the shoemaker, the baker, and the candlestick maker. Most painters and sculptors had to belong to a local guild to practice their craft, just as certain craftspeople today might have to belong to a labor union in order to find work. In Renaissance Florence, painters belonged to the guild of the *medici e speciali*, "doctors and pharmacists," because they bought most of their materials for pigments from the local pharmacist.

The workshops of many Renaissance artists were capable of producing not only painting and sculpture but also painted shields, banners, and chests or, in Verrocchio's case, altars, tombs, tabernacles, pulpits, medals, and fountains. All the members of the shop, in one capacity or another, collaborated on executing the master's designs. Eventually, the master would let an apprentice fill in parts of the master's design or copy the master's work for resale to another patron. The apprentice might develop a dozen different skills, as Leonardo certainly did.

For some unknown reason Leonardo opted out of the workshop system in 1482 to become an artist at court. Perhaps he disliked the tedium of running a shop while constantly searching for commissions; perhaps he wanted more independence to pursue his own interests. The wide range of Leonardo's interests stands out in the letter that the almost-thirty-year-old artist wrote to Duke Ludovico Sforza asking for a job at his court in Milan. In his "resume" Leonardo emphasized at length his skill at inventing instruments of war such as prefabricated bridges, siege machines, explosives, mortars, armored boats, mining techniques, primitive tanks, catapults, guns, and other firearms. "In time of peace," he concluded, "I can give perfect satisfaction and to the equal of any other in architecture and the composition of buildings, public and private; and in guiding water from one place to another." Then Leonardo added at the end, almost as an afterthought, "I can carry

LEONARDO DA VINCI [Italian, 1452–1519], Self-Portrait. C. 1512. Chalk on paper, 13 x 8 1/4 in. (33 x 21 cm.). Reale Library, Turin, Italy.

out sculpture in marble, bronze or clay, and also I can do in painting whatever may be done as well as any other, be he whom he may."[1] Leonardo got the job.

As a court artist, Leonardo did most of the things he wrote about and more. During his seventeen years in Milan he designed military fortifications; he offered advice and submitted architectural proposals for the cathedral and castle of Milan; he organized special court pageants with elaborate costumes of his own design; he painted portraits

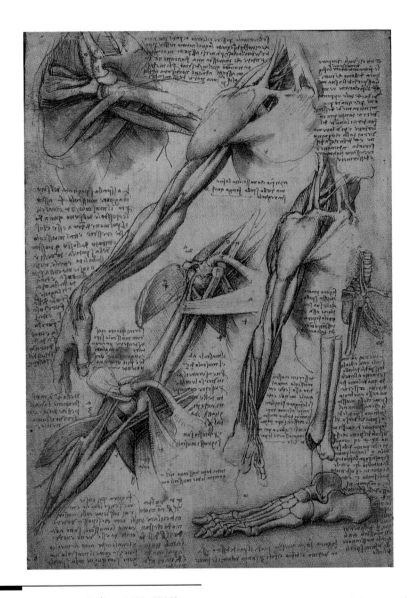

Leonardo went far beyond the ordinary painter's practical needs for representation and studied the mechanics of muscles, the flow of water, or the growth of plants for their own sake.

LEONARDO DA VINCI [Italian, 1452–1519], page from anatomy notebook. C. 1510. Royal Collection. Windsor Castle, London.

of members of the court and painted as well *The Last Supper* (FIG. 17-14); he set up an over-life-sized model in clay of an energetic horse and rider; and he began extensive research and study into anatomy, botany, geology, airborne flight, and hydraulics, much of which he recorded in hundreds of notebook pages. Because Leonardo's notebooks were not published until the nineteenth century, his inventions and discoveries had little effect on the history of science and technology. Leonardo did not wish to conceal his discoveries, but, as he was left-handed, he wrote backwards from right to left so that his handwriting has to be read in a mirror.

Like other Renaissance painters, his desire to capture the real world with his eye and reproduce it in art led him to scientific study of human anatomy and of nature. But Leonardo went far beyond the ordinary painter's practical needs for representation and pursued the mechanics of muscles, the flow of water, or the growth of plants for their own sake. He would have loved a modern computer graphics program capable of displaying change in a video animation! His scientific interests distracted him from ever completing many of his later paintings, and in the last years of his life he barely painted anything at all.

Some Renaissance artists, like Giotto or Donatello, were more famous than others, but they still maintained the same social status as other craftspeople of their time. Only at the beginning of the sixteenth century, with Michelangelo and Raphael and Leonardo, did people get the idea that an artist was a divinely inspired genius and a very special sort of person. Aloof and self-absorbed, Leonardo was no doubt the most mysterious of them all.

FIG 17-16 RAPHAEL [Italian, 1483–1520], *The School of Athens*. 1509–1511. Fresco. Stanza della Segnatura, Vatican Palace, Rome. Erich Lessing/Art Resource, New

overlooks a deep, mistfilled landscape, extremely rugged in contrast to the polite lady before it. Her left forearm, the one closest to us, rests on the arm of the chair. Her right hand relaxes on her left wrist. The gesture gently draws her shoulder around, and her head and its gaze follow the movement toward the front. Soft shadows round out her face and play around her mouth so that we can never be sure whether she is smiling or not. Leonardo painted her portrait in oil with transparent glazes that made the modeling so smooth and the contours so soft that his figure seems to emerge gradually from a twilight atmosphere.

The High Renaissance spirit of grace, ease, and harmony is also embodied in the work of the painter Raphael. His fresco *The School of Athens* (FIG. 17-16) is one of four large murals illustrating four branches of

learning—law, poetry, philosophy, and theology—in a room (or *stanza* in Italian) in the Renaissance papal apartments in the Vatican. *The School of Athens* illustrates philosophy through an imagined gathering of all the eminent thinkers of ancient Greece. Plato and Aristotle, framed by the arches in the center and set against the light of the sky, hold forth at the top of the steps as the most prominent of the school.

Raphael placed nearly sixty figures within a vaulted space that resembles the architecture that Bramante was contemplating at that time for St. Peter's. The figures are convincingly arranged throughout the space in two groups in the foreground and in two rows stretching into the distance above the steps. The figures contemplate, discuss, observe, and write in a variety of imaginative poses that often reveal the spirit of the individual's philosophy. The Greek philosopher Pythagoras, writing in a book, draws the attention of the group on the left. The philosopher Heraclitus, resting his elbow on a block in the center foreground, is lost in thought. He is said to be a portrait of Michelangelo. Euclid, on the right, who may have the features of Bramante, demonstrates a theorem to an avid group of students who pay him rapt attention. The balanced composition and the grace and ease with which the figures conduct themselves give *The School of Athens* the dignity and serious concentration of deep philosophical discourse.

In the High Renaissance, painting in the city of Venice developed a style that emphasized the application of color to build forms as opposed to the precisely outlined statuelike figures of the Renaissance in Florence and Rome. Despite that difference, the painter Titian, the leading master in Venice for nearly seventy years, was as inspired by the iconography and style of classical antiquity as were his central Italian contemporaries. Titian, who knew the work of Raphael through drawings, painted *Bacchus and Ariadne* (FIG. 17-17), and other mythological subjects, for the Alabaster Study of the duke of Ferrara, Alfonso d'Este. In the story derived from the Latin poets Ovid and Catullus, Bacchus, accompanied by his revelers, instantly falls in love with Ariadne, who had been abandoned by Theseus on the island of Naxos. Leaping from his cheetah-drawn chariot, Bacchus is caught suspended in midair before the startled Ariadne.

In addition to reflecting the influence of Raphael on his figures, Titian enjoyed contrasts of warm and cool colors for their own sake to enrich his painting. The vivid red scarf of Ariadne provides a strong warm accent against the predominantly cool blue and green on the left side. Titian observed the gleaming highlights of glossy materials and delighted in reproducing the value changes of colors as they disappear into the half-light of shadows. In *Bacchus and Ariadne* he employed some deeply saturated colors for their own sake. He also is known for veiling his colors in numerous colored glazes that attempt to unify different areas of color. Titian was perhaps the first Renaissance painter to exploit the sensuous appearance of richly applied paint and to exploit brushwork itself as a means of personal expression.

FIG 17-17 TITIAN (Tiziano Vecellio) [Italian, c. 1488–1576], *Bacchus and Ariadne*. 1523. Oil on canvas, 69 × 75 in. (175.2 × 190.5 cm). National Gallery, London. Erich Lessing/Art Resource, New York.

Michelangelo

In sixteenth-century Italy, Michelangelo was undoubtedly the greatest sculptor, and he is now probably the most famous sculptor who ever lived. In his hands the High Renaissance style went beyond a harmonious idealism and became a vehicle for psychological struggle. From the start, Michelangelo was recognized as a prodigy, a genius, someone who worked by different rules.

In his early twenties Michelangelo carved the famous *Pietà* (see page 183), the epitome of High Renaissance harmony and grace in sculpture. When he was twenty-eight years old, he carved the statue of

FIG 17-18 MICHELANGELO [Italian, 1475–1564], *David*. 1501–1504. Marble, about 161 in. (408.9 cm) high. Galleria dell'Accademia, Florence. Scala/Art Resource, New York.

David (FIG. 17-18) out of a giant block of marble that no one else could handle. Michelangelo had probably seen Donatello's much smaller bronze *David* (FIG. 17-8), created seventy years earlier. Unlike Donatello's David, Michelangelo's is thoroughly nude. Michelangelo reconceived the composition so that it might rival classical sculpture like Polyclitus's *Spearbearer*.

Michelangelo's David has yet to kill Goliath, and the gangling youth, almost a young man, is older than Donatello's. Michelangelo's David holds the sling over his left shoulder, and the fatal stone is in his right hand. As he looks sharply to the side, sizing up the enemy, his precisely defined muscles tense beneath the skin. As a result, his skin seems like an elastic covering stretched over his taut muscles and tendons. Every

inch of David conveys a feeling of pent-up energy ready to burst forth. Michelangelo gave classical nudity a psychological potency quite unlike the smooth and passionless idealization of Polyclitus's *Spearbearer*.

Michelangelo translated into paint the same sense of restrained force struggling within the human figure when he frescoed the ceiling of the pope's Sistine Chapel in the Vatican. Michelangelo covered the entire ceiling with illustrations of the biblical story of creation and of Noah's flood along with dozens of biblical and symbolic figures. In the section of the ceiling titled *Creation of Adam* (FIG. 17-19), it is not the nude figure of Adam that is alive with energy, but the flying figure of God the Father, who rushes in to inspire a soul into the human lump of clay that is Adam. The giant Adam's muscles are so flaccid he can barely raise his arm toward the outstretched hand of God. The contrast between the two figures, between passivity and action, can be read in the differing gestures of the hands, separated by a small gap between which sparks seem to fly from positive to negative energy. The dynamic shape of God and his companions sheltered under his billowing cloak visually overwhelms the reclining form of Adam. In this composition Michelangelo upset the nearly symmetrical balance that had become a key feature of the High Renaissance style. Confident of his own genius, he felt free to transform the Renaissance style of Leonardo and Raphael into the expression of his own personality.

Toward the end of his long life Michelangelo became more and more involved with architecture. It was Michelangelo who found a way to complete the Vatican church of St. Peter begun under Pope Julius II by the architect Bramante many years before (see FIG. 17-13). After years of delay and changed plans, Michelangelo, as soon as he took charge, returned to the design of Bramante, strengthening and simplifying it. To make the scheme work, Michelangelo greatly thickened the piers and the walls in most places. In contrast to Bramante's plan based on complex geometry, Michelangelo's church retains only the essential features of Bramante's symmetry: four barrel-vaulted arms of equal length radiate out in a cross shape from the central domed area, and a square ambulatory surrounds the four enormous piers supporting the dome.

Michelangelo did not live to see his own dome in place, and it was constructed with a pointed profile instead of in the hemispherical shape that he probably

Fig 17-19 Michelangelo [Italian, 1475–1564], *Creation of Adam.* 1508–12. Fresco. Vatican, Rome, Sistine Chapel ceiling. © Nippon Television Network Corporation, Tokyo, 1994.

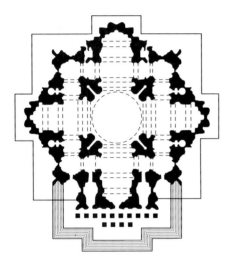

Michelangelo's Plan for St. Peter's

wanted (Fig. 17-20). Furthermore, in the next century, another architect added a nave to St. Peter's, which distorted the symmetry of Michelangelo's church and made his architecture virtually invisible from the front. But the rear of the church is still Michelangelo's.

Michelangelo the sculptor thought of architecture as the equivalent of a living human body. Therefore, in his hands St. Peter's expressed the same muscular tension as one of his nude figures. On the exterior of the building, Michelangelo placed pairs of giant pilasters against the walls, which he then pierced with an assortment of niches and windows. Along the exterior periphery of the cathedral, the wall curves and juts out at different angles as though it were kneaded out of clay. The vertical lines of the pilasters continue through the building and surge up through the ribs of the dome,

Fig 17-20 Michelangelo [Italian, 1475–1564], St. Peter's exterior, west end. 1546–1564. Vatican, Rome. Scala/Art Resource.

FIG 17-21 ALBRECHT DÜRER [German, 1471–1528], *Self-portrait.* 1500. Oil on panel, 25 5/8 × 18 7/8 in. (65.1 × 47.9 cm). Alte Pinakothek, Munich.

Dürer is praised as a printmaker who displayed a virtuoso's skill both in woodcutting (see *The Four Horsemen*, FIG. 9-4) and in engraving (see *Adam and Eve*, FIG. 9-11). Dürer displayed in the figures of Adam and Eve his knowledge of anatomy, of classical sculpture, and of proportions as the correct means of designing the human figure. His print also shows that he synthesized in his style these principles of Italian idealism with a wealth of significant detail that northern artists since Jan van Eyck had relished.

His extraordinary *Self-Portrait* (FIG. 17-21) reveals that he also cultivated Italian thinking about an artist as a divinely inspired genius. In his portrait his long hair and beard and the rigidly frontal and perfectly symmetrical pose make the artist look like Jesus Christ. By adopting the solemnity and formality of a portrait of Christ the Savior, Dürer was not being blasphemous but was indicating that, as a creator, the artist has a divine vocation and takes on almost divine powers. About the only thing to break the symmetry of his portrait is Dürer's rather tense looking hand, the instrument through which his inspired vision imparts new life in art.

Spanish Late Renaissance Art: El Greco

When Titian was a very mature artist, a young painter named Doménikos Theotokópoulos, from the Venetian island of Crete, worked for a short time in his studio in Venice. The young artist, who probably had some training in a very late Byzantine style at home, soon became known by his nickname El Greco ("The Greek") because of his ethnic origins. El Greco also studied the work of Michelangelo and his followers in Rome for several years. Sensing an opportunity for success at the court of the Spanish king Philip II, who favored Italianate artists, El Greco left for Spain in 1577. There he remained for thirty-seven years, not at court but in the city of Toledo, which for generations had been the spiritual center of Catholic Spain.

In Toledo the Italian-trained El Greco painted mostly religious art for the monasteries and churches in and around the city. With the color and brushwork of Venetian painters like Titian, with the expressionism of Michelangelo, and with his own colorful character and background, El Greco developed a unique

although Michelangelo's original plan for a hemispherical dome would have provided more contrast between horizontal and vertical lines than the building now possesses. With its unrestrained energy, St. Peter's creates new rules for Renaissance architecture.

Northern High Renaissance Art

During the period of the High Renaissance in Italy, a German artist named Albrecht Dürer set out to learn the lessons of classical art discovered by the Italian Renaissance. Convinced that he had a mission to bring an Italian style and Italian principles of art to northern Europe, he visited Italy twice and wrote his own treatises on measurements, proportions, and artistic theory. But it was the example of his own art, especially his prints, that carried Renaissance art to the north.

personal style, very evident in his painting *St. John the Baptist* (FIG. 2-15). Elongated far beyond normal proportions, the gaunt saint towers above the landscape. His contours and those of the clouds behind him writhe like tongues of flame, and light and dark flicker across the entire surface.

El Greco once painted his adopted city of Toledo with the same spiritual intensity (see FIG. 17-22). We view the city in the painting from across the steep river gorge that flanks Toledo where El Greco has rearranged some of the buildings to suit his composition. Lightning seems to flash in the sky, lining the edges of dark clouds with light and causing the city to glow with a ghostly phosphorescence. Land masses are clumped together into parabolic shapes that both roll along the surface and reach out beyond the painting into infinity. El Greco has given the city the character of a mystic—like the contemporary Spanish mystics Teresa of Avila and John of the Cross—a person on fire with divine illumination.

The Classic House, West and East

The architect Andrea Palladio expounded a more classical style of Italian Renaissance architecture than did Michelangelo at St. Peter's. Palladio employed the classical orders more correctly than Michelangelo, and he rejected Michelangelo's obvious self-expressionism in architecture. Just as important, Palladio returned to the rationalized system of mathematical proportions in laying out the dimensions of a building. Confident of the correctness of his principles, Palladio wrote a book about architecture, *I quattro libri dell' architettura (The Four Books of Architecture)*, illustrated extensively with his own work. Translated into different languages, the book gave his architecture international influence for generations.

His best known building, the Villa Rotonda (FIG. 17-23) in the suburbs of Vicenza, Italy, is perfectly symmetrical on all four sides. The central block is a cube, in a ratio of 1:1, within which sits a perfect circle and cylinder. Palladio arranged the rooms symmetrically according to another set of proportions. The Villa Rotonda may not be the most comfortable or convenient house to live in, but it is about as classically ideal as a piece of architecture can get. Its simple mass and serene harmony give it an authority that few other buildings possess.

FIG 17-22 EL GRECO (Doménikos Theotokópoulos) [Spanish, 1541–1614], *View of Toledo*. C. 1597. Oil on canvas, 47 3/4 × 42 3/4 in. (121.3 × 108.6 cm). Metropolitan Museum of Art, New York. Bequest of Mrs. H. O. Havemeyer, 1929. H. O. Havemeyer Collection (29.100.6).

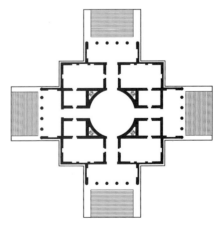

Plan of the Villa Rotonda

FIG 17-23 ANDREA PALLADIO [Italian, 1508–1580], Villa Rotonda. C. 1566–1570. Vicenza, Italy. Scala/Art Resource, New York.

The Villa Rotonda was a country house used by a wealthy gentleman for vacationing and entertaining. The four identical porches around the building provide pleasant views across the countryside and offer shelter from the sun at different times of day. Each porch looks like the front of an ancient Roman temple, and the combination of temple front and domed rotonda may remind us of Emperor Hadrian's temple, the Pantheon in Rome (FIG. 16-17). Palladio borrowed the dome motif also, from the tradition of Christian church architecture. He transferred elements of ancient and modern religious architecture to a private home because he believed (erroneously) that the Romans themselves first used these features on domestic architecture. Because of his mistaken idea, but captivating example, builders have been placing Roman temple porches on houses ever since.

The Japanese had a different idea of what a house should be. The Katsura Palace (figs. 17-24 and 17-25) outside Kyoto, Japan, has for centuries embodied their ideal of domestic architecture. The Katsura Palace was built for members of the imperial family as a country retreat, just as Palladio's smaller Villa Rotonda served as a place of relaxation in the country.

In both the East and the West, in the sixteenth and seventeenth centuries the main living area was nor-

FIG 17-24 [Japanese], Katsura Palace, exterior. C. 1615–1663. Kyoto, Japan. Shashinka Photo Library, New York.

nally on the second floor, not the ground level. Rooms in a house at that time were sparely furnished by our standards and could serve different functions. Neither the Japanese building nor the Italian building had plumbing or central heating—things that we now take for granted in our most modest homes.

The Katsura Palace is built of lacquered wooden posts using the post-and-lintel system, with merely paper screens set between the posts. In contrast, the Villa Rotonda has solid masonry walls that support vaults and the whole of the villa has an imposing blocklike appearance. In place of the symmetry of the Villa Rotonda, the three large halls and several dozen rooms of the Japanese palace are arranged in a more relaxed zigzag pattern. As in most Japanese buildings, the rooms are divided from one another by sliding screens, which when pushed aside or removed create a variety of new spaces and room arrangements. The palace has no central focus, no dramatic staircase and main entrance.

From the top of its four porches the Villa Rotonda commands the countryside around it. The Katsura Palace instead is integrated with nature. Winding paths leading to the house through extensive informal gardens provide glimpses of the structure. Many of the external walls of the palace slide open to reveal various views of the gardens. If the fluid spatial arrangement and sliding doors of the Katsura Palace seem more familiar to us than the formal grandeur of the Villa Rotonda, it is because these Japanese features were imitated by Frank Lloyd Wright and other Western architects in twentieth-century homes.

Fig 17-25 [Japanese], Katsura Palace, interior. C. 1615–1663. Kyoto, Japan. Shashinka Photo Library, New York.

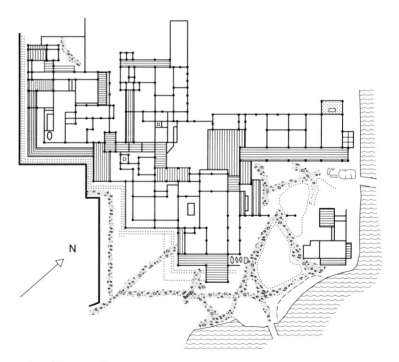

N

Plan of Katsura palace

FIG 17-26 CARAVAGGIO (Michelangelo Merisi) [Italian, 1573–1610], *The Calling of St. Matthew.* 1599–1600. Oil on canvas, 126 3/4 × 133 7/8 in. (322 × 340 cm). Contarelli Chapel, San Luigi dei Francesi, Rome. Scala/Art Resource, New York.

Baroque Painting

At the beginning of the seventeenth century, Italian artists invented a dynamic new style that years later became known as Baroque. *Baroque*, like the word *Gothic*, was originally intended to disparage this new style, which late-eighteenth-century critics considered bizarre and abnormal. But at its inception the new style suited the vigorous new age that was dawning. After generations of religious conflict in the sixteenth century, the boundaries between Catholics and Protestants in Europe became stable. Each group, assured of its religious beliefs, felt a sense of security in its political alliances. In this period great nation-states emerged, usually ruled by a monarch who claimed a God-given right to absolute authority. First Spain, then France, then England dominated European politics. It was an age of power and expansion, as the European nations sent their ships around the world to develop colonial empires. Discoveries in science and technology expanded humankind's horizon too. When Galileo built a telescope and revealed the true movement of the planets, the seventeenth century learned the meaning of immense space for the first time. The Baroque style savored these new vigorous attitudes and this new awareness of nature, and, in contrast to the Renaissance style before it, relished dynamic movement through space.

The Baroque painter Caravaggio, right at the turn of the century, started a revolution in painting by working directly from nature—even in his religious pictures. Caravaggio's *The Calling of St. Matthew* (FIG. 17-26) depicts Matthew as a disreputable tax collector surrounded by his accountants and sword-carrying henchmen at the moment when Jesus Christ called him to be his disciple. St. Matthew and his associates wear the striped clothing of contemporary liverymen and servants. Caravaggio reinforced his realism with an intense chiaroscuro that has been given the name Tenebrism. A strong light enters the scene from the upper right, causes a diagonal shadow across the wall, and illuminates only the body parts that face the light. This natural light, which might also be interpreted as the traditional symbol of divine grace, acts like a spotlight on a darkened stage. Using realism and dramatic light, Caravaggio reinvented the biblical event with a profound meditation on what it would have actually been like, had we been there. The truth to nature or naturalism that Caravaggio emphasized and his manipulation of light and dark for dramatic effects became key characteristics of the Baroque style.

Caravaggio's Tenebrist style became known at an early date in Spain, where a young artist from Seville, Diego Velázquez, experimented with a realist approach and strong contrasts of light and dark. In his later years in Spain, Velázquez also had ample opportunity to absorb the lessons of Titian, who was avidly collected there. At twenty-four years of age, Velázquez fulfilled his youthful ambitions as a painter when King Philip IV of Spain called him to Madrid to be the royal portrait painter.

Of all the portraits of the king and his court that Velázquez painted until the end of his life, none is more unusual than that of the royal family, now known by the title *Las Meninas*—Portuguese words for *Ladies-in-Waiting* (see FIG. 17-27). In *Las Meninas*, members of the court are portrayed in Velázquez's studio, where the artist himself stands poised, paintbrush at the ready, behind a very large canvas. They honor the painter by their presence. Velázquez, who was an educated gentleman, was surely aware that in antiquity Alexander the Great honored the famous painter Apelles by watching him at work in his studio.

The center of attention in *Las Meninas* is the five-year-old princess Margarita, to whom one lady-in-waiting is offering a cup of chocolate. It is impossible to tell whether Velázquez is supposed to be painting the princess's portrait on that large canvas or, more likely, the portrait of the king and queen, who are reflected in the mirror on the back wall. Just like Jan van Eyck in *The Arnolfini Wedding* (FIG. 17-5), the king and queen must be standing outside the painting in the viewer's space as they pose for Velázquez. Later, when the king looked at *Las Meninas* hanging in his study in the royal palace, he saw life at court re-created in his presence.

FIG 17-27 DIEGO VELÁZQUEZ [Spanish, 1599–1660], *Las Meninas*. 1656. Oil on canvas, about 125 × 108 in. (317.5 × 274.3 cm). Prado Museum, Madrid. Erich Lessing/Art Resource, New York.

In *Las Meninas* Valázquez demonstrated that he had mastered the perspective of the dim interior space where light and dark contrast help define his composition. He also displayed his thorough understanding of the style of Titian, now his favorite painter. The surface of *Las Meninas* has become fundamentally a texture of visible brush strokes of light and color. Rather than starting with a firm outline drawing that he then modeled with local color, Velázquez represented appearances by means of colored touches of light. Some touches are transparent, some are opaque. The seemingly haphazard dabs build solid forms in space with a kind of magic as one steps back from the painting. At the same time the soft and fuzzy edges of shapes

Text continues on page 482

Caravaggio (Michelangelo Merisi) (1573–1610)

*W*HEN MICHELANGELO MERISI—soon nicknamed Caravaggio—came from the small town of Caravaggio to Rome in 1593, the twenty-year-old artist had no connections, no patrons, and no work. He had to support himself painting cheap religious images or adding fruits and flowers to other artists' compositions.

Later in his life he remembered that one painter for whom he worked fed him only salad greens. Soon Caravaggio started painting, on his own, half-length images of provocative adolescents holding strikingly realistic fruits, flowers, or musical instruments.

A wealthy collector, a cardinal of the church, noticed these paintings, bought two of them, and furthermore let Caravaggio live and work in his town house. Without the sponsorship of this art-loving aristocrat, Caravaggio might never have succeeded as a painter. The patron introduced the artist to other collectors in the neighborhood and pulled strings to get Caravaggio a commission for religious paintings in the nearby church of San Luigi. Centuries ago, producing a successful religious painting—always on exhibition in a church—was about the only way artists could get their work before the public's eye.

Caravaggio's first public religious paintings, depicting the calling (FIG. 17-26), the martyrdom, and the inspiration of St. Matthew, were phenomenally successful. Everyone in the art world of Rome came to see them, and over the next several decades they were imitated by hundreds of artists. Whereas Caravaggio copied his figures from nature, the older generation of artists in Rome were still drawing and painting artificially posed and artificially proportioned human figures out of their imagination. Their models were frequently the extraordinary statutes and frescoes of Michelangelo, not living human beings. Caravaggio shocked his contemporaries by pointing out that the common people in the street were the models for the ordinary people who sometimes appear in his religious paintings. His religious characters were too real for some clerics, who complained that they were so coarse that they did not look like saints. These members of the clergy had several of his paintings removed from their churches. The rejected paintings were quickly purchased by eager collectors who recognized Caravaggio's genius.

Caravaggio's paintings also caused a stir because for his religious works, he painted with such strong contrasts between light and dark that outside the strongly lit parts was mostly darkness. A seventeenth-century critic compared his paintings to events taking place in a dark basement room illuminated by a single lamp up above. The stark contrast of light and dark combined with the realism of the painting makes the figure of his *Saint John the Baptist,* now in Kansas City, Missouri, almost spring from the canvas. Using an ordinary person as a model for his subject, Caravaggio depicted St. John, wrapped in a vibrant red cloak, as a brooding adolescent. A strong light strikes his left side, casting deep shadows under his brows and illuminating only the kneecap of his left leg.

Some critics complained that Caravaggio's skill was limited, that he could not paint more than a few figures at a time. For an artist of his era, Caravaggio's artistic skills were indeed narrow. Most of the great artists of his day made their reputation as fresco painters. Caravaggio either could not or would not do fresco because he developed a method of direct painting. As far as we know he never made preliminary drawings—or perhaps he never made drawings at all—but he began composing his images from the start right on the final canvas. Sometimes he would merely incise the outlines of the head and arms with a stick into the reddish brown underpainting, as he did in *St. John the Baptist.* Laboratory investigation of his work as well as direct observation demonstrate that he often changed his compositions while painting. This kind of direct painting has become standard procedure in modern times but was unheard of in

Whereas Caravaggio copied his figures from nature, the older generation of artists in Rome were still drawing and painting artificially posed and artificially proportioned human figures out of their imagination.

Caravaggio (Michelangelo Merisi) [Italian, 1573–1610], *St. John the Baptist.* C. 1605. Oil on canvas, 69 15/16 × 52 15/16 in. (172.5 × 134.5 cm). Nelson-Atkins Museum of Art, Kansas City, Missouri.

Caravaggio's day. Fresco painting did not suit his artistic talent because it demands methodical preparation and systematic execution.

Caravaggio painted the way he did probably because of his impetuous temperament. While he was going from success to success in Rome as a painter of religious subjects, he was appearing more and more frequently with the police and in court because of his fighting, slandering, and general contentiousness. Eventually he killed a man in a street brawl over a gambling debt on a tennis match. Caravaggio spent the last four years of his life as a fugitive, earning his way by rapidly painting even more startling, though less realistic canvases. Some of them are large, thinly painted, almost colorless images over which his brush, thick with paint, streaked only the highlights across the surface. Caravaggio's short life was truly tragic because the very impetuousness that drove him to succeed as a painter became the flaw in his character that led to his eventual undoing.

FIG 17-28 PETER PAUL RUBENS [Flemish, 1577–1640], *Venus and Adonis.* C. 1635. Oil on canvas, 78 × 96 in. (198.1 × 243.8 cm). Metropolitan Museum of Art, New York. Gift of Harry Payne Bingham, 1937.

give the impression of a palpable atmosphere surrounding the figures. Velázquez's manner of painting was especially admired by Manet and the Impressionists in the late nineteenth century.

Peter Paul Rubens, a Baroque artist trained in Antwerp in the north of Europe, observed Caravaggio's paintings firsthand during an extensive sojourn in Italy when he was a young artist. In fact, the incredibly fertile imagination of Rubens absorbed everything he could see in Italy, from classical sculpture to the works of the masters of the High Renaissance. On a trip to Spain he even copied El Greco.

In his depiction *Venus and Adonis* (FIG. 17-28) Rubens, like Valázquez, returned to the loose brushwork and vivid color of Titian, the High Renaissance master from Venice—in fact, it was Rubens who encouraged Velázquez to examine Titian. Rubens transformed Titian's colorful Renaissance style into something Baroque. He painted large, heroic figures, on the scale of Michelangelo's nudes. But they do not look like statues. Adonis and Venus are ruddy, full of life, and sensuous. The body of Venus and the arms of Adonis form a strong diagonal moving toward the rosy horizon, away from the darkness on the right.

Diagonal movements into space are another characteristic of the Baroque style.

Baroque Sculpture

When late-eighteenth-century critics first applied the word *baroque* to seventeenth-century art to condemn it as bizarre and irregular, they especially had in mind the sculptor Gianlorenzo Bernini. To them Bernini seemed to have made strange new works that broke the rules of art laid down by the Greeks and the Romans and by Renaissance artists like Raphael. Like Velázquez's painting, Bernini's sculpture energized not only the figures in the work but also the viewer's space.

Bernini's Shrine for the Chair of St. Peter (FIG. 17-29), in the apse of the church of St. Peter in Rome, mixes together architecture, sculpture, and painted glass instead of observing the traditional boundaries of each art form. The entire shrine overwhelms the viewer's space instead of resting comfortably in a niche or on a pedestal as might a Renaissance work.

By extolling the throne of St. Peter, the symbol of papal authority, Bernini glorified the renewed prestige and power of the papacy during the Catholic counterattack on the Protestant Reformation. Bernini put together a dynamic work, a mystical vision full of Baroque energy. The Holy Spirit, symbolized by the painted dove and by the light coming through the window, seemingly bursts through the rear wall of the church and miraculously sustains St. Peter's chair. Stucco clouds, swarms of angels, and gilded rays of light pour into and around the actual architecture of the church. SS. Anselm, Jerome, Augustine, and John Chrysostom sway ecstatically beneath the chair, which they help "support" with their fingertips. The robes they wear refuse to obey the laws of gravity and writhe about them in sympathy with their ecstasy. Light, color, rich materials, and rushing forms appeal to our senses and persuade us that a miracle is taking place before our eyes. Unlike Masaccio's *The Tribute Money* (FIG. 17-3), where the miracle occurs as a normal and natural event, Bernini's shrine shows a distant super-natural order exploding into our earthly space and dis-rupting the natural world—which by the seventeenth century has become much more secular and tangible.

Rembrandt and the Golden Age of Dutch Painting

If Bernini established a Roman Catholic Baroque vision of divine intervention on a grand scale, the great Dutch Baroque artist Rembrandt van Rijn set forth a distinctly Protestant image of a personal inner Christianity. During his lifetime Rembrandt made his fame and fortune as a portrait painter, until the public found his dark, penetrating insights into character unfashionable. But to the very end of his life Rembrandt was widely respected as a printmaker. In his prints and in his late paintings Rembrandt fre-quently explored biblical subject matter, even though Protestant churches in Holland, where he lived, would not allow religious art inside the church building. Like a good Protestant, Rembrandt believed that the mes-sage of the Bible came to each person individually when that person heard the word of God and experi-enced the presence of God within.

Rembrandt illustrated his beliefs in his large etch-ing of Christ preaching outdoors to a crowd of people (FIG. 17-30). Ever since a copy of the print sold for the high price of one hundred guilders, the etching has been called *The Hundred Guilder Print.* In this scene, Rembrandt combined several incidents that take place

FIG 17-29 GIANLORENZO BERNINI [Italian, 1598–1680], Shrine for the Chair of St. Peter. 1657–1666. Gilt bronze, marble, and stucco. St. Peter's, Rome. Scala/Art Resource, New York.

FIG 17-30 REMBRANDT VAN RIJN [Dutch, 1606–1669[, *The Hundred Guilder Print.* C. 1648. Etching. Cincinnati Art Museum. Art Resource, New York.

in the nineteenth chapter of the Gospel of St. Matthew. Reading from left to right, we see the Pharisees who cross-examine Jesus; the rich young man, head in hand, who ponders his vocation to follow Christ; the women who bring their little children to Jesus; and the apostle who attempts to restrain them. We see the poor, the sick, and the lame, and finally, in the gateway on the right, the camel that, in Christ's words, could pass through the eye of a needle easier than a rich man enter heaven.

Each person that Rembrandt depicted hears the words of Christ internally in his or her own way. No miraculous vision of celestial beings has to burst upon their life and overwhelm them, as in Bernini's conception of divine grace. And yet Rembrandt's use of light and dark leaves no doubt that something mysterious is going on. Rembrandt avoided the sharp contrasts of Caravaggio, although his print contains bright areas of light and sections of deep, velvety dark. Most of the print, however, is a subtle twilight zone where the softened shadows and hazy light build a feeling of mystery and of warm union between the devout faithful and Christ. The manipulation of chiaroscuro once again plays a key role in a Baroque style.

Although some artists, like Rembrandt, in Protestant Holland continued to illustrate religious iconography, the great majority turned to portraiture,

landscape, still life, and genre subjects—works that fit more appropriately in the ordinary homes of the burgeoning middle class of Holland. Dutch Baroque painters favored an iconography that viewers could actually see around them, and Dutch artists fostered a style that faithfully reproduced selected aspects of reality. Except for portraits, most Dutch paintings were not commissioned but were painted by the artist for the open market. Most Dutch painters specialized in a particular category so as to increase productivity and sales. The seventeenth-century Dutch art world was quite different from the rest of Europe at the time and foreshadowed some more recent developments in the production of art.

Of the many painters of genre subjects in Holland, Judith Leyster excelled in the depiction of a poetic mood. A pupil of Frans Hals in the city of Haarlem, Leyster produced the small painting *The Proposition* (FIG. 17-31), which shows a man offering a woman a handful of coins for her sexual favors. Tavern scenes and views of prostitution and brothel life were quite prevalent in Dutch Baroque art, but no other painting shows the woman ignoring an offer. Her feet resting comfortably on a foot warmer, the woman in Leyster's genre painting continues to sew by the light of an oil lamp. Unlike the main character in Emanuel de Witte's *Interior with a Woman Playing a Virginals* (FIG.

FIG 17-31   JUDITH LEYSTER [Dutch, c. 1610–1660], *The Proposition.* 1631. Oil on wood panel, 12 1/4 × 9 1/2 in. (31.1 × 24.1 cm). Mauritshuis, The Hague. Scala/Art Resource, New York.

2-22), she teaches a moral lesson in domestic virtue. The source of light located within the nighttime painting indicates that Leyster had seen the work of Dutch artists who had been to Italy and had copied the style of Caravaggio and Artemisia Gentileschi. Instead of the drama of the latter's painting *Judith* (FIG. 5-5), Leyster's work projects a mood of quiet introspection.

Baroque Architecture

The Italian Baroque architect Francesco Borromini towers above the other architects of his generation because he invented an exciting new style. His architecture broke all the classical rules of proportion beloved by the Renaissance, and, consequently, was one of the first to be labeled Baroque. In 1642 he fit a small chapel, dedicated to St. Ivo (FIG. 17-32), into one end of a courtyard of a college called the Sapienza (Wisdom). The dome of his chapel rises above the

FIG 17-32   FRANCESCO BORROMINI [Italian, 1599–1667], St. Ivo, exterior, view of cloister. Begun 1642. Rome. Alinari/Art Resource, New York.

curved courtyard wall and resembles nothing ever built before or since. The walls of the dome and the steps above them seem to ooze out from the pressure applied by the buttresses. The lantern above the dome is supported by protruding pairs of columns capped with an entablature that swings back between each pair. The lantern terminates in a spiral crowned with flames. Although the spiral can be explained as a symbol of wisdom, Borromini made it an integral part of an architecture that pushes and pulls and swirls with Baroque energy.

On the interior of St. Ivo (FIG. 17-33), instead of designing a building with perfectly proportioned squares and circles as in the Renaissance, Borromini

FIG 17-33 FRANCESCO BORROMINI [Italian, 1599–1667], St. Ivo, dome seen from below. Begun 1642. Rome. Foto Marburg/Art Resource, New York.

Plan of St. Ivo

used overlapping triangles to form a six-pointed star shape that becomes the basis of the floor plan of the chapel. He then rounded the six points of the star, first with a concave circle, then with a convex. As our eye runs along the walls of the interior, we see that one section of wall is straight and juts forward, the next section curves out. The next is again straight but at a different angle, the next curves away, the next is straight, and so on around the chapel. The dynamic energy of the walls can best be seen in the horizontal entablature running around the chapel. Underneath, the entablature is supported by giant pilasters. The charging vertical lines of these pilasters are continued, after only a slight horizontal interruption, right into the dome, which is not hemispherical in shape but irregular like the walls of the chapel beneath it. Magically, Borromini finally resolved the undulating shape of the chapel into a circle at the base of the lantern. The soaring vertical lines of the interior can legitimately remind us of Gothic architecture, which Borromini in fact admired. He also admired the architecture of Michelangelo. Indeed, the interior of St. Ivo resembles the energetic walls and vertical lines of the exterior of Michelangelo's St. Peter's, turned outside-in as it were.

Nothing like Borromini's flamboyant Baroque architecture ever took root in France. When France adopted the Baroque style in the seventeenth century, the country's innate sense of classical restraint modified the style. The French consider the late seventeenth century their golden age, a classical period when, under King Louis XIV, French political power and cultural life dominated Europe. Early in his reign, Louis XIV moved his royal residence and the government of France from Paris to his estate at Versailles, about eleven miles away. There he built an enormous palace (FIG. 17-34) to house himself and his court in a splendor that would declare to all the world the political power and elevated artistic taste of France.

The architecture of Versailles focuses on the king's own bedroom right in the center of the palace facing the rising sun in the east. Artistic imagery at court

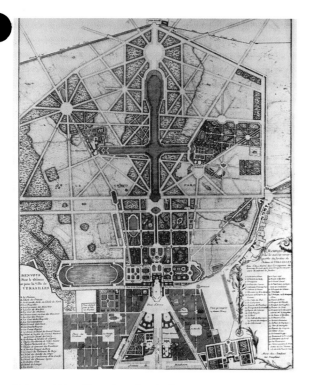

Palace of Versailles, plan of entire layout. Engraving from François Blondel. Foto Marburg/Art Resource, New York.

FIG 17-34 LOUIS LE VAU [French, 1612–1670] and JULES HARDOUIN-MANSART [French, 1646–1708], Palace of Versailles, garden and west facade, 1669–1685. Versailles, France. Giraudon/Art Resource, New York.

fashioned Louis as Apollo, the sun king. One of the greatest privileges at court was to attend Louis's rising in the morning as though it were a sacred ritual. On the opposite side of the palace, facing west, formal gardens spread out as far as the eye could see. Near the Palace of Versailles are flower beds arranged like embroidery patterns, reflecting pools, and sculpture-filled fountains. Away from the palace, avenues and canals extend in straight lines toward a distant focal point. In his design for the gardens the landscape architect André Lenôtre transformed nature into a rational plan that radiates from the center of the palace, the king's bedroom. Not even the grandeur of Versailles's architecture symbolizes the absolute authority of the king as well as its famous gardens.

FIG 17-35 NICOLAS PINEAU [French, 1684–1754], Varengeville Room, from the Hôtel de Varengeville, Paris, view of chimneypiece wall and adjacent mirrored wall to right. Original paneling commissioned from Nicolas Pineau by the Duchess de Villars. C. 1735. Carved, painted, and gilded oak; 18 ft. × 3 3/4 in. × 40 ft. 6 1/2 in. × 23 ft. 2 1/2 in. (5.6 × 12.4 × 7.1 cm). Metropolitan Museum of Art, New York. Purchase of Mr. and Mrs. Charles Wrightsman. Photo: Taylor and Dull.

Rococo Art

The Baroque style lasted well into the eighteenth century, during which time there appeared a flamboyant style of interior decoration that has a name all its own—Rococo. In the eighteenth century, the wealthy aristocracy in France avoided the formality of court life at Versailles and lived in town houses (hôtels) in Paris that grew ever more comfortable, convenient, and elegant. For a generation or two, roughly between 1720 and 1750, it was the rage among the well-to-do to decorate the rooms of their town houses with large mirrors in fancy frames, with sleek fireplace mantels, and with oak wall panels delicately carved with patterns formed by ribbons, scrolls, vines, and shells.

Since wooden paneling can easily be removed and saved, even when the building around it is destroyed, a number of Rococo interiors can now be found in museum collections in New York, Philadelphia, Cincinnati, and elsewhere. The oak panels that were carved from designs by French Rococo decorator Nicholas Pineau and that once delighted the Duchess of Villars at her town house in Paris (FIG. 17-35) can now be found in the Metropolitan Museum of Art in New York. Counterpoised C-shaped curves in all the decoration immediately identify the Rococo style. The gilded scrolls, ribbons, and moldings have the delicacy of embroidery and contribute to the light and gay appearance of the room. In the center of some of the carved panels, little still life compositions, forming "trophies," symbolize the four seasons and the arts. The Rococo style spread, as it were, from the walls and engulfed the design of chairs, tables, candlesticks, and other furniture in the room. This style betrays a clever and charming way of life dedicated to the pursuit of happiness.

A typical French Rococo interior leaves very little room for paintings on the walls. In fact, the paintings of playful cupids over the doors of the Duchess of Villars's room are housed in irregular frames that are actually part of the paneling. Painting in mid-eighteenth-century France had become in many cases a subordinate part of the interior decoration. The taste for small-scale works with an intimate iconography and a colorful style, suited to the pleasures and comforts of eighteenth-century living, was established early in the century by the artist Antoine Watteau. However, Watteau died very young just as the Rococo

Part IV: A History of World Art

FIG 17-36 ANTOINE WATTEAU [French, 1684–1721], *Pilgrimage on Cythera.* 1717–1719. Oil on canvas, about 51 × 76 in. (129.5 × 193 cm). Louvre, Paris. Giraudon/Art Resource, New York.

style of decoration was getting under way, and we now appreciate him as a more serious artist than his frivolous imitators.

Watteau's unusually large painting *Pilgrimage on Cythera* (FIG. 17-36), his most famous work, was submitted by him to the French Academy so that he might be accepted as a member. The Academy let him choose his own subject: a voyage by boat to the island of Cythera (Cyprus), where Venus was born. Young couples, who have come as pilgrims seeking favors to the island of the goddess of love, pay homage to her shrine at the right. Some of the couples, their prayers answered, now return happily; some are reluctant to go. Watteau clothed his small-scale characters in fancy-dress costumes adapted from the theater. To suggest also that the pilgrimage is a dreamy make-believe symbolizing the attraction between the sexes, he enveloped the scene and especially the distant shores in misty light reminiscent of the background of Leonardo's *Mona Lisa* (FIG. 17-15), which Watteau saw in Paris. Delightful and colorful, Watteau's fantasy about young love also strikes, in the imagination, deep chords about the human condition.

Neoclassical Art

In the second half of the eighteenth century Europe was captivated by the spirit of the Enlightenment. In this period, often called the Age of Reason, a number of bright and bold individuals dared to think for themselves, free from the restrictions of religion and traditional authority. In France and other countries cultural leaders like Voltaire used their clever wit to ridicule vice and superstition and at the same time to praise tolerance, democracy, industriousness, and sincere human feelings. Enlightened men and women felt confident that the human intellect by itself could solve all problems, even social and moral problems. Needless to say, a reaction set in against the irresponsible way of life of the aristocracy—a reaction that eventually led to political revolution in America, in France, and in other countries, under the banner of liberty and equality.

A similar moral revolution took place in the art world. Art was now supposed to move a person's deepest feelings and teach virtue—not cater to wasteful living. Artists and critics believed that it should once again serve the nation and be good for the people, just as it had for the ancient Greeks and Romans. Classical art had depicted serious subjects in a serious way, and so late-eighteenth-century artists and architects deliberately began imitating Roman and Greek art. Their work became known as Neoclassicism, a new imitation of classicism that was nevertheless conscious for the first time that Roman art was one style among many different styles in history.

The leading Neoclassical painter in France was Jacques Louis David (pronounced Dah-*veed*). His

Death of Socrates (FIG. 17-37) shows the famous Greek philosopher in prison surrounded by his followers. Socrates is about to drink poisonous hemlock because he was condemned to death, unjustly, for his beliefs. No one in France in 1787—two years before the outbreak of the French Revolution—was likely to miss the point that *Death of Socrates* was foremost a moral lesson in courage and sacrifice for the truth. David's painting encouraged those who saw it to stand by their convictions no matter what the consequences. By illustrating this subject, David obviously sided with many of the philosophers of the Enlightenment who also held that the human intellect, independent of the superstitions of the Christian church, could show the path to true morality and right living. A virtuous, thoughtful pagan like Socrates could set an example of martyrdom for truth and justice to rival that of any Christian saint.

David not only selected a serious subject from Greek history, he painted the story in an appropriately severe classical style. David created figures that resemble famous classical statues, and he arranged them across the surface of the canvas as in a classical relief. The architectural background is suitably stark. To bring out the dramatic presence of the characters, however, David resorted to Caravaggio's Tenebrism. He played a strong light on the precisely detailed figures and left the rest of the picture in darkness so as to sharpen the impact of the drama.

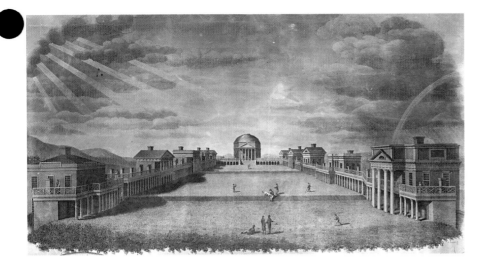

FIG 17-38 THOMAS JEFFERSON [American, 1743–1826], library and courtyard of the University of Virginia. Charlottesville, Virginia.

David invented his Neoclassical style with its serious moral iconography before the Revolution. He then became the leading painter of the French Revolution, reorganizing the art establishment in France, designing and directing new public festivals for the Revolution, and painting the portraits of its heroes.

Just as the Neoclassical painters criticized in their work the presumed frivolousness of Rococo art, architects of the Neoclassical period also condemned, in their search for a more serious architecture, the excesses and abnormality of the Baroque and Rococo styles. Since architects felt that classical architecture also taught lessons in virtue, they turned to the examples and principles of a classical style for their modern buildings. Everywhere in Europe and America architects wanted public buildings to be in a monumental classical style so that they would make manifest the courage and strength of the Roman republic, as though these virtues would rub off on the citizens of the new republics that used the buildings.

The American patriot and president Thomas Jefferson shared these feelings about architecture and expressed them in the design of a number of his buildings. He made the statehouse in Richmond, Virginia (FIG. 3-17), look like a Roman temple, and he designed his own house at Monticello (which is reproduced on the American nickel) after Palladio's Villa Rotonda and, ultimately, after the Pantheon in Rome.

Jefferson copied the Pantheon more closely when he designed the library as the centerpiece of the campus of the University of Virginia in Charlottesville (FIG. 17-38). Flanking the library on either side, two colonades connect a series of classroom pavilions, each in a different style of classical architecture so as to provide a lesson to the students. This new, close imitation of a classical style lets no one miss the point that the new republic in America shared the heroism and ideals of the past.

Romanticism

Whereas the Neoclassicists believed that human reason could discover the universal rules of morality and the arts, by the beginning of the nineteenth century a younger generation protested that their personal emotions and feelings were being slighted. Soon labeled Romantics, they were convinced that the heart was even more important than the head. As soon as they found ways to express their personal feelings in art, the Romantics encouraged artists to convey their deepest emotions in their work. Not only did Romantic works of art place subjective feeling ahead of reason; Romantic art itself was supposed to function like a serious religious belief that demanded a new way of life. Art was supposed to make a person whole because through it the inspired artist could join material reality with universal truth and thus integrate body and soul. Furthermore, art, because it was a spiritual activity,

Fig 17-39 Théodore Géricault [French, 1791–1824], *Raft of the Medusa.* 1818–1819. Oil on canvas, about 16 × 20 ft. (4.9 × 6.1 cm). Paris, Louvre. Erich Lessing/Art Resource, New York.

freed humankind from its slavery to material conditions. Art allowed the artist and viewer to find nothing less than the infinite in the finite, to find God in nature.

Typically, a Romantic artist chose an unusual and dramatic subject, a rare moment of tension that could be used to explore basic human feelings. Through exotic subjects from distant lands or from long ago, art would escape the humdrum of conventional daily life. Selecting an unusual and dramatic subject, the French Romantic painter Théodore Géricault explored in his enormous painting *Raft of the Medusa* (Fig. 17-39) humankind's emotional confrontation with the brute forces of nature and with unreasoning death. The incident he depicted, a recent scandal in the French government, took place far away off the west coast of Africa. French officers of the foundering ship *Medusa* had set 149 men and one woman adrift on a raft as they themselves sailed off in a lifeboat to safety. After days of facing raw nature on the seas and raw humanity among themselves, the fifteen survivors on the raft pull together to flag down a distant ship. Reduced to basic instincts, they find among themselves a common brotherhood.

Géricault's Romanticism used a dynamic Baroque composition of strong diagonals as the sea lifts the raft and as the figures surge up together toward their salvation. Ignoring probability, Géricault made the starving survivors as heroic in stature as Michelangelo's race of giants, and he boldly contrasted light and dark

throughout the scene. Géricault borrowed these elements of style to dramatize the Romantic confrontation of people and nature when life is lived according to subjective feelings.

The Spanish painter Francisco Goya had captured a similar Romantic theme several years earlier in his moving painting *The Third of May, 1808* (Fig. 17-40). Goya, who had been court painter for many years, had turned, in the eighteenth century, to the rationalism of the French Enlightenment to cure the social and moral problems of Spain. Soon after he satirized the superstitions, stupidity, and immorality of Spain in his series of etchings and aquatints *Los Caprichos* (Fig. 9-14), Spain was invaded by Napoléon's armies. The horrible devastation and inhumanity of that war aroused in Goya something like Géricault's Romantic attitude. Goya likewise imagined human beings stripped of all the restraints of civilization and of reason and relying only on their instincts.

The Third of May illustrates an incident at the beginning of the war when French troops, in retaliation for riots in the city, rounded up numerous suspects outside the gates of Madrid, where they were summarily shot by faceless soldiers. In the painting, bloody corpses already lie on the ground as more citizens file toward the place of execution. Of the group facing the firing squad, one man raises a fist in defiance, a monk tries to pray, the others cannot look. Only one man, prominent in his white shirt brightened by the square lantern on the ground, can stare down the barrels of

FIG 17-40   FRANCISCO GOYA [Spanish, 1746–1828], *The Third of May, 1808.* 1814. Oil on canvas, 104 × 135 in. (264.2 × 342.9 cm). Prado Museum, Madrid. Scala/Art Resource, New York.

the guns. He raises his arms like Jesus Christ on the cross, ready to sacrifice himself for his people. At the moment before death, the moment of truth, these men can only depend on themselves and live by their supercharged feelings. It is the supreme Romantic moment.

The Romantics developed a strong feeling for the beauty of nature and for the presence of Divine Providence in nature. The sensitive artist had the ability to intuit this presence and portray it for others to see. These romantic feelings rejuvenated landscape painting in the early nineteenth century. In America the painter Thomas Cole started a trend among artists to look upon the unspoiled American continent as being close to the biblical earthly paradise and thus closer to the revelation of the Divine in nature than the artificial landscapes of Europe. Cole founded what has become known as the Hudson River school of American landscape painting.

In Cole's 1838 painting *Schroon Mountain, Adirondacks* (FIG. 17-41), where the forest is blazing with autumn color, the Romantic artist saw nature as a revealing moral struggle. The distant mountain, shaped like one of the ancient pyramids, breaks through the clouds into the light of the heavens. Other hills closer to us bulge like muscular forces struggling to make the ascent. Several trees in the

FIG 17-41   THOMAS COLE [American, 1801–1848], *Schroon Mountain, Adirondacks.* 1838. Oil on canvas. The Cleveland Museum of Art, Hinman B. Hurlbut Collection.

foreground have risen above the forest only to be blasted by storms. Cole portrayed Schroon Mountain as a moralizing theater where nature's characters act out the drama with poses and gestures. The wilderness, so close to God, teaches lessons for the improvement of men and women.

When the Western world realized that a style belongs to the culture that produced it, many artists

FIG 17-42 RICHARD UPJOHN [American, 1802–1878], Trinity Church. 1839–1846. New York. Photo by Leo Sorrel.

tried to reverse that principle by attempting to imitate a past style and thereby reproduce the past culture. Neoclassicists had tried to associate the revival of a classical style with the heroism of ancient Rome and the ideals of ancient Greece. The Romantic revivers of the Gothic style in church architecture presumed that they would restore to the nineteenth century the confident Christianity of the Middle Ages. When Richard Upjohn and the members of Trinity Church in New York began to design a new building for their congregation in 1839, they expressed a desire to restore Christian worship by returning to a medieval style.

Although overall the building has a rather simple, boxy layout and the ribs in the nave vaulting are false, Trinity Church (FIG. 17-42) has pointed arches, clerestory windows, and an impressive tower and spire in a late-English form of Gothic known as the Perpendicular style. Upjohn's church was the first large-scale revival of the Gothic style in America, and

it succeeded in identifying that style with church building for generations to come. Nineteenth-century churchpeople believed that a Gothic style would restore the age of faith because Romantic feeling let them escape the harsh truths about secular modern urban life.

In the 1820s, 1830s, and 1840s in France, the Neoclassical and Romantic styles existed side by side. They were championed by two prominent artists, the Neoclassical painter J. A. D. Ingres and the Romantic painter Eugène Delacroix. Ingres asserted that line was the major element in all art; Delacroix maintained that the chief element was color. Other artists as well as the public took sides in this clash between the two forceful painters and their rival styles.

In the very large Romantic canvas *The Death of Sardanapalus* (FIG. 17-43) Delacroix illustrated a poem by the English poet Byron about an ancient Assyrian despot, Sardanapalus. At the defeat of his city by his enemies, Sardanapalus surrounds himself on his funeral pyre with all his possessions—his harem, horses, and jewels—rather than allow them to fall into the hands of the enemy. Reclining on the billowing mattress of his elephant bed, Sardanapalus calmly surveys the mayhem going on beneath him amid the objects of his sensual delight. He willingly, and in full control, meets his fate while indulging his every passion. Sardanapalus's conscious and deliberate confrontation with his emotions illustrates the nature of a Romantic artist.

Delacroix followed the example of Titian and Rubens by making color and chiaroscuro the basic elements of his composition. He applied the paint with passion and excitement, blurring contours by "drawing" with colored strokes of paint. A rich, saturated red, accentuated with cool color contrasts, runs throughout the composition. Delacroix observed the play of light on textures and the reflections of one color on another surface. He often experimented with touches of complementary colors, especially in the shadows, and with separate dabs of color to be mixed optically by the eye. He applied paint with a variety of strokes from thin and transparent to thick and opaque. The lush application of paint and contrasts of light and color intensify the emotional impact of the drama.

Ingres's Neoclassical painting *Odalisque with Slave* (FIG. 17-44) represents a curvaceous woman in a Turkish harem, languidly reclining as she listens to

Fig 17-43 Eugène Delacroix [French, 1798–1863], *The Death of Sardanapalus.* 1826. Oil on canvas, about 144 × 192 in. (365.8 × 487.7 cm). Louvre, Paris. Scala/Art Resource, New York.

Fig 17-44 J. A. D. Ingres [French, 1780–1867], *Odalisque with Slave.* Oil on canvas. Fogg Art Museum, Cambridge, Massachusetts.

music played by a slave. A eunuch stands guard at the door. The sensuous subject is as exotic as that in Delacroix's *Sardanapalus* but lacks entirely the intense emotional drama and the theme of a life-and-death struggle.

The three figures of Ingres's painting scarcely interact but are fitted into the composition, along with a profusion of objects and designs, like pieces of a mosaic or like the flattened components of a Persian minia-

ture. Ingres's painting sparkles with bright color and striking complementary contrasts, but each color remains within the boundary of a precise contour line. Ingres also emphasized the beautiful contour line of the twisting nude by downplaying the internal modeling of her nearly shapeless anatomy. His goal was to imitate the pure line drawing of Greek vase painting. Every kind of chiaroscuro in fact plays a minor role in Ingres's painting compared with Delacroix's. By his

Fig 17-45 Gustave Courbet [French, 1819–1877], *The Stone Breakers*. 1849. Oil on canvas, 63 × 102 in. (160 × 259.1 cm). Destroyed 1945. Giraudon Art Resource, New York.

perfect finish, by bringing his painting to an abstract perfection of line and tranquil harmony of design, the dispassionate Ingres cooled and hardened the sensuousness of his subject.

Realism

Around the middle of the nineteenth century a new and different kind of society emerged among most men and women in Europe and America. The most visible manifestation of the new age was the industrial revolution, which meant not only the proliferation of factories and mass-produced goods but also a network of railroads, cities exploding with large populations, and a wealthy middle class. Underlying these changes in the landscape, and stimulated by the changes themselves, were the fundamental ideas that practical business sense, technology, and science were the rules of life. In the real world, with the industrial revolution in full swing, business and science seemed to be laying the true foundations for a new society. Since progress in these fields depended on hard facts, artists likewise developed a factual and realistic style to depict modern life. By the mid–nineteenth century, artists themselves wanted to become part of the new real world and sought ways to depict it.

This next generation of artists shunned the Romantic movement because it seemed too much like an escape from reality. Some young artists, who declared themselves dedicated to "facts," felt that they should paint and immortalize only what they saw. Critics and collectors encouraged them to depict the world around them and to choose more relevant "modern" subjects. The discovery of photography by Daguerre (see *Parisian Boulevard*, Fig. 11-2) and others in 1839 and its rapid adoption resulted in good part from the growing desire to copy everyday reality. Photography in turn stimulated the growing desire for realism in other art forms.

The midcentury French artist Gustave Courbet claimed rather loudly that, since the people were better served when art was true to reality, he would paint only from nature. Courbet was inspired to create *The Stone Breakers* (Fig. 17-45) because he actually saw the young boy and old man breaking rocks at the side of a road. Brought to his studio, they resumed their poses for the artist—a little awkwardly perhaps. Although the painting no longer exists—it was destroyed in World War II—through photographs we can still study its iconography and style and the important place that Courbet's Realism has in the history of art.

Courbet sympathized with the stone breakers as faceless members of the exploited working class—whether or not this particular man and boy were actually being exploited. His painting was meant as an indictment of such backbreaking labor and showed his sympathy for the struggling worker. To emphasize their common fate, he bound them to the earth by raising the horizon far above their heads and hid their faces from the viewer. Although he depicted them as he saw them, he nevertheless enlarged their scale by having their figures fill the frame.

Viewers in 1849 complained not only about the socialist content of Courbet's painting but also about the crudity of its execution. It seems that the harsh dabs of paint on the surface insistently pressed home to them the materialism of Courbet's Realist point of view. The public wanted art with a polished surface that idealized reality in content and form, and it was not yet ready to abandon that desire.

The American artist Thomas Eakins also committed himself to painting from reality. To Eakins, realism meant the artist must study objects with virtually a scientific diligence. Thus, to paint the human figure, Eakins became an expert in anatomy. Skilled at mathematics, he made elaborate perspective studies for his compositions. And inspired by Eadweard Muybridge's photography (see *The Horse in Motion*, FIG. 11-7), Eakins also took photographs of the human body in motion for use in his work. Eakins studied art in Philadelphia and in Paris in the 1860s while Courbet painted there, but he also examined in Madrid the Baroque realism of Velázquez (see *Las Meninas*, FIG. 17-27).

The public sometimes reacted harshly to Eakin's realism, as they did when he exhibited his dramatic portrait of Dr. Gross performing surgery, *The Gross Clinic* (FIG. 2-6). His portraits were also sometimes rejected by the people who commissioned them because they were too truthful. In his painting of the thirty-seven-year-old Amelia Van Buren (FIG. 17-46), a dedicated art student who shared Eakins's interest in anatomy, Eakins re-created the still realism of a daguerreotype. He carefully balanced different kinds of

movement across the composition: the chair on the left is angled back toward the right. Miss Van Buren leans to the right but looks to the left, and her fan points in the opposite direction. She looks into a bright light that illumines her rose-colored dress, but the meaning of her reverie is as impenetrable as the darkness behind her head. Although Eakins did not flatter the woman, his realism makes her fascinating.

FIG 17-46 THOMAS EAKINS [American, 1844–1916], *Miss Amelia Van Buren*. C. 1891. Oil on canvas, 45 × 32 in. (114.3 × 81.3 cm). Phillips Collection, Washington, D.C.

Key Terms and Concepts

central plan
continuous narrative
module

18 ART OF THE EARLY MODERN WORLD: 1860 TO 1940

FIG 18-1 ÉDOUARD MANET [French, 1832–1883], *Déjeuner sur l'herbe (Luncheon on the Grass).* 1863. Oil on canvas, about 84 × 106 in. (213.4 × 269.2 cm). Musée d'Orsay, Paris. Art Resource, New York.

Late-Nineteenth-Century Painting

During the late nineteenth century a revolutionary new movement began in the history of European styles when new artists successfully challenged the art establishment. The art establishment began in France in 1737 when the government, through its Academy of Fine Arts, started holding an annual, sometimes biennial, exhibition of art in a large salon, or room, in the Louvre Palace in Paris. Thirty years later the British government established the same system of yearly exhibitions of art in London at the Royal Academy. Academy exhibitions, or the **Salon,** as it became known in France, had caused a profound change in the nature of art by the end of the eighteenth century. Instead of working directly for a wealthy and usually knowledgeable patron, artists now produced their work

to satisfy the general public who came by the thousands to the exhibitions. Artists also planned their work for the eyes of the often prejudiced critics and for the members of the Academy, who passed judgment on their work. When two of his paintings were rejected by the Salon jury, Gustave Courbet independently challenged this system in 1855 when he held his own exhibition of Realism apart from the official Salon.

In 1863 the French government, under pressure, held an exhibition of the many works that were rejected by the judges that year from the official Salon. Forewarned of official disapproval, the public came to scoff at this **Salon des refusés** (Salon of the Rejected), as it became known. The critics singled out as the most notorious offender of good taste *Déjeuner sur l'herbe (Luncheon on the Grass)* (FIG. 18-1), by Édouard Manet. In the painting a nude woman catches the viewer's eye while she sits at a picnic in the woods with two men in contemporary dress. It did not matter to the critics that the museums displayed plenty of paintings illustrating nude women associating with dressed men or that Manet borrowed the composition from a design by Raphael. The public and critics felt that *Luncheon on the Grass* was intended as pornography, not art, especially because the figures were real, not ideal.

It is hard to imagine that Manet was so naive that he did not realize what he was doing or foresee the objections his painting would raise. More likely, he was fully aware and fully convinced of the correctness of Courbet's Realistic approach and the need for modern subjects painted in the modern manner. Conscious of the tradition of European art, Manet worked with seeming indifference to it, asserting the right to paint as he saw. Inspired by the open brushwork of several famous Baroque artists—of Velázquez, for example (see *Las Meninas*, FIG. 17-27)—Manet painted with broad strokes of color. By illuminating the figures with a source of light from the front, he reduced modeling and all gradual transitions between values to a few distinct tones. Up close, his painting seems like a sketch of what the eye immediately sees: patches of colored light. Manet's handling of paint calls attention to itself and declares that the arrangement of colors on the surface is more important in art than a moral message. Manet's assertion of the primacy of the surface was the beginning of the revolution.

We have no name for the general style-period ushered in by this revolution other than **modern art.** This term generally refers to the art of recent times ever since the end of the nineteenth century. The phrase **contemporary art** means the art of the current generation, the last ten or fifteen years.

Impressionism

Photography in the nineteenth century both challenged painters to be true to nature and encouraged them to exploit aspects of the painting medium, like color, that photography lacked. This divergence away from photographic realism appears in the work of a group of artists who from 1874 to 1886 exhibited together, independently of the Salon. The leaders of the independent movement were Claude Monet, August Renoir, Edgar Degas, Berthe Morisot, and Mary Cassatt. They became known as Impressionists because a newspaper critic thought they were painting mere sketches or impressions. The Impressionists, however, considered their works finished.

Many Impressionists painted pleasant scenes of middle-class urban life, extolling the leisure time that the industrial revolution had won for middle-class society. In Renoir's luminous painting *Luncheon of the Boating Party* (FIG. 18-2), for example, young men and women eat, drink, talk, and flirt with a joy for life that is reflected in sparkling colors. The sun filtered through the orange striped awning colors everything and everyone in the party with its warm light. The diners' glances cut across a balanced and integrated composition that reproduces a very delightful scene of modern middle-class life.

Since they were realists, followers of Courbet and Manet, the Impressionists set out to be "true to nature," a phrase that became their rallying cry. When Renoir and Monet went out into the countryside in search of subjects to paint, they carried their oil colors, canvas, and brushes with them so that they could stand right on the spot and record what they saw at that time. In contrast, most earlier landscape painters worked in their studio from sketches they had made outdoors.

FIG 18-2 PIERRE AUGUSTE RENOIR [French, 1841–1919] *Luncheon of the Boating Party.* 1880–1881. Oil on canvas, 51 3/16 × 68 1/8 in. (130 × 173 cm). Phillips Collection, Washington, D.C.

FIG 18-3 CLAUDE MONET [French, 1840–1926], *Rouen Cathedral, Tour d'Albane, Morning.* 1894. Oil on canvas, 41 3/4 × 29 in. (106 × 73.7 cm). Galerie Beyeler, Basel, Switzerland.

that is now in Switzerland (FIG. 18-3) with the one that is now in Washington, D.C. (FIG. 5-27).

Realism meant to an Impressionist that the painter ought to record the most subtle sensations of reflected light. In capturing a specific kind of light, this style conveys the notion of a specific and fleeting moment of time. Impressionist painters like Monet and Renoir recorded each sensation of light with a touch of paint in a little stroke like a comma. The public back then was upset that Impressionist paintings looked like a sketch and did not have the polish and finish that more fashionable paintings had. But applying the paint in tiny strokes allowed Monet, Renoir, or Cassatt to display color sensations openly, to keep the colors unmixed and intense, and to let the viewer's eye mix the colors. The bright colors and the active participation of the viewer approximated the experience of the scintillation of natural sunlight.

The Impressionists remained realists in the sense that they remained true to their sensations of the object, although they ignored many of the old conventions for representing the object "out there." But truthfulness for the Impressionists lay in their personal and subjective sensations—not in the "exact" reproduction of an object for its own sake. The objectivity of things existing outside and beyond the artist no longer mattered as much as it once did. The significance of "outside" objects became irrelevant. Concern for representing an object faded, while concern for representing the subjective grew. The focus on subjectivity intensified because artists became more concerned with the independent expression of the individual. Reality became what the individual saw. With Impressionism, the meaning of realism was transformed into subjective realism, and the subjectivity of modern art was born.

Japanese Art of the Eighteenth and Nineteenth Centuries

Many Impressionist artists collected woodblock prints published in Japan in the eighteenth and nineteenth centuries. The Japanese call these works *ukiyo-e*, "images of the floating world," that is, images of the entertainment district of Edo (modern Tokyo). These popular prints illustrated famous actresses or courtesans (see Kitagawa Utamaro's *Three Celebrated*

The more an Impressionist like Monet looked, the more she or he saw. Sometimes Monet came back to the same spot at different times of day or at a different time of year to paint the same scene. In 1892 he rented a room opposite the Cathedral of Rouen in order to paint its facade over and over again. He never copied himself because the light and color always changed with the passage of time, and the variations made each painting a new creation. The differences are obvious when we compare the painting of Rouen Cathedral

500

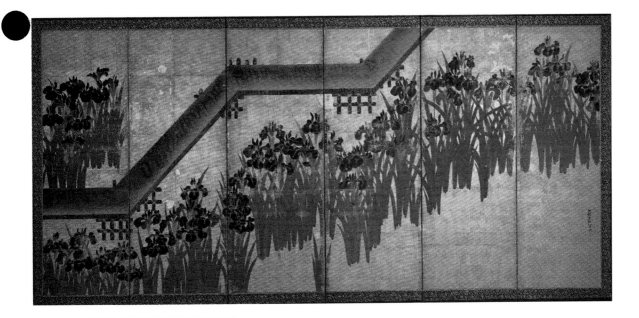

FIG 18-4 OGATA KŌRIN [Japanese, 1658–1716], *Iris and Bridge.* Early eighteenth century. Ink, color, and gold leaf on paper, 70 1/2 × 146 1/4 in. (179.1 × 371.5 cm). Metropolitan Museum of Art, New York. Louisa Eldridge McBurney Gift, 1953.

Beauties, FIG. 5-11), wrestlers, landscapes (see Katshushika Hokusai's *Great Wave,* FIG. 9-7), or scenes of contemporary life (see Torii Kiyonaga's *Woman's Bath House,* FIG. 6-18). The Impressionists and their followers were attracted to them because of their flat areas of color, their lack of chiaroscuro (they had no cast shadows, no modeling), their flattened perspective and different points of view, their bold designs, and their popular iconography.

Traditional Japanese artists and their upper-class patrons in the nineteenth century looked down on ukiyo-e prints as vulgar. Japanese art over the centuries had borrowed heavily from Chinese art with its high-minded spiritualism. Nevertheless, these popular woodblock prints in many ways represent the culmination of traditional Japanese art, which can be seen in the early-eighteenth-century painting *Iris and Bridge* (*Fig.* 18-4). This piece is one of a pair of folding screens, now in New York, painted on gold leaf by Ogata Kōrin. The Japanese had raised to a high art the painting of folding screens, which were used as space dividers in their homes.

Kōrin's painting alludes to a brief passage in a work of literature, the *Tales of Ise,* in which a character stops at Yatsuhashi, or Eight-Plank Bridge. The irises that he sees from the bridge make him nostalgic for home. Kōrin reduced the iconography of the screens to just the bridge and the irises; in another set of screens in Tokyo, the irises alone capture the literary allusion.

The composition and color of Kōrin's screen are as bold as the design of any of the ukiyo-e prints that nineteenth-century Western artists saw. The bridge, seen from two different points of view, becomes a zigzag line roughly parallel to the long row of irises. The bridge and irises become a flat design on the flat surface of the gold screen. Having reduced the composition to its quintessence, Kōrin painted the spiky leaves of the irises with vivid unmodeled green and the flowers in two shades of blue. Full of life and vitality, the irises virtually dance across the screen. Only Van Gogh succeeded in giving irises the same energy (see *Irises,* FIG. 20-1).

FIG 18-5 GEORGES SEURAT [French, 1859–1891], *Sunday Afternoon on the Island of La Grand Jatte.* 1884–1886. Oil on canvas, about 81 × 120 in. (205.7 × 304.8 cm). Art Institute of Chicago.

Post-Impressionism

Toward the end of the nineteenth century many people in the West grew dissatisfied with the materialism of modern industrial society. Important spiritual aspects of human nature were being denied or neglected. Eventually, many modern artists declared themselves prophets of a new age being born. Their art would not reflect the present age so much as challenge it and prod it into a new consciousness. Like many artists in modern times, they thought of themselves as an elite, and they purposely created art that was different, difficult in its symbolism, and ahead of its time. When they were scorned or neglected, many artists started to feel alienated from the masses of ordinary people who lagged behind. In this way their challenging art reflected the conflict of competing modern values as well as the pressures and stress brought on by rapid technological and social change in modern life.

At the eighth and final Impressionist exhibition in 1886, it was clear that many artists had grown dissatisfied with the formlessness of the style's bright-colored strokes and its limited significance. Artists wanted to regularize its design and application or give it more content or let it express more feeling. Many of the Impressionists themselves changed their style after 1885. These various new aims and new directions for Impressionism are now grouped together and labeled Post-Impressionism. The name does not denote a single distinct style; it only implies that a new movement came after Impressionism and that Impressionism was its starting point.

One Post-Impressionist artist, Georges Seurat, tried to make Impressionism scientific and systematic. He transformed the intuitive brush strokes of Impressionism into a regular system of separate colored dots. Seurat calculated his dots of paint, applied in accord with the laws of physics and psychology, so that they would produce the correct light and color sensation when mixed by the viewer's eye. His **Divisionism,** as he called it, or **Pointillism,** as it is also termed, works like the colored ink dots in modern magazine illustrations. The painstaking technique forced Seuart to paint indoors, not outdoors like Monet.

Seurat died young and painted only a few major works. The Art Institute in Chicago displays his most popular work, *Sunday Afternoon on the Island of La Grande Jatte* (FIG. 18-5). When a viewer looks closely at the painting, it is possible to see thousands of points of light and color. Any one area—a face, a dress, the grass—displays a rainbow of different colors and a variety of light and dark dots. In them Seurat tried to cap-

FIG 18-6 PAUL GAUGUIN [French, 1848–1903], *Fatata te mihi (Near the Sea).* 1892. Oil on canvas, 26 3/4 × 36 in. (67.9 × 91.4 cm). National Gallery of Art, Washington, D.C. Chester Dale Collection.

ture the most subtle color sensations of reflected and tinted light.

Something else happened to Seurat's painting while he was changing Impressionism into his own system. Since he was no longer capturing a fleeting moment in time with spontaneous brushwork, his orderly procedures made his figures appear frozen in time. In fact, he placed them carefully in the composition along parallel lines in frontal or profile poses. A friend said they looked Egyptian.

Seurat may not have intended to imitate the Egyptian style, but another Post-Impressionist painter, Paul Gauguin, deliberately rejected many European traditions of painting in order to incorporate other traditions in his work. In fact, he sailed away from France and lived for many years among the Polynesians of the South Pacific in his search for an unspoiled paradise where he hoped to find more genuine and immediate sources of inspiration. Gauguin believed that Western civilization had corrupted the spiritual revelation common to all people and that less developed societies were closer to the original truth. Ever since the eighteenth-century French philosopher Jean Jacques Rousseau praised the "noble savage," the myth had developed in the West that the early, primitive mani-

festations of a society were better than later, civilized developments because the primitive was more original, more inspired, and closer to the Truth. Admiration of and fascination with the nineteenth-century concept of primitive cultures was to have a profound effect on European and American art for many generations.

Gauguin first learned how to record sensations of color and light like an Impressionist, but he soon felt free to intensify colors and to manipulate lines and shapes according to the "music" of a painting, as he called it. Colors might even be used for symbolic reasons. When he depicted life in the South Pacific, he often injected symbolic motifs from other cultures. His *Fatata te mihi (Near the Sea)* (FIG. 18-6), in which two Polynesian women undress and walk into the sea, is far from an accurate depiction of life on a South Pacific island. Gauguin intended the pose of the more distant figure with raised arms to symbolize Buddhist Nirvana. The sea would thus represent the abyss. To back up his esoteric symbolism, Gauguin also made sure his painting had a corresponding musical part in the visual elements. The wavy forms in the foreground and the exotic scheme of secondary colors—green, orange, and violet— correspond to rhythms and harmonies in

FIG 18-7 VINCENT VAN GOGH [Dutch, 1853–1890], *Starry Night.* 1889. Oil on canvas, 29 × 36 1/4 in. (73.7 × 92.1 cm). Museum of Modern Art, New York. Acquired through the Lillie P. Bliss Bequest.

his imagination and do not necessarily imitate real appearances. Instead, they conjure up mysteries.

In Paris in the 1880s, the Dutch artist Vincent Van Gogh met Gauguin and some of the Impressionists, whose lessons he absorbed (see p. 11). Van Gogh then developed a style all his own that transformed Impressionism into something quite different. Van Gogh was a very intense man who in his paintings poured out his heart and soul. Seldom in the history of art has there been such direct communication of an individual psyche by a person so earnest and so forthright. His work has the power to speak to everyone directly. In his *Starry Night* (FIG. 18-7) in New York's Museum of Modern Art, Van Gogh painted in thick dabs and swirls of paint to express his feelings— instead of in the small, consistent touches of the Impressionists. Everything in *Starry Night*—hills, trees, sky, clouds—undulates with the same energetic line. The pulsating stars and writhing sky express his dynamic vision of time and eternity. Van Gogh day-dreamed of traveling to distant stars (his symbol of eternity) in the next life, just as pilgrims take a train to distant spots on a map.

Another Post-Impressionist, Paul Cézanne, sought to make out of the Impressionist style something sta-

ble and ordered like the old master paintings hanging in a museum. Like Monet, Cézanne went out into the countryside with his paints on his back to record his sensations before nature. Tied to the realist tradition, he had to look at what he painted. But Cézanne was disturbed by the formlessness of Impressionism. He worked for days on a still life or landscape, making subtle adjustments on his canvas to unify and balance his composition.

In his landscape paintings like *View of the Château Noir* (FIG. 18-8), he stayed in front of the same hills, valley, and trees day after day, trying to reconstruct the solid forms of objects and build up a tight composition using only the color sensations he perceived. In *View of the Château Noir* Cézanne knit together across the surface a grid of tree limbs that acts like a screen through which we see the rectangular planes of the distant building and landscape. In his hand, the small strokes and colored touches of Impressionism became flat rectangular patches that operate like building blocks. Contrasts of warm and cool colors give some feel for three dimensions. Cézanne's method of constructing a composition out of patches of color meant a lot to the next generation of artists, who ignored the remnants of Impressionist realism in his art.

Post-Impressionist Sculpture: Rodin

Auguste Rodin, more than any other artist at the end of the nineteenth century, transformed sculpture into a modern idiom. Until Rodin, most sculpture continued to reproduce the idealized images of heroes and heroines and saints. Rodin changed sculpture into a powerful means of personal expression and into a vehicle for profound symbolism. His statue *The Thinker* (Fig. 18-9) strikingly illustrates his achievement. Michelangelo's art obviously inspired the giantlike proportions and the nudity of *The Thinker*. The nudity also signifies a timeless universality. Rodin originally designed *The Thinker* for a position on the lintel of a large museum doorway that became known as the Gates of Hell. He intended his seated figure as Everyman contemplating scenes from Dante's *Inferno* illustrated in relief on the doors below.

Rodin may have adopted *The Thinker's* pose from printed images of Christ in distress during his passion, but the massive torso leans far forward through space in a thoroughly three-dimensional way. The figure's right elbow rests uncomfortably on his left leg. He does not quietly meditate. He hunches over, bites his knuckles, and claws at the rock with his toes as he ago-

Fig 18-9 Auguste Rodin [French, 1840–1917], *The Thinker*. 1880–. Bronze. Rodin Museum, Philadelphia. Vanni/Art Resource, New York.

FIG 18-10 DANIEL HUDSON BURNHAM [American, 1846–1912], Reliance Building. 1894–1895. Chicago Historical Society. ICHi-01066.

nizes over the human condition. The kneaded, irregular surface catches the light, and the vigor of the modeling reinforces the contortions and distress of the figure. Focusing the visual elements on this theme, Rodin made his sculpture express powerful human emotions.

Late-Nineteenth-Century Architecture

Rapid changes in society in the nineteenth century challenged architects as never before. Since the early 1800s, as urban life mushroomed, architects have had to provide new types of structures such as railroad stations, factories, and office buildings. At first architects tried to dress the new structures in the old styles of building: Greek, Roman, Gothic, Renaissance, or whatever else seemed appropriate. But the old styles say nothing about the technology and pace of modern life. Furthermore, styles suitable for Greek temples or Gothic cathedrals are generally inappropriate for the new types of building. All the while, new materials and technologies themselves have given architects the resources for a new architectural style.

The steel-and-glass office tower, born from the need for large modern bureaucracies and the economic demands of crowded urban space, takes its stylistic cue from modern materials and from the efficiency of the machine. Stripped to the essentials and dependent on technology—elevators, electricity, central heating, and air conditioning—the modern skyscraper has become *the* symbol of belonging to the advanced culture of industralized society.

After the Great Fire of 1871 leveled most of downtown Chicago, the booming city rebuilt itself with increased energy and freshness. Chicago architects became world leaders in new building technology and design. In 1884–85 William Le Baron Jenney built the first metal-frame skyscraper, the ten-story Home Insurance Building in Chicago, torn down in 1931. Another early skyscraper, the fourteen-story Reliance Building (FIG. 18-10), by Daniel Hudson Burnham, still stands. From the sidewalk to the tiny cornice at the top, slender vertical steel supports are left unmasked between large plate glass windows. (Movable sash windows were still needed to catch summer breezes.) Instead of placing on the exterior massive vertical supports that would look as though they were bearing the weight, Burnham created horizontal strips of glass subdivided by thin frames. Horizontal decorative bands of terra cotta panels separate the floors. The walls are truly a curtain hung from the skeleton and do not declaim the architectural forces at work. New materials and techniques permit a logical and honest new style of architecture.

Louis Sullivan was another pioneer of modern architecture in Chicago at the end of the nineteenth century. In the Guaranty Building (FIG. 15-8) in Buffalo, New York, he sought an organic style of architecture in which the verticality of the office building and the forces at work in the structure would be expressed on the exterior. In the Carson, Pirie, Scott Building (FIG. 18-11) in Chicago, Sullivan expressed on the exterior the steel cage construction. The equally emphatic horizontal and vertical lines of the exterior are covered with panels of white ceramic. Seen from an angle, the lines seem to wrap around the curved corner of the twelve-story department store.

Breaking free from the language of classical architecture, Sullivan did not cap the building with a cornice or rest the upper stories on some kind of heavy base. The entrance and the display windows of the first two stories are merely framed in a light wrought iron filigree design of Sullivan's own invention (FIG. 18-12). Delighting the eye of shoppers, this decoration stands in great contrast to the plain white ceramic above. Sullivan's filigree pattern, a fantasy of curvilinear vine and floral motifs, is a good example of the so-called **Art Nouveau** (New Art) style, which was quite fashionable by the end of the nineteenth century. The Art Nouveau style derived its love of swirling lines from the British Arts and Crafts movement (for example, William Morris's *Trellis* wallpaper FIG. 14-17) and from Japanese art (for example, Katshushika Hokusai's *Great Wave*, FIG. 9-7).

FIG 18-11 LOUIS SULLIVAN [American, 1856–1924], Carson, Pirie, Scott Building. 1899–1904. Chicago. Chicago Historical Society. ICHi-15065.

FIG 18-12 LOUIS SULLIVAN [American, 1856–1924], Carson, Pirie, Scott Building, detail of wrought iron decoration. 1899–1904. Chicago. Chicago Historical Society. Photo by Arthur Siegel.

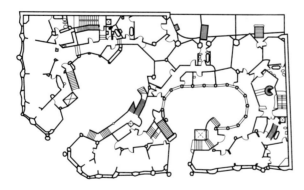

Plan of Casa Milà, Ground Floor.

Early-Twentieth-Century Architecture

Gaudí

The Art Nouveau style received monumental expression in the architecture of Antoni Gaudí. The massive stone facade of his Casa Milà (FIG. 18-13), an apartment house situated on a street corner in Barcelona, undulates like a serpentine growth or a surging wave. Up close, the rugged surface of the stone and its rounded forms seem like the weather-beaten rock of a steep cliff penetrated by numerous caverns where a primitive people have started to live. Gaudí, like Louis Sullivan, designed for the building decorative ironwork based on plant and vegetable growth. The iron railings of the exterior balconies of the Casa Milà look like clumps of seaweed that have been flung across the stone. Above the sinuous line of the tiled roof, bell-shaped chimneys spiral into the air as though they have been squeezed out of pastry dough. Each one is different.

The plan of the first floor reveals that Gaudí designed the rooms and corridors of the apartments with the same freedom as the exterior. Instead of a typical grid system, the irregular and often poly-sided rooms curve around two oval-shaped courtyards. The complex steel skeleton that Gaudí designed for the building finds no expression on the exterior. On the contrary, the Casa Milà seems like a fairy castle because its free-form fantasy and delicate waviness contradict the ponderous weight of the stone. For Gaudí a building was a living thing in which the architecture grows out of natural forms. Inspired by the revival of Gothic and Moorish architecture of his native Catalonia, Gaudí created a new expressionistic form of architecture. He gave the winding curves of his work a personal fluidity, force, and dynamism.

Wright

At the same time that Gaudí created Casa Milà in Barcelona, the architect Frank Lloyd Wright built the Robie House (FIG. 18-14) in Chicago. Another masterpiece of early modern architecture, the Robie House has a long, low roof and windows arranged in strips that accentuate the horizontal direction. These

FIG 18-14 FRANK LLOYD WRIGHT [American, 1867–1959], Robie House. 1907–1909. Chicago, Courtesy the Frank Lloyd Wright Foundation.

1. Porch
2. Living room
3. Dining room
4. Balcony
5. Guest room
6. Kitchen
7. Servants
8. Billiard room
9. Children's playroom
10. Entrance hall
11. Boiler room
12. Laundry
13. Garage
14. Court
15. Garden
16. Lavatory or bath
17. Fireplace
18. Bedrooms

Roof

Outdoor walls (garden, terrace, balcony, etc.)

Structures above or below plan level

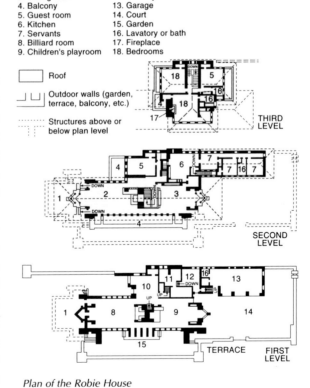

Plan of the Robie House

low horizontals mimic and hug the flat midwestern prairie—even though the house is sited on a residential street corner. Terraces extend the structure into the outdoors and integrate it with nature so that it seems to grow naturally out of the ground. Rather than break the horizontal lines of the building, Wright placed the street entrance on its short side and toward the back.

On the interior, the Robie House has an asymmetrical plan, in which the rooms of the main floor radiate out from the central focus, the fireplace. Even though his houses have separate kitchens and central heating, Wright made the hearth, the traditional source of heat, food, and light, the symbolic core of family living. Wright adapted the low horizontal roof, the fluid interior spaces, and the integration of the house with nature from Japanese architecture, (see the Katsura Palace, FIGS. 17-24 and 17-25), which he knew and admired. In the Robie House he declared to the rest of the twentieth century that the essential element in architecture was the experience of space.

Text continues on page 513

Frank Lloyd Wright (1867–1959)

*F*RANK LLOYD WRIGHT, a pioneer of twentieth-century architecture, was born, was educated, and grew to maturity in the nineteenth century. In many ways he retained, all his life, nineteenth-century ideas about American cultural life, its roots in the agrarian heartland, and the freedom of the individual—ideas that he embodied in his work.

Frank Lloyd Wright in his studio, 1946. Photo by Pedro E. Guerrero.

Raised in rural Wisconsin, Wright hated the congestion and mob behavior of cities. America remained for him the open spaces and broad plains of the Midwest. He championed the freedom of the individual to move and determine his or her own destiny.

Wright was a precocious child who was raised by his mother to become a famous architect. She hung prints of the great cathedrals about the house before he was born. She bought a set of building blocks designed by Friedrich Froebel, the inventor of kindergartens, for her son to play with. Wright himself always recognized the effect on his architecture of creative play with these rectangular blocks.

Wright studied engineering for two years at the University of Wisconsin, then went to work in Chicago at the architectural firm Adler and Sullivan, where Louis Sullivan became his inspiration. Wright quickly rose to prominence in the office, taking charge of designing the private homes of clients.

He left Adler and Sullivan in 1893 to develop his own ideas as an architect while building a series of large suburban homes outside Chicago. There, in the late 1890s and in the first decade of the twentieth century, Wright developed his Prairie style of architecture—the Robie House of 1907–9 (FIG. 18-14) is its classic example. These houses are characterized by the long horizontal lines of their low roofs, which extend far beyond the walls of the building and which cover and shelter the building from the elements. Their interior spaces flow freely one into another. Wright scorned buildings, old or new, in the shape of a box.

At a time when most of the architects in America were reviving past styles, Wright invented his own set of forms, which he eventually called organic or natural. His theory required that buildings be placed in their natural setting and be built with natural materials and with techniques drawn from nature. In 1910–11 a German publishing house, Wasmuth, issued two luxury volumes of drawings and plans of the houses and other architecture that Wright had designed until then. The

FRANK LLOYD WRIGHT [American, 1867–
1959]. Falling Water, exterior. 1936–1939.
Bear Run, Pennsylvania. Western
Pennsylvania Conservancy/Art Resource,
New York.

FRANK LLOYD WRIGHT [American, 1867–
1959]. Falling Water, interior. 1936–1939.
Bear Run, Pennsylvania. Photo by Bill
Hedrich, Hedrich-Blessing. Chicago
Historical Society. HB-04414G3.

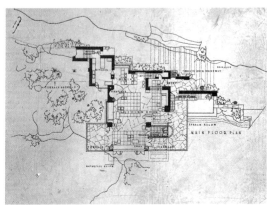

*Plan of Falling Water. Courtesy the Frank
Lloyd Wright Foundation.*

books made Wright internationally famous as his fluid mix of space and mass, his open plans, and other ideas influenced the course of European architecture.

Early in his career Wright discovered the potential of reinforced concrete and of cantilevering. For example, in the Unity Temple (1906–8) in Oak Park, Illinois, he left the concrete exposed; and cantilevering in the Johnson Wax Company tower (FIG. 15-22), Racine, Wisconsin, simulates the natural architecture of trees. *Falling Water,* the summer home he built for Edgar J. Kaufmann, the owner of a department store in Pittsburgh, illustrates Wright's principles in a memorable fashion.

Utilizing reinforced concrete and local stone, he built the house on a rock outcropping above a waterfall and amid the trees, thereby integrating the house with nature. The reinforced concrete terraces cantilever out from the cliff as though they were a natural growth. Their lines parallel the rock strata. The various rooms, without box-shaped walls, flow into one another. Large windows give the feeling that the house embraces the surrounding woods. Indeed, part of the rock cliff comes up through the living room floor to form the base of the fireplace, which Wright still considered the central focus of a home. In *Falling Water,* Wright proved that modern materials and techniques can produce, far from a machine-made look, an architecture organically related to nature.

FRANK LLOYD WRIGHT [American, 1867–1959]. Solomon R. Guggenheim Museum, original exterior. 1943–1959. New York. Photo by David Heald, © The Solomon R. Guggenheim Foundation, New York.

FRANK LLOYD WRIGHT [American, 1867–1959]. Solomon R. Guggenheim Museum, interior. 1943–1959. New York. Photo by David Heald, © The Solomon R. Guggenheim Foundation, New York.

During the Great Depression of the 1930s, Wright and the students of his Taliesen Fellowship (founded in 1932) near Scottsdale, Arizona, spent years developing plans for the utopian Broadacre City. In this urban setting every family was to have an acre of land, enough to live as individuals. Such low-density dispersal was made possible by the automobile and by telecommunications (radio, telephone, etc.). Wright predicted with foresight that America would build Broadacre City haphazardly, without anyone's help. It was to be a decentralized, horizontal, close-to-nature, self-sufficient community. The low-cost Usonian housing he planned for the city was adapted from elements of the Prairie style and had some influence on the popular ranch style of sub-

urban house. Although the city was never developed, Wright actually built a few of these modest and convenient open-planned houses.

After World War II Wright designed several buildings that still have the appearance of a science fiction fantasy. The Solomon R. Guggenheim Museum in New York, with its interior gallery spiraling down beneath its dome, looks like a fantastic movie set. Visitors to the museum are expected to take the elevator to the top of the ramp and to view the art along the walls on the way down. Many observers have complained that the architectural experience of the museum, with its tilted ramp and tilted walls, overwhelms the art on display. The Guggenheim Museum was one of the few buildings Wright ever designed

for a city street. Like many of his buildings, these personal expressions of a strong individual have had very few imitators.

Wright had a long and successful career, noted for numerous technical and stylistic innovations in his architecture. His early work had an international influence, and he proudly considered himself the greatest architect of the twentieth century. Articulate and outspoken, he wrote an autobiography and several books about architecture, while leading a colorful, sometimes flamboyant life.

Early-Twentieth-Century Painting

The twentieth century has been a century of enormous material progress and technological change. Great advances in education, social welfare, medicine, and mass communications have altered the meaning of life for billions of people throughout the world. The twentieth century has also produced two world wars of unprecedented devastation, dictatorial governments that practiced oppression on a massive scale, and for the first time in history the real threat of nuclear and environmental extinction for the human race. The century has a mixed record of achievement, to say the least. The discoveries of physics and of psychology and other behavioral sciences, and close contact with other cultures have radically changed the attitudes and values of the West. Modern artists, sensitive to the changing values around them, have reflected these upheavals in their work.

Twentieth-century artists did not invent a single, unified style—nor could there be a single modern style, since rapid change and personal freedom of expression are an overwhelming part of modern culture. In fact, the variety of stylistic possibilities within the modern movement is one of the century's strengths. Within the variety of modern styles, artists have time and again concerned themselves with the search for the essential, the primitive, and the inner self.

In the early years of the twentieth century, artists felt an exciting freedom to experiment and create one new style after the other. These pioneers of the modern movement, enlarging upon the achievements of the Post-Impressionists, developed several styles that laid the foundations for future generations to build on. Young artists at the opening of the century came to realize that Gauguin, Van Gogh, and Cézanne had won for them the freedom to use color as an expressive means and to let purely artistic considerations control lines and shapes. Early-twentieth-century Western artists borrowed freely from other cultures to find new ways of seeing with simplified forms, nonperspective space, and bold, overt designs.

Leading artists abandoned Western traditions because, as Europe headed toward World War I, they felt a growing frustration with traditional Western values. At the same time, they often hoped that their new art would lead the human race to a better future. Paradoxically, the modern styles they created sometimes became difficult for the public to understand

FIG 18-15 HENRI MATISSE [French, 1869–1954], *The Blue Nude*. 1907. Oil on canvas, 36 1/4 × 55 1/4 in. (92.1 × 140.4 cm). Baltimore Museum of Art, The Cone Collection.

because the artists attempted to return to such basic, simple forms of seeing and to such purity of means. These tensions and contradictions have not made modern art easy for the general public. But if a style of art is the exponent of the culture around it, it must be expected that twentieth-century art reflects the pace, the changing values, and the tensions of modern life, as well as its dreams of progress, equality, and individual freedom.

Expressionism

The early modern French painter Henri Matisse wanted his art to be an expression of his feelings. The styles of Van Gogh and Gauguin showed him the way. In 1905 Matisse so shocked the public with an exhibition of vividly colored and freely distorted work that he and his friends were labeled wild beasts (*Fauves* in French). Two years later Matisse painted *The Blue Nude* (FIG. 18-15) in the same brash and savage style. The subject was actually a traditional one among conservative painters: a reclining, life-sized female nude in a seductive pose. The drawing, however, has the intuitive simplicity of a child. Matisse gratuitously outlined the nude's shape in blue, a color that Cézanne often used for contours. The major key of blue clashes with the minor key of pinks, violets, and greens. Just as all the various shapes lie flat and decorate the surface, the round forms of the nude reverberate through-

FIG 18-16 ERNST LUDWIG KIRCHNER [German, 1880–1938], *Street, Dresden.* 1908. Oil on canvas, 59 1/4 × 78 7/8 in. (150.5 × 200.3 cm). Museum of Modern Art, New York.

FIG 18-17 WASSILY KANDINSKY [Russian, 1866–1944], *Improvisation Number 28.* 1912. Oil on canvas, 44 × 63 3/4 in. (111.8 × 161.9 cm). Solomon R. Guggenheim Museum, New York. Gift of Solomon R. Guggenheim. Photo by David Heald.

out the canvas. The bright fields of color, curved lines, and simple forms are the expression of Matisse's feelings, not the imitation of reality.

Fortunately for his viewers, Matisse had positive and happy feelings about life to express. His common practice was to paint his emotions intuitively and then refine his instincts by continually adjusting his lines and colors and planes to reflect his mental state. Matisse's emotional sensitivity and his artistic refinement make his art a pleasure to look at—at least, after the initial shock. He wanted his paintings to be as comfortable as an old easy chair, although *The Blue Nude* still bears traces of the harsh breakthrough of his earliest years as a Fauve.

Other Expressionists, close to Matisse in time, used similar stylistic means to portray, instead of Matisse's joy about living, the tensions and anxiety of life in the modern world. An outstanding group of young German Expressionists—including Ernst Ludwig Kirchner (see *Self-Portrait with Model*, FIG. 5-19) and Erich Heckel (see *Two by the Sea*, FIG. 7-4)—had strong feelings about the restlessness of modern urban life and its emptiness with the collapse of traditional moral and religious values. Meanwhile, they searched frantically for personal integrity amid the pressures of mass society. They identified their very nonconventional association with each other as *Die Brücke* (The Bridge).

In 1908 Kirchner depicted, in the large painting *Street, Dresden* (FIG. 18-16), a city thoroughfare filled with well-dressed women wearing broad-brimmed flowered hats. But Kirchner used a primitive style derived from Edvard Munch (see *The Scream*, FIG. 4-5) and the art of the Post-Impressionists, the Fauves, and the Middle Ages to elicit the smugness and apprehension looming in their complacent world. The German Expressionists embodied their anxiety-filled view of life in flattened perspective, harsh flat colors (the pink pavement in *Street, Dresden*), jagged lines, distorted shapes, and crude-looking features.

Even though artists for years had come to depend chiefly on visual elements such as lines and colors to express themselves, it was only about 1912 that a few of them took the plunge, eliminated all natural appearances from their work, and used only the visual elements. The Russian painter Wassily Kandinsky, in works like *Improvisation Number 28* (FIG. 18-17), was one of the first to make truly nonobjective art.

The theory of the correspondences among different sense perceptions helped Kandinsky take the final step toward creating a thoroughly abstract expressionism. Kandinsky believed, furthermore, that colors, lines, and shapes had symbolic or spiritual significance, so that by themselves they could convey the personal meaning he wanted. In 1913 he described his feelings and his beliefs in a book called *On the Spiritual in Art*. In it he wrote that he found blue restful and heavenly, the equivalent of horizontal direction. Yellow was vertical and aggressive. Each shape to Kandinsky had a particular spiritual perfume. Visual forms also had aural equivalents. The musical title *Improvisation Number 28* betrays his thinking. His abstract forms were far from meaningless scribbling; instead, they were intended to reproduce a spiritual aura. They also created a new sort of space, similar to Cubist space but without its rigid geometry and with color. Kandinksy's free-form lines and shapes seem to float in an ambiguous space appropriate for his vague spiritual message.

Cubism

Also in the years before World War I, Pablo Picasso, a Spanish artist living in Paris, invented a new style called Cubism, very likely with an eye to rivaling the bold steps taken by Matisse in his Fauvism. Picasso asserted the new style in *Les demoiselles d'Avignon (The Women of Avignon)* of 1907 (FIG. 18-18), the sudden and violent manifestation of a thoroughly new direction. The painting began as the representation of five prostitutes in a Barcelona brothel on Avignon Street displaying themselves before a curtain for two male viewers. Eventually, the specific narrative elements of the painting were eliminated from everything but the title. In keeping with the harshness of the subject, the figures twist so violently that they become regular geometric shapes lying flat on the surface. Picasso also fragmented the brown and blue drapes behind them into flattened shapes. Only distinctions made by differences in color isolate the pink flesh-colored figures from the ground.

By 1907 Picasso had discovered the color planes in Cézanne's paintings (see *View of the Château Noir*, FIG. 18-8), and he had heard that Cézanne wanted artists to see above all the geometry inherent in nature. He had also noticed that African artists make

FIG 18-18 PABLO PICASSO [Spanish, 1881–1973], *Les demoiselles d'Avignon*. 1907. Oil on canvas, 96 × 92 in. (243.8 × 233.7 cm). Museum of Modern Art, New York. Acquired through the Lillie P. Bliss Bequest.

even more radical reductions into geometry: the two faces on the right of Les demoiselles d'Avignon especially resemble African masks (see the Bushongo tribe dance mask in FIG. 18-22). Furthermore, Picasso rejected the Renaissance invention of perspective and, along with it, the static single point of view from which a traditional image was depicted. In the figures on the left in *Les demoiselles d' Avignon* Picasso showed the eye from one point of view, the nose from another—just as the ancient Egypitans did. The shifting point of view of Cubism actually has a basis in real-life experience, where we get to know objects by observing them from any number of angles. However, Picasso did not try to re-create the richness of real-life experience. The position of things and the shape of the patches on his canvas were governed by his desire to build a composition of forms arranged in a new kind of picture space.

triangle, and circle (see Braque's painting, *Musical Forms*, FIG. 10-19). Braque and Picasso also filled the entire surface with these Cubist shapes and fragments, as is evident in Picasso's painting *Ma jolie (My Pretty Girl)* (FIG. 18-19). The painting began as a portrait of Marcelle Humbert playing a guitar. She was Picasso's mistress, whom he called *ma jolie* after the title of a popular song.

In *Ma jolie* the surface is fragmented from top to bottom and from left to right so much that we cannot separate the human figure from the background. By breaking the entire surface into Cubist pieces, Picasso did away with the usual relationship between a dominant figure and the subordinate ground around it. To a Cubist's mind, the entire space is important. Any object to be painted exists with and within the surrounding space. Everything is seen as connected with everything else. Shapes as we perceive them in space are all relative—no one of them should dominate. The relativity of our perception is a very twentieth-century attitude. The relevance and assurance of Picasso's new forms and new space exerted a strong influence on a great deal of subsequent twentieth-century art.

Picasso himself offered an insight into the kind of spatial composition that Cubism created when he made some relief sculpture in a Cubist style. To make *Guitar* (FIG. 18-20) he cut ordinary scrap materials into simple geometrical shapes and assembled them into a shallow relief several inches deep. The pieces, which resemble the facets and planes of painted Cubism, lie this way and that. They overlap and intersect and in some places open up the interior of the object. Picasso never exhibited his Cubist reliefs, but a number of sculptors who visited his studio were deeply impressed with them. Every modern sculptor who welds or nails or glues shaped pieces together or assembles things in any way owes Picasso a debt.

African Art

A number of early-twentieth-century artists in addition to Picasso admired and collected pieces of African sculpture. They valued the bold expression of its designs and the essential nature of its forms as the means to wipe the slate clean and make a new beginning in art. Like Gauguin, they probably felt that African artists were closer to the essential truth of visual reality. Picasso and his contemporaries, however,

In this landmark painting Picasso here and there extended the lines of the regular geometric shapes of the figures right to the edge of the canvas. For example, the contours of the forearms of the figure in the upper right are the same lines as those for the edge of the blue curtain. The shapes of the figure's arms are projected into the surrounding space. The projection ties the figure and the surrounding space together, thus making it increasingly difficult to tell where the figure ends and the ground begins. The essential flatness of the surface is preserved, and equality among the shapes across the surface is maintained.

In the Cubist style that Picasso and his friend Georges Braque developed over the next several years, the essential features of their paintings are reduced to colorless patches or planes that are flat and that approach regular geometrical shapes like the square,

FIG 18-21 [Nok, African], head. C. 500 B.C.–A.D 200. Terra cotta, 14 1/4 in (36.2 cm) high. National Museum, Lagos, Nigeria. Werner Forman/Art Resource, New York.

FIG 18-20 PABLO PICASSO [Spanish, 1881–1973], *Guitar.* 1912. Sheet metal and wire, 30 1/2 in. (77.5 cm). Museum of Modern Art, New York. Gift of the artist.

may have had little idea about the range of African sculpture and its actual significance within African society.

Since much African sculpture was carved in wood, which perishes quickly in the climate of Africa, most examples seen in European and American collections date from the nineteenth and early twentieth centuries. Nevertheless, pieces in more durable terra cotta and bronze date back to centuries ago. A number of fully developed terra cotta heads have been found in the village of Nok and other areas in northern Nigeria. The life-sized specimen in FIG. 18-21, which may date as far back as the fifth century B.C., illustrates several characteristics of the Nok style. Within the overall naturalism of the rendition exist a few elements of abstraction: the upper eyelid is horizontal whereas the

lower lid is curved, and the lips, top and bottom, are symmetrical. It is quite possible that the sculpture carried out in the Nok area influenced the idealized bronze and terra cotta pieces of Ife (see the head of an *Oni of Ife* in FIG. 17-12) and then Benin.

Outside of Egypt and Nubia, African sculpture is found predominantly in Nigeria and the forests along the West African coast as well as in the Congo Basin (see the map on p. 464). Of all the many different peoples who inhabit those regions, the Yoruba of southern Nigeria seem to relish most the making of sculpture. These prolific artists work in a variety of materials, techniques, and types including masks, free-standing figures (see *Twin Figure*, FIG. 1-6), and architectural reliefs. Modern African sculptors generally avoid a very close likeness lest they be accused of mere copying. Instead, the Yorubans embody in their art the ideal of behavior they call cool, through the symmetry and the consistency of the masses within the body parts.

African art, like other arts around the world, usually served a function in society, so that divorced from its function, it loses a part of its meaning. African

sculptors carved many masks that were meant to be worn in rituals in which the wearer could be empowered with the spirit of the deity or person the mask expressed. The painted wooden mask in FIG. 18-22, of the Bushongo tribe among the Bakuba people of the Congo, was worn in a dance to promote an increase of some aspect of the life force. The exaggeration of the features of the face were intended to squeeze as much power as possible from the impersonation.

Most of the prominent artists living in Africa today are painters. Paintings on textiles, walls of buildings, or the human body existed in the past in Africa, but most of it has perished because of the impermanent materials. Modern African painters have had some contact with the Western art tradition, especially in the colonial period when art academies were set up in many countries. Today, unfortunately, the painters of most African countries receive little professional training and have no system of galleries, museums, and collectors to sustain them. The situation forces many

African artists to constantly repeat the same design for tourists, in what has been called the Hotel-and-Airport style. Furthermore, the ritual life that inspired much African art in the past is rapidly vanishing.

The Nigerian artist Prince Twins Seven Seven began painting in the 1960s when two Europeans set up an experimental workshop in Oshogbo. He has developed an original and personal style that is yet unmistakably related to the African tradition. A musician and dancer as well as a painter, Twins Seven

Seven paints in ink on wood panels. In his piece *Untitled* (FIG. 18-23) in which a many-armed hunter holds his rifle and prey, he combined illustrations of the myths and symbols of the Yorubans with stories that he invented himself. Within the wavy border of his painting he filled every square inch: masklike faces appear everywhere and a small village scene emerges at the top of the panel. His painting conveys a strong feeling of a spirit-filled world.

Dada and Surrealism

While World War I raged in Europe, a number of artists rebelled against a materialistic society engaged in mass slaughter on the battlefield, by emphasizing the absurd in life. A small group of them assumed the childish name Dada for their movement. In a famous incident, the prominent Dada artist Marcel Duchamp drew a moustache on a reproduction of the *Mona Lisa* and displayed it, as a protest and as a rejection of traditional values. He also exhibited everyday objects as works of art, which he called ready-mades. For example, in 1917 he tried to enter a urinal he named *Fountain* (FIG. 1-21) in an exhibition of art in New York. In another, earlier instance, just before the war broke out, Duchamp took a bicycle wheel, secured it to an ordinary stool, and exhibited the piece, called *Bicycle Wheel* (FIG. 18-24).

Underneath the social protest and the negative mockery of high art, Dada asserted, positively, that art resides in the creative intention of the artist. Duchamp's new intention for the wheel and stool forces us to look at those objects in a different way. Asked to view *Bicycle Wheel* as art, we become aware of the shapes and their relationship to one another. We notice the legs supporting the piece, the circular head, and the frustrated motion of the wheel—instead of ignoring such stylistic and iconographical elements as we do when the components are just utilitarian objects.

After the war, in the 1920s, the absurd element in Dada was put in a more positive light by the Surrealists, who also sought to transform reality into something extraordinary. Led by the poet André Breton, who wrote the movement's manifesto in 1924, Surrealism contended that true reality lies in the subconscious. The discoveries of Sigmund Freud's *The Interpretation of Dreams* (1900), which were just then

FIG 18-24 MARCEL DUCHAMP [French, 1887–1968], *Bicycle Wheel.* Third version, 1951; original, dated 1913, lost. Assemblage: metal wheel mounted on painted wood stool. 50 1/2 in (128.3 cm) high. Museum of Modern Art, New York. The Sidney and Harriet Janis Collection.

becoming popular, influenced Surrealism a great deal with the revelation that dreams were a fundamental avenue to explore the subconscious. Surrealist artists wanted to paint nothing less than the images of the unconscious mind, and therefore they depicted the often irrational combinations of things that seem very real at the time we are dreaming.

In *Two Children Are Threatened by a Nightingale* (FIG. 18-25) the Surrealist artist Max Ernst made the sweet and gentle songbird a source of terror in the same way that ordinary things become causes of fright in a nightmare. He combined traditional painting

FIG 18-25   MAX ERNST [German, 1891–1976], *Two Children Are Threatened by a Nightingale*. 1924. Oil on wood, with wood construction, 27 1/2 × 22 1/2 in. (69.9 × 57.2 cm). Museum of Modern Art, New York.

FIG 18-26   MAN RAY [American, 1890–1976], *Rayograph*. 1923. Gelatin-silver print, 11 1/2 × 9 3/4 in. Museum of Modern Art, New York. Gift of James Thrall Soby. Image © 1992 The Man Ray Trust–ADAGP–ARS.

with miniature real objects so as to destroy the distinction between illusion and reality. Objects lie within and in front of the deep, dark frame, obscuring the distinction between picture space and real space, between the dream world and real life. In the painted portion, one child lies dead and another threatens the bird with a knife—or perhaps she is running from her victim on the ground. On the rooftop a faceless man carrying a child runs toward an actual door buzzer to set off an alarm. Ernst's work makes no rational sense, but for that very reason it captures the feel of a dream as it stimulates hidden recesses of our unconscious imagination.

The Surrealist artists Joan Miró (see *Personages with Star*, FIG. 4-25) and Yves Tanguy (see *Indefinite Divisibility*, FIG. 5-4) explored the possibility of an abstract Surrealism in their work. Salvador Dalí (see *The Persistence of Memory*, FIG. 2-34) and René Magritte (see *The Birthday*, FIG. 7-11), with the nearly photographic realism of their work, have become pop-

ular exponents of Surrealism. The American photographer Man Ray, who was closely associated with Duchamp and the Surrealists, produced a Surrealist photography that exploited chance and the dislocation of things from everyday reality. To make his *Rayograph* (FIG. 18-26), a pun on his name, he randomly placed objects on a piece of light-sensitive paper in a darkroom and then exposed the paper momentarily to light. By means of his cameraless photography, the soft white silhouettes of real objects seem to float through space in a dreamy new existence.

Expressionism, Cubism, Dada, and Surrealism in the early years of the twentieth century became the basis for many new styles and new ways of seeing throughout the century. Cubism taught the twentieth century to see picture space in a new way. No longer a mirror of nature, pictorial space is now constructed afresh by each artist. Van Gogh and Matisse taught twentieth-century artists to express their feelings in color and form. They perpetuated the romantic celebration of subjectivity. Kandinsky pioneered pure subjectivity, painting nonobjective compositions of lines and colors. The Surrealists made the century aware of the subconscious and opened the door wide to the artist's free use of fantasy and imagination. Throughout the rest of the century other artists have adapted the achievements of these pioneers to their own needs. In many ways, twentieth-century artists have been working out the possibilities in the modern style established by Picasso, Matisse, Duchamp, and other artists at the beginning of the century.

Futurism

In 1910 several Italian artists, among them Umberto Boccioni and Giacomo Balla (see *Automobile Speed + Light + Noises*, FIG. 7-7), declared that they would reflect the dynamism of modern life in their art. They had read the *Manifesto of Futurism* of the poet F. T. Marinetti, who wrote that a "roaring automobile, which appears to run like a machine gun, is more beautiful than the *Victory of Samothrace*," the most famous Greek statue in the Louvre Museum.[1] Italian Futurist artists rejected all the representational art of the past and declared that museums ought to be swept clean of them. They set out instead to depict the movement of forms in space and the integration of all material bodies in space as revealed by modern science.

Boccioni illustrated these ideas in his bronze sculpture *Unique Forms of Continuity in Space* (FIG. 18-27). The masses of the powerful running figure flow out into the space around it, and space penetrates the figure's masses. The flowing curved masses indicate the different positions of the figure through successive moments of time. The sculpture is filled with lines of force that express dynamic motion, a key feature of Futurism. Many Futurist artists, like Boccioni in his painting *Dynamism of a Soccer Player* (FIG. 4-6) changed the flat facets of Cubism into something dynamic by repeating them rhythmically and by projecting them across the picture space as lines of force.

Constructivism

One of the most creative periods in the modern movement occurred in Russia between 1910 and about 1925. In the early years of the twentieth century

FIG 18-27 UMBERTO BOCCIONI [Italian, 1882–1916], *Unique Forms of Continuity in Space*. 1913, cast 1931. Bronze, 43 1/3 in. (110.1 cm) high. Museum of Modern Art, New York. Acquired through the Lillie P. Bliss Bequest.

Russia was in turmoil as new ideas from the West fanned the fires of revolution against the oppressive czarist regime. The avant-garde artists of Russia welcomed and celebrated the victory of the Russian Revolution of 1917, and many Russian artists dedicated their work to the service of the utopian communist state. Their modern art would help revolutionize society and help build the new socialist culture. In a short number of years before the revolution, Natalia Goncharova, Kazimir Malevich, and other Russian artists had absorbed the lessons of the Post-Impressionists and of Matisse and Picasso. In general, they combined the modern style from France with the colorful primitivism of their own folk art.

FIG 18-28 LYUBOV POPOVA [Russian, 1889–1924], *Constructivist Composition*. 1921. Oil on panel, 36 5/8 × 24 1/4 in. (93 × 61.5 cm). Courtesy private collection.

When the Russian Revolution began in 1917, the painter Lyubov Popova was practicing a dynamic form of Cubism that Russians also called Futurism. By the early 1920s she had moved from the investigation of Cubist space to the construction of nonobjective lines and planes, or Constructivism. In her *Constructivist Composition* (FIG. 18-28), diagonal lines crisscross the panel. They can be read as thin strips or the leading edges of intersecting planes. Since it exhibits no Cubist buildup toward the center, her painting seems like a fragment of a new kind of visual world.

Popova was concerned only with the material organization of the visual elements, in the belief that the solution of these design problems would contribute to the new socialist society. She and her Contructivist colleagues in fact soon gave up easel painting altogether and devoted themselves to theater, furniture, and textile design and to book illustration and graphic design. A few years after her early death, the Soviet Union under Stalin turned its back on the Russian artists who had struggled to create a new visual art for the Revolution. Some were persecuted; others fled the country.

De Stijl: Mondrian

The lessons of Cubism had a different effect on the Dutch painter Piet Mondrian, who was the theoretician for a group of Dutch artists and architects, founded in 1917, called De Stijl (Style). In a typical work of Mondrian's maturity, *Composition with Red, Yellow and Blue* (FIG. 18-29), the intuitively formed and ambiguously placed shapes of Cubism give way to a carefully thought-out choice of elements. Purging his style of personal expression, Mondrian reduced the facets of Cubism to the most basic of visual means. He distilled all lines to the intersection of only horizontal and vertical lines; he subsumed all shapes into the rectangle; he expressed every possibility of light by black and white, every color by the three primaries, red, yellow, and blue. To Mondrian these were the fundamental principles of nature, corresponding to essential mental antitheses such as active and passive, male and female. His paintings were not an imitation of nature—not even a reduction or abstraction of forms found in nature—but the re-creation of the reality of nature and the underlying forces of nature.

To express the dynamic harmony of reality, Mondrian arranged his essential elements in an asymmetrical balance. A large rectangle might play against several small rectangles. A rectangle of attractive color counterbalances the activity of a number of lines. The size, shape, and location of each element in a Mondrian composition is adjusted to the balance of the whole. No one element stands out and demands attention.

Mondrian was a mystic who looked for ultimate reality and who envisioned that the universally true harmony of the visual elements in his paintings would spread over all society and make the world a better place. His dream of universal community through art may not have come true, but a lot of modern architecture and modern design throughout the world speaks the language of his rectangular style.

FIG 18-29   PIET MONDRIAN [Dutch, 1872–1944], *Composition with Red, Yellow and Blue*. 1922. Oil on fabric, 16 1/2 × 19 1/4 in. (41.9 × 48.9 cm). Minneapolis Institute of Arts. Gift of Mr. and Mrs. Bruce Dayton.

Sculpture: Brancusi

The desire to simplify external reality in order to attain the essence of things also became manifest in twentieth-century sculpture. Likewise, the example of arts from around the world demonstrated to Western sculptors which forms to use in order to attain essential reality. When Constantin Brancusi, a true pioneer of twentieth-century sculpture, carved the portrait of the artist-dancer *Mademoiselle Pogany* (FIG. 18-30) in his Paris studio, he was striving to reduce the forms of nature to a basic egg-shaped mass, symbolizing the origin of all life. The wide eyes and arched brows of his bust portrait came from African masks. Brancusi's primitivism took him far from the emotional expression and rippling surface of Rodin's *The Thinker* (FIG. 18-9). Mademoiselle Pogany's tubular arms taper to her hands at the side of her head, and the curving, steamlined flow of the forms reproduce the lanky, long-necked grace of a dancer. Brancusi's witty and often elegant sculpture demonstrated to generations of artists how to shape elemental masses and portray primitive essences.

FIG 18-30   CONSTANTIN BRANCUSI [Rumanian, 1876–1957], *Mademoiselle Pogany*. 1913. Marble, 17 1/4 in. (43.8 cm) high. Philadelphia Museum of Art. Given by Mrs. Rodolphe Meyer de Schauensee.

The Bauhaus

In 1919, the year after the end of the First World War, the **Bauhaus,** the most famous school of art in modern times, was founded in Weimar, Germany, by the architect Walter Gropius. Over the years the Bauhaus had on its staff an illustrious group of teachers: Paul Klee arrived in 1921; Wassily Kandinsky joined in 1922. Josef Albers and others transformed the curriculum after 1923 into a systematic study of visual elements

Fig 18-31 Walter Gropius [German-American, 1883–1969], Bauhaus. 1926. Dessau, Germany. Vanni/Art Resource, New York.

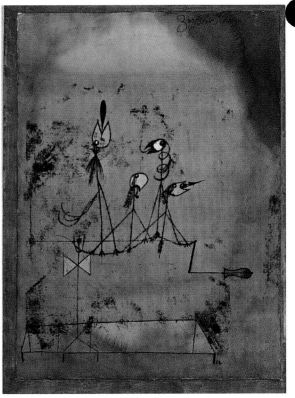

Fig 18-32 Paul Klee [Swiss-German, 1879–1940], *Twittering Machine*. 1922. Watercolor, pen and ink on oil transfer drawing, on paper mounted on cardboard, 16 1/4 × 12 in. (41.3 × 30.5 cm). Museum of Modern Art, New York.

and their application not only in painting and sculpture but also in the applied arts. In fact, those at the Bauhaus did not distinguish between the fine arts and crafts, and a community or team spirit united all the arts. During its turbulent fourteen-year history, ideas of every kind were put to the test, resulting in simple, unornamented household furnishings (see the side chair in Fig. 14-25) and graphic design.

In 1926 the Bauhaus moved to Dessau, Germany, where Gropius designed new buildings (see Fig. 18-31) that became the foundation for the **International style** of modern architecture. Constructed of reinforced concrete, the flat-roofed buildings contained classrooms, workshops, a cafeteria, a theater, and twenty-eight studio-dormitory rooms. The glass curtain wall that encased the workshop building stood free from the piers a few feet behind. A two-story-high bridge across a road connected the workshops with the administration building.

After Hannes Meyer, a militant Marxist, ran the school for a few years, the architect Mies van der Rohe was appointed director from 1930 to 1933, when the school closed under pressure from Fascists and Nazis who condemned the Bauhaus as a nest of Communists and Jews. Nevertheless, its art, architecture, design, and art theory influenced the course of modern art long after its closing.

The Swiss-German artist Klee helped direct several craft workshops at the Bauhaus and for years taught

the course in basic design. He gave formal lectures to his students from carefully prepared notes, which were later published, then encouraged them to experiment. He taught them not to copy nature in their art but to let art grow out of its basic elements: point, line, plane, space. In his own work—for example, *Vocal Fabric of the Singer Rosa Silber* (Fig. 6-4)—he often invented whimsical designs in which the clever title is very much part of the visual message.

In *Twittering Machine* (Fig. 18-32) Klee sketched in pen and watercolor a fantastic instrument for producing bird song by turning a crank. His delicate lines, tiny shapes, and artless style arouse in us disquieting questions. Why make a machine for something so natural? Is a machine for reproducing the sweet sound of birds serious or comic? Is the simple drawing the work of a child or a madman? Seldom do such simple means stimulate the imagination as much as they do in Klee's art.

Mexican Murals

In the 1920s, 1930s, and 1940s, the painters Diego Rivera, José Clemente Orozco, and David Alfaro Siqueiros led a resurgence of mural painting in Mexico. The new socialist government of Mexico offered the artists the walls of schools and government buildings for fresco paintings that would condemn the historical forces of oppression, glorify the people of Mexico, and illustrate the bright future promised through revolutionary social change. The artists were actively committed to the government's task of educating the people and winning their favor through art. They succeeded in creating a new image for the Mexican nation, which helped forge a new national identity.

Their fame also brought them work in the United States. In the early 1930s Rivera painted murals in San Francisco, Detroit, and New York. Orozco worked at Pomona College, California; in New York; and at Darmouth College, New Hampshire.

In his murals at the National School of Agriculture, Chapingo, Mexico, Rivera painted a secular chapel reminiscent of Giotto's Arena Chapel or Michelangelo's Sistine Chapel in the Renaissance. Rivera's style combines the lessons of Post-Impressionism, which he had learned in Paris; early Renaissance fresco painting; Mayan art; and the popular art of the Mexican printmaker José Posada (see *La calavera catrina*, FIG. 9-15). At the top of the main fresco, *The Fertile Earth* (FIG. 18-33), Rivera depicted a gigantic figure of Mother Earth, who greets the viewer with one hand and holds out new plant life with the other. At the bottom stands the family of New Man, who accepts fire from Prometheus rising out of the volcanic earth. The powerful River Goddess hides her face on the left. The mural proclaims that utopian progress harnesses the basic elements of the earth: earth, wind, water, and fire. In a forceful language of large simple forms, Rivera glorified the benefits of irrigation, electrification, and industrialization for the people of revolutionary Mexico.

1930s Art

The 1930s witnessed the rise of Fascism in Italy, Spain, and Germany, where Hitler ridiculed modern art as degenerate. The decade also witnessed the dictator-

FIG 18-33 DIEGO RIVERA [Mexican, 1886–1957], *The Fertile Earth (Frutas de la tierra)*. 1926–1927. Mural 11 1/2 × 11 1/2 ft. (3.54 × 3.53 m). National School of Agriculture, Chapingo, Mexico. Photo by James Prigoff.

ship of Stalin, which crushed every trace of revolutionary art in Russia. It saw the Great Depression and a world heading relentlessly to a second great war. While social realism characterized art in Mexico and the United States, in France Surrealism became the dominant artistic force. It even attracted Picasso, who used Surrealist principles of distortion and psychic investigation as a new means to express the crises in the world.

In 1937 Picasso painted the mural *Guernica* (FIG. 18-34). During the Spanish civil war the small town of Guernica, the capital of the Basque region of Spain, was the first city in history to receive saturation bombing from the air. Picasso rapidly painted the mural

FIG 18-34 PABLO PICASSO [Spanish, 1881–1973], *Guernica*. 1937. Oil on canvas, 11 1/2 × 25 2/3 ft. (3.5 × 7.8 m). Prado Museum, Madrid. Giraudon/Art Resource, New York.

illustrating this uniquely twentieth-century experience, for the pavilion of the ill-fated Spanish republic at the Paris World's Fair that year. It did not take much imagination in 1937 to see that the bombing of civilian populations by the Fascists was a nightmarish prediction of things to come.

Rather than illustrating the actual bombing, Picasso developed the iconography of *Guernica* from the ritual killing of the bullfight and other traditional sources. The scene is ineffectually illuminated by the harsh light of a bare bulb overhead. On the left a bull, the symbol of brute force and darkness, menaces a screaming woman holding her dead son—a reference to the *pietà*, the image of Mary mourning over the body of Christ in Christian art (see Michelangelo's *Pietà*, p. 183). The horse of the picador—the rider who stabs the bull's neck and shoulder muscles with a spear to weaken them—writhes in pain because it has

been wounded by the picador's spear. Picasso said the horse represented the people. At its feet lie the broken limbs of a warrior—perhaps the statue of a hero from a different time when warriors had faces. On the right a woman in flames leaps from a burning building. An elongated head and arm protrude from a window and try to illuminate the scene with a lamp.

Guernica, painted in black, white, and gray, has a fairly balanced and traditional composition—a triangle—that keeps the Cubist planes and ambiguous space organized across the compressed surface. But the gross distortion of the figures, especially of the human figures, aptly fits the madness of the event. In this painting Picasso successfully amalgamated the facets and shallow space of Cubism, the dreamlike and irrational connections of Surrealism, and the distortions of Expressionism into a powerful evocation of a very shameful practice of twentieth-century war.

Key Terms and Concepts

art nouveau	Die Brücke	Pointillism
Bauhaus	International style	Salon
contemporary art	modern art	Salon des Refusés

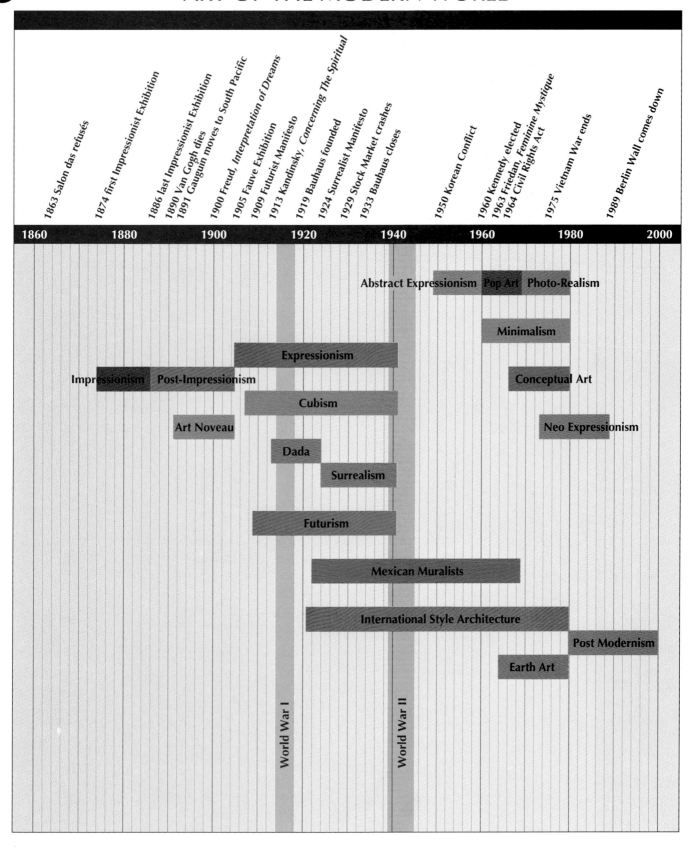

1863 Salon das refusés
1874 first Impressionist Exhibition
1886 last Impressionist Exhibition
1890 Van Gogh dies
1891 Gauguin moves to South Pacific
1900 Freud, Interpretation of Dreams
1905 Fauve Exhibition
1909 Futurist Manifesto
1913 Kandinsky, Concerning The Spiritual
1919 Bauhaus founded
1924 Surrealist Manifesto
1929 Stock Market crashes
1933 Bauhaus closes
1950 Korean Conflict
1960 Kennedy elected
1963 Friedan, Feminine Mystique
1964 Civil Rights Act
1975 Vietnam War ends
1989 Berlin Wall comes down

| 1860 | 1880 | 1900 | 1920 | 1940 | 1960 | 1980 | 2000 |

Abstract Expressionism Pop Art Photo-Realism

Minimalism

Expressionism

Impressionism Post-Impressionism

Conceptual Art

Cubism

Art Noveau

Neo Expressionism

Dada

Surrealism

Futurism

Mexican Muralists

International Style Architecture

Post Modernism

Earth Art

World War I

World War II

19

ART OF THE SECOND HALF
OF THE TWENTIETH CENTURY

FIG 19-1 JACKSON POLLOCK [American, 1912–1956], *Convergence (Number 10, 1952)*. 1952. Oil on canvas, 93 1/2 × 156 in. (237.5 × 396.2 cm). Albright-Knox Art Gallery, Buffalo. Gift of Seymour H. Knox, 1956.

Abstract Expressionism

When World War II ended, the world inherited the atom bomb, a divided Europe, and an arms race among powerful, cold warriors. America, the relatively unscathed victor, found itself the world's political leader and the dominant economic power. Migrations of large numbers of people in and out of cities as well as the spread of television and suburbia changed the nation's lifestyle. American culture quickly rose from a provincial status to an international force. During the war Mondrian and many Surrealists—Breton, Dalí, Tanguy—lived in exile in the United States. Stimulated by their work and impelled by their example, American artists asserted their independence of

Europe, and the New York school soon established its leadership in the art world.

Artists in New York—Jackson Pollock, Franz Kline (see *Buttress*, FIG. 8-7), and Willem de Kooning (see *Woman IV*, FIG. 2-36), to name a few—boldly asserted the new Abstract Expressionist style by making very visible, energetic gestures on relatively large canvases. Since their tangible brushwork reproduced the action of the painter in the process of creating, their style also became known as **Action Painting.** While becoming a hero of American art of almost mythic proportions, Pollock led the way with his notorious dripped-and-splattered paintings like *Convergence (Number 10, 1952)* (FIG. 19-1).

The Abstract Expressionists, who felt new freedom, energy, and self-assurance in postwar America, also built on styles invented before them. They expressed themselves in paint like any Expressionist. Like Wassily Kandinsky they created forms floating in space with their painted gestures. Like the Surrealists they found meaning in automatic painting where chance and accidents help reveal the inner person and create dreamlike images and shapes. They felt that their free and irrationally applied gestures and color fields were modern equivalent of the totems once worshiped by some cultures.

Other Abstract Expressionists—Mark Rothko (see *Orange and Lilac over Ivory*, FIG. 5-14) and Barnett Newman, for example—painted large areas of color in the exploration of their inner selves. Their style of Abstract Expressionism is called **Color Field Painting.** Newman's search to express his spiritual being led him to cultivate a style of large canvases painted uniformly in a single strong color and cut by thin stripes of another color. In *Covenant* (FIG. 19-2) two stripes of black and a light yellowish color subdivide the deep maroon canvas into three unequal parts. Newman called the stripes zips, perhaps because they opened up the uniform color field to new possibilities of perception. The large field of color has a mesmerizing effect, and the intuitive placement of the dissecting stripes sends ambiguous signals to our perceptions about space, color, and rhythmic pulsations.

The two stripes in *Covenant* seem symmetrically placed because the stronger value and color contrasts on the right balance the visual stimulation of the larger color field on the left. The two very different stripes thus bring the painting into agreement—the meaning of the word *covenant*. The stark assertion of the vertical stripes in a mysterious field of color evokes feelings

Text continues on page 532

FIG 19-2   BARNETT NEWMAN [American, 1905–1970], *Covenant*. 1949. Oil on canvas, 47 3/4 × 59 5/8 in. (121.9 × 152.4 cm). Hirshorn Museum and Sculpture Garden, Smithsonian Institution, Washington, D.C. Gift of Joseph H. Hirshorn Foundation, 1972. Photo by Lee Stalsworth.

Jackson Pollock (1912–1956)

*I*N 1947, just as Jackson Pollock was starting to drip and splatter paint on canvas laid on the floor, he wrote a brief statement about his technique. This artist of few words never described his working methods more fully than in these short paragraphs:

I prefer to tack the unstretched canvas to the hard wall or the floor. I need the resistance of a hard surface. On the floor I am more at ease. I feel nearer, more a part of the painting, since this way I can walk around it, work from the four sides and literally be in the painting. This is akin to the method of the Indian sand paintings of the West.

I continue to get further away from the usual painter's tools such as easel, palette, brushes, etc. I prefer sticks, trowels, knives and dripping fluid paint or a heavy impasto with sand, broken glass and other foreign matter added.

When I am in my painting, I am not aware of what I am doing. It is only after a sort of "get acquainted" period that I see what I have been about. I have no fears about making changes, destroying the image, etc., because the painting has a life of its own. I try to let it come through. It is only when I lose contact with the painting that the result is a mess. Otherwise there is pure harmony, an easy give and take, and the painting comes out well.[2]

Jackson Pollock at work in his studio at East Hampton, Long Island, 1950. Photo © 1990 by Hans Namuth.

When Pollock placed the canvas on the floor so that he could walk around and be in the painting, he was thinking of the painting as a landscape—a sprawling space like the American West where he grew up. Born in Wyoming, Pollock lived near Phoenix—where he may have seen Navajo sand painters—and in various places in California. Although the network of painted splatters and drips in his work tends to double back on itself and stays within the canvas, his designs could stretch endlessly. Pollock, who preferred large canvases, knew how to paint on a large scale because he was trained in New York by the muralist Thomas Hart Benton. In New York in the 1930s he also came in contact with Mexican mural painters like David Alfaro Siqueiros.

Pollock found it possible to drip and splatter paint and pour paint straight from the can thanks to his acquaintance with the ideas of a number of European Surrealist artists who were exiled in New York during World War II. They taught him that the source of art lies in the unconscious and that even accidental drips on a canvas could be signs of that unconscious life. European Expressionists, like Ernst Ludwig Kirchner (see *Street, Dresden*, FIG. 18-16), for years had also used visible brush marks and thick streaks of paint as symbols of their feelings and thoughts. Like the Expressionists, Pollock wanted to express himself in paint, but instead of describing or arranging his feelings he directly expressed his personality. The splattered and tangled lines of paint become not the representation but the equivalent of his feelings.

Pollock was an intense and troubled individual. He was an alcoholic—quiet and hardworking when he was sober; belligerent, aggressive, foulmouthed, and destructive when he drank. Whatever unshakable demon tormented his psyche, his driving personality expressed

itself in large, energy-filled paintings.

Pollock did not work from drawings, but the linearity of his drips and splashes has some of the characteristics of a drawing in paint. Moreover, like most drawings, each painting is a fresh creation. Pollock's work has been called Action Painting in the sense that it records the energetic gestures of his body in action.

When Pollock began a painting, he doodled, as it were. He may have had a general idea of what he was about, but at this initial stage of his work he came closest to Surrealist techniques of "automatic writing" that attempt to explore the unconscious. This stage was what he called his "get acquainted" period. Then the painting itself gradually took over in the sense that the forms already on the canvas suggested new forms: new lines, new drips and splashes to work with. The danger in painting as Pollock did is that the artist can lose control of the design and the canvas can become a mess and a muddle. If Pollock made some bad decisions about his design, his technique did not allow him to correct mistakes or make improvements. Instead, he abandoned and destroyed what he had done.

In 1949 *Life Magazine* published a double-page feature devoted to Pollock, asking whether he was "the greatest living American artist."[3] The words were those of the critic Clement Greenberg. Pollock knew success: each year between 1944 and 1952 he exhibited his work in a prominent New York gallery to general critical acclaim. Yet

Pollock directly expressed his personality in his paintings. The splattered and tangled lines of paint became not the representation but the equivalent of his feelings.

during his lifetime he sold only a handful of paintings and was quite poor. Crushed under the intense public pressure to produce something new and different, he painted nothing the last two years of his life before he died in a car accident. Despite the tragedy of his private and public life, Pollock was a pioneering art hero, not only in his innovative techniques but also because he broke the ice and won worldwide acceptance for American avant-garde art.

Fig 19-3   Isamu Noguchi [American, 1904–1988], *Woman with Child.* 1958. Marble, 44 in. (111.8 cm). Cleveland Museum of Art. Contemporary Collection (66.48).

of awe and power that have reminded critics of the eighteenth-century notion of the sublime in art. Many of Newman's paintings, like *Covenant*, have religious titles that point to the metaphysical significance that he sought to secure within his art.

In the 1950s, while Henry Moore (see *Reclining Figure: Angles*, Fig. 13-1) and David Smith (see *Cubi XVII*, Fig. 4-22) were emerging as leading sculptors on the international art scene, the career of Isamu Noguchi likewise continued to accelerate in accomplishment and fame. Noguchi's *Woman with Child* (Fig. 19-3) nicely illustrates his sculptural sensitivity. Born of an American mother in Los Angeles, Noguchi grew up in Japan, then studied sculpture in New York and in Paris with Brancusi. The roots of his imagination are truly international. For half a century, Noguchi was extremely successful especially in creating monumental public sculpture around the world.

Noguchi worked in a number of traditional and nontraditional materials, but he stood out for his ability to extend the potential of stone and coax new and modern feelings out of that medium. In *Woman with Child* he sawed, drilled, and polished the marble or left part of the stone unformed in its natural rough state. The contrast between the smooth cylindrical masses and the rugged block embracing them alludes to primitive feelings about woman and pregnancy and about male and female. Noguchi felt that because stone was a fundamental element of the earth, it was thus the primary natural medium to express the meaning of life.

Post–World War II Architecture: The International Style and Le Corbusier

After World War II the International style of architecture, evident in the Bauhaus and pioneered in the United States by Mies van der Rohe became the common language of modernity. Lever House (Fig. 19-4), designed by Skidmore, Owings, and Merrill, one of the largest architectural firms in the United States, makes an elegant variation on the idiom of the International style. An early example of the steel-and-glass office tower in New York City, it consists of a tall vertical glass slab rising on short stilts above a low horizontal slab that covers the building plot. The horizontal second floor is also raised on stilts, above a street-level

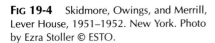

FIG **19-4**   Skidmore, Owings, and Merrill, Lever House, 1951–1952. New York. Photo by Ezra Stoller © ESTO.

plaza, and is open to the sky in its middle. Since the vertical window mullions form only a delicate netting over the tall vertical slab, horizontal bands of green material dominate the design. The poise and proportions of the two slabs in this structure have seldom been matched in countless subsequent International-style buildings.

Although the French architect Le Corbusier had been one of the inventors of the International style during the 1920s and 1930s, after World War II he proposed a very different alternative to it. Corbusier's pilgrimage church Notre Dame du Haut at Ronchamp in a remote part of eastern France challenged the rigid glass-and-steel box in every way. Abandoning the smooth machine-made appearance of the Inter-

national style's flat planes, Le Corbusier built a chapel of curved concrete forms that reflect the undulating hills of the site. As the pilgrim approaches the church from one angle, the structure appears to have a wedge shape like that of the prow of a ship cutting through space (see FIG. 19-5). (The wedge is actually one corner of an essentially rectangular plan.) On top of the curved and sloping thick walls rests an enormous roof that curves upward like a hollow shell. Le Corbusier molded the forms of the building as freely as sculptors model in clay or as freely as painters express their personality on canvas.

In many ways the building seems to have been constructed simply with the centuries-old thick-wall building techniques of rural southern Europe.

Although a framework of reinforced concrete lies hidden within them, the walls were made broad and massive with rough masonry, which was then coated with sprayed gunite (a mixture of cement, sand, and water). Randomly placed windows penetrate their depth. On the interior (FIG. 19-6) a subdued light enters the chapel through the deeply recessed windows and through a slit along the top of the walls. Separated from the walls by the strip of light, the bulging roof floats weightlessly overhead. Despite the massiveness of La Cobusier's forms, they do not oppress. They embody instead a feeling of intimacy and an aura of mystery.

The 1960s: Pop Art, Minimalism, and Conceptual Art

From the assassinations of John F. Kennedy and Martin Luther King to the divisive upheaval of the Vietnam War, the 1960s were a time of turmoil and change, in contrast to the apparent calm of the preceding decade and a half. American society was galvanized by the civil rights movement and convulsed by protests against the war. Hippies became the byword for dropouts from society and rebels against the establishment. When the Vietnam War gripped the nation, however, many artists recoiled from the moral dilemmas of American society into increased formalism. At the same time, the nation was reaping the fruits of life centered on television and mass marketing to suburbia. As the space race joined the arms race, the late 1960s saw economic boom and the increased commercialization of art as a commodity.

Even before the decade began, in the late 1950s Robert Rauschenburg (see *First Landing Jump*, FIG. 10-20) and Jasper Johns (see *Painting with Two Balls*, FIG. 10-5) had broken away from the heroic gestures of Abstract Expressionism by introducing representation and even real objects into their art. Then Pop Art made a consideration splash in the early 1960s with imagery drawn from advertising and the popular media. A leading Pop Artist, Andy Warhol, transformed the images of cult heroes like Marilyn Monroe and Elvis, or he painted deadpan images of a Campbell's soup can (see *Big Campbell's Soup Can, 19¢*, FIG. 19-7) and a box of Brillo pads in the flat colors of industrial design.

In complete revolt against the bold brush strokes and aggression self-expression of the Abstract Expressionists, Warhol remained passive in his art, like the millions of Americans who sit in front of their television set every night, watching the very same commercial imagery. Nevertheless, Pop Art restored the

FIG 19-7   ANDY WARHOL [American, 1927?–1987], *Big Campbell's Soup Can, 19¢*. 1962. Acrylic and pencil on canvas, 72 × 54 1/2 in. (182.9 × 138.4 cm). The Menil Collection, Houston. Photo by Paul Hester.

FIG 19-8   CLAES OLDENBURG [American. 1020–], *Three-way Plug, Scale A (Soft) Prototype in Blue*. 1971. Naugahyde, wood, chain, plastic, wire. 144 × 77 × 59 in. (365.8 × 195.6 × 150 cm). Des Moines Art Center. Purchased with funds from the Coffin Fine Arts Trust, Nathan Emory Coffin Collection. 1972.92.

importance of representational iconography to art after a generation dominated by abstraction. It asserted that advertising, comic strips, movies, and television had become the true visual reality of the second half of the twentieth century. The presentation of these commonplace images in Pop Art sometimes recalled the absurdity of Dada, yet in a positive vein Pop Art commented on the impersonality of consumer products and of the mass media and on the materialism that forms the basis of American society.

Claes Oldenburg developed a sculptural form of Pop Art by enlarging common household objects like a hamburger, a clothespin, or an electrical plug to an enormous scale. At such a gigantic scale, these items appear both comical and frightening. Oldenburg frequently translated them into a soft material that appears as pliant and friendly as flesh. The transformations both celebrate the forms of the commonplace

object and change it into something surprisingly different. For example, suspended from the ceiling, *Three-Way Plug—Scale A, Soft* (FIG. 19-8) floats like a parade balloon or walks on legs like a many-mouthed monster. On the floor, it slumps limply to the ground—its usefulness thoroughly contradicted. Another version of *Three-Way Plug*, made of steel and bronze, has been forced by gravity, as it were, to lie half buried underground. Oldenburg's cleverness recognized the mysterious nature of everyday reality that no one had thought to be art.

In the late 1960s another group of artists emerged, the Minimalists, who pared the visual elements down to a bare minimum. The Minimalists also rejected Expressionism for something like the cool detachment apparent in the attitude of the Pop Artists. However, the Minimalists remained in the mainstream of modern abstract art, since their work reflects earlier

FIG 19-9   AGNES MARTIN [American, 1912–], *The Tree.* 1965. Acrylic and graphite on canvas, 72 × 72 in. (182.9 × 182.9 cm). Albright-Knox Art Gallery, Buffalo. Gift of Seymor H. Knox, 1976.

FIG 19-10   DONALD JUDD [American, 1928–], *Untitled.* 1969. Galvanized iron and plexiglas (amber), 120 × 27 1/8 × 24 in. (304.8 × 68.9 × 61 cm). Albright-Knox Art Gallery, Buffalo. Edmund Hayes Fund, 1972.

Constructivist tendencies. In fact, they took the reduction to elemental and primary forms to its ultimate conclusion and produced elegant paintings and sculpture of the simplest geometric shapes.

Working in New York City, the Minimalist Agnes Martin went beyond Mondrian in reducing her forms to just the essentials. On a six-foot-square canvas that she called *The Tree* (FIG. 19-9), Martin drew hundreds of straight pencil lines creating thousands of thin rectangles. She employed no optical illusion to dazzle the eye. Her drawing simply broke the big square canvas into something mysteriously fragmented. The once powerful square now seems light in weight and tremulous. Her painting hints at fleeting experience.

The Minimalist sculptor Donald Judd created *Untitled* (FIG. 19-10), in which rectangular metal boxes defy gravity as they hover horizontally against a wall. The equally large gaps between them contradict the feeling that they are stacked on top of one another. Fabricated in an industrial foundry and painted with automotive colors, the smooth boxes are uniform

in manufacture, machine made, and devoid of any trace of the artist's hand. They have been called primary structures because they simply assert masses and voids in the most elemental and physical way. Judd's work contains no visual metaphors of personal or philosophical significance; it presents no illusion of space, only the real space and void of the piece itself.

In Minimalism, an important part of the modern movement reached an impasse in the sense that visual forms could not get much more pure or primitive without disappearing altogether. In fact, in the late 1960s several Conceptual Artists no longer made any objects. Often they merely documented their intentions with photographs and printed statements. Some

536

FIG 19-11 JOSEPH KOSUTH [American, 1945–], *One and Three Chairs*. 1965. Wooden folding chair, 32 3/8 × 14 7/8 × 20 7/8 in. (82.2 × 37.8 × 53 cm); photographic copy of a chair, 36 × 24 1/8 in. (91.4 × 61.3 cm); and photographic enlargement of dictionary definition of *chair*, 24 × 24 1/8 in. (61 × 61.3 cm). Museum of Modern Art, New York. Larry Aldrich Foundation Fund. Photo © 1994 The Museum of Modern Art, New York.

Conceptural Artists have been known to put their ideas for a new piece down on paper and leave it at that—without executing the work at all. Works in any media that call into question the very existence of the art object and our perception of art—often with clever wit—characterize the phenomenon of Conceptual Art.

In *One and Three Chairs* (FIG. 19-11) the Conceptual Artist Joseph Kosuth examined the nature of perception itself with the chair—the classic example used to discuss the nature of reality and the ideal. As installed in the museum, a real chair acts as a fulcrum balancing and equating a flat visual image of a chair and an abstract dictionary definition of the word *chair*. Or perhaps Kosuth has merely lined up the three chairs in a row and asked whether they are equal.

Conceptual Art began as a protest against the development of art as a high-priced, mass-produced commodity. In a positive vein, it also reaffirms the principle that art lies in the intention of the artist to transform perception rather than in the making of an object.

Likewise, artists in the 1960s staged happenings and performance art—works that are not collectible or salable objects (see the discussion at the end of chapter 13). Happenings cannot even be repeated because they depended on spontaneity. Tired of producing more objects to be consumed by an eager art-buying public, Michael Heizer (see *Double Negative*, FIG. 13-27) and other sculptors directed bulldozers to build one-of-a-kind earthworks in remote locations. Christo began wrapping buildings and transforming nature with temporary curtains across the land (see *Running Fence*, FIG. 8-10). Sculpture came out of the studio and off the pedestal to interact in an organic way with a specific site or situation.

The 1970s: Photo-Realism and Other Trends

The Vietnam War continued into the 1970s, only to be eclipsed by the Watergate scandal. Both events shook America's confidence in big government and raised concerns about the misuse of power. The oil embargo and energy crisis called into question limitless industrial progress and exposed the international nature of energy and the environment. The nation lost some of its naive idealism, and the me generation sought self-gratification instead of the solutions to social problems. Nevertheless, the feminist movement began to change

the consciousness of the entire population about the second-class status of half the population.

Even as Minimalism continued into the 1970s, a traditional realism returned to prominence in sculpture with the work of Duane Hanson (see *Woman with Dog*, FIG. 13-23) and several other artists. In painting, the new realism aspired to imitating the reality of the photographic image. Preceded by the realistic styles of Alice Neel and Philip Pearlstein, Chuck Close (see *Big Self-Portrait*, FIG. 7-10), Richard Estes, and other Photo-realists in the 1970s based their art on a photograph or the appearances of a photograph.

In general, a photograph freezes light reflections for the painter, and turns a fleeting moment into something permanent. In *Michigan Avenue with View of the Art Institute* (FIG. 19-12) Estes not only painted myriad details across the entire surface, as is typical of photography, he also imitated the range of highlights and value contrasts that give photography a distinctive appearance. The nearly deserted street scene on the right is mirrored in the glass on the left. The equiva-

lent reflections in the glass tend to flatten out the illusion of reality, call into question the very notion of solid objects in real space, and suggest the illusiveness of our perceptions. Photo-realism owes something to the Surrealists' premise that reality is not what it seems.

In the 1970s site-specific works that functioned organically with the space around them grew in importance. Mary Miss designed a characteristic work, *Perimeters/Pavilions/Decoys* (FIG. 19-13), in 1978. Her art was part sculpture, part architecture, and part landscaping integrally woven into a multisensory experience. Masses and voids were both artist-made and of the earth. Her site was a sloping meadow almost entirely surrounded and cut off by trees. The field was divided into two areas by a five-foot-high embankment of dirt. In the lower part were three wooden towers, standing like observation posts. In the upper part a ladder projected from a seven-foot-square hole in the ground. Under the ground was a larger space that contained corridors and openings beyond the wooden

FIG 19-13 MARY MISS [American, 1944–], *Perimeters/Pavilions/Decoys.* 1978. Nassau County Museum of Fine Arts, Roslyn, New York. Photos courtesy the artist.

walls of the pit. To experience *Perimeters/Pavilions/ Decoys*, the viewer had to move through the space and climb down the ladder and let the work unfold just as the experience of architectural space develops through time. Unlike architecture, however, Miss's work was a temporary installation, built of relatively ephemeral materials. Even while it lasted, there was something fragile and vulnerable about the piece, perhaps implying the transitoriness of experience.

The 1970s were an eclectric period in which many artists reacted in different ways against the lack of content in Minimal Art and against the impersonal objectivity of Photo-realism. Mixed media and shaped canvases, manifest in the work of Frank Stella (see *Agbatana III*, FIG. 4-28) and Sam Gilliam (see *Carousel Form II*, FIG. 10-16), grew in importance. The trend for outdoor murals arose from the public expression in graffiti and street murals of popular concerns about the pressing issues in society. Taking another approach, Miriam Shapiro (see *Personal*

Appearance #3, FIG. 3-1) and Joyce Kozloff (see *Homage to Robert Adam*, FIG. 3-21) found a vehicle to express their feminist interests in the Pattern and Decoration movement.

Another manifestation of the return of a content-based art was the emergence of African-American artists, such as Faith Ringgold, who had a message to communicate. In the 1960s Ringgold explored race relations in America in paintings that conveyed a pointed political message. Nothing could have been further from the cool detachment of Pop and Minimal Art. In the 1970s, in collaboration with her mother, Willi Posey, she stitched soft sculpture of masks and life-scale figures that explored the experience of the African-American woman in America. Bucking the commercial gallery system, she took her work to university and college art galleries across the country, where she often added a performance to the exhibition. In the 1980s Ringgold concentrated on painting story quilts like the charming *Tar Beach* (FIG. 19-14).

FIG 19-14 FAITH RINGGOLD [American, 1930–], *Tar Beach (Woman on a Beach Series #1)*. 1988. Acrylic on canvas bordered with printed and painted quilted and pieced cloth, 74 5/8 × 68 1/2 in. (189.5 × 174 cm). Solomon R. Guggenheim Museum, New York. Gift, Mr. and Mrs. Gus and Judith Lieber, 1988. Photo by David Heald.

Although her work now receives mainstream attention, she continues to be a political activist for women of color.

Ringgold paints on quilts because of their female tradition and because on them she can tell stories. *Tar Beach* is both an autobiographical recollection of pleasant summer evenings she spent with her family on the rooftop in Harlem and a symbolic paradigm of the power of a woman's imagination. It depicts Ringgold's actual experience of falling asleep under the stars, surrounded by the city's lights, as the great George Washington Bridge looms in the distance. The bridge also becomes the symbol of women's unstoppable courage, creativity, and freedom. *Tar Beach*, like her other story quilts, has a carefully crafted and printed narrative that not only describes the painted scene

but also extends its meaning. The simple text of an eight year old corresponds to the naive style of the painting, where the young girl dreams of flying among the stars above the bridge. Ringgold and several other contemporary artists forthrightly combine verbal and visual messages in their art to make their point.

The British architect Richard Rogers and the Italian architect Renzo Piano collaborated on the unusual Georges Pompidou National Center of Art and Culture (FIG. 19-15), completed in 1977, in the heart of Paris. The Pompidou Center completely reinterpreted the twentieth-century adage that a building is a functional machine for living, by exposing the machinery rather than covering it with a slick veneer. Rogers and Piano turned the body of the building inside out. Not only the skeleton but also the guts are visible on the exterior. Conduits for heating, plumbing, and electricity—painted in bright coded colors—are exposed. Escalators and corridors run through transparent tubes on the outside. The colorful and exotic building has a carnival atmosphere that in itself attracts people to the neighborhood and to the exhibits. The architecture of the Pompidou Center deliberately rejects the notion that art is a stuffy affair of high culture.

The 1980s: Post-Modernism

In political life, government took a conservative turn in the 1980s as baby boomers known as yuppies concentrated on the acquisition of money, power, and material possessions. The Chernobyl nuclear disaster, AIDS, and increasing famine in Africa taught sobering lessons to the modern world. While Communism grew liberalized and then collapsed in eastern Europe and the Soviet Union, artists around the world claimed independence from American trends. The connection between art and big money peaked in the late 1980s. Photography won recognition among museums and collectors as a significant modern art form. In the midst of these developments, many people began asserting that the modern style, begun a century ago, was now dead.

In the 1980s video and computer art came of age, and electronics became part of the creative process of art. Much of the technology had existed earlier, but more recent developments in the hardware and soft-

FIG-19-15 RICHARD ROGERS [British, 1933–] and RENZO PIANO [Italian, 1937–], Georges Pompidou National Center of Art and Culture, 1977. Paris. Photo by Charly Nes, Liason International.

ware of electronic art made it available to almost any artist. The Korean-born Nam June Paik has been the outstanding pioneer in America of video art. Trained in music and Eastern philosophy, Paik bought the first inexpensive video camera sold in New York in 1965 and has been experimenting with video ever since. Soon he and a colleague developed a "video synthesizer" so that he could twist, shrink, or break up the video image, change its color, or superimpose and manipulate it in a great variety of ways. By "painting" electronically this way on a videotape recording, Paik creates a time-collage, as he calls it—a visual montage that unfolds on the screen. Now that his expensive invention has become common computerized video equipment, many of the effects he pioneered appear frequently even on commercial TV.

In addition to individual videotapes, Paik has also assembled video sculpture, as in his *V-yramid* (FIG. 19-16). In this work he stacked over three dozen color television sets—some of them sideways or upside down—in a V-shaped pyramid over fifteen feet high. They were wired to play a synthesized videotape that he had produced. The pyramidal sculptural mass, housing fragile electronics, glows with colored video light. Along with the towering sculptural experience, Paik treats the viewer to a time-college of electronic sights and sounds.

FIG 19-16 NAM JUNE PAIK [Korean-American, 1932–], *V-yramid.* 1982. Color television sets and videotape, 186 3/4 in. (474.3 cm) high. Whitney Museum of American Art, New York. Purchase, with funds from the Lemberg Foundation, Inc. in honor of Samuel Lemberg.

FIG 19-17 GEORG BASELITZ [German, 1938–], *Die Verspottung (The Mocking)*. 1984. Oil on canvas, 120 × 100 in. (304.8 × 254 cm). Carnegie Museum of Art, Pittsburgh. Women's Committee, Washburn Memorial Fund and Carnegie International Acquisition Fund.

In the 1980s many artists and critics became convinced that the modern movement had lost its way and that art and architecture were in a state of crisis. Although it was not at all clear what the new period style should look like, many were convinced that they were already living in a Post-Modern world. Some reacted against the impersonal machine-made look of modern architecture and the mannered repetitiveness of modern painting. Many artists also felt that the time had come for a socially committed art that would make political and moral statements about race, gender, or the environment.

A key characteristic of the Post-Modern period is the resurrection of styles that were once thought to have been surpassed. In Germany and Italy as well as the United States, artists developed a Neo-Expressionist style to paint once again images from life with imagination and strongly felt emotions. The German Neo-Expressionist painter Georg Baselitz, for example, painted the human figure with crude, bold brush strokes, although unlike some earlier German Expressionists he did not illustrate his social environment. Baselitz often upset viewers by hanging the figures he painted upside down—a comment in itself on the topsy-turvy modern world. The title of his painting *Die Verspottung (The Mocking)* (FIG. 19-17) suggests that the figures represent, or at least refer to, the traditional iconography of the mocking of Christ as well as to modern interrogation and torture and to all forms of intimidation. Baselitz resurrected the devices of early-twentieth-century Expressionism—aggressive brushwork, crude and distorted drawing, and strong, clashing color—in order to make his work an expression of his inner feelings. Neo-Expressionists like him in the early 1980s injected new vitality into the traditional medium of painting on canvas.

Like the Pop Artists and Photo-realists before them, some artists in the 1980s merely appropriated their images from other visual sources. Sherrie Levine appropriates her imagery from the art of the recent past. Her small painting *After Piet Mondrian* (FIG. 19-18) challenges the modern thirst of artists and collectors for originality above all else. Like some Pop Artist, Levine hid her personality behind her matter-of-fact appropriation. Reproduced on the top of a small piece of paper, her picture has the quality of a

FIG 19-18   SHERRIE LEVINE [American, 1947–], *After Piet Mondrian*. 1983. Watercolor, 14 × 11 in. (35.6 × 27.9 cm). Collection of Eugene and Barbara Schwartz, New York. Photo courtesy Marian Goodman Gallery, New York.

museum shop postcard or a textbook illustration, rather than the real thing.

Martin Puryear is an appealing sculptor who emerged in the 1980s. His *Old Mole* (FIG. 19-19) illustrates at the very first glance that he has a sensitivity for working with old-fashioned wood—but not as a carver of wood and not even as a more modern assembler of wood like Louise Nevelson (see *Sky Cathedral*, FIG. 13-16). Puryear instead has developed a love and respect for the craft of woodworking as practiced by traditional cabinetmakers and furniture makers, wheelwrights, and coopers. Puryear makes sculpture by using their methods of bending and joining wood. In the pursuit of his art, he studied with traditional woodworkers and craftspeople in Sierra Leone, Africa, and in Scandinavia. In *Old Mole* wooden lathes are bent and ingeniously secured into a simple but irregular biomorphic mass. The conglomeration seems to grow from the ground and come to a head in a point at one side. The interwoven lathes create a deep network beneath the surface. Puryear's work has a refreshing simplicity and directness, and at the same time the skillful execution of the piece betrays the hand of an accomplished artist.

In reaction to the coldness and seeming indifference of the International style, Post-Modern architects believe that architecture should incorporate the traditional language of building with which people still feel a great deal of familiarity. They also believe that, unlike a typical International-style glass tower,

FIG 19-19   MARTIN PURYEAR [American, 1941–], *Old Mole*. 1985. Red cedar, 61 × 61 × 32 in. (154.9 × 154.9 × 81.3 cm). Philadelphia Museum of Art. Purchase of Samuel S. White III and Vera White Collection (by exchange) and gift of Mr. and Mrs. C. G. Chaplin (by exchange) and funds contributed by Marion Stroud Swingle and funds contributed by friends and family in memory.

FIG 19-20 MICHAEL GRAVES [American, 1934–], Humana Building. 1982. Louisville, Kentucky. Michael Graves, Architect.

architecture should not ignore the context in which a building stands. The Post-Modernist style has meant a return to mass instead of flat glass planes, to columns and arches, to a variety of rich materials, and to quotations of earlier architectural motifs. Architectural "symbols" on Post-Modern buildings may refer to traditional styles or to local traditions.

Michael Graves's headquarters for the Humana Corporation in Louisville, Kentucky (see FIG. 19-20), successfully displays these principles. The bulkiness of the Humana Building contrasts with the flat planes of the glass curtain walls of typical office towers nearby. The rich granite facing and the marble veneers of the formal lobby resemble elegant buildings of the 1920s and 1930s. The grand entrance, of almost Egyptian proportions, also declares the power and wealth of the modern corporation. The setback above the first few stories of the Humana Building respects the scale of the historic nineteenth-century buildings adjacent to it. The truss work underneath the terrace at the top symbolizes the bridges across the Ohio River a block away. The Post-Modern architecture of Graves tries to ingratiate itself to the people it serves and to integrate itself with its surroundings.

The 1990s: The Search for Identity

In the last decade of the twentieth century, the United States and the former Soviet Union struggle with their economies and with staggering debt inherited from the cold war. As America and Russia reduce their focus on the game of international power politics, ethnic groups around the world reassert themselves, stirring old hatreds of which the Serbian and Croatian fight for Bosnia is a vicious example. Instead of reinforcing the image of the melting pot, America is in the process of redefining itself as a multicultural society. Although white middle-class males of European origin have long dominated life in the United States, Americans now recognize the importance of Native American, African-American, Asian-American, and Latino cultures thriving within the country. In the 1990s communication technology and medical science continue to make stunning advances, but poverty, hunger, ignorance, and racial injustice still go begging for solutions. Artists likewise are struggling to

FIG 19-21   GUILLERMO GÓMEZ-PEÑA
[Mexican, 1955–] and COCO FUSCO
[American, 1960–], *Two Undiscovered
Amerindians Visit the West,* 1993. Whitney
Museum of American Art, New York. Photo
courtesy the artists.

find their identity in this new world and to actively address some of the problems.

Many artists in the 1990s are searching for their identity—just as people all over the world seek their own identity and freedom. This pursuit in art seems to be manifesting itself in at least two ways: first, the increased assertion and visibility of artists who because of their race, ethnic origin, or gender have been heretofore considered outsiders and excluded from the mainstream; second, the resurgence of performance and video art, perhaps because these media so readily lend themselves to self-examination by the artist.

The biennial exhibition of new American art held at the Whitney Museum of American Art in New York in the spring of 1993 emphasized these directions. The Whitney Biennial, the international Venice Biennial, and the exhibition called Documenta, held every four years in Germany, regularly attempt to confirm the trends that contemporary artists are setting. Instead of a general survey of the art of the previous two years, the 1993 Whitney exhibition deliberately focused on works concerned with gender, sexuality, racism, and ethnic and multicultural identity. The Whitney's choice in this exhibition implies that social commitment is a leading trend in current art. Many critics, no matter how much they sympathized with the themes, deplored the shallowness of some of the art and its one-dimensional solutions to complex social problems. Nevertheless, the

Biennial proclaimed that the new generation of artists are searching, through their work, for their cultural and sexual identity in a multicultural society.

The *kinds* of art work exhibited at the Whitney Biennial were perhaps of greater significance for the future of American art than the success of any single artist or work. The eighty-seven artists showed very few paintings and very little sculpture of a standard kind. Most of the works were photographs and found objects that had social or political significance. Many of the pieces were mixed media and installations. Artists' video was in abundance and given a prominent place. In fact, half the artists in the exhibition consider themselves video or performance artists. Furthermore, most were women, African-Americans, Latinos, Asian-Americans, or gays—members of groups that often feel excluded from the mainstream of American art.

For several days at the beginning of the exhibition, museum goers were treated to a performance piece titled *Two Undiscovered Amerindians Visit the West* (FIG. 19-21), by Guillermo Gómez-Peña and Coco Fusco. The two performance artists locked themselves in a gilded cage furnished with glitsy artifacts from Mexican and American culture. They impersonated two glamorous showbiz types, residents of the island of Guatinau, whom Columbus and subsequent generations had never discovered. Visitors could pose with the two natives and have their picture taken to take

Fig 19-22 Arnaldo Roche-Rabell [American, 1956–], *No solo de pan vive el hombre (Man Does Not Live by Bread Alone)*. 1993. Oil on canvas, 78 × 78 in. (198.1 × 198.1 cm). Galleria Botello, San Juan, Puerto Rico. Photo by Johnny Betancourt.

home as a souvenir. *Two Undiscovered Amerindians Visit the West* satirized the fantasies that Western culture perpetuates about colonization.

In their art, Gómez-Peña and Fusco examine not just the clash between Mexican and American cultures but the hybrid interpenetration and invasion of one culture into another. Rejecting the marginal status given to minority groups within the dominant white culture, Gómez-Peña wants to be active in the building of a new society. The ritual fantasies and parodies of Gómez-Peña and Fusco's performance art allows them to cross back and forth over the boundaries between the two cultures and begin the process of building. In the 1980s Gómez-Peña led the Border Arts Workshop/Taller de Arte Fronterizo in San Diego, where a collective of Mexican and American artists denounced ethnic stereotyping, injustice, and the artificiality of borders. They took their art out of the galleries and into the streets and staged perfor-

mances on the border itself. Born in Mexico City, Gómez-Peña was trained at the California Institute of the Arts.

Later, in the summer of 1993, the Museum of Modern Art in New York staged the exhibition *Latin American Artists of the Twentieth Century*. This show likewise confirmed the swelling tide of interest in artists living south of the United States and in Latino artists living in the United States. It included the work of the young Puerto Rican painter Arnaldo Roche-Rabell, who like Gómez-Peña, possesses two cultures. Trained at the University of Puerto Rico and the School of the Art Institute of Chicago, Roche-Rabell lives in both Chicago and San Juan. Painting with great emotional intensity, he struggles to capture his identity in self-portraits that communicate what he feels about himself.

In his painting *No solo de pan vive el hombre (Man Does Not Live by Bread Alone)* (FIG. 19-22) the figure

FIG 19-23 ALISON SAAR [American, 1956–], *Slow Boat*. 1992. Mixed media installation. Whitney Museum at Phillip Morris, New York.

(probably the artist himself) twists like a corkscrew as he floats above a lace tabletop and holds one foot. A cry of anguish barely escapes his enlarged head. Roche-Rabell paints in thick layers of yellow, red, and black; then he often draws on the canvas by scraping through the paint with a knife. Roche-Rabell pastes material like lace to the canvas, and he has been known to apply a canvas wet with paint to a model and produce an image through frottage (rubbing). This Latino artist, who learned his Neo-Expressionist style while in Chicago, sets his art squarely in the mainstream of the modern tradition to discover and expose his multicultural identity.

Alison Saar builds her provocative art out of the traditions of diverse cultures. Like many sculptors working today, she has turned more and more to installations such as her *Slow Boat* (FIG. 19-23). For *Slow Boat* she created an environment in a gallery by draping the walls with canvas painted like a camou-flage and by playing a recording of moving water. Into the top of a large wooden boat in the center of the installation Saar carved the negative impression of a life-sized human form. High above the boat she sus-pended a wooden door. Beyond the boat stood a large copper relief of a woman, which seems to have been

formed by being beaten into the hollow body mold carved in the boat. A visitor to the gallery could stand behind the figure, look out through the holes in its eyes, and see as she would see. To the side the artist suspended a pair of metal wings fitted with a harness so that they might be attached for flight. Drawing on archetypal imagery about death from religions around the world (wings, boat, door), Saar fashioned in the subbued light and sound of her environment a ritual space for the transmigration of souls from this life to the next. Visitors were also invited to write the names of their dead on yellow ribbons and thus actively par-ticipate in the spirit of *Slow Boat*.

The daughter of a White father and a Black moth-er who is also an established artist, Saar grew up in admiration of Simon Rodia's idiosyncratic Watts Tower in Los Angeles. Having studied the Black folk art of the United States and the Caribbean in college, she has always felt the strong influence of their iconography and style on her work. Most of all, she likes to find "junk," reuse it in her work, and thereby bring out the spiritual power hidden in it. Out of the images and symbols of various cultures she fuses together fascinating new cult objects.

FIG 19-24 JAMES INGO FREED [American, 1930–], United States Holocaust Memorial Museum, exterior. 1993. Washington, D.C.

FIG 19-25 JAMES INGO FREED [American, 1930–], United States Holocaust Memorial Museum, Hall of Witness. 1993. Washington, D.C.

One of the most talked-about and most admired works of architecture in the early 1990s is a museum that commemorates the ghastly effects of racial hatred, the United States Holocaust Memorial Museum in Washington, D.C. When James Ingo Freed received the commission to design the museum, he was daunted by the emotional needs of the task—to create a place to remember and to learn about the Nazi mass extinction of millions of Jews and other peoples deemed undesirable by Nazi policy. A visit to the death camps in Europe left Freed with haunting memories of steel and brick—heavy steel strapped around the brick furnaces at Auschwitz and the brick-and-steel watchtowers. He decided to design the museum building symbolically with the evocative forms of the death camps.

The east front entrance to the museum (FIG. 19-24) faced in limestone to fit in with the federal architecture of Washington, has the massive and solemn appearance of a 1930s railroad station. But its sedate appearance is a sham. The two steel doors set at different angles into the building lead on the left to an elevator lobby and on the right to the main hall, the Hall of Witness (FIG. 19-25). The doors set up the theme of ambiguity that runs throughout the building, where the visitor is constantly confronted with choices of up and down, left or right.

The two-story brick Hall of Witness is topped with industrial-looking steel truss work in which a skylight along the ridge of a glass roof runs diagonally across the room. The stairs within the room grow uncomfortably narrow as they approach the upper level. Their false perspective makes it impossible to tell the length of the stairs.

Freed did not intend the building to be "nice" or "easy"; he wanted the architecture to be unpleasant and disconcerting and the visual references to arouse gut feelings. He avoided a realistic theme park re-creation of a death camp, for only an emotional architecture could communicate something of the unspeakable horror.

Artists and architects of the twentieth century, like artists of earlier centuries, have searched for styles that would express themselves and the time in which they lived. The modern style is no exception to the rule that styles are related to the cultures that produced them. The rapid changes and greatly expanded freedoms of modern society perhaps make it more difficult than ever for artists to discover an original personal language with which to communicate their unique experience. The challenges of originality and the dangers of failure add excitement to the viewing of contemporary art, but most of all, like it or not, contemporary art is exciting because it belongs to us, speaks to us, talks about us, is us.

Key Terms and Concepts

Action Painting
Color Field Painting

CRITICAL ANALYSIS IV

In France in the mid-nineteenth century, an artist could achieve recognition and success only by exhibiting at the Salon. Virtually no other galleries or museums existed in which artists might show their work. Furthermore, the public and the critics expected artists to compete with one another at the Salon so that they might choose the best art produced that year. Not only did the system tend to reward crowd-pleasing mediocrity but the judges who accepted entrants and awarded the prizes were the professors at the Academy and naturally favored the work of their own pupils.

In 1874 the Impressionists invited the critics' scorn by staging an independent exhibition in a photographer's studio at the same time as that year's Salon. This Corporation of Independent Painters became known as Impressionists when a critic ridiculed their work as mere sketches or impressions. Despite the misleading implication that their work was unfinished, the name stuck, and over the next twelve years the Impressionists held eight independent exhibitions.

Independence from the Salon was not the only objective that brought the Impressionists

Mary Cassatt [American, 1845–1926], *Summertime: Woman and Child in a Rowboat*. 1894. Oil on canvas, 42 × 30 in. (106.7 × 76.2 cm). Terra Museum of American Art, Chicago.

together. All of them, Mary Cassatt included, wanted to be "true to nature" in their painting. In *Summertime: Woman and Child in a Rowboat* this meant that Cassatt concentrated on capturing the fleeting subtleties of color reflected from sur-

faces. Like many of the Impressionist painters, Cassatt painted *Summertime* out-of-doors where the motifs are filled with light and where even shadows are filled with color.

Since the Impressionists generally came from middle-class

backgrounds, they tended to reflect the interests of the French middle class in their work. Cassatt's family could be considered upper middle class; she always maintained a refined and proper household in Paris. She and the other Impressionists favored the depiction of leisure time activities—boating, picnicking, dancing, attending the theater, walking through the park—that the urban middle class could now enjoy on that new found phenomenon, the weekend. Although they were realists, they almost never represented physical labor, poor people, or slums. They never overtly espoused social causes in their work. Their iconography manifests the same joy in living as the bright colors and spontaneous brushwork.

The American Cassatt joined the Impressionists for their fourth exhibition in 1879, where she showed eleven works. Like many American artists after the Civil War, she had come to Europe—from Pennsylvania—to study the Old Masters in the museums and to study under leading painters of the day. She had begun exhibiting at the Salon, and deciding to make her career in France, she stayed there for the rest of her life. In fact, her sister and her parents eventually came to live with her in Paris. (She also had to care for them in their sickness and old age.) Her actions disclose the most striking aspects of her personality: her independence and her determination to become a successful artist. She went about her goal in a thoroughly professional way. She never married because mixing marriage and a professional career was out of the question for an American woman in the nineteenth century.

Cassatt had achieved some success at the government-sponsored Salon, when she boldly threw in her lot with the Independents, as she called them. Her decision made her feel free and alive. Among the Impressionists, Cassatt particularly admired Degas, since they both shared an interest in good drawing and Japanese art. As an Impressionist, she experimented with uncommon light sources and light-filled shadows, with asymmetrical compositions, with Impressionist subjects like women at the theater or women, absorbed in a conversation, sipping tea. It was only in the 1890s that she developed her specialty of mother and child.

Cassatt made a significant contribution to the history of Impressionism. Primarily a figure painter, she was able to breathe new life into the old categories of portrait and genre painting. By the beginning of the twentieth century she had realized her girlhood dream to be a great artist and to be recognized for her accomplishments. Despite all the conventional restrictions that society set about her life, Cassatt was one of a growing number of modern women who asserted their independence, built their own career, and added their personal vision to the history of the human imagination.

THE ART WORLD

FIG 20-1 VINCENT VAN GOGH [Dutch, 1853–1890], *Irises*. 1989. Oil on canvas, 28 3/4 × 36 5/8 In. (73 × 93 cm). J. Paul Getty Museum, Malibu, California.

The Australian businessman Alan Bond bought Irises at Sotheby's auction house in New York for $53.9 million. The painting had previously belonged to the John Whitney Payson family, which had exhibited it for some time at the art museum of Westbrook College in Portland, Maine. The purchase created a sensation when it was revealed that Sotheby's itself had financed it. Because it supplied the financing, the auction house was accused of pumping up the price. In any case, Bond was unable to pay for the painting and Irises was resold for an undisclosed price to the very rich J. Paul Getty Museum. Although the sale to Bond fell through, the event raised troubling questions. Should the bidding for other similar paintings by Van Gogh now start at $54 million? At what price should new owners expect to resell their Van Gogh? Rather than rejoicing in the price, dealers and museum directors were troubled by the sale.

THE ART WORLD

Every so often the news contains a feature about a painting that has sold for millions of dollars. In May of 1987, for example, *Sunflowers,* by Vincent Van Gogh, sold for $39.9 million; in November of the same year *Irises* (FIG. 20-1), by Van Gogh, sold for $53.9 million; and in May of 1990 Van Gogh's *Portrait of Dr. Gachet* sold for $82.5 million. The news item almost always recounts how the original owner once bought the painting for a few thousand dollars or how the artist who painted it lived in poverty and scarcely sold any work while alive.

Reading features like this, we cannot help question whether any piece of art is worth such a high price and cannot help wonder who determines that a work of art is deserving of such high esteem. To answer these questions requires some investigation of what has become known as the **art world**—a very informally structured society of artists, critics, dealers, galleries, museums, collectors, and educators who work in the business of art. In the late twentieth century especially, the art world appears to have increasing clout in the evaluation of art. It may even have indirect influence over what and how some artists create.

Like it or not, the visual arts have become big business in the second half of the twentieth century. Not every artist, collector, or museum curator is pleased with this turn of events, which can distort the nature of art, but the art business will not suddenly go away. It is a phenomenon that every contemporary artist and the public have to deal with.

Although art is often described as a revelation of the spiritual side of human nature, the visual arts have developed some very tangible human organizations that handle large sums of money and that guide the experience of art in contemporary society. The business of art provides many people, in addition to artists,

The Metropolitan Museum of Art, New York. Exterior, west facade. Photographed in April 1991.

with a livelihood and supports numerous large institutions. Although aspects of the art world have existed for some time, since 1950 phenomenal growth has occurred in every aspect of art in the United States and around the world.

The Art Market

One feature that distinguishes the visual arts from literature and the performing arts is that traditionally, the visual arts create objects that can be bought and sold on the **art market,** especially through galleries

FIG 20-2 REMBRANDT VAN RIJN [Dutch, 1606–1669], *Aristotle with a Bust of Homer*. 1653. Oil on canvas, 56 1/2 × 53 3/4 in. (143.5 × 136.5 cm). Metropolitan Museum of Art, New York. Purchased with special funds and gifts of friends of the Museum.

and auction houses. A best-selling author may sell a work to a publisher for an inflated price, but once the book is published, the original manuscript is generally neglected or if preserved, seldom attains a monetary value anywhere near that of a renowned painting. The visual arts, however, tend to produce unique or rare objects of great attraction that people want to possess.

Because objects of visual art continue to be bought and sold after the artist's work is finished, the ordinary economic laws of supply and demand come into play. Great demand for a small supply of goods inflates prices. Since a painting by Rembrandt, for example, will now rarely appear on the market for sale, dealers and museums who are eager for a Rembrandt will outbid each other when one is offered, and raise the price as high as they can afford to go. In fact, the sale of

Rembrandt's *Aristotle with a Bust of Homer* (FIG. 20-2) to New York's Metropolitan Museum of Art in 1961 for over two million dollars set the pace for runaway prices in recent times. Museums and art dealers interested in Rembrandt probably have a list of the few Rembrandt paintings still in private hands (the only paintings ever likely to be sold) and watch the obituaries and financial pages for circumstances that might bring those paintings into the market. Coincidentally, it was in Rembrandt's Holland in the seventeenth century that there first arose anything like the current art market, where artists painted in quantity for the open market and collectors speculated on works of art.

Needless to say, Rembrandt will not profit from the current market for his work. Even living artists may never see the big amounts of money involved in the resale of their work, although proposals and court rulings have required that a percentage of the resale price be given to a living artist. Indeed, only a small percentage of the thousands of artists living today are able to support themselves from the sale of their work. Most artists support themselves by teaching or by working in other art-related fields or by waiting on tables or by any means of employment they can find. Although they want to communicate their vision and would enjoy recognition, many artists prefer to pursue their art without the pressure of trying to achieve economic success through it. They refuse to concern themselves with the quantity or specific qualities that would increase marketability. They make art for the sheer joy of it and for the self-discovery found in their creative activity.

Sale prices for works of art, since they fluctuate for economic reasons, do not necessarily reflect the artistic value of any pieces. A price may instead reflect the scarcity of the artist's work, the quantity of collectors eager to buy, or the affluence of the current market, which, because of the economy, can or cannot afford to spend large sums for art. For economic reasons the art market prefers rare treasures and the original as opposed to derivations.

The art market also falls prey to collectors' fashions for certain artists or periods or styles. Impressionist and Post-Impressionist paintings are in the 1990s extremely popular with affluent collectors around the world, many of whom seem willing to pay any price for them. Other styles that have an admired place in the history of art may nevertheless be neglected by the same market and command low prices. In the mid-1990s, late-Baroque painting may be bought for bargain prices. In the 1950s, Victorian painting of the nineteenth century was so disregarded that it was virtually given away, but in the late twentieth century a new fashion for it has rocketed prices into the stratosphere.

Some speculative investors in the art world are eager to catch the first wave of a new fashion in the hopes that their original investment will earn huge profits. Speculation in art is far from a sure thing. Prices do not always go up—despite a myth to the contrary that few people in the art world want to puncture. The high prices that some works commanded in the mid-twentieth century have dropped, and fortunes spent on some schools of art have been lost when they went "out of favor." The art market, which during the economic boom of the late 1980s was driven to a fever pitch by speculation, experienced a significant decline in activity and in prices in the recession of the early 1990s.

The Institution of Art

Economics and fashion do not completely explain why collectors would pay thousands or millions of dollars to possess a work of art. People and events must stimulate a fashion and develop the taste of collectors toward certain works. (**Taste** is the kind or degree of appreciation for art that someone has gained through culture or education. By this definition, bad taste signifies a lack of exposure or education.) Indeed, certain consultants, critics, gallery and museum directors, journalists, and educators are in the business of building and guiding taste. Educators, for example, write art appreciation textbooks in the attempt to influence taste. All these people have extensive, though far from invincible, powers for deciding what works of art and which artists are worthy of attention.

The art world exercises its influence on the art of both the past and the present. Artists living in modern times have virtually complete freedom to use any material, adopt any technique, and declare that anything is art, yet someone in the art world must "ratify" their work before it becomes known and available as art. Although education in art is no guarantee of talent or

creativity, unless an artist receives "credentials" through training in a recognized art school, unless the work is given a "stamp of approval" through exhibition by art organizations and galleries, museums, and influential collectors—unless at least one of these events takes place—the work will probably not become known as art. At this very moment, countless artists in the United States and throughout the world are waiting to be discovered by a gallery or praised by an influential critic or purchased by a pace setting collector. If none of these events happen, most of those artists will eventually abandon the profession. Nevertheless, it is a myth that numerous great artists were ignored and neglected. The instances of neglected genius, subsequently discovered by a later generation, are quite rare.

The need for ratification by the art world held true for Marcel Duchamp's *Fountain* (FIG. 1-21) as it holds true for works of art produced today. If an ordinary plumber had displayed a urinal in a plumbing shop in 1917 and called it art, the results would not have been similar to those for *Fountain*. Duchamp, unlike the plumber, had been accredited as an artist by the art world when he trained as a student in a legitimate art school and when he exhibited his more traditional work as an artist. Furthermore, his *Fountain* was meant to be exhibited in a gallery, was reproduced in art publications and has been discussed by critics, historians, philosophers, and educators—most of whom have accepted his challenging work as art.

The Critics

The taste of the art world is influenced by **criticism**—by what is written about art and what "the experts" say is good or bad. Published criticism of contemporary work began to influence art in the eighteenth century when, for the first time, new art was shown to the general public in large-scale exhibitions. In many countries, art academies at that time began holding regular exhibitions open to the public. Before then, most artists, especially the best ones, worked for the satisfaction of a patron who commissioned each work. With the appearance of public exhibitions, artists now tended to produce work that might please the general public. Writers soon appeared in newspapers and magazines to educate and guide public opinion. The most

Fig 20-3 Pietro Martini [Italian, 1738–1797], *1787 Salon at the Louvre.* Engraving. Bibliothèque Nationale, Paris.

famous public exhibition was the annual *Salon* of the French Academy in Paris, portrayed in Pietro Martini's *1787 Salon at the Louvre* (Fig. 20-3). Success at a Salon, in the eyes of the critics, could make a career.

At the present time, it is rather unlikely that any critical review of an artist's work, appearing in a newspaper or magazine, could make or break that artist's career. The critics writing about art today are very likely either practicing artists or people trained in the history of art. They usually only review the work of artists who have already been recognized and are being exhibited in galleries or museums in major centers like Los Angeles, New York, or London. The attention an artist receives from a feature in the *New York Times* or the magazines *Artforum*, *Art News*, or *Art in America* might stimulate interest in new talent and help define new styles. Even a bad review might stimulate interest. For example, critical discussion—pro and con—about the work of Julian Schnabel in the 1980s aroused great interest in the artist and stimulated high-priced sales of his work.

Written criticism more likely affects the sale of work by artists who are already rather established and about whom a critical consensus is developing. Criticism of this sort appears in magazine features, exhibition catalogs, and books about the history of art. The Abstract Expressionists in New York were much discussed in newspapers and magazines in the 1940s and 1950s—for instance, a feature on Jackson Pollock,

appeared in *Life Magazine*. Nevertheless, despite the attention paid to them in print, sales of their work were modest until the Metropolitan Museum of Art gave its stamp of approval by paying the remarkable price of thirty thousand dollars for a Pollock. Since then the Abstract Expressionists have found such a hallowed place in discussions of modern American art that their best work now sells for millions.

Art Galleries

It is the dream of many if not most young artists in America today to be recognized and handled by an **art gallery** in Los Angeles or New York. Many cities around the United States—Chicago, Los Angeles, Washington, Houston—have several dozen business establishments that, through their showrooms, promote and sell art. But New York City outdoes them all because it has *hundreds* of galleries. At least until recently New York has been the indisputable capital of art in the Western Hemisphere if not the world. The New York art scene is not simply larger, it has the museums, communications media, and international connections to exert more influence on the art world than does any other place.

An artist living and working in another part of the country might have more talent than a New York artist and might do quite well in the region, but unless the artist is exhibited and sold in New York, he or she

will probably never become a superstar in fame or fortune. Because having a New York showing is such a mark of distinction, a growing number of "vanity galleries" in that city will rent an artist a wall or the entire facility for a brief exhibition. Galleries, nevertheless, have important functions. Even disregarding the nonsense of contemporary superstardom, some measure of financial success afforded by a legitimate art gallery in any city can give an artist the freedom, the time, the energy, and the resources to continue to create.

Whether the gallery system of recognizing, promoting, and rewarding creative talent is desirable is a difficult question to answer. Because those who run galleries are under some pressure to carry what is marketable, they may be limiting the public's access to really innovative or difficult work or to work that is not in favor. Artists who have success with an art gallery may find themselves under pressure to produce much more of the same sort of work that the gallery sells so well. There has been criticism that galleries, which have been run mostly by white males and sell mostly to white males, have discriminated against women and people of color. Organizations like the Guerrilla Girls have taken to protesting in public the unfairness of the system.

Located in New York or Los Angeles, an art gallery devoted to contemporary art typically handles the work of about fifteen or twenty artists. Gallery owners usually find it stimulating to recognize new talent and

The Guerrilla Girls are a group of artists and art professionals who since 1985 have been hanging posters to protest the art world's racism and unfairness to women. They wear gorilla masks to protect their anonymity and as a clever media ploy when they appear on panels and at public demonstrations. Photo by George Lange/Outline.

Text continues on page 562

Julian Schnabel (1951–)

*I*N MANY WAYS Julian Schnabel's life is the success story that many American artists dream about. Schnabel graduated with a bachelor of fine arts degree from the University of Houston in 1973. Soon after, he moved to New York on a grant from the Whitney Museum of American Art. For the next five years he alternately painted in New York, where he supported himself by working as a cook, and traveled in Europe.

Then, in 1979, the Mary Boone Gallery in New York held two Schnabel exhibitions, in February and December, presenting Schnabel's first expressionistic "plate paintings." Because of deft word-of-mouth preparation by the dealer, the exhibitions sold out at once. That same year Schnabel received critical attention in *The Village Voice* (twice), *Artforum* (three times), *Art in America*, and *Arts Magazine*—all prominent voices in the art world. His career was instantly in

JULIAN SCHNABEL [American, 1951–], Claudio al Mandrione (zona rosa). Oil and plates with Bondo on wood. 1985–86. 6 panels, 114 × 228 in. overall (289.5 × 579 cm.) Milwaukee Art Museum. Gift of Contemporary Art Society.

orbit. By 1982 major museums—the Stedilijk in Amsterdam and the Tate in London—were holding exhibitions of his work, and his pieces were soon reproduced in anthologies of contemporary art. As much a phenomenon as a painter, Schnabel was *the* New York superstar of the 1980s.

Critical analysis of Schnabel continues to flow, including some adverse criticism protesting the hype and self-promotion surrounding him. His own remarks about his work go from matter-of-fact to mysterious in the same sentence. Although some critics praise his brashness and inventiveness, others label his work bombast. The controversy only seems to increase his reputation.

Schnabel employs a wide range of imagery, techniques, and materials in his work. He is best known for his plate paintings, one of which is at the Milwaukee Art Museum, in which he glues shards of cheap ceramic tableware across large, thick wooden supports. Crudely painted images and abstract splashes of paint—like graffiti on city walls—go over and under this jagged mosaic surface. Since his bold self-expression in paint appeared at a time when Minimal Art and Conceptual Art were all the rage, Schnabel became the leading American in the Neo-Expressionist revolt that swept the country in the 1980s.

Often, like Robert Rauschenberg, Schnabel combines other real objects—a pair of antlers, for example, or driftwood—on the surface of a painting. He frequently and disconcertingly combines splashy amorphous abstraction with slick representational drawing. The imagery that he paints is sometimes

Since his bold self-expression in paint appeared at a time when Minimal Art and Conceptual Art were all the rage, Schnabel became the leading American in the Neo-Expressionist revolt that swept the country in the 1980s.

JULIAN SCHNABEL [American, 1951–], *Stella and the Wooden Bird.* 1986. Oil and tempera on muslin, 150 × 189 in. (381 × 480 cm). Private collection. Photo courtesy of Pace Wildenstein, New York.

appropriated from the history of art, sometimes simply suggested by an unknown personal experience. The juxtaposition of incongruous images, their irrational scale, and often their ambiguous forms remind the viewer of the devices of Surrealism.

His refusal to limit himself and his experiments with different kinds of modern painting make Schnabel's style hard to pigeonhole. Schnabel painted *Stella and the Wooden Bird* on the scale of a mural painting. A naked, breastless girl, presumably Stella wearing a crown, stands in a forest. She also wears a golden chain attached to a monstrous shape upon which Schnabel has drawn multiple breasts. Here Schnabel is explicitly referring to the famous Greek statute of Diana of Ephesus, which also has many breasts. A protuberance at the top of the monstrous shape wears a muzzle from which descends a shower of liquid over Stella, just as liquid flows from the breasts. Only the black outline of the wooden bird, emerging from its shell, appears against the landscape on the left. The bird's eye focuses on Stella.

The mysterious juxtaposition of images, the discrepancies of scale, and the monstrous blob have the irrationality of a dream whose message, even if Schnabel provided a key, probably lies too deep to really fathom rather than feel. In painting the figure of Stella, Schnabel employed expressionistic brushwork to make the modeling of light and dark look like bloody wounds. Quite different from his plate paintings, *Stella and the Wooden Bird* is perhaps even more disturbing and puzzling—traits that viewers either like or dislike in works of art.

Leo Castelli with Jasper Johns, 1988, New York. Photo © 1990 by Hans Namuth.

An art dealer since the mid 1950s, Leo Castelli has handled the work of famous artists such as Jasper Johns and Robert Rauschenberg. No other dealer has had as much influence on recent American art as Castelli has had for nearly four decades.

take the chance to promote the artist. Many galleries specialize in a certain kind of work like printmaking, crafts, or photography or in a certain kind of artist. Other galleries handle only Old Masters or operate like interior design agencies, fitting art into the patron's decor.

Artists are continually asking **art dealers** who run a gallery to handle their work, but dealers seem to accept new talent more on the recommendations of friends and other artists than on this direct solicitation. Dealers typically receive a 40 percent to 50 per-

cent commission from each sale. For that money, they are expected to promote the artist through advertising and regular exhibition of the artist's work. However, most sales in a gallery are made not to browsing visitors but to regular clients whose patronage the dealer has painstakingly nurtured. Dealers will in fact select and cultivate certain clients whose prestige will enhance the marketability of the gallery's artists. Dealers have been known to practice "creative pricing" by asking for inflated prices to increase the reputation of an artist they represent or by bidding up prices at an auction in order to maintain an artist's reputation in the market. When established artists go out of favor with collectors, dealers usually discourage them from selling their work at lower prices for fear that the deflation would undermine the whole marketing system.

Alternatives to the Gallery System

To counteract the gallery system, many artists, in New York and other cities, have for decades formed among themselves independent, nonprofit **artists' organizations** for showing their work. They have found **alternative spaces**—often places like storefronts, vacant warehouses, or empty churches—to exhibit new and experimental work not always commercially viable in most galleries. Artist have also taken to exhibiting in rock-music cafés, coffeehouses, restaurants, and even the streets and subway platforms (see Keith Haring's poster in FIG. 20-4) to try to get some exposure for their work. Some of these artists' cooperatives and alternative spaces, which now prefer to be called artists' organizations or artist-run organizations, have evolved into institutions with a director, a large staff, and a large budget. They function in the art world in a way similar to that of the galleries they revolted against.

Alternative spaces, artist-run organizations, and some university art galleries try to give new artists a chance to develop, break new ground, make mistakes, and receive criticism, stimulating or otherwise. A lot of experimental, temporary, and avant-grade activity takes place at these new exhibition spaces. They frequently have taken the initiative to exhibit art by women and by Native-American, Asian-American, Black, and Hispanic artists. Nevertheless, most of these artists, once they had made their mark, would

FIG 20-4 KEITH HARING [American, 1958—1990], poster. C. 1979. White chalk on black paper. © 1995 The Estate of Keith Harring.

Keith Haring, a superstar of the New York art scene in the 1980s, first received recognition when he began pasting his own art on empty advertising spaces in New York City subway stations. His very simple, heavily outlined white chalk drawings on black paper often satirized television or protested against pollution. His clever and witty style and iconography charmed the public.

jump at the chance to be represented by the right New York gallery because of the recognition it affords.

Artists without a gallery and independent art groups also often lean on government support for their activity, although agencies like the National Endowment for the Arts will seldom give grants to someone without a proven track record. Many groups have recently found that the government funding they depended on can shrink with economic recession and with adverse political pressure.

New forms of art—performance art, video, conceptual art, installations, site-specific work, and so forth—because they do not usually involve collectible objects, by their very nature attempt to break free of the gallery system and the marketplace. Video art is sometimes distributed by satellite to cable television's public access channels by groups like Deep Dish Television in New York or by Los Angeles Freeways. Artists' videos are more commonly distributed by mail-order houses—New York's Electronic Arts Intermix, for example—to museums and universities, which seem to be the only entities collecting them.

The Kitchen. An alternative space. New York. Photo by Kevin Noble, 1986.

Collectors

Dealers themselves insist that their influence in the art world is quite limited and that **collectors** have a greater effect on which works are more highly valued. Collectors, after all, by their purchases create the real demand for an artist's work. Collectors pay for and establish the success of artists in a world in which success is most often measured in terms of money. In addition to the thrill of speculation and the prestige of ownership, they have the delight of enjoying on a daily basis the art they own.

Today, with vast sums of disposable income, collectors from all over the world are eager to own modern American art, and American collectors show more and more interest in owning the work of foreign artists. Corporations like IBM, Phillip Morris, and Chase Manhattan Bank have also become very significant collectors of modern art. Companies invest in art to decorate their offices and places of business, to perform a public service, and to enjoy the prestige that collecting brings them.

Although collectors frequently ignore what is critically fashionable at the time and reach out on their own, nevertheless, the interest of well-heeled collectors seldom accounts for the sudden discovery of a living artist. This is unfortunate, since a purchase of the work of an unknown artist may keep that artist going at a crucial moment in his or her career. Collectors, rather, may have more effect on the fame of already established artists, whether living or dead. The purchase of a work by a collector, who is well-known in the art world for good taste, can raise an artist's reputation considerably.

Because of collectors' eagerness to possess original works of art, many people in countries around the world and even in the United States dig up and steal pieces of art from archaeological sites. By smuggling them out of the country and surreptitiously selling them to unscrupulous dealers, they are depriving their nation of its artistic treasures. Often such thievery damages the archaeological site and destroys the archaeological context that would have helped explain the art. The legal and social pressure is mounting to return art to its place of origin, even if a collector purchased it in good faith.

The history of collecting goes back to ancient times. The Romans, for example, avidly collected Greek art to display both the extent of their conquests and the extent of their culture. Throughout history many aristocrats defined their own importance, wealth, and fame in terms of the precious, rare, and finely wrought items they possessed. Beautiful art and luxurious surroundings distinguished them from ordi-

Fig 20-5   David Teniers [Flemish, 1610–1690], *The Picture Gallery of Archduke Leopold Wilhelm.* Oil on canvas, 27 1/2 × 33 7/8 in. (70 × 86 cm). Kunsthistorisches Museum, Vienna. Photo © Erich Lessing/Art Resource, New York.

nary people. David Tenier's painting *The Picture Gallery of Archduke Leopold Wilhelm* (FIG. 20-5) was intended as a display of the archduke's collection to reflect his wealth and good taste. The painting does not illustrate the way his collection was arranged in his palace in Brussels. In many cases aristocratic collections eventually became a national inheritance that now forms the core of many European museums.

Starting in the fifteenth century in Flanders and in Italy, collections of art were also formed by nonartistocratic individuals as an expression of the intelligence and refinement of the owner. By the late seventeenth century, collectors began to specialize in acquiring either antiquities and Old Masters, or contemporary art, rather than both. Today individuals and corporations collect art for the delight of it, for prestige, and sometimes for speculation. Since it has always taken a certain amount of money to buy art, it is no surprise that the wealthy upper classes or successful modern media personalities—like Oprah Winfrey, Jack Nicholson, Steve Martin, or Bill Cosby—have assembled large collections of art. Nevertheless, Herbert Vogel, a postal clerk, and his wife Dorothy, a librarian in Brooklyn, haunted the New York galleries for decades and diligently put together an outstanding collection of modern art, on a shoestring. Beloved by

Hubert and Dorothy Vogel with works from their collection in the 1994 exhibition From Minimal to Conceptual Art: Works from the Dorothy and Herbert Vogel Collection *at the National Gallery of Art, Washington, D.C.* Photo by Lorene Emerson. © 1994, National Gallery of Art.

FIG 20-6 JAN VAN EYCK [Flemish, before 1395–1441], *The Virgin with the Canon van der Paele.* 1436. Tempera and oil on wood, about 48 × 62 in. (121.9 × 157.5 cm). Musées Communaux, Bruges, Belgium.

the New York art world, they will eventually donate their collection to a museum for the general public to enjoy.

Patrons

For most of recorded history in the West, the arts have been produced for wealthy **patrons**—individuals or groups who have enough means to buy art and assist artists. Patrons in a sense make art possible; they also have had considerable influence upon the appearance of art. Perciles, the political leader of ancient Athens and the patron of the Parthenon, no doubt collaborated with Phidias on the program of the sculpture of the Parthenon. Medieval church officials, who closely directed the work of sculptors and architects, took credit for the art and architecture of the church. Throughout the Medieval, Renaissance, and Baroque periods almost all works of art were produced on commissions from a patron who sometimes had his or her portrait painted amid religious figures in the work, as in Jan van Eyck's *The Virgin with the Canon van der Paele* (FIG. 20-6). Artists and patrons in those times typically signed a legal contract that specified not only the iconography but also the number of figures, the

colors and other materials to be used, and even the quality of the work as reflected in the price.

The Medici in Florence, King Louis XIV of France, and other rulers took an active role in directing the arts to glorify the state. Costly materials, high quality work, and a uniform and distinct style reflected the power of the ruler. The emperor in China and the Oba, the king of Benin in Africa, also patronized this kind of art to enhance their rule. In the kingdom of Benin brasscasting was the exclusive right of the king. Heads of Benin kings, like the *Head of an Oba* (FIG. 20-7), were placed on altars dedicated to the more than thirty ancestors of the Oba. The royal art of Benin reinforced the legitimacy of the monarchy and functioned as a source of political and spiritual power.

By the nineteenth century in the West, a growing number of new, nonaristocratic patrons required small easel paintings and small-scale sculpture from artists and new kinds of iconography like still life and genre. Artists abounded who were glad to oblige them. Many artists in recent centuries may have felt drawn to large-scale religious and heroic themes, but the patronage of their time forced them to paint landscapes and portraits. In architecture, patrons, or clients, generally assume a considerable direction over

FIG 20-7 [African, Nigerian, Edo, Court of Benin] Head of an Oba. 18th century. Brass, iron. 13 1/8 in. (33.3 cm) high. The Metropolitan Museum of Art, New York. Gift of Mr. and Mrs. Klaus G. Perls, 1991. (1991.17.2)

Christies' auction house, New York. Photo by Eric Hartmann, Magnum Photos.

the design of a building. At the very least, they often get to have the building named after them.

Michelangelo occasionally defied the patronage system with his independent genius, but it was the Romantic movement in the nineteenth century that finally won freedom for the inspired artist to work as she or he liked—or, as some writers have put it, the freedom to starve. The French government throughout the nineteenth century helped artists by purchasing countless works of religious art for churches and secular art for public buildings. Government patronage in the United States supported hundreds of unemployed artists in all media through the Works Progress Administration during the Great Depression. Since the 1960s the National Endowment for the Arts has supported artists through grants.

Auction Houses

The buying and selling of art at auction is one of the most dramatic events in the art world. The two dominant **auction houses** in London and New York, Sotheby's and Christie's, were by the 1980s each selling over a billion dollars worth of art a year. During that decade the Japanese became major players in bidding wars that drove up prices. Auction houses continually set new record prices not only for Old Masters but also for the work of contemporary artists. Sotheby's and Christie's also have experts that handle and sell other areas like African art, Asian art, furniture, and decorative arts. There was a time when collectors went to an art auction to find a bargain. Today the auctioning of art has become instead a verifiable

FIG 20-8 JOHN ZOFFANY [British, 1734/1735–1810], *The Tribuna of the Uffizi.* 1772–1776. Oil on canvas. Windsor Castle, Royal Collection.

way of setting price levels in the art market.

The auctions at Sotheby's and Christie's are often played by such mysterious rules that only the highest rollers dare enter their game filled with secret codes and secret agents. For example, the auctioneer and the seller generally agree beforehand on a minimum price (known as a reserve), for an object, below which the work will not be sold. The buyers do not know this reserve price, nor do they always know that the auction house itself has bought back an object when the bidding did not meet the reserve price. Auctioneers try to keep this information hidden because unsold work is considered psychologically damaged or "burned" and will not elicit significant bidding when it again comes up for sale.

Museums

Among the most active collectors, deeply involved in the art market, are the many **museums** of art in the United States and throughout the world. (Although the name *museum* means "place of the Muses," there was no Muse of art among the nine Muses of Greek mythology.) Most of the famous museums of Europe, such as the Louvre in Paris or the Uffizi in Florence, were started from royal or aristocratic collections,

which remain the core of their holdings. Acquisitions by these museums in modern times are limited, in general, to examples of their own national heritage.

In America, the museums themselves or their millionaire patrons had to purchase everything they own on the market in fairly recent times. Although most items in most museums are gifts from wealthy donors, art museums in America are still keen on new acquisitions and will sometimes outbid wealthy collectors for a new prize. Museums, including new, well-endowed institutions like the J. Paul Getty Museum in Malibu, California, thus have a considerable effect on the art market. Museums sometimes run low on funds for maintenance and wages, but they often still have large sums earmarked for new acquisitions or will receive a gift of an expensive work from a donor. Dependent on corporate and government funding, these facilities run the risk of becoming the spokesperson of big business and government—or they may simply avoid taking risks and offending their patrons.

Museums exert more influence on art than do most collectors because the works they purchase go on public display and receive, as it were, the institution's seal of approval. A museum's acquisitions and even the display of its holdings imply a favorable critical attitude toward the art. Museums also greatly influence the esteem given a work of art by the special exhibitions that they hold. A work from a private collection exhibited in any museum and thoroughly documented and discussed in a catalog published by the museum's experts will surely rise in value from all the attention. Even a work not actually in the museum's exhibition will benefit from the museum's attention to the artist or the style. With such power comes an ethical responsibility for scrupulous fairness in exhibition and acquisition procedures.

Art museums began in the late eighteenth century when the collections of the pope in Rome, the French king in Paris, the Duke of Florence (see John Zoffany's *The Tribuna of the Uffizi,* FIG. 20-8), and other members of the nobility were opened to the public. To this day, most art museums, even in democratic America, retain the same paradoxical character: they are a collection of art paid for by the rich and famous but maintained for the benefit of the public. One goal in opening these collections was to allow artists to study more freely the works of the great masters. In the nineteenth century the public art museum became a temple dedicated to beauty and committed to the task of uplifting the spirit of the people and instilling virtue in the masses.

Organizational Structures of an Art Museum

Most art museums in the United States are private institutions that may or may not receive a portion of their operating expenses from the municipality in which they are located. Usually, a museum is governed by a board of directors made up of wealthy patrons who frequently have paid for the institution's acquisitions. A **museum director,** the chief administrator, sets the overall policies for the museum's financial, personnel, educational, and research operations as well as supervises the general nature of its displays and exhibitions. A director oversees public relations, courts past and future donors, answers to the board of directors, and keeps an ear to the ground of "popular" taste for ways to boost admissions.

A **curator** is usually an expert in one field, like European painting or Chinese ceramics, who investigates the objects in the museum's collection, attends

THOMAS KRENS. Director of the Solomon R. Guggenheim Museum. New York. Photo by David Heald.

As director, Thomas Krens presided over the Solomon R. Guggenheim Museum renovation in which a controversial slab tower was added behind Frank Lloyd Wright's spiral. Despite the increased gallery space that the renovation provided uptown, Krens opened a new Guggenheim annex downtown in SoHo (the area in Manhattan south of Houston Street where many galleries are located). He also struck a deal with the government of Bilbao, Spain, which will pay the Guggenheim Museum about twenty million dollars to exhibit art from the New York museum's collection in a new museum in Spain. Krens defends his plans because they will bring more of the Guggenheim's collection, usually kept in storage, to more people more of the time.

Shen C. Y. Fu. Curator of Chinese Art, Freer Gallery of Art/Arthur B. Sackler Gallery. Washington, D.C.

to the care and preservation of the objects, arranges exhibitions of work owned by the museum or borrowed from elsewhere, and publishes research and educates the public about art. The Fogg Art Museum at Harvard University has for years had a famous training program for museum administrators and curators.

A museum may also employ librarians, laboratory technicians, preparators who design and carry out displays, educators, maintenance staff, and security guards. Museum personnel, almost without exception, enjoy the opportunity to handle actual art objects.

Functions of an Art Museum

In the United States and Canada the local art museum is considered a vital *public* institution and an integral part of the community because it performs a number of public functions. The increasing millions of people who each year visit art museums have made those institutions an outstanding cultural resource. In addition to providing recreation and enjoyment to all the people through art, museums play an important educational role. They not only collect, maintain,

exhibit, and explain their own works, they frequently gather pieces from all over the world to hold special exhibitions in order to expand the viewer's awareness of an artist, a style, or a theme. Sometimes these become "blockbuster" exhibits, which attract enormous crowds. Museums investigate works of art and publish catalogs that communicate their research, which often becomes the definitive word about an artist. They run research libraries that are open to scholars and to the public. They hold lectures and show films that teach about art, and they train docents—volunteer tour guides—to instruct visitors of all ages, or record electronic tour guides. They run shops that sell books about art, souvenirs, and other art-related materials. Even though the public does not own the paintings on their walls, museums are enmeshed in the cultural life of their locality and thus indirectly contribute to the economic development of their region through tourism and by making the community a desirable place to live.

There are all kinds of art museums, some big, some small, some that attempt to cover every aspect of the history of art (like the Metropolitan Museum of Art in New York City), and some that are dedicated to only certain kinds of art (like the Museum of Contemporary Art in Los Angeles). The architecture of museum buildings is a fascinating subject to pursue. Museums have certain common physical needs of space and light to house art to the best advantage. But the attitude, expressed in the architecture, toward how to view art has changed over the years. Invariably, early museums were designed like the Philadelphia Museum of Art, as temples to the goddess of beauty, in which large spaces, grand staircases, and imposing classical columns would awe the viewer. The architects of the Pompidou Center in Paris (FIG. 19-15) decided that viewing art would be an adventurous and fun experience. The light and space of the Kimbell Museum (FIG. 4-9) in Fort Worth suggest that viewing art is a more intimate personal experience.

Most museums in the larger cities of the United States and Canada are general museums that can illustrate a broad range of styles and techniques. However, the Museum of Contemporary Art in Cincinnati, which only holds special exhibitions, has no permanent collection. Many universities run general museums, although few of them can rival the extraordinary

Arata Isozaki [Japanese, 1931–], Museum of Contemporary Art. 1984–1987. Los Angeles.

Charles Lewis Borie [American, 1870–1943], Horace Trumbauer [American, 1868–1938], Clarence Clark Zantinger [American, 1872–1954], architects, Philadelphia Museum of Art.

collections of the Fogg Art Museum at Harvard or the Yale University Art Gallery. Most campus museums are much smaller and are dedicated to the education of students.

Even municipal museums of a general sort are far from being mere repositories of past art, since many of them take part in the ongoing artistic life of the community. Painters, sculptors, printmakers—all artists can learn lessons from the distant and the recent past in the galleries of a museum. What was accomplished by others before them can challenge artists to emulate or rebel against the work in the museum. Furthermore, many museums stimulate the production of art by holding exhibitions of the latest work from artists of the region or around the country. The Whitney Museum of American Art in New York, through its biennial exhibition, has a long tradition of assessing for the community the best of recent art. Some museums, like the Art Institute of Chicago, run art schools to train artists.

Museums around the world offer the public a wealth of art to see and enjoy firsthand. Museums can be exciting places because nothing equals the direct experience of art, when we can finally see the true

A museum gallery with visitors experiencing art. Photo by Bert Glinn, Magnum Photos.

color, the correct scale, and the actual texture of a painting. In a museum we can walk around sculpture and sense its movement through space and its mass. But it is not always easy to visit a museum. Often, after traveling some distance to get there, we feel compelled to see everything at once and are confronted with

Chapter 20: The Art World

daunting, endless corridors arranged in a mazelike fashion. The art becomes a blur. Perhaps the best museum is our local museum. It may not have world-class objects, but we can return often. There is time to sit, relax, and let the mind and emotions start to work.

It can be deeply satisfying to see in a museum the actual work of some master that the experts of the art world have praised. It can be fascinating and illuminating to recognize and examine new and different examples of an artist's style. Unfamiliar works offer a special challenge. To see them we must open our eyes to the new; make our own judgments; puzzle out the iconography by ourselves; categorize the style; and, like an explorer seeing new territory for the first time, follow the lines, walk around the shapes, and discover the colors. Without engaging in direct communication with the work of art for ourselves, the opinions of the art world matter very little.

Conservation and Preservation

Many large museums have departments devoted to the **conservation** of works of art because they recognize their responsibility to preserve the works in their care and pass them on to future generations in the best possible condition. Conservation departments may attempt to clean works obscured with grime and to restore works that

have been damaged by vandalism or neglect. The Metropolitan Museum of Art in New York has extensive conservation laboratories. Together with the nearby Conservation Center of New York University, it teaches the science and techniques of examining, preserving, and restoring paint, wood, cloth, metal, stone, and other art materials.

The cleaning and restoration of works of art demands great familiarity with the style and techniques of the past so that the conservator does not falsify the work by imposing on it an alien style. Cleaning art often involves the risk of damaging the work permanently by removing delicate glazes and other essential features along with the grime. Despite the professional and technical expertise of the conservators, the cleaning and restoration of Michelangelo's Sistine Chapel ceiling aroused heated debate about the true nature of Michelangelo's style.

The success of art museums and the enormous increase of tourism around the world threatens works of art with another danger: too many people. A large volume of viewers increases the likelihood of accidental damage at some point; great numbers of people can simply wear down the floors or stairs of famous buildings; crowds can affect the environment where art is housed. In the 1960s the curators of the Lascaux cave, where prehistoric paintings had been preserved for fif-

JAN VERMEER [Dutch, 1632–1675] *Head of a Girl.* C. 1665. Oil on canvas, 18 1/3 × 15 3/4 in. (46.5 × 40 cm). Mauritshius, The Hague. Scala/Art Resource.

FIG 20-9 HAN VAN MEEGEREN [Dutch, 1889–1947] painting a Vermeer-style canvas. Photo by George Rodger, Life Magazine © Time Warner.

From 1937 to 1945 Han Van Meegeren fooled experts and collectors with his falsifications of Vermeer and another seventeenth century Dutch painter. A traditional and conservative painter, disgruntled by the critics' rejection of his original work, Van Meegeren wanted to prove that he was as great an artist as an Old Master. Cleverly, Van Meegeren chose not to forge Vermeer's mature style, as illustrated in Head of A Girl *at the left, but Vermeer's problematic early style which is still debated by art historians. He painted his forgeries on actual seventeenth-century canvas and he ground his own pigments, using only materials available to Vermeer. Most importantly, he found ways to harden his paint, as though it had been drying for centuries, and to reproduce the crackle or pattern of fine crack lines evident in most 300 year old paintings. Only after he confessed, did they submit his work to laboratory examination.*

teen thousand years, noticed green bacteria growing rapidly on the walls and threatening the art. A ventilation system introduced to eliminate the carbon dioxide and condensation caused by the breathing of increasing numbers of tourists had brought the bacteria into the cave. Since 1963 the Lascaux cave has been closed to tourists and a reconstruction of the cave has been built nearby.

Forgeries and Fakes

Museum laboratories also help determine the authenticity of works of art with scientific techniques of examination. A **forgery,** like the famous ones painted by Han Van Meegeren (FIG. 20–9), is the deliberate falsification of another artist's work for purposes of deceit. Forgeries have been made since ancient times whenever art has entered into commerce and thus offered the possibility of gain. Millennia ago, fake jewels and fake silver, gold, and other precious materials were fabricated to deceive the consumer. Sculptors

Problems of attribution to Rembrandt arise not only because Rembrandt had numerous pupils who imitated their master's style but also because Rembrandt is believed to have signed his own name to work painted by his students. The amount of participation by Rembrandt in any work painted entirely or in part by the pupils or assistants in his workshop probably varied. Such collaboration was common practice in Rembrandt's day and happens even today. The Rembrandt Research Project is trying to identify authentic Rembrandts by assigning to his students work that does not manifest Rembrandt's hand exclusively. It has set itself standards that even Rembrandt would likely disagree with.

who copied Greek statues for the Romans sometimes signed their copies with the names of the Greek sculptors Phidias and Polycleitos. Even Michelangelo is supposed to have carved a cupid and then buried it in a vineyard to make it look antique.

Modern forgers still concentrate on the re-creation of antiquities as well as pre-Columbian art where gaps in our knowledge of the range of that art allow the possibility of new "discoveries." Italy, Mexico, and East Asia have been home to veritable industries devoted to the deliberate production of fakes. Their diligence in the selection of materials, simulation of old techniques, and replication of the aging process have often fooled the experts.

A work that is merely false or inauthentic is different from a forgery. Since the beginning of the history of art, artists have made copies and reproductions of an original work without any intention to deceive. With the passage of time—even a short period of time—a copy may be confused with the real thing.

The buyer or the museum expert must decide, frequently without the aid of documentation, whether a work is genuine. Scientific analysis has only a partial

usefulness to disclose forgeries or false works. Tests can determine if the materials are old enough and whether the chemical components of certain colors are indeed those used at the period of time in question. Laboratory examination can judge if the techniques were those of the time or if the weathering of the stone or the cracking of the paint show sufficient age. An expert opinion still is needed to tell the scientists what to look for and to judge whether the work is in the style of the original and the hand of the master. Forgers and copyists tend to betray the taste of their own time in their replications and also betray their time-bound understanding of the original.

Since the early 1970s, five expert Dutch art historians have formed a committee to examine with an exhaustive thoroughness every painting claimed to be by Rembrandt. Known as the Rembrandt Research Project, they have published three volumes of their studies so far. Whereas, it was once believed that about six hundred Rembrandt paintings existed, the Rembrandt Research Project is expected to pare that number down to about three hundred. Using all the latest tools of scientific investigation and basing their findings on supposedly objective criteria, they have rejected several paintings that have long been considered to be among Rembrandt's most admired work. *Polish Rider* (FIG. 20-10) in the Frick Museum in New York is slated to be removed from the list and assigned to an imitator or student. Many owners of Rembrandt paintings and many other art historians disagree with the committee's decisions—despite the Research Project's claim of objectivity.

Forgeries and fakes puzzle many people not simply because they have fooled the experts who have at one time lauded the pieces as significant art but because they call into question some commonly accepted notions about the evaluation of art and the nature of art itself. It is difficult philosophically to understand why a nearly perfect fake Van Gogh is much less esteemed than a genuine Van Gogh. The art world rejects that fake Van Gogh partly because the modern cult of personality exalts originality, which the false can never have, and partly because the art market is interested in promoting the limited number of authentic works by Van Gogh or any artist. More important, instead of revealing the personality of the artist or the artistic attitudes of an ancient culture, a forgery reveals the ingenuity of the forger. It does not give us the true picture or the genuine imaginative experience of its artist or people.

Artists' Education

Approximately thirty-five thousand students graduate each year with advanced degrees from art schools in America. Most contemporary artists in America today have studied art at a university or an independent school like the Maryland Art Institute or the Cranbrook Academy in Michigan. The curriculum usually begins with foundation courses in the visual elements and principles of design. Drawing from a model is still required training at most art schools. More and more students also receive training in drawing and design through computer-generated programs incorporating multimedia technology. Students are encouraged to try a variety of art media and to begin a concentration in one. Upon graduation, they are ready to begin a lifetime of exploration for a style of

Students drawing and sculpting from the model at the Minneapolis College of Art & Design. Courtesy the Minneapolis College of Art and Design, Continuing Studies. Photos by Greg Helgeson.

personal expression. Rarely is a student established on graduation.

Although painters, photographers, and sculptors receive a very flexible kind of training, architects must complete a set course of instruction and graduate from an accredited school of architecture. The training is more regulated and stringent because the stability of buildings is without question a matter of public concern. Therefore, states license architects before they may practice. In general, future architects, with skills in mathematics, physics, and computer science, need to complete a five-year program at one of the approximately ninety accredited schools of architecture around the United States. Furthermore, they must spend a set amount of time as an intern at an architectural or engineering firm. Some architects are able to open their own office, but most work for a large architectural firm or for a business or government agency in a field such as planning or preservation. Also, many work in the interior design or industrial design field.

Art Careers

Not every artist living today is destined to achieve superstar status like that of a Rembrandt or Picasso. Most are happy to be doing something creative, to spend their lives exploring visual meaning, and to make statements about themselves or about the world through their art. A career as an artist also has a number of collateral advantages, ranging from personal independence and flexible hours to direct personal involvement with the product being made.

Training in the visual arts and in the history of art also qualifies a person for a number of careers related to the practice of making art. Teaching art at all levels from elementary to university challenges thousands of artists to pass on their knowledge and enthusiasm. Practicing artists in education teach by their example as well: most colleges and universities expect that their art instructors will produce a body of work while teaching.

Other art-related careers can be found in museums and galleries—in their curatorial and research staff, in their conservation and restoration departments, and in art administration and art education programs in museums. People with training in art often work in art criticism and journalism. An art background is needed for work in advertising and other kinds of graphic design; in industrial design; and in fashion, textiles, and interior design. Artists with photography and video skills often work in media production for a variety of agencies. Some of these careers require further training or experience in specialized skills, and all of them are competitive. Nevertheless, they afford the satisfaction of working with the visual arts in a meaningful way.

```
┌─────────────────────────────────────────────────────────────────────┐
│                     S U M M A T I O N   B O X                         │
│  ┌─────────────────────────────────────────────────────────────────┐ │
│  │                        THE ART WORLD                              │ │
│  └─────────────────────────────────────────────────────────────────┘ │
```

- The art world contains people and institutions that influence the production and evaluation of art.
- The art market buys and sells art as a commodity.
- Critics write about art and influence taste.
- Art galleries promote the work of a certain number of artists.
- Collectors own original works of art.
- Patrons support artists and often set a style.
- Auction houses sell art at public events that often establish prices for art.
- Museums collect, preserve, and display art to educate the public about art.
- Educational institutions train people for a variety of careers in the art world.

```
└─────────────────────────────────────────────────────────────────────┘
```

Key Terms and Concepts

alternative spaces	auction houses	museum director
art dealers	collectors	museums
art gallery	conservation	patrons
artists' organizations	criticism	taste
art market	curator	
art world	forgery	

Notes

Chapter 1

1. Stephen Halliwell, trans., *The Poetics of Aristotle* (Chapel Hill, N.C.: University of North Carolina Press, 1987).

2. Erwin Panofksy, *Idea: A Concept in Art Theory* (New York: Harper & Row, 1969), p. 60.

3. *The Encyclopedia of World Art*, vol. 5 (New York: McGraw-Hill, 1961), p. 31a.

4. Vincent Van Gogh, *The Complete Letters of Vincent Van Gogh*, vol. 3 (Greenwich, Conn.: New York Graphic Society, 1959), p. 64 no. 544a.

5. Ibid., p. 29 no. 533.

6. Ibid., p. 203 no. 604.

Chapter 2

1. John 1:29 Revised Standard Version.

2. Barbara Novak, *American Painting of the Nineteenth Century* (New York: Harper & Row, 1979), p. 200.

3. Roy Sieber, *African Art in the Cycle of Life* (Washington, D.C.: National Museum of African Art, 1987), p. 65.

Critical Analysis I

1. Nancy Mowll Mathews, ed., *Cassatt and Her Circle: Selected Letters* (New York: Abbeville Press, 1984), p. 259.

2. Ibid., p. 274.

3. For information about Cassatt's life and work, see Nancy Mowll Mathews, *Mary Cassatt.* (New York: Abrams, 1987).

Chapter 4

1. Paul Klee, *The Thinking Eye: The Notebooks of Paul Klee*, ed. Jürg Spiller (New York: George Wittenborn, 1961), p. 105.

2. Letter from Georges Seurat to Maurice Beaubourg, in William Innes Homer, *Seurat and the Science of Painting* (Cambridge: MIT Press, 1964), p. 199.

3. Edvard Munch, *La Revue blanche* (Paris) 2 (1895), p. 528, as quoted in George Heard Hamilton, *Painting and Sculpture in Europe, 1880-1940* (Baltimore: Penguin Books, 1967), p. 75.

4. Georgia O'Keeffe, "About Myself," in *An American Place* exhibition catalog (New York, 1939).

Chapter 5

1. Van Gogh, *Complete Letters of Van Gogh*, vol. 3, pp. 28-29 no. 533, p. 31 no. 534.

Chapter 6

1. Maurice Denis, "Definition of Neo-Traditionalism," in *Theories: 1890-1910* (Paris: L'Occident, 1912), as translated in Elizabeth G. Holt, *From the Classicists to the Impressionists* (Garden City, N.Y. Doubleday, 1966), p. 509.

2. Pablo Picasso, interview by Christian Zervos in 1935, as reprinted in Herschel B. Chipp, *Theories of Modern Art* (Berkeley and Los Angeles: University of California Press, 1968), p. 270.

Chapter 7

1. Peter Murray, *The Architecture of the Italian Renaissance* (New York: Schocken Books, 1986), p. 6.

Chapter 10

1. Michael Crichton, *Jasper Johns* (New York: Harry Abrams, 1977) p. 28.

Chapter 11

1. Julia Cameron, "Annals of My Glass House" (1874), as quoted in *Photographic Journal* 1 (July 1927).

Chapter 12

1. John Sayles, *Thinking in Pictures* (Boston: Houghton Mifflin, 1987), p. 118.

Chapter 13

1. Elizabeth G. Holt, *A Documentary History of Art*, vol. 1 (Garden City, N.Y.: Doubleday Anchor, 1957), p. 285.

2. Ibid., vol. 2, pp. 15-16.

3. Filippo Baldinucci, *The Life of Bernini* (University Park, Pa.: Pennsylvania State University Press, 1966), p. 79.

Chapter 15

1. Vitruvius, *The Ten Books on Architecture* (New York: Dover Publications, 1960), p. 17.

2. Ibid.

3. Ibid.

4. Ibid., p. 174.

5. Ibid., p. 73.

6. Mario Salvadori, *Why Buildings Stand Up* (New York: W. W. Norton & Co., 1990), p. 226.

Chapter 16

1. Quintilian, *Institutionum Oratoriarum*, XII, 10, 9.

2. Pliny the Elder, *Natural History*, 35.40, 147.L.

Chapter 17

1. Holt, *History of Art*, vol. 1, pp. 274–75.

Chapter 18

1. F. T. Marinetti, "The Foundation and Manifesto of Futurism," *Le Figaro* (Paris) 20 (February 1909), as reprinted in Chipp, *Theories of Modern Art*, p. 286.

Chapter 19

1. Jackson Pollock, "My Painting," *Possibilities 1* (winter 1947-48), p. 79, as reprinted in Chipp, *Theories of Modern Art*, pp. 546–47.

2. Dorothy Sieberling, "Jackson Pollock Is He the Greatest Living Painter in the United States?" *Life* 27 (August 8, 1949), pp. 42–43.

GLOSSARY

abstract art   Art that fragments, simplifies, or distorts reality so that the formal properties of lines, shapes, and colors are emphasized.

accent   A touch of a complementary color to enliven the other colors.

acrylics   A painting medium in which the vehicle is plastic (synthetic resin).

Action Painting   A form of Abstract Expressionism in which the artist uses forceful brushwork or drips and splashes the paint on the surface to express emotion. The dynamic brushwork or drips and splashes make evident the gestures employed in the act of painting.

additive sculpture   The use of clay, wood, or metal to build up sculptural forms.

aesthetics   A branch of philosophy that attempts to define the artistic experience.

aisle   A corridorlike space commonly running alongside the nave in a basilica.

alla prima   A method of painting directly onto the canvas or panel, without much preparatory drawing or underpainting.

allegory   A representation of two or more personifications performing some action that has a conceptual or moral message.

alternative space   An area, apart from the spaces of museums or galleries, in which artists can exhibit new and experimental work not always accepted by those institutions.

ambulatory   The semicircular aisle that surrounds the apse or sanctuary of a Christian basilica.

analogous colors   Several colors that are next to one another on the color wheel; also called adjacent colors.

applied arts   Arts concerned with the design of objects that perform some useful function, as opposed to fine arts, whose

objects have a purely aesthetic function.

apse   A semicircular extension of space in a building.

aquatint   A form of printmaking in which acid etches a metal plate around acid resistant particles attached to the plate, to produce areas of value.

arcade   A series of arches.

arch   An arrangement of wedge-shaped stones forming a span because they compress one another.

armature   A skeletal bracing within clay or wax sculpture, needed to support the soft and malleable material before it hardens.

art for art's sake   The aesthetic theory that the essence of art lies in perfecting and enjoying its purely formal properties rather than in creating something to serve a purpose.

Art Nouveau   A style of art, popular at the end of the nineteenth and beginning of the twentieth centuries, that employed curvilinear, swelling, plantlike forms.

artists' organization   An association for the exhibition and sale of art, run by artists themselves and functioning in ways similar to a commercial gallery.

Arts and Crafts movement   A late-nineteenth- and early-twentieth-century activity and tendency to replace machine-made goods with handcrafted objects.

asphaltum   The tarlike acid-resistant ground in the etching process that coats the plate and into which the design is made.

assemblage   A sculpture constructed from material that has been cut and pieced together and transformed into something new.

asymmetry   A design in which the visual elements on one side are rather different from those on the other side.

atmospheric perspective   The projection of three-dimensional space by observing that the intervening air causes distant objects to change in color and to diminish in sharpness of focus and to decrease in chiaroscuro.

auteur theory   In filmmaking, the belief that the director, like the author of a novel, is the person responsible for the artistic achievement of a film.

avant-garde   Artists who break away from accepted norms of style or iconography and invent new art.

balance   A principle of design in which the stimulation of the visual elements on one side of a work visually seems to "weigh" as much as the stimulation of those on the other side.

balloon frame   A construction technique in which the walls of a building are assembled from two-by-fours called studs and then covered with veneers both inside and out.

baren   A smooth, rounded pad about five inches in diameter that printmakers use to press the paper into the inked surface of a relief block.

barrel vault   A semicylindrical covering over an architectural space; also called a tunnel vault.

basilica   A Roman building type adopted for Christian churches.

basketry   The creation of handcrafted fibrous containers.

Bauhaus   An influential school of architecture and design located in Germany, first in Weimar (1919–25), then in Dessau (1925–32), and finally in Berlin (1932–33).

bay   The often square or rectangular subsection of a building, divided into similar multiple units by columns, arches, or vaults.

biomorphic Having an irregular shape and resembling a biological organism like a cell or tiny animal.

bistre A brown ink made from wood soot, popular before the twentieth century.

bronze An alloy of the metals copper and tin.

brush and ink A tool that uses colored liquid to create lines or areas of wash.

building type A group of buildings identified by their similar function and also by their conventional size and shape.

burin A small tool with a diamond-shaped steel tip, used to cut the lines of an engraving into a metal plate.

bust A representation of the head and shoulders of a person.

buttress A mass of masonry set against a wall to give it added strength or to counteract the forces of an arch or vault.

calligraphic Consisting of animated and decorative curved lines that create surface patterns that enhance a form; resembling the elegant flourishes of a fancy handwriting.

calligraphy A fancy or beautiful handwriting or printing, often with elegant flourishes; long considered an art form in China and Japan.

calotype The early photographic process invented by W. H. Fox Talbot in England. Calotype produced a negative from which copies could be printed.

camera obscura A box with a small hole in one wall. The light coming through the hole will project an upside-down image of the outside world on the opposite wall of the box.

cantilevering A construction technique in which a horizontal beam resting on vertical supports projects some distance beyond one of those supports.

capital The part of a column that rests above the vertical shaft and forms a transition between the vertical shaft and the horizontal beam.

caricature A drawing or other form of representation that exaggerates prominent or characteristic features of a well-known individual or a common type for either satirical effect or social commentary.

cartoon (1) The full-sized preparatory drawing used by a fresco painter to transfer to the wall the essential lines of a composition. (2) Often humorous drawing in a simple style that appears on the comic pages of most daily newspapers.

carving Cutting material away from blocks of wood, stone, ivory, or other material to create sculptural form.

caryatid A statute of the female figure that replaces the shaft of a column and actually performs an architectural function.

casting The process of creating sculptural forms by pouring liquid material into a mold, where it hardens.

cast shadow The dark shape projected onto another surface by objects as they intercept the light.

centering The wooden scaffolding that is situated underneath an arch during its construction until the last stone is in place.

ceramic Fired clay shaped into pottery or sculpture.

chalk Black, red, or white drawing material found naturally in the earth.

chancel The area of a church where the main altar is located.

charcoal Charred wood made into a soft, dry, granular drawing medium that easily smudges.

chiaroscuro Any contrast between light and dark.

chiaroscuro woodcut A form of printmaking popular in the sixteenth century, in which several colors printed from separate blocks indicate different values rather than local colors.

choir The area beyond the crossing of the transept and the nave in a Christian basilica, where the monks sang.

clerestory The upper part of the nave where windows placed above the aisles bring light into the center of a basilica.

cloisonné The technique of setting colored glass and semiprecious stones within thin borders of gold.

coffer A square or other polygon sunk into the ceiling of a dome or vault as part of its decoration.

collage The modern painting technique, developed by Pablo Picasso and Georges Braque, in which real or imagined materials are pasted upon the work's surface.

collagraph A printmaking process in which the printmaker fabricates a collage of different materials on the surface of the plate. It may be printed as a relief or as an intaglio.

collodian process A method of photography invented in 1851 by the English sculptor Frederick Scott Archer, in which he coated a glass plate with a film of chemicals and placed it in the camera while the plate was still wet.

color wheel The spectrum arranged in a circle so that red appears next to violet and complementary colors stand opposite one another across the diameter of the circle.

column A vertical and usually tapered cylindrical support in architecture.

complementary colors Hues that are completely opposite one another on the color wheel. The complementary colors provide the greatest color contrast.

composition A design of lines, shapes, or contrasts of visual elements across the picture plane or embedded in a three-dimensional work. A composition tends to build a structure or framework over the whole.

computer art Art that uses the digitized electronic impulses of a computer as a painting tool to create visual images.

conceptual artists Artists who depict what they have stored in their imagination, what they conceive or know an object to look like.

consistency A principle of design that helps integrate a work of art by making most of the lines or shapes resemble one another in some way, by treating the value contrasts in a uniform way, or by establishing homogeneous relationships between the color contrasts and other visual elements.

Conté crayon A stick of hard chalk compounded with an oily material so that the chalk adheres to the surface better.

contemporary art Art produced within the last ten to fifteen years.

contour line A line that surrounds the edge of a form; it limits and distinguishes one area from another.

contrapposto Movement in the human body displayed by placing parts of the body in contrasting positions; one part may turn in one direction, at the same time that a related part turns in another.

convention A device of representation or design that nearly all the artists in a culture accept and employ.

cool colors Hues that are near blue on the color wheel.

corbel arch An architectural span—not a true arch—in which stones laid horizontally protrude slightly beyond the stones beneath them until the two sides of the "arch" meet.

Corinthian order The most elaborate of the Greek and Roman systems of vertical building design; its column has a base and a large capital carved with acanthus leaves.

craft A special skill for making common practical objects; the revival of that skill to protest mass manufacture and to promote integrity of hand-made work; the use of traditional craft materials to create art.

crane shot A shot filmed by a camera borne aloft by a crane; it usually provides a dramatic revelation of the action.

crayon Colored sticks of paraffin made for children's drawings.

cross-hatching A printmaking or drawing technique for producing dark values by crisscrossing two or more series of parallel lines on top of one another.

crossing The space where the transept crosses the nave in a basilica.

cross vault A vault formed by the intersection of two tunnel vaults.

curtain wall The outside walls that are hung on the framework of a modern steel skeletal building.

cut The most common type of film editing procedure, in which one shot suddenly ends and the next shot immediately begins.

daguerreotype The photographic process announced to the public in 1839 by Louis Daguerre; it produced a finely detailed positive image on a metallic surface.

design The selection, arrangement, or organization of visual elements in a work of art.

Die Brücke (The Bridge) The community of German Expressionist painters formed by Ernst Ludwig Kirchner, Erich Heckel, and other artists in Dresden in 1905–6.

director The person who plots and supervises the shooting of a film and tries to guide the actors in interpreting their role. The director is usually credited with the overall responsibility for the outcome of the film.

diminishing size A method of spatial projection in which the small size of objects relative to others within a picture indicates that they are located farther back in space.

dissolve A type of film editing in which one shot gradually disappears from the screen while another shot gradually emerges.

Divisionism The late-nineteenth-century painting style in which separate colors are applied in a methodical series of touches of the brush according to the laws of color theory.

dome A normally hemispherical vaulting covering an architectural space.

dominance The emphasis placed on the main center of interest by giving it the brightest illumination, the main linear movements, the strongest color, the most detail, the most striking contrast, or a prominent location in space.

Doric order The most austere and weighty of the Greek and Roman systems of vertical building design; its column is baseless and has a simple cushion capital.

drapery The loose garments arranged on human figures in sculpture and painting.

drypoint A form of intaglio printmaking in which lines are made on a metal plate by scratching the surface directly with a sharp diamond-tipped or carbide steel needle.

earth colors Hues resulting from the mixing of secondaries. These mixtures—brick red, yellow ocher, olive green—mimic the colors of minerals found naturally in the earth.

earthenware Pottery fired at a low heat so that the clay remains grainy and porous.

earthwork Large-scale shaping of earth and rocks, often in remote places, into sculpture.

easel painting A painted work intended to be hung on a wall, whether it was painted on an easel or not.

editing Relating, coordinating, and connecting one shot of film with another.

edition The total number of prints that a printmaker pulls from a plate or a block.

egg tempera A painting medium in which the vehicle is egg yolk.

elevation A whole or partial view of the height and width of a building drawn to scale without the distortion of a spatial projection.

embroidery The decoration of cloth with needlework designs.

encaustic The process of painting in hot beeswax.

engaged column A column that seems to be partially sunk into a wall or a pier.

engraving A form of intaglio printmaking in which lines are cut into a metal plate with a burin.

entablature In classical architecture, the horizontal part of the building above the vertical columns.

entasis The slight swell of a column as it deviates from the straight line of its tapering.

environment A work of sculpture that transforms the whole of an interior space and then surrounds the viewer on all sides.

equestrian monument A work of sculpture that includes both horse and rider.

etching An intaglio printmaking process in which a drawing tool removes some of the acid resistant ground covering a metal plate and then acid cuts the exposed places of the plate.

eye-line An imaginary line between an eye and the object of its glance.

fabrication In photography, the process in which the photographer deliberately constructs or assembles the subject of a photograph instead of merely documenting existing reality.

fade A type of film editing in which the image of one shot disappears as the screen turns dark and then the image of another shot appears out of the darkness.

fantasy An illusion or a vision of something that exists only in the artist's imagination.

Fauves (Wild Beasts) A group of French Expressionist artists, around Henri Matisse, who exhibited together in 1905–7.

fiber arts Arts in which all sorts of fibrous materials are sewn, woven, or joined in any number of ways.

figure-ground relationship The perception that figures or objects in a foreground tend to dominate the shapes in the background.

fine arts Arts that have only an aesthetic function, as opposed to applied arts, which serve practical functions.

firmitas The Latin word for solid construction; one of Vitruvius's principles of architecture.

flying buttress In Gothic architecture, an arch that counters the lateral thrust of clerestory vaults by spanning the gap over the roofs of the aisles between the upper wall and the external buttresses.

folk art Traditional arts and crafts that were passed down within the confines of a culture.

foreshortening The projection of irregularly shaped, nonlinear objects like arms and legs into space.

found object sculpture Sculpture in which artists simply find objects that are already made and combine them, rather than shape raw material into sculptural form.

fresco Painting on plaster that is wet, so that the pigment soaks into the fresh plaster.

frieze A horizontal area of the entablature of a classical order, located below the cornice and above the beam that rests on the column capitals. It is often decorated with relief sculpture.

frottage The technique, exploited by the Surrealist Max Ernst, in which an image is created with a pencil or other drawing tool by rubbing a paper placed over a textured surface.

genre The depiction of scenes of everyday life, of anonymous, ordinary people doing ordinary things.

gesso Plaster of Paris or white chalk mixed with glue; the traditional ground for painting a wooden support.

Gestalt psychology The school of psychology that studies the natural tendency to perceive a unified whole or a pattern rather than its individual fragments or parts.

glaze (1) Paint that is applied in a thin, transparent layer. (2) In ceramics, a glasslike coating that is baked right onto the clay, normally coloring it and making it impervious to liquids.

golden section The relationship between two unequal lines such that the smaller is to the larger as the larger is to the whole (the addition of the two).

gouache An opaque form of watercolor.

graphic design The art of designing all printed and visual images that communicate messages appearing in print, film, and television, exhibitions and displays, packaging and informational systems.

groin vault A vault formed by the intersection of two tunnel vaults.

ground A layer of paint or gesso applied to a support so that the support will receive paint.

handheld shot A shot filmed by a camera operator who is moving.

handling The manner or method of production evident in a work of art.

happening A type of performance art, popular in the 1960s, in which loosely staged public events of all descriptions were organized by artists.

Hard-edge abstraction Shapes bounded by precise contours and resembling regular geometric forms like the square, circle, or triangle.

hatching A series of close, parallel lines that conventionally indicate darker values.

hieratic representation The depiction of important people in a larger scale than subordinate individuals in order to symbolize their significance.

highlight On any modeled surface, the area of the brightest light where the light might actually be reflecting its source.

historic preservation The protection and maintenance of what is good and meaningful from the architectural history of an area in order to ensure that the region can find its cultural roots through that history.

history painting A picture that tells a religious, mythological, or historical story and usually contains an inspiring or moral message.

hue A color such as red or green; the perception of a wavelength of light.

iconography The subjects and symbols of works of art.

ideal A state of perfection that is known or imagined in the mind.

illumination A miniature illustration or decorations painted in manuscripts and books especially in the Middle Ages.

impasto The thick buildup of paint on the surface of a canvas.

implied line An imagined line created by the eye, which tends to treat a series of many irregular forms and disjointed shapes as a line that moves in one comprehensible direction.

impression Each single sheet that the printmaker pulls from the plate, block, or stencil.

industrial design The art of creating for a mass-manufactured product a style that will enhance its appearance, increase its usefulness and efficiency, and raise its appeal to the consumer.

installation A large and complex work of sculpture that must be assembled and situated within the museum or gallery space.

intaglio Any printmaking process in which the image to be printed is created by cutting grooves in a plate and forcing ink into those grooves.

intensity The quality of purity of a hue; the true spectrum color; also called brilliance, saturation, or purity.

International Style A style of architecture, popular in the mid-twentieth century, characterized by cubic shapes, glass curtain walls, and a lack of ornament.

in-the-round A kind of freestanding statue that is finished both back and front.

Ionic order The Greek and Roman system of vertical building design in which a fluted column shaft rests on a base and has a capital elaborated with scrolls or volutes in the four corners.

isometric projection A representation of the three-dimensional character of a building or some object, in which parallel lines are depicted as always parallel to one another.

keystone The top stone in an arch, probably the last stone put into place.

kinetic sculpture Sculpture that actually moves because of wind, water, or a motor.

landscape art Art whose major focus is the depiction of elements of nature such as sky, mountains, valleys, rivers, fields, and trees.

light source The kind and direction of light that illuminates a work of art.

linear perspective A scheme for creating the illusion of three-dimensional space on a two-dimensional surface, in which parallel lines that move away from the viewer are drawn not as parallels but as diagonals that converge and meet at some point.

line A point in motion; a mark made to form a design on a surface.

linocut A reduction method of relief printmaking in which linoleum is gradually cut away after each new colored ink is printed.

lithography A planographic form of printmaking in which the flat surface of a block of stone is chemically treated to receive or reject printer's ink.

local color The color that an object is known to be, without any regard for temporary or accidental effects.

lost wax process A method of casting hollow metal sculpture by creating two molds, an inner core and an outer shell, kept apart by a suitable thickness of wax. When the molds are heated, the wax melts, runs out the bottom, and leaves a gap into which molten bronze is poured through a hole at the top of the molds. The bronze replaces the missing wax.

manipulation In photography, the control of photographic techniques and materials, often to the extent that the image is obviously changed from a straightforward reproduction of reality.

maquette A sculptor's small sketch in clay, wax, or other material.

mask A face covering that enables a person wearing it to obscure his or her features and assume the persona of another.

mass A solid, three-dimensional form that has weight and takes up a real space.

medium A distinct form of art such as painting or sculpture, or a distinct process within a form.

metalpoint A drawing stylus of gold, copper, tin, lead, or silver.

metalwork Art produced by the craft-related techniques of designing and fabricating all kinds of metals.

metope The nearly square panel alternating with triglyphs in the frieze of the Doric order; often decorated with relief carving.

mihrab A niche in the wall of a mosque that points to Mecca, the focus of prayer.

mimesis The imitation of nature by copying or reproducing what artists see before them.

minaret A slender tower, attached to a mosque, from which the muezzin chants a call to prayer five times a day.

mise-en-scène Everything that is put into each frame of a film; everything that appears on the screen at any given moment; all theatrical and photographic elements.

mixed media Different techniques combined in one work as in tempera combined with oil paint; different art media in combination, as in painting combined with photography.

mobile A form of kinetic sculpture, invented by Alexander Calder, in which the pieces are balanced from a wire suspended from the ceiling.

modeling (1) Gradual variations from light to dark across rounded surfaces like a face, an arm, or a leg. (2) Adding and manipulating clay or wax to create sculptural forms.

modern art The dominant art of the twentieth century that grew out of the radical ideas and bold experiments of the Post-Impressionists.

module A part of a building whose measurements govern the proportions of the rest of the building.

modulor "The module of gold"; Le Corbusier's system of architectural proportions based on the golden section.

monotype In printmaking, an impression made by simply pressing paper to a newly painted surface.

montage A French word for editing that stresses the positive aspects of connecting the shots to build a film.

morphing In film editing, the nearly imperceptible blending of one shot into another by means of computer technology.

mosque An Islamic place for worship, prayer, scripture reading, and preaching.

motif A recurrent theme or design that an artist employs.

movement (1) The paths that lines create in a work of art, for the eye to follow. (2) An essential characteristic of film art, including the activity of the actors and the changing position of the camera.

multimedia Works produced by a computer equipped with a sound card, a CD-ROM, and sufficient speed and capacity to combine text, graphics, sound, animation, and full-motion video.

mural A painting on a wall or ceiling where it becomes part of the architectural decoration.

nave The central space in a basilica.

negative shapes Subsidiary shapes surrounding the dominant figures or objects in a painting.

neutral A gray color produced when complements are mixed together in nearly equal proportions. Theoretically, mixing complements of full intensity should produce a black because one complementary color should totally absorb or subtract the wavelength of the other.

nonobjective art A work that reproduces no recognizable object in it.

nude An unclothed human figure in which the main emphasis is its beauty, grace, or ideal proportions.

oil A vehicle for painting; usually linseed oil.

optical color Color as the eye sees it with all the subtleties of reflected colors, filtering atmosphere, colored lighting, and simultaneous contrasts.

orthogonal Lines in linear perspective that move away from the viewer and are genuinely perpendicular to the picture plane.

outsider art The work of self-taught artists who, isolated from mainstream artistic culture, supposedly create with innocence, spontaneity, and honesty.

overlapping A fundamental method of spatial projection in which something obscures part of something else considered to lie behind it.

pace In film editing, a rhythm or tempo established by arranging shots to last on the screen about the same length of time throughout a sequence.

pan A camera movement in which the camera turns on its axis and sweeps horizontally across a scene.

paper A support for drawing and painting made from matted rag fibers.

parchment The prepared skin of animals such as sheep, goats, or calves used as a drawing support.

pastels Pure pigments that are dry (not mixed with oil) and lightly bound together by a gum into chalklike sticks for drawing.

patina The think layer of brown or greenish oxidation on bronze when it is exposed to certain chemicals or to the weather.

pediment The triangular gable at the end of a Greek or Roman temple.

pen and ink A tool that uses colored liquid for drawing.

pencil A thin shaft of graphite and clay sheathed in wood and used as a drawing tool.

pendentive The curving triangular area underneath a dome and between the arches supporting a dome.

pentimento A ghost like shape, once hidden by an artist under a layer of paint, that begins to reappear in time.

perceptual artists Artists who reproduce what they see before them.

performance art Works in which artists put themselves and their creative activity on display before an audience as a form of living art.

personification A human figure that stands for a virtue or some other abstract concept.

perspective See **linear perspective.**

petroglyph A drawing made by pecking or cutting a design into the stone face of a natural rock or cliff.

photographic moment The instant when all the technical and personal variables come together to form an image that will achieve a good photograph.

photographic realism The ability of photographic film to record an enormous amount of detail and an extraordinary range of values at a precise moment in time.

pictograph A visual image that represents a word or an idea.

picture plane The surface or imaginary window perpendicular to the line of vision on which the pictorial image appears to be inscribed.

pier A vertical support within a building; not a cylindrical column.

pigment The dry powdery substance that produces a color for painting.

pilaster A flattened vertical support along the wall of a building, normally designed in one of the classical orders.

plan A design of the spaces and masses of architecture, arranged over a horizontal area.

Pointillism Seurat's technique of painting in small dots of color.

porcelain Pottery produced by firing a highly refined clay mixed with kaolin at a very high temperature.

position A convention for representing on a flat surface the location of an object in the third dimension; the higher up the object is within the flat image, the farther back in space it is understood to be.

post-and-beam system See **post-and-lintel system.**

post-and-lintel system A method of construction in which horizontal beams are placed across vertical supports.

pottery Fire-hardened vessels made of clay.

primary colors Colors that cannot be formed by mixing other colors and from which all the other colors can be formed. The primary colors are red, yellow, and blue.

principles of design Guidelines that artists follow to bring unity and focus to their vision. The principles of design include dominance, consistency with variety, rhythm, proportions, scale, and balance.

proportions Mathematical relationships or ratios that govern the measurements and placement of the lines, shapes, and masses of a work of art.

quill pen A drawing tool made from the wing feathers of a large bird like the goose or swan or of a smaller bird like the raven or crow.

quilt A bed covering, stitched into a design with colored pieces of material.

recto The right-hand page of a book or the front of a piece of paper.

reed pen A drawing tool cut from a hollow reed.

reflected light Light from an indirect source.

reinforced concrete Concrete in which steel rods are embedded and tied at

their ends to the vertical supports to give the concrete the tensile strength of steel.

relief (1) Sculpture in which the back of the piece is not executed but is still attached to the block, slab, or wall. (2) Any printmaking process in which the image to be printed is raised from the surface of the plate or block.

rhythm A repetition of the visual elements in a work of art, in which they seem to flow to a steady beat across the picture plane or throughout a three-dimensional work.

Salon The annual or biennial exhibition of the French Academy in Paris in the eighteenth and nineteenth centuries, originally held in the Salon d'Apollon of the Louvre.

Salon des Refusés The exhibition of works rejected from the French Academy's Salon in 1863.

scale The relationship between the artistic image and the object in reality that it imitates.

screen printing A form of printmaking in which ink is pushed through a stencil attached to a porous screen of silk, polyester, or other material.

scumbling Brush strokes of paint dragged over, and only partially covering, a dry layer of paint underneath.

secondary colors The hues green, violet, and orange. They are called secondary because they can be created by mixing two primaries.

section A representation, in scale, of the dimensions of a building measured along a plane cut through the building.

semiotics The study of the communication between the artist and the viewer through the medium of the artist's signs and symbols.

sentimental art Art in which the means used to arouse feelings are exaggerated and the emotions aroused do not represent a normal or proportionate reaction to the subject.

sepia A brown ink made from secretions of the cuttlefish or squid.

sequence A portion of a film, normally lasting several minutes and consisting of a number of shots that are related to one another by some visual or conceptual coherence.

serigraphy A form of screen printing in which the screen is made of silk; also called silk screening.

shade A color produced by the addition of black to make it darker; adding some of the complement to any color will also produce a shade of that color.

shaft The cylindrical part of a column under the capital and above the base.

shaped canvases Canvases in which the traditional rectangular painting format is manipulated as though the shapes within the painting determine the shape of the format.

shape An area of the surface of a work of art that has a distinct form because it is bound by a contour line or because it has a different value, color, pattern, or texture.

shot The basic unit of a film; one continuous rolling of the camera.

significance The combination and interaction of style and iconography that result in new ways of seeing.

silhouette A darkened outline representation of something.

silk screening A form of screen printing in which the screen is made of silk; also called serigraphy.

silverpoint The most common metalpoint used for drawing.

simultaneous contrast The ability of a color to induce in its neighbor the opposite in value and hue.

single-point perspective A linear perspective projection in which the orthogonals meet at a single point, normally in the center of the composition and on the horizon line.

soft ground A form of etching in which the acid resistant asphaltum, mixed with petroleum jelly, remains soft and sticky so that a variety of materials and textured surfaces can be pressed into it in order to expose the metal plate underneath.

solid wall construction A building technique in which the firm mass of the wall holds itself up and supports the roof or the upper floors.

sound In filmmaking, the human speech, music, sound effects, and even ambient noise of the location, manipulated in relation to the visual images on the screen.

space (1) The illusion of a three-dimensional projection in a two-dimensional work. (2) The actual areas within architecture.

spatial relationship The appearance of close physical proximity established by connecting separate shots through film editing.

spectrum All the visible colors arranged by the size of their wavelengths, usually in a series of parallel bars of color.

spirit of the time The belief that a certain set of conditions at some period compels the art and architecture of that period into a uniform style.

steel cage construction A network of steel girders that forms an internal skeleton that supports a building.

still life Any deliberate grouping of small inanimate objects.

stoneware Pottery fired at a temperature higher than that of earthenware so that it becomes smoother and harder.

straight photography Photography produced under the conviction that the print should reproduce what the photographer saw through the camera lens when the picture was taken. Straight photography claims to document reality with a minimum of manipulation.

studio craft The work of many contemporary craft-artists who consider glass, clay, wood, fiber, or metal to be simply the means to create art.

study A drawing or painting in which the artist explores a part or an aspect of a work in order to resolve any problems in rendering that segment.

stupa A large hemispherical solid mound which may have originally contained relics of the Buddha.

style The formal properties of works of art and the ways artists use those properties; whatever answers the question How is it done?

subtractive sculpture A process of creating sculptural forms by taking away material from a block of something.

support The surface to which paint adheres.

suspension A construction technique in which a roadway, a floor, or a roof is held in place by a system of cables.

symbolic communication The transfer of a message through visual signs that have a rich, many-leveled, emotion-filled meaning similar to person experience.

symmetry A balance achieved when the formal elements on one side of a work resemble the formal elements on the other side, but reversed as in a mirrored image.

synaesthesia The theory that one sense organ in the body responds to the stimulus of another, as when a color evokes the sensation of a sound or a taste.

tapestry A wall covering woven into a pictorial design.

taste The appreciation of, and preference for, certain styles of art as a result of a person's background and education.

temporal relationship The appearance, established through film editing, that two or more shots are related in time. A temporal relationship can expand or contract time.

Tenebrism A strong and often dramatic contrast of light and dark; it emphasizes the space-creating property of chiaroscuro.

terra cotta Clay baked and made hard and permanent by being fired in a kiln.

tertiary colors Hues that are created by the mixture of a primary and a secondary.

texture A quality of the surface that calls attention to the physical presence of the material.

tilt In filmmaking, a camera movement in which the camera moves up or down in a sweeping motion.

tint A color produced by the addition of white to make it lighter.

tondo A circular shaped work of art.

tracking A camera movement in which the camera is pulled on a dolly, normally on small tracks, while it is filming.

transept A space similar in its proportions to the nave but set perpendicular to the nave in a basilica.

triglyph A rectangular panel decorated with three vertical cuts, forming part of the frieze in the Doric order.

trompe l'oeil Realism in art that nearly convinces the eye of the actuality of the objects represented.

truss A support beam of metal or wood designed with a very stable and rigid triangular configuration.

tunnel vault   A semicylindrical covering over an architectural space; also called a barrel vault.

tusche   The greasy medium used to create an image on a lithographic stone.

two-point perspective   A linear perspective projection in which the parallel lines of objects, which are not perpendicular to the picture plane, meet at two separate vanishing points.

tympanum   The area under an arch and over a doorway of a building.

typeface   A particular design, size, and style of letters and numbers.

typography   The visual appearance of letters and numbers.

ukiyo-e   "Pictures of the floating world"; Japanese woodblock prints from the eighteenth and nineteenth centuries that illustrate popular entertainments and views of daily life.

unity   A cohesion, a wholeness, and a completeness of the visual elements in a work of art.

urban environment   All the visible physical conditions in an urban area; a landscape of buildings, roads, open spaces, and facilities that humans have built over the natural landscape.

urban planning   The orderly arrangement and control of the growth and development of an urban environment on a rational basis.

utilitas   The Latin word for suitability, appropriateness, and practicality; one of Vitruvius's principles of architecture.

value   The amount of light reflected from the surface of an object; the name for the relative lightness or darkness or some area.

vanishing point   The position on the horizon where the lines of a linear perspective projection meet.

vanitas   The symbolism in a still life, often achieved by a skull, that all things must pass away.

variety   Differences, changes, and variations in the visual elements that break from the design principle of absolute consistency so that the elements do not look too static, dull, or monotonous.

vehicle   The liquid that suspends pigments and causes them to adhere to a surface.

vellum   Very fine calfskin or lambskin prepared as a drawing support.

venustas   The Latin word for beauty or the artistic expression of architecture; one of Vitruvius's principles of architecture.

verso   The left-hand page of a book or the back of a piece of paper.

video art   (1) An arrangement or installation of TV monitors in a gallery space. (2) Videotaped documentaries, interviews, and performances. (3) Video images electronically manipulated in a free and creative manner that is nearly impossible with ordinary film. The videotape can be colored, distorted, fragmented, combined, and abstracted.

visual relationship   The appearance established through film editing, that the lines, color, light, movement, or any part of the mise-en-scène of one shot is similar to—or, thoroughly different from—that of the next shot.

voids   The empty spaces between the masses of sculpture.

warm colors   Hues that are near red on the color wheel.

wash   Ink diluted with water and applied with a brush to produce values.

watercolor   A transparent painting medium whose vehicle is water and gum arabic (a thickener derived from the acacia tree).

wipe   A type of film editing in which a line moving across the screen removes one shot while introducing another behind it.

woodcut   A form of relief printing in which a design is drawn on a wooden block, then the part of the block that is not to be printed is cut away with woodcarver's tools such as knives, gouges, and chisels.

wood engraving   A relief method of printmaking using end-grain blocks of wood on which white lines normally are cut out by the printmaker.

zoom   An apparent camera movement caused by smoothly and rapidly changing the focal length of the camera's lens so that the camera seems to rush toward something on the screen.

BIBLIOGRAPHY

General References

Atkins, Robert. *Artspeak: A Guide to Contemporary Ideas, Movements, and Buzzwords.* New York: Abbeville Press, 1990.

Fleming, John, Hugh Honour, and Nikolaus Pevsner. *The Penguin Dictionary of Architecture.* New York: Penguin Books, 1991.

Holt, Elizabeth G. *A Documentary History of Art.* 2 vols. Garden City, N.Y.: Doubleday Anchor, 1957.

_____ . *From the Classicists to the Impressionists: A Documentary History of Art and Architecture in the Nineteenth Century.* Garden City, N.Y.: Doubleday Anchor, 1966.

_____ . *The Triumph of Art for the Public: The Emerging Role of Exhibitions and Critics.* Garden City, N.Y.: Doubleday Anchor, 1979.

_____ . *The Art of All Nations, 1850-1873: The Emerging Role of Exhibitions and Critics.* Garden City, N.Y.: Doubleday Anchor, 1981.

Mayer, Ralph. *The HarperCollins Dictionary of Art Terms and Techniques.* New York: HarperPerennial, 1991.

Piper, David, ed. *The Random House Dictionary of Art and Artists.* New York: Random House, 1988.

Chapter 1. What Is Art?

Alperson, Philip, ed. *The Philosophy of the Visual Arts.* New York: Oxford University Press, 1992.

Davies, Stephen. *Definitions of Art.* Ithaca, N.Y.: Cornell University Press, 1991.

Edwards, Betty. *Drawing on the Right Side of the Brain.* Los Angeles: Tarcher, 1989.

Fagg, William. *Yoruba: Sculpture of West Africa.* New York: Alfred A. Knopf, 1982.

Hall, Michael D., and Eugene W. Metcalf, Jr., eds. *The Artist Outsider: Creativity and the Boundaries of Culture.* Washington, D.C.: Smithsonian Institution Press, 1994.

Hammacher, A. M., and Renilde Hammacher. *Van Gogh: A Documentary Biography.* New York: Macmillan, 1982.

Panofsky, Erwin. *Idea: A Concept in Art Theory.* New York: Harper & Row, 1968.

Thompson, Robert Farris. "Yoruba Artistic Criticism." In *The Traditional Artist in African Societies,* edited by Warren L. d'Azevedo. Bloomington, Ind.: Indiana University Press, 1973.

Van Gogh, Vincent. *The Complete Letters of Vincent Van Gogh.* 3 vols. Greenwich, Conn.: New York Graphic Society, 1959.

Vogel, Susan. *African Aesthetics.* New York: Center for African Art, 1986.

Chapter 2. Subjects and Their Uses in Art

Elsen, Albert E. *Purposes of Art.* New York: Holt, Rinehart and Winston, 1981.

Furst, Peter T., and Jill L. Furst. *North American Indian Art.* New York: Rizzoli, 1982.

Gibson, Walter. *Hieronymous Bosch.* New York: Oxford University Press, 1973.

Hall, James. *Dictionary of Subjects and Symbols in Art.* New York: Harper & Row, 1979.

Sieber, Roy. *African Art in the Cycle of Life.* Washington, D.C.: National Museum of African Art, 1987.

Chapter 3. Styles and Cultural Expression

Mathews, Nancy Mowll. *Mary Cassatt.* New York: Abrams, 1987.

_____ , ed. *Cassatt and Her Circle: Selected Letters.* New York: Abbeville Press, 1984.

Schwartz, Gary. *Rembrandt: His Life, His Painting.* New York: Viking, 1985.

White, Christopher. *Rembrandt.* New York: Thames and Hudson, 1984.

Chapter 4. Line, Shape, and Mass

Carmean, E. A., Jr. *Helen Frankenthaler: A Paintings Retrospective.* New York: Abrams, 1989.

Klee, Paul. *The Thinking Eye: The Notebooks of Paul Klee.* Edited by Jürg Spiller. New York: George Wittenborn, 1961.

Richardson, John A., Floyd W. Coleman, and Michael J. Smith. *Basic Design: Systems, Elements, Applications.* Englewood Cliffs, N.J.: Prentice-Hall, 1984.

Rose, Barbara. *Frankenthaler.* New York: Abrams, 1971.

Chapter 5. Light and Color

Albers, Josef. *Interaction of Color.* New Haven, Conn.: Yale University Press, 1975.

Birren, Faber. *History of Color in Painting.* New York: Reinhold, 1965.

Hope, Augustine, and Margaret Walch. *The Color Compendium.* New York: Van Nostrand Reinhold, 1990.

Itten, Johannes. *The Art of Color.* New York: Van Nostrand Reinhold, 1973.

Weber, Nicholas F. *Josef Albers: A Retrospective.* New York: Solomon R. Guggenheim Foundation, 1988.

Chapter 6. Surface and Space

Dunning, William. *Changing Images of Pictorial Space: A History of Spatial Illusion in Painting.* Syracuse, N.Y.: Syracuse University Press, 1991.

Gill, Robert W. *Basic Perspective.* London: Thames & Hudson, 1980.

Hilton, Timothy. *Picasso.* New York: Thames and Hudson, 1989.

Chapter 7. Principles of Design

Ackerman, James. *The Architecture of Michelangelo.* Chicago: University of Chicago Press, 1986.

Hibbard, Howard, *Michelangelo.* Cambridge, Mass.: Harper & Row, 1985.

Lauer, David A. *Design Basics.* New York: Holt, Rinehart and Winston, 1985.

Maier, Manfred. *Basic Principles of Design.* 4 vols. New York: Van Nostrand Reinhold, 1977.

Ocvirk, Otto G., Robert O. Bone, Robert E. Stinson, and Philip R. Wigg. *Art Fundamentals: Theory and Practice.* Dubuque, Iowa: William C. Brown Co., 1981.

Pile, John F. *Design: Purpose, Form and Meaning.* New York: Norton, 1982.

Chapter 8. Drawing

Chaet, Bernard. *The Art of Drawing.* New York: Holt, Rinehart & Winston, 1978.

Hale, Robert Beverly. *Drawing Lessons from the Great Masters.* New York: Watson-Guptill, 1989.

Lambert, Susan. *Reading Drawings: An Introduction to Looking at Drawings.* New York: Pantheon Books, 1984.

Mendelowitz, Daniel M. *Drawing.* New York: Holt, Rinehart and Winston, 1967.

Rawson, Philip. *Drawing.* London and New York: Oxford University Press, 1969.

Tannenbaum, Judith. *Vija Celmins.* Philadelphia: Institute of Contemporary Art, University of Pennsylvania, 1992.

Chapter 9. Printmaking

Castleman, Riva. *Prints of the Twentieth Century.* New York: Thames and Hudson, 1988.

Peterdi, Gabor. *Printmaking: Methods Old and New.* New York: Macmillan, 1980.

Ratcliff, Carter. *Yvonne Jacquette: Paintings, Frescoes, Pastels, 1988-1990.* New York: Brooke Alexander, 1990.

Ross, John, Clare Romano, and Tim Ross. *The Complete Printmaker.* New York: Macmillan, Free Press, 1990.

Saff, Donald, and Deli Sacilotto. *Printmaking: History and Process.* New York: Holt, Rinehart and Winston, 1978.

Sander, David. *Wood Engraving: An Adventure in Printmaking.* New York: Viking Press, 1978.

Chapter 10. Painting

Anfam, David A. *Techniques of the Great Masters of Art.* Secaucus, N.J.: Chartwell Books, 1985.

Auping, Michael. *Susan Rothenberg: Paintings and Drawings.* New York: Rizzoli, 1992.

Chaet, Bernard. *An Artist's Notebook.* New York: Holt, Rinehart and Winston, 1979.

Cole, Bruce. *The Renaissance Artist at Work: From Pisano to Titian.* New York: Harper & Row, 1983.

Goldstein, Nathan. *Painting: Visual and Technical Fundamentals*. Englewood Cliffs, N.J.: Prentice-Hall, 1979.

Hall, Doug, and Sally Jo Fifer, eds. *Illuminating Video: An Essential Guide to Video Art*. New York: Aperture in association with Bay Area Video Coalition, 1990.

Mayor, Ralph. *The Painter's Craft: An Introduction to Artists' Methods and Materials*. New York: Penguin Books, 1991.

Truckenbrod, Joan. *Creative Computer Imaging*. Englewood Cliffs, N.J.: Prentice-Hall, 1988.

Wescher, Herta. *Collage*. New York: Abrams, 1968.

Chapter 11. Photography

Kirsh, Andrea. *Carrie Mae Weems*. Washington, D.C.: National Museum of Women in the Arts, 1993.

Newhall, Beaumont. *The History of Photography: From 1839 to the Present Day*. New York: Museum of Modern Art, 1982.

Rand, Glenn, and David Litschel. *Black and White Photography*. Minneapolis–St. Paul: West Publishing Co., 1994.

Rosenblum, Naomi. *A World History of Photography*. New York: Abbeville Press, 1984.

Smith, Joshua P. *The Photography of Invention: American Pictures of the 1980s*. Washington, D.C.: National Museum of American Art; Cambridge: MIT Press, 1989.

Warren, Bruce. *Photography*. Minneapolis–St. Paul: West Publishing Co., 1993.

Chapter 12. Film

Bordwell, David, and Kristin Thompson. *Film Art: An Introduction*. Reading, Mass.: Addison-Wesley, 1979.

Mast, Gerald. *A Short History of the Movies*. Indianapolis: Bobbs-Merrill Publishing, 1981.

Monaco, James. *How to Read a Film*. New York: Oxford University Press, 1981.

Sayles, John. *Thinking in Pictures*. Boston: Houghton Mifflin, 1987.

Chapter 13. Sculpture

Beardsley, John. *Earthworks and Beyond*. New York: Abbeville Press, 1989.

Goldberg, RoseLee. *Performance Art: From Futurism to the Present*. New York: Abrams, 1988.

Levine, Gemma. *With Henry Moore: The Artist at Work*. New York: Times Books, 1978.

Moore, Henry. *Henry Moore Sculpture*. New York: Rizzoli, 1981.

Padovano, Anthony. *The Process of Sculpture*. New York: Da Capo Press, 1981.

Rogers, Leonard R. *Sculpture*. New York: Oxford University Press, 1969.

Rubin, David S. *Petah Coyne*. Cleveland: Cleveland Center for Contemporary Art, 1992.

Weisberg, Gabriel. *Traditions and Revisions: Themes from the History of Sculpture*. Cleveland: Cleveland Museum of Art, 1975.

Wittkower, Rudolph. *Sculpture: Processes and Principles*. New York: Harper & Row, 1977.

Chapter 14. Applications of Design: Crafts, Industrial Design, Graphic Design, and Computer-Aided Design

Bowman, Leslie Green. *American Arts and Crafts: Virtue in Design*. Los Angeles: Los Angeles County Museum of Art; Boston: Little, Brown, Bullfinch Press, 1990.

Conover, Theodore E. *Graphic Communications Today*. Minneapolis–St. Paul: West Publishing Co., 1990.

Cumming, Elizabeth, and Wendy Kaplan. *The Arts and Crafts Movement*. New York: Thames and Hudson, 1991.

Davis, Virginia I. *Crafts: A Basic Survey*. Dubuque, Iowa: W. C. Brown, 1989.

Dormer, Peter. *The Meanings of Modern Design*. New York: Thames & Hudson, 1991.

——— . *Design since 1945*. New York: Thames & Hudson, 1993.

Frantz, Susanne K. *Contemporary Glass: A World Survey from the Corning Museum of Glass*. New York: Abrams, 1989.

Hall, Julie. *Tradition and Change: The New American Craftsman*. New York: E. P. Dutton, 1977.

Heskett, John. *Industrial Design*. New York: Oxford University Press, 1980.

Hurlburt, Allen. *The Design Concept*. New York: Watson-Guptill, 1981.

Klein, Dan. *Glass: A Contemporary Art*. New York: Rizzoli, 1989.

Lucie-Smith, Edward. *The Story of Craft*. Ithaca, N.Y.: Cornell University Press, 1981.

_____. *Furniture: A Concise History.* New York: Thames and Hudson, 1985. Reprint, 1990.

Rawson, Philip. *Ceramics.* Philadelphia, University of Pennsylvania Press, 1989.

Retzer, John P., and Florence H. Retzer. *Fiber Revolution.* Milwaukee: Milwaukee Art Museum, 1986.

Sparke, Penny. *An Introduction to Design and Culture in the Twentieth Century.* New York: Harper & Row, 1986.

Chapter 15. Architecture

Frampton, Kenneth. *Modern Architecture: A Critical History.* New York: Thames and Hudson, 1992.

Gauldie, Sinclair. *Architecture.* New York: Oxford University Press, 1969.

Salvadori, Mario. *Why Buildings Stand Up.* New York: W. W. Norton & Co., 1990.

Shay, James. *New Architecture San Francisco.* San Francisco: Chronicle Books, 1989.

Vitruvius. *The Ten Books on Architecture.* New York: Dover Publications, 1960.

Woodbridge, Sally. "A Regionalist Union," *Progressive Architecture* (June 1990), Vol. 71, pp. 106–113.

Chapter 16. Art of the Ancient and Medieval Worlds

De La Croix, Horst, Richard G. Tansey, and Diane Kirkpatrick. *Gardner's Art through the Ages.* Orlando, Fla.: Harcourt Brace Jovanovich, 1991.

Grodecki, Louis. *Gothic Architecture.* New York: Abrams, 1977.

Hartt, Frederick. *Art: A History of Painting, Sculpture, Architecture.* Englewood Cliffs, N.J.: Prentice-Hall, 1989.

Honour, Hugh, and John Fleming. *The Visual Arts: A History.* Englewood Cliffs, N.J.: Prentice-Hall, 1986.

Janson, H. W. *History of Art.* Englewood Cliffs, N.J.: Prentice-Hall, 1991.

Lee, Sherman E. *A History of Far Eastern Art.* Englewood Cliffs, N.J.: Prentice-Hall; New York: Abrams, 1982.

Stewart, Andrew. *Greek Sculpture: An Exploration.* New Haven, Conn.: Yale University Press, 1990.

Sullivan, Michael. *The Arts of China.* Berkeley and Los Angeles: University of California Press, 1984.

Chapter 17. Expanding Horizons of World Art

Cutler, Charles. *Northern Painting: From Pucelle to Bruegel.* New York: Holt, Rinehart and Winston, 1968.

Fagg, William. *Yoruba: Sculpture of West Africa.* New York: Alfred A. Knopf, 1982.

Hartt, Frederick. *History of Italian Renaissance Art.* Englewood Cliffs, N.J.: Prentice-Hall, 1987.

Hibbard, Howard. *Caravaggio.* New York: Harper & Row, 1983.

Miller, Mary Ellen. *The Art of Mesoamerica: From Olmec to Aztec.* New York: Thames and Hudson, 1986.

Murray, Peter. *The Architecture of the Italian Renaissance.* New York: Schocken Books, 1986.

Novak, Barbara. *American Painting of the Nineteenth Century.* New York: Harper & Row, 1979.

Pedretti, Carlo. *Leonardo: A Study in Chronology and Style.* Berkeley and Los Angeles: University of California Press, 1973.

Rosenblum, Robert, and H. W. Janson. *19th-Century Art.* New York: Abrams, 1984.

Willett, Frank. *African Art.* New York: Thames and Hudson, 1993.

Chapter 18. Art of the Modern World

Ades, Dawn. *Art in Latin America: The Modern Era, 1820-1980.* New Haven, Conn.: Yale University Press, 1989.

Arnason, H. Harvard. *History of Modern Art: Painting, Sculpture, Architecture, Photography.* New York: Abrams, 1986.

Blake, Peter. *Frank Lloyd Wright: Architecture and Space.* Baltimore: Penguin Books, 1964.

Chipp, Herschel B. *Theories of Modern Art.* Berkeley and Los Angeles: University of California Press, 1968.

Hamilton, George H. *Painting and Sculpture in Europe, 1880-1940.* New York: Penguin Books, 1983.

Hunter, Sam, and John M. Jacobus. *Modern Art: Painting, Sculpture, Architecture.* New York: Abrams, 1992.

Kandinsky, Wassily. *Concerning the Spiritual in Art, and Painting in Particular.* 1912. Reprint, New York: Dover, 1977.

Quirarte, Jacinto. *The Latin American Spirit: Art and Artists in the United States, 1920-1970.* New York: Harry Abrams, 1988.

Russell, John. *The Meanings of Modern Art*. New York: Museum of Modern Art and Harper Collins, 1991.

Wright, Frank Lloyd. *The Natural House*. New York: Mentor Books, 1963.

Chapter 19. Art of the Second Half of the Twentieth Century

The Decade Show: Frameworks of Identity in the 1980s. New York: Museum of Contemporary Hispanic Art; New Museum of Contemporary Art; Studio Museum of Harlem, 1990.

Frank, Peter, and Michael McKenzie. *New, Used, and Improved: Art for the Eighties*. New York: Abbeville Press, 1987.

Hoffman, Katherine. *Explorations: The Visual Arts since 1945*. New York: Harper & Row, 1991.

Landau, Ellen G. *Jackson Pollock*. New York: Abrams, 1989.

Lippard, Lucy R. *Mixed Blessings: New Art in a Multicultural America*. New York: Pantheon Books, 1990.

Lucie-Smith, Edward. *Art in the Seventies*. Ithaca, N.Y.: Cornell University Press, 1980.

Magnin, André. *Africa Now*. Groningen, The Netherlands: Groninger Museum, 1991.

O'Connor, Francis V., and Eugene V. Thaw. *Jackson Pollock: A Catalogue Raisonne of Paintings, Drawings, and Other Works*. New Haven, Conn.: Yale University Press, 1978.

Thompson, Jerry L., and Susan Vogel. *Closeup: Lessons in the Art of Seeing African Sculpture*. New York: Center for African Art, 1990.

Chapter 20. The Art World

Brommer, Gerald F., and Joseph A. Gatto. *Careers in Art: An Illustrated Guide*. Worcester, Mass.: Davis Publications, 1984.

Dyckoff, Wilfried. *Julian Schnabel*. New York: Pace Gallery, 1986.

Ito, Dee. *The School of Visual Arts Guide to Careers*. New York: McGraw-Hill, Visual Arts Press, 1987.

Michels, Caroll. *How to Survive and Prosper as an Artist*. New York: Henry Holt, 1992.

Schiff, Gert. *Julian Schnabel*. New York: Pace Gallery, 1984.

610